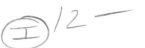

SPECIAL TASKS

SPECIAL TASKS

THE
MEMOIRS
OF AN
UNWANTED
WITNESS—
A SOVIET
SPYMASTER

Pavel Sudoplatov and Anatoli Sudoplatov

with Jerrold L. and Leona P. Schecter

Foreword by Robert Conquest

Little, Brown and Company
Boston   New York   Toronto   London

FOR EMMA

First Edition

ISBN 0-316-77352-2

Library of Congress Catalog Card Number 94-75737

10 9 8 7 6 5 4 3 2 1

MV-NY

Published simultaneously in Canada
by Little, Brown & Company (Canada) Limited

Printed in the United States of America

CONTENTS

APPENDICES

Photographs follow page 220

Robert Conquest

This is the most sensational, the most devastating, and in many ways the most informative autobiography ever to emerge from the Stalinist milieu.

It is perhaps the most important single contribution to our knowledge since Khrushchev's Secret Speech.

It is not quite true that Pavel Sudoplatov's name is little known, at least to historians. His role as organizer of the Trotsky murder had been established in a general way for some years. But full knowledge was indeed lacking even on this operation; and the rest of his multifarious career was obscure. A year or two ago the Moscow press printed some of his letters from prison, detailing the circumstances of the comparatively minor crimes for which he had actually been sentenced under Stalin's successors, and asking for amnesty. A hitherto secret list of the orders and medals awarded to those, including Sudoplatov, who carried out an unspecified "special task" — i.e., the murder of Trotsky — was also published at this time. And a couple of pieces appeared on his role in organizing operations in German-occupied territory during the war.

Later General Dmitri Volkogonov visited Sudoplatov with a view to arranging a full-scale interview. Sudoplatov refused; and Volkogonov published a not very informative account of the meeting, giving only the initial "S." (This was followed by a less inhibited, but also unsuccessful, try by an Italian paper.) Though nothing solid emerged at this stage,

Volkogonov left Sudoplatov with the suggestion that he write his memoirs. At the time it looked unlikely that this would come to anything. Nor would it have but for the strenuous and devoted efforts of Jerrold and Leona Schecter, for which we must all feel the gratitude due to the right people at the right time and with the right understanding.

Sudoplatov's activities were, of course, for the most part those of the criminal agent of a criminal regime. His original justification, in fact, lies at the heart of Communist ethics — in Lenin's theses that "our morality is completely subordinated to the interests of the class struggle of the proletariat," and that "everything that is done in the proletarian cause is honest." This was interpreted from the start as justifying "everything" that was done in the interests of the Communist party.

Sudoplatov has come to see that all this, and particularly the treating of all non-Communists as in principle enemies whose lives were forfeit, has proved false and destructive — though even after his release from prison he found it hard to stomach the views of his old terror-comrades, like the remarkable Leonid Eitingon, who concluded that the whole system was rotten.

In this foreword it will hardly be necessary to express general condemnation of the activities he records. They speak for themselves. Nowadays there are few who still fail to understand and condemn them and the whole Stalinist system of which they formed part. Today, surely, the main thing is to learn the lessons of this history, to discover as much as we can about its circumstances. In this context Sudoplatov is helpful, for he has not allowed occasional excuses or expressions of contrition to distort his narrative. Perhaps it is only such a temperament which could give us so cool a recital of the horribly criminal, but also often disgraceful and absurd actions of the government he served.

The range of Sudoplatov's activities, though consonant with his post-1938 position as NKVD (later MGB) officer in charge of special operations and espionage, is remarkable. To have headed the organization of both the Trotsky murder and the atomic spy rings in America is only part of his record. From the less than twenty years of his career in this post, ending in his imprisonment while still in his midforties, he also covers for us the wartime operations behind the German front, the actions against the Ukrainian nationalist partisans who fought against both Nazis and (until 1950) Communists, the Red Orchestra spy ring in Berlin, a set of murders of individuals in the USSR, the anti-Semitic campaign in the secret police itself, the fall and trial of Beria, and much else. Directly or at reliable second hand, he is also newly informative about the other key actions of the period — the Leningrad Case, the fall of Abakumov, the anti-Semitic operation in general — not only the Crimea Affair and the Doctors' Plot but also, for example, the murder of the great Yiddish actor-producer Solomon Mikhoels (the first full account we have).

Sudoplatov had direct contact, too, with most of the Stalinist leadership. He had a meeting with Yezhov, then about to fall. He had much to do with Beria. He saw Stalin himself several times, and received instructions from him on the murders of Konovalets and Trotsky, and later a plan to kill Tito. He met others in high position, including Khrushchev and Molotov.

His chapter on the Trotsky killing is far the fullest yet published, giving, for example, the reasons for the failure of the first attempt, and explaining why Trotsky's American bodyguard, Harte, had to be murdered.

Many readers will find his chapter on atomic espionage the most striking and informative. Using in the first place the ring set up to support the Trotsky operation, his men penetrated the Berkeley laboratory, and later (more importantly) Los Alamos itself. The physicists who wittingly or unwittingly then made their secrets available to Stalin have their activities depicted in detail: not a few readers will surely be shocked as well as enlightened (almost the only figure to emerge creditably is the much-maligned Edward Teller).

Sudoplatov had no links with GRU (military intelligence) operations. On these, in the United States in the 1930s, he does however report a conversation with an elderly colleague from that organization, whose information about the Hiss connection is of much interest.

His account of his own arrest, interrogation, and imprisonment, written, of course, from his own point of view, is remarkable testimony to the continuance of the petty legalisms and political distortions which accompanied the first attempts at de-Stalinization. Though they were not as bad as in the Stalin era itself, it is revealing to read how Sudoplatov was stopped when he mentioned the role of any of the post-Stalin (and post-Beria) leadership in the crimes he was charged with, and particularly that of Khrushchev; and how, when Molotov and Malenkov fell from power, the interrogators, hitherto suppressing reference to them, started to link them with the case.

Sudoplatov also gives us, almost in passing, useful insight into the nature of Soviet society. For example, he tells us, as if it were perfectly natural, that among the awards given to police operatives for good work was the right to send their children to higher education without taking the required examinations. This is not a matter of pull, or bribes, which might be met within other societies — and indeed, at a lower level in Soviet society too. No, here we find an official governmental (though unpublicized) award. Such attitudes thoroughly justify the concepts of the French scholar Emmanuel Todd — that the Soviet Union is to be considered a feudal society with, rather than a New Class, a New Caste — a priviligentsia deriving benefits, even (precariously) hereditary ones, not from their economic, but from their hierarchical status. Indeed, as the writer Konstantin Leontiev predicted for Russia a century ago, "Socialism is the feudalism of the future."

There has been for some years a tendency in certain academic circles of the more schematic type to reject personal reminiscences as almost by definition inferior to "documents." When this view was originally put forward about the USSR in the 1930s, and later again in the mid-1980s, Soviet official documents were in general highly unreliable, while some at least of the reminiscences were true, or contained truth. Western historical research of any value on the USSR was largely based on personal memoirs of defectors and others — and was largely validated when a mass of formerly secret Soviet documents appeared from 1989 on.

Now there is a mass of such documentation. But it still needs to be said, first, that even the most secret documents of the Stalin period often contain gross falsifications; second, that the highest category of secrecy — "word of mouth only" — is naturally not documented; third, that crucial documents are missing — as Sudoplatov notes of several he knows to have once existed.

Individual reminiscences must, indeed, be treated critically — but so must documents. Both are simply historical evidence, none of which is perfect, and none of which is complete. Evidence from individuals, given this caveat, is in fact often as important as, or even more important than, most documents — either cumulatively when it is a matter of mass experience, or singly in the case of high, or key, officials. Even in the spate of documentation now emerging in Russia, Sudoplatov's evidence is vastly informative in major but (as yet, at least) undocumented areas. One should add that, with the help of his security contacts, Sudoplatov has had access to useful documents. In fact, in those huge and often muddled and misleading archives, his special knowledge enabled him to track down material which no one was otherwise able to locate.

It is in the nature of autobiographies, however veridical in a general way, that they consist of various levels of evidence. First, the direct experience of the writer; second, information derived from direct and mutually confirmatory sources close to him (as with Sudoplatov's long imprisonment with Beria's closest assistants, including his secretary Ludvigov); third, more indirect material from areas beyond his or his immediate informers' real ken; and fourth, a penumbra of recollection, rumor, and speculation of variable reliability. To put Sudoplatov's work into perspective, we should note the limits of his experience. First, until 1938 he was a minor NKVD figure, with little access to, and no confidential contacts with, higher echelons, or with the political world. As a junior agent, he was sent on a mission to penetrate the Ukrainian nationalist organizations abroad. His success led to compliments from Stalin, and an assignment to murder the Ukrainian émigré leader Konovalets. Returning to Moscow in 1938 to further congratulations, he found the old NKVD heavily purged and its temporary survivors uncommunicative — its Foreign Department, in which he himself served, undergoing an almost total purge of the upper and middle ranks. Thus Sudoplatov was never close to secrets of the Yagoda-Yezhov period.

At the beginning of 1939, amid the disgrace and execution of all his seniors and even most of his lower-level colleagues, Sudoplatov was himself on the verge of arrest, and for some months was shunned by the replacements. Then as deputy head of the Foreign Department, he was called in by Stalin and given the Trotsky assignment. Over the next fifteen years he was privy to many but not all of Stalin's most secret actions (and learned much more about them later). Thus the areas in which he was not fully informed are twofold: in the period before 1939 and, to a much lesser degree, on certain secret plans of the later period. The absence of sensitive or communicative contacts in the earlier period arises in his treatment of the Kirov murder. He accepts one of the various long-rumored motives of the assassin (that it was a crime passionelle), but considers that it was therefore simply an individual crime. But it has always been clear that the murderer acted on his own. The question was if, and how, Stalin and others were involved in giving him his chance. Such a probability is high — and the absence of "documents," as with Hitler and the Holocaust, is meaningless when it is a matter of "word of mouth only." And when Sudoplatov writes that the jealousy motive has been suppressed because everyone wanted to protect Kirov's reputation, this consideration has been invalid now for several years.

On the patches of imperfect knowledge and imperfect deduction in the period of his own experience, he did not, for example, know of the secret protocols to the Nazi-Soviet Pact, and we may note his assertion that there were no plans to deport Jews in 1953. He bases this on the apparent absence of the transport plans necessary to such an operation. But the letter to Stalin, signed under heavy pressure, from leading Jews asking for their people to be deported is well attested; and all one can safely conclude is that the operational order had not been issued.

Such points need to be noted. But it will be seen that they are of little consequence compared with the solid substance Sudoplatov offers us. It is most fortunate that he changed his mind about recounting his career: the result is a unique document. He emerges, in fact, as one of the most valuable of all possible sources for important matters over the whole period of High Stalinism.

INTRODUCTION

Jerrold L. and Leona P. Schecter

The intelligence career of Pavel Anatolievich Sudoplatov coincided almost exactly with Stalin's thirty-year reign in the Soviet Union. For long years Sudoplatov worked in the Administration for Special Tasks, an elite unit of the Soviet intelligence service, becoming its wartime director. He defined the meaning of the word "special" with blood, poison, and terrorism. He and his colleagues forever after referred to their jobs as Special Tasks. In telling us his life story, he was torn between ingrained habits of secrecy and the desire to justify his operations within the ideological rationale of Stalin's communism.

Sudoplatov was eighty-five when we began to interview him in 1992. He had been ill with a recurring heart condition and marshaled his strength carefully; he prepared for the interviews and limited them to three-hour sessions. His back was stooped and he had lost the sight of his left eye while in prison, but his mind was alert and he spoke with the vigor and authority of a man who spent most of his life giving orders. Beneath his large head of wavy gray hair are the now wizened facial features of a handsome, even courtly man, with a strong sense of humor and keen analytical ability. He remains a believer in the dream of communism and attributes its fall to the lesser men who followed Stalin.

Pavel Anatolievich Sudoplatov's autobiography, recounting seventy years of manipulation and murder, is not an act of contrition or confession. He saw himself as "a soldier at war" in justifiable combat —

against Ukrainian fascists, Trotsky and Trotskyites, enemies of the people, German invaders, NATO and American imperialists. His good eye glistened with the pleasure of reliving battles won long ago. He assumed, incorrectly, that we shared the rationale behind all these operations. We were startled when Sudoplatov equated the agreements reached at Yalta with the Hitler-Stalin Pact, arguing that Yalta had confirmed what Hitler was the first to give the Soviet Union — recognition as a world power. Often he spoke of "being enemies then, but now having to work together." His son Anatoli told him, "Papa, let's get on with the story. Enough *mir i druzhba*" — citing the Soviet propaganda cliché, "peace and friendship."

Such slogans were used effectively by Sudoplatov's NKVD officers, posing as diplomats, to enlist the cooperation of Western atomic scientists in the 1940s. During our interviews Sudoplatov probed deeply into the differences between a traitor and a friend when discussing the cooperation of Western atomic scientists with the Soviet Union. None of the Western scientists who provided atomic secrets to the Soviet Union were controlled agents in the sense that they were paid or had signed recruitment contracts. Their fear that Hitler might produce an atomic bomb first was the initial motivation for sharing their knowledge with Soviet scientists. Later they believed that equality of superpower status for the Soviet Union would contribute to world peace. In dealing with them, Sudoplatov realized that the scientists saw themselves as a new breed of superstatesmen whose mandate transcended national boundaries; he and his officers exploited this hubris.

Why today's Russian intelligence service has chosen not to reveal full details of the atomic espionage activities of its predecessors is a matter of conjecture, but we believe there are two basic reasons. First, professional pride and obsession with secrecy are paramount. Even after the disintegration of the Soviet Union, the Russian intelligence service remains intact at the core, a world unto itself. The American and British intelligence services also classify "sources and methods" more than fifty years after the fact. The Federal Bureau of Investigation rejected our request for access to files on wartime espionage. Another major reason for Russian secrecy, Sudoplatov explained, is that the men and women who were most influential in acquiring atomic secrets for the Soviet Union were all later purged because they were Jewish. To reveal their success in atomic espionage, the Russian intelligence service would have to make heroes out of Jews, unlikely in the present political climate.

Thus far they are only willing to show that espionage was vital to the development of the first Soviet atomic bomb.

Complete details of wartime atomic espionage operations in America are not in the KGB files, Sudoplatov explained. Because of wartime urgency and the unique nature of the atomic bomb project, Sudoplatov's deputies Leonid Eitingon, Lev Vasilevsky, and Gregory Kheifetz were given permission to recruit agents on their own, without the usual prior approval from Moscow Center. Thus, according to Sudoplatov, they often did not send coded messages back requesting approval, and the absence of this traffic in the files makes it impossible for anyone other than Sudoplatov, who supervised their efforts, to put the full story together.

The Soviet Union of Sudoplatov's time was a very secret place in which journalists and diplomats were totally shut off from what was really happening in the country. The Soviet bureaucracy was a dangerous small town in which everyone knew everyone else and knew the rules of behavior. Survival required vigilance and extrasensory sensitivity to the whims of Stalin's favor. Communism was a social engineering experiment in which Stalin manipulated the levers of power, constantly discarding old comrades and adding new faces from the provinces to perpetuate his rule and to create a superpower from the ruins of a feudal dynasty. There were no economic, legal, or political institutions to balance the interests of competing groups. Stalin's favored method for the transfer of authority was death or exile. Seen through Sudoplatov's eyes, the process was even harsher and more corrupt than we have been taught. Those who served Stalin best were punished most.

There was regularity to the purges, Sudoplatov tells us. Whenever the country began to settle down and progress economically, Stalin created new tensions by fabricating imaginary crimes. A new purge was generated, sweeping any small center of bureaucratic power and its leaders into oblivion. Then new faces, inexperienced in Moscow, would pay obeisance to Stalin. Sudoplatov describes how after Stalin's death Khrushchev quickly adopted the same pattern for controlling his rivals.

Sudoplatov grew up in this environment and accepted it as a necessary cost. At one point he told us, "Stalin killed people who wanted to slow down reforms and the speed of industrialization. He destroyed people who opposed collectivization or put brakes on reforms. After all, the collective farms fed the country. He was also against people who pushed their own line, who were not really spies or traitors. People like

Gorbachev or Yeltsin would have been destroyed under Stalin because they pushed their own line."

After nearly all his friends were executed or imprisoned he began to question the efficacy of Stalin's socialist morality. In Stalin's final years, during the disruption brought about by the Doctors' Plot, Sudoplatov saw his position in the intelligence service erode and his privileged life threatened. He thought at first that it was the result of bureaucratic inefficiency and mistakes. Only when he was arrested and interrogated did he realize that the regime's real purpose was not a noble social experiment.

Sudoplatov's first outline for the book was directed to a Russian audience. His goal was to bring light to a dark period. He hoped to set the record straight about operations that at first won him praise and decorations but later targeted him for accusations of treason, then imprisonment. His suffering was not unusual; it followed a typical pattern of high-level Soviet service in which disinformation and murder, carried out under orders of the "highest authority," were warped into charges of conspiracy and treason.

The tales of betrayal were numbing, each adding a layer to the gruesome struggle. When Sudoplatov began to tell us yet another story of unlawful imprisonment, we wondered what it could add to the last such case. But by the time the victim stood outside Lubyanka in the Moscow winter without money or family and nowhere to go, we saw another man whose story took its place beside Arthur Koestler's *Darkness at Noon* and other classics depicting Stalinist terror.

What concerned Sudoplatov most was accuracy in the details. He insisted that the charges of treason against him, which cost him fifteen years in jail and forty more years of his life to prove untrue, were fabricated by Khrushchev and his followers in their deadly power struggle against Beria. The real "crime" for which he was jailed was having been subordinate to Beria.

Sudoplatov reveals the complex character of Lavrenti Beria, his mentor from 1939 to 1953. He was concerned with painting a full portrait of the Beria he knew: a man of vision and managerial brilliance who successfully presided over the creation of the first Soviet atomic bomb. Sudoplatov hoped that Beria would take over and turn his ruthlessness and drive to cleaning out the Augean stables of corruption. He would raise the Soviet Union's world stature. Sudoplatov describes with pride the corrective measures that Beria took in the months between Stalin's death and his arrest. He does not deny Beria's wily and criminal rise to the top of the intelligence service, his arrogance in the drive for Soviet aggrandizement after the Hitler-Stalin Pact, or his crimes against the Baltic peoples.

Beria, argues Sudoplatov, was an innovator who would have brought about the unification of Germany in the 1950s, avoiding the crises that led to the construction of the Berlin Wall. In the few short months between Stalin's death and his arrest by Khrushchev's supporters, Beria had begun emptying the Gulag and urged that political prisoners be released. Sudoplatov rejoiced in the freeing of his friends, mostly Jews who had been purged from the intelligence service during the so-called Zionist conspiracy. Sudoplatov's Beria is part monster and part reformer, too strong for Stalin's other heirs to let him live. Khrushchev successfully destroyed Beria and then created a historical image, still popularly held, that it was primarily Beria who shared with Stalin culpability for the crimes that preceded Khrushchev's leadership. Sudoplatov tells us, and documents, that Khrushchev and the other Politburo members were full participants in these crimes. Sudoplatov's original purpose in writing this book was to exculpate himself from an unfair trial and conviction. He also wanted to challenge Nikita Khrushchev's version of history, which, he said, whitewashed Khrushchev's own crimes when he dictated his memoirs from 1967 to 1971.

Sudoplatov's son Anatoli Pavlovich, now an Academician and a professor at Moscow University, struggled together with his mother, Emma, a retired KGB officer, to free his father from prison. Anatoli then encouraged and worked with his father to tell his story. Sudoplatov's secret career was first recorded in a letter of appeal written to the Central Committee of the Communist Party of the Soviet Union in 1960 while he was still in jail. He began his memoirs in 1970, two years out of prison, with an account of his career for the Party Control Committee. The vita was a requirement to become a member of the Writers' Association. In 1990 Sudoplatov wrote for the KGB an account of some of the most secret operations of the Administration for Special Tasks. Anatoli, who knew that Jerrold Schecter had accomplished the publication of Nikita Khrushchev's memoirs in 1970 with Little, Brown and *Life* magazine, and that Leona Schecter was a literary agent, approached us in Moscow in 1992 with a brief synopsis of his father's activities. When we explained that most of the names in the outline were unfamiliar to Western readers, Anatoli responded immediately by showing us his father's original appeal for rehabilitation, which contained the names Trotsky, Oppenheimer, Fermi, Fuchs, and Bohr. Others — the

Rosenbergs, Yalta, Prince Radziwill, and Tito — poured out. The
dam burst on long-held intelligence secrets. Why hadn't these episodes
been in the original proposal? For the simple reason that these were all
successful operations, cases long closed, which were not raised in
Sudoplatov's arrest, trial, and imprisonment.

We needed proof, and Anatoli had only limited access to archival
materials on his father's case. Thus began a search by Anatoli and his
father for documents and firsthand accounts to reconstruct and fill in
the details of Sudoplatov's memory of events and exploits beginning
more than a half-century ago. Fortunately, the KGB was trying to produce its own six-volume history of wartime operations, which led its
representatives to Pavel Anatolievich for his recollections. They brought
copies of documents that only he could interpret, and which were
also useful in telling his own story. He was asked to identify individuals behind code names and to describe the sequence of operations.
Sudoplatov is the surviving institutional memory of the Russian intelligence service's covert operations from the 1920s to 1953.

The scope of the material was not new to Anatoli. He had begun to
gather the record to prove his father's innocence while still a graduate
student in the 1960s. From his mother Anatoli acquired the analytical
intelligence skills to establish the shading and insights into otherwise
sterile documents and uninterpreted records. In soliciting testimonial letters from Pavel Anatolievich's wartime comrades, Anatoli heard firsthand their heroic feats against the Germans and their successes in
atomic espionage. He learned the tortuous nuances of the internecine
struggle for power in the Kremlin. Anatoli was forced to deal with a
legal system that equated justice with the politically motivated suppres-
sion of the real facts behind his father's indictment. In the process he
amassed a collection of newspaper accounts, memoirs, military journals,
KGB newsletters, and declassified documents relevant to his father's
career. When Anatoli got hold of archival materials, most of them
needed his father's professional validation and interpretation of personalities and context.

We interviewed Pavel Sudoplatov face-to-face and through Anatoli
for more than a year. Our filmmaker son, Steven Schecter, videotaped
twenty hours of Sudoplatov's reminiscences and answers to our questions. Through Sudoplatov's narrative we were introduced to his close
personal friends, now dead: Leonid Eitingon, Vassili and Elizabeth
Zarubin, and Lev Vasilevsky. The chronicle of their lives provided

details — some of them humorous — and insights into the most secret of Soviet intelligence operations. Their accounts, told and retold at dinners and lunches around the kitchen table after Sudoplatov was released from jail, were familiar to Anatoli. He has his own memories of their encounters with Robert Oppenheimer, Bruno Pontecorvo, Enrico Fermi, Leo Szilard, and other atomic scientists.

Sudoplatov had no direct cooperation or support from the KGB on the book. However, in relaxed meetings with former KGB officers who had obtained atomic secrets in the United States, England, Canada, and Western Europe, and with former GRU (Soviet military intelligence) colleagues, he filled in missing pieces of memory.

Sudoplatov's terse, official writings on wartime operations for the KGB archives served as the base from which he expanded the narrative with personal recollections. We used these, transcripts of twenty hours of taped reminiscences, and notes and documents Anatoli gathered for his father's defense, to prepare a first draft for Pavel Anatolievich's confirmation and approval. We compared this material with published sources to confirm dates. Finally, Sudoplatov made sure that nothing was lost or changed and, in the custom of the intelligence service, initialed the most sensitive pages.

Pavel Anatolievich Sudoplatov's sources are all named except for a former high-ranking Soviet military intelligence official who requested anonymity. We have added footnotes for clarity and to document sources. In most cases these sources are public and have appeared in Soviet or Western publications, but some are sources known to or seen by the Sudoplatovs or their friends which are not yet publicly available. Anatoli Sudoplatov did have limited access to his father's personal file through the cooperation of General Dmitri Volkogonov, who is in no way responsible for the text or its conclusions.

Anatoli gained access to the declassified archives of Soviet physicist Igor Kurchatov at the Ministry of Atomic Energy. Kurchatov's letters and reports amplified and confirmed KGB materials on the subject, and examples of both are reprinted as appendices. We were advised by a senior American physicist and former cabinet officer with long experience in national security affairs on which details of the atomic bomb have not yet been released in the Soviet Union or the United States. We have edited the appendices not to publish still classified material.

We wish to thank our editor, Roger Donald, for his dedicated involvement. He belies the canard that "nobody edits anymore"; he brings intellectual breadth, curiosity, and commitment to a demanding task. Peggy Leith Anderson's copyediting was a constant spur to clarity, consistency, and precision in the manuscript. Geoffrey Kloske in New York and Felix Rosenthal in Moscow were outstanding in providing research. Dmitri Linnik translated technical documents.

EVOLUTION OF
THE SOVIET SECURITY
AND INTELLIGENCE
SERVICE

The Lubyanka or Dom Dva (House Number 2) are the names for the Russian security service headquarters located at number 2 Lubyanka Street, in what was long ago the offices of the Rossia Insurance Company. From 1917 until the abortive coup of August 1991, the building was the headquarters of the Soviet security service. It faced onto a square named after Feliks Edmundovich Dzerzhinsky, a Polish intellectual who became the first head of the CHEKA, the acronym for Extraordinary Commission to Combat Counterrevolution and Sabotage. When the 1991 coup failed, Dzerzhinsky's statue was removed and the square's name was changed to Lubyanka Square.

The CHEKA was the first Soviet security service, lasting from 1917 to 1922, when it became the GPU (State Political Administration) and then the OGPU (Unified State Political Administration). In 1934 the security police service was renamed the GUGB (Main Administration of State Security) and made part of the NKVD, People's Commissariat of Internal Affairs, which was expanded to carry out Joseph Stalin's purges and run the vast chain of labor camps.

Throughout the 1930s there were within the GUGB/NKVD parallel intelligence services: the Foreign Department, known by the Russian acronym INO (Inostrannye Otdel), and the Administration for Special Tasks. The INO was responsible for running the *rezidenturas* (intelligence stations) abroad and was headed first by Mikhail Abramovich Trilisser

(1921–1929) and then by Artur Khristyanovich Artuzov (1929–1934), hero of the so-called Trust operation, which attacked members of the White (anti-Bolshevik) Army who emigrated abroad and organized an opposition to the Communist regime.

The Administration for Special Tasks was set up by Vyacheslav R. Menzhinsky, who succeeded Dzerzhinsky in 1926. This separate intelligence center was primarily responsible for acts of diversion (sabotage) and for deep illegal penetration into the West. Its premise was that war was inevitable. Special Tasks was small in the 1920s and 1930s, but it grew in importance in World War II, when it took on the job of preparing Soviet "illegals" for military operations in Germany and the countries of Eastern Europe. "Illegals" is a term for spies who operate without diplomatic immunity and who live in a foreign country under false identity.

During World War II the security service went through occasional bureaucratic transformations, sometimes standing as an independent agency, the NKGB (People's Commissariat for State Security), and sometimes as an agency (the GUGB) within the larger NKVD. After the war, it was upgraded to the status of a ministry, as the MGB, Ministry of State Security. Following Stalin's death (March 1953), Lavrenti Beria placed the security services in an enlarged Ministry of Internal Affairs (MVD), which he ran until his arrest in June 1953. In 1954 the security apparatus was made a separate committee, the KGB (Committee for State Security), under the Council of Ministers.

After the August 1991 coup attempt against the government of Mikhail Gorbachev, the KGB was restructured. The First Chief Directorate, in charge of foreign intelligence, was made an independent agency and renamed the Foreign Intelligence Service. The Second Chief Directorate, devoted to counterintelligence, was renamed the Ministry of Security, and it absorbed other directorates dealing with transportation security, economic crimes, fraud, and corruption. In December 1993 Russian president Boris Yeltsin abolished the Ministry of Security and replaced it with the Federal Counterintelligence Service in an effort to assert his control over internal security.

1917–1922	CHEKA	Extraordinary Commission to Combat Counterrevolution and Sabotage (Chrezvychaynaya Kommissiya po Borbe s Kontrrevolyutsiey, i Sabotazhem)
1922–1923	GPU/NKVD	State Political Administration (Gosudarstvennoye Politicheskoye Upravleniye), within People's Commissariat of Internal Affairs (Narodny Kommissariat Vnutrennikh Del)
1923–1934	OGPU	Unified State Political Administration (Obiedinyonnoye Gosudarstvennoye Politicheskoye Upravleniye)
1934–1941	GUGB/NKVD	Main Administration of State Security (Glavnoye Upravleniye Gosudarstvennoye Bezopasnosti), within NKVD
Feb.–July 1941	NKGB	People's Commissariat for State Security (Narodny Kommissariat Gosudarstvennoye Bezopasnosti)
July 1941–1943	GUGB/NKVD	
1943–1946	NKGB	
1946–1953	MGB	Ministry of State Security (Ministersvo Gosudarstvennoye Bezopasnosti)
1953–1954	MVD	Ministry of Internal Affairs (Ministersvo Vnutrennikh Del)
1954–1991	KGB	Committee for State Security (Komitet Gosudarstvennoye Bezopasnosti)
1991–1993	MB	Ministry of Security (Ministersvo Bezopasnosti)
1991–	SVR	Foreign Intelligence Service (Sluzhba Vneshnei Razvedki)
1993–	FSK	Federal Counterintelligence Service (Federal Sluzhba Kontrazvedki)

SPECIAL TASKS

REVEALING
A SECRET

My name is Pavel Anatolievich Sudoplatov, but I do not expect you to recognize it, because for fifty-eight years it was one of the best-kept secrets in the Soviet Union. You may think you know me by other names: the Center, the Director, or the head of SMERSH (the acronym for Death to Spies), names by which I have been misidentified in the West. My Administration for Special Tasks was responsible for sabotage, kidnapping, and assassination of our enemies beyond the country's borders. It was a special department working in the Soviet security service. I was responsible for Trotsky's assassination and, during World War II, I was in charge of guerrilla warfare and disinformation in Germany and German-occupied territories. After the war I continued to run illegal networks abroad whose purpose was to sabotage American and NATO installations in the event hostilities broke out. I was also in charge of the Soviet espionage effort to obtain the secrets of the atomic bomb from America and Great Britain. I set up a network of illegals who convinced Robert Oppenheimer, Enrico Fermi, Leo Szilard, Bruno Pontecorvo, Alan Nunn May, Klaus Fuchs, and other scientists in America and Great Britain to share atomic secrets with us.

It is strange to look back fifty years and re-create the mentality that led us to take vengeance on our enemies with cold self-assurance. We did not believe there was any moral question involved in killing Trotsky or any other of our former comrades who had turned against us. We believed we were in a life-and-death struggle for the salvation of our grand experiment, the creation of a new social system that would protect and provide dignity for all workers and eliminate the greed and oppression of capitalist profit.

We believed that every Western country hated us and wished to see our doom. Therefore, anyone who was not for us was against us. In the Great Patriotic War against Hitler, the struggle between good and evil was simplified. All anti-Nazis knew that we were the only hope of destroying the fascist regime. Good men and women of every nationality became pro-Communist and gave their lives in this clear-cut cause for human freedom. There was no doubt in our minds that we had to learn how to build an atomic bomb before the Germans. We resented that the Americans moved ahead in this field without us, even though they were our wartime allies against Germany. Therefore, every theft of atomic secrets was a heroic act. Every scientist who handed over diagrams and formulas for building a bomb was counted a Soviet hero working for world peace.

After Hitler was defeated, it became less clear who was against us and who was merely critical of our methods. We had no time or patience for these distinctions. Good men who had risked their lives and suffered torture by the Nazis spent years in the cells of Lubyanka for merely doubting that we knew best. The result was that we created a weakness in ourselves that we never overcame. We never learned how to incorporate and deal with diversity. You in the West have your weaknesses as well. The diversity in America, the plethora of foreign-born immigrant communities within your population, are the pride of your melting pot. Yet within these communities we were able to enlist thousands of agents ready to destroy you in case war broke out between us.

During World War II, more than ninety percent of the lonely soldiers spread throughout Western Europe who sent us crucial information that enabled us to beat back the German invasion were Jews whose hatred of Hitler spurred them to risk their lives and families. Yet when the Western tide of sentiment turned against the Soviet Union after World War II and our own internal conflicts within the leadership weakened us, we turned against the Jews who had served us loyally.

My wife, Emma, a lieutenant colonel in the KGB, who was a Jew, had served proudly. She retired in 1949, just in time to avoid the new purge of Jews from the security forces that was a result not of any disloyalty, but merely of their identification as Jews in intelligence work.

I was a witness to the purges of the 1930s, 1940s, and 1950s and saw how they affected the development and history of my country. The truth of the past fifty years is still being subordinated to politically self-serving interpretations of the events. Those claiming to write our history cannot whitewash the czarist empire and Lenin simply to expose Stalin as a criminal — that is too easy, given his intellect and vision. Victorious Russian rulers always combined the qualities of criminals and statesmen. In this regard it is overlooked that Stalin and Beria, who played tragic and criminal roles in our history, at the same time played a constructive one, turning the Soviet Union into an atomic superpower. It is that accomplishment which determined how events in the world would unfold. So we must ask, How did these individuals perform as statesmen? What were the rules of the game in the inner development of the Soviet superstate from the 1930s until Stalin's death in 1953, and afterward, under his heirs?

My conclusions are based on my own personal involvement with these people and events. Unfortunately, due to its political sensitivity, this book is being published first in the West in order to assure its access to Russian readers. I hope historians will find the events I recount and my explanations helpful. I am not going to whitewash anybody, and I do not intend to justify what I did as a member of the foreign intelligence service from the 1920s to the early 1950s. That was a different time, a different historical period. What is needed is to understand the mechanism of the power struggle and how this mechanism developed into present-day Russia.

O N E
BEGINNINGS

was born a Ukrainian in the town of Melitopol in 1907. Part of a rich fruit-growing area, Melitopol then had a population of about twenty thousand. My mother was Russian, and my father, a grain miller, was Ukrainian. I was baptized in the Russian Orthodox church, as were all the five children in our family. My early education included the Old and New Testaments and the fundamentals of the Russian language, since it was forbidden in czarist times to teach the Ukrainian language at school. It was used only as a spoken dialect. I led a normal childhood until my father died, when I was ten, and our relatives had to support us. That same year the Bolshevik Revolution began.

At first little changed, but when basic food supplies ran out chaos overtook the city and gangsters terrorized us. We owned only our small single-story house, and my attitude was typical of that of needy families who had no property. We had nothing to lose, and it was natural for me to believe, when I read *The ABC of Communism* written by Bukharin,[1] that public ownership would mean the building of a just soci-

---

1. Nikolai Ivanovich Bukharin (1888–1938), the leading theorist of the Bolshevik party, was called "the darling of the party" by Lenin. In the inner party struggle after Lenin's death, Bukharin sided with Stalin, first against Lev Trotsky and then against Grigori Zinoviev and Lev Kamenev. He replaced Zinoviev as head of the Communist International in 1925 but fell out with Stalin and opposed him in 1928–1929. Stalin

ety where everyone would be equal, that the representatives of the peasant and working classes would run the country for the benefit of the common people, not for the landlords.

My elder brother Nikolai joined the Red Army in 1918 and in 1920 became a member of a CHEKA battalion. In 1919, as a twelve-year-old, I ran away from home and joined the Red Army regiment that was retreating from Melitopol in the face of a White offensive.[2] Our regiment was defeated, and small groups of soldiers from the Melitopol regiment managed to join the detachments of the 44th Infantry Division of the Red Army near Kiev.

Since I had attended elementary school, and could read and write, I was assigned to the signal company. I later fought in the battle for Kiev. In 1921, when I was fourteen, the special department of the division, its security organization, suffered heavy losses in an ambush by Ukrainian nationalist forces. At that time we were fighting not the Whites, but the army of the Ukrainian nationalists led by Simon V. Petlura and Yevhen Konovalets, the commander of an infantry rifle division, the Sitcheveye Streltsi.[3] (When the Civil War broke out, the Ukrainian nationalists declared an independent republic and formally declared war against Russia and the Ukrainian Bolshevik leadership. During two later periods, in the 1930s and again in the 1940s, I found myself a fighter in that war, which formally ended only in January 1992, when the Ukrainian government-in-exile and the rest of the world acknowledged President Leonid Kravchuk as the head of the legitimate government of Ukraine, a sovereign nation.)

As a result of heavy losses from the ambush, there was need for a telephone operator and cipher clerk in the intelligence department of the division. I was sent there, and that is how my career in the security service began.

---

won, and Bukharin lost all his positions. Bukharin was a central figure in the Stalinist purges of the 1930s. After a show trial based on fabricated evidence of an anti-Soviet conspiracy, he was executed in 1938. Bukharin was not rehabilitated until 1988, when his widow, who had memorized his last will and testament protesting his innocence, finally broke her fifty-year silence.

2. The White Army was the pro-czarist, antirevolutionary force supported by the United States, Great Britain, Japan, and others in the Civil War of 1918–1922.

3. The Ukrainian nationalists were fighting for independence from Russia, regardless of whether its rulers were czarists or Communists. Sitch was the name of the independent fiefdom that later became the Ukraine.

In our division there were Poles, Austrians, Germans, Serbs, and even Chinese fighting together with us. The Chinese were very disciplined and fought to the last soldier. It was a bitter fight in which whole villages were destroyed by the Ukrainian nationalists and over a million people were killed. The atrocities of the Civil War were regarded as natural by my generation. The country had been in a state of war from 1914, so people gradually became accustomed to losses and hardship. The tragedy of Russia is that until the Civil War ended in 1922 the country lived constantly on the edge or in the midst of war, and a traditional, stable society was not possible. At that time the fighting was brutal, and the population looked upon the Red Army as saviors who would bring a measure of order.

My duties as a telephone operator and later as a cipher clerk were useful in my future career. I typed sensitive documents sent to the military high command and deciphered cables received directly from Feliks Dzerzhinsky, head of the CHEKA, in Moscow.

In 1921 there was a turning point in my life. The division was transferred to the city of Zhitomir, eighty miles west of Kiev. The main task of our special department was to help the CHEKA office there penetrate the Ukrainian nationalists' guerrilla underground headed by Petlura and Konovalets. Their armed resistance groups sabotaged Soviet administrative centers. The local CHEKA managed to establish a dialogue with the local guerrilla leaders and held informal talks. We met them in Zhitomir in a safe house set up by the CHEKA. As a junior technician I was assigned to live in the safe house and guard against outbreaks of violence during the talks. That experience of dealing with guerrilla leaders who were local dictators helped me in my future work as a case officer. I got a taste and feel of what it was like to deal with conspiracy and underground operations through these meetings with the Ukrainian nationalist gangsters.

The nationalist warfare lasted for almost two years and ended finally in a compromise when the local leaders accepted an amnesty from the Soviet Ukrainian government. This happened only after the battle group of two thousand cavalry troops sent by Konovalets to Zhitomir was surrounded by Red Army units and surrendered. Konovalets was defeated. In those clashes my elder brother Nikolai, who served in the CHEKA frontier troops on the Polish border, was killed. I asked for a transfer to Melitopol so I could be near my family and help them.

For the next three years in Melitopol I was a junior case officer responsible for a network of informers operating in the local Greek and

German settlements. In 1927 I was promoted to the Secret Political Department of the Ukrainian OGPU[4] in Kharkov, then the capital of the Ukraine. At the age of twenty I met my future wife, Emma Kaganova, two years older, who had come from Gomel, a Jewish settlement in Byelorussia.

Emma was a good student, one of the few Jews admitted to the gymnasium in the two percent quota. After graduation she had become a typist-secretary for Mendel M. Khatayevich, secretary of the Bolshevik district organization in Gomel. Later, when her boss was transferred to Odessa to be secretary of the Bolshevik organization there, Emma accompanied him. It was in Odessa that Emma was recruited by the OGPU. She was assigned to work with the German communities scattered around the city. With her blond hair, blue eyes, and knowledge of Yiddish, she could pass for German.

She had been transferred to Kharkov a year before I arrived and was far more influential than I in the OGPU. Because she was an educated and attractive young woman, well read and poised enough to be at ease with writers and poets, Emma was put in charge of the informers in the Ukrainian Writers Union and the theater. We met on the job, and I was impressed with her mind and beauty. Emma's father had died when she was ten, and she was the only member of her family of eight children earning money. We had much in common: we were both the only support for our families, and had to become adults at an early age.

Our life was intensely busy, but Emma encouraged me to begin law studies at Kharkov University. I only managed to attend ten lectures and pass one exam in economic geography because of my work schedule. My day began at 10:00 A.M. and lasted until 6:00 P.M., with a meal break. Then we resumed work, meeting informers in the safe apartments at 7:30 P.M. I returned to my office around 11:00 P.M. to report what the informers told us and pass on operational material to our bosses.

Under Lenin's decree of 1922, the GPU was the principal source of information for every segment of Soviet society. Even today, security offices and administrative agencies provide the leadership with a

4. The CHEKA became the GPU, State Political Administration, in 1922; a year later the GPU was attached to the Soviet Council of People's Commissars and renamed OGPU, meaning it was now a "unified" administration operating both at the all-union level and in the constituent republics. OGPU was reorganized as GUGB (Main Administration of State Security) and placed within the NKVD (People's Commissariat of Internal Affairs) in 1934; the term NKVD was commonly used to denote the security apparatus.

monthly report on developments in the country. This report includes a summary of internal difficulties and failures of performance at various institutions and enterprises, based on informers' reports. Under Stalin's rule it was almost impossible to meet an informer during the daytime; we met our sources almost every evening. Stalin worked late into the night and, naturally, we all followed his example.

Ironically, the head of the information section was a former czarist army officer, Stanislav Kozelsky, who came from a family of minor Polish-Russian nobility. Even though he had served in the czarist army, his sympathy during the Revolution earned him a place with us. He committed suicide in 1937, when facing arrest in the purges.

For me Emma was an ideal woman, and we were married in 1928, but we never registered our union until 1951. This was the way we and many of our colleagues lived, not registering our marriages for years. I was assigned an unusual but important duty in the OGPU under the direct supervision of the party and OGPU bosses: I was appointed the commissar of a special colony for homeless children. After the Civil War these colonies were an effort to end the blight of orphaned teenagers who engaged in crime and vandalism in our cities. All chekists had to deduct ten percent of their salary for the maintenance of these colonies, which set up workshops and training centers. That work was regarded as a top priority; I succeeded in winning the children's confidence and establishing a shoe factory that soon became profitable.

Thanks to my wife's position in the Ukrainian party establishment I twice met S. V. Kossior, then secretary of the Ukrainian Communist party, in the apartment of Khatayevich, Emma's boss, where we were guests. This made an enormous impression on me, because Khatayevich and Kossior displayed a sophisticated outlook on the future of the Ukraine. They regarded the economic difficulties and the tragedy of collectivization as temporary obstacles to be overcome by all possible means. They said it was necessary to raise a new generation, totally devoted to the cause of communism, free from obligations toward the old society. They paid particular attention to developing and nurturing a new Ukrainian intelligentsia hostile to nationalist ideas.

Only now do I understand that the moral basis of the Revolution could not be absolute, that the cause of Ukrainian nationalism, although doomed to failure for another sixty years until the collapse of the Soviet Union, deserved at least sympathy and understanding. In those years each side was determined to annihilate the other, and I was flattered when Kossior and Khatayevich spoke to us as members of the Revolution. Emma and I were still only Komsomol (Young Communist League) members. We became candidate members of the party in 1928.

In 1933 V. A. Balitsky, the director of the Ukrainian OGPU, was appointed deputy director of the all-union OGPU. When he went to Moscow to assume his new post he took several of his people along, including me. I was appointed senior inspector, supervising promotions and the filling of vacancies in the Foreign Department of the state security administration, what was later to become the First Directorate of the NKVD.

It was in this new post of senior inspector in 1933 that I began to meet regularly with Artur Artuzov, then director of the Foreign Department, and his deputy, Abram Slutsky. In 1933 the case officer supervising surveillance and actions against Ukrainian exiles in the West asked to retire because of poor health. Artuzov, learning of my Ukrainian origin and experience, suggested that I be given the job. Emma was also transferred to Moscow and assigned to work in the Political Department dealing with networks of informers in the Union of Writers and the intelligentsia.

In 1934 the Ukrainian OGPU reported its success in penetrating the inner circle of the Ukrainian military organization in exile. This was a breakthrough for us, because we were smarting from the assassination of a Soviet diplomat in Lvov by a Ukrainian terrorist in 1934. The order came from the chief of the OGPU to develop a plan to neutralize terrorist activities of the Ukrainian nationalists.

Abram Slutsky, who had become head of the Foreign Department, told me of the new directive and asked me to become an illegal officer[5] serving abroad. At first it seemed improbable to me, because I had no experience with foreigners and was ignorant of life in the West. My knowledge of German, which I would need in Germany and Poland, where I was to operate, was nil. But the more I thought about it the more fascinating and challenging it appeared. I accepted the offer and was taught German five days a week at a safe apartment; I learned hand-to-hand combat and the use of weapons from expert instructors. Most important were meetings with Sergei Shpigelglas, then deputy director

5. Illegals operate without diplomatic cover under false identity. There are two types of illegal operations. One is to live undercover in the West awaiting assignment from the Center (security service headquarters) and building a network of agents. This is a long-term assignment and can last from five to fifteen years. Another, more dangerous, illegal role is to penetrate hostile intelligence services, posing as a sympathizer coming from the Soviet Union.

of the Foreign Department of the NKVD. Shpigelglas had wide experience abroad; he had been an illegal in China and Western Europe. As a cover for his operations in Paris in the early 1930s, he had owned a fish store near Boulevard Montmartre whose specialty was lobsters.

After eight months of training I was ready for my first trip abroad, accompanied by Vassili Lebed, the chief representative of the Ukrainian nationalists, but actually our agent for thirteen years. Together with Yevhen Konovalets, Lebed spent three years in a Russian camp for military prisoners near Tsaritsyn, from 1915 to 1918. He became Konovalets's deputy and commanded an infantry rifle division fighting against the Red Army in the Ukraine. After Konovalets's forces retreated from the Ukraine to Poland in 1920, Lebed was sent by him to the Ukraine to organize an underground network but was captured. He did not have much choice: either join us or die.

Lebed became a major fighter for us in suppressing banditry in the Ukraine in the 1920s, but his nationalist reputation abroad remained high because Konovalets saw him as the man who could prepare for a takeover from the Soviets by the Ukrainian Nationalist Organization (OUN). From Lebed, whom we allowed to travel to the West in the 1920s and 1930s using illegal channels, we knew that Konovalets had plans to recapture the Ukraine in a future war. Lebed met in Berlin with Colonel Alexander, Admiral Wilhelm Canaris's predecessor as chief of German intelligence in the early 1930s, and learned that Konovalets had twice met with Hitler, who offered to train several of his followers in the Nazi party school in Leipzig.

I posed as a nephew of Lebed assisting him in his work. My wife was transferred to the Foreign Department to act as a courier with the Center. She was to pose as a student from Geneva and meet agents occasionally in Western Europe, for which she was given special courses in espionage tradecraft.

Lebed was unaware that we also ran another agent, who was Konovalets's chief representative in Finland, Kondrat Poluvetko. He lived under a false identity in Helsinki, arranging contacts between the Ukrainian nationalists in exile and their underground in Leningrad. The Ukrainian nationalists hid their archives in the famous Shadrin Library in Leningrad, and even though we knew this we could not find them until after World War II, in 1949.

I was sent to the west via Helsinki, accompanied by Lebed, who immediately returned to Kharkov via Moscow. I was turned over to Poluvetko, who was not told of my real identity. Thus he regularly reported on me to his NKVD case officer, Zoya Vozkresenskaya Rybkina. At one point Poluvetko suggested I be eliminated, but luckily for me the decision was not his to make. My living standard in Finland (and later in Germany) was extremely low. I had no pocket money at all and was constantly hungry. Poluvetko regarded me as the enemy and allowed me only ten Finnish marks a day so I had money for lunch and one coin to be inserted in the gas meter to heat my room. At clandestine meetings between us, for which a schedule had been arranged before I left Moscow, Zoya Rybkina and her husband, our *rezident* — station chief — in Finland, brought me sandwiches and chocolate. Then they checked my pockets to see that I did not carry away any food with me, which would have given away the game. To let the Center know I was well, I wrote a note to my "girlfriend" and then tore it up and threw it in my wastebasket. Poluvetko, unwittingly my accomplice, collected these pieces and handed them over to Zoya. After I had waited two months in Helsinki, couriers from Konovalets arrived.

We took a steamer to Stockholm, where I was given a false Lithuanian passport. When we arrived in Stockholm the waiter in the dining room where we were lined up for our passports to be returned to us was reluctant to give mine back. He said the photo in the passport was not mine. The waiter was right. I had been given the passport of a Ukrainian activist. Poluvetko indignantly intervened and intimidated the waiter, who handed over the passport. After a week in Stockholm we went by boat to Germany, where I had no trouble with the passport. Then we went on to Berlin, in June 1935, where I met and was interviewed by Konovalets in an apartment of the Central Museum of Ethnography provided for him by German intelligence. In September I was sent to the Nazi party school in Leipzig for three months, where I met the elite of the Ukrainian Nationalist Organization, all of whom were interested, naturally, in checking my identity. However, I had no problems with my cover story.

My discussions with Konovalets became serious. He wanted to set up administrative networks to run certain areas of the Ukraine in the near future, when they would be liberated by Ukrainian nationalists allied to the Germans. I was told that they already had at their disposal two brigades, a total of about two thousand men; they would act as a police force in Galicia (in Western Ukraine, then controlled by the Poles) and in Germany.

The Ukrainians tried to involve me in the power struggle between their two main factions, the old generation represented by Konovalets and his deputy, Andrei Melnick, and the young faction headed by Stepan Bandera and Kosterev. My primary task was to convince them that prospects for successful terrorist activities in the Ukraine were nil because the NKVD would immediately crush small pockets of resistance. I recommended that we hold our forces and underground network in reserve, ready to operate once war broke out between Germany and the Soviet Union.

Most disturbing were the terrorist connections of this organization. They had contracted with Croatian nationalists to carry out the assassination of King Alexander of Yugoslavia and Minister of Foreign Affairs Louis Barthou of France. It was a revelation to learn that all these terrorists were financed by the Abwehr, the intelligence and counterespionage organization serving the German high command. It also came as a complete surprise to me that the assassination of the Polish minister General Bronislaw Pieracki, by the Ukrainian terrorist Matsekov, was undertaken contrary to the order of Konovalets and was carried out on the command of Bandera, his rival. Bandera had wanted to seize control of the organization by capitalizing on the natural enmity of Ukrainians against Pieracki, who was responsible for repression of the Ukrainian minority in Poland. Konovalets told me that the Germans and Poles had just signed a treaty of friendship and the Germans for the time being were in no way interested in acts against the Poles. The Germans were so outraged by the assassination that they turned over Bandera and his followers to the Poles, but the assassin, Matsekov, managed to escape.

Matsekov had planned to kill Pieracki with a grenade, but it did not explode so he shot him to death. The crowd ran after him, but he darted in front of a tram that cut off his pursuers. Matsekov managed to slide into the entryway of a building and climb the stairs. He took off his hat and raincoat, discarded his revolver, and exited unnoticed. The Polish Okhrana (security force) ambushed all the safe apartments of the Ukrainian nationalists in Warsaw, but Matsekov did not go to the designated one. Instead, he spent the night with his girlfriend, another Ukrainian terrorist, who arranged his escape through the Carpathian Mountains to Czechoslovakia. There he was given a false Czech passport, with which he traveled to Paris and Le Havre. From France he sailed for Argentina, where he died in 1950.

Despite Bandera's stirring defense of the Ukrainian cause at his trial, he was sentenced to death by hanging. In the end, German pressure on the Polish authorities saved him. His sentence was reduced to a prison term. After the German invasion of Poland, they promptly released him. Then bloody warfare developed between the two Ukrainian factions.

I acted absolutely confident and superior to my colleagues in the Nazi party school because I was representing the head of their underground network in the Ukraine, while they were just emigrants living off German subsidies. I had the right to veto their suggestions because I was carrying out the instructions of my uncle (*vuiko*) and their leader, Lebed. If I didn't like something, I would say "*Vuiko nevelel*" — "My uncle would not allow that."

That was how I rejected the suggestion that I meet Colonel Lahausen from Abwehr headquarters. To be directly involved with German intelligence would have been very risky, as they would have tried to recruit me forcibly as an agent. I repeated my opposition to meeting anyone from Abwehr when my colleagues secured a snapshot of me while I was walking in the street with Konovalets. A street photographer approached, took a picture, and handed the film to Konovalets, who paid him two marks. It was a brazen act. They were determined to get a picture of me for their files so they could identify and track me down if it later became necessary. I protested strongly to Konovalets right there on the street that it would be a mistake to reveal my real photo to the Germans, which is what I assumed he had in mind. Konovalets tried to calm me and said there was nothing wrong with having our picture taken together in the streets of Berlin by an ordinary photographer who was just earning his living. I later learned I was right. In the 1940s SMERSH (Soviet military counterintelligence) captured two guerrilla fighters in Western Ukraine, one of whom had this photo of me on him. When asked why he was carrying it, he replied: "I have no idea why, but the order is if we find this man to liquidate him."

I gained Konovalets's trust by revealing a confidence to him. Kosterev and other young Ukrainian nationalist students at the Nazi school said Konovalets was too old to run the organization and should be used only as a figurehead. When they asked my opinion I indignantly replied: "Who are you to suggest such an idea? I knew nothing about you before coming here. Our organization not only has full trust in Konovalets, but regularly receives adequate support from him. You have been doing nothing but studying in the Nazi school for the past year." When I repeated this to Konovalets his face turned white, and it was not by accident that Kosterev was later eliminated.

The Center had decided that once I arrived in Germany I would be completely on my own and would have no contact with our rezidentura or illegals. After my stay at the Nazi party school in Leipzig I returned to Berlin, and Konovalets took me under his wing. I lived in a small rented room near the ethnographical museum and ate lunch in the museum cafeteria. Konovalets frequently visited me, and we walked around the city. Once he took me to a performance of the Berlin opera, but life was dour. The Ukrainian community was very poor and there were no luxuries. It had become customary to bring your own lumps of sugar if you were invited for tea. The Ukrainians whom I met were either sons of priests of the Uniate church or low-level city bureaucrats, who ludicrously believed they could finance the organization with income from a shoe polish factory run by their relatives in Poland. They did not understand that only all-out war by Germany against Poland and the Soviet Union could help their cause. We were all waiting for war to begin.

Konovalets grew to like me and suggested that I accompany him on an inspection tour of his Ukrainian emigrant supporters in Paris and Vienna in early 1936. In Paris we stayed in a good hotel since Konovalets had money from the Germans and was playing his role as the leader of a powerful organization. I was overwhelmed by Paris and remain under its spell to this day. This was a city of history, and it occurred to me that the French Revolution lasted for a hundred years, until the Paris Commune of 1871. What the French went through in the nineteenth century, we Russians are enduring in the twentieth. There was a general strike in Paris while I was there, and Konovalets had to take me to Versailles to lunch because all the restaurants were closed in Paris and the subway was not operating. I remember we took an expensive taxi.

The Center knew that Konovalets and I were to spend three weeks in Paris. They used the opportunity to arrange a rendezvous with my courier. My instructions from Moscow included a possible meeting in Paris, and a rendezvous in Vienna. I was to appear twice a week from 5:00 P.M. to 6:00 P.M. at the corner of Place de Clichy and Boulevard de Clichy. My instructions were that the courier would be someone known to me, but true to the rules of tradecraft I was not given the name; the courier could have been one of any number of people. The first time I went to the meeting place I spotted my wife dressed in fashionable clothes and sipping coffee in a sidewalk café. I was overcome with conflicting emotions. I forced myself to check on possible surveillance before approaching her. I quickly realized that the meeting site had been badly chosen. There was no way to rule out surveillance in the passing crowd.

My experience as a counterintelligence officer in Kharkov was that in almost all cases that were blown it was the fault of badly chosen meeting arrangements. I controlled myself and in bad German asked for permission to join her at the table. We were both very tense. I sat down, and she said she assumed everything was all right with me. "Although you've lost some weight you look fine." She added with a smile, "You are well shaven." In Russia I would often shave only once every two days.

The café was too open for a meeting, so we quickly left. As we walked toward the boulevard we noticed two gendarmes moving toward us. Instinctively, we crossed the street to avoid them, quite foolish in retrospect.

Emma's hotel, a few blocks away, was cheap and fitting for a student on vacation in Paris. Although I was delighted to be with my wife after a separation of six months, I was also deeply fearful of her being compromised through meeting me. We embraced, and then I told her that she should report my demand to the Center that in no way should she be involved with me. I was not permanently settled in the West, and I was certain that all my contacts were being studied and analyzed both by Ukrainian nationalist security and by the Germans. If the Germans, or even French counterintelligence, traced her to me they would seize her and subject her to the most ruthless interrogation. I ordered her to return immediately to Switzerland and then home. For me to feel safe and not worry about her, it was necessary to reject her. She assured me she would leave Paris and return to Bern as quickly as possible. I briefed her on the situation in the Ukrainian émigré community and its strong German support. She found interesting the conflicts emerging within the Ukrainian organization. I told her that Konovalets and I planned a trip to Vienna and strongly urged that she not appear at the assigned courier meeting place near the Schönbrunn Palace.

One day Konovalets invited me to visit the grave of Petlura, the Ukrainian nationalist leader, who was defeated by the Red Army and fled to Paris, where he died in 1926. Konovalets revered Petlura, "our leader and our favorite teacher. We will preserve his memory." I was pleased to accompany him, but what to do about flowers? When you go to a cemetery you have to lay flowers on the grave, but I did not have any pocket money. Konovalets was very senior and to remind him would have been tactless and improper. It should have been he and not I who was offering the flowers. What should I do? I was thinking, thinking all the way there.

We walked across the cemetery and stood before Petlura's small gravestone. Konovalets crossed himself and so did I. We stood silently, and then I pulled out my handkerchief and wrapped a handful of dirt from the grave site in it. "What are you doing?" asked Konovalets. I explained that I wanted to take some dirt from Petlura's tomb back to the Ukraine and plant a tree in his memory. We would sprinkle this earth around the tree. Konovalets was thrilled. He hugged and kissed me, and praised me for thinking of this idea. Our friendship and his trust in me were strengthened.

Konovalets revealed to me in Paris that they suspected one of his assistants, Gribevsky, of cooperating with Czechoslovakian counterintelligence and asked me to meet and assess him. The Czechs, after the assassination of General Pieracki in Warsaw by the Ukrainians, managed to round up in one day all the safe houses of the Ukrainian organization in Prague and seize many of the files, which were guarded by Gribevsky. Then Konovalets told me a story I already knew. My close friend and colleague Ivan Kaminsky, who served in Germany two years before me as an illegal, had tried to recruit Gribevsky as an informer, supposedly for the Slovakian police but actually for us. Gribevsky on his part planned to seize Kaminsky at the rendezvous, but Kaminsky spotted the surveillance and evaded the trap by jumping on a tram. Konovalets accurately suspected that Kaminsky was not a Slovak agent but a Bolshevik agent. I objected to meeting Gribevsky, saying he might be controlled by the Bolsheviks (after all, he might have deliberately failed to capture Kaminsky) and could abort my mission by revealing me to them.

After we arrived in Vienna I went to the rendezvous site and found Major Pyotr Zubov waiting for me. He was a master craftsman in espionage, and I was a willing journeyman who learned from his tutelage. I brought him up to date on Konovalets's activities and told him that we were going to the opera on the following evening. Pyotr managed to buy a ticket just behind us so he could overhear my conversation with Konovalets. When we were leaving the opera house, I deliberately tripped over him in a foolish act of bravado and apologized for bumping him.

After Vienna I returned to Berlin, and for several months we were engaged in useless talks about the possible deployment of our underground forces in the Ukraine when war broke out. I also twice traveled to Paris from Germany during this period, where I met with leaders of the Ukrainian government-in-exile. Konovalets warned me about them. He did not take them seriously; he said the rules of action and life would be dictated by his military organization, not by these café politicians in Paris.

By that time my uncle Lebed, our agent, sent instructions through Finland recalling me to the Ukraine, suggesting that I take over the job of radio operator on board a Soviet steamer that frequently visited foreign ports. Thus I would be a regular courier from the Ukraine to the nationalist organization abroad. Konovalets liked this idea and agreed for me to return to the Soviet Union.

I made my way back to Finland with false papers, escorted by Roman Sushko, a leader of the Ukrainian military organization, to the Soviet-Finnish border. Konovalets wanted to make sure that I returned safely. Sushko accompanied me to what appeared to be a safe border crossing point and left me in the forest. As I made my way to the frontier I was intercepted by a Finnish border patrol, arrested, and sent back to jail in Helsinki. I was interrogated there for a month. I said that I was a Ukrainian nationalist trying to return to the Soviet Union under the orders of my organization.

Throughout the entire month the atmosphere in the Center was tense because Zoya Rybkina had reported from Helsinki that I was on my way back. When I failed to appear, Zubov and Shpigelglas went to the frontier to search for clues to my whereabouts.

Emma was distraught over my fate and lost thirty pounds. Everybody suspected that I had been eliminated by Sushko. Finally, after three weeks, Poluvetko, the official Ukrainian representative in Helsinki, was contacted by the Finnish police and Abwehr officers with inquiries about a certain Ukrainian who was trying to enter the Soviet Union. The Abwehr and Finnish intelligence had an agreement to monitor the Soviet border and jointly study whoever tried to cross it into the Soviet Union. I was handed over to Poluvetko, who then accompanied me to Tallinn. There I was given another Lithuanian false passport and obtained a tourist visa in the Soviet consulate office for a short visit to Leningrad. Now I crossed the border without incident; my passport was stamped by the frontier guard, and I escaped from the Intourist guide waiting for me in Leningrad, causing, I am sure, quite a commotion in the local Intourist office. The militia was put on the alert to find the Lithuanian tourist who disappeared in Leningrad.

My successful journey to Western Europe changed my status in the intelligence community. My mission was reported to Stalin and to Kossior, then the general secretary of the Ukrainian Communist party, and to Grigori Ivanovich Petrovsky, chairman of the Supreme Soviet of the Ukraine. I was summoned to Slutsky's office, where I related the details of my trip to two people whom I had not met before: Yakov Serebryansky, director of the Administration for Special Tasks,[6] and Vassiliev, a junior case officer in Stalin's secretariat in the Central Committee.

Later, I was awarded the Order of the Red Banner and received it from President M. I. Kalinin. Also present to receive a medal was Vassili Zarubin, who had returned from his illegal journey to Western Europe almost simultaneously with me. It was our first meeting, but not the last. Our families became closely tied to each other for the rest of our lives, although Zarubin was much older than I.

At a cocktail party in honor of Zarubin and me at Slutsky's apartment, I was obliged, for the second time in my life, to drink a glass of vodka. The first time was when I was seventeen years old, in Odessa, and I had had a terrible reaction — headache and nausea. Although I was healthy, doctors diagnosed a rejection by my system of alcohol stronger than twenty percent. Slutsky and Shpigelglas ordered me to drink, and the next day I was incapacitated.

Throughout 1937 and into 1938 I traveled to the West as a courier on a cargo ship under the cover of a radio operator. I was appalled at a meeting with Konovalets when he told me that his organization reported to the Germans that the Red Army commanders in the Ukraine (who were subsequently executed by Stalin) sympathized with the Ukrainian cause. Konovalets's people concocted these stories to impress the Germans and extract more money from them. Later I read in the Ukrainian émigré press that the loyalty of Ivan Dubovoy, Ivan Fedko, and other Red Army commanders was divided between the Soviets and the Ukrainian nationalists. Konovalets made up his mind to tell me about the disinformation because he knew that as an organizer of the Ukrainian underground I would know the truth.

When I reported this to Shpigelglas in Moscow in 1937, he sug-

6. Its nickname in the West is Wet Affairs, a shortened translation of Mokre Dela Osobaya Grup.

gested that it was not impossible that there had been contacts by Dubovoy and others with the Ukrainian nationalists and Germans. I think that Shpigelglas just wanted to protect me against reporting information that might displease the leadership, who had already decided the fate of these commanders.[7]

In November 1937, after the celebrations of the October Revolution, I was summoned to the office of Nikolai Ivanovich Yezhov, head of the NKVD, accompanied by Slutsky. It was my first meeting with Yezhov, and I was shocked by his unimpressive appearance. He asked incompetent questions about elementary matters of intelligence tradecraft. He didn't know basic techniques of working with a source of information. Moreover, he did not seem to care about splits in the Ukrainian émigré organization. Yezhov was both people's commissar of internal affairs and a secretary of the Central Committee. I sincerely believed I was incapable of understanding the intellectual qualities that had placed him in such high positions. Although a tested professional, I remained naive about what to expect from the leadership, because the ones I had met, Kossior and Petrovsky, Communist party leaders of the Ukraine, were intelligent and sophisticated.

Yezhov listened to my report about the schedule of future meetings with the Ukrainian leadership and then abruptly suggested that I accompany him to the Central Committee. I was surprised when our car entered the Kremlin through the highly restricted Borovitsky gate and Yezhov announced that Comrade Stalin would receive us personally. This was my first meeting with Stalin. I was thirty years old and still could not control my emotions. I was overwhelmed and could not believe that the leader of the country would meet with a rank-and-file case officer. When Stalin shook my hand I could not collect myself to report to him succinctly. Stalin smiled and said: "Young man, don't be so excited. Report the essential facts. We have only twenty minutes."

"Comrade Stalin," I replied, "for a rank-and-file party member to meet with you is a great event in life. I understand I am summoned here for business. In a minute I will control my emotions and report the essential facts to you and Comrade Yezhov."

Stalin nodded and asked me about the relationships between the political figures in the Ukrainian émigré movement. I briefly described the fruitless discussions among Ukrainian nationalist politicians over who would play what role in a future government. Konovalets, however,

7. See Chapter Five for a discussion of the army purges.

was a real threat because he was preparing for war against us, backed by the Germans. His weak point was the constant pressure on him and his organization from the Poles, who wanted to eliminate the Ukrainian national movement in western Galicia.

"What are your suggestions?" asked Stalin.

Yezhov remained silent; so did I. I said I was not prepared to answer.

"Then in a week," said Stalin, "you should prepare your suggestions."

The audience ended. We shook hands and departed.

On our return to Lubyanka, Yezhov instructed me to work quickly with Shpigelglas to prepare a proposal. The following day in Yezhov's office, Slutsky and I presented a plan for intensive penetration into the Ukrainian organization, especially in Germany. We suggested that three candidates from the Ukrainian NKVD be placed in the Nazi party school for further training. We also felt it necessary to send with them one real Ukrainian nationalist with limited intellectual potential, just to be on the safe side. Yezhov did not comment or ask any questions, but told us that Comrade Stalin had given his consent for us to consult Comrades Kossior and Petrovsky, who might have their own ideas. I should get on a train to Kiev and meet with them the next day, then immediately return to Moscow.

In Kossior's office in Kiev, he and Petrovsky displayed interest in this deception game, but their main concern was with the imminent proclamation of the independent Carpathian-Ukrainian Republic. Back in Moscow a week passed, and then at 11:00 P.M. Yezhov brought me to Stalin's office again. This time I was not surprised to find Petrovsky there. In five minutes I summarized the plan for operational activities against the Ukrainian nationalist movement, stressing that the primary goal was to penetrate the Abwehr through Ukrainian channels, since it was the nationalists' main source of support.

Stalin asked Petrovsky to comment. Petrovsky solemnly announced that the Ukrainian socialist state had, in absentia, condemned Konovalets to death for grave crimes against the Ukrainian proletariat when he personally ordered and supervised the hangings of revolutionary workers of the Kiev arsenal in January 1918. Konovalets, said Petrovsky, was at war against Soviet Russia and the Ukraine.

Stalin interrupted him and said: "This is not just an act of revenge, although Konovalets is the agent of German fascism. Our goal is to behead the movement of Ukrainian fascism on the eve of the war and force these gangsters to annihilate each other in a struggle for power."

Then Stalin asked me: "What are the personal tastes of Konovalets?" He said, "Try to exploit them."

"Konovalets is overly fond of chocolate candies," I replied, noting that wherever we went Konovalets would not fail to purchase a box of chocolates.

Stalin suggested I think about that. Throughout the whole audience Yezhov remained silent. When we parted, Stalin asked me whether I understood correctly the political importance of the mission entrusted to me.

"Yes," I replied, and I assured him that I would not spare my life in fulfilling this assignment.

"I wish you success," said Stalin, and he shook my hand. I had been ordered to kill Konovalets.

After my meeting with Stalin, Abram Slutsky and Sergei Shpigelglas prepared a series of plans for assassinating Konovalets. The first proposal was for me to shoot him, but Konovalets was always accompanied by his aide, Jaroslav Baranovsky, code-named Mr. Engineer. It seemed impossible to find a way for me to be alone with Konovalets. Another plan was to present him with a gift that would be a disguised bomb. That idea seemed to hold the most promise because, if the bomb's timing device worked properly, there was a chance for me to escape.

The director of the technical bureau, Mosiev Paulkin, was ordered to create a bomb disguised as a box of chocolates. On the outside cover there was to be a traditional Ukrainian decoration. The problem was that I had to press a hidden switch to activate the timing device. I did not like this idea, because the attractive box would draw attention or Konovalets might hand it to Baranovsky to hold.

Using my cover as a radio operator aboard the cargo ship *Shilka,* I met Konovalets in Antwerp, Rotterdam, and Le Havre, where he traveled under a false Lithuanian passport posing as Mr. Novack. The game that had now lasted for more than two years was about to end. The prospect of war was regarded to be inevitable by the spring of 1938, and we knew he would fight for the Germans.

On my way to Antwerp and Rotterdam I inspected our illegal network in Norway operating against German and Japanese ships that supplied arms and raw materials to the Franco regime in Spain. The head of this network, Ernest Wollweber, known to me at that time as Anthony, led a group of Polish miners who were trained in the use of explosives. Because there was no work in Poland, they had emigrated to France and Belgium, where we recruited them for sabotage operations in case of war. The order I brought was to run a test of these miners. Wollweber did not speak Polish, but my Western Ukrainian languages were similar enough to Polish for me to direct the test. When we stopped over in the Norwegian port of Bergen, I met with a team of five Polish agents. On orders from the Center, the Polish cargo ship *Stefan Batory*, loaded with strategic materials for Spain, sank in the North Sea when a fire broke out in its hold. A bomb placed by our team had done the damage.

Wollweber impressed me. He was a German Communist who had been in the German navy and led an uprising in 1918. He had been condemned to death by a military tribunal but managed to escape to Scandinavia. After our encounter he was arrested by the Swedes, and the Germans demanded his extradition; but before he could be handed over to the Germans, the Soviet government granted him Soviet citizenship. He was transferred to Moscow on the eve of the war, in time to recruit German prisoners of war for NKVD operations.

After the war he was rewarded with the post of minister of state security in the German Democratic Republic. He was ousted by Ulbricht when he ran afoul of Khrushchev in 1958.[8] Wollweber had told Ivan Serov, then the head of the KGB, of disagreements in the East German leadership, claiming that this was a manifestation of pro-Western sentiments contrary to the Communist party line. Serov reported the conversation to Khrushchev. At a dinner accompanied by heavy drinking, Khrushchev asked Ulbricht, "Why should you have a minister of security who reports to us on ideological divergences in your party? This is in the tradition of Beria and Merkulov,[9] whom Wollweber frequently visited in the 1940s when he came to Moscow." Ulbricht got the message and immediately fired Wollweber for antiparty behavior. He died in 1961 or 1962.

Finally, the bomb in the candy box was prepared with a timing device that did not depend on a hidden switch. The bomb was to explode thirty minutes after the position of the box was changed from

8. Walter Ulbricht ruled East Germany as first secretary of the Socialist Unity (Communist) party (1953–1971) and chairman of the Council of State (1960–1973). Nikita S. Khrushchev was first secretary of the Communist party from 1953 to 1964 and Soviet premier from 1958 to 1964.

9. Lavrenti Pavlovich Beria and Vsevolod Nikolayevich Merkulov followed Yezhov as head of the Soviet security service.

vertical to horizontal. I had to keep the box in an upright position in the inner pocket of my jacket. I was to present the gift to Konovalets and leave before it exploded.

Shpigelglas brought me to Yezhov and then saw me off. He told me, "You are supposed to act as a man if the attempt fails." He meant that I was to use the Walther automatic pistol he supplied me, rather than be seized by the police or the Ukrainian nationalists. This was an order to die with dignity, but Shpigelglas spent more than eight hours discussing various plans for my escape. He gave me a railway ticket valid for two months for a trip to any city in Western Europe during May and June 1938. He supplied me with a false Czechoslovakian passport and $3,000, which was a great deal of money in those days. Shpigelglas told me to change my appearance by buying a hat or a raincoat in the nearest store as soon as I began my escape.

Before my ship left Murmansk I read in *Pravda* that Slutsky had died from a heart attack. I regretted his untimely loss. I held him in high regard as a skilled professional intelligence officer, and he had been attentive to Emma and me. It was Slutsky who had stolen the design for ball bearings from Sweden. The acquisition of the designs was a coup for our industry, and Slutsky was awarded the Order of the Red Banner. He and Aleksandr Nikolsky (later known as Orlov), chief of the division for foreign economic intelligence, in 1930 or 1931 met with a Swedish match monopolist, Ivar Kreuger, and threatened to flood the Western market with cheap Soviet matches unless he paid the Soviet government industrial blackmail of $300,000. Orlov got the money.[10]

I had carefully studied escape routes in all the cities in which I might meet Konovalets and had worked out a detailed plan for each. The final trip to meet Konovalets began with logistical problems. After I called him from Norway, Konovalets suggested we meet in Kiel, Germany, or that I fly to Italy using a German plane that he would send for me. I said that I was short of time. Although the captain of the ship was part of the Ukrainian organization, I said I could not leave the ship for more than five hours in the course of this trip. We arranged to meet in Rotterdam at the Atlanta restaurant, not far from the central post office, only a ten-minute walk from the railway station. Before I left the ship in Rotterdam I told the captain, who was instructed to follow my orders,

10. Kreuger's industrial empire collapsed from blatant bond forgeries and bookkeeping dishonesty, and he shot himself through the heart in 1932. His worldwide monopoly of match production did not include Russia. See Duncan Norton-Taylor, *For Some, the Dream Came True* (Secaucus, N.J.: Lyle Stuart, 1981).

that if I did not return to the ship by 4:00 P.M. he should depart without me. The technician who designed the bomb, Aleksandr Timashkov, had accompanied me on the voyage; he loaded the bomb ten minutes before I left the ship and remained on board. (Later he became the director of the division for the production of special explosive devices and prepared the magnetic bomb that killed Gauleiter Wilhelm Kuba in Byelorussia in 1943. He also served as an adviser to the Greek guerrillas in the civil war after World War II.)

The weather was warm and sunny after rain in the morning. At ten minutes to twelve on May 23, 1938, I arrived in the side street near the Atlanta restaurant and noticed that Konovalets was sitting at a table near the window, waiting for me. This time he was alone. I joined him at the table, and after a brief chat we agreed to meet again at 5:00 P.M. in downtown Rotterdam. I presented him the gift of chocolates and told him I had to return to the ship. I laid the box near him on the table in a horizontal position. We shook hands and I left, carefully controlling my desire to run.

I remember how I turned to the right when I left the restaurant and walked along a side street lined with shops. I entered one that sold menswear and purchased a hat and a light raincoat. When I left the shop I heard a bang that sounded like the blowout of a tire. People were running toward the restaurant. I hurried to the railway station and boarded the first train to Paris.

I was supposed to be met at a subway station in Paris the next morning by a man who would be known to me. So that railway employees would not remember me, I left the train at a stop an hour out of Rotterdam and ordered lunch in a restaurant near the Belgian border, but I was unable to eat because of a terrible headache. I crossed the border by taxi, and the border guards paid no attention to my Czech passport. The taxi took me to Brussels, where I had just missed a train to Paris, but another one left shortly, and I arrived in Paris late at night without incident. In Paris I was cheated at the railway exchange office when I changed $100 for French francs. I decided not to register in any hotel because the Dutch stamps in my passport from when I crossed the border might be useful to the police. The counterintelligence service might check all those who entered France from Holland.

I spent the night walking the boulevards that circle the center of Paris. I went to a movie to kill time. Early in the morning, after hours of walking, I found a barbershop for a shave and a shampoo. Then I hurried to the subway station for my rendezvous at 10:00 A.M. When I emerged on the platform I noticed Ivan Agayants, who was under cover as the third secretary of the Soviet Embassy in Paris. He was leaving the platform when he suddenly noticed me and doubled back. He signaled me to follow him. We took a taxi to the Bois de Boulogne, where we had breakfast and I handed him my revolver and a small note that was supposed to be cabled to Moscow. It read: "The gift was presented. The parcel is now in Paris and the tire of the car by which I traveled had a blowout while I was shopping." Agayants, who had no idea of my assignment, accompanied me to a safe house in the suburbs of Paris, where I stayed for two days.

There was nothing in the papers about an incident in Rotterdam; however, the émigré Russian newspapers reported that the fate of Yezhov was clear: he was doomed to be purged. I laughed to myself, thinking how stupid these articles were. Only two months earlier he had wished me success on my mission, and I myself had observed that Comrade Stalin had full confidence in him.[11]

From Paris I traveled to Barcelona by car and train, using forged Polish documents. There the newspapers carried reports about an obscure incident in Rotterdam in which the Ukrainian nationalist leader Konovalets, while traveling under a false identity to meet a trusted agent, was blown up in the street. The newspaper accounts speculated on three possibilities: the Bolsheviks had killed Konovalets, a rival Ukrainian group had eliminated him, or he had been assassinated by the Poles in retaliation for the murder of General Pieracki.

By luck, Baranovsky was traveling from Germany to meet Konovalets and arrived in Rotterdam one hour after the blast. He was arrested by the Dutch police, who suspected him of the crime. When he was taken to the hospital and shown the body, he cried, "My führer," which together with his railroad ticket, convinced the police he was innocent.[12]

On the day after the fatal explosion, the Dutch police, accompanied by Baranovsky, inspected the crew members of all Russian ships in the port, looking for the man in a photo they had. It was the picture of me taken on the street in Berlin. Baranovsky knew that Konovalets was sup-

11. The story of Yezhov's fate is told in Chapter Three.

12. After Konovalets's death, the Ukrainian Nationalist Organization split into two sections, one headed by Andrei Melnick (OUN-M) and one by Stepan Bandera (OUN-B). Baranovsky was shot to death by Bandera men in Zhitomir in 1943, according to P. A. Sudoplatov.

posed to meet a courier who used to appear in Western Europe under the cover of a Soviet ship's radio operator, but he was not sure it was me. The Dutch police knew there had been a telephone call to Konovalets from Norway and naturally suspected it was from his agent, but nobody was sure with whom Konovalets had had his last meeting. When the bomb exploded in the street he was alone. His identity remained unknown to the police until late that night, and my ship, the *Shilka,* had already departed.

I remained in Spain for three weeks acting as a Polish volunteer in the foreign guerrilla warfare group run by the NKVD, attached to the Republican Army.

SPAIN: CRUCIBLE FOR REVOLUTION AND PURGES

t was during my stay in Barcelona that I first met Ramon Mercader del Rio, a young lieutenant who had just returned from a guerrilla mission behind Franco's line. Mercader was a charming young man, twenty years old. I learned that his elder brother had been killed in battle when he tied grenades to his body and threw himself under a German tank advancing on the Republicans. His mother, Caridad, also had a high reputation in the guerrilla task force, because she was wounded during an air raid and displayed courage in combat operations. I had no idea then what the future held for Mercader, that he would become Trotsky's assassin and that I would direct the operation.

From 1936 to 1939 there were two life-and-death struggles in Spain, both of them civil wars. One pitted nationalist forces led by Francisco Franco, aided by Hitler, against the Spanish Republicans, aided by Communists. The other was a separate war among Communists themselves. Stalin in the Soviet Union and Trotsky in exile each hoped to be the savior and the sponsor of the Republicans and thereby become the vanguard for the world Communist revolution. We sent our young inexperienced intelligence operatives as well as our experienced instructors. Spain proved to be a kindergarten for our future intelligence operations. Our subsequent intelligence initiatives all stemmed from contacts that we made and lessons that we learned in Spain. The Spanish Republicans lost, but Stalin's men and women won. When the Spanish Civil War ended, there was no room left in the world for Trotsky.

In Barcelona I encountered Leonid Aleksandrovich Eitingon, whom I had first met five years earlier when he headed the section for illegal operations in the Foreign Department. In Spain, Eitingon was a major of state security directing guerrilla operations behind Franco's lines under the pseudonym General Kotov. At the Center he was known by the names Tom and Pierre. On the instructions of the Center, Eitingon was responsible for arranging my return to Moscow. He accompanied me to Bordeaux and put me on board a Soviet ship. I still remember his appearance, that of an ordinary French street peddler without a necktie, wearing his cap no matter how hot it was.

According to his NKVD personnel file, Naum Isakovich Eitingon was born on December 1, 1899, in the city of Sklov in the Mogilov district of Byelorussia, not far from Gomel, the big Jewish center where Emma was from. In the Lubyanka and among friends we always called him Leonid Aleksandrovich, because in the 1920s Jewish CHEKA officers adopted Russian names so as not to attract attention to their Jewish origins while working with Russian informers and officers.

His branch of the Eitingon family was poor, but Eitingon told me that they had prosperous relatives in Europe. To my knowledge, he had two sisters, one of whom, Sonia, a well-known cardiologist, I knew personally, and a brother, Isaak, a respected professor of chemistry who made major contributions to explosives research during the war.

Eitingon joined the Socialist Revolutionary party in 1917.[1] Then, in 1918, at age nineteen, he joined the Red Army and was transferred to the CHEKA. In 1919 he was appointed deputy chief of the CHEKA for the Gomel area. He abandoned the Socialist Revolutionary party and joined

---

1. The Socialist Revolutionary party was established in 1902, advocating a federal structure for the Russian state, self-determination for non-Russian peoples, and socialization of the land. It had an autonomous "fighting organization" whose tactics included assassination of leading government personalities. A section of the party, the Left Socialist Revolutionaries, supported the Bolshevik seizure of power in 1917 and took part in the Bolshevik government until the Brest-Litovsk treaty in 1918, which removed Russia from World War I. The Socialist Revolutionaries formed the majority of the Constituent Assembly, which was forcibly dissolved by the Bolsheviks after one session in 1918. The Civil War followed, and the party was suppressed in 1922.

the Bolsheviks in 1920. Eitingon's career took off after he helped crush a rising of White Army officers against the Bolsheviks in Gomel when they seized the city briefly in 1920.

Dzerzhinsky took note of him and sent him to Bashkiria, near Tatarstan, as head of the CHEKA, to enforce discipline in the area. There he was slashed in the leg by a saber during a battle with local forces, and for years he often complained to me about his leg. In 1921 Eitingon was transferred to Moscow for training in the military academy, where he studied strategy and tactics together with future marshals of the Soviet Union. I remember him showing me his photograph with V. I. Chuikov, later Marshal Chuikov, the defender of Stalingrad.

After military training he was assigned to the Foreign Department of the OGPU. His distant European relatives declined his request to provide him recommendations, papers, and money for travel and cover for operational work in Western Europe. Instead, he was sent to China, where he served as the OGPU rezident, first in Shanghai, where he worked with the GRU network that included Richard Sorge,[2] and then in Harbin. Eitingon obtained the release of Soviet military advisers who had been seized by a Chinese warlord in Manchuria. He also successfully crushed an attempt by Chiang Kai-shek's agents to seize the Soviet consulate office in Shanghai. After that he was recalled to Moscow.

For a short time in 1930 he became deputy director of the Administration for Special Tasks under Yakov Serebryansky. The Administration for Special Tasks was established in 1926 by Vyacheslav Menzhinsky, Dzerzhinsky's successor, as a parallel intelligence service to prepare sabotage operations in Western Europe and Japan in case of war. In this capacity Eitingon placed agents in California, moving them there from Western Europe. His personal relations with Serebryansky were poor, and in 1932 he was shifted to chief of section, coordinating the operation of illegals in the Foreign Department under Artur Artuzov and later Abram Slutsky. He was also in charge of supervising the production of forged passports for illegal operations abroad.

When we first met in Moscow in 1933, I was the new inspector of the personnel department. We were not close back then, as his position was much senior. For me, he was an important official, respected for his

2. After spending the early 1930s running an espionage network in China, Richard Sorge was sent to Tokyo in 1933. There, operating as a Nazi journalist, he headed the Soviet general staff's military intelligence (GRU) in the Far East until he was arrested a few weeks before Pearl Harbor. Sorge is best known for sending Stalin the date of the German invasion of Russia in time for Stalin to have acted.

career achievements and mastery of tradecraft. He headed the most sensitive section for illegal operations. In those years illegal operations were of the highest priority, because we had few official diplomatic-based rezidenturas to operate from abroad and we wanted to establish organizations with agents whose trails would not lead to the Soviet Embassy if they were caught.

Eitingon's intelligence shone from his handsome face and gray-green eyes. He had a penetrating look and a heavy head of black hair. A scar on his chin from a car accident (most people thought it was a battle scar) gave him an air of bravado. Eitingon was a charmer who recited Pushkin by heart to illustrate both the folly and heroism of everyday life. He never drank much — one glass of cognac would last him for the evening. His hobby was hunting, but he did not shoot animals; he only liked to spot and track them. What struck me immediately was that he had none of the pretensions of a high-ranking bureaucrat. His favorite weapons were humor and ridicule.

I remember bringing him the file of a midlevel chekist from a province near the Polish border to add to his section. There was a note in the file from the Ukrainian deputy director of the GPU, fully endorsing the candidate for a job near his home. Eitingon didn't want him stationed in Poland too near the border, where he might be recognized. Eitingon commented, "If this guy with no experience gets caught during a routine check, whose head will roll? If I follow these recommendations there should be a special basket for collecting heads." I thought that the matter was closed, that he didn't want to be bothered further with the fellow's fate, but suddenly Eitingon phoned Abram Minsker, who was in charge of our operations in the Far East, and suggested he take the young officer.

Our next operational meeting occurred in Spain, where he smuggled me into France in 1938 after the elimination of Konovalets. Eitingon had been sent to Spain in 1936 as deputy rezident in charge of guerrilla operations, including sabotage against railways and airfields. When Nikolsky, alias Aleksandr Orlov, who was the rezident there, disappeared in July 1938 Eitingon took over as rezident. I appreciated the skill with which he adapted to local conditions. His lack of interest in money was amazing. He never had any savings, and all the furniture in his flat was state owned. His salary went to his wives and children, whom he adored.

Eitingon's first wife had died after the birth of their son Vladimir. Vladimir became an officer in the security service, but was fired twice, in 1951 and in 1953, because of his Jewish origin. He was chief of the counterintelligence section dealing with America and Great Britain in Leningrad. He became a full professor and chairman of the economics department at Voronezh University.

In Harbin, China, Eitingon fell in love with the wife of Vassili Zarubin, Olga Naumova, whom he met in the rezidentura and later married. Zarubin was a case officer under Eitingon at that time. In the 1930s, without divorcing his second wife, Eitingon took with him to Spain as his wife an officer from the third section, responsible for visas. She was Aleksandra Kochergina, an attractive brunette of Russian origin. Eitingon never bothered to register his second and third marriages and lived alternately in two households. Svetlana, his daughter from his second marriage, followed the career of her aunt Sonia and became a cardiologist.

His children adored him despite his relations with their mothers. Emma regarded him highly as a professional but was critical of his personal lifestyle. She was close friends with Aleksandra (Shura), who had accompanied him to Spain. Eitingon sensed Emma's disapproval and always appeared in our apartment with a bouquet of flowers to win her favor.

After the Spanish Civil War was lost to the fascists in 1939, Eitingon fled to France, where he stayed for a couple of months reorganizing what was left of his network and running Guy Burgess, code name Mädchen, a member of the Cambridge ring. Burgess was then shifted to the control of Anatoli Gorsky in England.[3] In 1938 the Center was in a frenzy

---

3. The Cambridge ring was recruited by Soviet intelligence among students at Cambridge University in the 1930s. Its members were Harold Adrian Russell (Kim) Philby, Donald Maclean, Guy Burgess, Anthony Blunt, and John Cairncross. Eitingon, say John Costello and Oleg Tsarev in *Deadly Illusions* (New York: Crown, 1993), was Moscow Center's link with Burgess from August 1938 until March 1939, meeting him periodically in Paris (p. 237).

Recently available KGB files reveal that Aleksandr Orlov headed the London rezidentura from summer 1934 to fall 1935. Orlov traveled to England on a false American passport. During his time in England, Orlov was in charge of the recruitment of the Cambridge ring. Costello and Tsarev, in their effort to enhance Orlov's role, credit him with recruiting Philby, Burgess, and Maclean, but Sudoplatov notes that the Cambridge ring was already in its early stages thanks to the work of Arnold Deutsch, who recruited Philby. Orlov had to return to Moscow prematurely because his cover was broken during a chance meeting.

The Cambridge five worked their way into posts in British intelligence, the Foreign Office, and other government agencies and spied for the Soviet Union until the early 1950s. Burgess and Maclean escaped to Moscow in 1951 when they learned they

because the former rezident in Spain, Aleksandr Orlov, was missing. The NKVD soon learned he was on the run because he feared he was to be purged. Eitingon suggested that despite the defection of Orlov, contacts with the Cambridge group should be continued, because Orlov, living underground in the United States, would not reveal his involvement with them but rather would do everything he could to avoid coming to the attention of American authorities. Eitingon argued that since Orlov had used a forged American passport in England he would avoid all mention of this episode. Revealing the use of forged documents would have made Orlov liable to prosecution by American authorities or led to his deportation. Eitingon knew this because of his own use of forged American documents in the early 1930s.

A year after the death of Aleksandra Kochergina in 1941, Eitingon was dispatched to Turkey, where he arranged to be accompanied by a champion parachutist, Muza Malinovskaya, with whom he had a son and a daughter. Eitingon stayed in Turkey for about eight months in 1942 under the name Leonid Naumov — his second wife's maiden name — planning the assassination of Franz von Papen, then German ambassador to Turkey, who was rumored to succeed Hitler if a separate peace accord was signed by Britain and the United States with Germany. The assassination attempt failed when the Bulgarian assassin lost his nerve and exploded the bomb prematurely, killing himself. Von Papen suffered only slight injuries.

In later years, Emma and Leonid proved to be more cynical than I was. Leonid said that the party was no longer an association of people devoted to socialist ideas and justice but had become the machinery for ruling the country. His jokes at the expense of the leadership at first upset me. Later I got used to them, and I came to realize how right Eitingon was in his view that the leaders placed their own self-interest above the needs of the people and the Soviet state. Emma always rebuked Eitingon when he complained about the inordinate privileges

---

were about to be arrested. Philby, who by then had become the British intelligence representative in Washington, was recalled to England and forced to resign. He avoided arrest, however, and in 1963 fled to Moscow from Beirut, Lebanon, when a former intelligence colleague tried to extract an admission of guilt and offer immunity from prosecution in exchange for a full and secret confession. Anthony Blunt was unmasked in 1964 but was given a grant of immunity from prosecution for full disclosure of his treachery. He remained Keeper of the Queen's Pictures until 1972. He was publicly exposed in 1979 and stripped of his knighthood; he died in 1983. Burgess died in Moscow in 1963, Maclean died there in 1983, and Philby in 1988. Cairncross was never arrested and is living in France writing his memoirs.

of the Kremlin leadership. She said, "I agree with you in one respect. There are too many of them, and most of them receive their privileges for nothing, certainly not for hard work. Don't forget that in those years you had two dachas for your two families and received similar privileges."

Eitingon smiled and insisted he was different.

After he was imprisoned with me in the waves of arrests that followed Beria's fall from power in 1953, he asked Zoya Zarubina, his stepdaughter from his marriage to Naumova, to look after his other children. After his release in 1964 he returned to Olga Naumova, who was seriously ill. She died in 1966.

By the time I was released from prison in 1968, Eitingon had remarried. His new wife was Yevgenia Puzirova, the only KGB woman officer decorated with a British military medal, for her role in providing assistance to convoys from Britain to the Soviet Union during the war. Simultaneously, she was part of the support team for clandestine agents such as the Cambridge ring. Although she won both British and Soviet medals and the ship on which she was returning to the Soviet Union in 1943 was sunk by a German submarine, she was denied the privileges of a war veteran because of her marriage to Eitingon. He died in 1981, still considered a released criminal. She is still alive and received the certificate of Eitingon's rehabilitation only in April 1992.

Leonid was a talented man, and if he had not gone into the intelligence business he would no doubt have become either a prosperous administrator or a professor in the sciences. I still remember how he joked, "There is one small guaranteed way not to end up in jail under our system. Don't be a Jew or a general in the state security service."

Earlier Western accounts which attribute to Eitingon an instrumental role in the operation to kidnap General Yevgeni K. Miller, head of the White Russian Military Union in Paris, in 1937 are incorrect. The truth is that General Miller was abducted by General Nikolai Skoblin, code name Farmer, operating under the direction of Sergei Shpigelglas. Skoblin kidnapped General Miller by luring him to an NKVD safe apartment, supposedly to meet German intelligence officers. The French authorities protested the disappearance of Miller to the Soviet ambassador, insisting he had been kidnapped and placed aboard a Soviet ship. They threatened to send a French destroyer to intercept the vessel and search for Miller. Our ambassador vigorously denied any Soviet involvement and warned the French they would be held responsible if a peaceful

Soviet vessel was halted and searched in international waters. General Miller would not be found, the ambassador insisted. The French failed to stop the ship, which sailed from Le Havre. On arrival in Moscow, Miller was interrogated, tried, and shot. His kidnapping was a cause célèbre. Eliminating him disrupted his organization of czarist officers and effectively prevented them from collaborating with the Germans against us.

Skoblin escaped from Paris to Spain on an airplane chartered by Orlov. (When Orlov fled in 1938, he kept Skoblin's gold ring as proof of his involvement in the case.) Skoblin was killed during an air raid on Barcelona during the Civil War. His wife was the famous Russian singer Nadezhda Plevitskaya. She did not know Shpigelglas was controlling the Miller operation but thought him a friend of her husband. Plevitskaya was arrested in France and convicted of complicity in Miller's disappearance. She was sentenced to twenty years of hard labor and died in prison in 1944.

In April 1988 Theodore Draper in the *New York Review of Books* unraveled the mistaken identity between Eitingon and his alleged brother Max, a prominent German psychiatrist who was a member of Freud's inner circle.[4] In Draper's exemplary research on the Eitingon family, he includes material from Plevitskaya's trial, in which she acknowledged receiving money from the wife of Max Eitingon; the doctor's wife was a former actress who supported the arts. To the best of my knowledge, Plevitskaya's connection to Max Eitingon was an accident of fate that had nothing to do with Leonid. His relatives named by Draper are not listed in Leonid Eitingon's NKVD personnel file. He never contacted them or mentioned a brother named Max.

In 1992 Eitingon's daughter Svetlana telephoned me and asked me to receive her distant relative from England, who came to Moscow to research a book about Eitingon. When we met, in May 1992, it became clear to me that there existed many branches of Eitingon's family in Byelorussia, Moscow, New York, and Leipzig; but these relatives played no role in his professional career, and he did not maintain contact with them even after his release from Vladimir prison.

Now let me return to events of 1938. Shpigelglas had summoned Emma to his office when he received my message from Paris and congratulated

4. John J. Dziak, *Chekisty: A History of the KGB* (New York: Ivy Books, 1988), suggests that Max Eitingon was the brother of Naum I. Eitingon, but that was not the case.

her. He said, "Andrew" — my code name — "is safe. The mission is accomplished. He saw people running to the place of the incident, and realized that in Western Europe people do not run to look when a car tire explodes."

In July 1938 the ship on which I was traveling anchored in Leningrad. I took the night train to Moscow and was met there by Pasov — who had been appointed to replace Slutsky — Shpigelglas, and my wife, Emma. There were congratulations and embraces. I was exhilarated to return to Moscow and resume my life. I believed my assassination of Konovalets was justified in every way, and I was proud that no innocent people were hurt by the explosion. There were no clues for the Abwehr or the Ukrainian nationalists to use to find the real reasons for Konovalets's death. They could suspect me, but they had no proof against me or the people who arranged my mission.

One more thing convinced me I was serving the right cause. The leaders whom I had met in Berlin and Warsaw were the so-called westernized Ukrainians, and I often had to correct their usage of the Ukrainian language, which they spoke very poorly. I sincerely believed these people were historically doomed; they were totally isolated from life in Kiev and did not have any understanding of the performance and strength of the Soviet system. They were not aware of the cultural upsurge of Ukrainian literature and arts. They had received their education mostly in Austria or Prague, and Ukrainian culture in Poland's Galicia was ruthlessly suppressed by the Polish administration. Although they regularly monitored our daily newspapers and journals, they could not explain the differences between collective farms and state farms or the various interrelations between government and public organizations responsible for social services in the Ukraine. They claimed they were relying on entrepreneurs for support in the villages, unaware that in real life these traders were being replaced by cooperatives.

The next day I appeared at Lubyanka early in the morning and was summoned to meet the new chief of the Main Administration of State Security of the NKVD, Lavrenti Beria, of whom I knew absolutely nothing except that he had been the head of the GPU in Georgia in the 1920s and then became secretary of the Georgian Communist party. Pasov took me to Beria's office on the third floor, next to the grand office of Commissar Yezhov, the head of the NKVD. My first meeting with Beria lasted for four hours. Pasov remained silent, but Beria asked question after question, wanting to know about every detail and element in the operation against Konovalets and the Ukrainian nationalists from the very beginning.

After an hour he ordered Pasov to bring the file code-named Stavka (High Command), where all the details of the operation were recorded. From Beria's questions I realized that he was highly competent in intelligence tradecraft and methods of implementing sabotage operations. Beria continued asking questions, I understood later, in order to increase his understanding of how I became accustomed to life in the West and adapted myself as an illegal.

In particular, Beria was impressed with the simple procedures for buying railway tickets that permitted me to travel freely throughout the continent. I remember him asking how the sale of railway tickets was arranged so as to divide the lines of passengers for local and foreign journeys. In Holland, Belgium, and France, those buying tickets for foreign travel approached the ticket counter one at a time when summoned by the clerk, who rang a bell. We assumed that this was to better allow the ticket salesman to remember those who purchased tickets. He asked me whether I had checked the number of exits, including the reserve exit, in the safe house in the Paris suburbs, and was very surprised I had failed to do so because I was too tired when I arrived. This made me realize that Beria probably had had some experience in illegal tradecraft during his career in the Georgian CHEKA.

I remember distinctly that Beria was dressed in a very modest suit. It seemed odd to me that he wore no necktie, and although the shirt was of good quality, the sleeves were too long and he had rolled them up. This made me feel a bit ill at ease, because during my one-day stay in Paris I had ordered three fashionable suits, an overcoat, shirts, and ties. The tailor took my measurements and Agayants picked them up and sent them to Moscow in the diplomatic pouch. At the time, I believed that would be my last visit to the West.

Beria showed great interest in the guerrilla group with which I had stayed near Barcelona. He knew one of the guerrilla commanders, Lev Vasilevsky, who served under his command in the counterintelligence department of the Georgian GPU. Beria spoke fluent Russian with a slight Georgian accent and was extremely polite to me, but he did not remain calm during the interview. He grew agitated reliving my arguments with Konovalets over whether to initiate terrorist acts against the Communist administration in Ukraine. I had objected on the grounds that this would destroy the organization because the NKVD would trace the assassins and then crush our network; Konovalets argued these actions could be undertaken by isolated groups. He insisted the image of heroic struggle should be fostered in the people's imagination.

Wearing pince-nez because of his nearsightedness, Beria gave the appearance of being an ordinary Soviet minor official. It occurred to me that he deliberately fostered that appearance because no one knew him in Moscow, and people would pay no attention to an ordinary-looking man visiting a safe apartment to meet an agent. It must be remembered that at that time some of the NKVD safe apartments in Moscow were communal flats. Later I learned that the first thing that Beria had done when he was appointed Yezhov's deputy was to take over from the chiefs of the departments the most important agents and informers and run them personally.

Beria gave me five days' leave to visit my mother, who still lived in Melitopol. When I returned I was supposed to resume my work in the Foreign Department. Shpigelglas and Pasov were delighted with my meeting with Beria and assured me when they saw me off at the Kiev railway station in Moscow that an important job was awaiting me on my return.

During the train trip Emma told me about the extraordinary and sad developments in the country and the NKVD. As a result of ruthless purges — Yezhov purged the counterintelligence service of NKVD in 1937 and the Foreign Department in 1938 — many of our close friends, people in whom we had absolute trust, had been arrested on charges of treason. We assumed that this was the result of Yezhov's incompetence, which was becoming increasingly evident even to rank-and-file NKVD personnel.[5]

Here I want to reveal an important fact overlooked in books devoted to the history of the Soviet security police. Before Yezhov headed the NKVD, there was no special department for internal investigations. That meant that the case officer was supposed to investigate personally any alleged crime committed by the people he was responsible for. Yezhov created a Special Investigation Department in the NKVD

5. Yezhov was named head of the NKVD in September 1936, and the Great Terror, also known as the Yezhovshchina (Yezhov's Reign), intensified. Yezhov was removed from office in December 1938; however, even before that, from July to December, all his orders had to be countersigned by Beria, according to P. A. Sudoplatov. Yezhov was arrested in 1939 and executed in 1941. In his Twentieth Party Congress speech denouncing the crimes of Stalin, Khrushchev described Yezhov as a degenerate.

that operated not with real information, but with materials received from forced confessions of suspects. To our professional officers this system was an abuse that unleashed a wave of arrests based on the imaginations of investigators and forced confessions. We hoped that the appointment of Beria as Yezhov's deputy in July 1938 might help correct the evident mistakes. Naturally, we were naive, since we sincerely believed in the decency and honesty of our leaders. We knew, for example, that Slutsky and Shpigelglas had the wives and children of some of our colleagues who had been arrested immediately moved out of Moscow, so that they, too, would not be jailed.

Our reunion with our families was deeply moving. Emma and I were the sole supporters of both our families, sending them half our salaries. We spent two days in Melitopol and then went to Kharkov, where Emma's family lived. After our trip to the Ukraine I returned to Moscow perplexed with the rumors of atrocities revealed to us by our relatives. I could not possibly believe that Khatayevich, by then the secretary of the Ukrainian Communist party, was an enemy of the people. Allegedly involved in connections with Polish Communists, Kossior was ruthlessly purged in Moscow. I thought perhaps the real reasons for these arrests were some mistakes in their practical work. It was known that Khatayevich, to improve the food supply in Ukraine in the desperate years of hunger, consented to selling the flour that was reserved for mobilization in case of war. For that he received a party reprimand from Moscow in 1934. Probably, I thought, he had made another, similar mistake. I repeat, I was too naive.

When I returned to Moscow, Pasov and Shpigelglas informed me that I was to be appointed special assistant to the director of the Foreign Department. This nomination had to be endorsed by the Central Committee since it was a designated *nomenklatura* appointment.[6] From August 1938 until November, although there was no official order for my appointment, I served in an acting capacity.

My new job did not begin well. I quickly realized that my boss, Pasov, had absolutely no experience in intelligence tradecraft and had no idea what it was like to recruit and run an agent in the West. He trusted any piece of information he received from his agents, without

6. The nomenklatura was a list of appointments approved by the Communist party to important posts at all levels of the bureaucracy, in effect constituting the ruling class. Members of this elite received privileges of special food, clothing, medical care, and vacations at exclusive resorts.

the slightest idea of how to check it. This was natural, because his only experience was forcing confessions from the accused. I was dismayed when he endorsed the directive allowing every operational case officer to use his own cipher and bypass the rezident, reporting directly to the Center if he had reason not to trust his superior. Only later was the reason for this directive clear. The Central Committee plenary session in March 1937 demanded the purge of the Foreign Department of the NKVD, using information about shortcomings in its work gathered from honest rank-and-file personnel abroad. The criminality of this resolution was that it was a ruse to disguise the leadership's desire to get rid of the top echelon of the intelligence directorate.

In 1937 the Spanish Republicans had agreed to ship most of Spain's gold bullion reserves — half a billion dollars' worth — to Moscow. In the summer of 1938, Agayants sent a cable from Paris to the Center claiming that not all the Spanish gold, along with other precious metals and diamonds we had amassed during the Spanish Civil War, had been sent to Moscow. He suspected embezzlement of some of these funds by the Republican government and the Spanish Communist party. The news was reported to Stalin and to Vyacheslav Molotov, chairman of the Council of People's Commissars, who ordered Beria to investigate immediately. However, when we asked Eitingon for clarification and details about the transactions, he replied with an indignant cable using obscene language. Emphasizing that he was not an accountant or clerk, he said the gold and treasures were smuggled out of Spain in full cooperation with Dolores Ibarruri, the prominent Spanish Communist leader.[7] The transfer had taken place under extreme conditions. The cable from Eitingon greatly impressed Beria, who suggested that before undertaking any actions against our rezidentura in Spain we should first look into the relationships between the officers in the field.

I was personally instructed by Beria to look into the files of these transactions in the Central Administration for the Preservation of Treasures (GOKHRAN). That was easier said than done because the permission to study the files of GOKHRAN had to be signed by Molotov. His assistant declined to have the document signed without the signature of Yezhov, the people's commissar of the NKVD. Beria's signature was not enough. I

---

7. Dolores Ibarruri, known as La Pasionaria (the Passionflower) after a pseudonym she used for newspaper articles, was a celebrated Spanish Communist who fled to Moscow after the Republican cause failed in Spain in 1939. She returned to Spain in 1977 and died in 1989.

had not been aware of these bureaucratic rules. I passed the document for Yezhov's signature to his secretariat. The following morning it remained unsigned. Beria cursed me on the telephone for my sloth, but I said it was impossible for me to reach Yezhov, who was not in Lubyanka. Beria said indignantly, "You are supposed to reach him for urgent government business; this is not a private matter. Take a courier, who will carry the document in his briefcase, and go to Yezhov, who is unwell and in his dacha."

With a courier I was driven to Yezhov's dacha in the suburbs of Moscow. His appearance was rather strange. I had the impression that I was presenting the document for signature to a person who was either fatally ill or had spent the night drinking heavily. Without any questions or comments he signed the order, and I left for the Kremlin to deliver it to Molotov's secretariat. From there I proceeded to Gokhran accompanied by two accountants, one of whom, Abram Berenzon, had been the chief accountant of NKVD since 1918. Before the Revolution he had served as the chief accountant of the Rossia Insurance Company, whose offices were taken over by Dzerzhinsky. We worked for two days checking the records and found that there had been no thefts, and the gold and treasure had not been used for operational purposes by NKVD rezidents in Spain or France. It was then that I learned that the document for the transfer of the gold had been signed by the prime minister of the Spanish Republic, Francisco Largo Caballero, and Deputy Commissar for Foreign Affairs Nikolai Krestinsky, who had been shot as an enemy of the people after Bukharin's show trial in March 1938. The gold had been taken from Spain in 1937 by Soviet cargo ships loaded in Cartagena, the Spanish naval base, and sent to Odessa. From there it was deposited in the vaults of the state bank. At that time it was valued at $518 million. Other treasure, intended for operational purposes by the Spanish Communists and the Republican government to finance clandestine operations, was smuggled from Spain to France and then taken as diplomatic cargo to Moscow. We concluded that these funds were sufficient to support Spanish emigrants and refugees, who began to appear in Moscow.[8]

Two months before the safe shipment of the Spanish gold, Nikolsky/ Orlov, our rezident and the agent responsible for security operations in

---

8. Peter Wyden, *The Passionate War* (New York: Simon and Schuster, 1983), offers a lively and detailed account of the gold transfer. Spain ended up owing a final total of about $50 million to the Soviet Union when the war ended (Wyden, p. 155). The final accounting is still shrouded in mystery and secret negotiations.

Spain, disappeared. At the time, it had been rumored that he would succeed Pasov as head of the Foreign Department. Orlov was a natural candidate to be appointed director of the Foreign Department, but his brother-in-law, Zinovy B. Katznelson, deputy director of the Ukrainian NKVD, was purged in 1937 or 1938, leading Orlov to believe his brilliant career was doomed.

Nikolsky's real name was Aleksandr Feldbin. He used the alias Schwed and the nickname Lyova, but he was known in the West by the name Aleksandr Orlov. I knew Orlov in the West and when he served in the Center, but only in passing. It is important that I explain a few things about Orlov, whose revelations in the 1950s and 1960s were responsible in large measure for American understanding of developments in the Soviet Union. He was never a general in the NKVD, as he claimed. He had the rank of major — a special rank then equal to the current rank of colonel.[9] In the 1930s Orlov headed economic intelligence and was involved in clandestine relations with Western businessmen; he was instrumental in bringing new technology from Sweden into the Soviet Union.

Orlov was also a very talented journalist. In 1935 and 1936 he had nothing to do with the purges in Moscow, but his later version of the purges has been accepted by the public and is even used by our writers now to describe the atrocities of the regime. To a certain extent what he wrote is true, but he had little knowledge of the real circumstances behind what he described.[10]

Orlov was one of the section chiefs of the intelligence directorate, and he held the rank of major of state security. He was known for his good command of English, German, and French, and for his success in the German bond market, where, in the early 1930s, he had made considerable sums of money. Orlov had published a book for our special school on clandestine work abroad. My good friend Raisa Sobel worked

9. P. A. Sudoplatov adds: "At the time Orlov defected, there was no rank of general in the NKVD hierarchy. In 1945 a decree by Stalin converted NKVD ranks into ordinary military ranks; but Orlov's rank of senior major of state security was lower than the rank of commissar of state security, which in accordance with the decree became equal to the rank of major general, a one-star general in the Red Army."

10. In 1953, after spending fifteen years underground in the United States, Orlov published *The Secret History of Stalin's Crimes* (New York: Random House) and in 1962 *A Handbook of Intelligence and Guerrilla Warfare* (Ann Arbor: University of Michigan Press).

under him in the economic department of the GPU in the 1920s and held him in high regard. He managed to establish among his informers an informal auditing group that disclosed the true incomes of New Economic Policy enterprises in the 1920s. Abram Slutsky personally supervised Orlov's penetrations into illegal accounting books. Then Slutsky transferred him to the Foreign Department, and in 1934–1935 he was rezident in London.

In July 1936 Orlov was sent to Spain after a tragic love affair with Galina Voitova, a young NKVD operator, who shot herself in front of Lubyanka because Orlov left her and refused to divorce his wife. Slutsky, who was his close friend, immediately transferred him abroad before Yezhov took over as head of the NKVD in September 1936. While in Spain, Orlov directed guerrilla warfare. More important, he was in charge of such operations as kidnapping and terrorism against Trotskyites and people whom the special service wanted to neutralize. He was also responsible for security operations and successfully shipped the Spanish Republic's gold to Moscow. For this daring operation he was promoted to the rank of senior major of state security. *Pravda* reported that Senior Major of State Security Nikolsky was awarded the Order of Lenin for fulfilling an important government assignment. In the same issue of *Pravda* it was also stated that Major of State Security Naumov (Eitingon's alias) was decorated with the Order of the Red Banner and Captain of State Security Lev Vasilevsky was decorated with the Order of the Red Star. Shpigelglas also had great respect for Orlov. He frequently visited Spain and told me that Orlov did a good job of eliminating Trotskyites there. Orlov managed to publish an anti-Trotskyite pamphlet over the signature of Andreu Nin, who had already been shot by Orlov's assassination team on Stalin's orders. Orlov wrote the pamphlet to compromise Trotsky, as if Nin, who had once been Trotsky's secretary in Moscow, had recanted because of the defeats and treacherous behavior of the Trotskyites in Spain. It was a successful piece of disinformation reported to Stalin directly by Yezhov.

In July 1938, Shpigelglas was supposed to meet Orlov on board a Soviet ship in French waters for consultations. Shpigelglas suspected that his identity had been compromised to the French police because some of his agents had been arrested after the kidnapping of General Miller, the White Russian leader, a year earlier. For this reason Shpigelglas feared to go ashore. But Orlov had his own suspicions that he was being set up to be seized and purged. He did not go to meet Shpigelglas.

Orlov fled and only in November did we learn that he had arrived in America. Before that I signed a formal *orientirovka,* or briefing, on the case to be channeled to every rezidentura. This bulletin contained a full description of Orlov and his habits, and a description of his wife and daughter, who had last been seen with him in France; and it suggested that he had been kidnapped by the British, German, or French special services. In particular I stressed the fact that Orlov was known to the French and British authorities because he twice participated in sessions of the International Committee for Nonintervention in the Spanish Civil War as an expert in the Soviet delegation. We also speculated that he might have defected; $60,000 in operational funds was missing from the safe of the rezidentura in Barcelona. His disappearance was of concern to us because Orlov was also aware of our NKVD network in France and Germany. He even knew of Philby, Maclean, Burgess, and Blunt and the start of their cooperation with us. His defection raised serious doubts whether Philby and his friends had been compromised. Yet in November of 1938 Beria summoned me and among other instructions ordered me to stop any efforts to locate Orlov. I was to resume the search only on his direct order. The reason was that Orlov had sent a personal letter to Stalin from America explaining his defection on the grounds of his imminent arrest on board the Soviet ship.

The letter stated that if he found any attempts to discover his whereabouts or traces of surveillance he would order his lawyer to disclose a letter he had deposited in a Swiss bank which contained information about falsification of materials for the International Committee for Nonintervention in the Spanish Civil War. He also threatened to tell the full story of the Spanish gold that was deposited secretly in Moscow and provide lists of the shipment. This story would have been an embarrassment for the Soviet government and Spanish Civil War refugees in Mexico, because Soviet military support for the Republican cause was supposedly given in the name of socialist solidarity. The payment in gold and treasures was a secret. Orlov asked Stalin not to persecute his aged mother left behind in Moscow and said that if his terms were met he would remain silent about all NKVD secrets known to him.

I don't believe that loyalty to the Soviet system was the reason Orlov did not expose the Cambridge group or the kidnapping of General Miller in Paris. Orlov was simply struggling to survive.

The order from Beria was that the Central Committee had decided to leave him alone.

*   *   *

In August 1938 I first learned about the kidnapping and assassination of Trotskyites and defectors that had been carried out in Europe in the 1930s. The case of Ignace Reiss deserves correction. Reiss, alias Poretsky, was an illegal stationed in Western Europe. He had received large sums of money that he had failed to account for and feared that he would be a victim of the purges. Reiss decided to make use of operational funds to defect, and so he deposited money in an American bank. Before defecting in 1937 he wrote a letter to the Soviet Embassy in Paris denouncing Stalin. This letter found its way into a Trotskyite publication. This was a fatal error. From Reiss's file it was clear that he never sympathized with Trotsky or any of the groups supporting him, but after the letter appeared Stalin marked him for elimination.

Reiss had a careless lifestyle and was soon detected by Shpigelglas's network in Paris. Actually, his assassination was carried out by a Bulgarian illegal in our employ, Boris Afanasiev, and his brother-in-law, Victor Pravdin. They had found him in Switzerland and sat down at his table in a small restaurant in the suburbs of Lausanne. Reiss drank heavily with the two Bulgarians, who pretended they were businessmen. Afanasiev and Pravdin staged a quarrel with Reiss and hustled him out of the restaurant into their car and drove away. Three miles from the restaurant they shot him and left him on the roadside.

I received Afanasiev and Pravdin in a safe apartment in Moscow when they returned from their mission. With them was Shpigelglas, their mentor. Afanasiev and Pravdin were awarded the Order of the Red Banner. Under a special decree of the government the mother of Pravdin, who lived in Paris, received a pension. Afanasiev became a junior case officer in the intelligence directorate and Pravdin joined the Moscow Foreign Languages Publishing House, where he worked until he died in 1970.

Claims that Sergei Efron, the husband of the famous Russian poet Marina Tsvetayeva, was involved in betraying Reiss to the NKVD are false. Efron, who did work for the NKVD in Paris, had no idea of Reiss's whereabouts.

The case of Georgi Agabekov also needs clarification. In the 1920s Agabekov was the OGPU rezident in Istanbul, Turkey. He defected because he was close to Yakov Blumkin, who had been unmasked as a sympathizer of Trotsky. Agabekov, we believed, fell in love with the daughter of a British intelligence officer in Istanbul, and his romance with this woman and British intelligence lasted for five years, until she left him. Desperately needing money, he published two books in the

West. He also became involved in risky deals with émigrés from the
Caucasus, claiming he could smuggle hidden family treasures from the
Soviet Union.[11]

It was reported that Agabekov was assassinated in the Pyrenees
Mountains on the Spanish border, but in fact Agabekov was killed in
Paris, after being lured to a safe house where he was supposed to arrange
a clandestine deal to smuggle diamonds, pearls, and precious metals
belonging to a wealthy Armenian family. The Armenian, whom he met
in Antwerp, was a plant who lured Agabekov to the safe house with
appeals to national feelings. In the safe house a former officer of the
Turkish army, our assassin, awaited him, together with a young illegal,
Aleksandr Korotkov, who would later become chief of the illegal department of the First Chief Directorate in the 1950s. The Turk knifed
Agabekov and killed him. Agabekov's body was stuffed into a suitcase,
thrown into the sea, and never found.

The Turk and Korotkov carried out another terrorist mission in
1938. Our young agent Ale Taubman, code-named Youngster, a Lithuanian Jew, gained the confidence of Rudolf Klement, the head of
Trotsky's European organization and the secretary of the so-called
Fourth International. Taubman was Klement's assistant for a year and a
half. One night Taubman suggested that Klement join him for dinner
with his friends and led Klement to an apartment on Boulevard St.
Michel on the Left Bank. The Turk and Korotkov were waiting for him.
The Turk stabbed Klement to death, cut off his head, and put his body
into a suitcase and threw it into the Seine. Klement's beheaded body was
found and identified by the French police, but by then Taubman, Korotkov, and the Turk were far from Paris, on their way to Moscow.

When they arrived they were decorated, and I had to arrange their
future employment. The Turk was put in charge of a safe house in Moscow. Taubman's name was changed to Semyonov and he was sent to
study at the Institute of Chemical Machinery to be trained as an engineer. Korotkov remained a case officer in the directorate and rose
rapidly.

---

11. Gordon Brook-Shepherd presents a different account of Agabekov's defection in
The Storm Petrels: The Flight of the First Soviet Defectors (New York: Harcourt,
Brace, Jovanovich, 1977), pp. 95–138.

    Agabekov's books were published in Russian in Berlin in 1931. *GPU: Zapiski
Chekista* (*Memoirs of a CHEKA Worker*) was translated into English as *OGPU* (New
York: Brentano's, 1931); the other book, *CHEKA Za Raboty* (*CHEKA Is Operating*),
was not translated as far as we know.

Walter Krivitsky, an intelligence officer who defected in 1937 and emerged in America in 1939, wrote a book, *In Stalin's Secret Service,*[12] and in February 1941 was found dead in a hotel room in Washington, D.C. It was assumed that he was assassinated by the NKVD, although the police verdict was that his death was a suicide. There was an NKVD order issued to look for Krivitsky, but this was routine for all defectors. We were not sorry to see him go, but it was not through our efforts that he died. We believed he shot himself in despair as a result of a nervous breakdown.

12. New York: Harper & Brothers, 1939 (reprinted in 1985 by University Publications of America, Frederick, Md.).

PURGE YEARS

hen a defector dies or a political figure is assassinated, the moment is ripe for exploitation. Therefore, various versions and motives may appear. The most natural reason for a death, or the most logical motive for a murder, may be unacceptable politically and therefore buried under layers of nuance, deception, and accusation.

The death of Sergei M. Kirov, the Leningrad party leader, in 1934, is a classic example. His murder was exploited to the fullest by Stalin in purging his opponents and unleashing a campaign of terror. The idea that there was a Trotskyite plot against Kirov was fabricated from the very beginning by Stalin. Kirov was shot by Leonid Nikolayev, the estranged husband of Milda Draule, who worked as a waitress in Kirov's secretariat in the Smolny Institute. It was natural for the guards to allow Nikolayev, a relative of a worker and a regular visitor there, to enter. There was no system of special passes, and it was sufficient for Nikolayev to show his party card to enter restricted areas.

I learned these details from Emma, who worked in the Secret Political Department (culture and ideology) of the NKVD, in the group that supervised the Bolshoi Theater and the Leningrad Ballet (later to be named for Kirov). When Kirov was assassinated, Emma's team investigated Kirov's personal relationships with the ballets' members. It turned out that Kirov had a string of mistresses both in the Bolshoi and the Leningrad ballets and that Milda Draule had served at some of Kirov's parties. Milda Draule, an attractive Jewish girl, was also one of Kirov's girlfriends, although she was married to Nikolayev, a minor official in one of the Leningrad party districts. He had quarreled with his superiors and been expelled from the party, and had his wife ask Kirov for help. Kirov agreed and arranged for Nikolayev to be reinstated, but in a minor party position. Milda was about to divorce him when he shot Kirov.

Stalin and later Khrushchev, Gorbachev, and Aleksandr Yakovlev,[1] each for his own reasons, wanted to preserve Kirov's reputation as an unflawed hero. The Communist party, which required of all its members absolute personal morality, could not afford to announce that one of its icons, the head of the Leningrad Communist party, was a lecher, involved in a string of marital infidelities. All official versions of the assassination published in the press are fabrications. Stalin's version is that Kirov was killed by Nikolayev, assisted by leaders of the Leningrad NKVD, Filipp D. Medved and Ivan V. Zaporozhets, on Trotsky's and Zinoviev's order.[2] For Stalin, Kirov's death created the myth of a secret rebellion that allowed him to purge his enemies and rivals. Khrushchev's version is that Kirov was shot by Nikolayev, assisted by Medved and Zaporozhets, under orders from Stalin. Khrushchev recounted the story of Kirov's being urged by other leaders to run against Stalin for the post of general secretary at the Seventeenth Party Congress. When Stalin found out about the opposition, he was determined to eliminate Kirov,

---

1. Aleksandr N. Yakovlev, former Soviet ambassador to Canada, was brought back by Mikhail Gorbachev in 1985 to become a Politburo member and Gorbachev's closest domestic and foreign policy adviser. (The Politburo was the chief policy-making body of the Communist party and thus the center of power in the Soviet Union.)

2. Grigori Yevseyevich Zinoviev was a key organizer of the Bolsheviks under Lenin and a leading theoretician in the 1920s who strongly opposed Stalin. In the internal power struggle after Lenin's death, Zinoviev, whose power base was in Leningrad, was ousted by Stalin and deprived of all his offices. He was sentenced to ten years in prison for "moral complicity" in the assassination of Kirov and was tried again at a show trial before his execution in 1936.

according to this version.[3] For Khrushchev, this sealed another charge in the long list of crimes he attributed to Stalin. This version was later endorsed by Gorbachev and Yakovlev as part of their anti-Stalin campaign. By not revealing what actually happened, Gorbachev and Yakovlev tried to salvage the reputation of the Communist party and lay the blame for its failure on Stalin's criminal behavior.

The documents prove that Zaporozhets, allegedly the key plotter and case officer for Nikolayev, was on leave in the Crimea with a broken leg when Kirov was murdered. Nikolayev's whole family and Milda Draule and her mother were shot by a firing squad two or three months after Kirov's death. Milda and her innocent family were not rehabilitated until December 20, 1990, when their case was raised in the Soviet press.

Senior officers in the NKVD, especially those who were knowledgeable about Kirov's personal life, knew a husband's jealousy was the reason for his murder; but none would even discuss the case, because the story of a conspiracy against the party had been promulgated by Stalin and could not safely be challenged. Before the murder of Kirov, Stalin, accompanied by Vlasik[4] and only two bodyguards, used to walk on the Arbat[5] to visit Demyan Bednyy, the well-known poet. It was enough for a party member simply to produce his party card to enter even the Central Committee headquarters. It was enough for an NKVD officer who wore a badge with the chekist sword and shield to enter Lubyanka headquarters. Party members had the right to go anywhere except a prison. The whole system was abruptly changed after Kirov's murder. It was an excuse to tighten controls that were never again relaxed.

The use of Kirov's murder by Stalin's successors is a classic example of the party's attempts to preserve the myth that Stalin had been opposed by healthy elements in the leadership, led by Kirov, and to make the case that Kirov would have been a good alternative to Stalin. In fact, Kirov

3. Kirov was approached by Lenin's old comrades and told that the time had come to fulfill Lenin's testament, a letter he wrote in 1923, proposing "to the comrades to find a way to remove Stalin" from the position of general secretary of the party and appoint another man "more tolerant, more loyal, more polite, and more considerate to comrades, less capricious." Kirov told Stalin of the proposal to oppose him as general secretary at the congress. Stalin was said to have listened and thanked Kirov. See *Khrushchev Remembers: The Glasnost Tapes,* translated and edited by Jerrold L. Schecter with Vyacheslav V. Luchkov (Boston: Little, Brown, 1990), pp. 20–21.

4. Lieutenant General N. S. Vlasik was Stalin's chief bodyguard.

5. Arbat was an old section of Moscow favored by writers and artists.

was one of the essential components of Stalin's system; he was a staunch Stalinist who took an active part in purging party opposition groups. Kirov gave no quarter to the opposition; he was no different from the others in Stalin's inner circle.

Speculations on his death continued in the 1960s. I remember anonymous letters claiming that the real assassin had escaped. Dmitri Yefemov, the minister of state security in Lithuania in the 1940s, after the war told me that he received an order to search for Kirov's assassin, said to be hiding in a small town in Lithuania. They found the author of the anonymous letter, who was an alcoholic.

The report on Kirov's death by the Party Control Commission has never been released. The case was closed only on December 20, 1990, when members of Nikolayev's family were formally rehabilitated by the Supreme Court of the USSR. The decision of the court established that there was no plot to kill Kirov and that all of the so-called collaborators with Nikolayev were simply rivals of Stalin or witnesses to his excesses. However, it was only after the Party Control Commission on the Kirov case had been disbanded in July 1990, and despite strong objections of Aleksandr Yakovlev, that the procurator's office filed its appeal for the family's rehabilitation to the Supreme Court of the USSR. Even then, in this system of so-called justice, Medved and Zaporozhets were not cleared of charges of high treason, including the plot to kill Kirov and collaborate with German intelligence. Why? The procurator's office is afraid to raise this subject because unofficially Medved and Zaporozhets are regarded as guilty of other crimes in the purges. As to Khrushchev's charges, there are no documents implicating Stalin or NKVD personnel in Kirov's murder.

Professor Sergei Lavrin, professor of Communist party history at Moscow University, at a meeting of party activists in 1986 discussing the rewriting of history, said that the Kirov affair was clear to those who worked in the party machinery. Milda Draule's affair with Kirov proved fatal because her jealous husband, Nikolayev, was a known neurotic with a reputation as a troublemaker. A fresh look at the famous murder case would only reveal dirty linen in Kirov's personal affairs and violate the party rule of no disclosure of the private life of Politburo members.

On November 4, 1990, *Pravda* published a report from the commission investigating the Kirov Affair, charging that the motive for Kirov's murder was personal, but giving no details as to the circumstances or motives. *Pravda* never mentioned Milda Draule. The report accused Yakovlev, who had retired as chairman of the party commission investigating Stalin's crimes, of blocking the rehabilitation of Nikolayev's family and innocent people accused in the conspiracy.

Yakovlev indignantly replied (*Pravda,* January 28, 1991) that he still believed in a conspiracy to kill Kirov, and that there were several versions of how the murder was planned and executed. Yakovlev did not refer either to Milda Draule or to the alleged attempt to nominate Kirov instead of Stalin as the party leader at the Seventeenth Party Congress.

In his book *Stalin: Triumph and Tragedy,*[6] Dmitri Volkogonov refers to a rumor of Kirov's affair with Milda Draule but dismisses it as slander. The incriminating materials about "special relations" between Milda Draule and Kirov, told to me by my wife and General Leonid F. Raikhman, then head of counterintelligence in Leningrad, were concealed in the operations reports of NKVD informers from the Leningrad Ballet. The ballerinas who had been Kirov's mistresses considered Draule a rival for his affections. Some who were indiscreet with their opinions were sent to labor camps for "slanderous anti-Soviet agitation."

Kirov's name and memory were sacrosanct. My feelings at that time were simple. I never doubted the need to protect the prestige of the ruling party by not revealing the true facts of Kirov's murder. We chekists were known informally as the dirty workers of the revolution. It was a role we accepted with conflicting emotions. Kirov symbolized the leadership of the country. He was a staunch Stalinist. Naturally only the enemy could kill him. I sincerely believed at the time, and still believe now, that Zinoviev, Kamenev,[7] Trotsky, and Bukharin were real enemies of Stalin; and, within the framework of the totalitarian system in which they operated, this meant they were enemies of the state. Regarding them as enemies and feeling no pity for them, I considered exaggerated accusations against them to be minor details. Being a Communist idealist, I did not realize until later the crucial importance of what seemed to be minor discrepancies at the time. From that point of view I regret how wrong I was.

6. New York: Grove Weidenfeld, 1991.

7. Lev B. Kamenev worked closely with Zinoviev as a Bolshevik party organizer and supporter of Lenin. Although he opposed the Bolshevik seizure of power in October 1917 he held high government positions and sided with Stalin against Trotsky. Together with Zinoviev he headed the opposition to Stalin. He was twice expelled from the Communist party but readmitted; then, in 1935, he was again expelled and jailed. He was executed in the 1936 purge after a show trial with Zinoviev.

We must feel repentant for the innocent, because knowingly or unknowingly we were involved in the operation of a monumental, oppressive machine in a backward country; the magnitude of the repression still shocks me. Historically assessing the purges, I think they can be compared in their proportions, affecting the army, the peasantry, and the bureaucracy, with the purges of Ivan the Terrible and Peter the Great. It is tragic that this country has such cruel traditions of massive purges.

The "conspiracy" against Kirov was gradually expanded by Stalin from acquaintances of Nikolayev to the family of Draule, then to Zinoviev and Kamenev, who at first were accused of moral responsibility for the murder and then of actually planning it. Nikolayev's colleagues were linked to Zinoviev's opposition. Then Stalin wanted to get rid of Yagoda[8] and NKVD officials who knew the truth; they, too, were connected to the case and eliminated. Yagoda was accused of being the chief organizer of Kirov's murder. Stalin, General Raikhman told me, even ordered that Kirov's widow, until her death, be placed under close day-to-day surveillance.

The whole affair was manipulated by Stalin for his own purposes and continued to be covered up for political reasons. Kirov's murder was used to divert public opinion from the worsening economic and political crises. The truth about Kirov's murder was unthinkable in this context. No one at the top had the strength to face up to Stalin's use of the murder for his own ends, and because of that every investigation compounded the lies and made it more difficult for future generations to reconstruct the events.

There is no evidence that Stalin ordered the murder of Kirov to eliminate him as a rival center of power; rather, Stalin, when he learned of Kirov's death, saw an opportunity and used it. Stalin decided to fabricate a grand conspiracy against Kirov and himself; he exploited the situation to eliminate all those he suspected as rivals or disloyal opponents, which he could not tolerate. I am convinced that the murder of Kirov was a personal act, but the revelations of this personal motive would have been so damaging to the party, the ruling instrument of power and moral exemplar for the Soviet people, that to this day the true story has been suppressed. No compromising material is ever revealed against a mem-

8. Genrikh G. Yagoda headed the NKVD from 1934 to 1936. He stage-managed the treason show trial of Zinoviev and Kamenev in 1936 and introduced the forced labor system to build the infamous White Sea Canal. In September 1936 Yagoda was arrested and charged with conspiracy, espionage, and treason. He was shot in March 1938.

ber of the Politburo unless he is publicly purged, and Kirov remains a
Communist saint.

In 1938 fear was in the air. Sergei Shpigelglas, deputy director of the
NKVD Foreign Department, grew more grim with each passing day. He
stopped his habit of spending weekends with me and other friends in
the directorate. Suddenly, in September 1938, NKVD chief Yezhov's secretary reportedly shot himself while boating on the Moscow River. A
puzzling directive was handed down declaring that no arrest order was
valid without the signature of Beria, first deputy to Yezhov. It was
rumored that Beria used to call Yezhov *dorogoy* Ezoick, dear Yozick, an
intimate and friendly diminutive of his family name, and pat him on the
back. But their friendly behavior was all show. It was hard to explain,
but I felt something ominous in the air. In the headquarters at Lubyanka,
people were constrained and reluctant to discuss anything. There was
no joking or gossip. It was rumored that a commission from the Central
Committee of the Communist party was examining the operations of
the NKVD.

I clearly remember the extraordinary developments that followed.
In November, on the eve of the anniversary celebrations of the Revolution, I was awakened by a telephone call at 4:00 A.M. Vladimir Kozlov,
head of the secretariat of the Foreign Department, was on the line speaking in a formal but terribly agitated manner.

"Pavel Anatolievich, you are immediately summoned to Comrade
Merkulov, first deputy director of the state security administration. The
car is waiting for you. Come as soon as possible. Shpigelglas and Pasov
have just been arrested."

Emma was extremely worried, and I expected that my turn had
come.

At Lubyanka I was met by Kozlov, who accompanied me to
Merkulov's office on the third floor. Vsevolod Merkulov greeted me as
usual, in a polite and sympathetic manner, and suggested we go imme-
diately to see Lavrenti Pavlovich — Beria himself. Nervously, I expected
some sort of interrogation about my connections with Shpigelglas, but
Beria startled me. In a very official tone he announced that Pasov and
Shpigelglas had been arrested on charges of deceiving the party and that
I should immediately take over as the acting director of the Foreign
Department. He told me to report directly to him on any urgent matters.
I told Beria that Pasov's office was sealed and I could not enter it.

"Then remove the seal immediately, and in the future don't bother me with elementary questions typical of a schoolboy," said Beria harshly.

Ten minutes later I was looking through the documents in Pasov's safe. They were amazing. The first document was a *spravka,* or fitness report, on Gregory Kheifetz, at that time our rezident in Italy. The report stressed his connections with elements sympathetic to ideological deviance in the Comintern,[9] where he used to work. Also, it suggested that his connections with former graduates of the Jena Polytechnical Institute in Germany in 1926 were suspicious. I still remember Yezhov's note on the report: "Recall to Moscow. Arrest immediately."

Another document was a recommendation to the Central Committee and the Presidium of the Supreme Soviet that the Order of the Red Banner be awarded to me, Pavel Anatolievich Sudoplatov, for fulfilling an important government assignment abroad in May 1938. It had been signed by Yezhov. There was also an unsigned order to make me assistant director of the Foreign Department. I took these documents to Merkulov, Beria's deputy, who smiled and, to my great surprise, tore them up before my eyes and threw them in a wastebasket to be destroyed. I remained silent but felt cheated out of the commendation I was to receive for risking my life and succeeding in a dangerous task. I did not understand at that moment how lucky I was to lose a medal and a promotion.

Later that day my phone rang. It was Georgi M. Malenkov's deputy in the Central Committee, Kiselov. He indignantly reprimanded me for the delay in delivering the funds for Comintern clandestine operations in Western Europe. He was even more angry that no one from the NKVD had appeared for a meeting of the Spanish Commission at the Central Committee. I tried to explain that I had no knowledge of any funds and did not know who was responsible for the transactions. "There was no one present at the meeting at the Central Committee because Pasov and his deputy have been arrested as enemies of the people," I said.

I told him I had taken over only two hours before his call. Kiselov did not reply but slammed down the receiver, and the line went dead.

9. The Comintern, or Communist International, was an association of Communist parties throughout the world established by Lenin in 1919 to promulgate Soviet policy. It was a tool in the hands of the Soviet leadership, and its internal struggles reflected those within the Bolshevik leadership. Most of its leaders, Russians and foreign Communists living in exile in Moscow, were executed during Stalin's purges of 1936–1938, and the Comintern was dissolved by Stalin in 1943.

During the three weeks I was acting director of the service I learned the structure and organization of our clandestine intelligence operations abroad. There were two foreign intelligence services in the NKVD. The Foreign Department, which was headed by Artuzov, then Slutsky, and then Pasov, was organized to combine at the Center in Moscow the intelligence operations of legal channels — personnel under diplomatic cover and trade missions — and the illegal networks. Their primary task was to monitor governments and business corporations clandestinely financing activities aimed against the Soviet Union by Russian emigrants and White Army exiles in Europe and China. The Foreign Department had geographical sections, a section for scientific and technological intelligence, and one for economic intelligence. These sections processed the material from our legal and illegal rezidenturas abroad. The predominance of illegal penetrations was natural because there were not many Soviet diplomatic and trade missions abroad. Thus, the share of intelligence operations arranged through illegal channels was very significant.

We also had another intelligence service, the Administration for Special Tasks, subordinated to the head of the NKVD, a reserve network designated to carry out sabotage operations in case of war. For this reason Special Tasks did not have any slots in our diplomatic and trade missions abroad. The Administration for Special Tasks consisted only of twenty officers in the Center, who did the planning and organization. All other Special Tasks officers worked abroad under various illegal covers. At that time there were about sixty illegals. I soon understood that the head of the NKVD had the option to use either the resources of the Foreign Department or the Administration for Special Tasks to carry out assassinations. Both were used, depending on the circumstances.

Special Tasks, also known as the Yasha Group, was headed for more than ten years by Yakov Serebryansky, who had organized the kidnapping of General Aleksandr Kutepov, head of the White Russian Military Union in Paris in 1930. Serebryansky was a former member of the terrorist organization of the party of Socialist Revolutionaries in czarist Russia. He was responsible for the assassination of police and counterintelligence officers of the czar who organized Jewish pogroms in Mogilov in Byelorussia. The Yasha Group had established its networks in the 1920s in France, Germany, and Scandinavia. It chose its members from people in the Comintern underground who were not involved in any open propaganda activities and who had kept secret their membership in national Communist parties. By November 1938 Serebryansky had been arrested. He was sentenced to death but not shot. He was released in 1941 when the war broke out and on my initiative served as the chief of a section recruiting German prisoners of war; he planted agents in Western Europe until 1946.

In 1946, when Viktor S. Abakumov was appointed minister of state security, it was time for Serebryansky to retire. Abakumov had been in charge of his case in 1938, and had brutally interrogated him and forced him into a false confession. Serebryansky could no longer remain on the job. He retired as a colonel and received his pension, but unfortunately after Stalin's death he was appointed one of my deputies in the enlarged MVD (Ministry of Internal Affairs), under Beria. He was arrested with his wife for the second time in 1953 on charges of being one of Beria's conspirators, planning to assassinate the Presidium of the Central Committee.[10] He died in jail under interrogation in 1956 and was posthumously rehabilitated in 1971 by Yuri Andropov,[11] who learned about his fate when he ordered the first history of Soviet intelligence to be written.

Only in 1963 did I learn the real background of the drastic reshuffle and purge of the NKVD in the latter months of 1938. The full story, which has never been revealed, was related to me by Stepan Mamulov and Boris Ludvigov, the heads of Beria's secretariat, when they were in jail with me in Vladimir. They told me how the purges were rigged. Acting on the urging of Beria, two regional directors of the NKVD departments in Yaroslavl and Kazakhstan wrote to Stalin in October 1938, falsely alleging that Yezhov had hinted to them imminent arrests of members of the Soviet leadership on the eve of the November celebration of the Revolution. Beria's plan to eliminate Yezhov succeeded. Within weeks, Yezhov was charged with plotting to overthrow the government and removed as head of the NKVD, and the Politburo passed a resolution denouncing all senior NKVD officials as "politically unreliable." This led to a full-scale purge, and I was lucky that Yezhov's order promoting me to a senior rank had remained unsigned in Pasov's safe.

Beria now took over as official head of the NKVD and Vladimir G. Dekanozov became the new head of the Foreign Department; he had

10. Presidium was the name given to the Politburo during the years Khrushchev headed the Soviet government (1953–1964).

11. Yuri Andropov was head of the KGB from 1967 to 1982 and then president of the USSR and first secretary of the Communist party until his death in 1984.

experience working in the Azerbaijan GPU under Beria as a supply officer. Later, in Georgia, Dekanozov was the people's commissar of the
food processing industry, where he was notorious for his lust for luxuries. As the outgoing acting director of the Foreign Department, I
explained to him the most elementary details about our agent networks
in Western Europe and China, but he interrupted me. He ordered me to
trace Orlov's suitcases and household goods that had been shipped from
Barcelona to Moscow and bring them all to his office for examination.
He wanted to pick over the contents.

The next day Beria introduced Dekanozov to the staff of the intelligence service. In an official and stern voice Beria announced that a
special commission had been set up under Dekanozov to look into the
activities of the service to expose traitors and adventurists who were
deceiving the Central Committee of the Communist party. Beria
announced the nomination of Aleksandr Garanin, Pavel Fitin, A.
Lyonenko, and Viktor Liagin to key positions and stressed that all
remaining personnel would be investigated. The new officials were chosen as a result of the purges. The Central Committee stuffed the ranks
of the NKVD with party activists and graduates of the Frunze Military
Academy. I was demoted to assistant director of the Spanish section, and
all other veterans of the intelligence service were similarly demoted to
assistant chiefs of sections.

Beria personally questioned every case officer at that meeting,
harshly asking whether or not they were double agents, making his point
that everyone was under suspicion. Emma was one of only four women
case officers in the intelligence directorate. He impudently looked her up
and down and asked whether she was German or Ukrainian. "Jewish,"
she replied, to Beria's surprise. From that day Emma warned me repeat-
edly that there was something evil about Beria and that he was a man
without feeling. Assuming our apartment was bugged, she invented a
code name for him so we would not have to refer to him by name at
home. She called him Shadiman, after the hero of a novel about the war
in Georgia in the middle ages. Prince Shadiman of Mingrelia fell victim
to a power struggle between Georgian feudal lords. Emma's vision of
Beria's fate and her constant advice to steer clear of him and his clique
were prophetic.

Beria's meeting was followed by a party meeting, the next level in
the hierarchy, at which a senior operational officer, the Armenian Grand
Gukasov, whom I had known in Kharkov, suddenly suggested that the

Party Bureau investigate me.[12] He said I had been brought to Moscow
by Balitsky, an enemy of the people, who had been executed. Gukasov
charged that I was on friendly terms with other newly exposed enemies
of the people — Shpigelglas; Raisa Sobel and her husband, Mikhail
Revzin, an NKVD case officer; and Mikhail Yarikov, deputy rezident in
China, who was famous for his sarcastic adages. (I remember one: "In
the fourth year of a five-year plan, corrupt connections are decisive in
fulfilling the plan" — "*V chitvortom zavershaushem blat yavleitsy
recheaushim.*")

The Party Bureau set up a commission to investigate me. A good
friend of mine, Lev Heselberg, chief of the photographic laboratory, and
responsible for clearing photographers to photograph Stalin, began to
interrogate me by asking stupid questions. Heselberg claimed that I was
defending my innocence as "a typical Trotskyite double-dealer."

(I hold no grudges against Gukasov and Heselberg. Three years
later, Gukasov, then Soviet consul in Paris, was awakened as the
Gestapo was storming the building. Our cipher clerk, Marina Serotkina,
started burning the codebooks, and when one of the Gestapo ripped
Stalin's portrait from the wall, Gukasov used it as the pretext to start a
fight. He was brutally beaten, but he bought enough time for the codebooks to be burned. Gukasov was deported to Turkey by the Germans
in exchange for the release of the German diplomatic mission in Moscow. Later Gukasov was put in charge of the department in the intelligence directorate supervising surveillance of Soviet emigrants. He died
in Moscow in 1956.)

Heselberg prepared a resolution for the Party Bureau on the instructions of Dekanozov, calling for my expulsion from the Communist party
for connections with enemies of the people and failure to expose
Shpigelglas. In the same document Slutsky, although he had died in February 1938 and had been buried with honors, was also named a people's
enemy.

The Party Bureau passed the resolution with one abstention. Pavel
Mikhailovich Fitin, the editor of an agricultural journal and the man
recommended to be deputy director of the Foreign Department,
abstained, because, he said, I was completely unknown to him. His

12. The Communist Party Bureau in the NKVD was the party organization charged
with conducting agitation and organization work, carrying out party appeals, recruiting new members, organizing political education, developing criticism and self-criti-
cism. The Party Bureau enforced party discipline.

integrity, unusual under the circumstances, did not hurt his career. Fitin became chief of the Foreign Department in 1939. He died of natural causes in 1971.

My expulsion was proposed by the Party Bureau in December 1938, but before it took effect, it had to be endorsed at a general party meeting of the intelligence service that was scheduled for January 1939. Until that meeting I did nothing but appear in the office every day and sit at my desk. The newcomers refused to have anything to do with me for fear of being contaminated. I remember the chief of our section, Garanin, whispering to his deputy about operational problems for fear that I might overhear them. I decided to educate myself with files from the archives, which I examined laboriously while awaiting my fate.

I felt depressed, and Emma also believed that we were under serious threat. By that time, for all we knew, we might have been compromised by forced confessions from our friends. Emma argued strongly against my plan to approach the Central Committee Party Control Commission to appeal my case. She said that was a last resort; instead we should prepare a letter addressed to Stalin that should be mailed by her — or by my mother if we were both arrested.

We felt that a terrible injustice was being committed. When our friends were arrested, we thought mistakes had been made. But when Dekanozov was appointed chief of the Foreign Department, we realized for the first time that not only were mistakes being made, but there was a policy of appointing inexperienced people who would definitely commit more mistakes. For the first time we feared for our lives and faced the threat of being exterminated by our own system. At that time I began to think about the system, which sacrificed those devoted to its service. I accepted the brutality and stern order that characterized our centralized society; it appeared to be the only method of preserving the country when it was surrounded by German, Polish, and Japanese enemies.

I hoped that since I was personally known to the NKVD leadership as a devoted comrade, they would not sanction my arrest. In these years I lived under the illusion that injustice to a party member, especially if the person making the decision was highly placed in the Communist party organization and was fully trusted by Stalin, could only be committed by incompetence or a genuine mistake.

Another old friend, Pyotr Zubov, was about to be devoured by the meat grinder. In 1937 Zubov had become the NKVD rezident in Prague, working under diplomatic cover for the first time in his career. There he met with President Edvard Beneš and on Stalin's instructions passed him

$10,000 to arrange his escape from Czechoslovakia to Great Britain by a clandestine route with the full assistance of the NKVD network. The receipt for the money was signed by President Beneš's secretary. Beneš fled to England in 1938. Zubov did a good job. Before Beneš appeared in France, the British and French authorities had no idea by what route he would travel from Czechoslovakia. But after Beneš left Prague, Zubov was recalled to Moscow and arrested on the direct order of Stalin.

The reason was that Beneš had suggested to Stalin through Zubov that the Soviet Union subsidize a coup against the king of Yugoslavia in order to establish an anti-German military regime, easing pressure on Czechoslovakia. Beneš asked for $200,000 in cash for the Serbian military officers who would carry out the coup. Zubov obtained the money from the Center and journeyed to Belgrade to check out the situation. To his dismay he found that the officers were unreliable adventurists who were unlikely to carry out a coup. He refused to pay them in advance, returned to Prague with the money, and reported to Moscow. Stalin was furious because Zubov had not obeyed orders. On Zubov's cable explaining his actions Stalin wrote: "Arrest immediately." (I saw this cable in 1941 when I was shown Zubov's file.)

When Zubov returned I was in a very awkward position, because at this time the Party Bureau was about to consider my expulsion. I was delighted to see Zubov in the corridor of the seventh floor of Lubyanka the day he returned from Czechoslovakia. We agreed to meet the following day, but he did not appear. I suspected him of avoiding contact with me, but Emma met Zubov's wife on the street and learned he had been arrested. I had no idea of what he was accused; these were perilous times in which I could only watch carefully and maintain hope.

Then an unexpected thing happened. The meeting set for January 1939 at which my expulsion from the party was to be endorsed was postponed. In March, Yezhov, who had been relieved of his duties as people's commissar in December, was arrested. Beria and Bogdan Kobulov, one of his deputies, I learned later, personally handled the case of Yezhov. Kobulov told me years later that Yezhov was arrested in Malenkov's office in the Central Committee. While being escorted to his execution, he sang the "Internationale." I still regard Yezhov as responsible for grave crimes, but even worse, he was an incompetent criminal. I am sure that the crimes of Stalinism acquired such mad dimensions at least in part due to Yezhov's professional incompetence in intelligence and police matters.

To understand the Yezhovshchina we need to look into this backward country's political traditions. Political campaigns in a dictatorship acquire absurd proportions to mobilize a political result. The criminality of Stalin derived not only from the crimes committed under his direct orders but also from the fact that he allowed his subordinates, in his name, to eliminate people who were unwanted by local party bosses. Party and NKVD bosses settled normal joustings for leadership and day-to-day disagreements by eliminating rivals.

In those days I didn't know the whole story, but I knew enough to fear for my life. Logically, I expected to be arrested by the end of January or the beginning of February. I did absolutely no work; each day I appeared in my office expecting to be arrested. Then one day in March 1939 I was summoned to Beria's office, where he accused me of doing nothing for the past two months. I said I was simply obeying the orders from the chief of my section. He did not bother to answer and told me to accompany him to an important meeting. I thought that he would take me to a meeting at a safe apartment with an agent he was running personally. I had twice accompanied him in September on such missions. The car drove us to the Kremlin through the Spassky gate and stopped at a dead end off Ivanovsky Square. I suddenly realized that I had been summoned to see Stalin.

F O U R

THE ASSASSINATION
OF TROTSKY

The entryway into the Kremlin building was familiar to me from my first meeting with Stalin. We took a staircase to the second floor, where we walked down a long, wide, carpeted corridor past offices with high doors, like rooms in a museum. The same guard who had admitted Yezhov and me to the building was on duty. This time he offered his military salute and the traditional greeting to Beria: *"Dravia zalayu,* Tovarich Beria" ("Good health to you, Comrade Beria"). Otherwise, everything was the same. The same empty corridors. My feelings were the same. I was apprehensive and tense with enthusiastic excitement.

I felt I could hear my heart beating when Beria opened the door and we entered a reception room so huge it made the three writing tables seem tiny. There were three people, one in military uniform and two in tunics the same style as Stalin's. The short, dumpy-appearing man in a green tunic greeted Beria in a low, emotionless voice. Later I learned that he was A. N. Poskrebyshev, chief of Stalin's secretariat. It appeared to me that there was a strict unwritten rule banning emotions in this room. Poskrebyshev led the way into Stalin's office and closed the door behind us without a sound.

It was my third meeting with Stalin. He rose from his desk to greet us. We shook hands in the middle of the office and Stalin motioned us to sit at the long table covered with a green baize cloth. Only a few feet from this table, but not against the wall, was Stalin's personal desk, and I noticed that the files on his desk were arranged in perfect order. Behind his desk hung a portrait of Lenin and on the adjacent wall were portraits of Marx and Engels. Everything in the office appeared the same as when I'd last seen him, but Stalin looked different. He was focused, poised, and calm. He was not putting on a show for us, but radiated a natural self-confidence and ease that were impressive. He focused on his visitors and made us feel he was listening attentively to every word and weighing it carefully.

Was it really so? I cannot be certain, but Stalin listened intently to Beria, who told him: "Comrade Stalin, having exposed on the party's orders the NKVD Foreign Department's former leadership's treacherous attempts to deceive the government, we suggest that Comrade Sudoplatov be appointed a deputy director of the NKVD Foreign Department in order to assist recently mobilized party activists to comply with the orders of the government."

Stalin frowned. His pipe was in his hand, but although full of tobacco it was not lit. Then he struck a wooden match with a gesture known to all who watched newsreels, and moved an ashtray close to him. He did not address my nomination but urged Beria to outline the priorities for intelligence operations abroad. While Beria talked, Stalin rose from the table and began to pace back and forth across the room slowly and silently in his soft Georgian boots.

Although he moved around the room, there was no impression that he was not fully absorbed; on the contrary, his concentration on Beria's words could be felt. I am still impressed by the simplicity of Stalin's reactions. It was hard to imagine that such a man could deceive you, his reactions were so natural, without the slightest sense of him posing. I also noticed a certain harshness in his remarks, which he did not try to conceal. This gruffness was the most typical feature of his dealings with anybody summoned for an audience, an inseparable component of his personality, just like the stern look that came from smallpox marks on his face.

Beria said he thought that foreign intelligence should change its traditional priorities on the eve of war in Europe and the Far East. He suggested that a great role should be played by our agents of influence, people whose positions in government and business circles gave them access to leaders who could affect the course of events. Beria's idea was that we should use these agents of influence to implement our policy goals. However, most of them were left-wing sympathizers, and the left movement was in serious disarray because of Trotskyite efforts to infiltrate and take it over. Trotsky and his followers were a significant challenge to the Soviet Union, competing with us to be the vanguard of the world Communist revolution. Beria suggested I should be put in charge of all anti-Trotskyite NKVD operations so as to inflict the decisive blow on the headquarters of the movement. This was the reason he had nominated me to be a deputy head of the Foreign Department under Dekanozov. My task would be to mobilize all available NKVD resources to eliminate Trotsky, the worst enemy of the people.

"There are no important political figures in the Trotskyite movement except Trotsky himself. If Trotsky is finished the threat will be eliminated," Stalin said, and returned to his seat opposite us. Then slowly he began to speak of his dissatisfaction with the present state of our intelligence operations, which he said were not active enough. Stalin stressed that the elimination of Trotsky had first been assigned to Shpigelglas in 1937, but he had failed to fulfill this important government mission.

Then Stalin stiffened, as if giving an order, and said, "Trotsky should be eliminated within a year, before war inevitably breaks out. Without the elimination of Trotsky, as the Spanish experience shows, when the imperialists attack the Soviet Union we cannot rely on our allies in the international Communist movement. They will face great difficulties in fulfilling their international duty to destabilize the rear of our enemies by sabotage operations and guerrilla warfare if they have to deal with treacherous infiltrations by Trotskyites in their ranks.

"We have no historical experience in building the industrial and military might of the country while we consolidate the dictatorship of the proletariat," Stalin said, giving voice to the theory of revolutionary defensism, defense of the revolution in Russia. This idea of revolution in one country, versus Trotsky's internationalism, advocating revolution of all working classes simultaneously, was the heart of the ideological struggle between Stalin and Trotsky. Stalin concluded his short elaboration of the state of the world with an order for me to head the team of *buyeveke*, shock troops, to implement the action against Trotsky, who was in exile in Mexico. Stalin preferred indirect words like "action," noting that if the operation was successful the party would forever remember those who were involved and would look after not only them, but every member of their family. Stalin remained calm when I replied that I was not totally fit for the assignment in Mexico because I spoke no Spanish at all.

I asked for permission to draw on veterans of guerrilla operations in the Spanish Civil War for the mission. Stalin replied, "It is your job and party duty to find and select suitable and reliable personnel to carry out the assignment. You will be provided with whatever assistance and support you need. Report directly to Comrade Beria and nobody else, but the full responsibility for carrying out the mission remains with you. You should personally make arrangements to dispatch a task force to Mexico from Europe and report it only in your own handwriting."

We shook hands and Beria and I left Stalin's office. After the meeting with Stalin I was immediately appointed a deputy director of the Foreign Department and put in charge of the new operation against Trotsky in Mexico. I was given a new office on the seventh floor, room 735 of Lubyanka, formerly occupied by Slutsky.

Emma was ill at ease with my promotion and said I would have been better off to remain a junior case officer. Emma correctly sensed that my swift promotion to acting head, even though it had been temporary, was the reason for the denunciations against me. I was not an enemy of the people but an enemy of jealous colleagues. Such was the standard pattern of denunciation during the purges.

The heady pace of events swept me along, and my new assignment left me little time to brood over my nearly fatal denunciation. The party meeting never voted on my case. Two days later I was informed that the Party Bureau had reconsidered its decision to expel me from the party and instead reprimanded me for failure to unmask hostile elements in the directorate.

The following day when I arrived at my new office Eitingon, who had returned to Moscow from Spain, called me from his apartment. "Pavlusha, for ten days I have been in Moscow doing nothing but being under close surveillance by the Operations Department. I am sure my telephone is tapped. You are one who knows my real work, so please report immediately to your superiors that if they decide to arrest me they should do it now without these childish games."

I told Eitingon it was my first day on my new job and I knew of no plans to arrest him. I suggested that he come to see me immediately at Lubyanka. I called Merkulov and reported the conversation to him. Merkulov laughed and said, "Those idiots put Eitingon and his team under their surveillance without realizing that they were dealing with professionals." Ten minutes later Beria rang me on the direct line connecting his office to mine and suggested that since Eitingon had now joined my team we should come to his office at the end of the day.

When Eitingon arrived I ordered tea and suggested he join the operation against Trotsky. He agreed without hesitation. He was a natural choice to head the task force in Mexico because the approach to Trotsky was through our Spanish network and he was the one who knew it best. Working together we became close friends. The order to eliminate Trotsky did not surprise us, because for more than ten years the OGPU and NKVD had been engaged in a war with Trotsky and his organization. For us, enemies of the state were personal enemies.

By 1939 Trotsky was in exile in Mexico. He had been forced to leave the Soviet Union in 1929, and after living in Turkey, Norway, and France, he moved to Mexico as the war approached. Before he was exiled, Trotsky had already lost the power struggle to succeed Lenin; from exile, his efforts to split and then control the world Communist movement was damaging to Stalin and the Soviet Union. His challenge to Stalin kept the Communist movement in turmoil and weakened our position in Western Europe and Germany in the 1930s.

Eitingon suggested that the operation against Trotsky should be code-named Operation Utka (Duck).[1] In Russia, "duck," aside from its normal meaning is a term for disinformation. "When the ducks are flying" means that the press is publishing disinformation.

Leonid knew our agent networks in the United States and Western Europe, so he was able to come up with a realistic estimate of whom we could rely upon. Unfortunately, Maria de la Sierra, our best agent, whom we had successfully placed as Trotsky's secretary while he was in Norway and was still with him in Mexico, had to be recalled immediately. She was known to Orlov and we did not want to take the chance

1. There are two types of operational files in the Soviet intelligence service, according to P. A. Sudoplatov. The *delo formular,* or service record, contains an individual agent's file. These files are also coded, but they contain only an agent's biography, his reports and verification of their information, and an assessment of the agent or his sources by the case officer.

The *liternoye delo,* or operational case file, contains the overall summary of agent reports and case officers' comments as well as the detailed operational plan, all cables, necessary orders, and reference notes. Sometimes the cables from the minister are in the operational file signed with his alias — in Beria's case Pavel (Paul) — rather than his full name. Duck was the name given to this overall operational file.

that she would be exposed by him. We were right. Two months after he arrived in America, Orlov wrote to Trotsky warning him that there were plans to assassinate him and not to trust anyone who came to visit him from Spain. At the time we did not know of Orlov's warning, but we anticipated that one might come.

Eitingon's idea was to use agents in Western Europe or Latin America who had never been involved in operations against Trotsky and his followers. We had to rely on a task force led by David Alfaro Siqueiros, the Mexican painter, who was personally known to Stalin. A veteran of the Spanish Civil War, he had moved to Mexico and was one of the organizers of the Mexican Communist party. We also decided to establish another illegal network, headed by Caridad Mercader, a Spanish aristocrat. Among her wealthy ancestors were former governors of Cuba, and her grandfather had been the Spanish ambassador to the czar. Caridad had deserted her husband, a Spanish railroad magnate, and fled to Paris with their four children in the early 1930s. She earned a living by knitting. When the Spanish Civil War broke out in 1936 she returned to Barcelona, joined the anarchists, and was wounded in an air raid. Her eldest son was killed in action. Her middle son, Ramon, served in a guerrilla detachment. The youngest son, Luis, and her daughter came to Moscow in 1939 with other children of Spanish Republicans who fled from Franco. As Ramon was totally unknown among Trotskyites, Eitingon, who was still stationed in Spain at the time, had decided to send him to Paris from Barcelona in the summer of 1938, posing as an adventurous young businessman with a profligate lifestyle who from time to time supported political extremists because of his hostile attitude toward all governments.

Thus by 1938 Ramon and his mother, Caridad, both living in Paris, had become agents for the Soviet Union, formally recruited by Eitingon.[2] In September, Ramon first met Trotskyites in Paris: Sylvia Ageloff, who later became Trotsky's secretary, and the Rosmers.[3] Following orders from Eitingon, he refrained from any political activities. His role was to be a friend who occasionally provided funds but who played no political

2. Eitingon and Caridad were lovers, assert Christopher Andrew and Oleg Gordievsky in *KGB: The Inside Story* (New York: HarperCollins, 1990), p. 168. Sudoplatov insists this would have violated good professional tradecraft. He says they were close but not physically intimate friends, despite Eitingon's deserved reputation as a man of many affairs with women.

3. Alfred and Marguerite Rosmer were French socialists who became disciples of Trotsky, founded the French Trotskyite movement, and traveled with him to Mexico.

role. He took no interest in and rejected their proposal for him to join their work. Ramon Mercader's code name was Mother.

In addition to Mercader we had an important agent code-named Harry, actually an Englishman, Morrison, who was not known either to Orlov or to Shpigelglas. Harry was instrumental in stealing the operational records of the Trotsky organization in Europe in December 1939. He also had good connections in the Seventh Arrondisement gendarme headquarters in Paris and was able to assist us in obtaining real French police stamps for forged passports and permissions for our agents to remain in France.

Eitingon suggested that the task force should operate absolutely autonomously from local NKVD rezidenturas in the United States and Mexico. I agreed with him, but said that it would be impossible to move the entire group from Western Europe using our regular support organization. We estimated we would need $300,000 to set up and equip the group and establish a cover for its operations in Latin America and the United States.

We laid out our options before Beria, stressing that we had no one in Trotsky's entourage capable of assassinating him. We said we felt we would have to storm Trotsky's residence. Beria surprisingly suggested that we use Orlov's connections, and approach him on behalf of Beria personally. Beria had known Orlov when he was serving in Georgia as a commander of a frontier brigade in 1921. Eitingon objected strongly for personal reasons. He had not been on good terms with Orlov in Spain. I agreed with Eitingon and reminded Beria that there was a government order that he himself had issued not to have anything to do with Orlov. Eitingon noted that as a professional intelligence officer Orlov would quickly learn of any attempts to contact him through his relatives in America and would regard them as an effort on our part to assassinate him, thus jeopardizing the operation against Trotsky. Reluctantly, Beria was forced to agree with us.

Beria seemed preoccupied with using his own old personal connections. He had a string of Georgian princes in the West who fed him rumors about unbelievable treasures in remote hiding places in the Caucasus. His wife, Nina, had two uncles, one a staunch Bolshevik, and another who was in the Menshevik[4] government of Georgia, in exile in

---

4. The Mensheviks were a political party of social democrats who advocated a broad proletarian constitutional government. They at first collaborated with the Bolsheviks, then broke with their authoritarian rule. Because of splits within the party, they could not stand up to the Bolsheviks, who took power and suppressed them in 1922.

Paris. Later this formed the basis for the charge that Beria was associated with imperialist intelligence circles. But Beria realized as we spoke that we would need a new network not subject to betrayal. He told us to proceed and not worry about operational funds. Beria said that after we had established the task force, he wanted to add agents who were known to him.

Beria ordered me to accompany Eitingon to Paris to assess the group we would send to Mexico. In June 1939 George Miller, an Austrian emigrant who was director of the NKVD forged passport office, provided us with false papers. When we left Moscow, Eitingon was delighted that one of his sisters, a chronic complainer, did not come to see us off. There was a superstition in his family that any mission that departed with her blessing was doomed to failure. We left Moscow for Odessa, where we boarded a ship sailing to Athens. There we changed our identities and boarded another ship for Marseilles.

We took the train to Paris, where I met first with Ramon and Caridad Mercader and then separately with members of the Siqueiros group; the two working groups did not meet and neither was aware that the other existed. They all appeared quite reliable and, even more important, had been involved before in high-risk military operations, experience that would prove valuable in action against Trotsky. I suggested that Eitingon spend about a month training Caridad and Ramon in intelligence tradecraft, because they were not competent in such basics as operational methods, recognizing surveillance, or changing their appearance. While this training helped them evade the attention of a small group of Trotskyite counterintelligence forces when they arrived in Mexico, the delay was almost fatal for Eitingon.

In August 1939 Caridad and Ramon sailed from Le Havre to New York. Eitingon was supposed to follow them soon after, but by that time the Polish passport with which he had arrived in Paris was no longer valid. After the German invasion of Poland, igniting World War II, he was supposed to be mobilized into the French army as a Polish refugee or interned as a suspected element. Furthermore, tight restrictions on foreign travel for Poles were put into effect, and Eitingon had to go into hiding.

I had returned to Moscow, where I cursed myself for the delay caused by the training period, but there had been no other way. We instructed our rezident in Paris, Lev Vasilevsky, who served as consul general under the alias Tarasov, to undertake all measures to provide

Tom, the code name for Eitingon, with valid travel documents for America. It took Vasilevsky almost a month to fulfill this assignment. Meanwhile, he placed Eitingon in a mental hospital run by a Russian émigré and, under my instructions, he used Morrison's connections to supply Tom with a forged French internal passport of a Syrian Jew suffering from a mental illness. He was now clearly unfit for military service, and this internal document allowing him to reside in France was used to obtain a passport for foreign travel. Vasilevsky was certain that the passport was valid — the French officials had been bribed — but there remained the problem of an American visa and how to get it stamped in the passport.

Our only connection with the American consulate was through a respectable businessman from Switzerland, who was in fact our illegal Maksim Steinberg. But there was an additional problem. Steinberg had refused to return to Moscow when recalled in 1938; he had written a letter pledging his loyalty but saying he feared being unjustly purged. Vasilevsky now sent a case officer to meet Steinberg in Lausanne. After a tense meeting at which Steinberg was prepared to shoot the case officer, who he feared might be an assassin, Steinberg agreed to arrange the visa for the Syrian Jew. Steinberg did not recognize the passport photo of Eitingon, who had grown a moustache and changed his hairstyle. Within a week Steinberg obtained the visa and the case officer returned with it to Paris.

Eitingon arrived in New York in October 1939 and established an import-export company in Brooklyn which we used as a communications center. Most important, it provided cover for Ramon Mercader, now established in Mexico with a forged Canadian passport under the name Frank Jacson, to make frequent trips to New York to meet Eitingon and receive money from him.

In Mexico the cover for the Siqueiros task force was gradually developed. We had two illegal radio operators, but unfortunately radio communications were not effective, because the equipment was poor. Eitingon correctly developed parallel and separate efforts to penetrate Trotsky's villa in Coyoacán, outside Mexico City. The villa was owned by the Mexican painter Diego Rivera, who loaned it to Trotsky. The Siqueiros group was planning to storm the building, while Ramon Mercader was unaware of their existence. His primary goal was to use his love affair with Sylvia Ageloff to become friendly with the people around Trotsky.

Ramon was handsome; his appearance was not unlike the smooth good looks of the French actor Alain Delon. He also had a magnetic charm to which Sylvia had first succumbed in Paris. Sylvia traveled to New York with Ramon, who carefully kept her away from Eitingon. On occasion Eitingon observed Ramon and Sylvia at a restaurant, but he was never introduced to her.

Ramon behaved independently in Trotskyite circles, making no attempt to win their confidence through sympathy with their cause. Rather, he remained a businessman who was supporting Trotsky for his own eccentric reasons, not as a devoted follower.

The Siqueiros group had to rely on a floor plan of Trotsky's villa that had been smuggled out by Maria de la Sierra before she was recalled to Moscow. She made an assessment of Trotsky's bodyguards and gave me a detailed character analysis of his secretariat. This very useful information was forwarded to Eitingon.

At the end of 1939, Beria suggested we strengthen our illegal network in Mexico. Beria brought me to a safe apartment and introduced me to Joseph Grigulevich, code name Padre, who came to Moscow from illegal work in Western Europe. He was known in Trotskyite circles to be politically neutral and was not suspected of trying to infiltrate their organization. His presence in Latin America was natural because his father owned a large drugstore in Argentina. Grigulevich arrived in Mexico in January 1940 and under Eitingon's instructions established a third reserve illegal network to operate in Mexico and California. He also cooperated with the Siqueiros group. Grigulevich managed to meet one of Trotsky's bodyguards, Sheldon Harte, and when Harte was on duty in the predawn hours of May 23, 1940, Grigulevich knocked on the gate. Harte made the fatal mistake of half opening the gate, and the Siqueiros battle group stormed the building. They machine-gunned the room where Trotsky was, but because they shot up the room through a closed door — neglecting to open it — they missed Trotsky, who was hiding under the bed.

Harte was liquidated because he knew Grigulevich and could have exposed us. The incident ended with the arrest of Siqueiros, which provided good cover for the continuation of the efforts of Grigulevich and Mercader, who were still unaware of each other's existence.

The attempt failed because the assault team were not professional assassins experienced in direct personal attack. Unfortunately, Eitingon did not take part in the raid. He would have checked the plan and ensured that Trotsky was eliminated. Among the Siqueiros group there was no one with experience in conducting a search of an apartment or home. They were peasants and miners with only elementary training in guerrilla warfare.

Eitingon reported by coded radio message that the raid was unsuccessful. The report was delayed in reaching us because it came via a Soviet ship in New York. Then it was forwarded in coded form by the radio operator to Vasilevsky in Paris. He relayed it to Moscow, but he was not aware of the importance of the message because he could not decipher it. Because of the delay in transmitting this report, Beria and Stalin learned that the raid was unsuccessful from TASS, the news agency. I don't remember the exact date, but I know it was a Sunday in May 1940. I was summoned to Beria's dacha. He sent his car and driver for me, and when I arrived at the dacha I found two other guests, Ivan Aleksandrovich Serov, then commissar of state security in the Ukraine, and Sergei Nikforovich Kruglov, Beria's permanent deputy. They were in the middle of lunch when I arrived.

Beria did not want to discuss the case in their presence. He gestured for me to wait for him in the garden, where he had planted rare semi-tropical vegetation that he hoped to keep alive in the severe Moscow climate. His wife, Nina, an agronomist, and his son Sergei, to whom he introduced me, were in charge of the garden. He left the table and accompanied me alone to a corner of the garden. Indignantly, he asked about the composition of the team I had approved in Paris and what I knew about the plan for eliminating Trotsky. I said that the professional level of the Siqueiros team was low but they were devoted comrades and ready to sacrifice their lives. I was expecting a full report from Mexico within a day or two via radio. We returned to the dining room and Beria suggested that I immediately return to the office and inform him of any further developments.

Two days later Eitingon's report arrived via Paris and I briefed Beria. Eitingon stressed in the message that with the approval of the Center he would turn to an alternative plan. The alternative plan would mean the end of agent penetration into Trotskyite circles in Mexico. If some of our agents were arrested trying to kill Trotsky, the whole network might be exposed. I briefed Beria on the situation. At first he did not respond to Eitingon's proposal to pull out our agent penetration of Trotsky's secretariat and use one of our outside agents to assassinate Trotsky. Shutting down this network meant giving up the eyes and ears we had in Trotskyite circles in the United States and Mexico. I sensed this was a decision too important to be taken by me and Eitingon; it had to be made by Beria and Stalin. Penetration of Trotskyite groups abroad was still one of the highest priorities for Soviet intelligence in 1940. How would we know what was going on inside the Trotskyite movement after we managed to kill Trotsky? Would the Trotskyites still be powerful and a threat to Stalin without their leader? Stalin regularly read reports that came from our agent who had infiltrated the Trotskyite newspaper in New York. From him we obtained the plans and priorities of the movement and worked to counter them. Often, Stalin read Trotskyite documents and articles even before they were published in New York. I returned to my office on the seventh floor to await word.

I didn't wait long. In two hours I was called to Beria's office on the third floor. "Come with me," he said. This time we drove to Stalin's *bliznye,* or nearby dacha, thirty minutes west of Moscow. The meeting was very short. I reported the failure of the Siqueiros attempt to assassinate Trotsky, and explained that the other option meant that, with the elimination of Trotsky, we would lose our anti-Trotskyite network in the United States and Latin America. Stalin asked only one question: "To what extent is our agent network in the U.S. and Mexico under Ovakimian involved in the operation against Trotsky?"[5] I replied that Eitingon's operation was completely separate from Ovakimian, whose spying efforts under cover of the trading company AMTORG had in no way been compromised.

Stalin remained steadfast with his previous analysis and said, "The elimination of Trotsky will mean the total collapse of the entire Trotskyite movement, and we will have no need to spend any money on combatting Trotskyites and their attempts to undermine the Comintern or us."

Stalin ordered the approval of the alternative plan and, despite the failure of Siqueiros, ordered a cable to Eitingon expressing his full confidence in him. I prepared the cable and added a postscript, "Pavel sends his best regards." Pavel was Beria's code name.

When I was arrested in 1953, the investigators looked into the Operation Duck file, which was kept in my safe, and asked me for the real name of Pavel. I told them it was my name, added to ensure the

5. Gaik Badalovich Ovakimian, who operated out of AMTORG, the Soviet Trade Mission in New York, arrived in the United States in 1933 to head Soviet espionage operations. A short, lively Armenian who was educated as an engineer, Ovakimian specialized in industrial espionage. He was arrested but allowed to leave the United States in July 1941. See Robert J. Lamphere and Tom Shachtman, *The FBI-KGB War* (New York: Random House, 1986), pp. 25–27.

cable's authenticity. I saw no need to emphasize that Eitingon was highly respected by Beria, who by that time had been arrested and executed.

Stalin suggested that Beria and I stay for supper since it was about 11:00 P.M. I remember that it was a simple meal. Stalin displayed his humor and suggested that I taste Georgian wine, but in a very peculiar manner. The glass was filled half with wine and half with Logidzy, a Georgian lemonade. This lemonade was flown daily to Stalin. Contrary to what was later written by General Volkogonov, who was not in the room that night, Stalin did not rage over the failure of the assassination attempt. If he was angry, he masked it in his determination to proceed with the elimination of Trotsky. Certainly, he was displeased that the attempt had been botched, but he appeared to be patient and prepared to play for higher stakes, putting his whole agent network on the line in a final effort to rid himself of Trotsky.

Eitingon later told me that Ramon Mercader was prepared to carry out his mission relying on his training as a guerrilla fighter in Spain. In the course of the war, he had not only used his rifle, but had engaged in hand-to-hand combat with a knife. He was prepared for three alternatives: to shoot Trotsky, stab him, or beat him to death. Without any special laboratory at his disposal, this was the inevitable range of options. Caridad gave her blessing to her son. When she and Eitingon met with Ramon to analyze the security in Trotsky's house, they decided that it would be best to use a knife or a club, as it would be easier to conceal from the guards and members of the household and because there would be a minimum of noise. Ramon was strong enough and had once stabbed a sentry to death at a bridge that was about to be blown up.

It was important to suggest a motive for the act that would undermine Trotsky's image and discredit the movement. The murder would be made to appear to be personal revenge by Mercader for Trotsky's alleged attempt to discourage Sylvia Ageloff from marrying him. If caught, Mercader also was to claim that the Trotskyites wanted to use his financial contributions personally instead of for Trotskyite activities. He would also allege that Trotsky had tried to convince him to join an international terrorist group planning to assassinate Stalin and other Soviet leaders.

On a snowy day early in 1969 I met with Ramon Mercader at the Union of Writers club in Moscow for lunch. It was my first meeting with him after almost thirty years. There Ramon told me the full details of his deed of August 20, 1940. Ramon had known, naturally, that he was a member of the team to combat Trotskyism in Mexico, but he did not expect that he would be the assassin. He told me that when he met with his mother and Eitingon in a safe apartment in Mexico City, it was suggested that Eitingon, Caridad, and a team of five guerrillas attempt to storm Trotsky's house when Mercader was already inside. Their attack would engage the guards, enabling Mercader to shoot Trotsky. "I did not agree with this plan and told them I would carry out the death sentence by myself," Mercader told me.

Contrary to what has been written about the murder itself, Ramon did not close his eyes before striking Trotsky with a small, sharp mountain-climbing pickax he had hidden under his raincoat. Trotsky was alone at the desk in his study. He knew Mercader, who had asked him to read an article he had written defending Trotsky against his critics. Trotsky agreed. At the last moment, just when Mercader was about to strike, Trotsky, who had been absorbed in the article, moved his head. That changed the direction of the blow, weakening its impact. That is why Trotsky was able to scream for help and was not killed instantly. Ramon was too excited and could not stab Trotsky, although he carried a knife. "Imagine, although I was a trained guerrilla who had stabbed a guard to death during the Spanish Civil War, Trotsky's scream almost totally paralyzed me," Ramon explained. When Trotsky's wife appeared with the guards, he was immobilized and could not use his revolver. Anyway, that turned out not to be necessary. Trotsky died in hospital the next day from the pickax blow.

"I was knocked out with the butt of a pistol by one of Trotsky's guards. Later my lawyer used this episode to prove that I was not a professional assassin. I stuck to the story that I was motivated by love for Sylvia and that the Trotskyites were embezzling funds I had given to the movement and were trying to involve me in terrorist operations. I stuck to the prearranged legend that my actions were an internal affair within the Trotskyite movement," Ramon told me.

The plan was that Trotsky would die in silence and before his body was found Ramon would be able to escape, since the bodyguards knew him as a frequent visitor there. Eitingon and Caridad, who were waiting for Ramon in a car parked nearby, were forced to flee when the alarm in the villa became evident. At first they fled to Cuba, where Caridad used her family connections to remain in hiding. Grigulevich escaped from Mexico City to California, where he was not well known.

The first report reached us in Moscow via TASS. Then Eitingon sent a coded radio message from Cuba a week later, once again via Paris. The reaction in Moscow was approval for a job well done. I was too busy at that point with our takeover in Latvia to give any more thought to Trotsky. Beria asked me if Caridad, Eitingon, and Grigulevich had escaped and were in hiding. I told him they were under good cover, unknown to Mercader, who had been arrested on the spot and remained in jail in Mexico City. Mercader was arrested as Frank Jacson, Canadian businessman, and his real identity remained unknown for six years.

Ramon also reminded me of the advice I had given the team in Paris. "If you are caught, try a hunger strike in jail, but do it in such a way that you do not arouse the suspicions of your jailers. At first just eat less and less, preparing yourself for a hunger strike. Eventually they will feed you artificially, and the whole investigation will be delayed." Mercader did this for two or three months and then kept to his story that he was a disgruntled supporter of Trotsky. Ramon said that before his identity was discovered he was beaten by the Mexican police twice a day for six years and was kept in a windowless cell.

Beria said to spare no funds to defend Mercader and to protect the legend that the assassination resulted from chaos and internal conflicts in the Trotskyite movement. Eitingon and Caridad were ordered to remain in hiding. For six months they stayed underground in Cuba. Then they took a ship to New York, and there Eitingon used his connections in the Jewish community to obtain new papers and identity. They traveled across America to Los Angeles and San Francisco and sailed for China in February 1941. Eitingon took advantage of the trip to resume contacts with two agents he had planted in California in the beginning of the 1930s. They were to become couriers in the network obtaining American atomic secrets from 1942 to 1945. In May 1941, on the eve of the Great Patriotic War, Eitingon and Caridad returned to Moscow on the Trans-Siberian Railroad.

Only when one of Ramon's relatives, who was distantly related to Fidel Castro, defected to the West from the Soviet Union was Mercader's real identity unmasked to Western intelligence services. The fact that this information ever came out was the fault of his mother, Caridad, who, after arriving in Moscow, went to live in Tashkent for two years during the war, from 1941 to 1943. There she confided Ramon's role as Trotsky's assassin to her relative, a minor official in the Spanish Communist party who had fled to the Soviet Union at the end of the Spanish Civil War. She thought her secret was safe.

After World War II ended, Caridad made repeated attempts to free Ramon, one of which was to arrange a wife for him, but Stalin ruled against a bride because Ramon's identity was still not known. Caridad traveled to Mexico and then to Paris, looking for help in her cause to get her son out of jail.

Help came unexpectedly when the Spanish Communist party official, Caridad's confidant in Tashkent, defected to the West in 1946 and blew Ramon's cover. Ironically, this saved Ramon from his daily beatings and solitary confinement in prison. When he was confronted with evidence that he was Ramon Mercader, from a wealthy family, and his record in the Spanish police archives was brought to Mexico, he had to admit his real identity. But he never admitted he assassinated Trotsky on the orders of Soviet intelligence. In all his statements, he stressed a personal motive for killing Trotsky.

Conditions in jail improved because of Caridad's indiscretion; once the defector exposed his identity, Ramon was allowed outings to Mexico City to have lunch with the warden. The woman looking after Ramon in jail fell in love with him and came to see him every week. Later he married her and took her with him to Moscow after he was released on August 20, 1960. He had served twenty years.

KGB chairman Aleksandr Nikolayevich Shelepin received Mercader and presented him with the medal of Hero of the Soviet Union, but later when Mercader requested a personal meeting with KGB chairman Vladimir Yefimovich Semichastny, he was refused.[6] Mercader became a Communist party member through a special decision of the Central Committee, and at the direct request of Dolores Ibarruri, La Pasionaria, he was made a senior research fellow of the Institute of Marxism-Leninism. He and his wife were given a party dacha in Kratovo, near Moscow. Mercader received money from the Central Committee and from the KGB, a pension equal to that of a retired major general. But his relations with the KGB were strained in the 1960s because Mercader demanded that Shelepin and then Semichastny arrange the prompt release of Eitingon and me from jail. He pressed this matter with Dolores Ibarruri

6. Aleksandr N. Shelepin, born 1918, was chairman of the KGB from December 1958 to November 1961. Until Khrushchev's ouster in October 1964, he served in high party and government posts and was a Politburo member. Leonid Brezhnev, who succeeded Khrushchev as first secretary, feared him as a rival, and gradually demoted him out of office and power. Semichastny succeeded Shelepin as KGB chairman until April 1967. He played an instrumental role in the ouster of Nikita Khrushchev from power.

before Mikhail Suslov, the senior Politburo member. Suslov was unmoved and outraged that Mercader should try to appeal to him. Suslov told Mercader, "We have decided the fate of these men once and for all."

At first, Mercader lived in the Leningradskaya Hotel near the Leningrad railroad station. Then he received an unfurnished four-room apartment near the Sokol metro station. Vasilevsky, although expelled from the party, was the only one of those involved with Mercader still not under arrest or jailed. He intervened on Mercader's behalf, and adequate furniture was allotted for the apartment. Mercader's wife, Raquelia, worked as an announcer for Radio Moscow Spanish broadcasts. In 1963 they adopted two children, a boy, Arthur, age eleven, and a girl, Laura, six months old. Their parents had been friends of Mercader's. The father, a Spanish Civil War refugee who had fled to Moscow, had been shot by the Franco government in Spain after he returned there as an illegal agent and was captured. The mother had died giving birth to the baby girl in Moscow.

Mercader was a professional revolutionary, proud of his role in the struggle. He told me, "If we were to relive the 1940s I would do the same thing, but not in the present-day world [of 1969]." He did not repent his murder of Trotsky. He quoted the Russian saying, "One does not choose the time to live and die," and said, "I would add to that. One does not choose the time to live, die, or kill."

Mercader left Moscow in the mid-1970s for Cuba, where he worked as an adviser to Fidel Castro. He died in 1978, and his body was returned secretly to Moscow. His widow tried to contact me, but I was out of Moscow at the time. However, Eitingon managed to attend his funeral at the Kuntsevo Cemetery, where he is buried under the alias Ramon Ivanovich Lopez, Hero of the Soviet Union.

It is clear to me now that present morals are incompatible with the cruelty of revolution, civil war, and the power struggles that follow them. Stalin and Trotsky opposed each other, resorting to criminal methods to achieve their ends. The main difference was that during his exile abroad Trotsky opposed not only Stalin, but also the Soviet Union. This confrontation was a state of war that had to be resolved through victory or death. There was no way for Stalin to treat Trotsky in exile as merely a writer of philosophical books; Trotsky was an active enemy who had to be destroyed.

Maria de la Sierra, Trotsky's secretary, code-named Africa, our agent who had been recalled to Moscow when Aleksandr Orlov's defection threatened her cover, was a legendary figure. She parachuted behind German lines to be a guerrilla fighter in World War II, and after the war she was active in the KGB illegal network in Latin America, where she served as a radio operator. She was an illegal for more than twenty years, returning to the Soviet Union only in the 1970s. She died in 1988.

Trotsky's son, Lev Sedov, who took his mother's name, was closely watched by our agents. He was the chief organizer of the Trotskyite movement in the 1930s after he left Turkey and moved to Paris in 1933. We used two independent networks. One was headed by Mark Zborowski, alias Etienne and Tulip, and another was headed by Serebryansky. Zborowski gave us the lead, and Serebryansky used that information to obtain Trotsky's archives, hidden in Paris, and smuggle them out to Moscow with the help of Harry, his agent in Paris. Serebryansky used his agent in the French police to smooth the way. Zborowski had no idea how his tip was used. Volkogonov, however, claims in his biography of Trotsky that Zborowski arranged the smuggling and also helped to kill Sedov in a French hospital, where he died in February 1938 under mysterious circumstances after his appendix was removed.[7]

Sedov definitely died in Paris, but I found no evidence in his file or in the file of the Trotskyite International that he was assassinated. If that were the case, somebody would have been decorated or claimed the honor. At the time, there were accusations that heads of intelligence were taking false credit for elimination of Trotskyites, but no details or examples were provided. The conventional wisdom is that Sedov's death resulted from an NKVD liquidation operation. In fact the record shows that Shpigelglas reported Sedov's death from natural causes to Yezhov, who commented: "A good operation. We did a good job on him, didn't we?" Shpigelglas was not about to argue with Yezhov, who tried to take credit for Sedov's death when reporting it to Stalin. This contributed to the belief that the NKVD did away with Sedov.[8]

---

7. In 1948 Zborowski was questioned by the FBI in New York, where he had settled as a member of the White Russian émigré community. According to Lamphere, "Zborowski gave the FBI excellent information on the KGB's interest in Russian émigrés in the United States, which led to the shutdown of the activities of other KGB agents. For his own illegal activities, Zborowski himself was sent to prison for five years." *The FBI-KGB War*, p. 88.

8. Costello and Tsarev quote from the transcript of Shpigelglas's confession in May 1939 in *Deadly Illusions*, pp. 469–470.

When Eitingon and I discussed with Beria the plan to eliminate Trotsky the death of Sedov was never raised. It is easy to assume that Sedov was assassinated, but I do not believe that to be the case, and the reason is very simple. He was so closely watched by us and so trusted by Trotsky that his presence in Paris kept us informed about Trotskyite plans to smuggle agents and propaganda materials to the Soviet Union via Europe. His liquidation would have lost us control over information about Trotskyite operations in Europe.

After Trotsky's assassination, some members of the illegal network I had set up in the United States and Mexico were integrated with other illegals already in place. This enlarged network would later become invaluable in collecting the secrets of America's first atomic bomb. Our illegals, who had false papers and no official government positions, had begun operating in the late 1920s and early 1930s. We trained and assigned our officers to live abroad and gather information or work their way into positions of access to information. In other cases we simply told them to go abroad, become good members of their communities, and wait to be called upon to serve.

In the beginning of the 1930s Eitingon had been sent to the United States as an illegal to recruit Japanese and Chinese emigrants who might be useful in military and sabotage operations against Japan. By that time the Japanese had seized the central and northern areas of China in Manchuria and we feared war with Japan. At the same time, he planted two moles, Polish Jews, whom he arranged to bring from France.

Another chief task of Eitingon's was to assess the intelligence potential of Americans involved in Communist activities. He was shrewd enough to suggest that recruiting operations should concentrate on people who were sympathetic to Communist ideas but were not true members of the party.

Eitingon was joined by Isak Akhmerov, who, despite Eitingon's strong objections, married the niece of Earl Browder, founder of the American Communist party. For the Center, operations in the United States and the establishment of an illegal network there were not considered high priorities, because at that time intelligence information from the United States did not affect any major decisions in the Kremlin. However, Eitingon asked some of his confidential contacts to focus on U.S. policy toward China. He managed to locate the journalists who later formed the so-called Amerasia Lobby, which influenced State Department policy decisions on Asia.[9]

One of the agents Eitingon recruited was a well-known Japanese painter, Miyagi, who later became part of the Sorge team in Tokyo.[10] Eitingon and my good friend Ivan Vinarov, who later became the director of Bulgarian intelligence in the 1940s under Georgi M. Dimitrov, contacted Sorge in Shanghai at the end of the 1920s. Sorge's information throughout the 1930s was treated as valuable but with the caveat that he was regarded by the Germans and Japanese authorities as a double agent.

In 1932 Eitingon left California and returned to the Soviet Union via Shanghai. He was appointed deputy to Serebryansky, but quarreled with him and was nominated instead to be chief of the section in the Foreign Department responsible for illegals and fabricating false passports.

After we established diplomatic relations with the United States in 1934, the Center believed that war with Japan was inevitable. We required intelligence capability in the western states of the United States. For that purpose the choice was natural, Gregory Kheifetz, who had first worked in the Comintern and was one of the organizers of the American Communist party. He personally knew many prominent American Communists. After his Comintern experience, Kheifetz had been transferred to the Foreign Department of the GPU. He had set up illegal networks in Germany and Italy in the mid-1930s, posing as a student from India. Kheifetz was a Jew, but because of his dark skin he gave the impression

9. *Amerasia* magazine was started in 1936–1937 and supported a pro-Soviet united front and coalition between the Chinese Communists and Nationalists. *Amerasia* was co-owned and edited by Philip Jaffe and Frederic Vanderbilt Field and followed a pro-Soviet line. In June 1945 Jaffe was arrested by the FBI when seventeen hundred classified documents were found in the magazine's office. Jaffe pleaded guilty to the charge of removing confidential material from government files but denied he worked for Soviet intelligence. See David J. Dallin, *Soviet Espionage* (New Haven: Yale University Press, 1964), pp. 445–450.

10. Yotoku Miyagi was born in 1903, the second son of a peasant family in Okinawa. His father emigrated to California, and Miyagi, suffering from the first signs of tuberculosis, joined his father in June 1919. Miyagi graduated from the San Diego Public Art School and established the Owl restaurant in Los Angeles. He joined a Marxist study group and was recruited as a member of the Communist party in 1931. In September 1933 Miyagi returned to Japan and became a member of the Sorge spy ring. He was arrested and died in prison in 1943.

of being an Asian emigrant, even though he had blue eyes. In America he was known as Mr. Brown.

When Kheifetz served in Italy, he established valuable contacts there; he met Bruno Pontecorvo, then a young student in Rome. Kheifetz recommended that Pontecorvo contact Frédéric Joliot-Curie, the famous French physicist, who was close to the leadership of the French Communist party. Pontecorvo would later act as the conduit supplying atomic secrets to us from Enrico Fermi.

Kheifetz was lucky not to have been purged in the 1930s. He was summoned to Moscow and Yezhov ordered his arrest in November 1938, but as I explained earlier, Merkulov tore up the arrest order that I found in Yezhov's safe. Then Kheifetz was sent to the United States to monitor scientific and technological developments and to assess the intelligence potential of the American Communist party. Kheifetz cleverly made it appear that he was only collecting routine information on the activities of American Trotskyites, of no interest to the FBI. He was told about the moles Eitingon planted for possible use in case of war between the Soviet Union and Japan. The original plan was to set up our illegal network in American ports, similar to what we had done in Scandinavia, to destroy ships transporting strategic raw materials and fuel to Japan. Not knowing the Japanese intentions to attack Southeast Asia or Pearl Harbor, we assumed they would go to war with us first.

Kheifetz's deputy in the San Francisco consular office, Viktor Liagin, was assigned the special task of procuring technological information from the West Coast. Liagin was an engineer, a graduate of the Leningrad Shipbuilding Institute. His primary task was to monitor American naval programs. I remember his report emphasizing the great interest attached to the aircraft carrier program.

Liagin recruited an agent in San Francisco who described to us antimagnetic devices being developed to protect ships against mines. Liagin kept away from all contacts with American pro-Communist circles.

Liagin did not serve long in San Francisco. He was summoned to Moscow and appointed a deputy director of foreign intelligence when he was only thirty-two years old. Later I sent him to the Black Sea naval base in Nikolayev as an illegal rezident when it was occupied by the Germans. He conducted sabotage actions while pretending to be friends with the German head of the naval base. The Germans discovered his dual role, and he and his radio operator were arrested by the Gestapo and shot. In 1945 we awarded him the title of Hero of the Soviet Union.

Kheifetz in San Francisco was provided with funds to support the two moles established by Eitingon. They led normal lives, one a dentist, the other posing as the owner of a medium-sized retail business. They were both Jewish emigrants from Poland. The dentist was known to Serebryansky and, in fact, we had given him the money to receive his dental degree from a French medical college. The two moles were in place, ready for their next assignment, which might come in one year or ten. Soon enough the American Southwest came into Moscow's focus. From Mexico City our illegals fanned out into California and New Mexico. From this seedbed we made our first contacts with Robert Oppenheimer and the builders of the American atomic bomb.

STALIN AND HITLER: PRELUDE TO WAR

n late May 1937 a group of eight high-ranking Soviet generals were accused of high treason, espionage, and secretly plotting to overthrow the government by means of a military coup. They were promptly arrested, and after two weeks, following a closed military trial, they were executed. Thus began Stalin's purge of the military, which cost us thirty-five thousand of our best officers and men and left us without their experienced leadership when Hitler attacked.

The most famous and highest ranking of the eight senior officers was Marshal Mikhail Nikolayevich Tukhachevsky, chief of staff of the Red Army from 1925 to 1928 and at the time of his death the deputy commissar for military and naval affairs and chairman of the Revolutionary Military Council.

From files that are now being published we know that the criminal charges against Tukhachevsky and other high-ranking military leaders were consciously fabricated. The real reasons behind Stalin's and Marshal Voroshilov's orders to Andrei Vyshinsky (the chief prosecutor) and Yezhov to liquidate these people have not been widely written about, then or now.

Currently there are three versions of the reasons for their fall. The first states that they were compromised by German and Czechoslovakian disinformation that convinced a suspicious Stalin and his defense minister, Kliment Y. Voroshilov, that the generals were maintaining secret contacts with German military commanders. This was the version repeated by Khrushchev in his address denouncing Stalin to the Twentieth Party Congress in 1956.

The German connection must be understood against the background of a close relationship between German and Soviet strategic thinkers. In 1933, Stalin ended a long period of cooperation between the military leadership of Germany and the Soviet Union under the fabricated pretext that the Germans were leaking information to the French about secret Soviet-German military contacts.[1] A group of Soviet generals, led by Marshal Tukhachevsky, had wanted to continue it, hoping to utilize Germany's technological leadership. There was similar interest, but for different reasons, on the German side, especially among high-ranking East Prussian officers, followers of the Wehrmacht's founder, General Hans von Seeckt. After defeat in World War I, Von Seeckt spent years rebuilding German military strength and studying its strategic options. He demanded that the German leadership improve relations with the USSR to avoid the danger of war on two fronts.

The second version alleges that the victims were the intellectual superiors of Voroshilov and had a stronger, more professional military overview. They disagreed with Stalin and Voroshilov on issues of strategy and military reform, the theory goes, and therefore Stalin got rid of them, fearing they would become rivals to power.

The third version states that they were eliminated because of a long-simmering hostility between Tukhachevsky and Stalin over blame for military mistakes during the Civil War and the war against Poland in 1920. The Red Army was defeated on the outskirts of Warsaw because Stalin and Voroshilov blocked the transfer of cavalry troops to assist Tukhachevsky in the battle of the Vistula River.

My own view differs from these three versions. I recall being startled

---

1. In a secret message to the German Embassy in Moscow in June 1933, Nikolai Krestinsky, deputy commissar of foreign affairs, falsely accused German vice chancellor Franz von Papen of disclosing the top-secret Soviet-German military contacts to French officials and canceled further cooperation. The Soviet note was unexpected because in May Voroshilov and Tukhachevsky had received a top-level German military delegation. Stalin's decision was dictated by his belief that the Germans had served their purpose, helping to lay the foundations for Soviet tank and aircraft production. N. Roshchin, writing in *Voyennoi Istoricheski Zhurnal* (*Journal of Military History*), August 1993, p. 41.

when I examined the reports coming from Germany in August 1939 that revealed the German high command's rather high assessment of the Red Army's potential. I remember, as well, a document of the German high command intercepted by us that postulated the causes for Marshal Tukhachevsky's fall as his ambitions and basic disagreement with the quiet Marshal Voroshilov, who was wholly subservient to Stalin's views. Beria underlined one sentence in this document: "The fall of Tukhachevsky decisively shows that Stalin tightly controls the Red Army."

This statement was quoted by Beria in the summary of intelligence information he forwarded to Stalin, probably to please Stalin with fawning affirmation of his good judgment in getting rid of Tukhachevsky.

I remember Beria's comments on this case and especially those of Viktor Abakumov, who was in charge of military counterintelligence during the war, supervising the political and combat reliability of the armed forces. Both men remarked on the impudence of Tukhachevsky and his subordinates, who, they said, planned to demand that Stalin dismiss Voroshilov. This, Beria explained, clearly indicated that the highest military ranks were behaving contrary to party rules, daring to make proposals totally beyond their authority. The Politburo, according to Beria, was the only institution that could initiate any move to substitute or change a people's commissar of defense. Besides, Abakumov noted several times, Tukhachevsky and his crowd had behaved immodestly, in a manner not befitting senior officers. They had ordered the military orchestra to stage private concerts for them and to play for parties at Tukhachevsky's dacha.

I learned what was proper behavior from a conversation in October 1941 with Marshal Boris Mikhailovich Shaposhnikov, who succeeded Tukhachevsky. In the urgency of wartime, I had suggested that to speed up the general staff's reaction to information from highly placed agents, we should channel it directly to him. He replied in a self-effacing manner: "Golubchick [Little Pigeon, a common term of endearment among Russians], important military intelligence should always first be sent to the political leadership of the country. Most urgent messages should be sent simultaneously to Stalin, as people's commissar of defense, and to Beria as your direct superior, with a copy to me. Remember, these are the strict rules which we are in no way authorized to modify." The marshal was a seasoned bureaucrat.[2]

---

2. Shaposhnikov was forced to step down because of poor health in 1942, and he died in 1945.

Another element in his downfall: Tukhachevsky was on bad terms with General Shaposhnikov. At the end of the 1920s, Tukhachevsky had conspired to get Shaposhnikov demoted and had taken his place as chief of the general staff. Significantly, Shaposhnikov was a member of the special military court that sentenced Tukhachevsky. He and the chief judge, V. V. Ulrikh, were the only members of this court to survive the purges.

My belief is that Tukhachevsky and his group were probably tempted by Stalin, who met with them frequently, to criticize Voroshilov. Stalin was always receptive to what he called constructive criticism and discussion of alternatives. He was willing to consider various approaches to military, industrial, and foreign policies. Tukhachevsky took this liberty beyond closed doors and spread rumors about imminent changes in the Ministry of Defense. He and his colleagues went too far. They became a matter of concern when the NKVD reported these rumors to the leadership. Even historians eager to expose the crimes of Stalinism admit that Tukhachevsky's file contains evidence of rumors and stories of plans to reshuffle the military leadership.

In the published archives of the Red Army there is a letter to Voroshilov, signed by the chief of the secretariat of the Ministry of Defense, I. V. Smorodinov, dated June 5, 1937, asking Voroshilov's permission to provide the NKVD with copies of Tukhachevsky's letters to Stalin and Voroshilov on military matters. No resolution to this request is revealed, but it is clear to me that in the course of the investigation against him, Tukhachevsky protested vigorously, referring to documents that proved lack of serious disagreements on military matters among him, Voroshilov, and Stalin.

Tukhachevsky argued that he maintained contacts with German military representatives only under instruction of the government. He struggled to prove that he was obediently and loyally fulfilling orders in every aspect of military policy.

Bolstering Khrushchev's version of this affair, that Stalin swallowed German disinformation designed to destroy Tukhachevsky, is a legend that Stalin was warned of a conspiracy with the Germans. In 1939 the Soviet defector Krivitsky, who had worked for the NKVD and GRU in Western Europe, published his book *In Stalin's Secret Service,* in which he claimed that the NKVD received secret information about such a conspiracy from Czech president Edvard Beneš and from its agent Nikolai Skoblin, code name Farmer, who had been a White general in our Civil

War. Krivitsky accused Skoblin of providing the Soviets with disinformation from the Germans about secret contacts with Tukhachevsky. Later General Walter Schellenberg, chief of Hitler's foreign intelligence service, in his memoirs[3] also claimed that the Germans fabricated documents pointing to Tukhachevsky as their agent. Before the war, he said, they passed these documents to the Czechs, and Beneš reported the information to Stalin.

For me, this is a self-serving fairy tale. The documents have never been found in the KGB or Stalin archives. The criminal case against Tukhachevsky is based entirely on his confession, and there is no reference to any incriminating evidence received from German intelligence. If such documents existed I, as deputy director and the man responsible for the German desk in the intelligence directorate, would have seen them or found some reference to their existence. The only mention of German intelligence connections in Skoblin's file is in reference to the pretext he used in Paris to lure General Miller to the safe apartment. According to his file, Skoblin's "German" contacts for the operation to kidnap the White Russian leader were in fact NKVD Paris rezident Kislov (code name Finn) and Shpigelglas (code name Douglas).

(Contrary to versions of events by Christopher Andrew and Oleg Gordievsky, John J. Dziak, and Krivitsky, Skoblin was not involved in eliminating Miller's predecessor, General Aleksandr Kutepov. This job was done in 1930 by Yakov Serebryansky, assisted by his wife and his agent in the French police. Dressed in French police uniforms, they stopped Kutepov on the street on the pretext of questioning him and put him in a car. Kutepov resisted the kidnapping, and during the struggle he had a heart attack and died, Serebryansky told me. They buried Kutepov near the home of one of our agents on the outskirts of Paris.)[4]

In reality, the archives show nothing about any involvement of Tukhachevsky in suspicious connections with the Germans. The files show only a routine compilation of foreign sources' comments about him, including some nonincriminating remarks by Beneš.

In July 1937 Aleksandrovsky, the Soviet ambassador to Czechoslovakia, reported President Beneš's reaction to the execution of the generals. There have been contradictory interpretations of the remarks of

3. *The Labyrinth* (New York: Harper & Brothers, 1956).

4. See Andrew and Gordievsky, *KGB: The Inside Story*, pp. 152–153 and 163–164; Dziak, *Chekisty: A History of the KGB*, pp. 111–113; and Krivitsky, *In Stalin's Secret Service* (Frederick, Md.: University Publications of America, 1985), pp. 237–240.

Beneš, who is portrayed by Soviet historians as a man who "sincerely and with good intentions betrayed Tukhachevsky to Stalin, being unaware of the German falsification of the materials he was passing to the Soviets." The documents tell quite a different story.[5]

According to Aleksandrovsky, Beneš emphasized that he didn't believe that Tukhachevsky was a spy and saboteur; nor did he believe that the marshal was plotting the overthrow of Stalin. He stressed that Tukhachevsky was only capable of overthrowing Stalin in alliance with Yagoda. Tukhachevsky, according to Beneš, referring to information from the Czech ambassador in Berlin, simply favored continued Soviet-German military cooperation, despite this cooperation having been severed when Hitler ascended to power. It is clear that Beneš didn't seriously believe in the guilt of Tukhachevsky, but sensed that for some reason the marshal had lost favor with the Stalinist regime. He added to the criticism of Tukhachevsky because he needed Stalin's support and, like Beria, wanted to heap approval on Stalin's decision. Aleksandrovsky's diary quoted Beneš as saying Tukhachevsky was an adventurer, unreliable. The sum total was that Beneš enthusiastically supported the purge of Tukhachevsky but in no way played a role in his removal and arrest.

It is clear from the NKVD archives file Remote Farm that Beneš, on April 24, 1937, the eve of Tukhachevsky's downfall, hinted to Ambassador Aleksandrovsky and NKVD rezident Pyotr Zubov that he did not rule out a possible agreement between Germany and the Soviet Union over their current differences, in part because of the good relationship between the Red Army and the Wehrmacht established by Tukhachevsky in the 1920s and 1930s. However, not until July 4, 1937, after Tukhachevsky's execution, did Beneš tell Aleksandrovsky about obscure contacts of the Czech ambassador in Berlin with German military officials, which had allegedly taken place in January 1937.

Beneš had received from his ambassador in Berlin reports of vague hints by German generals that they were maintaining confidential relations with the Red Army leadership. The purpose of this German disinformation was to frighten the Czechs into believing that they could not count on the support of the Red Army in a confrontation with Germany over the issue of Sudetenland. This was in July 1937, one year before the ultimatum from Hitler to Beneš demanding that the Sudeten-

5. Central Archive of the Red Army, file 33987, summary 3, case 1028[1], pp. 107–114.

land, with its ethnic German population, must be ceded by the Czechs to Germany.[6] In his diary, Beneš records his apology to Aleksandrovsky for not sharing with the Soviet leadership information that suggested there were secret contacts between the Wehrmacht command and Red Army headquarters, information that would have been one more reason for Tukhachevsky's downfall.

Also from the Remote Farm file comes the real purpose of the July meeting between Ambassador Aleksandrovsky, Zubov, and Beneš. Beneš wanted support from Stalin in overthrowing the government in Belgrade, which was hostile to the Czech leadership. This move was thwarted by our rezident Zubov, who doubted the reliability of Beneš's connections and ties in Belgrade. Beneš wanted Stalin's all-out support of Czech policy in the Balkans and in Europe. That is why, in contrast to the British and French, he did not disapprove of the execution of Tukhachevsky and Stalin's purge of the Soviet military command.

I have heard that there are still secret files on Tukhachevsky in the archives of Stalin's secretariat, based on materials received from abroad. I would venture that these files are nothing more than a reader's clipping service of the foreign and domestic press, plus reports from TASS correspondents, diplomats, heads of trade missions, and NKVD and GRU rezidenturas on the way Tukhachevsky was perceived abroad. These were called the Special Foreign Mail File, which compiled the reactions of foreign public opinion to Soviet ambassadors and heads of our government delegations. They included German, French, or British minutes of meetings with high-level Soviet officials, reported through intelligence channels, which were valuable because they revealed the thoughts of people with whom we were negotiating.

The tragedy was that Stalin, and later Khrushchev, Brezhnev, and Gorbachev, used materials from the Special Foreign Mail File to compromise their rivals during internal power struggles. These collections of clippings were usually discounted and ignored, but Stalin established the rule that foreign press assessments of individuals could be used as incriminating material. This rule, formalized by special enactment of the Central Committee, was used in 1989 to discredit Russian leader Boris Yeltsin when he visited the United States for the first time and was accused in the press of drunken behavior. In 1991 the clipping service again became a weapon in the conflict between Gorbachev and Eduard

---

6. The region, in western Czechoslovakia along the German border, was annexed by Hitler in September 1938 as a result of the Munich Agreement.

Shevardnadze, his former foreign minister. The use of the clippings was abandoned by Gorbachev only in November 1991, on the eve of his downfall. Vitaly Ignatenko, head of TASS and an ally of Gorbachev, put an end to this long-established procedure.

In the 1930s it seemed to me that anyone who was exposed as disloyal to the government or to party leaders, such as Stalin and Voroshilov, was undoubtedly an enemy of the state. Only later did I realize the cynicism of Beria's and Abakumov's comments on Tukhachevsky; the top leadership knew the accusations were fabricated. They preferred the story of a military plot because it would have been damaging to themselves and to the party to admit that the targets of their purges were in fact rivals for leadership.

What had been a grave crime in 1937, spreading critical remarks about Voroshilov, which indeed Tukhachevsky had done, suddenly in 1957, when he was rehabilitated, was no longer a crime. There was no change in the law and no apology. There were only vague references to "mistakes" in the official party documents.

On April 8, 1938, the NKVD rezident in Finland, Boris Rybkin, was summoned to the Kremlin, where Stalin and other members of the Politburo, in a formal way, entrusted him with the mission of acting as informal envoy of the Soviet government in Finland. Rybkin donated money, on Stalin's orders, to the formation of the Small Farmers party, which propagated a neutral stand for Finland. Rybkin was ordered to offer the Finnish government a secret deal, sharing interests in Scandinavia and economic cooperation with the Soviet Union, on the conditions of their signing a pact of mutual economic and military assistance in case of aggression by third parties. The pact was to guarantee Finland eternal safety from attack by European powers and mutual economic privileges for the two countries on a permanent basis. Included in the proposals was a division of spheres of military and economic influence over the Baltic areas that lay between Finland and the Soviet Union.

Rybkin expressed his doubts that the Finns would agree to a treaty contrary to their historic hostility toward their eastern neighbor, but Stalin stressed that these proposals should be offered orally, without the involvement of our ambassador. Rybkin did as he was told, and the proposals were turned down by the Finns; however, they caused a split in the Finnish leadership that we later exploited when we managed to sign a separate peace treaty with Finland in 1944, with the Swedish Wallenberg family acting as intermediaries.

While I have no knowledge whether or not similar proposals were made informally to the Germans, I believe that Marshal Carl Gustaf Mannerheim, chairman of Finland's defense council, informed Hitler about our overtures. Therefore, Hitler, when he sent his foreign minister, Joaquim von Ribbentrop, to Moscow in August 1939 to negotiate a nonaggression treaty, was not relying just on the spontaneous reaction of Molotov and Stalin. He knew that we were open to such suggestions because we had already sought a similar deal with Finland that had failed.

The Finns refused the deal in April 1938 because for them it was more important to remain allied with Britain, Sweden, and Germany. They saw no benefit in becoming the buffer zone between East and West. Later this role was forced on them by their defeat in the border war between us and then in the German-Soviet war. For attacking the Soviet Union jointly with the Germans, Finland reaped the war's bitter harvest. As a consequence, Finland had to live with a less advantageous form of the original plan offered by Rybkin in 1938.[7]

The intelligence traffic was intensive in August 1939. After Donald Maclean was transferred from London to Paris,[8] we received reliable reports that the French and British governments were reluctant to commit support to the Soviet Union in case of war with Germany. This dovetailed with information we had received three or four years before from the Cambridge ring — Philby, Maclean, and Burgess — that the British cabinet, namely Neville Chamberlain and Sir John Simon, were consid-

7. Formal negotiations with the Finns to move the Soviet-Finnish border on the Karelian isthmus farther away from Leningrad and, to protect the city from attack by sea, for the Soviet Union to take over all the islands in the Gulf of Finland, broke down as the Finns refused Stalin's demands. On November 30, 1939, the Winter War began as Soviet troops from the Leningrad military district attacked. What the Soviets thought would be an easy victory turned into a humiliating and costly little war, with heavy Soviet losses. The Finns in camouflage white on skis were better prepared for winter warfare, and it was not until February 17, after a massive artillery bombardment followed by 1,000 tanks and 140,000 troops, that the Mannerheim Line was breached and the Finns ran out of reserves. The Finns were forced to agree to tougher terms from Stalin and cede 22,000 square miles of their territory to end the war on March 11, 1940. See Alan Bullock, *Hitler and Stalin: Parallel Lives* (New York: Alfred A. Knopf, 1992), pp. 659–662.

8. After more than two years in a London posting, Donald Maclean had been routinely reassigned by the British Foreign Office and by late fall 1938 was in place as third secretary in the Paris embassy.

ering a secret agreement with Hitler to support him in a military confrontation with the Soviet Union. We also gave special attention to the
information from three reliable sources in Germany. They said that the
Wehrmacht generals strongly objected to any war on two fronts.

We received instructions to look quickly into possible options for
nonaggression cooperation, not only with the British and French, with
whom we were already cooperating, but also with Germany. In Germany only East Prussian aristocrats and influential military figures supported a peaceful settlement with the Soviet Union. These were the same
ones who had given credence to cooperation between the Wehrmacht
and the Red Army, encouraged by Tukhachevsky.

Having been ordered to look into the alternatives, either an agreement with the English and French or a settlement with Germany, it did
not occur to me that a separate deal between Berlin and Moscow was
already afoot. When I was informed of the imminent arrival of the German foreign minister in Moscow on August 23, 1939, just hours before
it took place, it came as a surprise to me. When Ribbentrop arrived and
the nonaggression pact was signed in the Kremlin thirteen hours later,
at 2:00 A.M. on August 24, it became evident that this was not a sudden
decision. The strategic goal of the Soviet leadership was to avert war on
two fronts, in the Far East and in Europe, at any cost. This pattern of
diplomatic relations not governed by ideological considerations had
already been established in the 1920s, when the Soviet Union carried on
economic cooperation and normal relations with Italy after the fascist
regime of Benito Mussolini came to power in 1922. The Kremlin leadership was ready for a compromise with any regime, provided it guaranteed stability for the Soviet Union. The first priority of Stalin and his
aides was the fulfillment of their geopolitical aspirations to transform
the Soviet Union into the largest superpower of the world.

The country had developed more or less steadily only after the end
of the collectivization drive in 1934. Up until then it had undergone civil
war and chaos, turmoil, and upheavals. Only by the mid-thirties did
industrialization begin to bear fruit. The growing might of the country
was displayed in successful military confrontations with Japan in Mon-
golia and Manchuria. Although the country had established diplomatic
relations with all the major powers and was thus seemingly accepted as
a member of the international community, it was nevertheless kept in
isolation when the world powers settled their interests among themselves. All cardinal agreements on the future of Europe and Asia were

undertaken by the Western powers and Japan with no concern for the interests of the Soviet Union. The Anglo-German agreement of 1935, accepting German naval rearmament, and the subsequent agreements between major powers in the naval arms race, did not include the Soviet Union.

The French and British delegations that arrived in Moscow in August 1939 to probe the possibility of an alliance against Hitler were headed by secondary figures. Stalin's policy of appeasing Hitler thus was based on the reasonable belief that hostility against Soviet communism by the Western world and Japan would forever keep the USSR in isolation from the international community.

Looking back, all three future allies — the Soviet, British, and French governments — were guilty of letting Hitler unleash World War II. Mutual suspicion ruled out compromise agreements between the British and French on one side and the Soviet Union on the other that could have halted Hitler's aggression against Poland. It is overlooked by historians of World War II that only President Franklin D. Roosevelt's initiative started British, French, and Soviet negotiations in May 1939 in an attempt to stop Hitler's aggression. Donald Maclean reported that Roosevelt had sent an envoy to Prime Minister Chamberlain warning that the domination of Germany in Western Europe would be detrimental to American and British interests. Roosevelt urged Chamberlain to enter into negotiations with Britain's European allies, including the Soviet Union, to contain Hitler. Our intelligence sources reported that the British government reacted reluctantly to this American initiative and had to be forced by Roosevelt to start negotiations with the Soviets on military measures to stop Hitler.

Nevertheless, the nonaggression treaty with Hitler came out of the blue for me, because only two days before it was signed I was receiving orders to look into options for peaceful settlement with Germany. We were still sending these strategic propositions to Stalin and Molotov when the treaty was signed. Stalin had handled the negotiations on his own in total secrecy.

I did not know about the secret protocols of the Molotov-Ribbentrop Pact,[9] but such protocols are a natural feature of diplomatic relations regarding sensitive issues. On the eve of outbreak of war, the

9. The secret protocols of the pact spelled out how Germany and the USSR would divide the territory of Poland and the Baltic states between them.

British government signed secret protocols with Poland concerning its obligations for military assistance to Poland if war broke out between Poland and Germany. Similarly, in 1993 the German weekly *Wecht* published secret protocols and minutes of confidential meetings between Gorbachev and Chancellor Helmut Kohl on the eve of the unification of Germany. When I look now at the Molotov-Ribbentrop secret protocols, I find nothing secret in them. The directives based on these agreements were definite and clear, and were known not only to the intelligence directorate but to the heads of military, diplomatic, economic, and border guards administrations.[10] In fact, the famous map of the division of Poland, which was attached to the protocols in October 1939, was published a week later in *Pravda,* without Stalin's and Ribbentrop's signatures, for the whole world to see. By then, of course, Poland had fallen to Germany, and Britain and France had entered the war.

In October 1939, together with Pavel M. Fitin, director of intelligence, and Vsevolod Merkulov, Beria's deputy, I attended a meeting in Molotov's Kremlin office that included the director of the operational department of the general staff, Major General Aleksandr M. Vasilevsky (minister of defense in the 1950s); Deputy Commissar of Foreign Affairs V. P. Potemkin; Deputy Chairman of the State Planning Committee Borisov; the deputy chief of the navy, Admiral Ivan S. Isakov; the chief of the Border Troops, General Ivan I. Maslennikov; and the chief of the GRU, Major General I. V. Panfilov.

The agenda of the meeting was to put forward recommendations for defending our strategic interests in the Baltic states. Our troops were already deployed there under pacts with the governments of Lithuania, Latvia, and Estonia. Molotov, who opened the meeting, stated, "We have agreement with Germany that the Baltic zone is to be regarded as an area of most important geopolitical interest to the Soviet Union. It is clear, however," continued Molotov, "that although the German authorities accept that in principle, they would never agree to any 'cardinal social transformations' that would change the Baltic states into constituent republics of the Soviet Union. On the contrary, the Soviet leadership believes that the way to defend the geopolitical interests of the Soviet Union in the Baltic zone in the most lasting manner would be to help the proletarian internationalist movement in the area. That would change this region into a reliable frontier of the Soviet state."

10. The full texts were released from the Presidential Archives in 1992.

From that comment it was clear how we intended to interpret the terms of the agreement with Hitler. In the late autumn of 1939, however, there was a new impetus for activating our political, economic, military, and intelligence operations in the Baltic republics. From our rezidenturas in Sweden and in Berlin we received checked and reliable information that the Germans were planning to send top-level economic delegations to Riga and Tallinn to make long-term agreements with these regimes to include them under Germany's political and economic umbrella. The cables from Berlin and Sweden were each dispatched under two signatures, the rezident's and the ambassador's, which was unusual and meant high priority. On arrival the cables were countersigned by Molotov and then Beria, and then normally forwarded with Beria's orders to Fitin and me in the NKVD for action. Whenever top-level cables were signed by both ambassadors and rezidents, they were also channeled to several top members of the Politburo as well as to the minister of foreign affairs.

Fitin routed the cables to Gukasov, chief of the section dealing with nationalist and emigrant organizations settled in areas near our borders. It was Gukasov who had called for the Party Bureau to investigate me a year earlier. Now, still suspicious of my loyalty and probably holding a grudge, he didn't pass on Beria's instructions to me. On his own, Gukasov prepared inadequate recommendations to counter German intelligence in Latvia, Lithuania, and Estonia, and then routed them back to Fitin, bypassing me. His plan was to use only agent networks comprised of Russian and Jewish emigrants in the three Baltic republics. A scandal ensued.

Beria summoned Fitin and me to his office, and when Fitin reported Gukasov's recommendations Beria asked my opinion. I answered honestly that I had no opinion, never having received any instructions and being unaware of German intentions in Riga. I had been busy with other matters. He exploded with rage; the cables were once again brought into his office. He saw that my signature was missing; the standard rule was that any secret paper passing through the hands of an official in the intelligence bureau should be signed by that official. Gukasov was then called on the carpet and Beria threatened to take his head off for not complying with his order. Gukasov said he had not shown me the cables because — he dropped his voice in a confidential manner — he was informed by the chief of the Investigation Department, Sergienko, that there was incriminating evidence of my suspicious contacts with the former leadership of the intelligence bureau, exposed as dangerous enemies of the people. Beria replied that Gukasov should overcome his stupid haggling mentality and realize once and forever that his orders should be implemented immediately, without hesitation.

Now, with Europe at war, intelligence priorities had greatly changed, Beria said. He quoted Stalin, who demanded active involvement of intelligence operatives in political manipulations and exploitation of conflicts in ruling circles of foreign powers. "This," underlined Beria, "is the key to success in bringing down the current governments of the semipuppet states that proclaimed so-called independence in 1918 under the patronage of German bayonets" — a scathing reference to the Baltic states. "These states were at that time and are still regarded by German administrations as provincial outskirts and colonies of the German empire," emphasized Beria. "But we must play on the conflicts of British and Swedish interests in this area," he said, turning to me. "Think it over, summon Chichayev to Moscow immediately, and report your suggestions, along with the required logistical support you will need, in three days."

This cocky and arrogant thinking reflected the way Stalin, Molotov, and Beria were exploiting the pact with Hitler. It was a sea change in their self-confidence. More important, we began to proceed with active measures to influence "in a cardinal manner" the internal situation in the areas that had come under our geopolitical sphere of interest.

When Ivan Chichayev, NKVD rezident in Riga, arrived in Moscow, he reported a sharp split in the Latvian government, namely between President Karlis Ulmanis and Minister of Defense Janis Balodis. This conflict undermined the stability of the Latvian regime, which was already under double pressure from us and from the Germans. Naturally, the Germans relied on their strong supporters in the Latvian economic administration and in the business community, while we were influential in left-wing groups connected with the Communist party and trade unions. However, Latvia and the other Baltic states were in fact a buffer zone between us and Germany. The plan to form a broad coalition government, in which German and Soviet interests would be equally represented, was discussed in Molotov's Kremlin office. Ulmanis, when he heard of it, opposed this idea, while Minister of Foreign Affairs Wilhelm Munters unexpectedly supported it. Meanwhile, labor unrest, instigated with our support, was spreading; an economic crisis brought on by the war was deepening because the Baltic states' trade links with Britain and Western Europe were severed.

Chichayev and Mikhail Vetrov, the counselor of the Soviet Embassy in Riga, came to my office, and Vetrov suggested that we exploit the personal ambitions of Munters, whose reputation in Berlin was bolstered by his frequent meetings with Ribbentrop. Ulmanis's government was unpopular as a result of its economic failures and for its tolerance of chauvinistic behavior by German businessmen in Riga. The Germans bought up prime property and took advantage of the cutoff of Western trade to direct some seventy percent of all Latvian exports to Germany for prices no better than dumping. The government, I reported to Beria and Molotov, relied for support not on the regular army and military machinery, but rather on Latvian auxiliary police forces composed of sons of farmers and small businessmen, a home militia.

Foreign Minister Munters presented himself as the ideal figure to lead the new government, acceptable to both the Germans and the Soviets. When he ordered the main Latvian newspaper to publish a photograph of Molotov in honor of his fiftieth birthday, this signaled his eagerness to establish personal relations with Molotov. Our reaction was swift and prompt: I was given a diplomatic passport, with the name Matveyev. Munters was informed that a certain Matveyev, special adviser of Molotov, through whom he could channel his most important informal messages to the Soviet leadership, would see him in Riga. I didn't take the train; I was put on board an SB bomber and dispatched to Riga in June 1940. Together with Vetrov I paid a secret visit to Munters and expressed our government's wish to accelerate the reshuffle of the Latvian administration, with the understanding that he would lead the coalition government.

This was a complex operation, to seize control of the Latvian government. Merkulov, first deputy to Beria, was in charge and had been secretly dispatched to Riga ahead of me to coordinate the plan. In Riga posing as an adviser to Molotov, I was reporting to Merkulov. He had a personal telephone line to Molotov and Beria. An ultimatum was issued and President Ulmanis was forced to resign; our troops occupied the country and Ulmanis was arrested. Originally, we intended to make Munters head of the coalition government, but then the rules of the game changed. The Germans had become too deeply involved in military operations in the West to pay attention to Latvia. Molotov and Stalin decided to place in the key Baltic positions not mutually acceptable figures like Munters, but reliable ones close to the Communist party. Some of the conditions of the original proposal to form a coalition were kept; Latvian and Estonian generals were given equivalent ranks in the Red Army, and Munters was not immediately arrested.[11]

Together with Vetrov, I went to his residence and we made arrangements for his quiet removal with all his personal goods and family to Moscow, and then to Voronezh, where he was given a post in the university. We officially notified the Germans that Munters was still regarded by us as a figure of political importance. Under our control he met with German diplomatic officials at lunch in Moscow, but his role as even a puppet head of state was finished. After the war with Germany broke out in 1941, he was arrested and sentenced to long-term imprisonment for activities hostile to the Soviet government. By a strange coincidence, I met Munters in Vladimir jail at the end of 1958 or early 1959. When he was released he remained in Vladimir, living as a pensioner, publishing articles in *Izvestia* on the inevitability of Latvia's alliance with the Soviet Union.

The fate of the Baltic states, which was originally decided in the Kremlin and in Berlin, was similar to the fate of the East European states decided at Yalta. There are striking similarities: the preliminary agreement was to set up coalition governments friendly to both sides. We needed a buffer between us and the spheres of influence of the other world powers, and we were willing to face harsh confrontations in those areas where the Red Army remained in place at war's end. Once again, for the Kremlin, the mission of communism was primarily to consolidate the might of the Soviet state. Only military strength and domination of the countries on our borders could ensure us a superpower role. The idea of propagating world Communist revolution was an ideological screen to hide our desire for world domination. Although originally this concept was ideological in nature, it acquired the dimensions of realpolitik. This possibility arose for the Soviet Union only after the Molotov-Ribbentrop Pact was signed. In the secret protocols the Soviet Union's geopolitical interests and natural desires for the enlargement of its frontiers were for the first time formally accepted by one of the leading powers in the world.

After the incident with Gukasov, but prior to the takeover of Latvia, Beria unexpectedly summoned me to his office and without explanation ordered me to accompany him to a soccer game at Dynamo Stadium.

11. Similar coalition governments acceptable to the Soviet Union were imposed on Lithuania and Estonia.

This game between Spartacus, the trade union team, and Dynamo, the NKVD team, was in those years an event in itself. I thought Beria wanted to meet some agent in the Dynamo Stadium restaurant, an ideal place to meet agents, since its private rooms were equipped with listening devices. When we arrived at the stadium and got out of the car, I followed Beria at a respectful distance because he was immediately surrounded by Kobulov, Lavrenti F. Tsanava, Maslennikov, and his other deputies. He turned back and made a gesture for me to join him, and thus I found myself in the government loge of the stadium. There Beria introduced me to Malenkov and other party and government officials. I remained in this deluxe loge throughout the game but felt uneasy because I did not even dare to enter in their discussion of the players' performance. I didn't utter a word, but my mere presence in that elevated place signaled Kruglov, Serov, Tsanava, and others to stop spreading rumors about evidence against me in the archives of the Investigation Department. I was now a person trusted by the leadership of the country.

I was lucky that all my personal meetings with Beria, whether in his flat or at his dacha, were in fact business occasions. This was true even when I joined him at the wedding of his former protégée Vardo Mataradze, an attractive woman who had been coached by Emma in intelligence tradecraft. It was rumored that she became Beria's mistress when she was still a medical student in Tbilisi; he moved her to Moscow and employed her in his secretariat. He then arranged her marriage to a rank-and-file NKVD officer, also a Georgian. My invitation to the wedding was to assess her and her husband's manners and inclinations. For example, were they drinking too much? It was necessary to know this before they were dispatched to Paris to work in the Georgian émigré community there.

After a year or two in Paris she returned to the intelligence directorate in Moscow, where she served as an officer until 1952, when she was arrested. She was charged with conspiring with Georgians in Paris against the Soviet state, under instructions of the influential anti-Soviet Mingrelian organization of Georgians, meaning Beria.[12] She was put in

12. Beria was a Mingrelian, a nationality from the area in western Georgia north of the River Rioni adjacent to the Black Sea. In 1952 an alleged Mingrelian nationalist organization, which included leading Communist party officials, was liquidated. (Sudoplatov discusses this in greater detail in Chapter Eleven.) In his Twentieth Party Congress speech Khrushchev implied that the Mingrelian Affair was engineered by Beria, but in his memoirs Khrushchev says, "My feeling that Stalin was afraid of Beria

custody at the direct order of Stalin and remained in prison until Stalin died in 1953. Then Beria had her released, but she was promptly re-arrested after his downfall. She spent two years in jail, then was released and went back to her medical career. To her troubles we must add another: in 1939 or 1940 she and her husband received from the Moscow city government, Mossoviet, the apartment that once belonged to the famous theater director Vsevolod Meyerhold, who had been executed on Stalin's orders. This apartment had also been used as an NKVD safe apartment. After a new de-Stalinization campaign launched by Gorbachev, Vardo was pressured to move out of the apartment. It was difficult for Mossoviet to evict her, because she produced documents to show that she had been a victim of political repression. To avoid a row, since her case had already been reported on television without naming her, the KGB moved her into an equally good apartment.

Another result of the Molotov-Ribbentrop Pact was the takeover of Western Ukraine. After Poland was invaded and defeated by the Germans, our troops moved into Galicia and eastern Poland. Galicia had always been the stronghold of the Ukrainian nationalist movement, supported by leaders such as Hitler and Canaris in Germany, Beneš in Czechoslovakia (before he became our agent in 1938), and Chancellor Engelbert Dollfuss in Austria (before his death in 1934).

Lvov, the capital of Galicia, became the center for refugees from Poland trying to escape the German invasion and occupation. Polish intelligence and counterintelligence evacuated to Lvov its most important prisoners, those suspected of playing double roles in the Polish-German confrontations of the 1930s. I learned about events in Galicia only in October 1939, when Lvov was occupied by the Red Army. Khrushchev, then first secretary of the Ukraine, and his commissar of the interior, Ivan Serov, moved there to Sovietize Western Ukraine. Emma was dispatched to Lvov with Pavel Zhurovlev, director of the German section of the intelligence directorate. I worried about her on this trip because her section was to deal with German agents and guerrilla organizations of Ukrainian nationalists who had gone underground. The atmosphere was very different from Soviet Ukraine.

---

was confirmed when Stalin concocted the Mingrelian Affair." *Khrushchev Remembers*, edited and translated by Strobe Talbott (Boston: Little, Brown, 1970), p. 312.

In Lvov there was still a capitalist Western mode of life, with wholesale and retail trade in the hands of businessmen who would soon be wiped out by Sovietization. The influence of the Ukrainian Uniate Catholic church was immense. The Ukrainian nationalist organizations, headed by followers of Bandera, were active, influential, and very strong and enjoyed significant support from the local population. Besides, they were very experienced in conspiracy, while Serov's team, dispatched from Kiev, which included Emma and Pavel, had no such experience. The security service of Ukrainian nationalists quickly traced some of the safe apartments of the Ukrainian NKVD in Lvov. Their method was simple: they organized a surveillance post near the NKVD headquarters and followed every man coming out in civilian clothes wearing high boots, the normal gear of military dress. Ukrainian chekists tried to cover their uniforms with coats, but forgot to change their boots. In Russia and Soviet Ukraine, everyone wore high boots; in the Soviet Ukraine, short boots were not available. But in Western Ukraine everyone except military people wore short boots.

The compromise of the safe apartments was reported to the Center; Emma moved into the Central Hotel, first posing as a refugee from Warsaw, then as a journalist from *Izvestia,* using her experience with Polish refugees in Byelorussia in the 1920s. She could speak Polish fluently and managed to establish friendly contacts with a family of Polish Jews from Warsaw. She dispatched them to Moscow, where we provided them financial support and arranged their further move to the United States to join their relatives, with an understanding that "friendly relations" would be maintained, meaning that they would remain an asset for Soviet intelligence. They did not know Emma was an intelligence operative, but they agreed to stay in touch. Later, after my arrest, a Jewish-American tourist, a relative of this family, came to Moscow in 1960 and looked for Emma at the *Izvestia* publishing house, where she had told them she worked as a translator. Emma received the relative cordially, but he was not developed for intelligence purposes.

Serov and Khrushchev ignored Zhurovlev's warnings to be patient with local Ukrainian leaders and cultural figures who were well known in Prague, Vienna, and Berlin. Serov arrested Kost-Levitsky, once president of the former independent nationalist Ukrainian People's Republic. Khrushchev promptly reported this arrest to Stalin, taking credit for neutralizing the potential leader of the Ukrainian government-in-exile. Kost-Levitsky was deported from Lvov and jailed in Moscow. By that time he was an old man in his eighties, and his arrest greatly compromised our image among Ukrainian intellectuals.

The Molotov-Ribbentrop Pact put an end to Ukrainian nationalist plans, supported by Britain and France in 1938, for setting up an independent republic of Carpathian Ukraine. This initiative was torpedoed by President Beneš, who agreed with Stalin that Carpathian Ukraine, which included some Czechoslovak territory, was to be given to the Soviet Union at the time of the pact. Konovalets, who perished in 1938, was the only Ukrainian leader with direct access to Hitler and Göring; as a former colonel of the Austrian army, he was to a certain extent respected in Nazi ruling circles. The remaining Ukrainian nationalist leaders had Nazi connections only at lower levels, mainly intelligence operatives of Abwehr and Gestapo, and in this situation they had no political value to British or French authorities once the war began. So Khrushchev's claim in his message to Stalin that the detention of Kost-Levitsky was important in defeating Western plans to set up a Ukrainian provisional government-in-exile was nothing but misleading self-aggrandizement.

I sensed that, and when ordered to assess the importance of Kost-Levitsky's detention in Moscow I emphasized in my report to Beria, which was then sent to Molotov, that his detention was in no way justified. On the contrary, I wrote, we should grant special status to Galicia in order to neutralize anti-Soviet propaganda there, which was being enthusiastically received. I suggested we promptly release Kost-Levitsky, apologize to him, and send him back in good health to live in comfort in Lvov. This should be done, naturally, with the understanding that he would support the idea of sending an influential and respected delegation from Western Ukraine to Kiev and Moscow to negotiate a special status for Galicia in the Soviet Ukrainian Republic, giving due respect to the traditions of the local population. Molotov agreed; Kost-Levitsky was released and sent back to Lvov in a special railway carriage.

This satisfactory conclusion coincided, however, with my first open confrontation with Khrushchev and Serov. Under the confidential protocol between Molotov and Ribbentrop, it was agreed that the USSR would not hamper German citizens and persons of German origin inhabiting our spheres of interest should they wish to move to Germany or spheres of German interest. We decided to take advantage of these terms.

We sent the team of Captain Adamovich and Lieutenant William

Fisher, aka Rudolf Abel,[13] to Chernovtsy, near the border between Buko-
vina, Galicia, and Polish territory occupied by the Germans. Our team
was to finalize contacts with agents recruited by us from German, Polish,
and Ukrainian ethnic minorities. They would settle themselves, pretending to be refugees from communism, in territories controlled by the Germans. Captain Adamovich left for Chernovtsy from Moscow, taking
with him photographs of our agents and operatives in Poland and in
Germany, which he was to show to four agents who were to recognize
these people at prearranged rendezvous in Warsaw, Danzig, Berlin, and
Krakow. The photos were of officers who worked under diplomatic,
trade mission, or journalistic cover in those cities. Fisher was to provide
elementary training in radio communications to these four men.

However, after Adamovich visited Serov's deputy, probably in
Chernovtsy, and made arrangements with him for the necessary logistic
support to train the agents in radio communications, Adamovich disappeared. Serov, unable to find him, cursed Fisher and reported the disappearance to Khrushchev. Fisher, although second in command, was
inexperienced in bureaucratic intrigues; he thought that if he reported
Adamovich's two-day absence to the local NKVD chief, there was no need
for him to report directly to me in Moscow as well. Imagine how I felt
when Beria summoned me to his office and ordered me to report the
progress of Adamovich's mission. To his dismay, I was unable to present
him with anything concrete. My information was a week old.

Then the telephone rang and Khrushchev was on the line, indignantly reproaching Beria for sending incompetent people and traitors
who interfered in the work of the Ukrainian NKVD. His people were
capable of doing the job themselves. Khrushchev kept asking Beria,
"Who is that scoundrel Adamovich?" The high-frequency telephone line
made it possible to hear his angry voice across the desk. Beria wanted
to avoid answering in the same rude manner in my presence. Instead he

13. William Fisher, aka Colonel Rudolf Ivanovich Abel (1903–1971), whom the FBI
called the highest-ranking espionage agent ever caught in the United States, was
arrested in 1957 in New York, where he had worked undetected for ten years undercover as a retired photofinisher and amateur artist. In February 1962 Abel was
exchanged for Gary Powers, pilot of an American U-2 spy plane shot down over the
Soviet Union in 1960. He began his career as a radio operator and worked for Sudoplatov during World War II, directing radio deception games against the Germans.
Fisher took the name Abel only when he was arrested in the United States. (His postwar espionage mission is discussed in Chapter Eight.)

said, "Nikita Sergeyevich, here is Major Sudoplatov, deputy director of our intelligence service, in charge of the operation of Adamovich. He will explain this case directly to you." I took the telephone receiver and began to say that Adamovich was an expert in Polish affairs, but Khrushchev didn't bother to listen. He cut me short and, suspecting that Adamovich had defected to the Germans, said that this scoundrel should be arrested or kidnapped from German territory. Khrushchev then added he would put an end to my career if I continued being sympathetic to bandits like Kost-Levitsky and Adamovich. He hung up on me.

Beria's reaction was cold and official. "In two days," he said, "Adamovich should be found alive or dead, and if alive, immediately brought to Moscow. If you don't comply with this order of a member of the Politburo, you will bear full responsibility for the grave consequences of this incident, with due regard for your past association with enemies of the people in the former leadership of the intelligence directorate."

I left his office very upset. After ten minutes my telephone began to ring continuously. Counterintelligence, the frontier troops administration, directors of all district NKVD administrations in the Ukraine and Byelorussia, were demanding photos of Adamovich. An all-union search had begun, under a personal directive signed by Beria. Two days passed but the whereabouts of Adamovich remained unknown. I began to feel I was in serious trouble. However, I decided to phone Adamovich's wife in Moscow, because surveillance reports noted nothing suspicious in her behavior. I asked her casually when she had last spoken with her husband. To my great surprise, she thanked me for the call, saying that her husband for the past two days had been at home suffering from a concussion. The doctors from the NKVD polyclinic had instructed him to stay in bed for at least ten days. I immediately phoned General Ivan I. Novikov, head of our NKVD medical service, who confirmed Adamovich's condition.

I was greatly relieved, and in my regular report to Beria at the end of the day I told him that Adamovich was in Moscow. "Under custody?" asked Beria. "No," I answered, beginning to explain the situation. We were alone in his office. He cut me short and began to berate me in language I did not expect from a member of the Politburo. He paced in circles in his large study, cursing me and Adamovich, calling us naive, irresponsible youngsters who were compromising him and the whole NKVD in the eyes of the party leadership. After ten minutes he stopped and said, "Why are you silent?" I replied that I was suffering from a terrible headache, and that in fact it was caused by his reprimand. "Then leave my office immediately," said Beria, "and as you are sick, go home immediately."

Before I left the NKVD building, I filled in an order for Adamovich's arrest and went to Merkulov for him to sign it. However, when I explained the case to him, he laughed and tore the order into shreds in my presence. At that moment my headache became unbearable, and I was accompanied home by a medical officer. The next morning the telephone rang in my apartment, and Beria's secretary connected me with him. He was businesslike and brief, ordering me to stay at home for three days for medical treatment and announcing that he was sending me lemons from Georgia.

The investigation into Adamovich's disappearance revealed that after heavy drinking in Chernovtsy, he got into a fight in a restroom, was hit hard, and received a concussion. In this condition he managed to board a train for Moscow, forgetting to inform Abel about his departure. In the course of the fight, he had lost the pictures he was to show to the four agents. The pictures were later found in the restroom by a Ukrainian NKVD team, which suspected that the fight was an attempt by the Abwehr to kidnap Adamovich. The incident ended with Adamovich's being discharged from the NKVD and then assigned to the post of deputy and later minister of foreign affairs of Uzbekistan. I saw him once again in a theater in Moscow in the early fifties, but we did not greet each other.

Unfortunately, my conflict with Serov and Khrushchev did not end there. Serov was involved in a love affair with a famous Polish opera singer, Wanda Bandrovska, whom he reported to Moscow he had recruited. Everybody was delighted with this news, because Bandrovska was a celebrity who frequently visited Moscow and other European capitals before the war. However, the euphoria ended when Bandrovska departed for Romania with Serov's consent and then declined to meet our rezident in Bucharest, the counselor of our embassy there. I remember that several officers of the Ukrainian NKVD wrote a letter to Khrushchev and Beria saying that Serov was having love affairs under the cover of operational duties.

Serov was summoned to Moscow, and I happened to be in Beria's office when Beria asked him to justify his actions and answer the accusations in the NKVD letter. Serov told Beria that he had received permission for the flirtation with Bandrovska from Khrushchev himself, on the grounds of operational requirements. He got permission from Beria to telephone Khrushchev, but when he told Khrushchev that he was speaking from Beria's office, Khrushchev cursed him. "You prodigal son of a bitch, trying to prove your innocence by getting me involved in your love affairs. Pass the telephone to Comrade Beria." I heard Khrushchev telling Beria: "Lavrenti Pavlovich, do whatever you want with this green graduate of the military academy with no experience in serious matters. It's up to you to use him further in his job or punish him adequately, but please keep me out of this affair and your intrigues with Ukrainian émigrés."

Beria began to curse Serov, threatening him with discharge and disgrace, calling him a petty womanizer and in every way abasing him. I felt awkward standing in the midst of this tirade. Then Beria ordered Serov to discuss with me finding a suitable way out of his troubles. We decided that Serov should make no further attempt to contact Bandrovska, for operational or any other reasons. Her departure was significant, because her performances in Lvov or Moscow in late 1939 and 1940 would have helped produce the impression on Polish and West European opinion makers that the situation in Galicia was normal and healthy. Her escape to Romania was a setback for Khrushchev, who regularly reported to Moscow the satisfactory Sovietization of Western Ukraine, with alleged support from Polish and Ukrainian cultural figures.

The image of Khrushchev was badly shaken by two other episodes. In 1939 one of the commanders of our guerrilla detachments, Captain Nikolai Prokupuk, arrived from Spain. He was an experienced operator, suitable to be appointed chief of the Ukrainian NKVD section preparing for guerrilla activities in case of war with Poland or Germany. When he heard about it, Khrushchev telephoned Beria, who immediately summoned Kruglov, director of personnel, and me, because I had signed the order for Prokupuk to be appointed. Khrushchev categorically objected to the appointment because in 1938 Prokupuk's brother, a member of the collegium of the People's Commissariat for Education, had been executed as a Polish spy. Khrushchev heard Beria berate Kruglov and me for sending to Kiev a man who, although competent in his job, was not acceptable to local party authorities.

Let me tell you about the kind of person Khrushchev thought acceptable. A. I. Uspensky, the man whom Khrushchev had earlier brought to the Ukraine to be head of the NKVD there, had been director of the NKVD office of Moscow district and had worked directly for Khrushchev when he was first secretary of the Moscow party organization. In the Ukraine, Uspensky conducted the 1938 purges, and only three members of the Central Committee of the Ukrainian Communist party survived.

As soon as he arrived in Kiev, Uspensky summoned all NKVD officers and said he would suppress such traditions as synagogue gatherings. Anyone who did not want to work with him could leave, and some of Emma's friends took advantage of the offer. In the presence of a large audience, Uspensky signed their applications for transfer into the reserve for appointments to vacancies at lower levels in other republics. Uspensky was responsible for mass tortures and repressions, and Khrushchev was one of the few top Politburo members who personally joined Uspensky in interrogating prisoners.

During the 1938 purge, when Yezhov, head of the NKVD, lost the confidence of Stalin and the hunt began for "traitorous" chekists, Uspensky tried to escape abroad. Uspensky took several blank passports from his office and staged a mock suicide, pretending that he had drowned, but no body was found. Khrushchev panicked and appealed to Stalin and Beria to find Uspensky at once. The search was intensive, and it turned out that Uspensky's wife knew that he had gone into hiding. Finally he gave himself up in Siberia, after he detected surveillance teams that arrived in Omsk. His wife did not actually betray him, but her behavior indicated that he was alive somewhere. Henceforth, whenever a question arose about the use of Ukrainian officers, the NKVD leadership always referred to Uspensky, quoting Khrushchev that no chekists who had worked under him should be trusted. Under interrogation, however, Uspensky tried to attach himself to Khrushchev, claiming that they were friends and maintained close relations between their families. He wanted to show that he was an obedient soldier of the party. That claim proved fatal for his wife; she was arrested three days after he surrendered and was sentenced to death by firing squad for assisting his escape. Khrushchev intervened in her case, Kruglov told me, but only to recommend turning down her appeal for clemency to the Presidium of the Supreme Soviet.

The whole affair shook my confidence. I learned for the first time from Kruglov, who knew how the Central Committee operated because he formerly worked there, that high-ranking party leaders could personally intervene in the fate of a condemned criminal's family — not with the purpose of saving someone innocent, but to get rid of an unwanted connection. In the archives, the list of wives of important condemned government, party, military, and NKVD officials whose order for execution had to be endorsed by the party leadership contains Uspensky's wife's name.

After my appointment as a deputy director of the intelligence service in March 1939, I reminded Beria about Pyotr Zubov, who was still in jail for failing to carry out a coup in Yugoslavia, saying that he was a devoted, experienced officer. Beria, who had known Zubov for seventeen years, pretended not to hear me, even though Zubov had been the linchpin in Beria's rise to power. In 1922 Zubov was in charge of monitoring clandestine connections between rebel Georgian Mensheviks and their agents in Turkey. When Beria reported to Dzerzhinsky and Lenin, relying on Zubov's information, about the planned revolt and how he succeeded in suppressing it, his letter was discussed at the plenary of the Central Committee of the CPSU (Communist Party of the Soviet Union). The letter, based on Zubov's work, led to Beria's promotion to head the GPU in the Caucasus. Zubov had long been on friendly terms with Beria and his deputy Bogdan Kobulov, who stayed in Zubov's Moscow apartment when he visited from Georgia.

In the autumn of 1939, after the German conquest of Poland, we seized Colonel Stanislas Sosnowski, previously head of Polish intelligence in Berlin, and Prince Janusz Radziwill, a wealthy and politically powerful Polish aristocrat. We transferred the two men to Lubyanka in order to actively develop them for our use as agents.

To save Zubov, I suggested to Beria that he should be planted in the same cell as Colonel Sosnowski. Zubov spoke fluent French, German, and Georgian. Beria agreed and Zubov was moved from Lefortovo prison, where he had been mercilessly beaten on the orders of his former houseguest Kobulov. His torturer was the infamous B. V. Rodos, who had tried to force him to confess by smashing his knees with a hammer, Zubov became an invalid but he refused to confess.

The director of the Investigation Department, Sergienko, objected to Zubov's transfer from Lefortovo, even though I explained to him that my interest in Zubov was operational, under Beria's orders. Sergienko refused and said, "I will personally report that case to Beria. That scoundrel Zubov refuses to confess although he committed the grave crime of not fulfilling the direct order of the country's leadership."

I told Beria that Sergienko refused to obey orders. Beria, in my presence, switched on his direct communication panel and started to curse Sergienko. Beria said he would have his head if within the next fifteen minutes he failed to comply with any orders coming in his name. Sergienko tried to justify his actions, but Beria cut him off without listening to his reply.

In general, Beria was extremely rude in his remarks to high-ranking officials. While speaking to rank-and-file officers unknown to him he was always polite and attentive. Later I learned that these were the rules in the Soviet system. Rudeness was displayed only toward top-level personnel. Before ordinary people, members of the Politburo behaved like respectable comrades.

Zubov successfully recruited Sosnowski, convincing him that as neither the German nor Polish intelligence service held any future for him, he should cooperate with Russian intelligence. Sosnowski had run an effective agent network as the Polish rezident in Berlin in the 1930s. He was a Polish aristocrat who owned a stable of horses in Berlin and planted his agents, mostly attractive women, in the headquarters of the Nazi party and the secretariat of the Ministry of Foreign Affairs. The Gestapo rounded up most of his agents in 1935 and arrested Sosnowski on charges of espionage. He told his interrogators at Lubyanka that his agents were beheaded in the Plötzensee jail before his eyes. He was exchanged for the leader of the German ethnic community in Poland, who had been accused of espionage by the Poles.

In 1937 the military court in Warsaw convicted Sosnowski of embezzlement of state funds, and he was sentenced to prison in eastern Poland. He was captured by the Red Army in 1939 when the prison was liberated by our troops and turned over to the NKVD.

From Sosnowski we learned that two of his agents remained operative, and it was he who first gave us the idea that Prince Radziwill might serve as a go-between with the Polish leadership and Hermann Göring, Hitler's chief deputy. Sosnowski started collaborating with us when confronted with the evidence of his Berlin network, which convinced him that we knew everything about him. He was a man who knew too much and therefore would not be allowed to escape without cooperating with his new controllers. Two of his sources of information in Germany were useful to us in 1940 and in the first two years of the war.

Once Zubov had assessed Sosnowski's potential intelligence value and helped turn him, I suggested that Zubov be used as a cellmate for Prince Radziwill. Beria agreed, and Zubov stayed with Radziwill for one month. By that time the conditions of Zubov's detention allowed him to lunch and dine in my office, on food ordered from our restaurant. Still under guard, he was escorted to the NKVD hospital for medical treatment. He was released as an invalid and made chief of a section in my directorate. He was in the service throughout the war, but when Abakumov was nominated minister of state security in 1946, Zubov was allowed to retire. Abakumov had been in charge of the investigation against Zubov and given orders for him to be beaten.

Prince Radziwill was handled personally by Beria, who, over the course of several meetings, convinced Radziwill to act as a go-between for the Soviet government with Göring for probes on sensitive issues. We had kept our eye on Radziwill from the middle of the 1930s and knew that he had entertained Göring at his hunting estate near Vilnius, then a part of Poland. In his memoirs Radziwill confirms his meetings with Beria, who when parting with him said, "People like you, Prince, will always be needed by us."[14]

After Beria recruited him for use as an agent of influence, I arranged for Radziwill to return to Berlin in 1940, responding to requests from British, Italian, and Swedish royalty to free him. We had reports on Radziwill from our rezidentura in Berlin. He was seen at diplomatic functions there and in the company of his former hunting companion Göring. I was ordered to establish procedures for contacting him there in 1940. It was decided not to use any unnecessary clandestine techniques since he was a public figure who could visit the Soviet Embassy under what would appear to be normal business reasons, such as concern for his properties in occupied areas.

In 1940, Radziwill was received twice by the Soviet rezident in Berlin, Amayak Kobulov, who reported the contacts to the Center. However, no instructions were given to Kobulov to use Radziwill in operational contacts with the Germans. We doubted Radziwill's sincerity and decided not to try to use him because his political contacts were of no immediate value to us. Before the Germans invaded in June 1941, there was no problem in our relations with Germany and its allies in which he might be used to probe into delicate matters, since Molotov was maintaining confidential ties with Ribbentrop.

We knew that Radziwill had no access to strategic military information. We decided to be patient and wait; we planned to make contact only if he appeared in Switzerland or Sweden. As far as I know, he did not go there. After Hitler invaded, Radziwill faded into the background,

14. See entry on Janusz Radziwill (1880–1967) in *Polski Slownik Biograficzny* (Warsaw: Polish Academy of Sciences, Institute of History, 1987), vol. 30, pp. 215–225.

but we knew he remained in Germany and Poland enjoying life. Then in 1942 we lost track of him for a time. In retrospect it is clear that we overestimated Radziwill's personal ties and influence on Göring.

Olga Chekhova, a niece of the writer Chekhov, was a well-known actress who reported regularly to the NKVD and had access to Radziwill and Göring. Originally it was planned to contact Radziwill through her since she was also close to Göring. We had a plan to assassinate Hitler that called for Radziwill and Olga Chekhova to approach their friends in the German aristocracy to obtain access to Hitler for our team, led by illegal officer Boris Miklashevsky, who arrived in Germany in December 1941.

Miklashevsky was joined by three other agents, who were parachuted into Germany and remained undercover in Berlin. A former boxing champion, Miklashevsky posed as a Soviet defector and was popular in Berlin after he took part in a boxing match with German champion Max Schmeling, in 1942 or 1943, and defeated him. Under his cover as a defector, Miklashevsky remained in Berlin until 1944.

Miklashevsky's uncle had defected from the Soviet Union at the outbreak of the war and had become active in the German anti-Bolshevik committee for the liberation of the Soviet Union. He received his nephew proudly and provided him with support as a fellow defector. In 1942 Miklashevsky managed to meet Olga Chekhova at a social occasion. He reported to Moscow that it would be easy to assassinate Göring, but the Kremlin had no interest in this. In 1943 Stalin abandoned his original orders to try to eliminate Hitler; he feared that if Hitler was killed his Nazi henchmen would be purged by the German military and a separate treaty would be signed with the Allies without Soviet participation.

Such a fear was not without foundation. We were aware that in the summer of 1942, on the initiative of Pope Pius XII, the Vatican's representative in Ankara had approached the German ambassador, Franz von Papen, urging that he exert his influence to bring about a separate peace between Britain, the United States, and Germany. In addition to this report from our rezident in Ankara, our rezidentura in Rome reported that the Pope met with Myron Taylor, President Roosevelt's envoy to the Vatican, to discuss the meeting between Cardinal Roncalli (who later became Pope John XXIII) and Von Papen. Such an accord would limit Communist influence in Europe and exclude the Soviet Union from a future European economic union. Nobody in the Kremlin wanted to make it easier for this to be consummated at our expense. Stalin was so angry he ordered that Von Papen be assassinated, since he was the key figure around whom the Americans and British would build an alternative government to Hitler if they signed a separate peace. However, as I mentioned earlier, the attempt failed when the Bulgarian assassin botched the job, killing himself and only slightly wounding Von Papen. We also had reports, without details, of a direct American approach to Von Papen in Istanbul.[15]

Miklashevsky escaped to France in 1944 after liquidating his uncle. He remained in France for two years when the war ended, hunting the remnants of the renegade Russian army led by Colonel General A. A. Vlasov that escaped to the West. In 1947 he returned to the Soviet Union and was awarded the Order of the Red Banner and resumed his career as a boxer until he retired.

Much has been written about intelligence information that was gathered on the eve of the Great Patriotic War, showing the inevitability of the German attack upon us. Stalin's stupidity in waiting for the invasion before counterattacking is frequently offered as one of the reasons for the defeats and heavy losses suffered by the Red Army in 1941. In general I agree that the leadership of the country did not assess the intelligence information correctly, but we must look into the content of this intelligence information.

We were in a state of alert from November 1940. By that time, Pavel Zhurovlev and Zoya Rybkina had initiated the operational file (liternoye delo) named Zateya (Venture), which gathered the most important information on German military moves against Soviet interests into one place. This file would make it easier to monitor events and inform the leadership about trends in German policy. Information from this file was regularly reported to Stalin and Molotov, and they tried to use it in their policy of both appeasing Hitler and cooperating with him. The Venture

15. In October 1943 Theodore A. Morde, the Middle East representative of *Reader's Digest*, met with Von Papen in Istanbul and tried to persuade him to organize a revolution against Hitler, hand the Führer and his top leadership over to the Allies, and make a separate peace with the United States and Great Britain. Morde's meeting with Von Papen and the document with terms for peace were reported to President Roosevelt. Anthony Cave Brown, *The Last Hero: Wild Bill Donovan* (New York: Times Books, 1982), p. 367, says, "There is clear evidence that [William J.] Donovan and the OSS [the U.S. Office of Strategic Services] were involved . . . but it is impossible to resolve who gave Donovan and the OSS orders to undertake the operation." Morde died with his secret in 1953.

file contained disturbing reports that caused the Soviet leadership to seriously suspect the sincerity of Hitler's proposals for a division of the world between Germany, the Soviet Union, Italy, and Japan — a proposal he made to Molotov in Berlin in November 1940.

Although our intelligence disclosed Hitler's intentions to attack the Soviet Union, the reports were to a certain extent contradictory. They didn't contain assessments of the potential of the German tank force and air force units or their capability of breaking the defense lines of the Red Army units deployed on our borders. No one in the intelligence service examined the real balance of forces on the Soviet-German frontiers. Thus the strength of Hitler's strike came as a surprise to our military commanders, including Marshal Georgi Zhukov, the Red Army chief of staff at the time, who admits in his memoirs that we did not foresee an enemy able to unleash large-scale offensive operations by mass tank formations simultaneously in several directions.

What was overlooked in the intelligence information was the qualitative force of the German blitzkrieg tactics. We believed that if war broke out the Germans would first try to seize our Ukrainian regions, which were rich in food supplies and raw materials. We knew from their military strategic games that a prolonged war would demand additional economic resources. This was a big mistake: GRU and NKVD intelligence did not warn the general staff that the aim of the German army in both Poland and France was not to seize the territory but rather to destroy the military might of the opposing army.

When Stalin learned that the German military games showed the German general staff the logistical problems of waging a prolonged war, he ordered that Hitler's military attaché in Moscow be shown our industrial military might in Siberia. Sometime in April 1941 the German attaché received a tour of new plants producing planes, engines, and the most advanced tanks. Through our rezidentura in Berlin we also tried to spread rumors in the Ministries of Aviation and Economics that the decision to wage war against the Soviet Union would be tragic for Hitler's leadership. Our rumors promised that it would be a prolonged war on two fronts; its outcome would be fatal to Germany and to its geopolitical interests.

In early 1941 there were contradictory signs concerning peace and war. On January 10, Molotov and Friedrich Werner von der Schulenburg, the German ambassador in Moscow, signed a secret protocol on territorial issues in Lithuania. Germany gave up its interest in certain areas of Lithuania in return for 7.5 million American dollars in gold. At the time, I didn't know about this protocol; I was only briefly informed that we had reached an agreement with the Germans on territorial issues in the Baltic area and on economic cooperation throughout 1941. From Britain we also received reliable messages that any German offensive against the Soviet Union depended on their rapprochement with the British government, because they could not risk fighting a war on two fronts.

From K. A. Umansky, our ambassador in Washington, and Ovakimian, our rezident in New York City, we received reports that Montgomery Hyde, an MI-6 (British Secret Intelligence Service) officer working for William Stephenson's British Security Coordination in the Empire State Building, had planted a choice bit of disinformation with the German Embassy in Washington. If Hitler invaded England, the Germans were told, the Russians planned to wage war on Hitler.

Analyzing the information that was received by both the NKVD and GRU from trusted sources, it becomes clear that half the data before May and even June 1941 contained confirmation that war was inevitable; but it also showed that a clash with us depended on whether or not Germany invaded England. Philby reported the plans of the British cabinet to stimulate tension and military conflict between Germany and the Soviet Union to distract the Germans and bring about their defeat. In the liternoye delo file Black Bertha,[16] in NKVD archives, there is a reference to information coming from either Philby or Cairncross that British agents through contacts in the United States were spreading rumors that war between Germany and the Soviet Union was imminent and would be started by the Soviet Union in a preemptive strike in southern Poland. The thickness of this file grew day by day, as we received further reports of British activity to stimulate fear among the German leadership that the Soviet Union was coming into the war. There were also reports of increased serious contacts between British and German informal representatives in search of peaceful solutions to the European war.

Meanwhile, Stalin and Molotov, Beria told me, had decided to at least postpone the military conflict and better our situation by resorting to a scheme they had abandoned in 1938. This was the plan to

16. This file, says P. A. Sudoplatov, was called Black Bertha because that was Rudolph Hess's nickname among homosexual circles of Nazis in the 1920s in Munich. Hess, deputy leader of the Nazi party and Hitler's close confidant, fled to Scotland on May 10, 1941, on an unauthorized peace mission.

overthrow the Yugoslav government. In March 1941 GRU and NKVD rezidenturas actively supported a coup d'état against the pro-German government in Belgrade. Molotov and Stalin hoped to strengthen the USSR's strategic position in the Balkans. A new anti-German government in Belgrade, they reasoned, could impede and prolong Italian and German operations against Greece.

Major General Solomon R. Milshtein, deputy director of the GRU, was sent to Belgrade to assist the military action in the overthrow of the pro-German government. We also sent two experienced illegals: Vassili Zarubin and A. M. Alakhverdov, an Armenian. By this time in Moscow, with the help of the Ministry of Foreign Affairs, we formally recruited as our agent the Yugoslavian ambassador to the Soviet Union, Gavrilovich. Peter Fedotov, director of the Counterintelligence Department, and I ran him together. However, we suspected him of playing a double game in the interests of the British, because every week he contacted British representatives in Moscow.

A week after the coup, we signed a pact of mutual assistance with the new government in Belgrade. On April 6, the day after the signing, Hitler attacked, and in two weeks the Yugoslavian army ceased to exist. The reaction of Hitler to the coup was prompt and effective, and I admit we didn't expect such total and rapid military defeat of Yugoslavia. We were shocked.

Hitler clearly showed that he was not bound to official and confidential agreements, because the secret protocols of the Molotov-Ribbentrop Pact included prior consultation before any military move. Even though both sides were involved in active consultations on the division of spheres of influence from November 1940 until March 1941, mutual distrust was in the air. Hitler was surprised by the events in Belgrade, and we were surprised by his invasion of Yugoslavia.

Following these events, on April 18, 1941, I signed a directive to all rezidenturas in Europe ordering activation of our agent networks and lines of communication for conditions of war. The GRU sent similar warnings to its networks in Europe. We also planned to send to Switzerland a group of experienced operators, including the Bulgarian Boris Afanasiev, to act as links with reliable sources, using their cover from neutral Switzerland. There was no direct land travel to Switzerland; our agents had to take a train through Germany, changing in Berlin. It was decided to strengthen our rezidenturas in Berlin and in other German and Polish areas; some of our operatives were summoned to Berlin from France and Italy. Belgium was already occupied. We did not cope fast enough with the speedy developments; we did not get radio equipment, batteries, and spare parts to our German agents fast enough, and even worse, they had not been sufficiently trained either in intelligence trade-craft or in the art of clandestine radio communications.

We began to pay more attention to the possibility of using political refugees who had come to Moscow from the countries occupied by the Germans. Before escaping to Britain, Beneš ordered young Lieutenant Colonel Ludvik Svoboda to Moscow to act as his secret military repre-sentative. Svoboda was given the status of a secret envoy and lived com-fortably in a safe apartment and at my dacha in the outskirts of Moscow. In May and June, just before the war, we started discussing with him the idea of forming Czech units in the Soviet Union and parachuting them into the rear of the German army to wage guerrilla operations in Czechoslovakia. I vividly remember him, always polite, always dignified.[17]

At the same time, Stalin and Molotov transferred substantial num-bers of army units from Siberia in April, May, and early June to protect our western borders. In May, on the eve of Eitingon's appearance in Moscow from China, together with Caridad Mercader, I signed a direc-tive to prepare Russian and other national emigrant groups in Europe for their involvement in wartime intelligence operations.

We now know that secret consultations between Hitler, Ribbentrop, and Molotov, searching for a strategic alliance among Germany, Japan, and the Soviet Union, led Stalin and Molotov to the illusion that they could come to terms with Hitler. They believed until the last moment that their authority, coupled with the military might displayed to Ger-man experts, would stave off the war for at least a year while Hitler searched for a peaceful formula to settle his disputes with Britain. Stalin and Molotov were annoyed with opinions that contradicted their stra-tegic plans to avoid military conflict, which explains rude notes written by Stalin on the report sent by Merkulov on June 16, warning of signs

---

17. During World War II Svoboda led a Czech battalion against the Germans. After the war General Svoboda was the pro-Communist minister of defense under Beneš and played an active part in the overthrow of parliamentary democracy in Czechoslovakia. He joined the Communist party in 1948 but was regarded with deep suspicion by Stalin, who had him demoted. After Stalin's death, Khrushchev, who had known Svo-boda during World War II, helped to rehabilitate him. Svoboda became president of Czechoslovakia after Antonin Novotny's fall in 1968. He put up gallant resistance to Soviet bullying when the liberal regime was suppressed by the USSR. He died in 1979.

of imminent war. That Stalin relied on his personal contacts with Hitler and was confident he could convince Hitler not to launch the war is revealed by the fact that he appointed himself prime minister, the formal head of the government, in May 1941. The famous statement by TASS on June 14 indicated that he was ready for negotiations and that this time he would lead them directly. Although large-scale military preparations for war were under way in Germany for a long time, Stalin and Molotov knew that Hitler had still not made the final decision to attack, and that there was serious disagreement among German military leaders. The archives show that the TASS statement appeared on the day Hitler fixed the date of the invasion.

Two other little-known matters remain to be mentioned. In May 1941, a German Junkers 52 intruded into Soviet airspace undetected by Soviet air defense and landed safely at the central airfield in Moscow near Dynamo Stadium. This caused an uproar in the Kremlin and led to the purge of the military command; first came dismissals, then the arrest and execution of top figures in the administration of the air force and in the command of the Red Army. To Hitler, this spectacular landing signaled that combat readiness of the Red Army was low.

Second, the military leaders and Stalin's entourage were under the illusion that the Red Army's might was equal to the German units deployed along our western frontiers. Why the miscalculation? First, although the Red Army had tripled in numbers, this had happened only recently, because military conscription was not introduced until 1939. Given that more than thirty-five thousand officers had been purged in the 1930s, there was a lack of personnel experienced in even elementary military arts. The mobilization and a large network of military colleges and schools established in 1939 were impressive but in no way adequate. Even though some purged officers were returned from jail and the Gulag camps, they could not cope with the large numbers of recruits. Zhukov and Stalin overestimated the strength of our combat units; the inadequately trained army and air force cadre did not have a system for creating combat readiness. They had not yet perceived what modern warfare meant in terms of the coordination of air force, tank units, communication troops, and ground forces. They believed that their numbers were enough to halt any onslaught and to prevent significant German incursion onto Soviet soil. Contrary to the leadership, Admiral N. G. Kuznetsov, commander of the navy, correctly assessed the weakness of his forces. Based on his experience in Spain as naval attaché, he introduced in spring 1941 a modern system of combat readiness. That's why the navy, although under surprise attack in the Baltic and in the Black Sea, repelled the enemy.

The NKVD and GRU should be blamed for underestimating the striking potential of the German armed forces; they were too preoccupied with political intentions and decisions, instead of the Wehrmacht's tactics.

I remember clearly the final days before the war. Eitingon had just returned from America and China. He and I, together with Mercader's mother, were decorated in the Kremlin by President Kalinin for the assassination of Trotsky, and this coincided with the wedding party of Zoya Zarubina, Eitingon's stepdaughter. The atmosphere was enthusiastic and confident. But on June 16, Fitin returned from the Kremlin with Merkulov, people's commissar for state security,[18] looking concerned. Fitin summoned me and Nikolai D. Melnikov, his deputy for the Far East, and said that the Hozyain (the Master, meaning Stalin) found Fitin's report contradictory, and ordered him to prepare a more convincing and conclusive summary of all intelligence information about the timing of military conflict with Germany.

Contrary to what General Petr I. Ivashutin[19] and other writers say in their memoirs, I don't remember any angry notes by Beria on the reports of an agent Eagle saying, "This is British disinformation. Find out who is the author of the provocation and punish him." I do not recall any agent code-named Eagle, and there was no tradition in the intelligence and security service of writing such lengthy notes. I believe this story is fabricated. Also improbable is Beria's alleged resolution to recall and punish our ambassador in Berlin, Dekanozov, the former head of the Foreign Department, who was bombarding him with "disinformation." Some people claim that Beria wrote to Stalin on June 21 sug-

18. In February 1941, the foreign intelligence and security services were detached from the NKVD and made an independent agency, the NKGB, People's Commissariat for State Security, headed by Merkulov. (The NKVD remained under Beria and handled primarily internal police matters and large-scale construction projects with forced labor.) At this time, the Foreign Department of the NKGB was upgraded to become the Foreign Directorate, a status it maintained when the intelligence and security services were again incorporated into the NKVD in July 1941. The head of the Foreign Directorate was Fitin.

19. Former deputy chairman of the KGB and head of the GRU from 1962 to 1986.

gesting Dekanozov's recall, but this was beyond his authority since Dekanozov reported directly to Molotov.

Intelligence estimates on the timing of the invasion were contradictory. Sorge reported from Tokyo that the invasion was planned for June 1. Our rezidentura reported from Berlin that the invasion was planned for June 15. Prior to that, on March 11, GRU had reported that the invasion was planned for spring. There was no clear picture, and it was further muddled by ongoing negotiations.

Zoya Rybkina, attending a cocktail party in the German Embassy in Moscow a few days before the war, noticed that some decorations and paintings had been removed. Trying to find new places to install listening devices, she discovered that the embassy personnel were packing for evacuation. This worried us.

In the Hotel Metropol, Abram Yakovlev and Raikhman, who were coordinating counterintelligence operations, intercepted the German couriers guarding the diplomatic pouch. One was blocked in the elevator at the same moment that the other was locked in the bathroom of their hotel suite. When the courier in the elevator could not open the door he pressed an alarm button; he was released by the counterintelligence agents, who in the five minutes available to them had opened his diplomatic attaché case in the suite and photographed its contents. Among the documents was a letter from Ambassador Schulenburg to Ribbentrop stressing his confidence in the peaceful intentions of the Soviet leadership and his strong support for solving growing differences between Germany and the Soviet Union through negotiations. At the same time, Schulenburg reported that instructions for curtailing the embassy staff to the minimum were fulfilled and diplomats were departing to Germany on schedule. This report, I think, added to the controversy because, although signs of approaching war were evident, Schulenburg's stand and high reputation meant that the door to peaceful settlement with Hitler was not yet closed.

On the day Fitin returned from the Kremlin, Beria summoned me. Beria ordered me to reorganize the Administration for Special Tasks, directly under him, to be the apparatus of intelligence operations and diversions (sabotage) in case of war. At that moment our first task was to establish an experienced strike force to counter any frontier incident that might be used as an excuse to start a war. He stressed that we must not allow German provocateurs to stage actions like those against Poland in 1939, when they seized the radio station in Gleiwitz (then in

Germany). They took it over, broadcast anti-German statements, and then killed common criminals whom they had pulled from jails and dressed in Polish military uniforms, making it look like the Polish army had attacked the station.

I immediately suggested that Eitingon be appointed my deputy. Beria agreed, and on the eve of the war we began to look for people to serve as the backbone of a special-purpose brigade that could be airlifted to trouble spots on our European or Far East borders. Eitingon's military experience was superior to mine, and therefore I relied heavily on him in assessing military matters and in relations with military headquarters. Eitingon and I made plans to destroy the supply infrastructure of the German motorized and tank units that had already begun clustering on our borders.

On June 20 Eitingon reported to me that he was displeased by a talk he had with General Dmitri Pavlov, commander of the Byelorussian military district. Because they had known each other in Spain, Eitingon asked his friendly advice on what trouble spots Pavlov foresaw in his territory. Eitingon said that Pavlov either was drunk or understood nothing about the coordination of various fighting services in modern warfare. Pavlov anticipated no problems and believed that even if the enemy at first seized the initiative on the border he had enough strength in reserve to counter any major breakthrough. He saw no necessity for subversive operations to cause disorganization among the attacking force.

On June 21 I remained in my office all night, even though Emma and I had agreed that I would take her to our dacha late that evening. In 1940 she had decided to quit operational work in the Center and found a job in the NKVD training college as an instructor of agent operational work. She left the NKVD college on Saturday, the twenty-first, approximately at three. Fitin was meeting with Gavrilovich, the Yugoslavian ambassador, at his dacha in the evening, so I was the only one on duty this fatal night. The rules were that you left your office only when the secretary of the people's commissar or the minister informed you that the boss allowed you to go home. Heads of departments usually left at eight, went home or to safe apartments to meet agents, and then returned to their offices at ten or eleven to register their agent reports and lock them in their safes. On Saturdays, as a rule, nobody returned after leaving at eight.

This time I received no word from either Beria's or Merkulov's secretary allowing me to leave, so I stayed and called Emma to say that I would be late. She agreed to wait for me, and fell asleep. While waiting I went through documents, but no mail or news came after six. Only the commander in chief of Border Troops, Maslennikov, phoned. He was disappointed when I said that the special-purpose brigade would not be ready for action sooner than ten days. I knew that Beria and Merkulov were not in the building but their secretariat expected them at any moment. They had been summoned to the Hozyain. I remained in my office, edgy and impatient to leave, not expecting calamity to strike. I sensed the danger of military provocation or conflict but not the magnitude of the full-scale invasion that followed. I had an inner feeling that we were capable, despite everything, of controlling events.

At 3:00 A.M. the telephone rang and Merkulov told me to come immediately to his office. There I found the chiefs of all major departments already gathered. Merkulov formally announced that the war had broken out, that the German forces had attacked on all fronts. He ordered all personnel summoned to headquarters under the alarm signal; by nine o'clock, he said, each department head should propose war measures to be implemented immediately. I phoned Emma and sent a car to bring her to the Lubyanka to report for duty. Fitin arrived around nine. In the conference room of the intelligence directorate we held a formal meeting of personnel, announcing the start of the war. There was no panic, but automatically the orders and the comments of all officers suddenly became harsh. Even our jokesters, and Eitingon especially, refrained from their usual gibes on this first tragic Sunday of the war.

THE GREAT PATRIOTIC WAR: DECEPTION GAMES AND GUERRILLA WARFARE

The war completely changed my position in the NKVD headquarters. I was formally appointed director of the Administration for Special Tasks by Beria's order on July 5, 1941, and named Eitingon my deputy; later Serebryansky and Mikhail Maklarsky became section chiefs. Without exception, the head of every department of the NKVD network was obliged to provide all the personnel and equipment required to fulfill my duties. Special Tasks became the principal unit responsible for intelligence operations against Germany and its satellites, organizing guerrilla warfare, establishing illegal networks in the German-occupied territories, running secret operations in the Soviet Union to deceive the enemy, and planting disinformation rumors.

We immediately organized the Special-Purpose Motorized Brigade, the operational arm of Special Tasks. Under a decree of the Central Committee and Comintern, all political immigrants in the Soviet Union were mobilized for active duty in the Special-Purpose Brigade. We had under our command a force of twenty thousand men and women, including two thousand foreigners, among them Germans, Austrians, Spaniards, Americans, Chinese, Vietnamese, Poles, Czechs, Bulgarians, and Romanians. The quality of the brigade was predetermined by the fact that we also had at our disposal the best athletes in the Soviet Union, including champions in boxing and track and field. They became the backbone of guerrilla units sent to the front and to the enemy's rear.

In October 1941 the Administration for Special Tasks was enlarged and reorganized into Independent Department Two of the NKVD, still reporting directly to Beria. I remained a deputy chief of the Foreign Intelligence Directorate. In February 1942 Department Two became Independent Directorate Four for Special Tasks and Guerrilla Warfare of NKVD.[1] At this time I was promoted from senior major (equivalent to colonel in the army) to the rank of commissar of state security third grade (equivalent to lieutenant general). The Fourth Directorate comprised sixteen sections, two of them monitoring developments in the Far East and China, the rest concerned with Germany, Scandinavia, Hungary, Czechoslovakia, Turkey, and the Middle East.

When the war broke out we were in desperate need of qualified personnel. I suggested that a group of about 140 former intelligence and security officers be released from jail, a request that revealed Beria's cynicism and simplicity in dealing with the fate of men. Beria did not question the guilt or innocence of the people I recommended; he only asked, "Are you sure we need them?"

I replied, "Yes, I am absolutely certain."

"Then contact Kobulov for arrangements to release and use them immediately."

After that I was given the files of all those people to review. The files showed that they had been arrested under the initiative and direct orders of the top leadership, namely Stalin and Molotov. Unfortunately Shpigelglas, Karin, and Maly, the Hungarian priest, had already been shot.[2]

After their release, several of these intelligence officers who were my most intimate friends had no place to stay in Moscow because their families had been evacuated from the city. They moved into my apartment in Gorky Street, above the sports store Dynamo. On the next floor up lived Merkulov, Beria's first deputy, who sometimes came down to

1. Letter of Beria to Stalin on Setting Up Guerrilla Detachments and Diversion Groups for Operations in the Rear of the Enemy, August 8, 1941. In *Izvestia CC CPSU* (*News of the Central Committee, Communist Party of the Soviet Union*), no. 9, 1990, pp. 197, 198, 215.

2. Aleksandr Karin was a deputy to Artuzov, head of the Foreign Department in the 1930s, and then head of the GRU illegals department until he was arrested and executed in 1937. Theodor Maly ran Maclean and Philby in London until he was recalled to Moscow in July 1937 and shot late that year.

visit me if there were pressing issues to discuss. Our two flats were also used as safe apartments for meetings with foreign diplomats. While my friends were in the apartment, Merkulov telephoned that he was coming there for urgent business. To avoid a clumsy situation, in which a minister of the state walked in upon four recently released felons, my friends hid in the bedroom.

The only experienced agent among the four was Ivan Kaminsky, who stayed in the apartment until he was dispatched to Zhitomir, to the German rear. We sent him as illegal rezident. Emma couldn't hide her tears when we saw him off. He looked like a French businessman in his spectacles and three-piece suit and was overflowing with optimism, saying he was happy that now he was considered a real patriot. He said he was armed with luck even if he had to die, and tried to calm Emma with French jokes. He was betrayed only one day after he landed, by the priest agent of the local NKVD, who by that time was collaborating with the Gestapo. Kaminsky was experienced enough to sense the ambush when he entered the safe apartment, and shot himself. We learned his fate within three or four months. The men with him were surrounded and died in the firefight.

The other released men returned to work in junior positions, and most of them were sent as heads of task forces behind the German lines. Some of them perished, but some, like Dmitri Medvedev[3] and Nikolai Prokupuk, became Heroes of the Soviet Union for their successful guerrilla operations against the Germans.

Having learned from the 1938–1939 purges, I was not so naive as to sign the rehabilitation documents for my friends released from prison in 1941. I had already been tainted by association with them when they were arrested. To appear objective in their rehabilitation, I asked Fitin to sign the necessary documents giving them back their citizenship. This turned out to be a farseeing precaution, because in 1946 and 1953, when I was accused of releasing friends who were enemies of the people, I could point to Fitin's signature. For Serebryansky, my personal interven-

3. "Dmitri Medvedev, a veteran NKVD officer, formerly Emma's chief in Odessa, had been purged before the war because his elder brother was one of the leaders of the Trotskyite opposition. I obtained his release when the war broke out and immediately sent him to the German rear. At Bryansk, he outsmarted the Abwehr and kidnapped from the Germans Prince Lvov, son of the first prime minister of the Russian provisional government after the fall of the czar. The prince was to be appointed governor of the Moscow district by the Germans when they captured Moscow," recalls P. A. Sudoplatov.

tion for his reinstatement in the party in 1941 proved fatal, because in 1953 he was charged with escaping the highest measure of punishment only through my treacherous intervention. He died in prison in 1956.

On June 26, 1941, I was also appointed deputy chief of the NKVD staff for combatting German parachutists and sabotage. In 1942, an elite detachment of paratroopers was assigned to my command; with them came a squadron of transport planes and long-distance bombers. Throughout the war we maintained close cooperation with General (later Marshal) of Aviation Aleksandr Evgenievich Golovanov, who had been a good friend of Eitingon's from the time they studied together at the military academy.

Our situation after the invasion was disastrous. The thrust of the German tank force was beyond our calculations; the magnitude of the defeat of the Red Army in the Baltics, Byelorussia, and the Ukraine stunned us. Before August we undertook sabotage operations, mainly in an attempt to save Red Army units surrounded by the Germans. But this didn't work; the units were destroyed and could no longer support guerrilla operations.

Then, in cooperation with district and local party organizations, we began to send guerrilla units with experienced intelligence officers and radio operators behind enemy lines. During the course of the war, we placed 212 guerrilla detachments and units comprising 7,316 men to the rear of the enemy. We trained a thousand officers and technicians in sabotage for the Red Army. We also sent 3,500 civilian saboteurs and agents. The parachutists' unit dropped an additional 3,000 guerrillas behind enemy lines. Twenty-three of our officers were decorated with the highest honor, Hero of the Soviet Union, and more than 8,000 people received lesser decorations with orders and medals. Marshals Georgi Zhukov and K. K. Rokossovsky made special appeals to Beria for detachments of the Fourth NKVD Directorate to destroy enemy communications and support offensive operations of the Red Army in Byelorussia and the Caucasus.[4] Detachments of the Fourth Directorate and the Special-Purpose Brigade annihilated 137,000 German officers and soldiers, killed 87 high-ranking German officials by individual terrorist operations, and liquidated 2,045 agents and police officers who were Soviet collaborators in the service of the Germans. For Western readers the names Kuznetsov, Medvedev, Prokupuk, Vaopshasov, Karasyov, and

4. A cable from Rokossovsky requesting guerrilla support to destroy German communications is on display in the KGB Museum.

Mirkovsky mean nothing, but for Soviet and Russian readers they are
the symbols of resistance to Germany in the occupied territories.

I was in charge of all these operations. This chapter in NKVD history
is the only one that was not officially rewritten, since its accomplishments stood on their own merit and did not contain Stalinist crimes that
had to be covered up.[5] At every official gathering for the anniversary of
the Battle of Moscow or Stalingrad, or the liberation of Byelorussia,
there is always a reference to a dozen guerrillas who were under my and
Eitingon's command. Approximately 5,000 Soviet books and articles on
the war were published from 1945 to 1992 — while I was still on active
duty, after I was arrested and imprisoned, and after my release, but
before my rehabilitation. In none of them is my name, Eitingon's, or
Serebryansky's mentioned. Where my name was on a document, only a
series of dots appears. First I was not mentioned for security reasons,
and then my name was excluded because I was a convicted criminal and
an unwanted witness.

In one of our operations Medvedev and Nikolai Kuznetsov detected that
Otto Skorzeny, chief of SS special operations — whose paratroopers
later freed Mussolini from a mountain prison in the Gran Sasso — was
training units to attack the American Embassy in Tehran, where the first
U.S.-British-Soviet summit was to take place in 1943. Skorzeny's German assassination team was being trained in the Ukraine near Vinnitsa,
where Medvedev's guerrilla detachment operated, in the captured territory where Hitler had set up his subsidiary headquarters for the conduct
of the war. Kuznetsov, a young intelligence officer posing as a senior
lieutenant in the German army, managed to establish friendly relations
with a German intelligence officer, Oster, who was looking for personnel
with experience fighting against Russian guerrillas. He needed such men
for an operation against the Soviet high command. Oster offered to pay
Kuznetsov's debts with Iranian carpets that he would bring to Vinnitsa
after returning from a "business trip" to Tehran. This intelligence,
promptly reported to Moscow, coincided with other bits of information
and helped us wipe out the assassination team in Tehran.

Kuznetsov, code name Fluff (Pookh in Russian), is known as a hero
who personally liquidated several governors of the German administra-

5. Document 278 of the publication *Vnutrennie Voiska v Gody Otechestnennoi Voiny*
(*NKVD Troops in the Great Patriotic War, Documents and Materials*) (Moscow: Yuri-
dichiska Literatura, 1975), pp. 517–524.

tion in Galicia. He undertook these terrorist acts boldly, in daylight, in the streets of Rovno and Lvov. Dressed in German military uniform, he directly approached his victims and announced their death sentence to them before shooting them. Each carefully planned act was supported by a battle group. Once he was received by a close aide of Hitler's, Gauleiter Erich Koch, administrator of Poland and Galicia, who was also to be one of Kuznetsov's targets. But when Koch warned him to return to his unit because a major offensive near Kursk would begin within ten days, Kuznetsov opted not to shoot Koch so he could return immediately to Medvedev and radio the news to Moscow.

Rumors persist about Kuznetsov, raising doubts about how he could successfully pose as a German officer for so long, and claiming that he had been sent to Germany before the war. The activists of Memorial, the organization of Gulag survivors dedicated to exposing the crimes of Stalin and preventing their repetition, have tried to associate him with the extermination of Germans who lived in Siberia and along the Volga and who were deported to Kazakhstan. In reality, Kuznetsov was a Russian born in Siberia and spoke fluent German because he had lived among Germans there. He was recruited by the local NKVD and sent to Moscow for training in 1939. He was trained not as an officer but as a special agent to be used against the German Embassy in Moscow. He was blond and handsome and could pass as half German, a Soviet citizen of German ancestry. He ran the network of informers among Moscow ballet dancers and, as a friend of the ballerinas, was introduced to foreign diplomats. Gradually, German diplomats took a special interest in him because of his Germanic good looks, language skills, and his established position in the Moscow art world. General Leonid Raikhman, deputy chief of the Counterintelligence Directorate, and Viktor Ilyin, commissar of state security for cultural affairs, supervising the artists and writers section of the NKVD, were his control officers. The famous ballerina Lepishinskaya, star of the Bolshoi, was married to Raikhman and, well aware of Kuznetsov's role, she introduced him as an expert on the Bolshoi to high-ranking German diplomats. Kuznetsov made the most of his assignment and his friends. His agent file listed him as the lover of most of Moscow's ballet stars, some of whom he shared with German diplomats for the good of our cause.

We were able to intercept German diplomatic mail because occasionally their couriers stayed in the Metropol and National hotels instead of the German Embassy. Through his diplomatic connections

Kuznetsov was able to tip us off when couriers would be arriving and vulnerable to theft for quick copying of their documents by teams we placed in the hotels with photographic equipment.

In 1942 Kuznetsov was parachuted into Rovno in Western Ukraine. He appeared dressed in a German supply corps officer's uniform. He claimed that he had been on leave after being wounded at the front, and was reassigned to arrange shipments of food supplies and warm clothing to his division stationed near Leningrad. According to his cover story, which I approved, Kuznetsov claimed he was a German who had lived for a number of years in the Baltic states and was mobilized from there. He said he had returned to Germany only in 1940 as a repatriate. The war was on, the traffic of people was intensive, and for the Abwehr or Gestapo to check his story would have been a matter of prolonged search.[6]

I spent long hours with Kuznetsov preparing him for terrorist missions. I remember him as a rare personality capable of remaining calm while performing combat duty, realistic and reasonable in his actions. He had nothing to do with the relocation of Siberian and Volga Germans that occurred when the war broke out.

Gradually, he began to believe too much in his luck and made the fatal mistake of trying to cross the front lines to join Red Army units. He and his team were captured by Bandera's men, Ukrainian nationalists who cooperated with the Germans, in one of the villages near Lvov. Our investigation revealed that Kuznetsov blew himself up with a hand grenade in 1944. Later, in the Gestapo archives we found the cable indicating that Bandera's men reported to the Gestapo that they had captured a team of Red Army officers, one of whom was disguised in German military uniform. They believed that this man, who was killed in the battle, was the one for whom the Germans had been searching throughout Poland and Galicia. They passed to the Germans some of the forged documents prepared by us in the name of Oberlieutenant Paul Zibert, his alias, and part of Kuznetsov's report to his headquarters in Moscow, indicating remarkable and startling details of the assassinations of high-ranking German officials in the Ukraine. Posthumously,

6. P. A. Sudoplatov adds: "Kuznetsov's forged documents were supplied by George Miller, the chief of the NKVD illegals passport bureau. Miller's documents indicate that Kuznetsov was not permanently living in Vinnitsa and Rovna in Galicia, as is claimed in some accounts of his life. He only visited there when coming on leave from the front."

Kuznetsov was decorated with the Hero of the Soviet Union medal. He was not married, and his brother received the decoration. In 1991 at the KGB Club on Dzerzhinsky Street, although still not rehabilitated, I was invited to address a memorial meeting honoring what would have been Kuznetsov's eightieth birthday.

Guerrilla warfare played an important role in the disruption of German communications, which acquired strategic importance when the Soviet counteroffensive in Byelorussia began in 1944. This operation of the Fourth Directorate was known as the Railway War, or Operation Concerto, because on the eve of our offensive we simultaneously put out of operation all the principal railway communications of the Germans, blocking their attempts to send reinforcements.

We provided vital support to the Red Army during the battles on the outskirts of Moscow. When the Germans approached the outskirts of the city, in the fall of 1941, the Special-Purpose Brigade was put in charge of the defense of downtown Moscow and the Kremlin. Our troops were stationed opposite the Kremlin in the House of Columns building. In this critical period, the Special-Purpose Brigade appeared to be the only unit deployed around Moscow equipped with a large number of mines and the technicians to plant them. Under direct orders of Zhukov, we effectively blocked major highways around the city; our motorized unit helped wipe out the German motorcyclists and armored personnel carriers that approached the bridge over the Moscow River near Sheremetievo airport by mining the road. This was the closest the Germans got to Moscow. Today this landmark is memorialized with a huge sculpture symbolizing an antitank trap.

We were responsible for mining the most important installations in and around Moscow in case the Germans occupied the city. We also mined some VIP dachas, but not Stalin's. One young engineer, Igor Shorse, my section chief, who enlisted in NKVD service in 1940, was briefed by Maklarsky and me, provided with forged documents, and assigned the job of chief water and sewage engineer in the suburbs of Moscow near Stalin's dacha. If the Germans occupied this area, he was to use these water and sewage tunnels for sabotage and hiding agents. Bombing had damaged part of the system, affecting the water supply to Stalin's dacha. Shorse supervised the repairs, which were made by Stalin's bodyguard troops, within three hours. Under the name he used as an agent, he was awarded the Order of the Red Star, but he was unable to accept it because he was still working for the KGB and not allowed to use his real name. In 1945 Shorse was sent to Bulgaria to supervise the extraction and shipment of uranium to the Soviet Union for our atomic bomb.

When I was arrested in 1953, the indictments included charges that I planned to use the mines planted in the VIP dachas to murder the leaders of the Soviet government. Investigators falsely claimed that these mines were still usable and could be detonated by remote control on orders of Beria to eliminate the successors to Stalin.

By October 1941 the danger to Moscow was serious, and Beria ordered us to set up an intelligence network in the city in case it was captured by the Germans. Our families were evacuated, as was the bulk of the NKVD apparatus. We removed from Lubyanka, in central Moscow, to the northern suburbs near Comintern headquarters, into the school for firefighters. I shared an office with Serov, Ivan I. Chernyshev, and Kobulov, Beria's deputies, but we stayed there only one day, testing communications facilities and our ability to control operational NKVD units in the Moscow area.

We established two independent networks to remain in Moscow. One was to be headed by an old friend of mine from the Ukraine, Viktor Aleksandrovich Drozdov, then a major, later a general, who was appointed deputy director of a Moscow pharmaceutical factory as a cover. He was to offer medicine to the German command to earn their confidence. He was not known in Moscow, as he had been appointed deputy director of the Moscow militia only a few months before the war. Another undercover agent chosen by Beria was Pavel Meshik, who was later shot with Beria in 1953. Apart from these two networks we set up another autonomous group to assassinate Hitler and his entourage if they appeared in Moscow when it fell. That task was assigned to the composer Lev Knipper and his wife, Margareta, who were relatives of Olga Chekhova, the famous actress, who lived in Berlin and was a favorite of Göring and the German leadership.

In his memoirs, Khrushchev portrays Stalin's panic and confusion in the first days of the war and later. I saw no such behavior. Stalin did not isolate himself in his dacha until June 30, 1941. The Kremlin diary shows he was regularly receiving visitors and monitoring the deteriorating situation.[7] From the very beginning of the war, Stalin received Beria and Merkulov in the Kremlin two or three times a day. They usually

7. See Appendix One.

returned to NKVD headquarters late at night, or sometimes called in their orders directly from the Kremlin. It appeared to me that the administrative mechanism of command and control was functioning without interruption. In fact, Eitingon and I maintained a deep belief in our ultimate victory because of the calm, clear, businesslike issuance of these orders.

I must say that sometimes it was very difficult to implement them. In October 1941 I was summoned to Beria's office and found Malenkov there. They ordered me to mine the most important installations in Moscow, such as Dynamo Stadium and the principal railway stations, and to find the necessary explosives within twenty-four hours. We worked feverishly day and night to accomplish this. Malenkov and Beria worked without rest in the NKVD office in Lubyanka, displaying a cool and confident manner in contrast to Beria's usual excited style.

On November 6, 1941, I received an invitation to attend the October Revolution anniversary gathering in the Mayakovsky subway station. Traditionally, these celebrations were held in the Bolshoi Theater, but this time, for security reasons, it was arranged on the subway platform. We went down the escalator and entered the platform, one of the longest in Moscow. On one track stood a train with open doors, where sandwiches and soft drinks were being served. At the end of the platform was a rostrum for the Politburo. My seat was in the second row of benches.

The government arrived in a subway train. Stalin emerged, accompanied by Beria and Malenkov. Mikhail I. Pronin, chairman of the Moscow Soviet, opened the meeting. Stalin spoke for about thirty minutes. I was deeply moved, because his confidence and self-assurance symbolized our ability to resist the Germans. The following day there was the traditional parade on Red Square, performed with great enthusiasm despite a heavy snowfall. My pass to the parade was stamped Prokhod Vsidy, which meant I was allowed access to the leadership standing in review on top of Lenin's tomb.

Beria and Merkulov warned me that if anything important occurred I should report immediately to them on the rostrum. The situation was critical: the German advance was only thirty miles from Moscow. I brought along with me to Red Square a young captain, William Fisher, chief of the radio communications section of my department, and a field radio operator with his equipment. We stayed in touch with NKVD headquarters and the brigade defending Moscow. It was snowing so heavily that the Germans could not send aircraft to bomb Red Square. However, the order for the troops participating in the parade was very strict: no matter what happens, stay calm and maintain discipline. The parade strengthened our belief in the defense of Moscow and our inevitable victory.

Even in that dangerous hour, we began to assess German weaknesses that could turn the tide of war in our favor. According to information from Count Neledov, a former officer of the czarist army who was living in Berlin and who was an agent of Admiral Canaris, the Germans were losing the war even while they advanced on Moscow. Count Neledov was our agent by pure luck. On the eve of the German invasion of Poland, he was sent by the Germans to Warsaw on a reconnaissance mission and was captured by Polish counterintelligence. When we seized Western Ukraine in 1939 we found him in the Lvov prison and brought him to Moscow. Vasilevsky, deputy director of the operations department of the general staff,[8] and General Filipp Golikov, director of military intelligence, dressed in civilian clothes, arrived at NKVD headquarters to interrogate Count Neledov. They were impressed with his knowledge and contacts and the way he was able to portray the mentality of the German high command.

Zarubin, Zoya Rybkina, and Pavel Zhurovlev, chief of the German section of the intelligence directorate, worked with him. Count Neledov had been asked by Canaris to participate in the German general staff's strategic war games in 1936 and 1937, in which the Germans tested General von Seeckt's theory of the possibility of a blitzkrieg against Russia. Another source had earlier confirmed that these games played a serious role in developing the German war plans against Russia. Neledov revealed that the games showed the Germans had the potential to defeat us only within the first two or three months of the war. If they failed in that time frame to capture Leningrad, Moscow, the Donbas, Kiev, and the Northern Caucasus, including the Baku oil fields, the invasion was doomed to failure.

The reason was clear. The huge tank and motorized forces needed for a blitzkrieg could perform effectively over a limited territory. The Germans had no reserves of oil and gasoline for a prolonged war. A critical amount of oil was needed to sustain the German navy, especially

8. Marshal Aleksandr M. Vasilevsky (1895–1975) was appointed chief of the general staff in 1942 and held this post until the end of the war. He served as minister of the armed forces from 1949 until Stalin's death in 1953 and then was first deputy minister of defense until he retired in 1957.

its submarine fleet. In October and November 1941, we received reliable information from Berlin that the German army was running out of ammunition and oil and gas reserves. Our source was Arvid Harnack, code-named Corsican, a secret anti-Nazi who advised Germany's Ministry of Economics.[9]

In March 1939, when I became a deputy director of the NKVD Foreign Department, one of my principal tasks was to supervise the planting of illegals in Western Europe and develop an agent network run by NKVD officers under diplomatic cover, especially in Germany, which was a primary target. After the purges of 1937 and 1938, new faces appeared in charge of the German desk, and the decision was made to reactivate our contacts with agents who had been suspended. The defection of Aleksandr Orlov in 1938 and the purge of Shpigelglas, Maly, Aleksandr Belkin, Serebryansky, and other key figures who controlled our agent networks in Western Europe had a debilitating effect on our intelligence-gathering abilities. When I took over, I had to send new and often inexperienced men into the field.

As a result, from November 1938 until March 1939 the flow of intelligence from Western Europe was halted. The decision of Beria and Stalin at the beginning of 1939 to establish a special intelligence school to train officers meant that we would not have graduates until the end of the year. Demands were pressing, and I was desperate for more men; Hitler was preparing for the takeover of Poland. The prospects for war in Europe were growing. Stalin demanded full details on Hitler's order of battle and political plans from Beria.

Since those who had been in charge of the network in Western Europe had either defected (Orlov in Spain, Krivitsky in Holland, Reiss and Steinberg in Switzerland) or been purged in Moscow, it was difficult to convince Beria and Merkulov to risk reactivating the networks they had run. Fortunately, not all the spotters and recruiters for our networks were purged. Some, such as Stefan Lange and M. Gershfeld, were temporarily placed on active reserve while their fate was being decided. We

9. Arvid Harnack, a member of a famous family of writers and philosophers, was forty years old when Germany's war with Russia started. His opposition to Hitler had led to his recruitment as an agent by Comintern leaders Otto Kuusinen and Osip Piatnisky during a visit Harnack made to the Soviet Union in 1932. From then on, for a full decade, he served Soviet intelligence until he was exposed, tried, and hanged in December 1942. His American wife, Mildred Fish Harnack, whom he had met and married while studying at the University of Wisconsin, was also arrested, and was tried and beheaded in 1943 for her anti-Nazi activities.

still had people in place in Berlin and Paris. The Cambridge ring in England, whom we feared might have been compromised by Orlov, began operating again. I convinced my chief, Pavel Fitin, that we had to risk compromise and get our networks running. We made the case to Beria and he agreed. The difficult decision to resume contacts with our agents after a suspension of six months, during which they might have been captured and turned against us, was finally made at the end of April 1939, driven by the specter of war.

Lev Vasilevsky was dispatched to France to become the new head of our rezidentura and reactivate contacts. A group of new officers was assigned to Germany, Finland, Poland, and Czechoslovakia. It took them nearly six months to check the status and bona fides of our agents who had been out of touch and control.

In 1939 and 1940 we resumed contacts and active work. This organization became known in the West as the Red Orchestra, the clandestine Soviet intelligence network that existed throughout World War II. It got its name from the German secret service term for the head of a spy network, *Kapellmeister*, or orchestra leader. The agents communicated with us by radio, tapping out their coded messages back to the Center.

Let me explain how it worked. The GRU (military intelligence) had its own network in Germany, France, Belgium, and Switzerland. In 1938–1939, prior to the war, they were smart enough to dispatch two case officers, Leopold Trepper and Anatoli Gurevich, to France and Belgium, together with radio operators to run their agent network in wartime.[10] By that time the GRU also had its own illegal rezidentura in Switzerland, run by the Hungarian Comintern official Aleksandr Rado, and Ursula Kuczynski, code-named Sonia, who later was a courier for the German physicist Klaus Fuchs in England in 1941.

These GRU networks operated independently of the NKVD network, which was run clandestinely from our embassy in Berlin. On the eve of the war, we had developed a powerful network in Germany, run by Aleksandr Korotkov and Pavel Jurovlov. The GRU also had two important agents in Germany, Ilsa Sturbe, in the press department of the Ministry of Foreign Affairs, and Rudolf Shelia, a high-ranking German

---

10. Anatoli Markovich Gurevich was a GRU officer incorrectly identified in the West as Viktor Sukolov. This was the name used by the Gestapo to identify Gurevich, who traveled with a Uruguayan passport issued to Vincent Sierra. See Ronald Seth, *Encyclopedia of Espionage* (London: New English Library, 1975), p. 640.

diplomat. When the Germans attacked us in June 1941, there was no centralized control of these networks, which all reported independently — there was no single conductor for the Red Orchestra. However, the GRU was better prepared for switching from couriers and diplomatic pouch to clandestine radio communications because it had equipment in place. Although I had issued a directive in April 1941 to Amayak Kobulov and Korotkov in Berlin to expedite the training of radio operators, and provided the accelerated supply of radio equipment to the Berlin rezidentura, we ran out of time.

During the period when our agent contacts were broken in 1938–1939, our agents in Berlin, Harold Schulze-Boysen (code-named Starshinya, Senior Warrant Officer, or Senior), Arvid Harnack (Corsican), and Adam Kukhov (Starik, Old Man) had gotten to know each other, a violation of basic tradecraft that jeopardized the whole network. If one were detected the others would fall. Another basic weakness we faced was that all three agents were using the same radio operator, Rudolf Koppie, because nobody else was available.

The effort to reestablish radio traffic from our Berlin group was made with the help of the GRU in Belgium. The GRU headquarters ordered its illegal rezident in Brussels, Anatoli Gurevich (code-named Kent), to travel to Berlin at the end of 1941 with radio transmission equipment for Corsican and Senior, which he delivered personally. On his return to Brussels, Kent confirmed the successful accomplishment of his mission and transmitted to Moscow information he received from them. On December 13, 1941, in Brussels, Kent's radio operator and a cipher clerk were seized with their codes by the German Abwehr and Gestapo.

On August 5, 1942, we parachuted two of our agents, Arthur Hoessler and Albert Barth, into Germany while the group was under surveillance and they were captured. Barth was turned by the Gestapo and began to play a radio deception game against us. During his interrogation, Barth revealed the existence of our agent Willy Lehmann (code-named Breitmann and Dike), who had been recruited by the NKVD rezident Belkin and NKVD officer Elizabeth Zarubina in the 1930s. Lehmann was a Gestapo officer and provided us with valuable information on the methods used by German counterintelligence to track down dissidents and Polish agents in Berlin. He was arrested secretly and executed without any announcement. The Gestapo informed his wife that he had disappeared and that they were looking for him. After the war we found only his registration card in the archives in the Plöt-zensee prison in Berlin. There were no other traces of him. Lehmann was the only Gestapo officer who cooperated with us.

Although Barth is mentioned by the Gestapo in its chart of the Red Orchestra, Lehmann is omitted, probably in an effort to avoid embar-rassment to the Gestapo for harboring a Soviet spy. Barth was taken prisoner by the British and turned over to us in 1946. He was returned to Moscow, tried, and executed for treason.

Thus, by August 1942 the GRU and NKVD Red Orchestra networks in Berlin were destroyed. The networks in France and Switzerland were still operating. Our group in Hamburg was not connected with the three agents in Berlin and survived the Gestapo hunt, but they were forced to remain out of contact.

Vasilevsky in early 1941 targeted his illegal network in France on Lieu-tenant Colonel Schmidt, deputy director of the radio communications section of the Abwehr. Vasilevsky learned that in the beginning of the thirties Schmidt had been recruited by French intelligence. French Com-munists who were assisting Vasilevsky's men learned that Schmidt was also being used by the British; his British contact in France had been identified to us by Maclean as early as 1939. From the material Schmidt gave Vasilevsky we knew that the British were intercepting and deci-phering German messages. We did not know they had a copy of the German coding machine Enigma.[11] The Germans detected Schmidt's activities and he disappeared without a trace. Since he had worked for the British too, we knew they were feeding us German material through the Red Orchestra.

Stalin distrusted the British, and he had more reason than ever when we compared the intelligence on Germany coming to us from our agents in Switzerland and in London. Thousands of radio messages to Moscow from the Red Orchestra in Switzerland from 1941 until October 1943

11. Enigma was the German coding machine that the British replicated and used throughout World War II to decipher German radio messages, thus enabling them to anticipate German troop and naval deployments, capabilities, and intentions. In 1938 a Polish mechanic who had worked in a German factory making the Enigma machine reconstructed it for British intelligence in Paris. The decoded material, called Top Secret Ultra, made a significant, often vital contribution to the Allied victory. See Peter Calvocoressi, *Top Secret Ultra* (New York: Ballantine, 1981), and F. W. Winter-botham, *The Ultra Secret* (New York: Harper & Row, 1974). Nigel West, *The SIGINT Secrets* (New York: Quill/William Morrow, 1990), offers an updated overview of the Ultra contribution.

revealed the orders of the German high command and troop movements, as well as a wealth of operational details on how the Germans were conducting the war. The information came from Rudolf Rossler (code-named Lucy), but he refused to disclose where he got it to the Soviet GRU illegal rezident in Geneva, Aleksandr Rado.[12]

A double check of the material in Moscow revealed that the reports from the GRU network in Switzerland, given to Rado by Rossler, were similar to information being received from members of the Cambridge ring in London. This coincidence was striking. However, the reports from London contained more details and clearly indicated that they were based on deciphered messages of the German high command. Unlike the Lucy ring, which was sending material that purportedly came from the German opposition to Hitler but was actually edited and provided by British intelligence, the Cambridge ring was providing the same material unabridged. At that time we were unaware that the British possessed the Enigma machine, which facilitated their deciphering the German codes, and were trying to guard this secret. We thought they were trying to protect an agent source of information in the German headquarters.

John Cairncross, who worked for a time at Bletchley Park, the British code and cipher center, periodically provided decoded messages to our London rezidentura. In later years I discussed his contribution with Konstantin Kukin, one of my colleagues who ran him in London during the war. Kukin, with whom I was very friendly, was rezident from 1943 to 1947 and was in charge of the Cambridge group. Cairncross was the group's so-called Fifth Man, and the materials we received from him were of great value in revealing German operational plans. With the unabridged decoded messages given to us by Cairncross we were able to

12. Anthony Read and David Fisher, in *The Deadly Embrace* (New York: W. W. Norton, 1988), pp. 608–609, reveal Churchill's attempts to warn Stalin of Hitler's decision to attack the Soviet Union without compromising Enigma sources. Lieutenant Colonel Claude Dansey, vice chief of the Secret Intelligence Service, passed carefully edited materials to Alexander Allan Foote, an RAF aircraft fitter recruited by Dansey. Foote had fought in the Spanish Civil War, was recruited by the GRU, and became the radio operator and second in command of the Lucy ring, named after Lucerne, the hometown of Rudolf Rossler, an émigré German antifascist publisher. Foote remained the channel for the edited Enigma messages until the ring was closed down by the Swiss authorities in October 1943. Also see Read and Fisher, *Colonel Z* (New York: Viking, 1985), pp. 243–255, which describes Rossler's role and how the British, who did not know the Russians were getting the Enigma material direct from spies in London, thought Moscow Center accepted the Lucy ring's reporting as authentic.

trace the British penetration of the Rado group of the Red Orchestra in Switzerland.

In spring of 1943, several weeks before the Battle of Kursk, our rezidentura in London sent a message by radio describing the intentions and specific objectives of a planned German offensive, code-named Operation Citadel. This detailed message contained the number of German divisions and stressed that Operation Citadel was aimed at Kursk, three hundred miles southwest of Moscow, not Velikiye Luki, three hundred miles west, where we suspected an attack would take place.[13] The NKVD channeled this information to the Soviet high command on May 7, 1943.[14] The London message was a more precise version of the plans for the German offensive than was described in a GRU report via the Lucy network from Geneva. It became clear to GRU and NKVD intelligence chiefs that the British were rationing the information. We knew they wanted to protect their source and yet were interested in our halting the German advance. But because they didn't share all the information they had, we believed they were not concerned about a decisive victory for us.

Early in 1943 the GRU chief, General Leonid Ilychov, wrote a letter to the NKVD and General Nikolai Selivanovsky, the deputy head of military counterintelligence, reporting that the Red Orchestra had been penetrated by German counterintelligence. A coded warning had been received from their agent in Brussels, Gurevich (Kent), that he was under German control, and we assumed from this that Barth was in the same position. The GRU decided to continue the radio game with the Germans. In the fall of 1943 the Swiss arrested the GRU Red Orchestra radio operators in Geneva and Lausanne, but we still continued to receive the information from London from rezident Kukin, who succeeded Anatoli Gorsky (aka Gromov).

Although the British have not admitted that they planted edited Enigma messages with our network in Switzerland, I strongly believe this was the case, and that is what the Center believed. Therefore, the

---

13. The Battle of the Kursk Salient in July 1943 was the greatest tank battle in history, engaging some six thousand tanks and self-propelled guns on the open steppes southwest of Moscow. The Soviet strategy conceived by Marshals Zhukov and Vasilevsky was ruthlessly executed by Marshal Rokossovsky and General N. F. Vatutin, who halted the German advance and destroyed the offensive potential of Hitler's forces in the Soviet Union.

14. Document No. 136/M, signed by Merkulov.

performance of the Red Orchestra was viewed with suspicion in Moscow. Neither the NKVD or GRU intelligence received credit from their superiors for the Red Orchestra's heroic performance in Germany, France, and Switzerland. No one made these operations top priority, because we believed they produced no hard documentary evidence, only intercepted oral information.

The Red Orchestra was perceived in the West as the primary source of the Soviet Union's wartime intelligence, but its supply of information during the war was secondary for us. Nevertheless, its agents acted with courage and a high degree of professional skill; many died heroically. But the leaders of the Red Orchestra, Trepper (Big Chief), Gurevich (Little Chief or Kent), and Rado (Dora) were treated as traitors by the GRU. When they reported to the Center in 1945, expecting praise for their sacrifices and bravery, they were jailed in Lubyanka.

Trepper and Rado each spent ten years in prison before being released and rehabilitated at the end of the 1950s. In their memoirs they presented Gurevich as a traitor, but it was he who brought the chief Gestapo investigator of the Red Orchestra to Moscow in 1945.

When Gurevich was captured by the Gestapo in November 1942 and managed to send the message indicating he was under German control, one of the instructions he received told him in code to continue to play the radio game, which he did. When the war ended, Gurevich convinced SS officer Friedrich Panzinger, in charge of breaking the Red Orchestra, to contact us. Gurevich told him he would be a valuable asset for Soviet intelligence, since he possessed information enabling us to identify our sympathizers and enemies. This would assure Panzinger's amnesty and a job with Soviet intelligence. Shocked by the German defeat, Panzinger accepted Kent's suggestion for a clandestine meeting with a Russian representative in France. He was detained, and together with Gurevich quickly sent to Moscow.

Panzinger's revelations had only limited historical interest to the GRU and the NKVD, and his notorious background made him of little future use. Since he could identify Gestapo informers who were still being hunted by the NKVD, the GRU, and British intelligence, it was decided not to liquidate him but to keep him in prison. Trepper, Rado, and Gurevich were treated in the same manner. They remained alive because they were witnesses whose testimony might be called upon.

In 1946 Rado and Trepper alleged that the fall of the Red Orchestra was due to Gurevich's defection. After Stalin's death in 1953, Comintern veterans lobbied for the rehabilitation of Rado and Trepper. Their cases were reconsidered and both were cleared of treason charges in 1955, although the GRU took note of their misconduct in violating the rules of tradecraft and unauthorized expenditures of funds. After ten years in prison, Panzinger was repatriated to Germany. Gurevich was freed in 1955 under an amnesty for those who had collaborated with the Germans.

Gurevich appealed to Khrushchev to examine his case, but the GRU was determined to make him the scapegoat for the destruction of the Red Orchestra. In 1958 Gurevich was rearrested on the grounds that the amnesty had been erroneously applied to his case. The order was signed by Ivan Serov, then the head of the KGB, and Procurator General Roman Rudenko. Gurevich was sentenced to twenty-five years in prison, but in accordance with the new Soviet penal code the term was reduced to fifteen years. Since he had already served almost ten years in jail, he was released after another five years in confinement.

After serving his term Gurevich settled in Leningrad, where he worked as a translator. Every year he appealed for reconsideration of his case, but the GRU opposed him, determined not to permit his rehabilitation or the reopening of his case. In the official history of Soviet military intelligence, Gurevich is presented as a traitor whose actions led to the exposure of the Red Orchestra in France and Germany. In the West, Gilles Perrault in *The Red Orchestra*[15] presents the same view.

In 1990 the Office of the Military Procurator consulted me on the case of Gurevich, who persisted in demanding his rehabilitation. Only in 1990 did the procurator's office find the key message from the GRU to the NKVD that approved the radio game Kent was playing with the Germans. When Gurevich's case was reopened, it became clear that he had committed only one act of misconduct: he had married Margarete Barcza in France without the consent of the Center and established a family in the West. However, the GRU leadership, namely Admiral N. Bardaiev, opposed all legal moves. After Gurevich's rehabilitation was announced in 1991, the GRU continued to refuse to pay him compensation and denied his right to a military pension and war veteran status.

Gurevich is still alive. Although Gurevich's wife died in Europe, his son brought his own wife and children to St. Petersburg to meet Gurevich in 1992. The story of Gurevich was obscurely reported in the Rus-

15. New York: Simon and Schuster, 1969, p. 499.

sian press, and no questions were raised about who on the GRU staff had laid the blame on Gurevich.

For us, Stalin's directive to stand firm to the end, and to block any movement of the enemy, appeared sound and reasonable given our knowledge of German supply problems. In hindsight, the tragic defeat of the Red Army units in Byelorussia and the loss of millions of lives and men taken prisoner by the Germans were only tactical victories for the Wehrmacht. The Germans still faced the prospect of a prolonged war which they lacked the resources to sustain and win.

In the middle of July 1941, we received two pieces of information, one by radio from Berlin and another from our diplomats and intelligence officers who had been interned by the Germans in Berlin and Italy when the war broke out. En route to the Soviet Union after being exchanged for German diplomats interned in Moscow, USSR Embassy first secretary Valentin Berezhkov and NKVD rezident Amayak Kobulov, younger brother of Beria's deputy Bogdan Kobulov, reported that Baron Botman from the German Ministry of Foreign Affairs had hinted that because of prolonged battles on the Soviet-German front, the two countries would probably have to come to terms.

By this time Corsican (Arvid Harnack) reported from Berlin that there was growing disillusion in the German high command with the rate of advance by the German army in July. The tank force of General Heinz Guderian had been halted in the exhausting battles near Smolensk. On July 25, 1941, Beria ordered me to contact our agent Ivan Stamenov, the Bulgarian ambassador in Moscow, and induce him to spread a rumor among diplomats close to the Germans that Moscow was ready for a peaceful settlement with Germany. The rumor was intended to weaken German resolve by saying that the blitzkrieg the enemy thought would conquer Moscow, Leningrad, and Kiev within a month had failed and a prolonged war was inevitable. Beria warned me that this task was top secret and it was essential that Stamenov report these rumors to Sofia on his own initiative to make the disinformation sound plausible. The aim of this disinformation operation was to play for time and to assemble our resources while the Germans expended theirs.

Stamenov had been recruited in 1934 in Rome, where he had been the third secretary of the Bulgarian Embassy. He was sympathetic to the Soviet Union and cooperated with us for entirely patriotic motives. He was not a Communist but was convinced of the necessity of a firm alliance between Bulgaria and the USSR. He saw close ties between the two countries as the only guarantee of Bulgaria's influence in the Balkans and in European politics.

When Beria ordered me to meet Stamenov, he was speaking with Molotov. I could hear from their phone conversation that Molotov consented not only to the meeting but also to finding Stamenov's wife a job in the Institute of Biochemistry at the Academy of Sciences. Molotov forbade Beria to meet Stamenov personally, claiming that Stalin ordered the meeting to be handled by Stamenov's case officer so as not to ascribe unusual importance to the conversation. Since I was his case officer, I met Stamenov at Eitingon's flat, and then again at the Aragvi restaurant. In the restaurant our private room was equipped with listening devices, and the conversation was taped. Stamenov did not express surprise at the rumors. I told him about possibilities for a peaceful settlement based on territorial concessions and the prolonged character of the military operations at Smolensk in Byelorussia, where the backbone of the German tank force had suffered heavy losses. To Stamenov these rumors appeared reasonable. He said that everyone knew that the German invasion was not progressing in accordance with Hitler's plans and that the war naturally would be long, but he was convinced of our final and inevitable victory over the Germans. I told him, "A war is a war. Maybe it is worth putting out a feeler about negotiations."

"I doubt anything will come of it," replied Stamenov.

I had been instructed not to suggest to him whom he might talk to about this, to let him decide himself how to communicate with the Germans. It was the same as what the Germans did, testing the waters. Our man in Berlin, Berezhkov, was approached in the same way by a German functionary.

We effectively monitored the mail and radio communications out of the Bulgarian Embassy because we had access to all the ciphers, nicknamed by us "Bulgarian verses." Monitoring their communications revealed that Stamenov did not repeat our conversation; he did not report the existence of peace rumors in Moscow diplomatic circles. Shura Kochergina, Eitingon's third wife, who worked as my assistant in the directorate, checked with her contacts in Bulgarian diplomatic and émigré groups in Moscow, and found no steps had been taken by Stamenov to verify the rumor.

That is how the story ended in late July and early August 1941. In 1953, however, Beria was accused of secretly planning "to overthrow Stalin and the Soviet government by approaching Hitler's agents and offering them a treacherous separate peace on the conditions of territorial concessions." Beria testified on August 26, 1953, under interrogation, that he was acting under Stalin's orders, with the full knowledge of Molotov, minister of foreign affairs, and that the aim of the probe was to pass on to the Germans disinformation that would provide time for the Soviet government to mobilize its reserves.

Two weeks before Beria was interrogated, I was summoned to the Kremlin with Stamenov's agent file, and reported full details of the episode to Khrushchev, Bulganin,[16] Molotov, and Malenkov. They listened attentively without comment, but later I was charged with being the liaison officer between Beria and Hitler in attempting to use Stamenov for striking a peace deal with Hitler. Wanting to present Beria as a German agent and to compromise him, Malenkov ordered that the secretary of the Presidium of the Supreme Soviet, Nikolai Pegov, should go to Sofia, accompanied by interrogators from the procurator's office, to bring back evidence and confessions from Stamenov that would expose Beria's plans for cooperating with Hitler. Stamenov, however, declined to provide any written statement to his interrogators.

In oral form he confirmed that he was an NKVD agent cooperating with Soviet intelligence, with the aim of opposing Hitlerism, fascism, and their allies. Attempts to blackmail him and threats to deprive him of the special pension he received from the Soviet government for his services during the war also led nowhere. According to the testimony of Dmitri Sukhanov, Malenkov's assistant, and the revelations of my younger brother's former wife, Nina Sudoplatova, who worked in Malenkov's secretariat, Pegov returned from Sofia with empty hands: no proofs or confessions. The whole episode was kept secret, although it was included in Beria's indictment and in mine.

However, Khrushchev in his memoirs, although aware of these details, preferred to stick to the version of negotiations between Beria and Hitler, resulting from Stalin's panic and desire to capitulate. In my view, Stalin and the leadership sensed that any attempt at capitulation —

16. Nikolai A. Bulganin (1895–1975) was a member of Stalin's inner circle. An early chekist, he was chairman of the Moscow City Council from 1931 to 1937 and prime minister of the Russian Federation. During World War II he served on the Western front, and he was defense minister from 1947 to 1949. He became a Politburo member in 1948 and was deputy premier and defense minister from 1953 to 1955. In 1955 he became prime minister; he was ousted in 1958 for his opposition to Khrushchev as a member of the "antiparty group." He is known in the West as the straight man for Khrushchev during their world travels together when Bulganin was premier.

in a war that was so harsh and unprecedented — would automatically ruin the leadership's ability to govern the country. Apart from their true patriotic feelings, of which I am convinced, any form of capitulation was for them unacceptable. As experienced politicians and as leaders of a superpower, they frequently exploited intelligence probes for their own purposes and for blackmailing competitors and even allies. An example is the success of NKVD intelligence probes through the Wallenberg family in Finland and through King Michael of Romania in 1943–1944 that led to separate peace treaties with these countries and their removal from Hitler's coalition.

During the war I participated in major military decisions entrusted to the NKVD, and I had to learn fast. Especially important were contacts with the chief of staff of the navy, Admiral Ivan S. Isakov, and officers of operational directorates of the general staff. In August 1942, Beria and Merkulov — Malenkov was also present — ordered me to equip 150 mountain climbers for combat operations within twenty-four hours.

When the mountain climbers were ready, Beria ordered me to accompany him and Merkulov on the mission. We took 150 men with us in several planes and left for the Caucasus. The route was very long because we flew to Tbilisi through Central Asia on lend-lease American C-47s. Our mission was to halt the German advance into the Caucasus on the eve of the crucial battle near Stalingrad. In Krasnovodsk, where we first landed, and then in Baku, Colonel M. S. Shtemenko, chief of the Caucasian branch of the operational department of the general staff, briefed us. It was decided that our special troops would attempt through sabotage to block the mountain routes and halt the advance of the German mountain rifle divisions.

Right after us, an experienced guerrilla group arrived in Tbilisi, headed by one of my deputies, Colonel Mikhail F. Orlov. They blocked the Germans from coming into Kabardino-Balkaria, the autonomous district near Nalchik. Now these are areas of ethnic unrest and instability, but then they were loyal to the Soviet Union. Our guerrillas inflicted heavy losses on the Germans while they were still preparing for attack, and our Georgian alpinists were successful in blowing up oil tanks and German motorized units. On the eve of the final thrust at Stalingrad the Germans lacked adequate fuel for their offensive.

Our losses were also heavy, because the skilled mountain climbers did not have enough combat experience. Their advantage lay in their professionalism as mountaineers, their knowledge of the local territory, and the active support they received from local mountain men. Only in the Chechen area was the local population reluctant to cooperate with the Red Army.

At staff meetings in Tbilisi, headed by Beria, Stalin's chief representative on the high command, I was at a loss when questioned on purely military matters and redirected these questions to Shtemenko, saying, "I'm incompetent to discuss military strategy." Beria cut me short and said, "You must seriously study military matters, Comrade Sudoplatov." Beria continued, "You should not have said that you are incompetent. You will be sent to a military academy after the war." Later, after the war, that's exactly what happened. I began evening and correspondence studies in 1946 and was then sent to the Military Juridical Academy.

The critical battle in the Northern Caucasus came in August and September 1942, the period I was there. Together with Merkulov, my mountaineers were responsible for mining oil fields and rigs in Mozdok. To prevent the Germans from using that fuel, we blew up the rigs just when German motorcycles were approaching. Merkulov and I joined our task force, retreating to the mountains at the last moment. Later we intercepted — from Sweden, oddly enough — a cable from the German high command and learned we had succeeded: they were unable to use the oil deposits they seized in the Northern Caucasus.

The criticism we received for our success made a lasting impression on me. When we returned to Tbilisi, Beria announced that Stalin had formally reprimanded Merkulov for taking the unnecessary risk of personally supervising the mining operation and exposing himself, Beria's deputy, to capture by the German advance guard. He reprimanded me for not convincing Merkulov to entrust the whole operation to his subordinates. During the course of German air raids, several ranking officers of our high command in the Caucasus were killed. Lazar Kaganovich, a Politburo member close to Stalin, who happened to be with them, was badly wounded, and so was Admiral Isakov. In this air raid one of the most experienced Georgian NKVD operatives, Sadjiah, was killed.

There was the danger that Tbilisi and the entire Caucasus could be conquered by the enemy. One of my tasks was to supervise the deployment of Georgian NKVD agents in an underground network if Tbilisi should fall. Professor Konstantin Gamsakhurdia (the father of Zviad Gamsakhurdia, the principal opponent of Georgian president Eduard Shevardnadze in the early 1990s) was a candidate to lead the NKVD agent network. He was a veteran NKVD informer, having been forced to cooperate with Beria after several arrests for alleged anti-Soviet statements and nationalist separatism. Ironically, he was known before the war for his pro-German statements and hints that the prosperity of Georgia would depend on cooperation with the Germans. I wanted to take advantage of these rumors about him, and Beria agreed, so together with Sadjiah, I interviewed Professor Gamsakhurdia in the Intourist Hotel in Tbilisi. He appeared to me unreliable, and besides, his experience as an agent was not in influencing people, only informing on them. He was too preoccupied with writing verses and what he believed to be great novels in the Georgian language, such as *Abduction of the Moon,* a saga of medieval Georgian history; he also wrote Georgian biographies of Stalin. Gamsakhurdia was a man inclined to intrigue and tried to capitalize on Beria's sympathy for him, a fellow Mingrelian from western Georgia.

Sadjiah and I decided to use him in some minor role. The basic work was entrusted to Georgi Machivariani, a dramatist with a solid reputation in Tbilisi. He was an honest man to whom we entrusted large sums of currency and gold and silver objects that could become currency if necessary to finance the underground. Machivariani kept all this treasure in a safe place and returned it without loss.

Much later, one of my cellmates in jail, Academician Pyotr A. Sharia, an assistant to Beria who had been in charge of party propaganda in Georgia, told me that Beria had lost interest in Gamsakhurdia. Still, he remained influential in Georgia as a cultural icon, and Stalin personally forbade his arrest. In 1954, after Beria had already been shot, the Georgian authorities wanted to get rid of Gamsakhurdia, and the Georgian KGB demanded of Moscow that he be arrested as an accomplice of Beria, one who capitalized on his personal relations with this vicious enemy of the people. The charges were that he had received orders from Beria to blackmail the Georgian intelligentsia into establishing secret relations with German intelligence and was rewarded by Beria and Mikoyan with large sums of money and an American Jeep.

Sharia told me that finally they left Gamsakhurdia in peace, and I learned that he died a natural death in the seventies in Tbilisi. His son became the first president of independent Georgia but was overthrown in 1992 and reportedly committed suicide at the end of 1993.

In 1953 Beria was also accused of undermining our defense in the battle for the Caucasus. Shtemenko was dismissed from the army because of his close ties with Beria. However, it was not in the interests of the party propagandists to pursue Beria's alleged treachery in this episode. Marshal Andrei A. Grechko, then deputy minister of defense, had fought under Beria's command in the Caucasus. Such accusations might reflect poorly on the current high command. Therefore, in the press release of Beria's indictment there was no reference to any treachery in the battle for the Caucasus.

Sadjiah had been killed in an air raid and Shtemenko did not mention his good relations with me, so I was not interrogated on this episode of the Beria case. Later, my interrogators lost all interest in the subject, although they commented that, by working with Beria in deceiving the government, I was undeservedly decorated with a medal for the defense of the Caucasus.

After the defeat of the Germans at Stalingrad, at the beginning of 1943, Moscow blossomed. Theaters reopened one by one. Performances by major actors and ballerinas reminded us that the war had taken a turn for the better. Emma returned with our infant sons, Andre and Anatoli, from Ufa, Bashkiria, where she was an instructor in the NKVD training college. We moved into the Moskva Hotel because the heating system at our apartment no longer worked, and later in 1943 we moved to a small building containing nine apartments in a side street near Lubyanka, where the NKVD leadership was housed.

At that time Moscow was closely watching the romance between Konstantin Simonov, a popular poet, and the popular actress Serova, and the public suffered with them when he went to the front. In fact it was not a happy marriage, and after the war Simonov divorced Serova. Emma and I met the couple several times in the Moskva Hotel in the canteen for VIPs. Ilyin, commissar of state security in charge of cultural affairs, complained that among other pressing duties he was personally responsible for the safety of twenty-five-year-old Simonov, a wild driver who enjoyed a free and privileged life. Simonov was a friend of Vassili Stalin, son of the Hozyain, a heavy drinker also known for dangerous pranks. Ilyin told me Stalin's reaction to Simonov's famous verses, which shook public life when they were published in 1942. *With You and Without You,* dedicated to Serova, was difficult to buy because it was so popular. Complaints about a shortage of the book were reported to Stalin, who asked, "How many copies were printed?" Merkulov replied,

"Two hundred thousand copies." "I read it," Stalin joked. "I think it would have been enough to print only two copies, one for her and one for him."

At this time Stalin was preoccupied with his daughter Svetlana's infatuation with the Jewish film writer Aleksei Yakovlevich Kapler; she was sixteen and he was in his thirties. Kapler was the director of the famous films *Lenin in October* and *Lenin in 1918*, which until 1991 were used for educating generations of Communists. Later, Beria was accused of plotting to have Kapler beaten up on the street, which, if true, would have been done on Stalin's order. This plan to attack Kapler was not known to me until I was arrested. Kapler eventually was arrested and sentenced to the Gulag for depravity, seduction of a minor, and telling anti-Soviet anecdotes.

One of our most successful deception games of the war was Operation Monastery, which was originally designed by the Administration for Special Tasks and the Secret Political Department of the NKVD in close cooperation with the GRU in July 1941. Monastery was intended to be a counterintelligence operation aimed at penetrating the agent network of the Abwehr (German intelligence) inside the Soviet Union. For this we decided to create a supposedly pro-German, anti-Soviet organization seeking contacts with the German high command. Despite the sweeping purges in the 1920s and 1930s, some representatives of the Russian gentry and their relatives remained untouched, though kept under permanent surveillance. Some of these former gentry and their children became our informers and agents.

Analyzing the materials and agent networks that were given to us by NKVD counterintelligence, we decided to use as bait Glebov, the former chairman of the Gentry Assembly in Nizhni Novgorod. By that time, Glebov was in his seventies; he was an old man well known in Russian aristocratic society because he greeted the Romanov family in Kostroma in 1913 on the occasion of the 300th anniversary of the Romanov dynasty, and his wife had joined the court of the last Russian empress, Czarina Alexandra. No other living person in the Soviet Union had had such an honor. By July 1941 Glebov, practically a beggar, lived under the patronage of the Russian Orthodox church in Novodevichy Monastery.

Of course, he had no skills for intelligence work. It was decided that he and a fellow aristocrat, our trusted agent, should enter into the Germans' confidence. Our agent, Aleksandr Demyanov, and his wife, also a veteran NKVD agent, visited Novodevichy Monastery ostensibly to buy him a special Orthodox cross before he left for the front to serve in the cavalry. Most of the monastery staff were NKVD informers. In the process of getting the cross blessed by the archbishop of Novodevichy, Demyanov made his first contact with Glebov. An easygoing, warm relationship full of reminiscences of the old days began to develop between the old man and the young one. Glebov enjoyed Aleksandr's company and Aleksandr brought other sympathizers who were either trusted by the NKVD or indeed operatives, because Mikhail Maklarsky, his case officer, carefully orchestrated every gathering.

Aleksandr Demyanov, code-named Heine, had an impressive heritage: his grandfather was the founder of the Kuban Cossacks, and his father was an officer of the czar's army, killed in action in the war against Germany in 1915. The younger brother of Demyanov's father was chief of counterintelligence for the White Army in the Northern Caucasus. He was captured by chekists but died of typhus on his way to Moscow under arrest. Demyanov's mother was a famous beauty, a graduate of Bestuzhevsky Institute in Smolny and well known in St. Petersburg society. She received and rejected several invitations to emigrate to France and was known personally by the leader of White Russian émigrés, General Sergei Ulagai, who cooperated with the Germans from 1941 to 1945. Aleksandr's childhood had been brutalized by scenes of White and Red terror he witnessed during the Civil War, when his uncle fought under Ulagai.

After his mother refused to emigrate they returned to St. Petersburg, where he began working as a junior electrical technician. His gentrified origin blocked his attempts to receive a higher education and he was expelled from the polytechnical institute. In 1929 the OGPU in Leningrad (St. Petersburg's new name), in response to a letter signed by one of Demyanov's friends, arrested him for possessing illegal weapons and anti-Soviet propaganda. It was established, however, that the gun found in his apartment belonged to his friend, and Aleksandr appeared to be sincere in his explanations. It was decided not to sentence him to administrative exile, but to recruit him. His family's reputation in émigré circles could make him useful. He agreed to cooperate because he was told that his role would be to neutralize possible terrorist acts by White emigrants returning to the Soviet Union, and he had witnessed the blowing up by White terrorists of the Party Club in Leningrad in 1927. Demyanov would work for us using his family connections.

He was soon transferred to Moscow, where he got a job as an electrical engineer at the Central Cinema Studio, Moscow's Hollywood. Filmmaking was the center of cultural life in the capital then. Aleksandr's impressive bearing allowed him to join easily into the company of famous actors, writers, and poets; he shared a communal apartment in downtown Moscow with an actor from the MXAT (Moscow Academic Art Theater). We arranged for him the rare privilege of keeping a horse at the central stables, the Manezh, which broadened his contacts with diplomats. Aleksandr socialized with Michael Rohm, film director, and Irina Golovna, translator of British and American dramas. The NKVD allowed this group of cultural leaders and former gentry to flourish; some were recruited, the others were under careful watch, to be used when necessary.

Demyanov was controlled by Ilyin and Maklarsky, who did not use him as a petty informer; rather, they encouraged him to make friends with foreign diplomats and journalists who frequented the Hippodrome, Moscow's racetrack, and the theater. His appearance in the company of actors, directors, and writers was so natural that he managed to establish easygoing relationships. He never concealed his origins, which could be easily traced through Russian emigrants in Paris, Berlin, and Belgrade, so officials of the German Embassy, both Abwehr and Gestapo, began to take an interest in him.

On the eve of the war, Aleksandr reported that a member of the German trade mission in Moscow had casually referred to Russian emigrants who had been close to Aleksandr's family before the Revolution. On the instructions of Ilyin, he showed no interest; this was the sign that the Germans were really starting to recruit him and he should not appear overeager. At that stage, Aleksandr was assigned the code name Max in the Abwehr's Berlin files.

This first contact with German intelligence in Moscow changed his fate. In his NKVD agent file, Maklarsky placed a special stamp to indicate that in case of war with Germany, Demyanov could become one of our principal intelligence lures. By the beginning of the war Aleksandr had almost ten years of experience as an agent in serious counterintelligence operations, frequently contacting people who did not conceal their anti-Soviet inclinations. When the war broke out, he enlisted in the cavalry, but in July 1941 he was among the most important agents placed at my disposal to be used against the Germans for Special Tasks. In July Sergei Gorlinsky, then director of the NKVD's ideological arm, the Secret Political Department, and I asked Beria's approval to team Aleksandr with Glebov in Operation Monastery.

Our concept was to set up a fictitious pro-German underground organization called Throne (Prestoll) that would offer the German high command support on condition that the leaders of Throne would be assigned appropriate roles in the German administration of the Soviet Union. We hoped to uncover German agents and penetrate their intelligence network in the Soviet Union. We presumed the Germans would set up a provisional government when they had occupied considerable territory. Through Throne we would have our own men and women in place in such a puppet government. Throne's central secret file quickly grew into a multivolume case, which is now stored in the Central Archives of the Russian Ministry of Security. Despite its having been initiated and approved by Beria, Merkulov, Kobulov, and other executed security ministry officials, it remains the classic classified textbook in counterintelligence tradecraft for cadets of the security schools. It is used without reference to the names of the agents involved.

The deception operation, planned originally as a means of exposing Russian collaborators with Hitler, expanded into a bitter confrontation between NKVD and Abwehr. Aleksandr, our agent Heine, crossed the front line as an emissary of the pro-German organization in December 1941. He was on skis, pretending to be a deserter from the Red Army, near Gzhatsk, 120 miles southwest of Moscow. To make the crossing, he skied over a recently laid minefield, unaware of the danger. The Abwehr group at the front did not trust him, and as a deserter he was treated with contempt. They were most interested in how he had made it across the minefield; they couldn't believe he could do it without knowing the pattern of the mines in advance. The Abwehr officers took no interest in Throne, the mighty organization he claimed to represent. Disappointed because he knew or revealed nothing about the deployment of troops at the front line, they staged a mock execution to compel him to admit cooperation with the OGPU. That failing, they transferred him to Abwehr headquarters in Smolensk. There, to Aleksandr's surprise, they took no interest in his political motives but instead recruited him as a fulltime agent of Abwehr, German military intelligence, with the task of setting up a spy ring based on his connections in Moscow. They were reassured of his bona fides when they checked his background among Russian émigrés and also learned that he was already code-named Max in the Abwehr's Berlin files. Planting Aleksandr in the German community in Moscow before the war bore fruit when the Abwehr found that he had been contacted before the war by their own agents for development as a source. It all fit together.

The White Guards, consultants to the Abwehr, took credit that they had found Max in Moscow before the war and that on their recommendation he developed confidential relations with older officers in the secretariat of Marshal Shaposhnikov, the man who replaced Tukhachevsky in 1937 as chief of the Soviet general staff. These officers supposedly shared with Max promonarchist sympathies.

To this day some Western publications state that NKVD double agents in the émigré community in Western Europe established the bona fides of Heine/Max/Aleksandr. These émigré leaders allegedly took credit with the Germans for finding them such an impressive source of information in Moscow. In fact, these leaders were never double agents. They were simply exploiting a good opportunity to verify a name for the Abwehr and thus justify their financial support by the Germans.

After the war, when the Americans analyzed the Abwehr archives, they concluded that Max was planted in German intelligence by Russian émigrés. In fact, Max was chosen by the Germans themselves; they used their émigré networks to check his credentials. The Germans only began to use Max intensively when they were convinced he was not involved in the prewar intelligence operations of the Russian émigrés. The Germans were quite right in not trusting the prewar efforts of Russian emigrants to set up an underground in Soviet Russia, because Russian emigration had been effectively infiltrated by the NKVD. All White attempts at assassination and subversion came to naught. For the Germans, Max was their own new venture, a clean slate. Abwehr decided not to use Max in the political intrigues of Russian émigrés, and he quickly sensed that the Germans would not offer him or Glebov any political role. They were not planning any centralized political organization as a future anti-Soviet government. Their primary goal was to exploit Max's and his colleagues' intelligence potential.

When Demyanov crossed the front line as our agent he was confident of his success in his deception game with German intelligence. He enjoyed the full support of his entire family, which was rare. Every detail of his intelligence operation was revealed to his wife and father-in-law. Although this was against the rules, our reason for doing it was simple and made good sense: his wife Tatiana had an undisputed reputation in Moscow cinema and theater circles for her technical work at Mosfilm. More important, her father, the well-known physician Professor Berezantsov, was regarded as a medical god in the Moscow academic community and in diplomatic circles. He was a primary consultant to the

Kremlin clinics and was one of the few top-level doctors allowed a private practice. In his fifties, he spoke fluent German — he had been educated in Germany — French, and English. His flat was used as the safe apartment for the underground organization Throne, and later for contacts with the Germans. The NKVD understood that the Germans could easily check who lived in the apartment, and it seemed natural that the whole family, with its intensive relations with the czarist past, could be involved in anti-Soviet conspiracy. The only difficulty for Aleksandr/ Heine in the course of his Abwehr training was to conceal his ability to type radio code messages. He had to hide what he already knew. The Germans were delighted that they had recruited such a naturally skillful operator, a man who could act independently of his German radio assistant. For us it was an advantage because we did not have to recruit his assistant.

In February 1942, after his Abwehr training, Aleksandr was parachuted back to Moscow with two assistants. The Germans chose the timing for the landing badly; the three men lost contact with each other in a snowstorm near Yaroslavl and had to reach Moscow independently. Aleksandr quickly contacted us and became the underground rezident of German intelligence in Moscow. The two assistants were soon arrested. The Germans began to send couriers to contact Aleksandr's community; most of these couriers we turned into double agents, but some of them were kept in custody. In total we received more than fifty Abwehr agents.

As we developed alleged sources of information for the Germans among elderly ex-czarist officers, the operation turned into an important channel of disinformation. Aleksandr managed to create the impression that his group sabotaged Russian railways near Gorky. Railway accidents were falsely reported in the press in a campaign to step up vigilance and to make Aleksandr look good.

I suggested that the first Abwehr group that arrived in Moscow be left at liberty for at least ten days, to check their contacts, and to see if they were depending only on Aleksandr. Both Beria and Kobulov personally warned me that they would take out my innards if any terrorist act or sabotage was committed in Moscow by them. Aleksandr's wife dropped knockout pills into their tea and vodka to make them fall asleep in her apartment, allowing a team of experts to disable their hand grenades, ammunition, explosives, and poisons. Some of their equipment had remote control devices, but in effect these men were disarmed. These

disarming sessions at Aleksandr's apartment were risky because the
guests were physically strong and on several occasions, in spite of the
drugs, suddenly recovered in a dizzy state. Some of the German couriers,
especially those of Baltic origin, were allowed to return to Abwehr
headquarters, where they reported that the network was functioning
successfully.

Aleksandr himself, according to his cover, was assigned the post of
junior communications officer for the Red Army high command in Moscow. The exchange of information accelerated. William Fisher was put
in charge of radio control of the deception game in mid-1942.

In the American archives the story of the deception game Monastery is known as the case of Agent Max. In his memoirs, *The Services*,[17]
Reinhard Gehlen, chief of German military intelligence, gave high
marks to the role of Agent Max as the primary source of strategic military information for the German high command throughout the crucial
years of the war. He reproaches Hitler for ignoring the valid warnings
radioed by Max from Moscow to Berlin about Soviet military intentions. The Americans, to their credit, did not believe Gehlen, and in
some publications correctly established that the German intelligence service was deceived by the NKVD. However, Gehlen sticks to the story of
Max as one of the major achievements of German intelligence in the
war years. Max was decorated by the Germans with the Iron Cross,
while we in turn awarded him the Order of the Red Star. His wife
received a medal from us for military services, and so did her father for
taking such risks.

Operation Monastery created major defeats for the Abwehr. From
the archives we know that the German high command made fatal mistakes because it relied too much on Abwehr's efforts to penetrate the
Soviet high command. The information supplied by Max was used in
critical situations by the German high command because it always contained elements of truth, but in each case we had more troops than were
predicted by Max in his radio messages. The offensive operations he
described were auxiliary diversions, not the main battles. Max as a
source of information, although impressive, was taken too much on
faith.

Max predicted on the eve of the Battle of Stalingrad that the Red
Army would unleash a major offensive in the North Caucasus and in

17. New York: World, 1972.

the areas to the north of Stalingrad. The reality, however, was different. The offensive predicted by Max, on the central front near Rzhev, was planned by Stalin and Zhukov to divert German efforts away from Stalingrad. The disinformation planted through Aleksandr was kept secret even from Marshal Zhukov, commander of the Rzhev front, and was handed to me personally by General Fedor Fedotovich Kuznetsov of GRU in a sealed envelope. When Aleksandr's information about Zhukov's intention to mount an offensive proved to be true, his credibility with the Germans rose. In fact, the real action was near Stalingrad, and Aleksandr's information turned their attention in the wrong direction. Zhukov, not knowing this disinformation game was being played at his expense, paid a heavy price in the loss of thousands of men under his command. In his memoirs he admits that the outcome of his offensive was unsatisfactory, but he was never told that Stalin had pointed the Germans in his direction. He knew his offensive was an auxiliary operation, but he did not know he had been targeted in advance by the Germans. The Germans, alert to our offensive moves, beat us back, but we accomplished our intention, the disaster for them at Stalingrad and the total defeat of Field Marshal Friedrich von Paulus and General Fritz Erich von Manstein in January–February 1943.

In the case of the Battle of Kursk, Max in April and May 1943 sent a false report to Berlin saying that while we had strong reserves to the east and south of Kursk district, they lacked maneuverability. He reported that the Russian command was planning military operations to the north of Kursk and in the Ukraine, on the southern front. Max's disinformation contributed to our surprising victory at Kursk. These battles turned the tide of the war for us.

Former ss general Walter Schellenberg confirms in his memoirs that the Germans were deceived by Aleksandr/Heine/Max. He refers to having an officer spy in the entourage of Marshal Rokossovsky, who was, according to Schellenberg, hostile to Stalin because he had been imprisoned in the purges of the thirties for almost two years. Max worked in Rokossovsky's headquarters as a communications officer when Rokossovsky was commander of the Byelorussian front.

Using the Enigma machine, and with the help of the German communications officer Lieutenant Colonel Schmidt, the British managed to learn the content of some of Max's radio messages to Berlin, because the German high command used the information from Max to orient the commanders of the German forces in the Balkans. The British picked up the messages going out of Berlin back to the Balkans, and then they were played back to us by Blunt, Cairncross, and Philby. This route proved to us that our disinformation operation was working. (In Switzerland, British intelligence, as I said earlier, gave modified interceptions taken from Enigma to their agent there who was in contact with Rossler, who in turn gave the information to the Red Orchestra, which played it back to us. Thus we were getting two versions of the effects of Max's disinformation.)

In February 1943, we received from London a modified version of Aleksandr's report to Berlin together with an indication that German intelligence had a source in military circles in Moscow. Later the British officially warned us through our rezident in London, Chichayev, that they had reason to believe the Germans had an important source leaking military information to them in Moscow. We, of course, knew it was Aleksandr.

Alongside Monastery, our department was engaged in forty minor radio deception games with the Abwehr and Gestapo. In 1942 we began to feed the Germans disinformation prepared by the GRU under supervision of Colonel General Kuznetsov. Then bureaucratic intrigues began within SMERSH (army counterintelligence), NKVD, and the GRU high command. Suddenly Viktor Abakumov, head of SMERSH, appeared in my office and said that in accordance with instructions from the high command I was to turn over to him control of all radio deception games against the Germans. He insisted that this was the province of military counterintelligence, which was at that time part of the Commissariat of Defense, not the NKVD. I agreed, provided there was an order from my superior officer to do so. The order came within one day, but it excluded Monastery and Couriers, another deception game. Abakumov was displeased, knowing that the results of the Monastery and Couriers operations were reported directly to Stalin.

The Couriers operation had been developed under the cover of an anti-Soviet clerical underground supported by the Russian Orthodox church in Moscow. Archbishop Ratmirov was the head of this network. From his post in Samara (Kuibyshev), in the Volga area, he sent two couriers, posing as novices, to Pskov Monastery, southwest of Leningrad, carrying information for the monastery's head, who was collaborating with the German occupiers. The two novices were Ivan Mikheev and Vassili Ivanov, young professional NKVD officers, one of them trained by Emma. Archbishop Ratmirov had worked under the control of Zoya Rybkina in Kalinin when it was occupied by the Germans.

Later, when the city was liberated, he had been transferred to Samara, where he ostensibly headed an anti-Soviet clerical organization, establishing branches in all German-occupied territory and proclaiming the formation of one unified Orthodox church. The novices had earlier worked with him in Kalinin and therefore were familiar faces to the Germans.

The Germans sent to Samara radio operators who were Russian prisoners of war; we soon recruited them. Our officers, the two novices, operated freely among a wide network of NKVD agents in the religious communities. The Germans thus thought that they had another intelligence stronghold in Samara, and regularly maintained radio communications with their intelligence bureau near Pskov, receiving disinformation on the transport of raw materials and ammunition from Siberia to the front. Meanwhile, we effectively thwarted attempts by the Pskov church and the Germans to set up a unified Orthodox organization against us.

Mikheev returned to Moscow in 1943 and presented a credible report on the Orthodox church's patriotic stand against the Germans. This convinced Stalin to satisfy Western requests for a milder approach to the church and was decisive in his taking a most unexpected step, the reestablishment of the patriarch in the Russian Orthodox church. Stalin realized that in the course of the war the church had become his political ally. The government officially consented to the election of a patriarch in 1943, a remarkable event the ceremony of which Emma and I attended.

The Western view was that the church had made a bargain with the devil, but the church simply was following Russian traditions. Peter the Great had abolished the post of patriarch when the religious leader opposed Peter's reforms. He dissolved the office and proclaimed himself chairman of the synod, a situation that remained in force nearly two hundred years, until 1917. After the overthrow of the monarchy, the provisional government allowed the election by the clergy of the patriarch Tikhon, and when he died under house arrest, the government did not allow election of another patriarch. It was not until Stalin sensed the usefulness of a united church in wartime, albeit fully infiltrated by the NKVD, that he reinstated the election of the patriarch.

After the war Stalin ordered that Archbishop Ratmirov be awarded a gold watch and a medal. Mikheev, one of the novices, became deputy chairman of the state commission for administering religious affairs in Moscow in the 1960s. His career as a priest during the war under German occupation helped him later establish undisputable authority among churchmen, and he became one of the principal advisers of the Russian patriarch.

When he failed to pick up the political plum of the deception games Monastery and Couriers, Abakumov warned me, "I will not forget this. I've made my decision not to cooperate with you." At that time, more important than his quarrel with me was Abakumov's conflict with no less than Beria himself. In 1943, without the sanction of Beria, Abakumov arrested Commissar of State Security Viktor Ilyin, who since 1942 had been director of the Secret Political Department of NKVD (which included both ideology and cultural affairs). According to rules that were only abolished by Gorbachev, you were not supposed to arrest any high-level official without his superior's agreement. It could be done, but it would then be treated as an extraordinary affair. Although the procurator signed orders for arrests, in the left lower corner was supposed to be a stamp, *Soglasovenno* (Agreed), placed next to the signature of the detainee's superior. Beria never signed it.

The professorial, mild-appearing Ilyin was highly respected in the NKVD because of his indisputable honesty. Ilyin had run Aleksandr as an agent for five years before Operation Monastery began, and had participated in the initial phase of this grand operation. He had survived the purges because he was responsible for monitoring the Mensheviks, who were of no interest by that time to Stalin or Yezhov.

Late in 1938 he had been sent by Beria to Orel and Rostov to investigate a plot by Trotskyites to sabotage railroads. The conspirators were supposedly in the local government and party hierarchy. He returned to Moscow horrified by the primitive nature of these falsified accusations, and reported that the Orel and Rostov NKVD directorates had fabricated these cases for self-aggrandizement and promotion. The cases were reviewed and Ilyin was assigned the job of deputy to the head of the Secret Political Department. In this capacity he initiated the arrest of two important informers who were feeding the NKVD disinformation.

Ilyin simply summoned the informers to Moscow and ordered them to develop cases against two targets. When Ilyin received their reports he knew that they had learned during the purges how to slander subjects of surveillance. The informers were arrested and sentenced to ten years in prison camp. Ilyin was decorated with a badge of Honorary Chekist and his cases were used to portray the NKVD to its own men as a fair and honest organization. Because of Ilyin's personal contacts with writers like Aleksei Tolstoy, and prominent musicians and composers, he was often received by Beria and was on good personal terms with Merkulov.

In 1943 Ilyin's career was destroyed following a confrontation with Abakumov. During the Civil War, Ilyin had made friends with Boris Teplinsky while they both served in the cavalry. Later Ilyin joined the OGPU and Teplinsky rose in the air force. In 1943 Teplinsky had risen to major general and was chosen for promotion to chief of the headquarters department of the Red Army Air Force in the Ministry of Defense. At that time, for two years during the war, Stalin was minister of defense. He had military counterintelligence, SMERSH, transferred from the NKVD to the Ministry of Defense under him and appointed Abakumov, on Beria's recommendation, to head it. That made Abakumov Stalin's deputy, enhancing his status, giving him direct access to Stalin, and making him independent of Beria. He went from being a subordinate of Beria's to being a rival.

Teplinsky's promotion was delayed, and he heard that the security services objected to his promotion. He turned to Ilyin to check on what was wrong. Ilyin quickly found that the only incriminating evidence against Teplinsky was his alleged attendance at a cocktail party at the military academy in 1936, prior to the arrest of Tukhachevsky, where he praised the officers and generals who later fell victim to the purges. Ilyin cautioned Teplinsky to be careful in his statements, but made the mistake of doing so over the telephone.

Abakumov quickly learned about this warning and indignantly demanded that Beria dismiss Ilyin. Instead, Beria ordered Merkulov simply to reprimand Ilyin in a friendly manner, because by that time relations between Abakumov and Beria had deteriorated. Abakumov decided to use this episode to compromise Beria and Merkulov, and reported to Stalin that Commissar Ilyin was blocking SMERSH security checks of promotions in the high command of the air force. This was extremely important, because one of Stalin's reasons for placing SMERSH under his personal control was to rule out any interference by Beria's NKVD with military promotions. Stalin promptly ordered Abakumov to arrest first Teplinsky and a week later Ilyin. Even in the war years, Stalin was obsessed with exercising his personal control over any institution he headed, in this case the Ministry of Defense.

Teplinsky, under intensive interrogation, including beatings by Abakumov, who broke his two front teeth during the first night, confessed that Ilyin had coached him on how to avoid exposure as a sympathizer to enemies of the people. Besides, he admitted he had told Ilyin two years earlier of his sympathies to highly placed officers who were purged in 1938. Reporting these confessions to Stalin, Abakumov filled out an order to arrest Ilyin. Stalin signed it without the signature of Beria or Merkulov, Ilyin's superiors, whose agreement was supposedly required.

Abakumov arrived at Merkulov's office at Lubyanka and ordered him to summon Ilyin, a major general and commissar of state security, who was disarmed and placed in custody downstairs in the internal Lubyanka jail. Ironically, this was the NKVD jail but the NKVD was deprived of the right to interrogate him because he was under supervision of SMERSH. The next day Abakumov had Teplinsky and Ilyin confront each other. Teplinsky, already beaten, repeated his confession, but Ilyin indignantly slapped Teplinsky, cursing him for not behaving like a man.

Abakumov was unable to find any other witness for Teplinsky's tales, and according to the rules, two independent testimonies were required for sentencing. Since no one in the military hierarchy close to Teplinsky was even aware of Ilyin's existence, or could identify him, it was problematic for the prosecution to find a second witness against Ilyin and to prepare his case for hearings at the Military Collegium. Despite severe beatings and denial of sleep by Abakumov, Ilyin refused to confess or even sign the protocol of interrogation. To prosecute a commissar of state security, the investigative reports would have had to go back for Stalin's ruling; Abakumov feared to appear before Stalin without a convincing case. Abakumov's failure to make a case, however, did not get Ilyin out of jail.

Ilyin was interrogated for four years, 1943 to 1947, beaten periodically to try to obtain a confession, and kept alone in his cell. Then they gave up and left him in jail for five more years, with occasional cellmates such as Minister of Aviation Aleksei Shakhurin, Marshal of Aviation A. A. Novikov, and the Romanian minister of foreign affairs. Ilyin never admitted he was a chekist security officer; he said only that he was a technician in the documentary film industry. He realized that he was a victim of a power struggle and promised himself not to confess and to die with his honor intact. He managed to keep a sense of humor. Once he asked one of his interrogators what the ribbon on his chest meant. The officer replied that it was the Order of Lenin. Ilyin said he was glad that his case was so important.

In July 1951 Ilyin was transferred to Matrosskaya Tishina (Sailor's

Silence) jail and placed in the special block run by the Party Control Commission, which investigated cases involving party members and security officers. The director of the jail warned him of serious consequences should he not confess his guilt before the party. A new interrogator appeared in the tunic of a major general, the deputy military prosecutor of the Soviet Union, Yuri Kitayev. To Ilyin's shock, Kitayev demanded testimony on treacherous activities by Abakumov. Ilyin asked for proof that these questions were not a provocation. Then the warder pushed him along the corridor to the peephole of Abakumov's cell, and Ilyin could see that his archenemy was in custody.

Nevertheless, he refused to testify against Abakumov, shrewdly understanding that Abakumov had reported to Stalin, and if he, Ilyin, were in the position now to say that he then knew about cases Abakumov had fabricated, he could be accused of abetting these crimes. Ilyin testified that in his work he had no contacts with Abakumov after 1933, and only occasionally met him at Lubyanka headquarters and when he went on an inspection tour to Rostov in 1938. Kitayev was unhappy with this statement and transferred Ilyin back to Lubyanka. His interrogation started again, but the tone changed. He was now accused of not adequately complying with his duties and maintaining contacts and friendly relations with suspicious elements. This lasted for another six months, at the end of which he was informed by the head of the Kommandatura[18] of the Ministry of State Security (MGB), Major General Nikolai N. Blokhin, that for maintaining friendly relations with suspicious elements, which was incompatible with obligations and duties of a chekist, he was sentenced to nine years' imprisonment, which had now expired. He had to fill in some documents in the next room for the formalities of his release. Ilyin told me that because Blokhin was not only chief of the Kommandatura Service but also supervisor of executions in important cases, who personally carried out death sentences, his whole life passed through his mind in one or two seconds. He was sure he would soon be in the next room, the Kommandatura, for execution. The next room, instead, was a standard bureaucratic office, where he filled in the release form with an oath not to reveal the terms and conditions of his confinement. He was given temporary papers and his old uniform, now shabby and shorn of his major general's insignia.

Put out on the street at night, without any money, Ilyin decided to

18. The Kommandatura Service was responsible for management of the internal jail of Lubyanka and for executions.

seek refuge in the reception room of the MGB, on Kuznetsky Most Street across from Lubyanka, where citizens could go to register complaints of MGB abuses. He knew that the war was over, but he didn't know how the war had changed people's lives, that new money had been issued, or whether or not he still had a family. In the morning he learned that his wife, a Bolshoi Theater ballerina, had divorced him because his whereabouts were unknown and he was presumed dead. She had taken their daughter and remarried.

Ilyin tried to reach Merkulov, now minister of the State Control Commission, but Merkulov's secretary answered that the name Ilyin did not sound familiar to Vsevolod Nikolayevich. He had no place to go but back to Kuznetsky Most. He made an attempt to contact his successor as director of the Secret Political Department, Mikhail Shubnikov. He did not have the telephone number or a coin, therefore he dialed the old number from the internal phone in the MGB reception room. He had the wrong number, so he turned to the officer on duty, who recognized him and in a sympathetic manner, because his reputation was still high among NKVD veterans, told him to go as far from Lubyanka as his feet would carry him. His successor, Shubnikov, had been arrested in the purge following the arrest of Abakumov. He loaned Ilyin five hundred rubles, then a large sum, and told him to leave Moscow immediately.

Ilyin took the train to Ryazan, where his cousin lived. There he started working as a freight loader at the railway station. He reported his arrival to the railway security office and within two months they helped him get the position of head of the loaders. They then demanded that he tell his fellow workers that he'd been jailed for abuse of power and embezzlement of funds, not for anti-Soviet activities. Ilyin refused, fearing that this might be used against him and twisted into a crime of concealing his past. They finally came to agreement not to lie in his local registration documents, and he began a new life at age forty-eight. He married a junior research fellow of the local institute of medicine.

After Stalin's death he appealed for rehabilitation, which was at first turned down, but he was allowed to return to Moscow with his wife. He took a job in the transportation department of the Moscow city government and finally was rehabilitated in 1954 after Beria's fall and my arrest. For a year he was refused full KGB pension by Serov because he was compromised by his relationship to Teplinsky, who was still serving his term as an enemy of the people.

Three days after I was released from jail in 1968, Ilyin came to visit me at my apartment. He had been in touch with Emma since 1960. I learned that he had made a remarkable recovery of fortune. In 1956, his former boss at the Ministry of State Security had become deputy director of the Department of Culture of the Central Committee. He was looking for an experienced and honest official to become organizing secretary of the Moscow branch of the Union of Writers. Ilyin's past experience as commissar for cultural affairs made him the right man. He was supported by the writers Konstantin Fedin and Konstantin Simonov. The party officials wanted someone who knew everybody, including the informers. Ilyin was perfect for the job, and he served well until he retired in 1977. He died in 1990.

In 1944 Operation Monastery began to develop into a new venture. On the eve of the Red Army offensive in Byelorussia, I was summoned to the Kremlin with Merkulov, Abakumov, and Colonel General Kuznetsov, director of the GRU, to discuss Monastery, which was going well. A month earlier, Eitingon and I had received the Order of Suvorov for successful strategic combat operations behind German lines. It was a high and unusual award for an intelligence officer, usually given only to commanders of front-line troops for a decisive battlefield victory. Therefore, I entered the meeting feeling confident, and Merkulov was also in high spirits because of his part in the operation.

However, Stalin received us coolly. He was businesslike and asked us how we could use Monastery to help our troops at the front. Traditional deception techniques would not do, Stalin said. Kuznetsov suggested that we should plant disinformation about an alleged offensive in the Ukraine through Aleksandr. I was not prepared for such a turn in the discussion. I was absolutely unaware of the plans of the high command; Kuznetsov was close to Stalin's headquarters. I remembered Marshal Shaposhnikov's advice: never be involved in business beyond your competence. With this in mind I remained silent, while Abakumov resumed his efforts to subordinate Monastery to SMERSH, arguing that his organization had closer ties to the general staff than NKGB had.

Stalin reproached us for not understanding the realities of the war. He ordered us to enlarge Monastery's role as a strategic instrument in the deployment of forces of both sides. General M. S. Shtemenko, deputy chief of the general staff, was summoned to Stalin's office and read out an order obviously prepared prior to our conversation. We were directed to create the impression that German units, already surrounded by the Red Army in Byelorussia, still had the ability to hamper Soviet communications and supply lines. Stalin's intention was to trick the Germans into expending their resources in supporting and trying to break through to their besieged forces. We were impressed with the scope and daring of our new mission. I was excited and concerned because the assignment went well beyond the usual limits of our disinformation efforts.

Eitingon, Maklarsky, and Fisher were promptly dispatched to Byelorussia. In July 1944 Aleksandr/Max radioed the Germans that he had received a new assignment, in the communications department of the Red Army headquarters in Byelorussia. On August 19, 1944, Gehlen reported to the German high command a message from Max that the German brigade headed by Lieutenant Colonel Heinrich Scherhorn, numbering 2,500 men with artillery and a small tank force, was surrounded and blocked by the Red Army near the Berizina River.

In reality, the Scherhorn group had been taken prisoner by the Red Army, with only 1,500 men left. Eitingon, Maklarsky, and Serebryansky recruited Scherhorn and his radio operators. We added to this group German prisoners of war we had already turned, which created an impression of a real German force in the rear of the Red Army. From August 19, 1944, to May 5, 1945, we conducted the most successful radio deception game of the war.

Scherhorn was feeding the German high command in Berlin reports of sabotage against Red Army units; his reports were written by Eitingon and Serebryansky. Max received orders from Berlin to check the reliability of Scherhorn's reports and operations behind Red Army lines, which he confirmed. On March 28, 1945, Scherhorn received a message signed by General Guderian, chief of the German general staff, congratulating him on his promotion to the rank of colonel and on being awarded the Knight's Cross. He was ordered to break through the Red Army lines and proceed to Poland, then to East Prussia, with his unit. Scherhorn demanded that Polish collaborators be parachuted to him behind Red Army lines to guide his men in the breakthrough. Berlin complied, and we seized the Polish rescuers. Hitler planned to send ss General Skorzeny and his crack assault team, but the plan was abandoned because of the Germans' deteriorating military situation in April.

The German high command had ordered sixty-seven transport planes to supply Scherhorn in September 1944. Some were allowed to land and return safely to Germany to keep the ruse alive, some dropped supplies, radio equipment, and ammunition. We confiscated thirteen portable radio sets and 10 million rubles in cash, sent for Scherhorn's use. We captured twenty-five German intelligence agents, who parachuted in or were flown in to assist Scherhorn.

On May 5, 1945, Scherhorn and Max received their last messages from Abwehr. The messages informed them that the war was lost, and the army group should rely on its own resources; Max was ordered to return to Moscow and lie low to conserve his connections. Scherhorn and his group were interned under house arrest near Moscow until all prisoners of war were released in the late 1940s and early 1950s.

At first I toyed with the idea of using Scherhorn for the purpose of recruiting Grand Admiral Erich Raeder, chief of the German navy, dismissed by Hitler in 1943; Raeder was in Moscow, a prisoner of war. Later, in accordance with his request, his wife was brought to Moscow to join him. He appeared cooperative in exchange for our not indicting him as a war criminal at Nuremberg, although the British were anxious to try him because of his U-boat operations against the British fleet and unarmed merchant ships.

I kept him and his wife at my dacha, but I soon realized that Raeder and Scherhorn were incompatible. Serebryansky, posing as a German businessman also being held prisoner at the dacha, was more effective in dealing with Raeder. He was better able to suggest possible approaches to acquaintances and connections in Germany. Raeder enjoyed outings along the Moscow River in a captured Horch limousine similar to the one he had in Germany.

We returned Raeder to Germany late in 1945 after the British pressed for his trial as a war criminal. It is my understanding that there was an exchange agreed upon with the Americans and British.[19] Raeder, other naval officers, and a group of German generals were turned over to them, and we received the former czarist general Pyotr N. Krasnov, head of the White Cossacks in the Civil War, who served on the Wehrmacht staff, and Russian officers who fought with the Vlasov army.[20]

19. Raeder and his wife were taken to Moscow from Germany in July 1945, and he remained there until October 17, 1945, when he was flown to Berlin and handed the indictment from the Allied International Military Tribunal for trial as a war criminal. His wife was returned to a Russian prison camp near Berlin until 1950. See Erich Raeder, *My Life* (Annapolis: United States Naval Institute, 1960), pp. 384–387 and 399–400. Raeder was convicted at Nuremberg in 1946 and sentenced to life imprisonment. He was released in 1953 and died in 1960.

20. Colonel General Andrei A. Vlasov, highly regarded by Khrushchev and Stalin, boldly escaped encirclement in the defense of Kiev and Moscow but was captured by the Germans in the spring of 1942. Vlasov was turned and created an army of Russian

Scherhorn was also returned to Germany, and my connections with them came to an end.

Aleksandr Demyanov, the double agent Heine/Max, returned to Moscow, where he worked as an electrical engineer in a research institute. We tried to reactivate him after the war to operate in Paris, but the émigrés there were not interested in him, so he and his wife returned to Moscow without engaging in any significant intelligence work. He died of a heart attack while on a boating trip on the Moscow River in 1975 at the age of sixty-four.

Our Special Tasks brigade and directorate suffered heavy losses in the war. Especially hard for me were the losses of Ivan Kaminsky, the man I got out of jail who shot himself when ambushed by the Germans; Joseph Friedgood, our illegal in Europe, killed in action; and three of our rezidents — in Odessa, Kiev, and Nikolayev — who were captured by the Germans. Viktor Liagin, operating behind enemy lines in Nikolayev, the shipbuilding port on the Black Sea occupied by the Germans in 1941, was captured and died in silence, declining to escape because there was no chance for his radio operator to get out with him. Ivan M. Kudrya, our rezident in German-occupied Kiev (he had been trained by Emma), penetrated the Abwehr network there and passed important information to Moscow before he was betrayed. Vladimir A. Molodtsov, our rezident in occupied Odessa, captured by the Romanians, became famous because of his and his group's trial, widely publicized in the Romanian press. When he and his group were sentenced to death by firing squad, the chairman of the court suggested that they appeal for clemency to the king of Romania. Molodtsov answered that he would never sign a petition of clemency to the representative of a foreign power that stood on our land, and would not ask for mercy from our enemies. On my petition, Liagin, Kudrya, Molodtsov, and Nikolai Kuznetsov (Fluff) were posthumously awarded the title of Hero of the Soviet Union after the war. Until my arrest, I personally supervised regular support to their families.

The end of the war is still vivid in my memory as a glorious event that washed away all my doubts about the wisdom of Stalin's leadership. All heroic and tragic events, losses and even purges, seemed to be justified

---

prisoners of war to fight for Hitler. Vlasov's troops were used for punishment expeditions against partisans in the Balkans and in Poland against the Warsaw ghetto uprising of 1944. Vlasov surrendered to the Americans in May 1945 and was handed over to Soviet authorities, who tried and executed him by hanging.

by the triumph over Hitler. I remember the grand reception in the Kremlin where I had the privilege of being seated in the Georgian Hall at table number nine together with Admiral Isakov, deputy commander of the navy; General Shtemenko, deputy chief of the general staff; Fitin, head of the intelligence directorate; General Ilychov, director of the GRU; and Colonel General Kuznetsov, director of intelligence for the army. I remember when Stalin came to our table to greet Isakov, who had lost a leg in a German air raid in the Caucasus in 1942, and pronounced a toast in his honor. Isakov could not appear before an audience on crutches, and we were all moved by Stalin's gesture.

You must realize the emotion of every officer in the high command when Stalin admitted in his speech to us that mistakes were made and that we had been helpless in dreadful situations in the war. He said that another people and another nation would have asked the government to conclude a peace treaty with the Germans, but the Russian people had displayed confidence and patience in their government, and he thanked the Russian nation for that confidence.

Stalin was quite a different man that night from the one I had met in his Kremlin office. This time he displayed deep emotion, and it seemed to me that he looked at us young generals and admirals as the generation he had raised, his children and his heirs.

In retrospect, what is remarkable is that Stalin displayed such emotion and devoted such special attention to the mid-level military leaders who were much younger than Zhukov, Voroshilov, and others of the old guard. He was definitely addressing himself to my generation, which had come of age in the war, and we were thrilled to bask in his proud and approving glances in our direction.

ATOMIC
SPIES

The most vital information for developing the first Soviet atomic bomb came from scientists designing the American atomic bomb at Los Alamos, New Mexico — Robert Oppenheimer, Enrico Fermi, and Leo Szilard.

Oppenheimer, Fermi, Szilard, and Szilard's secretary were often quoted in the NKVD files from 1942 to 1945 as sources for information on the development of the first American atomic bomb. It is in the record that on several occasions they agreed to share information on nuclear weapons with Soviet scientists. At first they were motivated by fear of Hitler; they believed that the Germans might produce the first atomic bomb. Then the Danish physicist Niels Bohr helped strengthen their own inclinations to share nuclear secrets with the world academic community. By sharing their knowledge with the Soviet Union, the chance of beating the Germans to the bomb would be increased.

As early as 1940, a commission of Soviet scientists, upon hearing rumors of a superweapon being built in the West, investigated the possibility of creating an atomic bomb from uranium, but concluded that such a weapon was a theoretical, not a practical, possibility. The same scientific commission recommended that the government instruct intelligence services to monitor Western scientific publications, but no government funds were allocated for research. However, Leonid Kvasnikov, chief of the NKVD scientific intelligence desk, sent an order to all stations in the United States, Great Britain, and Scandinavia to be on the lookout for information on the development of superweapons from uranium.

A major shift in our intelligence priorities occurred just as Vassili Zarubin, aka Zubilin, was posted to Washington, ostensibly as secretary of the Soviet Embassy but actually as our new NKVD rezident. Stalin met with Zarubin before his departure for Washington on October 12, 1941, just as the Germans were on the outskirts of Moscow. Until then, our political intelligence collection in America had been minimal because we and the United States had no conflicting geopolitical areas of interest. Now we realized we needed to know American intentions because America's participation in the war against Hitler would be decisive. Stalin ordered Zarubin to set up an effective system not only to monitor events, but to be in a position to influence them through friends of the Soviet Union. Over the next year and a half, however, intelligence reports from Britain, America, Scandinavia, and Germany concerning the development of nuclear weapons would drastically alter our priorities once again.

Less than a month before Zarubin's departure, Donald Maclean, code-named Leaf, who was part of our Cambridge ring, reported from London that the British government was seriously interested in developing a bomb with unbelievable destructive force based on atomic energy.[1] When France fell to the Germans in June 1940, Maclean, third secretary in the British Embassy in Paris, returned to the Foreign Office in London. He reported on September 16, 1941, that the uranium bomb might be constructed within two years through the efforts of Imperial Chemical Industries (ICI) with support of the British government. The project to build a uranium bomb was called Tube Alloys, code-named Tube. Maclean sent us a sixty-page report, minutes of the British Cabinet Committee on the Uranium Bomb Project.[2]

1. In the archives of the NKVD/KGB file, number 13676, vol. I, are Donald Maclean's messages reporting on the first British efforts to build an atomic bomb. According to Sudoplatov: "Maclean was under the operational control of Anatoli Veniaminovich Gorsky, our rezident in London. Gorsky used Vladimir Borisovich Barkovsky as the case officer for Maclean because as an engineer, Barkovsky was capable of dealing with the technical details."

2. The British cabinet report from Maclean and the assessment of it by Igor Kurchatov, the physicist who headed Soviet atomic research, are on pages 20–38 of the operational file (liternoye delo) code-named Enormous. See Appendix Two, Document 2.

We also had a source in ICI, however, who reported that the company's management considered the possibility of building an atomic bomb as theoretical, not realistic. To confuse matters more, we also had information that on September 20, 1941, the British Chief of Staff's Committee decided to start immediately building a plant to manufacture uranium bombs.[3] Maclean's report on the bomb submitted on September 24, 1941, contained the top-secret report of the war cabinet on the "development of a method for the utilization of the nuclear energy of uranium for the production of explosive substances."

It is clear now that Maclean's reports contained only intentions and general discussions about the uranium bomb. Since our scientists believed only in the theoretical possibility of an atomic weapon, we were not surprised that reports about nuclear research were contradictory.

Our intelligence activities in the United States continued to focus on efforts against Germany and Japan. Gregory Kheifetz, our NKVD rezident in San Francisco, was trying to recruit agents in the United States to be used in intelligence work for us in Germany, but failed because his connections were mostly in the Jewish community. Kheifetz's other priority was to neutralize anti-Soviet statements by White Russians in the United States, men such as Aleksandr F. Kerensky, briefly prime minister of Russia in 1917 before the October Revolution, and Viktor Mikhailovich Chernov (1873–1952), once chairman of the Socialist Revolutionary party, who was exiled by Lenin in 1922. Lend-lease was beginning, and it was critical to change our image. The American administration was very sensitive about criticism of its ties with the Soviet Union. We wanted to know to what extent this criticism was inspired by the White Russian émigrés.

These concerns paled in comparison when Kheifetz reported on the full-scale development of an American atomic bomb. Kheifetz advised us by cable, sent in code from our embassy in Washington, of a piece of information that changed Moscow's skeptical attitude about the atomic project. Kheifetz and Robert Oppenheimer, a brilliant American physicist at the University of California, had met in December 1941, and Kheifetz reported that the outstanding physicists in the Allied world, including Nobel Prize winners and scientific giants like Albert Einstein, were involved in a secret project. The concentration of such eminent scientists could not be accidental nor of no practical significance.

As a deputy director of foreign intelligence, I saw these cables from

3. See Appendix Two, Document 1.

the United States. Kheifetz reported that Oppenheimer and his colleagues were planning to move from Berkeley, California, to a new site to conduct research in nuclear weapons. Kheifetz further informed us that the American government would spend around twenty percent of all the money allocated for military research and development on the atomic project. At this very dangerous period of the war, the decision to spend so much money on the nuclear project convinced us it must be vital and feasible. That sentence in the cable was underlined by our analysts, calling to Beria's attention the project's importance.

Kheifetz's first contact with Oppenheimer came at a party to raise money for Spanish Civil War refugees on December 6, 1941. Kheifetz was known to Oppenheimer as Mr. Brown, vice consul of the Soviet consulate. Brown had an outgoing personality and spoke good English, German, and French. He had been sent to America from Italy, where in the 1930s as deputy rezident in Rome he targeted the physicist Enrico Fermi and his younger colleague Bruno Pontecorvo as dedicated antifascists and potential sources. I had known Kheifetz over the years when he visited Moscow and was attracted by his personal charm and professional skill. Kheifetz had served as a secretary to Nadezhda Krupskaya, Lenin's widow, and was also a veteran of the Communist movement and one of the founders of the American Communist party through his work in the Comintern. While living as a Comintern illegal in Germany, he had received a diploma from the Jena Polytechnical Institute.

He mixed easily in San Francisco social life and was deeply respected by Communist and left-wing circles who knew of his Comintern background. Kheifetz told me that he twice met Oppenheimer and his wife at cocktail parties. Then he managed to meet Oppenheimer alone for lunch later in December 1941. Kheifetz had heard rumors of a secret atomic weapons project, but Moscow still doubted its importance and urgency. Oppenheimer expressed his concern to Kheifetz that the Nazis might succeed in building atomic weapons before the Allies. Kheifetz reported that in their conversation Oppenheimer revealed Albert Einstein's then still secret letter, written to President Roosevelt in 1939, urging the United States to investigate the possibility of using nuclear energy to make a weapon of war. Oppenheimer felt frustrated that there had been no prompt or adequate response to Einstein's letter, which had been initiated and drafted by Leo Szilard, a Hungarian-born physicist who had emigrated to the United States in 1938.

Kheifetz was an experienced professional and knew better than to approach such a jewel of a source with the usual money or threats.

Instead, he created a common ground of interest and idealism, drawing on stories of his travels and cosmopolitan view of life that the two men could discuss and compare. Oppenheimer, Fermi, and Szilard could not be run as traditional agents.

From Moscow we instructed another agent in the United States, Semyon Semyonov, to follow up on Kheifetz's report. He was to identify the major scientists involved in the project and try to establish their specific contributions. Semyonov, known as Sam, was a graduate of the Massachusetts Institute of Technology and personally knew several of the scientists involved. His old MIT friends were unaware that their amiable Russian colleague was collecting information to be reported back to the Center.

Semyonov's code name was Twain, after the American writer, and he is now known in America as the man who ran Harry Gold, the atomic spy who worked closely with Klaus Fuchs. Semyonov was a graduate of the Leningrad Institute of Mechanical Engineering whom I had recruited in 1938 to work in the intelligence directorate when he was still a minor clerk in one of the district party offices in Moscow. He was sent to study at MIT in 1939 and to integrate himself into American life. An active and effective case officer, he worked under the control of Gaik Ovakimian, who operated out of AMTORG, the Soviet Trade Mission in New York. Semyonov worked for the NKVD in the United States from 1939 to 1944.

Semyonov set off his own chain reaction in Soviet intelligence when, through his MIT connections, he identified most of the prominent scientists involved in the Manhattan Project, as the American atomic bomb project came to be known. Independently of Kheifetz — whose information concurred — Semyonov reported in the spring of 1942 that the uranium bomb was being taken seriously not only by scientists, but by the American government. One of Semyonov's reports stated that among the scientists involved was the well-known expert in high explosives George B. Kistiakowsky, of Ukrainian origin. We immediately cabled back, instructing Semyonov to use our agents among Russian emigrants to approach Kistiakowsky, but they never managed to attract him.[4]

4. P. A. Sudoplatov recalls two important agents among the emigrants. One was General Yakhontov, a former czarist officer, married to the sister of Merkulov's wife. Merkulov at that time was people's commissar for state security. Yakhontov, his wife, and her sister had fled to America. After World War II, Yakhontov returned to the Soviet Union and published his memoirs, never admitting that he was spying in the United States.

Semyonov was the case officer of Julius and Ethel Rosenberg after Ovakimian recruited them. The Rosenbergs were never more than minor couriers and were never involved with our major networks, but their later arrest had global repercussions.

In March 1942 we received another message from Maclean, which supported his original report and confirmed that the British were proceeding with their atomic energy project. Then in May 1942 Stalin received a letter from George Florev, a professor of physics who had long been engaged in nuclear research, warning that an atomic bomb conceivably could be built during the war, and that the Germans might be the first to develop one.

As director of Special Tasks, my main work was to organize guerrilla warfare and intelligence operations against the Germans and the Japanese. The reports on atomic developments were sent to me with an order to investigate whether the Germans were engaged in such research. The information we received from our agent in Sweden, a businessman, was confusing. There were rumors about secret weapons being built in Germany, but no specifics. In retrospect it is clear that the top German priority was the V-2 two-staged rocket, which they unleashed on London in 1944 and whose range they hoped eventually to lengthen so it could be used against the United States. From Norway we received reliable information that the only plant producing heavy water — a component considered essential to creating a nuclear weapon — was not closely guarded and was not regarded by the Germans as a strategic facility.

Still, we took the atomic matter seriously when the reports from Kheifetz, Maclean, and Semyonov coincided. Further confirmation came from Lise Meitner, a prominent physicist who fled from Germany to Sweden, where Niels Bohr had arranged for her to work at the Physical Institute of the Academy of Sciences. Our agents in Sweden run by Zoya Rybkina approached Lise Meitner and she confirmed the feasibility of a uranium bomb.[5]

The other agent was Sergei Kurnakov, a veteran GPU agent who emigrated to America in the 1920s, after the Civil War. He was helpful in finding people, checking bona fides, and acting as what was called a spotter, someone who could be used as a contact or cutout. Kurnakov returned to the Soviet Union in 1943.

5. Lise Meitner was forced to flee from her work on nuclear physics and chemistry at the Kaiser Wilhelm Institute in 1938. Slight, shy, but formidable, Meitner played a major role in experiments on transmuting natural elements under neutron bombard-

On March 10, 1942, Beria channeled all this information to Stalin in a letter, saying, "In a number of capitalist countries, in connection with work under way on the fission of the atom nucleus with a view to obtaining a new source of energy, research has been launched into the utilization of the nuclear energy of uranium for military purposes." Enclosed were "top-secret materials . . . obtained by the NKVD through intelligence gathering."[6] Nearly a year later, in February 1943, when the British sabotaged the heavy water installation at Vemork in southern Norway, Stalin was convinced that the atomic bomb project was an authentic venture. Details of the successful British operation against the German occupiers were reported by our sources in Norway and by the Philby group in London. I had paid only routine attention to these reports because the damage seemed insignificant. I was surprised when Beria told me to look more carefully, and to note in particular that the British, although they knew about our agent networks in Scandinavia, and were working with us on a plan for joint sabotage operations in Western Europe, did not ask us for any help in the raid against Vemork. This further convinced us it must have been of great importance.

ment with Otto Hahn and Fritz Strassmann. See Richard Rhodes, *The Making of the Atomic Bomb* (New York: Simon and Schuster, 1986), pp. 233–236.

According to P. A. Sudoplatov, contacts with Niels Bohr and Meitner were arranged through the daughter of the famous Finnish writer Hella Wuolijoki (1886–1954), known for her novel *Naiset Niskavuoren* (*Women of Niskavuori*). Sudoplatov recalls that Wuolijoki was controlled by Zoya Rybkina and that Wuolijoki's daughter was married to the deputy foreign minister of Sweden.

6. See Appendix Two, Document 3, for the text of Beria's letter. In 1991, a special issue of the KGB publication *Kurier Sovietski Razvedke* (*Courier of Soviet Intelligence*) reproduced a copy of the first page of this letter. On the document are contemporaneous handwritten notes saying that another version of the letter, with additional information, was the actual one sent to Stalin. Its file number is crossed out and replaced with a different number. In *Voprossi Istorii Estestvoznania i Tekhniki* (*Questions of History of Natural Science and Technology*), no. 3, 1992 (see the notes to Document 3, Appendix Two), the disappearance of the expanded letter is affirmed and Anatoli A. Yatskov, who was the New York control officer for the atomic research intelligence operation, is cited as suggesting that the only extant copy of it is in Beria's archive.

One of the difficulties for anyone trying to piece together the story of Soviet atomic espionage is that crucial documents are missing or misplaced. The example of this letter helps to confirm Sudoplatov's belief that the Enormous (atomic espionage) file was reshuffled and part of the material was placed in the archives of Beria or of the Special Committee on Atomic Energy.

In 1940 the State Defense Committee rejected a proposal from a young nuclear physicist at the Ukrainian Institute of Physical and Technical Studies in Kharkov and a German scientist who had emigrated to the Soviet Union, F. F. Lange, to begin work on a "superexplosive device." This suggestion was channeled to the department of inventions of the People's Commissariat of Defense but was rejected as being premature.

In his March 10 letter Beria suggested to Stalin that the State Defense Committee should consider establishing a scientific consultative committee, composed of well-known scientists and other responsible officials, to coordinate the efforts of scientific institutions in the USSR dealing with atomic energy. He also asked Stalin for permission to show information on atomic developments received from our agent network to prominent scientists for their evaluation. Stalin agreed, but also suggested setting up a second committee to investigate independently.

The Special Committee on Atomic Energy proposed and headed by Beria in 1942 included Communist Party personalities such as Mikhail Georgievich Pervukhin, deputy chairman of the Council of People's Commissars; Georgi Maksimilianovich Malenkov; Nikolai Alekseyovich Voznesensky; and other members of the Politburo.[7] Beria took the responsibility of running the committee, but Molotov and Pervukhin, as deputy prime ministers, were formally in charge. I was attached to the committee as its director of intelligence. Attendance at the committee's sessions made me realize that personal relations were often the critical element in decision making. Likes and dislikes, personal notes, and jokes played an inordinate role in determining policy. The ministries that stood behind every participant in this state committee were struggling to maintain power, defend their own bureaucratic turf, and expand their influence. The resulting shouting matches and acrimony were resolved by Beria, who had Stalin's mandate and the NKVD organization throughout the Soviet Union to implement his commands.

At that time a special commission of the Academy of Sciences to examine atomic energy, among other things, already existed. It had been set up in November 1940 by the Academicians Abram Ioffe and V. I.

7. Although this state committee contained Politburo members, i.e., leaders of the Communist party, it was government run. The two parallel hierarchies of government and party ruled together, but decisions of the party always took precedence over the government.

Vernadsky, and was chaired by Academician Vladimir Khlopin, an expert in radiochemistry. Academician Vernadsky, the patriarch of Russian science, was now consulted, and he suggested that Academician Ioffe, our leading physicist in Leningrad, also be called in. Ioffe was well known in the West; in the 1920s and 1930s he had been invited to visit major Western laboratories, and he turned down proposals to settle in the United States. But physicists from Moscow University strongly resented any attempts to use colleagues from Leningrad. Later one of them asked me, "Why are you consulting with those gangsters from the Leningrad Physical Technical Institute and the Academy of Sciences? They are a group of hooligans."

An old rivalry had now come between scientists who were needed to work for the same cause. The group that Vernadsky and Ioffe assembled to consider the question independently, as Stalin had suggested, without the aid of intelligence information, was headed by Academician Pyotr Kapitsa at the Academy of Sciences[8] with Academician Dmitri V. Skobeltsin of Moscow University and Professor A. A. Slutsky at the Kharkov Physical Technical Institute.

Ioffe's and Vernadsky's evaluation took six months. In September 1942, Pervukhin summoned Academicians Ioffe and Kapitsa to Moscow. Skobeltsin and Slutsky continued to believe that building an atomic bomb was improbable in the near future; Kapitsa said only that the problem was a challenge facing contemporary physics and that the most important fundamental research in this area was being undertaken in Great Britain and the United States.

Stalin preferred to meet only with Vernadsky and Ioffe, and in October he received them at his dacha in Kuntsevo. Academician Ioffe was the first to sense the validity of the information supplied by the NKVD on American nuclear developments. After that meeting, I was later told by Boris L. Vannikov, who headed our weapons industry, we began to believe that a nuclear weapon was possible. We were ready to react.

---

8. Pyotr Leonidovich Kapitsa (1894–1984) worked under Ioffe until he went to England in 1921, where he worked under Ernest Rutherford and from 1924 was deputy head of the Cavendish Magnetic Research Laboratory at Cambridge University. Induced to visit the Soviet Union in 1934, he was refused permission to return to England. After a period of tension, Kapitsa agreed to remain in Moscow, and his laboratory equipment was brought to the Soviet Union for him as head of the new Institute of Physical Problems, which he headed from 1936 to 1946 and again after Stalin's death in 1953. He was awarded a Nobel Prize in physics in 1978.

Taking into account the British reports that ICI was working on the Tube project, Stalin had already assigned Pervukhin to consider the logistics of a Soviet atomic weapon.

Vernadsky suggested to Stalin that we approach Niels Bohr and the American and British governments about sharing their information with us. Stalin told Vernadsky, "You are politically naive if you think that they would share information about the weapons that will dominate the world in the future." However, Stalin did agree that the idea of privately contacting prominent Western scientists through our own scientists could prove very useful.

A year later, in 1943, when Bohr moved to London from Denmark, Kapitsa bombarded Stalin and Beria with suggestions that they invite him to head our atomic project and even wrote to Bohr asking him to come to the Soviet Union for just that purpose, guaranteeing him the best conditions.

Bohr was then invited to the Soviet Embassy in London to meet Anatoli Gorsky, the NKVD rezident, listed as a counselor of the embassy. Bohr avoided any direct discussion of nuclear developments, but later on several occasions he urged President Roosevelt to share atomic secrets with the Soviet Union.[9]

Ioffe helped overcome the rivalries between scientists in Moscow University (Skobeltsin's group) and the Academy of Sciences (Kapitsa) and was influential in settling the question of who should direct the three major atomic research centers that would be established in 1943 for developing our nuclear programs. Following his meeting with Stalin in the autumn of 1942, Ioffe contended that he was too old and suggested his young protégé, Igor Kurchatov, to lead the Soviet project. Until then Kurchatov had been engaged in research efforts to counter German magnetic mines planted in the Black Sea near Sevastopol and in the Barents Sea near Murmansk. Ioffe brought Kurchatov to Moscow to organize a full-scale Soviet nuclear project. Kurchatov assembled a talented and energetic team, including Academicians A. I. Alikhanov and I. K. Kikoin, and they prepared a research and development plan and budget.

That Oppenheimer, a relatively young scientist, then age thirty-eight, was being put in charge of the American project influenced our decision to appoint Kurchatov, then forty, to head ours. This was a controversial decision, as our older scientists did not, or could not, believe

9. See Rhodes, *The Making of the Atomic Bomb*, pp. 526–527, 529.

that Niels Bohr and Enrico Fermi, world-famous figures, could be sub-ordinate to Oppenheimer in Los Alamos.

At the end of January 1943 we received through Semyonov a full report on the first nuclear chain reaction from Bruno Pontecorvo, describing Enrico Fermi's experiment in Chicago on December 2, 1942. A few hours after the pile of graphite went critical, Semyonov had received a prearranged telephone message saying, "The Italian sailor reached the new world." The written report that followed was the first documentary information that verified progress in making a bomb. It was written by scientists, not administrators, not from oral discussions or cabinet minutes. Early in 1943 Pontecorvo met Lev Vasilevsky, trav-eling as an elegantly dressed Soviet diplomat, Tarasov, in Canada and New York and informed him that Fermi was prepared to provide information.

Contrary to strict standard rules, when Eitingon went to the United States in 1939 he had been allowed to recruit agents without approval of or consultation with the Center. Early in 1943 Pontecorvo met with illegal moles whom Eitingon had planted in the United States and Mex-ico in 1940 and 1941. These moles were controlled by Vasilevsky, who was the only one in the Center informed about them in 1942.

On February 11, 1943, Stalin signed a decree organizing a spe-cial committee to develop atomic energy for military weapons, with Molotov in charge. Beria, acting as his deputy for the procurement of intelligence, gave me permission to invite Kurchatov, Ioffe, and Kikoin to my office in Lubyanka and to show them the scientific materials gath-ered by our agents, but without disclosing the sources. They came and were shown what we had received, translated into Russian. Kikoin was excited about the report on the first nuclear chain reaction and, although I had not told him who had done the work, said immediately, "This is Fermi's work. He is the only one capable of producing such a miracle." I showed some of the material to them in the original English.

I was in my thirties and hesitant to share secrets; I put my palm over the signatures and enumeration of the sources. Kurchatov, Ioffe, and Kikoin were astonished and said to me, "Look, Pavel Anatolievich, you are too naive. You read the material to us and we will tell you who the authors are." Then Ioffe identified Otto Frisch as the source of another document. I reported this incident to Beria and from that time was allowed to disclose to them all scientific sources of information.

On April 12, Special Laboratory Number Two of the USSR Acad-emy of Sciences was organized. Kurchatov, on March 22, 1943, after receiving our report on the chain reaction at the University of Chicago, asked Deputy Prime Minister Pervukhin to have the intelligence organs clarify what was being accomplished in the United States.

Kurchatov and his team often visited Beria, the intelligence procurement director, in his office on the third floor of Lubyanka. Then they would come to my office on the seventh floor for lunch and to formulate assignments for the acquisition of information from abroad. The scientists, obviously, were particularly interested in nuclear projects in the United States. In a memo to Pervukhin, Kurchatov expressed the tremendous impact of intelligence information from the West on Soviet research:

> To Deputy Chairman of the Council of People's Commissars of the Union SSR Comrade M. G. Pervukhin
>
> The examination of the materials I have done shows that obtaining them has immense, indeed incalculable, importance for our State and science.
>
> On the one hand, the materials furnished evidence of the importance and intensity of the research work in Britain on the uranium problem; on the other, they provided a chance to obtain most important guidelines for our own research, enabling us to bypass many very labor-consuming stages of the problem's development and to learn about new scientific and technological ways of tackling it.[10]

The information, especially that regarding separation of isotopes, surprised Kurchatov and his colleagues and significantly altered the direction of Soviet research.

By July 1943 our agents in the United States had already provided us with 286 classified publications on scientific research in nuclear energy. In March and April of 1943, Kurchatov identified in particular seven research centers, twenty-six scientists, and specific technical information on which we should concentrate our intelligence efforts. Kurchatov wrote to Pervukhin requesting that he "instruct intelligence Bodies to find out what has been done in America" about the materials and shapes of certain parts used in the U.S. nuclear reactors, as well as some questions about the physics of the fission process. He further specified locations where this work was being done and identified the

10. See Appendix Two, Document 4.

American scientists whose work was essential to the development of an atomic bomb. He said their efforts should be checked, because "more precise definition" of technical details "requires painstaking work of a great number of specialists," whom he then proceeded to name.[11] In operational terms, this meant the development of these scientists as sources of information. In December 1943, by direct order of Stalin, Kurchatov became a full member of the Academy of Sciences.

Two months later, in February 1944, Beria summoned me to his office and appointed me to be the director of the new autonomous Department S. This was one of the results of a major reorganization of our intelligence services undertaken in part to accommodate the importance of atomic espionage. In previous years atomic espionage had been the responsibility of two sections: scientific intelligence in the GRU, and the Foreign Intelligence Directorate of the NKVD, where I was a deputy director until 1942. In July 1943 the foreign intelligence and security services of the NKVD were detached as a separate commissariat, the NKGB. That same year it was decided to coordinate the activities of the intelligence services monitoring atomic projects. Special Department S — at first the department was called the Sudoplatov Group, but later Beria suggested we simply call it Department S — was organized to supervise atomic intelligence activities of both the GRU and NKGB.

Department S was responsible for direct contacts with the leaders of the Soviet atomic project and the dissemination of information to them from abroad. It was formally established by written orders of the government in 1944. Uniting sections from the GRU and NKGB into Department S was an effort to improve the gathering, utilization, and dissemination of atomic intelligence. This explains why Klaus Fuchs, who was first run by the GRU, was transferred to the NKGB network.

At the same time, I was appointed head of the Special Second Bureau of the newly set up State Committee for Problem Number One, whose aim was the realization of an atomic bomb through uranium fuel. We had progressed from the research to the production phase. In this capacity I had full authority to supervise all activities of the Soviet special services relating to efforts to obtain information on the atomic

11. See Appendix Two, Document 6. A number of Kurchatov's letters are reproduced in Appendices Two and Three.

bomb. My function in both Department S and the Special Second Bureau was the same, but wearing two hats made coordination between the NKGB and the GRU, which had been separate and often competitive, easier to achieve. My position on the Committee for Problem Number One underscored the importance of my role in unifying our intelligence efforts to solve the problem of building a bomb.

I was not very pleased when Beria put me in charge of atomic intelligence, because my primary duties were still to direct guerrilla warfare in the rear of German armies. Besides, I had no background in physics. The only positive aspect was my absolute trust in Semyonov; Zarubin and his wife, Elizabeth; Eitingon's moles; and in Kheifetz, who came back to Moscow in 1944 and described his impressions of Oppenheimer and other important people involved in nuclear research. Oppenheimer and his colleagues were deeply troubled by the possibility of the Germans building an atomic bomb before America.

Beria told me, "The time has come for more systematic efforts in our work with scientists." To improve the atmosphere with the scientists, who were suspicious and nervous around NKGB officers, and to assess their strengths and weaknesses, Beria suggested I invite some of the scientists on the project to dinner. I was ordered to become their good friend, someone on whom they could rely in daily business and personal matters. On one such evening we ate in the sitting room behind my office. My waitress served us tea and brandy. I do not drink at all because alcohol causes me severe headaches, and I imagined that scientists, like academicians, drank in a refined manner. Since I had placed a bottle of the best Armenian brandy in front of them, Kikoin and Kurchatov assumed that it was a practical joke on my part that I poured the brandy into a teaspoon and placed it in the tea. They hesitated a moment, laughed at me, and filled their glasses.

Kikoin soon realized how lucky he was to be on good terms with the NKGB. Beria ordered that all surveillance reports on the project personnel and their relatives be turned over to me. In two weeks I received an agent report that Kikoin's younger brother kept in his desk a Trotskyite pamphlet smuggled into the Soviet Union in 1928. Even worse, he had been foolish enough to show it to one of his colleagues, who reported him immediately to an NKGB case officer. Now you may wonder what was wrong with saving historical rarities, but in those days it was different. The counterespionage people wanted to arrest Kikoin's relatives, which would have meant the end for Kikoin in academia.

I informed Beria, who told me to call Kikoin in, brief him, and suggest that he discipline his brother "to stop this stupid business." Instead I went to see him at the laboratory and told him about his brother's indiscretion. Kikoin promised to beat his brother, who, he explained, collected historical manuscripts and leaflets. Later Kikoin telephoned to say that he had slapped his brother in the face and was convinced he had destroyed the Trotskyite pamphlet.

The next day Beria appeared in Kikoin's laboratory to allay his fears. He convened the troika of Kurchatov, Alikhanov, and Kikoin and told them in my presence, "General Sudoplatov is attached to you to provide you all necessary assistance. You have the absolute trust of Comrade Stalin and me personally. Whatever information is shared with you is to help you accomplish the mission of the Soviet government, on which depends the survival of the Soviet state. I repeat that you have absolutely no reason to be concerned for the fate of people you trust or your relatives. We guarantee in every way to you and to them absolute security and a standard of living that will enable you to concentrate entirely on matters strategically important to our state."

On Beria's initiative all atomic project personnel were given access to special foods and high-level medical care. They were provided with apartments, dachas, and special shops where they could buy goods for coupons. In 1945 the personnel files of all scientists and officers working on the project were removed from the American section to Department S and later centralized under the control of Beria's secretariat. Without his permission, no one could have access to these files, thus enhancing security. By then Beria had displaced Molotov as head of the atomic project because Molotov lacked the managerial ability needed for an undertaking of such magnitude.[12]

When it became clear that the atomic project was a heavily guarded, top-secret American priority, Eitingon and I suggested that we use our

---

12. In contrast to dissatisfaction with Molotov, Beria's instrumental role was noted by Academician Yuli Khariton, who wrote: "Beria understood the necessary scope and dynamics of the research. This man, who was the personification of evil in modern Russian history, also possessed great energy and capacity for work. The scientists who met him could not fail to recognize his intelligence, his will power, and his purposefulness. They found him a class administrator who could carry through a job to completion. It may be paradoxical, but Beria — who often displayed great brutishness — could also be courteous, tactful, and simple when circumstances demanded it." See Yuli Khariton and Yuri Smirnov, "The Khariton Version," *Bulletin of the Atomic Scientists,* May 1993, p. 26.

networks of illegals as couriers for our sources of information. Vassili Zarubin, our Washington rezident, instructed Kheifetz to divorce all intelligence operations from the American Communist party, which we knew would be closely monitored by the FBI, and to have Oppenheimer sever all contacts with Communists and left-wingers.[13]

Eitingon and I also instructed Kheifetz and Semyonov to turn over

13. Steve Nelson, aka Steve Mesarosh, an emigrant from Yugoslavia and a member of the Communist party since 1925, in January 1942 attempted to take over atomic espionage in Berkeley through the traditional method of utilizing party cells. His efforts conflicted with Zarubin's instructions to divorce intelligence operations from the American Communist party. Nelson had studied at the Lenin Institute in Moscow, worked for the Comintern in China in 1933, and been a member of the International Brigade in Spain. Since 1940 Nelson, a member of the American Communist party's national committee, served as a Communist organizer in San Francisco.

David J. Dallin, in *Soviet Espionage,* pp. 468–469, writes: "In December 1942, on instructions from Nelson, the Communist professor Haakon Chevalier approached Oppenheimer; he used the standard argument of Russia's moral right to share American atomic secrets. 'Since Russia and the United States are allies, Soviet Russia should be entitled to any technical data which might be of assistance to that nation.' Oppenheimer not only refused but called the effort outright treason; later he informed General [Leslie] Groves, head of the Manhattan Engineering District [the Manhattan Project], of the incident. It was not long before United States security agencies were informed of the activities of Steven Nelson and his Communist cell in Berkeley." It is unclear from Sudoplatov's account whether Oppenheimer in doing this was acting on the suggestion of Zarubin and Kheifetz that he establish a record of separation from his Communist friends.

Nelson continued his efforts and opposed the Moscow order for the American party to cease its espionage efforts. Between January and March 1943 Nelson established close relations with Joseph W. Weinberg, a research physicist at Oppenheimer's Berkeley laboratory, who provided highly confidential information that Nelson turned over to Peter Ivanov in the Soviet consulate in San Francisco. Nelson's meetings with Weinberg and visits to the consulate were observed by the FBI, according to Dallin.

In April 1943 Vassili Zarubin came to San Francisco from Washington to receive a report from Nelson on his work. At that meeting, according to Dallin, Nelson proposed a compromise: that "the Soviets choose in each important city or state where espionage activities might be necessary, a trustworthy contact and allow that person to handle direct contacts with the Communist members to be given special assignments." Zarubin agreed to this compromise. Nelson's scheme, however, never materialized, according to Dallin.

In July 1952 Steven Nelson was convicted in Pittsburgh and sentenced to a twenty-year prison term for violating the Smith Act, which forbids advocating the overthrow of the government by force. His conviction was overturned in 1957 when the Supreme Court ruled that proof of intent was lacking and that "mere teachings" of the Communist party, party activity, or party membership were not illegal. Nelson died in December 1993.

to our old moles all their confidential contacts with friendly sources around Oppenheimer in California. Vasilevsky took part in this operation. Under Beria's direct orders we forbade Kheifetz and Semyonov to tell anybody from the American section of the Foreign Directorate about this transfer of contacts. Later, in the purges of 1950, Kheifetz and Semyonov were accused of losing these contacts, which was untrue.

Meanwhile, there were multiple intelligence approaches, some of which worked and some of which did not. Our principal targets of penetration were Los Alamos and the research labs servicing it, and the Oak Ridge, Tennessee, plant. We also attempted to get into the companies doing the actual manufacturing work for the government.

In 1943 a world-famous actor of the Moscow Yiddish State Art Theater, Solomon Mikhoels, together with well-known Yiddish poet Itzik Feffer, toured the United States on behalf of the Jewish Antifascist Committee. Before their departure, Beria instructed Mikhoels and Feffer to emphasize the great Jewish contribution to science and culture in the Soviet Union. Their assignment was to raise money and convince American public opinion that Soviet anti-Semitism had been crushed as a result of Stalin's policies. Kheifetz made sure that the message they brought was conveyed to Oppenheimer. Kheifetz said that Oppenheimer, the son of a German-Jewish immigrant, was deeply moved by the information that a secure place for Jews in the Soviet Union was guaranteed. They discussed Stalin's plans to set up a Jewish autonomous republic in the Crimea after the war was won against fascism.[14]

Although they were unaware of it, Oppenheimer and Fermi were assigned code names, Star and Editor, as sources of information. Star was used as the code name not only for Oppenheimer, but also for other physicists and scientists in the Manhattan Project with whom we had contact but who were not formally recruited agents. Code names were changed from time to time for security reasons; Oppenheimer and Fermi were also jointly known as Star.[15]

14. See Chapter Ten.

15. Anatoli Yatskov, in an interview in October 1992, before his death in March 1993, said the FBI uncovered "perhaps less than half" his network. He referred to Perseus as a code name for a major source still alive. Says Sudoplatov: "I do not recall that code name or such a source, but I remember a cable from New York reporting the date of the first nuclear blast which referred to information passed by three moles and friendly sources — Charles (Klaus Fuchs), Mlad (Pontecorvo), and Star (meaning Oppenheimer and Fermi). The three moles, whose names I do not remember, worked

In developing Oppenheimer as a source, Vassili Zarubin's wife, Elizabeth, was essential. She hardly appeared foreign in the United States. Her manner was so natural and sociable that she immediately made friends. Slim, with dark eyes, she had a classic Semitic beauty that attracted men, and she was one of the most successful agent recruiters, establishing her own illegal network of Jewish refugees from Poland, and recruiting one of Szilard's secretaries, who provided technical data. She spoke excellent English, German, French, Romanian, and Hebrew. Usually she looked like a sophisticated, upper-class European, but she had the ability to change her appearance like a chameleon. She came from a family of revolutionaries related to Anna Pauker, the founder of the Romanian Communist party. Elizabeth's elder brother had been the head of the military terrorist section of the Romanian party. Twice he had escaped from a military court while being tried, but finally, in 1922, he was killed in a firefight.

Elizabeth became part of the intelligence system in 1919 as a junior case officer in Dzerzhinsky's secretariat. While working for Dzerzhinsky, Elizabeth met and fell in love with Yakov Blumkin, the assassin of Count Mirbach, the German ambassador in Moscow in 1918. Blumkin was a key figure in the plot of the Socialist Revolutionaries against Lenin in July 1918. When the plot failed, Blumkin was pardoned and continued to work for Dzerzhinsky and Trotsky.

In 1930 Elizabeth and Blumkin were posted as illegals in Turkey, where he was to sell prized Hasidic manuscripts from the Central Library in Moscow. The money was intended to support illegal operations in Turkey and the Middle East, but Blumkin gave part of the funds to Trotsky, who was then in exile in Turkey. Elizabeth was outraged, and exposed her husband. She contacted Eitingon and Pyotr Zubov, who were on a mission in Turkey, and they arranged for Blumkin to be recalled to Moscow via a Soviet ship. Blumkin was immediately arrested and executed by a firing squad.

After Blumkin's execution, Zarubin promptly married Elizabeth, and they traveled and spied together for nearly seven years, using the cover of a Czechoslovakian business couple. One of their accomplishments was the recruitment of the deputy director of a Gestapo section,

in their laboratories. Vasilevsky knew the details, as he was the first intelligence officer to approach Pontecorvo directly in 1943. It should not be excluded that Perseus is a creation by Yatskov or his colleagues to cover the real names of the sources."

Willy Lehmann (Breitmann, Dike), who became one of our most valuable sources in Germany in the 1930s.

In 1941 Elizabeth Zarubina was a captain in the NKVD. After her husband's posting to Washington, she traveled to California frequently to cultivate the Oppenheimer family through social contacts arranged by Kheifetz. Kheifetz provided Elizabeth Zarubina with a rundown on all the members of Robert Oppenheimer's family, known for its left-wing sympathies, to enable her to approach them. He then introduced Elizabeth to Oppenheimer's wife, Katherine, who was sympathetic to the Soviet Union and Communist ideals, and the two worked out a system for future meetings. Katherine Oppenheimer was not mentioned by name in the reports, but we worked through a woman close to Oppenheimer, and it was my understanding then and is now that the woman was his wife.

Through Katherine, Elizabeth Zarubina and Kheifetz convinced Oppenheimer to refrain from statements sympathetic to Communist or left-wing groups in order not to call the attention of the FBI to himself. Zarubina and Kheifetz persuaded Oppenheimer to share information with "antifascists of German origin," which provided a rationale for taking Klaus Fuchs to Los Alamos. Oppenheimer agreed to hire and promote these people, provided he received confirmation of their opposition to Nazism before they came to the project. Oppenheimer, together with Fermi and Szilard, helped us place moles in Tennessee, Los Alamos, and Chicago as assistants in those three labs. In total there were four important sources of information who transmitted documents from the labs to the New York and Washington rezidenturas and to our illegal station, which was a drugstore in Santa Fe.

The material that reached Anatoli Yatskov, the control officer in New York, came from Fuchs and one of the Los Alamos moles and was carried by couriers, one of whom was Lona Cohen. Her husband, Morris Cohen, was recruited during the Spanish Civil War, when he served as a volunteer in the American Abraham Lincoln Brigade under the name Israel Altman. While recovering from a leg wound in Barcelona in 1938, he was transferred to a spy school in a villa in Madrid, where he demonstrated a special aptitude for undercover work. On his return to New York City, Cohen married Lona, an old high school sweetheart, and recruited her for Soviet "secret work." In Cohen's KGB file he is quoted as saying, "Moscow has already decided on Lona and me fulfilling its assignments together. There is nothing like a good and reliable married couple." Lona's first reaction to their secret work was that it might be treason; Morris responded that he was "upholding and fighting for universal truth and justice" and this, by definition, "was not treachery at all."[16]

When Morris was drafted into the U.S. Army in July 1942, their controller in New York, Anatoli Yatskov, aka Yakovlev, used Lona as a courier to Los Alamos to pick up information. Lona's trips to New Mexico were explained as visits to a sanatorium for a tuberculosis cure. Yatskov, code name Johnny, recounted in 1992 his work with Lona Cohen, a "pretty young woman." On one of her trips, August 1945, she traveled to Albuquerque shortly after the first atomic bomb was dropped on Hiroshima. She anxiously awaited a contact, who gave her a "thick wad" of tightly written pages that were "priceless" to Moscow Center.

As she left the security-infested town, she demonstrated her trade-craft. Carrying a suitcase, a purse, and a box of Kleenex tissues, she arrived at the railroad station just as the train was supposed to leave. She dropped her suitcase and started rummaging nervously through her purse, searching for her ticket. She handed the Kleenex box to the con-ductor to hold while she looked for and found her ticket. Delighted, Lona boarded the train, leaving the box of tissues with the conductor. "I felt it in my skin, that the conductor would return the box of Kleenex, and indeed later he handed it to me." When Yatskov met her in New York City, Lona told him, "You know, Johnny, everything was all right except for one thing. The police held these materials in their hands." The Kleenex box contained a detailed description and drawing of the world's first atomic bomb.[17]

The Cohens fled to Moscow when Julius and Ethel Rosenberg were arrested in 1950 for atomic espionage. They were trained as illegals and given New Zealand passports with the names Peter and Helen Kroger. They settled in London and established an antiquarian book business. From their house in Ruislip, outside London, they provided radio and technical support for the KGB illegal Konon Molody, alias Gordon Lonsdale. They were arrested with Lonsdale in 1961, when their net-work was exposed, and were sentenced to twenty years in jail. After

16. Ronald Radosh and Eric Breindel, "Bombshell," *New Republic*, June 10, 1991, pp. 10–12.
17. Anatoli Yatskov, in *Voprossi Istorii Estestvoznania i Tekhniki*, no. 3, 1992, p. 103.

their release they settled in Moscow, where Morris Cohen survives Lona, who died in 1992.

There was one respected scientist we targeted with both personal threats and appeals to his antifascism. George Gamow, a Russian-born physicist who defected to the United States in 1933 when he was permitted to leave the Soviet Union to attend an international meeting of physicists in Brussels, played an important role in helping us to obtain American atomic bomb secrets. Academician Ioffe spotted Gamow because of his connections with Niels Bohr and the American physicists. We assigned Sam Semyonov and Elizabeth Zarubina to enlist his cooperation. With a letter from Academician Ioffe, Elizabeth approached Gamow through his wife, Rho, who was also a physicist. She and her husband were vulnerable because of their concern for relatives in the Soviet Union. Gamow taught physics at George Washington University in Washington, D.C., and instituted the annual Washington Conference on Theoretical Physics, which brought together the best physicists to discuss the latest developments at small meetings.

We were able to take advantage of the network of colleagues that Gamow had established. Using implied threats against Gamow's relatives in Russia, Elizabeth Zarubina pressured him into cooperating with us. In exchange for safety and material support for his relatives, Gamow provided the names of left-wing scientists who might be recruited to supply secret information.

On some occasions Gamow had essential data in his house for several days, in violation of security regulations. Scientists on the bomb project asked him for his comments on the data, which he then verbally repeated to our illegals by arrangement with Zarubina. Gamow took nothing, and violated security only through mutual consent of his colleagues. He also described to us the political infighting among the American scientists and their conflicts with the government bureaucracy.

Another route was from the mole who worked with Fermi and Pontecorvo. The mole in Tennessee was connected with the illegal station at the Santa Fe drugstore, from which material was sent by courier to Mexico. These unidentified young moles, along with the Los Alamos mole, were junior scientists or administrators who copied vital documents to which they were allowed access by Oppenheimer, Fermi, and Szilard, who were knowingly part of the scheme.

The Santa Fe drugstore was an illegal station left over from the Trotsky operation. In 1940, on Beria's orders, I had sent Joseph Grigulevich to Mexico to assist Eitingon in assassinating Trotsky. Grigulevich, who had been recruited by the NKVD in 1934 or 1935, had made a name for himself liquidating Lithuanian police informers, fighting a Trotskyite network there, and, in 1937, taking part in the Spanish Civil War. He had visited Argentina, where his father was a successful pharmacist.

As I related in the chapter on Trotsky, Grigulevich's assignment in Mexico was to organize a parallel illegal network, independent of the Spanish emigrants whom Eitingon was using to target Trotsky. While organizing this group, Grigulevich opened a drugstore in New Mexico as a safe station for his illegals; before leaving Mexico and the United States in 1941, he transferred ownership of the pharmacy to one of his agents. It was simply good luck that a previous mission left us with a safe house in Santa Fe.

Elizabeth Zarubina gave a code word — in fact, a code sentence — to a member of Oppenheimer's circle to pass to Oppenheimer. Its use would identify someone friendly to their cause: "My escape from Germany was similar to the escape of Lise Meitner." Oppenheimer had suggested to the Roosevelt administration that it invite to America top-level scientists from Europe. In 1943, under the influence of Kheifetz and Elizabeth Zarubina, he suggested that Klaus Fuchs be included in the Los Alamos British team.[18] Fuchs, a German Communist who was forced to seek refuge in England in 1933 and who completed his education as a physicist at Bristol University, had offered his services to the Soviet Union when approached in 1941.[19] He was instructed to tell Oppenheimer the code sentence and to emphasize that he was spiritually close to the ideals of Lise Meitner. When Fuchs appeared, he was to identify himself as the only one on the British team who had escaped from a German prison camp, and thus gain the respect and absolute confidence of

18. Aleksandr Feklisov, who was Fuchs's case officer in England from 1947 to 1950, wrote that "by the end of 1943 Robert Oppenheimer, the leader of the work on the creation of the American atomic bomb, who highly appreciated the theoretical works of Fuchs, asked to include Fuchs as part of the British scientific mission coming to the U.S.A. to assist the project." "Geroicheski Podvig Klaus Fuks" ("The Heroic Deed of Klaus Fuchs"), *Voyennoi Istorischeski Zhurnal*, December 1990, p. 25.

19. Fuchs was recruited through the German Communist Juergen Kuczynski who fled to England and also worked for the OSS during the war. Kuczynski, according to Sudoplatov, informed Soviet ambassador Ivan Maisky of Fuchs's work. Maisky instructed Soviet military attaché Simon Davidovich Kremer, known to Fuchs as Aleksandr, to recruit him. In the summer of 1942 Fuchs was transferred from Kremer to Kuczynski's sister Ursula (aka Sonia and Ruth Werner). For Fuchs she was Mrs. Brewer, a Jewish refugee from Germany living near Oxford.

Oppenheimer.[20] In this way, under Oppenheimer's initiative, Fuchs was given access to material that he had no right to look at. We received reports of the bitter conflicts between Oppenheimer and General Groves, who objected to allowing summaries of applied experiments to be made available to scientists unconnected with these experiments.

One agent report cites Oppenheimer's stressing that information should be leaked in a way that was not traceable to those who worked in Los Alamos. Rather, it should be done through someone not on the permanent staff of the Manhattan Project who, due to illness or personal reasons, would leave when the work of producing a bomb was finished, perhaps even leave the country.

Elizabeth Zarubina's other mission was to check on the two Polish Jewish agents established on the West Coast as illegals by Eitingon in the early 1930s. They had remained under deep cover for more than ten years. One of these agents was a dentist with a French medical degree that the OGPU had subsidized. His code name was Chess Player. The dentist's wife became a close friend of the Oppenheimer family, and they were our clandestine contacts with Oppenheimer and his friends, contacts that went undetected by the FBI. To the best of my knowledge, even Elizabeth was not identified by the FBI as a Soviet case officer in America until 1946, after she had returned to Moscow.

We received reports on the progress of the Manhattan Project from Oppenheimer and his friends in oral form, through comments and asides, and from documents transferred through clandestine methods with their full knowledge that the information they were sharing would be passed on. In all, there were five classified reports made available by Oppenheimer describing the progress of work on the atomic bomb.

Another source of information was the Radiation Laboratory at the University of California in Berkeley. From there we received general information, not precise classified material on the actual engineering aspects of bomb production, and not on the operation of the first atomic power reactor.

We learned that military experts and managers from the field of high explosives were supervising the engineering aspects of the American project. That led us to decide to follow the American example and appoint Vannikov, our ammunition expert, to head the project when the

20. Actually Fuchs escaped arrest, but his father was imprisoned by the Gestapo. See Robert Chadwell Williams, *Klaus Fuchs, Atom Spy* (Cambridge, Ma.: Harvard University Press, 1987), pp. 15–19.

use of hardware was needed. Vannikov was our equivalent of the American General Leslie Groves.

Not only were we informed of technical developments in the atomic program, but we heard in detail the human conflicts and rivalries among the members of the team at Los Alamos. A constant theme was tension with General Groves, director of the project. We were told of Groves's conflicts with Szilard.[21] Groves was outraged by Szilard's iconoclastic style and his refusal to accept the strictures of military discipline. The "baiting of brass hats" was Szilard's self-professed hobby. Groves believed that Szilard was a security risk and tried to prevent him from working on the Manhattan Project despite Szilard's seminal contributions to the development of the first chain reaction with Fermi.

Kheifetz described Oppenheimer as a man who thought of problems on a global scale. Oppenheimer saw the threat and promise of the atomic age and understood the ramifications for both military and peaceful applications. We always stressed that contacts with him should be carefully planned to maintain security, and should not be used for acquiring routine information. We knew that Oppenheimer would remain an influential person in America after the war and therefore our relations with him should not take the form of running a controlled agent. We understood that he and other members of the scientific community were best approached as friends, not as agents. Since Oppenheimer, Bohr, and Fermi were fierce opponents of violence, they would seek to prevent a nuclear war, creating a balance of power through sharing the secrets of atomic energy. This would be a crucial factor in establishing the new world order after the war, and we took advantage of this.

The line between valuable connections and acquaintances, and confidential relations is very shaky. In traditional Russian espionage terminology, there is a special term, *agenturnaya razvedka,* which means that the material is received through a network of agents or case officers acting under cover. Occasionally the most valuable information comes from a contact who is not an agent in the true sense — that is, working for and paid by us — but who is still regarded in the archives as an agent source of information. Our problem was that the atomic espionage business required new approaches; we used every potential method to pen-

21. The continuing struggle between Groves and Szilard is skillfully recounted by William Lanouette in his biography of Leo Szilard, *Genius in the Shadows* (New York: Scribner's, 1992), especially pp. 305–313.

etrate into a unique area of activities that was intensively guarded by the American authorities.

I was pleased that the worldview of the Western scientists was strikingly similar to that of our own leading scientists — Kapitsa, Vernadsky, Ioffe — who were quite sincere in suggesting that our government approach the British and Americans to share with us information about atomic research. They suggested the organization of a joint team of Soviet, American, and British scientists to build the bomb. This was also the ideal of Bohr, who had greatly influenced Oppenheimer, both as a scientist and in his political worldviews. While Bohr was in no way our agent of influence, his personal views were that atomic secrets should be shared by the international scientific community. After meeting with Bohr, Oppenheimer suggested that Bohr visit President Roosevelt and try to convince him that the Manhattan Project should be shared with the Russians in the hope of speeding up its results. Our sources in England told us that Bohr not only made this suggestion to Roosevelt but allegedly, on the instructions of Roosevelt, returned to England to try to win British approval of the idea. Churchill, we were told, was horrified, and urged that all efforts be taken to prevent Bohr from contacting us.[22] If the development of atomic weapons had been left totally to the scientists, they might have changed the course of history.

In the KGB files there is a report that the Swedish government received detailed information from its intelligence service on the technical design of the atomic bomb in 1945 or 1946. The Swedes rejected the idea of building their own nuclear weapons because of the huge resources required, but the fact that they knew enough to reach such a decision leads to the conclusion that Niels Bohr had the data after leaving Los Alamos.

The Zarubins, despite their success, did not stay long in Washington. It was not their fault or the prowess of the FBI. One of Vassili Zarubin's

22. Bohr saw Churchill on May 16, 1944, for thirty minutes at 10 Downing Street with his son Aage, who described the meeting as "terrible." "We did not speak the same language," Bohr said afterward. While he was in London waiting to see Churchill, Bohr was invited to the Russian Embassy to receive a letter from Pyotr Kapitsa inviting him to the Soviet Union, "where everything will be done to give you and your family a shelter and where we now have all the necessary conditions for carrying on scientific work." See Rhodes, *The Making of the Atomic Bomb*, pp. 528–531.

subordinates who worked in the NKVD rezidentura in the Soviet Embassy, Lieutenant Colonel Mironov, sent a letter to Stalin denouncing Zarubin as a double agent. He had followed Zarubin to some of his clandestine meetings with American agents and in his letter to Stalin specified the dates and hours of these meetings, alleging that Zarubin was contacting the FBI. It was either in 1943 or 1944 when Mironov's letter caused Zarubin's recall to Moscow. The investigation against him and Elizabeth lasted six months and established that all his contacts were legitimate and valuable, and that he was not working with the FBI. Mironov was recalled from Washington and arrested on charges of slander, but when he was put on trial, it was discovered that he was schizophrenic. He was hospitalized and discharged from the service.

By 1943 it was agreed at the Center that all contacts with Oppenheimer would be through illegals only. Lev Vasilevsky, our resident in Mexico City, was put in charge of running the illegal network after Zarubin left. But Vasilevsky was directed to control the network from Mexico City, not to move to Washington, where the FBI could more easily monitor our activities. Our facilities in Washington were to be used as little as possible.

Vasilevsky told me that on one occasion in 1944 he visited Washington in order to pass to the Center materials received from Fermi. To his dismay, the embassy radio operator, who was supposed to encode his message, was missing. The next day the clerk was brought to the embassy by the American police, who had picked him up dead drunk in a nearby bar. Vasilevsky decided on the spot not to use the Washington embassy to transmit any of his sensitive messages; he would rely on Mexico City.

In 1945, for his work in handling the Fermi line in the United States, Vasilevsky was appointed deputy director of Department S. For a short period in 1947 he was the director of the department of scientific and technological intelligence in the Committee of Information, which was the central intelligence-gathering agency from 1947 to 1951. Vasilevsky was ousted in the anti-Semitic purges of 1948 and permitted to retire on pension. He died in 1979.

A description of the design of the first atomic bomb was reported to us in January 1945. In February, although there was still uncertainty in the report, our rezidentura in America stated that it would take a minimum of one year and a maximum of five years to make a sizable bomb. The experimental test of one or two bombs would take only two or three months.

By this time our intelligence efforts to penetrate the project were intensified because uranium ore had been found in the Belgian Congo, Czechoslovakia, Australia, and Madagascar. The GRU penetrated the Canadian firm Canadian Radio and Uranium Corporation in Port Hope, Canada. Colonel F. Muravitz, chief of Czech intelligence in their government-in-exile in London, reported that the British were interested in the processing of uranium ore and in shipping it from the Sudeten Mountains in Czechoslovakia after the war. He had access to the minutes of the British-Czech talks on exploration for uranium.

In the beginning of 1945, as the war drew to a close, we organized a full-scale search in the Soviet Union for uranium deposits. Our proven reserves were limited and the quality of our uranium was unsatisfactory. In February 1945 we received information from captured German documents that high-quality uranium ore was available in Bukovo, a rural area forty miles from Sofia, Bulgaria, in the Rodopi Mountains. We approached Georgi Dimitrov, the former Comintern leader, who headed the Bulgarian government, and he agreed to cooperate in building facilities to mine the ore.

A Soviet-Bulgarian Mining Association was established, headed by NKGB lieutenant colonel Igor Shorse, who had coal-mining experience. Bukovo uranium deposits were the primary source for the first Soviet reactor in 1945. The ore in Czechoslovakia's Sudeten Mountains, which we had hoped to exploit at the end of the war, turned out to be of low uranium content. Our top priority was to arrange rapid shipment of the Bulgarian ore to the Soviet Union for processing.

Dimitrov personally visited the ore-mining site once a month to ensure that all was going according to schedule. We assigned three hundred engineers from the Red Army with coal-mining experience to manage the operation. We used our troops and local Bulgarian labor to mine the ore. It was hard to keep such a large-scale operation a secret. Through informers we soon learned that the local population was aware that the ore was being shipped to the Soviet Union for an atomic bomb. Two American diplomats and their wives were detained at the mine site when they attempted to photograph the facilities. There was an attempt by local Bulgarian nationalists to kidnap Shorse, but it failed.

The mine was producing 1,500 kilos (3,300 pounds) of ore a week, packed in metal cans with wooden covers and flown to the Soviet Union for processing. To Shorse's surprise he received American data for determining the uranium content in the ore. Although Dimitrov paid regular visits to the mine throughout 1945 and until July 1946, it was forbidden to disclose to him the details of the uranium's quality. There were several attempts to sabotage the mine by accidents, but they proved ineffective.

From knowledge of the quality of the uranium and the amount mined, the Americans could estimate the time we would need to process enough uranium to produce a bomb. In 1946, when huge, high-quality uranium deposits were found in the Urals, the decision was made to set up a disinformation operation based on the Bulgarian mining operation and make it appear that we would not have enough uranium for a bomb until 1952 or 1953.

Eitingon and a team were sent to Bulgaria to create the story that Bukovo was our primary source of uranium ore. An official Soviet delegation headed by Beria's deputy A. P. Zavinyagin came to Sofia to sign a formal agreement with the Bulgarian authorities to increase the capacity of the Bukovo mine, thus indicating its vital importance to us.

Our counterintelligence services detected that the Bukovo installation continued to be of great operational interest to American and British intelligence officers in Bulgaria. The British and Americans used members of the Turkish minority in Bulgaria as a source for agents. A game developed in which some of these Turkish agents were fed with carefully inflated figures of the mine's production which supported the view that we would not be able to produce a weapon until the mid-1950s. In reality our new uranium source in the Urals ensured a stable supply for our needs and was sufficient to produce our first bomb in 1949.

On February 28, 1945, we presented Beria a summary on the progress of atomic bomb accomplishments in the United States, describing in detail the leading American centers, such as the Oak Ridge plant in Tennessee, twenty miles from Knoxville. We also described the activities of the American firms Kellex (subsidiary of the design firm Kellogg in New York), Jones Construction, Du Pont, and Union Carbide and Chemical Company. The American investment of $2 billion and the employment of 130,000 people in construction of the plants were included. The report contained a description of the Los Alamos facilities.[23]

On April 6, 1945, Kurchatov received from my department mate-

---

23. See Appendix Two, Document 7.

rials "of great value . . . on atomic characteristics of the nuclear explosive." He also received details on the method of activating an atomic bomb, and on the electromagnetic method of disintegration of uranium isotopes. The material was so important that he assessed it the next day.[24]

On April 25, 1945, Kurchatov presented our report to Stalin on the prospects of atomic energy and the necessity of creating an atomic bomb.

Twelve days before the first atomic bomb was assembled in Los Alamos, we received a description of the device from both Washington and New York. I saw two documents relating to the intelligence information received from America a short time before the first atomic bomb explosion at Los Alamos. One cable came to the Center on June 13 and another on July 4, 1945.[25] A week later it was reported to Beria that two intelligence sources, unconnected to each other, reported almost simultaneously the imminent explosion of a nuclear device.

At that time there were parallel scientific efforts in Leningrad and Moscow to develop a nuclear reactor. Only when it became clear in June 1945 that the Americans were ready to test their first atomic device did a sense of urgency arise. Kurchatov appealed to Stalin to appoint Beria as head of the atomic project. Pervukhin was an expert at organizing heavy industries. He understood how to turn Stalin's directives into the reality of steel and smokestacks, but when it came to building an atomic bomb, which required vast coordination of resources, Pervukhin lacked the management scope to be the head of it. He was an administrator without broad vision. Although he was deputy prime minister, and held the rank of deputy chairman of the Council of People's Commissars during the war, Pervukhin did not have enough personal power to mobilize all the resources of the country. What was more important, he did not have at his disposal the machinery of state control to implement an atomic program.

These cables that came from our rezidenturas in New York and Washington have by now probably been deciphered by American code breakers, although I do not quite believe it. However, I can verify that the sources described in the cables as Charles and Mlad (Youngster) were Klaus Fuchs and Bruno Pontecorvo.

24. See Appendix Two, Document 10.
25. See Appendix Four. The first test firing of the atomic bomb took place on July 16.

A detailed report from Fuchs (Charles) came from Washington via the diplomatic pouch after he met his courier, Harry Gold, on September 19. I remember that later in September we received a detailed report from Pontecorvo (Mlad), passed on by a mole to Lona Cohen. I do not remember which one was which, but both these reports contained a thirty-three-page design of the bomb. I believe that this material was, in fact, the chapter on the bomb's construction that for security reasons was omitted from the official publication for the American Congress, the Smyth Report, published August 12, 1945.[26] Oppenheimer and General Groves edited the report, making rough notes on what should be deleted in the official publication. Fuchs reported that Oppenheimer declined to sign the Smyth Report because he believed it contained a piece of disinformation that would impede the progress of scientific research in other countries. What we received in September was the deleted parts, which included photos of the facilities in Oak Ridge, Tennessee. The photos were helpful because at that time we had started building our first nuclear reactor. I remember that a twelve-page summary of the report, with a description of the bomb, compiled by Semyonov and signed by Vasilevsky, was channeled by me to Beria and Stalin. This document became the basis for our own program of work on the atomic project over the next three or four years.

The information we received from our sources in America and Britain was extremely valuable in enabling us to develop our own atomic program. The detailed reports contained specifications for the design and operation of nuclear reactors and for the production of uranium and plutonium. Fuchs's contributions were substantial. In 1944, through him we knew the timing, scope, and progress of the Manhattan Project. From him we learned the principles of atomic bomb detonation and why the method used had been chosen. He gave us:

- the principle of the lens mold system and dimensions of the high explosive on which it worked;
- a discussion of the principle of implosion developed at Los Alamos;

---

26. The report, *Atomic Energy for Military Purposes*, was a year in preparation by Princeton physicist Henry DeWolf Smyth. Richard Rhodes describes it as "another faded echo of Niels Bohr's appeal for openness. It appalled the British, enlightened the Soviets on which approaches to isotope separation not to pursue." *The Making of the Atomic Bomb*, p. 750.

- details about plutonium 240, multiple-point detonation, time and sequence of construction of the atomic bomb, and the need for an initiator to set off the device.[27]

He also provided a comparative analysis of the operation of air- and water-cooled uranium nuclear reactors. He gave us plans for a plant to refine and separate uranium isotopes, which greatly reduced the amount of raw uranium to be processed.

On July 20, 1945, ten days after the information on the imminent explosion of the American nuclear bomb was reported to Stalin, he made up his mind to set up the Special State Committee on Problem Number One, making it a more powerful, Politburo committee.[28] On August 20, 1945, two weeks after the Americans dropped the first atomic bomb on Hiroshima, we once again reorganized our atomic project. Beria was appointed chairman of the new Special State Committee. There were still two schools in Russian physics, one centered around Ioffe and the other around Kapitsa. Stalin suggested that both should be made full members of the Committee on Problem Number One. However, Ioffe suggested Academician Kurchatov be made a full member of the committee. Ioffe became a member of the scientific and technical council attached to the committee.

I maintained friendly relations with both Ioffe and Kapitsa. At Beria's request I presented Kapitsa with an inlaid Belgian shotgun. When Kapitsa complained about the poor condition of a book written by his wife's father, I used the facilities of the special government printing house to print two copies on high-quality paper. Kapitsa sent one copy to Stalin as a souvenir, seeking a personal interview with him.

There was open rivalry between Kapitsa and Kurchatov. At meetings of the Special State Committee, Kapitsa was a marvelous tactician. He commented on every report with jokes and anecdotes, and once even suggested a break to listen to the radio broadcast of a soccer game our team was playing in Britain in 1945. Everybody was stunned by this suggestion, but when our team won everybody was in high spirits. Right after the break, Kapitsa suggested that due to the contradictory nature of Kurchatov's experiments, Kapitsa should be consulted by Kurchatov prior to reporting results to the plenary session of the committee. Per-

27. Lamphere and Schactman, *The FBI-KGB War*, pp. 155–157.

28. By upgrading it to the status of a Politburo committee, under the aegis of the Communist party, Stalin stressed the urgency of its task and increased its power to complete the bomb.

vukhin supported Kapitsa, saying that joint consultation would save time and henceforth they should jointly submit scientific proposals to the committee. However, Beria and Voznesensky did not agree. Beria, in particular, suggested that Kapitsa and Kurchatov should table contradictory proposals and Kapitsa should use his Institute of Physical Problems to duplicate some of the research efforts of Kurchatov.

Kapitsa was indignant, claiming that the reorientation of his institute would ruin the development of theoretical physics in the Soviet Union. About a month later, in October 1945, Kapitsa asked Beria and Voznesensky why he had not been consulted on the decision by the Special State Committee, then endorsed by the government, to open three additional training and research centers in nuclear physics separate from the Academy of Sciences. These were the Institute of Nuclear Physics in Moscow University (a rival to Kapitsa's and Kurchatov's research centers) and two training institutions, the Institute of Engineering Physics and the Physical Technical Institute (Moscow). The guiding figures in establishing these institutions were Kurchatov and the three outstanding scientific figures closest to him, Kikoin, Alikhanov, and Ioffe. Pervukhin retained the rank of deputy chairman of the committee. Full members of the committee were Malenkov, Voznesensky, Pervukhin, Kurchatov, V. A. Makhnev, Kapitsa, Vannikov, and A. P. Zavinyagin. Its mission was to accelerate the development of our bomb. The administration of Problem Number One was entrusted to the Special First Chief Directorate of the USSR Council of Ministers.

The committee had the power to requisition resources from all sectors of the economy, including electrical energy. In practice this meant diverting energy to plants producing equipment for the bomb. I recall violent arguments and exchanges of obscene remarks between Voznesensky, then chairman of GOSPLAN,[29] and Pervukhin, who had become minister of chemical industries, over what plants would receive electric power. There was not enough to go around, and the demands for power to refine uranium strained our capacity.

Stalin was fascinated by the potential of the bomb. In late October 1942, he had suggested that the plan for our offensive to surround the Germans at Stalingrad be called Uranium. In all his suggestions and pronouncements Stalin had some hidden inner motive. Marshal Zhukov and Marshal Vasilevsky, to whom Stalin assigned the task of creating

---

29. The State Planning Committee, responsible for the command economy's allocation of resources.

the plan for the offensive, were not even aware of our plans for building an atomic bomb.

Throughout the year following the war, atomic espionage was our primary preoccupation. In December 1945, Beria moved from his post as people's commissar for internal affairs, NKVD, into a new office in the Kremlin. The meetings of the Special State Committee on Problem Number One were also transferred from NKVD headquarters to the Kremlin. As director of the Special Second Bureau of this committee, for the first time I received a permanent pass to the Kremlin, allowing me to enter at any time.

Meetings were usually in Beria's study; heated discussions erupted from time to time. I remember Pervukhin, deputy prime minister, indignantly reprimanding and attacking Voznesensky, a member of the Politburo and his superior, for his reluctance to reconsider allocations of supplies of nonferrous metals for the needs of chemical processing plants that were engaged in the project. I had always assumed that members of the bureaucratic structures were subordinated to each other in accordance with their status. A member of the Politburo was always beyond criticism, at least by a person in a lower rank. It was not so in this special committee, where Politburo members and key ministers behaved almost as equals. It also startled me that Pervukhin was Beria's deputy in this committee, in which Voznesensky and Malenkov, members of the Politburo and far outranking Pervukhin, were ordinary members. Most impressive at these sessions was the secretary of the committee, Major General Makhnev, who during the war years was deputy minister of ammunition supplies.

I frequently went to General Makhnev's study with information about the progress of the Manhattan Project that came from open sources that I ordered through TASS. Makhnev was thankful to me for preparing digests of the foreign press and from our economic missions abroad describing the facilities of American industrial companies involved in the production of the atomic bomb.

Only then did I understand the particular interest of Beria in economic and industrial matters. I learned that as deputy chairman of the all-powerful State Defense Committee, which combined executive and legislative functions during the war years, Beria was responsible for the production of weapons, ammunition, and fuel supplies. Oil refineries were his particular passion. In his office he kept three scale models of oil refineries. On his initiative, Dmitri F. Ustinov, Vannikov, and Nikolai Baibakov, still in their early thirties, were promoted to the posts of people's commissar of armaments, ammunition, and oil processing, respectively.

The twice-a-month meetings in the Kremlin, chaired by Beria, revealed a new world to me. I understood that intelligence issues were crucial to foreign policy and national security, but the real postwar priority was the restoration of the national economy. Selection of sites and managers for industrial plants was fascinating. It was a far more interesting business than running agent networks in peacetime. This was a heady new world of activity where people displayed their talents and skills in dealing with shortages of supplies and equipment. We were remobilizing for a new kind of war, to rebuild our economy.[30]

Beria was harsh and rude to his subordinates but at the same time attentive and supportive in every way to the people doing the real work. He protected them from the intrigues of the local NKVD and party bosses. Beria always warned every manager about his total responsibility for the fulfillment of his assignment. Beria had the singular ability to inspire both fear and enthusiasm. Naturally, for industrial managers he was associated with the might of the security police. As this was their first encounter with him, fear dominated their behavior, but gradually, for those who worked with him over several years, fear was replaced by confidence. Beria would not betray them if he felt they were right in taking an independent stance to accomplish their mission. He derived these qualities from Stalin.

A pivotal moment in the Soviet nuclear program occurred in November 1945. The first Soviet nuclear reactor had been built, but all attempts to put it into operation ended in failure, and there had been an accident with plutonium. How to solve the problem? One idea, which proved unrealistic, was to send a scientific delegation to the United States to meet secretly with Oppenheimer, Fermi, and Szilard. Another suggestion to solve the problem of the balky reactor was to send Kapitsa to see Bohr in Denmark. Kapitsa by that time was no longer a member

30. There is a growing revisionism of Beria's historical role in Russia and the West. Deputy Prime Minister Viktor Novikov, in his short article in the book *Beria: Konets Karierie* (*Beria: The End of His Career*) (Moscow: Polizdat, 1991), describes Beria's outstanding performance as an economic administrator during the war years and praises his role in building the Soviet military-industrial complex. Amy Knight, in *Beria, Stalin's First Lieutenant* (Princeton, N.J.: Princeton University Press, 1993), discusses Beria's efforts to institute reforms after Stalin's death by reducing the power of the party apparatus and giving the non-Russian minorities a greater share in decision making.

of the Committee on Problem Number One because of his conflict with Beria, Voznesensky, and Kurchatov. Since Bohr had turned down Kapitsa's invitation to the Soviet Union in 1943, and because of the internal conflicts in the scientific community, we decided to rely on scientists already in the project who were also intelligence officers.

There was not a big choice. The scientists suggested Professor Yakov Borisovich Zeldovich, a member of the Kurchatov team with high professional skills. But Zeldovich was not aware of all the developments in the West because his access to the information we received was limited. We had only two officers who were both physicists and fluent in English. One was Arkady N. Rylov, who was less a physicist than an intelligence officer; the other was Yakov Petrovich Terletsky, who had a reputation as a real researcher. Most important, he was the man who had processed and edited all the scientific information that was gathered by our intelligence networks and reported personally to the closed sessions of the scientific technical committee for the project. With the exception of Kurchatov, he was the most knowledgeable, and would be able to hold his own with Bohr.

Terletsky made his own scientific analyses of intelligence materials we received. That sometimes created problems, because we received atomic information twice a day and sometimes Terletsky was late with his assessments. I would then be reprimanded for lack of discipline in my department, but I recognized that we were operating not with ordinary agent reports but with complex theoretical scientific formulations. Traditional discipline might be detrimental to the end result.

We decided that Terletsky should be sent to see Bohr in the guise of a young Soviet scientist working on a project supervised by Academicians Ioffe and Kapitsa. He was to explain the problems in activating the nuclear reactor to Bohr and to seek his advice. Terletsky could not be sent alone on such a critical assignment, so he was accompanied by Lev Vasilevsky, who had run the Fermi line from Mexico and now was my deputy director of Department S. He would lead the conversation with Bohr while Terletsky would handle the technical details. The meeting was arranged with the help of the Danish writer Martin Andersen Nexø, a friend of Zoya Rybkina.

I met with Terletsky in 1993, just before he died. He recalled that at first Bohr was nervous and his hands trembled, but he soon controlled his emotions. Bohr understood, perhaps for the first time, that the decision that he, Fermi, Oppenheimer, and Szilard had made to allow their trusted scientific protégés to share atomic secrets had led him to meet

agents of the Soviet government. Bohr had sent official confirmation to
the Soviet Embassy that he would meet with a delegation and now he
realized that the delegation contained both a scientist and an intelligence
officer.

Thus, after this first contact with Vasilevsky, Bohr preferred to
speak only to Terletsky, his scientific counterpart. There was no choice
but to let Terletsky meet Bohr alone with our translator. Terletsky
thanked Bohr in the name of Ioffe, Kapitsa, and other scientists in Russia
known to him, for the support from and consultations with their Western colleagues. Bohr readily explained to Terletsky the problems Fermi
had at the University of Chicago putting the first nuclear reactor into
operation, and he made valuable suggestions that enabled us to overcome our failures. Bohr pointed to a place on a drawing Terletsky
showed him and said, "That's the trouble spot." This meeting was essential to starting the Soviet reactor, and we accomplished that feat in
December 1946.

My relations with Kurchatov, Alikhanov, and Kikoin became especially friendly when Terletsky returned from his meeting with Bohr in
Denmark. Together with Emma we spent several weekends at a special
rest house with the scientific troika and their wives. At my flat near
Lubyanka I hosted lunches and cocktail parties in the Western style for
them and their subordinates at the suggestion of Vasilevsky, who toyed
with the idea of using Terletsky and other Soviet nuclear experts to lure
Western scientists to the Soviet Union.

In Western Europe, Vasilevsky took advantage of the charms of
Lubov Orlova, the famous film actress, and Gregory Alexander, her husband, a film producer, as the cover for meeting Bruno Pontecorvo, Frédéric Joliot-Curie, and other well-known Western scientists. Vasilevsky
also relied on professionals. He took with him three key figures: Vladimir Barkovsky, who handled Fuchs in Britain from 1944 to 1947; Anatoli Yatskov, who handled Fuchs in the United States and Britain; and
Aleksandr Semyonovich Feklisov, who took over Fuchs in Britain from
1947 to 1950.

Vasilevsky's successful trips to Denmark, Switzerland, and Italy
coincided with the start of the Cold War. Beria awarded him a choice
apartment and $1,000 — a considerable sum at that time — for his
expenses abroad. After our reactor was put into operation in 1946, Beria
issued orders to stop all contacts with our American sources in the Manhattan Project; the FBI was getting close to uncovering some of our
agents. Beria said we should think how to use Oppenheimer, Fermi, Szi-

lard, and others around them in the peace campaign against nuclear
armament. Disarmament and the inability to impose nuclear blackmail
would deprive the United States of its advantage. We began a worldwide
political campaign against nuclear superiority, which kept up until we
exploded our own nuclear bomb, in 1949. Our goal was to preempt
American power politically before the Soviet Union had its own bomb.
Beria warned us not to compromise Western scientists, but to use their
political influence.

Through Fuchs we planted the idea that Fermi, Oppenheimer, and
Szilard oppose the hydrogen bomb. They truly believed in their positions
and did not know they were being used. They started as antifascists, and
became political advocates of the Soviet Union.

Beria's directive was motivated by information from Fuchs in 1946
saying there was serious disagreement among leading American physicists on the development of a hydrogen bomb. In a panel that met in
April 1946, Fermi objected to the development of the superbomb, and
Oppenheimer was ambivalent. Their doubts were opposed by fellow
physicist Edward Teller. Fuchs, who returned to England in 1946 and
declined the offer of Oppenheimer to work with him at the Institute for
Advanced Study at Princeton, continued to supply us with valuable
information. From the fall of 1947 to May of 1949, Fuchs gave to Colonel Feklisov, his case officer, the principal theoretical outline for creating
a hydrogen bomb and initial drafts for its development, at the stage they
were being worked on in England and America in 1948.

Most valuable for us was the information Fuchs provided on the
results of the test explosions at Eniwetok atoll of uranium and plutonium bombs. Fuchs met with Feklisov six times, usually every three or
four months, in London. Feklisov was assisted in preparations for these
clandestine meetings by three experienced MGB officers who checked for
hostile surveillance. Every meeting was carefully planned and usually
lasted for no more than forty minutes. Fuchs's meetings with Feklisov
remained undetected by British counterintelligence. It was only after
Fuchs came under suspicion and he himself offered that he might
become a security risk when his father was appointed to a professorship
in theology at the University of Leipzig in East Germany that he was
accused of giving secret information to the Soviet Union. When he was
arrested in 1950, the indictment mentioned only one meeting in 1947,
and this was based on his confession.[31]

31. In 1949 the FBI notified British counterintelligence (MI-5) that Fuchs was a prime
suspect. The process by which William Skardon of MI-5 obtained Fuchs's confession

The information Fuchs gave us in 1948 coincided with Maclean's reports from Washington on America's limited nuclear potential, not sufficient to wage an all-out and prolonged war. Maclean had become first secretary and acting head of chancery at the British Embassy in 1944.

Looking back, one may say that in every scientific team, both in the Soviet Union and in the United States, there were politically motivated figures, Kurchatov in the Soviet Union, Edward Teller in America. Kurchatov always kept the interests of the state first in his mind. He was less stubborn and less independent than men like Kapitsa or Ioffe. Beria, Pervukhin, and Stalin immediately sensed that he was different from the scientists of the older generation; they saw that he was young, ambitious, and fully prepared to subordinate academic traditions to the interests of the state. When the government wanted to speed up the test of our first atomic bomb in 1949, Kurchatov went along with copying the American design. However, parallel work continued on the Soviet-designed bomb, which was exploded in 1951. In the United States, Edward Teller assumed a similar role later, when he was put in charge of the hydrogen bomb project.

Oppenheimer reminded me very much of our classic scientists who tried to maintain their own identity, their own world, and their total internal independence. It was a peculiar independence and an illusion, because both Kurchatov and Oppenheimer were destined to be not only scientists but also directors of huge government-sponsored projects. The conflict was inevitable; we cannot judge them, because the bomb marked the opening of a new era in science, when for the first time in history scientists were required to act as statesmen. Initially neither Oppenheimer nor Kurchatov was surrounded by the scientific bureaucracies that later emerged in the 1950s. In the 1940s, neither government was in a position to control and influence scientific progress, because there was no way to progress except to rely on a group of geniuses and adjust to their needs, demands, and extravagant behavior. Nowadays no new development in science can be compared to the breakthrough into atomic energy in the 1940s.

Atomic espionage was almost as valuable to us in the political and diplomatic spheres as it was in the military. When Fuchs reported the

is described by Alan Moorehead, *The Traitors* (New York: Scribner's, 1952). Also see Robert Chadwell Williams, *Klaus Fuchs, Atom Spy*. Lamphere and Schactman, *The FBI-KGB War*, have the best account of how Fuchs's spying was discovered.

unpublished design of the bomb, he also provided key data on the production of uranium 235. Fuchs revealed that American production was one hundred kilograms of U-235 a month and twenty kilos of plutonium per month. This was of the highest importance, because from this information we could calculate the number of atomic bombs possessed by the Americans. Thus, we were able to determine that the United States was not prepared for a nuclear war with us at the end of the 1940s or even in the early 1950s. This information might be compared with Colonel Oleg Penkovsky's information to the Americans during the early 1960s on the size of the Soviet ICBM (intercontinental ballistic missile) arsenal.[32] Just as Fuchs enabled us to determine that the United States was not ready for nuclear war against the Soviet Union, Penkovsky told the United States that Khrushchev was not prepared for nuclear war against the United States.

Stalin pursued a tough policy of confrontation against the United States when the Cold War started; he knew he did not have to be afraid of the American nuclear threat, at least until the end of the 1940s. Only by 1955 did we estimate the stockpile of American and British nuclear weapons to be sufficient to destroy the Soviet Union.

That information helped to assure a Communist victory in China's civil war in 1947–1948. We were aware that President Harry Truman was seriously considering the use of nuclear weapons to prevent a Chinese Communist victory. Then Stalin initiated the Berlin crisis, blockading the Western-controlled sectors of the city in 1948. Western press reports indicated that Truman and Clement Attlee, the British prime minister, were prepared to use nuclear weapons to prevent Berlin's fall to communism, but we knew that the Americans did not have enough nuclear weapons to deal with both Berlin and China. The American government overestimated our threat in Berlin and lost the opportunity to use the nuclear threat to support the Chinese nationalists.

Stalin provoked the Berlin crisis deliberately to divert attention from the crucial struggle for power in China. In 1951, when we were discussing plans for military operations against American bases, Molotov told me that our position in Berlin helped the Chinese Communists. For Stalin, the Chinese Communist victory supported his policy of confrontation with America. He was preoccupied with the idea of a Sino-Soviet

32. Penkovsky was the highest-ranking Soviet military officer to cooperate with the West during the Cold War. See Jerrold L. Schecter and Peter S. Deriabin, *The Spy Who Saved the World* (New York: Scribner's, 1992).

axis against the Western world. Stalin's view of Mao Tse-tung, of course, was that he was a junior partner. I remember that when Mao came to Moscow in 1950 Stalin treated him with respect, but as a junior partner.

In August 1949 the Soviet Union exploded its first atomic device. This event, for which we had worked a decade, was not announced in the Soviet press; therefore, when the American media announced our explosion on September 23, Stalin and the Soviet security establishment were shocked. Our immediate reaction was that there had been an American agent penetration of our test; but in a week our scientists reported that nuclear explosions in the atmosphere could be easily detected by planes sampling air around Soviet borders. This scientific explanation relieved us of the burden of proving there was no mole among us.

Kurchatov and Beria were honored by the government for outstanding contributions and services in strengthening the might of the country. They received medals, monetary awards, and certificates granting them lifetime status as honored citizens. Free travel, dachas, and the right of their children to enter higher education establishments without exams were granted for life to all key scientific personnel on the project.[33]

In assessing all the materials that were processed by Department S, we must take into account the views of Academician Yuli Khariton and Academician Anatoli P. Aleksandrov, president of the Academy of Sciences, who said that Kurchatov (1903–1960) was a genius who had made no major mistakes in the design of our first atomic bomb. They made their comments on the eighty-fifth anniversary of Kurchatov's birthday, in 1988. They noted that Kurchatov, having in his possession only several micrograms of artificially produced plutonium, was brave enough to suggest the immediate construction of major facilities to refine plutonium. The Soviet bomb was constructed in three years. Without the intelligence contribution, there could have been no Soviet atomic bomb that quickly. For me, Kurchatov remains a genius, the Russian Oppenheimer, but not a scientific giant like Bohr or Fermi. He was certainly helped by the intelligence we supplied, and his efforts would have been for naught without Beria's talent in mobilizing the nation's resources.

When Niels Bohr visited Moscow University in 1957 or 1958 to take part in student celebrations of Physicists Day, the KGB suggested

33. The children of illegal officers serving abroad were also admitted to universities without entry examinations. In 1960 Khrushchev canceled free travel for the scientists.

that Terletsky, then a full professor at the university and a corresponding member of the Academy of Sciences, should not meet with Bohr. Terletsky saw Bohr, who seemed not to recognize him. I was under arrest and Vasilevsky had been expelled from the party for "treacherous antiparty activities in Paris and in Mexico." There was no desire to remind Bohr of his past connections with Soviet intelligence.

Vasilevsky had been wise enough to foresee the inevitable disclosure of Bruno Pontecorvo's contacts with Soviet intelligence. He met him several times in Italy and Switzerland in 1946 and arranged his escape route to the Soviet Union, which was used in 1950 after Fuchs was arrested and tried. Pontecorvo's escape was a major success for Soviet intelligence because it kept the FBI and MI-5 from discovering other sources of our atomic intelligence. This was, in fact, the reason Pontecorvo had to leave the West.[34]

In the Soviet Union, Pontecorvo did nuclear research at Dubna in the International Institute of Nuclear Physics of the Socialist Countries. I heard that he wrote a marvelous autobiography published in Italy about his work with Fermi, never revealing his contacts with Soviet intelligence.

Although Vasilevsky was in disgrace for seven years, from 1953 to 1960, he maintained his ties with Pontecorvo in the 1960s and 1970s, regularly having lunch with him at the restaurant in the Union of Writers on Hertzen Street. After I was released from prison in 1968, Vasilevsky suggested that I, too, lunch with Pontecorvo, but since the restaurant was under regular KGB surveillance and they objected to Vasilevsky's contact with Pontecorvo, I preferred not to accept.

When I became a member of the Writers Professional Association after my release from prison, Vasilevsky and I had lunch with Ramon

34. "In 1949 a Communist friend of Pontecorvo who had broken with the Party reported Pontecorvo to United States authorities, giving a complete picture of his activities and connections. No action was taken. The information, however, was turned over to the British authorities (Pontecorvo was working at Harwell at the time), but again nothing happened," according to David J. Dallin in *Soviet Espionage*, pp. 465–466. In the summer of 1950, Pontecorvo and his family traveled to Europe for a vacation, and in September 1950 they went to Finland, allegedly for a vacation; there they disappeared. On March 1, 1965, Pontecorvo published an article in *Pravda*, and a few days later he answered questions at a press conference. Pontecorvo said he worked on atomic projects of a nonmilitary nature and praised the Soviet Union for its "peace policy." He died in Dubna, the nuclear research center outside Moscow, in 1993.

Mercader, Trotsky's assassin, at the writers union restaurant. I strongly suggested that Ramon not wear his Hero of the Soviet Union medal on his jacket, since I did not want to attract attention to our meeting. But Ramon and Vasilevsky had fun scandalizing the authorities. Until his last days, Vasilevsky sent letters to the Central Committee exposing the shortcomings of General Aleksandr Sakharovsky, then the director of the KGB First Chief Directorate.

Julius and Ethel Rosenberg were recruited by Gaik Ovakimian, our rezident in New York, in 1938. The irony is that the Rosenbergs are portrayed by the American counterintelligence service as the key figures in delivering atomic secrets to the Soviet Union, but actually they played a very minor role. They were absolutely separate from my major networks gathering atomic secrets. The New York rezidentura from 1943 to 1945 was run by Leonid Kvasnikov, working with Yatskov and Semyonov. In the summer of 1945, shortly before the first nuclear test explosion, a report had been prepared by David Greenglass, code name Caliber, the brother of Ethel Rosenberg. Greenglass was an army sergeant working in a Los Alamos machine shop on parts for the test. The courier scheduled to pick up his report could not make the trip, and Yatskov, eager to supply the report to Moscow, and authorized by the Center, ordered Harry Gold, Klaus Fuchs's courier, to substitute. Gold met Fuchs in Santa Fe and then went to Albuquerque to pick up the report from Greenglass. The Center had broken the first commandment: never allow an agent or courier from one cell to have contact with or know the members of another group. When Gold, having been implicated by Fuchs, was arrested in 1950, he identified Greenglass, who incriminated the Rosenbergs.

I first learned of the arrest of Julius and Ethel Rosenberg in 1950 from a TASS report. I was not concerned about it. This might strike some as odd, but it is important to note that as well as being responsible for the thousands of fighters behind German lines during the war, we had hundreds of agents in the United States, not including illegals, sources, and informers. As the director of Department S, I was familiar with our personnel, though not with any but their most important sources; the Rosenbergs were not important or significant sources of information. It occurred to me that they might have been related to our intelligence operations, but they were not major players in my atomic intelligence networks. I considered the whole affair to be routine business.

The following summer, I was surprised when General Sergei Savchenko, then deputy chief of the Foreign Intelligence Directorate, came to see me looking worried. Savchenko told me that the new minister of state security, Semyon Ignatiev, who took over after Abakumov's arrest in July 1951, had ordered all materials relating to the failures of our operations in the United States and Great Britain turned over to a special commission appointed by the Central Committee of the Communist party. Savchenko told me he feared possible accusations of negligence following the arrests of Gold, Greenglass, Morton Sobell,[35] and the Rosenbergs.

I had known Savchenko since the 1920s.[36] He had been deputy chairman of the Committee of Information before becoming deputy head of the Foreign Directorate. He personally endorsed all intelligence operations in the United States and Great Britain, but Savchenko told me he was uncertain of his conclusions about the American cases, because they went back to intelligence operations conducted before and during World War II. Anatoli Gorsky (or Gromov, as he was known in the United States), along with Vasilevsky, Vassili Zarubin, and Elizabeth Zarubina — all of whom ran the American network — had been ousted from the intelligence service in new purges. Gregory Kheifetz was in jail after being arrested in 1948, accused of taking part in the Zionist conspiracy. There was no one to turn to for an interpretation of the files for the commission.

Zarubin, who had been fired at age forty-six in 1946 with the rank of general, called Savchenko a son of a bitch and refused to see him, insisting he would speak only to a member of the Central Committee. Yatskov and Viktor Sokolov, from the American section of the Foreign Directorate, appeared to be the only case officers who could provide an assessment of the real damages from the arrests, but they were interested parties.

Savchenko and I were summoned to the Central Committee to establish who was responsible for the fatal cable allowing Harry Gold to meet David Greenglass in Albuquerque.

The results of that inquiry appeared in a report to the special com-

35. Morton Sobell, a college friend of Julius Rosenberg and a member of his group, was convicted of conspiring to commit espionage and sentenced to thirty years in prison.

36. Savchenko was then chief of the operational department of frontier troops on the Moldavian-Romanian border, and Sudoplatov worked with him on several cases.

mission, prepared by Savchenko and others in the American section. It said that the failures were due to mistakes committed by Semyon Semyonov, the recruiter of Harry Gold. The Rosenbergs, Sobell, and Gold, said the report, were not properly instructed by Semyonov in conducting clandestine meetings and maintaining correspondence. Semyonov had left New York to return to Moscow in 1944. The summary presented to the Central Committee concealed the fact that contact between Greenglass and Harry Gold was authorized in a special message from the Center. The report recommended that Semyonov and Ovakimian, head of the American desk when the fatal permission was sent, be discharged from the service. I strongly disagreed, because Semyonov was a professional operator who was the only one to actually build a network of technological intelligence in the United States. I was overruled, and Semyonov was discharged. Ovakimian was demoted. It was the Center that violated the rules of tradecraft, but Semyonov was the scapegoat because of his Jewish origin. All of us who disagreed with the verdict contributed money to support Semyonov until he found a job in the Institute of Technical Information as a translator.

The following year, another scandal erupted. I was summoned to the Central Committee to appear before Malenkov's assistant, Kiselov. To my surprise I found Savchenko in his office. Kiselov was rude and repeated accusations similar to those I had heard before, in 1938 and 1939, when the purges began. "The Central Committee has exposed attempts by MGB [Ministry of State Security] operators to deceive it. To what extent were the Rosenbergs involved in providing atomic secrets to us?" he demanded. Kiselov said the Central Committee had received an anonymous letter from an MGB officer stating that the summary report of the special commission contained a treacherous attempt to minimize the role of the Rosenberg family in intelligence operations. The letter said the Rosenbergs had supplied valuable information until 1950.

Savchenko categorically objected; he said that atomic espionage operations in the United States were effectively blocked by the end of 1946 and therefore we had had to rely on our sources in Great Britain. Kiselov accused me of not reporting to the special commission the importance of the Rosenbergs' contacts with Harry Gold. I replied that our priority was to concentrate all agent sources on penetrating the Los Alamos project. The validity and usefulness of agent sources varied greatly. The involvement of the Rosenbergs in atomic spying was the outcome of our efforts to utilize any and all possible sources of information, but the Rosenbergs were never a significant source. They were a naive couple overeager to cooperate with us, who provided no valuable secrets. I said that I was completely unaware of their providing technological information of high value to Semyonov. They were spies recruited by Ovakimian who worked for us because of their ideological motivations. Their contributions to atomic espionage were minor.

Kiselov said he would report my answers and Savchenko's information on the Rosenbergs to Malenkov, who would instruct the Party Control Commission to determine who was guilty of criminal negligence in handling the failed intelligence operation. No scapegoat was needed, because the Rosenbergs behaved heroically and did not admit their guilt. It was clear from the very beginning that the case had acquired a political character far out of proportion to their actual role as spies. More important than their spying activities was that the Rosenbergs served as a symbol in support of communism and the Soviet Union. Their bravery to the end served our cause, because they became the center of a worldwide Communist propaganda campaign.

The fact that the Rosenbergs were arrested promptly after Greenglass confessed indicates that the FBI was not seriously determined to discover the extent of the Rosenberg spy ring. The FBI appeared to be acting just like the NKVD, following political orders rather than handling the case professionally, which would have required continued surveillance of the Rosenbergs to determine the identity of their controller and the extent of their role in Soviet intelligence operations in America. The FBI's haste prevented it from detecting our illegal William Fisher (Colonel Rudolf Abel), who entered the United States in 1948 and was not arrested until 1957. The code name of Helen Sobell, the wife of Morton Sobell, a member of the Rosenberg group, was found in Fisher's wallet when he was arrested.[37] It struck me how both the NKVD and the FBI, in political cases like the Rosenberg case, relied on confessions of the accused. I was fascinated to read that the defense counsel of the Rosenbergs complained that Gold and Greenglass were coached by the FBI before they were brought to court. To me that seemed the natural thing for them to do. The FBI did not fulfill its primary task of revealing the true role of the Rosenberg family in providing technical intelligence for

37. Lamphere and Schactman, *The FBI-KGB War*, pp. 275–276, describe how, after Abel was tried and convicted in 1957, the FBI found an old microfilm message in his wallet implicating Helen Sobell.

the Soviet Union. Greenglass's alleged diagrams remain a vague episode in the work that continued for six years. Greenglass's contributions were minimal, and he was never developed further after his contact with Harry Gold.

The Rosenbergs were victims of the Cold War. Both sides did their utmost to exploit the political implications of their trial. At the height of the so-called Zionist conspiracy in 1952 and 1953, we claimed that the Rosenberg case proved the United States had a consistent policy of anti-Semitism. At the same time, Soviet propaganda insisted there was nothing anti-Semitic in exposing the Zionist conspiracy, while actually a very real anti-Semitic campaign was gaining momentum in the Soviet Union.

In the United States the Rosenberg trial heightened anti-Semitism; the writer Howard Fast exposed it in his plays and stories, which were promptly translated and published in the Soviet Union. The case of the Rosenbergs became a major cause for the peace movement.

There were four agent networks in the United States during the war years. Three of the networks operated from the San Francisco consular office, the Soviet Embassy in Washington, D.C., and the AMTORG trading company in New York City. The fourth network was run by our chief illegal, Isak Akhmerov, who was married to the niece of the American Communist leader Earl Browder. Akhmerov was the control officer of Yakov Golos, the chief organizer of espionage activities through the American Communist party.[38] In addition, there was Vasilevsky's network run from Mexico City.[39]

I remember that the defection of the Soviet code clerk Igor Guzenko in Canada in September 1945 had deep repercussions. He gave the American and Canadian counterintelligence services clues to our agent networks in the United States and Canada during the war. More important, he revealed a list of key scientists we had targeted for development. They were not our agents, but we had given them code names as possible sources of information from the atomic project. For the FBI to utilize the disclosures by Guzenko and later by Elizabeth Bentley, an American

---

38. He died in America in 1943 of natural causes.

39. This differs from the structure of Soviet espionage in America as portrayed in Lamphere and Schactman's *FBI-KGB War*, which is incomplete, according to P. A. Sudoplatov.

NKVD agent, to penetrate and destroy our agent networks was not an easy job.[40] Every lead to Guzenko's notes, no matter how obscure, had to be checked; this took years of patient work. By the time these revelations bore fruit for the FBI we already had the information we needed to build the bomb. The FBI claims that Guzenko's revelations and the breaking of coded intercepted cables was how they finally traced Harry Gold, Alan Nunn May,[41] and Klaus Fuchs.

I do not think that American codebreakers played the decisive role in unmasking our espionage effort. In December 1941, our agent Senior Warrant Officer in Berlin reported that the Germans had seized our codebook in Petsamo, Norway, and were trying to decipher our cables. Naturally, we changed our codebooks.[42] By the time the Petsamo book had fallen into American hands we had stopped using it entirely.

Ovakimian told us in 1944 that he believed the FBI had managed to penetrate our agent network in America. When Zarubin was recalled to Moscow in 1944, falsely charged by his assistant with being a double agent working for the FBI, all cipher codes were changed again and a new system introduced. The FBI has never publicly discussed its sources and methods. However, former FBI agent Robert Lamphere, in Chapter Six of his book *The FBI-KGB War,* presents a complicated story of how the FBI re-created our codebooks by using the old one as a starting point. That may be true. I cannot absolutely exclude that codebreaking might have played a role in exposing our agents in the United States and Canada. But we have reason to believe that the FBI, wanting to hide its agent source of information, invented the story of codebreaking.

In 1944, when the question arose of whether to share our codes with Yugoslavs sent by Tito to our special training school, Ovakimian, director of the American section of the intelligence directorate, objected in my presence. I remember him saying, "We drastically changed our

40. Elizabeth Terrill Bentley, a Vassar graduate, joined the Communist party in the 1930s and served as a courier for the NKVD during World War II in New York and Washington. In the fall of 1945 she turned herself in to the FBI and named more than eighty people as Soviet sources or agents in the OSS, air force, War Department, War Production Board, Foreign Economic Administration, and Departments of Treasury, Agriculture, and Commerce.

41. Alan Nunn May, a British scientist working on the Anglo-Canadian nuclear research project, was a member of the GRU espionage network in Canada.

42. In 1944 the OSS obtained 1,500 pages of an NKVD codebook captured by the Finns from the Soviets. Secretary of State Edward Stettinius urged President Roosevelt to return the codebook. OSS chief General William Donovan handed it over, after making a copy. See Andrew and Gordievsky, *KGB: The Inside Story,* pp. 284–285.

codes following our setback with underground networks in Germany in 1942. Why should we share our experience with students sent by Tito if we have every reason to suspect them of playing a double game with us and with British intelligence?" His objection was accepted.

In September 1992, while I was in a KGB clinic for a medical checkup, I met with retired colonel Anatoli Yatskov, who had run Harry Gold in 1945 and 1946. We recalled the controversy over the cable that was intercepted from the Soviet rezident in New York to Moscow that allegedly was the basis for American decoders to break our cipher security.[43] The Americans claim that with this cable they learned of the connection between Harry Gold and Klaus Fuchs.

Yatskov and Feklisov still believe that the FBI produced a falsified version of the cable, from our consulate office in New York to the Center, reporting on the meeting of Gold and Fuchs in January 1945 at the home of Fuchs's sister Kristel. As Feklisov has written in *Voyennoi Istorischeski Zhurnal* (*Journal of Military History*), the evidence against Fuchs was a map of Santa Fe, New Mexico, near Los Alamos, on which the meeting place between Gold and Fuchs was indicated. That map had Fuchs's fingerprints on it when it was found in Gold's apartment during an FBI search.

From an intelligence point of view the FBI's failure to detect our espionage rings is understandable. The personnel in the Manhattan Project were assembled hastily and included foreign scientists. There was no time for the FBI during the year and a half it took to organize the Manhattan Project to establish a strong counterintelligence network of agent informers among the scientific personnel of the project. That was absolutely necessary for detection of mole penetration. In our case the selection of personnel was an easier task, because all their records were at hand.

We must also take into account the historical circumstances. At the beginning of the war, the primary concern was to rule out leakage of information to the Germans. My theory is that the FBI was checking for German connections of the scientists at Los Alamos. Pro-Soviet sympathies were on the record, but they only began to acquire importance in the eyes of the administration of the project in the final stage, in 1945. A directive to intensify the search for Communist sympathizers was issued at the end of 1944, after an initial check of left-wingers in the Radiation Laboratory in Berkeley. Although we managed to penetrate

43. Andrew and Gordievsky, *KGB: The Inside Story*, pp. 373–374, discuss the decrypted traffic code-named Venona.

the project by planting scientists close to Oppenheimer, Fermi, and Szilard, and through Fuchs, we never stopped our efforts to use the initial channel at Berkeley because of its connection to Los Alamos. The FBI probably detected these efforts but overconcentrated on figures at the Radiation Laboratory, who played a lesser role. The most successful penetration and most valuable stream of information came in the last phase, prior to the production of the bomb in 1945. By the time American counterintelligence efforts were strengthened, we had ceased contacts with our agents. None of our agents was caught red-handed.

*Pavel Sudoplatov (right), age
fourteen, a CHEKA apprentice in
Western Ukraine, with brother
Nikolai, a CHEKA officer, two weeks
before Nikolai's death in 1921.*

*Sudoplatov in 1942, head of the
NKVD's special tasks operations.*

Sudoplatov in 1935.

Emma Kaganova, 1935, in prewar NKVD *uniform.*

V. N. Merkulov, head of the People's Commissariat for State Security, 1943–1946. (Acme Photo)

Nikolai Yezhov, NKVD *chief, 1936–1938. (Sovfoto)*

Sudoplatov's pass allowing him access to any part of the Kremlin, dated November 7, 1941.

*Lavrenti Beria, commissar
(later minister) of internal
affairs, 1938–1953.
(Sovfoto)*

*Invitation to a Kremlin reception to
honor Red Army commanders of
World War II.*

Pass to Stalin's funeral.

Sudoplatov, director of the atomic intelligence bureau, in 1945.

Lev Vasilevsky (left) at a guerrilla training camp near Barcelona in 1938. Aleksandr Orlov's deputy Grigori Syroyezmkin is in the front row, without uniform.

Zoya Rybkina (right) with Ambassador Alexandra Kolontai in Sweden in 1942.

Boris Rybkin in Finland, 1938.

Vassili Zarubin, 1946.

Elizabeth Zarubina at a military health resort near Moscow, 1946.

Aleksandr Demyanov, alias Heine and Max, in Moscow in 1943.

Solomon Mikhoels, director of the Moscow Yiddish State Art Theater and chairman of the Jewish Antifascist Committee of the USSR, shakes hands with Helen Hayes in New York, 1943. (World Wide Photos)

Ramon Mercader, alias Frank Jacson,
awaits treatment of head wounds
inflicted by Trotsky's bodyguards.

Ramon Mercader in Moscow, 1962.

Leonid Eitingon in 1950 with
daughter Svetlana, born in
California.

This photo taken by security agents of the Manhattan Project shows San Francisco rezident Gregory Kheifetz, right, with his replacement, Gregory Kasparov, left. Between them is Dr. Martin Kamen, staff chemist at the Radiation Laboratory of the University of California. (International News Photo)

Igor Kurchatov. (Sovfoto)

Robert Oppenheimer. (Los Alamos
National Laboratory)

Enrico Fermi. (Argonne
National Laboratory)

Leo Szilard. (Argonne National
Laboratory)

Sudoplatov with Eitingon in 1977.

Pavel Sudoplatov in 1993. (Joseph Kogan)

THE COLD
WAR

The conventional wisdom is that the Cold War started with Winston Churchill's "iron curtain" speech in Fulton, Missouri, on March 6, 1946, but for us, confrontation with the Western allies had begun when the Red Army liberated Eastern Europe. The conflict of interest was evident. The principle agreed upon with Roosevelt at Yalta, providing for multiparty elections, was acceptable to us only for the transition period after the defeat of Germany, while the fate of Eastern Europe was in the balance. I remember the remarks of Foreign Minister Molotov and Beria, saying that coalition governments in Eastern Europe would not last long. Later, at the gatherings of the Committee of Information, which Molotov headed in 1947, these statements of Molotov's acquired new significance. From 1947 to 1951, the Committee of Information was the central decision-making group that collected all foreign intelligence and acted upon it.

The road to Yalta, strange as it may seem, was opened by the Molotov-Ribbentrop Pact. Without claiming any high-minded moral principles for that deal in 1939, it was clearly the first time the USSR was treated as a superpower. Following Yalta, Russia became one of the political power centers in determining the future of the world. Nowadays many analysts point to the similarity of Stalin's and Hitler's approaches to dividing the world. Stalin is bitterly attacked for betraying principles of human morality in signing a pact with Hitler; it is overlooked that he also signed a secret deal to divide Europe with Roosevelt and Churchill at Yalta, and later with Truman at Potsdam.

Principles of ideology are not always decisive in secret deals between superpowers; this is one of the rules of the game. I met Ambassador Konstantin Oumansky in Beria's office in December 1941, when he returned from Washington after the Japanese attack on Pearl Harbor. He told me that to defuse the opposition and give Roosevelt a stronger hand in providing us lend-lease aid, Harry Hopkins had insisted on the dissolution of the Comintern and on our rapprochement with the Orthodox church. These informal recommendations came from Roosevelt via Hopkins, his close friend and personal envoy on many important missions, and were accepted by Stalin. As the time neared for the Yalta Conference, all these requests had been met.

At the end of 1944, in preparation for the Yalta Conference in February 1945, there was a meeting of the intelligence services, chaired by Molotov. The goals of this meeting were to assess what strength Germany had left to continue the war and to analyze areas of future peace settlements with America and Britain. We were not informed of the dates of the Yalta meeting, but Molotov said that the summit would take place in the Crimea within two months.

After that meeting Beria appointed me the chief of the special team to set up a group to present information to Molotov and Stalin. Beria went to Yalta but did not take part in the conference. In preparation for what we could expect at Yalta from the Allied leaders and their aides, we provided him with psychological portraits of the American delegation. We knew that neither the American nor British delegation had a coherent program for postwar policy in the countries of Eastern Europe. There was no agreement between them and no organized program. They were just seeking to restore to power the Polish and Czechoslovakian leaders of governments-in-exile in London.

The reports from military intelligence and our directorate indicated that the Americans were ready for a compromise and that a flexible position on our part would ensure a fair division of influence in postwar Europe, and probably the world as a whole. To the Allies, this "flexibility" meant that the Polish government-in-exile should be given some important posts in the postwar government; but Churchill and Roosevelt's demands at Yalta were very naive, because from our point of view the composition of the Polish government would be decided by the power structures that were receiving their support from the Red Army.

In the period before Yalta, the Red Army was fully engaged in combat operations against the Germans and had liberated large areas of Poland. The political turn of events in our favor in all the countries of Eastern Europe was easy to predict, especially in the areas where the Communist parties were active in national salvation committees, which were de facto provisional governments under our control.

We could be flexible and allow democratic voting because the governments-in-exile could not challenge our influence. Beneš, for example, escaped from Czechoslovakia to Britain using NKVD money and was highly influenced by us. Ludvik Svoboda, who later became president of Czechoslovakia, was a supporter of the Soviet government and the Red Army. The head of Czech intelligence, Colonel Muravitz, was a full-time NKVD agent, recruited by our rezident in London, Chichayev. In Romania, young King Michael relied on Communist combat troops to arrest General Ion Antonescu and implement his anti-Hitler coup d'état when he joined the antifascist coalition. The situation in Bulgaria was advantageous to us because of the strong presence and influence of the legendary Georgi M. Dimitrov, former chairman of the Comintern. At the time of the Yalta Conference, we were secretly taking uranium ore from the Rodopi Mountains in Bulgaria for our atomic project.

In 1945 I met Averell Harriman, the ambassador of the United States to the Soviet Union, in the Ministry of Foreign Affairs. I was introduced as Pavel Matveyev, an official from Molotov's secretariat in the Kremlin, in charge of preparations for the Yalta Conference. After the first formal meeting, I invited Harriman to lunch at the Aragvi, a restaurant famous for its Georgian cuisine. Harriman seemed pleased to accept the invitation. I brought with me to the lunch Prince Janusz Radziwill, to act as my interpreter. He was introduced as a Polish patriot living in exile in Moscow, but at that time was, in fact, our controlled agent.[1]

When Harriman and Radziwill met in the Aragvi, it was a reunion of old friends. Harriman owned a chemical plant, a porcelain factory,

1. The meetings with Matveyev are not included in Harriman's daily diary for 1945, but the presence of an NKVD lieutenant colonel is mentioned in Harriman's top-secret memorandum of conversation with K. I. Novikov, chief of the Second European Division of the Ministry of Foreign Affairs, on January 13, 1945. Sudoplatov recalls that his first meeting with Harriman took place with Novikov in the ministry on the eve of the Yalta Conference.

two coal mines, and two zinc mines in Poland. More important, Radziwill and Harriman jointly owned Spulnata Intersuv, a coal mining and metallurgical enterprise that employed forty thousand workers. Janusz Radziwill was an important political figure in Poland. He was a senator and chairman of the commission on foreign affairs of the Sejm, the Polish parliament. In the 1930s he had assisted Harriman in acquiring shares of Polish businesses in fierce competition with French and Belgian entrepreneurs.

As I've previously related, we had kept our eye on Radziwill from the middle of the 1930s; and after we had seized him in 1939, following the invasion of Poland, Beria recruited him for use as an agent of influence. I then arranged for him to return to Berlin, where for a time our rezidentura reported on him. He was spotted at diplomatic functions there and in the company of his former hunting companion, Göring, who had been a guest at the Radziwill estate near Vilnius.

In late 1944 or early 1945 I was summoned to Beria's office and informed that Radziwill had been arrested by SMERSH, military counter-intelligence, in Poland or Lithuania and would be transferred to Lubyanka in two days. At that time our relations with the Polish authorities were very tense. The pro-Communist Lublin Provisional Committee proclaimed itself the government of Poland in opposition to the Polish government-in-exile in London. We were prepared to use Radziwill in a very active manner to soothe the pro-British Poles. In the meantime, British and American authorities made inquiries into Radziwill's whereabouts.

A routine check of his prewar connections revealed Radziwill's business association with Harriman. On hearing this, Beria ordered Radziwill moved from Lubyanka, where he had spent a month, into a safe house in the outskirts of Moscow under house arrest. He was to be used as an intermediary with Harriman.

At the lunch with Harriman and Radziwill, I was ready to express our tolerance of Catholics, Protestants, and Orthodox priests, even those who had collaborated with the Germans in the occupied territories during the war. (I myself received Archbishop Slipi, later the cardinal of the Ukrainian Catholic church; although he had collaborated with the Germans, he was allowed to return to Lvov. A year after Yalta, however, he was arrested and exiled to a labor camp on the orders of Khrushchev.) At lunch I was prepared to discuss the fate of Russian Orthodox priests and to assure Harriman that no leaders of the Orthodox church were being persecuted by the Soviet government.

When I raised this subject at the lunch, Harriman said that the recent meeting to elect a patriarch for the church had produced a favorable impression on American public opinion. That was as far as we got with my agenda. Harriman quickly sensed that Radziwill was serving as interpreter in an informal role and proceeded to discuss with him possible business ventures in the Soviet Union after the war. I was not prepared for that kind of overture. Harriman said that business opportunities were the logical outcome of the defeat of Germany. He was interested in mines and railways.

I told him that we were impressed by the information provided to us by American agents in Switzerland who had contacts with the German underground, in particular with the Halder group and General Ludwig Beck's group, who had tried unsuccessfully to overthrow Hitler. I mentioned that we had informed the State Department about our clandestine meetings with the Finns to achieve a peace pact and the mediation role of the Wallenberg family.

Finally, I asked Harriman what the Americans hoped to accomplish at Yalta. My purpose was to prepare responses to the American positions on sensitive issues such as the future of Poland, the future boundaries of Europe, and the fate of Yugoslavia, Greece, and Austria. Harriman was not prepared to explore any of these problems. Clearly, he wanted to receive instructions on how to proceed. Harriman was interested to know how long Radziwill was planning to stay in Moscow. I assured him that Radziwill was free to travel to London, but he preferred to go directly to Poland as soon as it was liberated from the Germans.[2]

Harriman was interested in problems relating to the involvement of Jewish capital. Informally, he assured full support by the American administration for plans to use Jewish funds for the restoration of the Gomel area in Byelorussia, which was totally destroyed by the Germans and was one of the primary areas for Jewish settlements in prewar Russia.

I tried to divert his attention from investments by talking about a personal matter. In a very gentle manner, I advised Harriman to look closer at the adventures of his daughter in Moscow, because her relationships with certain Russian young men could lead her to trouble. Moscow was full of hooligans and gangsters in this last year of the war,

2. Radziwill was kept under house arrest with his wife until permitted to leave the Soviet Union in 1947.

but Harriman did not respond to my warnings. He was concerned with assurances about the supply of vodka and caviar for the participants at the Yalta meeting. This warning about his daughter was very friendly; I emphasized that our government "in no way would permit any dubious actions of any of its institutions" against Harriman or his family, and stressed that he was highly respected by our leader. This meant that the warning was in no way a threat of blackmail; our purpose was to show that he was beyond any provocations by us. We showed by this that we could discuss any delicate matters, both personal and diplomatic.

Harriman pointed out to Radziwill that Yalta would give the green light for interesting business ventures in postwar Eastern Europe and in the Soviet Union. I said that the purpose of Radziwill's stay in Moscow in hiding was to rule out rumors that a friend of Göring's was about to appear in Sweden or Britain as a courier from Hitler for peace overtures. Radziwill not only translated my remarks but supported them, confirming his desire to appear in Europe only after the end of the war. Since I was supposed to be a high official of the Council of Ministers, I presented Harriman with a tea service, a gift on behalf of our government.

My conversations with Harriman at the Aragvi restaurant and later at the Sovietskaya Hotel, which was once the residence for Western delegations, were taped. We listened to these conversations to pick up revealing remarks that would help develop our psychological profiles of American delegates, which were more important to Stalin than intelligence information. From this he knew that the personal deals and relations he would establish with Roosevelt and Churchill at the conference would be decisive. These personal relations would predetermine all the formal documents and agreements.

In November 1945, when Stalin was on leave in the Crimea, Harriman tried in vain to meet him personally to discuss plans for economic and political cooperation. I was told that he came to see Molotov, saying that he was a friend who for a number of years discussed very sensitive issues with various Soviet officials and with Stalin personally, but Molotov remained strictly official at that meeting. This signaled an end to Harriman's high-level access and thus his effectiveness as the ambassador.[3]

In the summer of 1941 Harry Hopkins suggested to our ambassador in Washington, Oumansky, that they establish confidential relations.

3. Harriman left Moscow the third week of January, 1946.

Oumansky told me that President Roosevelt had directed Hopkins to make the approach to him. In December 1941 Stalin replaced Oumansky with Maksim Litvinov, and Hopkins quickly established a close personal relationship with him, to the point that Litvinov would visit Hopkins at home. Litvinov told me how he sat on Hopkins's bed to discuss problems while Hopkins was ill.[4] Oumansky and Litvinov, with whom I frequently met in Moscow, also established these informal relations with other officials of the State Department and the White House. Zarubin and later his replacement, Anatoli Gorsky, expanded these contacts during our wartime alliance. Gorsky, officially a first secretary of the Soviet Embassy, was acting rezident from 1944 to 1945.

Before any official visit, a list of participants was handed to the NKVD (or NKGB), in this case to me, which described every person and their possible relationship, plus attitudes, to us. The materials I received for preparing the psychological profiles of all the members of the American delegation to Yalta contained information on their personalities and indicated if they were under our control as agents.

One of the officials we had established confidential relations with was Alger Hiss, a member of the American delegation. I had the feeling that Hiss was acting under the instructions of Hopkins. In conversation, Hiss disclosed to Oumansky, and then Litvinov, official U.S. attitudes and plans; he was also very close to our sources who were cooperating with Soviet intelligence and to our active intelligence operators in the United States. Within this framework of exchange of confidential information were references to Hiss as the source who told us the Americans were prepared to make a deal in Europe.

On our list of psychological profiles, Hiss was identified as highly sympathetic to the interests of the Soviet Union and a strong supporter of postwar collaboration between American and Soviet institutions. However, there was no indication that he was a paid or controlled agent, which I would have known or would have been marked.

In June 1993 I talked with a former colleague who had served as rezident for GRU, the intelligence directorate of the Soviet general staff, in New York and London. According to my old friend, Hiss was a source

4. At a Kremlin meeting in September 1941, Stalin asked American special envoy Averell Harriman his impression of Oumansky. Harriman told Stalin that Oumansky was zealous to a fault, talked too much, and ran around Washington creating more irritation than good will. In a matter of weeks, Stalin sent Litvinov to Washington and Oumansky to Mexico. W. Averell Harriman and Elie Abel, *Special Envoy to Churchill and Stalin, 1941–1946* (New York: Random House, 1975), pp. 93–94.

of agent information for the Silvermaster spy cell[5] in Washington in the early and middle thirties. The network was composed of both agents and confidential contacts, but no documents exist since none of them had registered their relationship by signing formal obligation documents. Contrary to the myths about General Yan Karlovich Berzin, founder of GRU, the registration of documents and the bureaucracy handling agent files were unstructured. Only in the 1940s were the documents received from agents subjected to systematic evaluation. The rule before then was just to report a document to the Central Committee or Stalin, translated into Russian without comments. The only attachment to a document would be a statement that the source was trusted, but it would not attest to the veracity of the document. Hiss's code name as a source of information was Mars, but he might not have known that. Probably he was in close contact with people from GRU, because when Whittaker Chambers testified against Hiss we considered this to be a setback for GRU intelligence activities in the United States.[6]

---

5. Nathan Gregory Silvermaster, a Russian-born economist who worked for the Farm Security Administration, established a network of friends in government to provide secret materials to aid the USSR during World War II. Among those in the group were White House counselor Lauchlin Currie and Assistant Treasury Secretary Harry Dexter White. In testimony before the House Un-American Activities Committee in 1948, Silvermaster dismissed Elizabeth Bentley's charges that he supplied material to the Soviet Union, but he invoked the Fifth Amendment when asked if he was a Communist. On August 13, 1948, White acknowledged to the committee that he knew Silvermaster but vigorously denied being a Communist or knowing Bentley. White died of a heart attack three days later.

6. Testifying before the House Un-American Activities Committee in 1948, Whittaker Chambers, a former spy for Soviet military intelligence (GRU), accused Hiss, a former high-ranking official in the U.S. Department of State, of having given him secret government documents in the 1930s. Hiss went before the committee to deny the charge, but Chambers responded by producing microfilms of classified documents he had hidden in a hollowed-out pumpkin on his Maryland farm to support his case. Because the statute of limitations had expired on his purported espionage activities, Hiss was charged with perjury. The jury could not agree on a verdict, but at a second trial the government introduced new evidence in its efforts to prove that Hiss's personal typewriter was used to copy classified documents, and on January 21, 1950, Hiss was found guilty on two counts of perjury and sentenced to five years in prison. After serving three years and eight months he was paroled, and he continues to declare his innocence, claiming that the evidence against him was forged. New evidence on Hiss's connections to Soviet military intelligence has emerged from Hungarian secret police files on Noel Havilland Field, who worked with Hiss in the State Department in the 1930s and was allegedly run by the same Soviet control officer. See Sam Tanenhaus,

What GRU records do reflect is that the Silvermaster group was affected by internal divisions. Contrary to the rules of clandestine operations, members of the group knew one another, and their relations were strained.

Because of the purges of intelligence officers in 1937–1938, contacts with the Silvermaster group were temporarily severed. When the GRU attempted to resume contacts with Hiss in the 1940s, after war broke out, he preferred not to meet with anyone who referred to connections with the Silvermaster group. The GRU station officers in Washington who succeeded Boris Bykov (who had run the Silvermaster group) were not aware of the splits, divisions, and conflicts in the group. When they approached Hiss, referring to his earlier cooperation, he turned away from them.

When Hiss was accused at the end of the 1940s, his behavior followed instructions he may have learned in the 1930s: never admit anything. Or perhaps he might have been tempted not to admit anything because he thought he could prove that the evidence was forged. My old friend, now eighty-one, believes Hiss was chosen by Hopkins and Roosevelt for confidential contacts with Soviet diplomats and intelligence officers, knowing that he had contacts and was pro-Soviet.

The retired GRU officer remembers that there was a controlled agent source of information in Roosevelt's office. He was Roosevelt's assistant on intelligence affairs, and he was on bad terms with William Donovan and J. Edgar Hoover, heads of the OSS and the FBI, respectively. My friend strongly believes that Roosevelt and Hopkins were also ill disposed toward Donovan's bureau and the FBI. GRU files reflect that Roosevelt set up his own informal intelligence network during the war, used by him for sensitive missions. My friend is certain that Hiss, Hopkins, and Harriman were in this trusted group.

That could be why Hiss was not immediately disowned by Truman. The mild sentence he received, the incoherent accusations against him, and the neutral stand of the administration in the case could indicate that he knew too much that was damaging to the prestige of both Roosevelt and Truman. The old GRU veteran believes that the FBI had more material on Hiss than was revealed, and that perhaps there was a deal between Truman and Hoover that the charges should be confined to perjury.

"Hiss: Guilty as Charged," *Commentary*, April 1993, pp. 32–37, and Maria Schmidt, "The Hiss Dossier," *New Republic*, November 8, 1993, pp. 17–20.

Some eighty percent of intelligence information on political matters comes not from agents but from confidential contacts. Usually these contacts are detected by counterintelligence services, but it is always problematic to prove the case of espionage. Indeed, the policy of Soviet intelligence in 1942 was to cut off any connection between Communist party members and intelligence activities. If the source of information was important enough, he was ordered by us to publicly declare his severance from the party to show that he was disillusioned with communism.

It is interesting to observe shifts in the history of diplomatic contacts between American and Soviet representatives. Throughout the war Hopkins and Harriman maintained personal, informal, and diplomatic relations with Soviet leaders, and I believe they were fulfilling instructions of Roosevelt. Stalin resorted to informal diplomacy only in the first period of the war, using Oumansky and Litvinov. When he himself established relations with Roosevelt at Tehran, he no longer needed Litvinov, the skillful negotiator with fluent English, French, and German, in America. Andrei Gromyko's appointment as ambassador in 1943 was a clear sign of the establishment of a personal link between Stalin and Roosevelt. Stalin no longer needed a strong intermediary such as Litvinov or Oumansky.

Later Stalin got rid of all who engaged in informal contacts with Roosevelt's envoys. This explains why he dropped Litvinov. Our last effort to ensure friendly ties with Americans before Yalta was our disclosure to them that Roosevelt's interpreter was the son of one of the leaders of Oberleague, the White Russian terrorist organization. This happened just two days before the start of the Yalta Conference. The news was channeled to Beria, and on his instructions Sergei Kruglov, who chaired the guards for the conference, informed the chief of the American guards. The interpreter was immediately evacuated from Yalta to one of the American ships anchored near Crimea.[7]

Originally, Soviet intentions were to participate in the Marshall Plan. I remember meeting Molotov's assistant, Mikhail Vetrov, on the eve of his

---

7. Sudoplatov offers this final, personal note about Yalta: "Gorbachev and KGB chairman Viktor M. Chebrikov in 1986, before the summit meeting with President Reagan in Reykjavik, asked for files on the NKGB preparation for Yalta. I sent a letter on my reminiscences on this matter and was rewarded with medical treatment in the KGB hospital but not real assistance in my rehabilitation, which did not come until 1992."

departure to Paris with Molotov to participate in talks about rebuilding Europe in June 1947. Vetrov was an old friend with whom I had worked in Riga in 1940. He told me that the directive was to cooperate with the Western allies in the implementation of the Marshall Plan, giving special attention to restoring the devastated industrial facilities in the Ukraine, Byelorussia, and Leningrad.

Then, in a sudden turn of policy, I was summoned to meet with Deputy Foreign Minister Andrei Vyshinsky and Peter Fedotov, his deputy in the offices of the Committee of Information. Vyshinsky explained that they had received a cable from an agent, code-named Orphan, who was Donald Maclean. As first secretary of the British Embassy in Washington and acting head of chancery, Maclean had access to all of the embassy's classified traffic. He stated that the goal of the Marshall Plan was to ensure American economic domination in Europe. The new international economic organization to restore European productivity would be under the control of American financial capital. The source for Maclean's report was British foreign secretary Ernest Bevin. This fateful report decided the future disparity between the economic levels of Eastern and Western Europe.

Vyshinsky knew he must immediately report this message to Stalin. However, before doing that he wanted to double-check the credibility of Maclean and the agents in his group — Philby, Burgess, Cairncross, and Blunt. Vyshinsky was frightened that Aleksandr Orlov, who had defected to the West, had been in contact with these agents and might have compromised them. Vyshinsky asked me and Fedotov to what extent Philby, Maclean, and Burgess might be engaged in a double game.

I was the one responsible for giving orders to resume contacts with Philby and Maclean in 1939 after Orlov's defection. Since my signature was on the formal order registered in Maclean's file, Vyshinsky created an awkward moment when he asked if I was still confident of Maclean's reliability. I told him that I was responsible for the orders I signed, but that I was aware of Maclean's work only until 1939 and it had not been reported to me since 1942. At the same time I added, "Every important source of information should be subjected to regular checks and evaluation, with no exceptions for Philby, Burgess, and Maclean." Vyshinsky, clearly distressed, was relieved by my final remark: "But Comrade Stalin personally ordered the NKVD not to track down Orlov or persecute members of his family." This convinced Vyshinsky that there was no reason to withhold the information from Stalin pending a new check on Maclean. If Maclean's information was tainted, Vyshinsky could wash his hands with Stalin's own order to leave Orlov alone. Besides, I told all this to Vyshinsky in the presence of Fedotov, so he could use him as a witness against me in case the Maclean information was proven false.

The message revealed a crucial point: the Marshall Plan was intended to be a substitute for the payment of reparations by Germany. This was a serious concern for the Soviet leadership, because at that time war reparations were the sole source of foreign capital to restore our economy.

At Yalta and Potsdam it had been agreed that German reparations in the form of equipment, manufacturing machinery, cars, trucks, and building supplies would be sent to Russia regularly for five years. This was essential for modernizing our chemical and machine tool industries. It was not to be regulated by international control. That meant we could use these supplies for whatever purposes we found necessary.

The Marshall Plan was quite different, because all its economic projects would be under international or American control. The scheme would have been attractive if it were an additional element to the regular flow of reparations from Germany and Finland. However, the Maclean report indicated that the British and American governments wanted to replace reparations to the Soviet Union and East European countries with international aid, based not on bilateral agreements but on international control.

This was totally unacceptable because it would obstruct our consolidation of control in Eastern Europe. It meant that Communist parties already established in Romania, Bulgaria, Poland, Czechoslovakia, and Hungary would be deprived of economic levers of power. Six months after the Marshall Plan was rejected by the Soviet Union, multiparty rule in Eastern Europe came to an end.

On instructions from Stalin, Vyshinsky sent a coded message to Molotov in Paris which summarized the Maclean report. Based on Maclean's information, Stalin instructed Molotov to obstruct the implementation of the Marshall Plan in Eastern Europe.

This was carried out in various ways. Vyshinsky personally conducted negotiations with King Michael of Romania for his abdication, guaranteeing part of his pension in Mexico.

In Bulgaria the situation was unique. During the war, I met frequently with Georgi Dimitrov, the head of the Comintern until it was disbanded in 1943. For a year he was the first director of the international department of the Central Committee of the CPSU. When Dimitrov returned home to Bulgaria in 1944, he allowed the czarina and her son, the heir apparent, to leave the country with their personal wealth and property. Sensing the danger that might come from monarchist émigrés, Dimitrov decided to eliminate the entire political opposition; he purged and liquidated all key figures in the former parliament and government of czarist Bulgaria. As a result of this action, one which today would be considered a terrorist act, Dimitrov was the only Communist leader in Eastern Europe who did not face the existence of an émigré organization in the West. Dimitrov's followers exploited the absence of a political opposition for more than thirty years. The former minister of defense of Bulgaria, General Ivan Genarov, who worked under my command in the Fourth Directorate during the war years, told me later, when we met in Moscow in the 1970s, that Bulgaria "is the only socialist country without any dissidents in the West because we ourselves learned the lesson from you and wiped them out before they were able to escape to the West."

Czechoslovakia was different. In 1948, on the eve of the crucial transfer of power from Edvard Beneš to Klement Gottwald, under the instructions of Molotov, I was dispatched to Prague with four hundred Special-Purpose troops — whom I thought unnecessary — all dressed in civilian clothes. The troops were flown to an airfield used by our military command outside Prague.

Boris Rybkin, our rezident in Prague at the end of 1947, had set up an illegal network disguised as an export-import company producing costume jewelry. His assignment was to use the new Czech firm as a base for sabotage operations in Western Europe and the Middle East. Czech costume jewelry was world famous, which made it easy for Rybkin to create subsidiary distribution companies in the most important capitals of Western Europe and the Middle East. An immediate objective was to use Kurdish resistance against the shah of Iran and the rulers of Iraq, King Faisal II and Prime Minister Nuri Said. Rybkin was killed in Prague in an automobile accident at the end of 1947, but by then his organization was in place.

When Molotov summoned me to his office in the Kremlin, he directed me to go to Prague and arrange a secret meeting with Beneš to ask him to retire with dignity and hand over power to Gottwald, the Communist party leader. I was to use the receipt for $10,000 signed by Beneš's secretary in 1938 for his safe passage to Great Britain to remind him of his intimate, informal relations with the Kremlin. Otherwise, we would reveal our financial support for his escape and the involvement of Beneš in the political coup and assassinations in Yugoslavia in 1938–1940.

Molotov stressed that I did not have the authority to negotiate on any issues of Czech politics, only to pass the message on clearly, leaving it to Beneš how to accomplish the end we sought. Molotov repeated my instructions in a very strict manner, peering intently at me through his eyeglasses. I replied that it would be better for someone who knew Beneš personally and had been directly involved with him to conduct such a sensitive conversation. That man was Zubov, our rezident in Prague before the war, whom Stalin had jailed because he had not carried out the coup suggested by Beneš in Yugoslavia. Molotov said I should handle the matter as I saw fit. It was clear that he wanted no responsibility for how I operated; his only concern was the results. My instructions were to leave Prague within twelve hours after passing the message to Beneš, not to await his reply.

When I arrived in Prague by train with Pyotr Zubov in January 1948, we avoided our embassy and stayed in a modest hotel as members of a Soviet trade mission. Zubov had been a pensioner since September 1946. He was virtually an invalid as a result of his torture in prison by Rodos. He walked with a pronounced limp, using a cane. When Zubov was our rezident in Prague, he had been Beneš's control officer and savior on the eve of the war.

Beneš was under considerable pressure from our official representatives in Prague, and we were to add even more. We stayed in Prague for a week while Zubov, using his skill and past connections, managed to meet with Beneš for fifteen minutes at his residence in the Grachansky Palace in the center of Prague. He passed the message unequivocally, stressing that "cardinal transformations" would occur inevitably, with or without the present-day leadership of the country, but that Zubov's personal view was that Beneš was the only man who could accomplish a smooth and bloodless path to change. This was a meeting between two sick men for the last time in their lives.

We boarded the earliest train for Moscow. Following my instructions, Zubov had said to Beneš that he did not expect to receive an answer; he was just giving him an informal message. Zubov told me his impression was that Beneš was a broken, ailing man who would do what he could to avoid the outbreak of violence and turmoil in Czechoslovakia. When we crossed the border, I followed orders and used the facilities of the local party district committee to send a coded message to Molotov, with a copy to Abakumov, then minister of state security, that Zubov, code name Leo, had been granted an audience and conveyed the message. In a month the political crisis in Prague ended with Beneš peacefully handing over power to Gottwald.

The end of the war marked a strengthening of my position in the security apparatus bureaucracy. The Fourth Directorate, which I headed, had contributed greatly to our victory. Among twenty-eight chekists who were awarded the highest decorations in the war, twenty were officers of the Fourth Directorate. I was given the rare privilege in December 1945 of addressing the annual NKGB/NKVD gathering on the anniversary of the founding of the CHEKA. I presented the official report, and was elected a member of the party committee of the newly formed Ministry of State Security (MGB). In the spring of 1946, the NKGB became the MGB, what had been a commissariat becoming a ministry. Stalin's renaming it meant a coming of age and streamlining of the intelligence bureaucracy.[8]

In July 1945, right after the war, on the eve of the Potsdam Conference, Stalin signed a decree converting all NKGB/NKVD ranks into military ranks similar to those in the Red Army. Fitin and I were given the rank of lieutenant general (two stars) by the Council of Ministers. Eitingon, under the same decree, was confirmed in the rank of major general (one star). That was the first and last time my family name was mentioned in the Soviet press.

The hostilities of the Cold War became dangerous in late 1946, leading to an important reorganization of Soviet intelligence structures. The army and navy intelligence services were not adequately evaluating data. Molotov, who before Yalta chaired several conferences of intelligence service directors, suggested they be merged into a new centralized intelligence board. Stalin agreed, and the Committee of Information was set up, comprising Fitin's First Directorate (foreign intelligence) from the MGB and the parallel intelligence directorate of the Ministry of Defense, the GRU. It was decided to keep in the Ministry of Security a special service for diversions (sabotage) and intelligence in case of war or local military conflicts in the Middle East, Europe, the Balkans, or Asia. A similar reserve unit was set up in the Ministry of Defense. Thus

8. At the same time, the NKVD became the MVD, Ministry of Internal Affairs.

operations were split between the ministries and the Committee of Information.

To me it is clear in retrospect that the rational idea of setting up a unit for analysis of intelligence information was implemented in the wrong way. Operations should have been left where they were, and the new Committee of Information should have restricted its activities to analysis and functioned as a clearinghouse for secret information from all government agencies. In 1946 and 1947, the Committee of Information seemed like a simplification, but ultimately it weakened the existing intelligence structures.

MGB and GRU operations depended on the integration of these services into the bigger military and security structures under which they worked. The MGB intelligence service relied on cooperation with counterintelligence units; and the GRU cooperated with other departments of the general staff. Neither the GRU nor the MGB intelligence directorate was by itself capable of setting priorities and goals of intelligence penetrations. Both were professional servants of military or security leadership. Under the new system, initiatives from the military high command and from the Security Ministry went first to Stalin and then to Molotov, head of the Committee of Information, adding miles of red tape to the process of decision making.

The old NKVD/NKGB intelligence directorate, which acted as the primary arm of national security interests abroad, now became in effect a subsidiary component of the Ministry of Foreign Affairs, which was primarily occupied with diplomacy, and which was also controlled by Molotov. The former highly successful NKVD/NKGB activities — penetration of émigré organizations, penetration of British and American intelligence services, and coordination with internal security forces combatting nationalist movements in the Baltics and Western Ukraine — began to lose effectiveness. The Committee of Information was set up simultaneously with the creation in the United States of the CIA, the Central Intelligence Agency, in a mistaken attempt to meet its challenge.

Even now, after the collapse of the Soviet Union, I still think that in Russia the effective operation of the intelligence service depends on its integration with the security institutions. Currently there are no independent institutions to perform security operations like taxation and drug and customs control. In the West, all these systems have long-established authority and hold serious controlling levers in the society. In Russia these services are only emerging. An evaluation and analysis unit should process intelligence information independently, and not be hampered by the bureaucratic interests of influential politicians. We gradually came to this idea in 1951 and 1952, when Stalin ordered operational intelligence work concentrated in the GRU and the new First Chief Directorate (foreign intelligence) in the Ministry of State Security. The Committee of Information was retained as a subsidiary department of the Ministry of Foreign Affairs, and it was there that Burgess and Maclean started to work in 1952, after their defection from the West.

In 1991, after the failed coup, instead of working out a mechanism of parliamentary and public control over the security services, Gorbachev and Yeltsin made the same mistake, mixing analysis and operations, creating the Foreign Intelligence Service, which still relies on the former KGB for its activities abroad. Coordination of its day-to-day business with internal security interests remains its weakest element.

The Committee of Information was first chaired by Molotov, then by Andrei Vyshinsky, and then Valerian Zorin, who later became the Soviet ambassador to the United Nations. I attended several meetings. Vyshinsky chaired the committee for only three months, and until his last day on the job managed not to sign any sensitive documents, entrusting that responsibility to his deputies. He kept saying, "In this serious business I have no competence."

Vyshinsky said that he had twice told Comrade Stalin of his incompetence in intelligence matters. Vyshinsky's style was always to bring his deputy with him when he visited Stalin. He clearly wanted to share the responsibility for decisions and prepare a way to disclaim them if they didn't work out. Vyshinsky was far more competent than he pretended to be; in an informal moment he told me that "the intelligence business is associated more often with unpleasant results than with positive accomplishments." It was not a place to feel secure in one's achievements — the risk was too great. Vyshinsky convinced Stalin that he should be transferred, and after three unhappy months he was removed from heading the Committee of Information and replaced by Zorin.

In the midst of these changes, in June 1946, Merkulov was dismissed from his post as minister of state security. There were vague hints that the security service had made mistakes in the arrangements for traditional May Day demonstrations in Moscow, causing traffic snarls. However, I soon realized that traffic snarls were a pretext for ousting Merkulov.

With the end of the war, the first task was demobilization of the army; after that Stalin ordered the Politburo to consider new priorities in national security policy. Later I was told by Stepan Mamulov and

Boris Ludvigov, chiefs of Beria's secretariat, that Merkulov was formally ordered to submit a plan to the Politburo for reorganization of the Security Ministry. Beria cursed Merkulov for being unable to explain coherently the priorities for counterintelligence work after the war, and Stalin joined in, bitterly attacking Merkulov for unpreparedness. The meeting, with Merkulov's deputies present, was to discuss the new role of the Ministry of State Security. Military counterintelligence, SMERSH, which had been headed by Abakumov in the war years, was being returned to the Ministry of Security from the army because Stalin had given up his role as people's commissar for defense. Bulganin, former party apparatchik and chairman of GOSBANK (the state bank) and Mossoviet (the city government of Moscow), never a professional military officer, was promoted to the rank of marshal and appointed defense minister.

There was an interesting scene. Stalin said he didn't understand why the director of military counterintelligence shouldn't have the right to act as the deputy minister of security. Merkulov said he believed Comrade Stalin was absolutely right, Abakumov should be appointed first deputy minister of security. To this Stalin sarcastically replied that Merkulov was being two-faced and therefore he felt it expedient to replace him as head of the ministry. It appeared that Merkulov had made a mistake agreeing so readily, but in fact Stalin was looking for any excuse to dismiss him. Stalin suggested that Comrade Sergei Ogoltsov, a provincial but honest man who had never worked at the Center and only six months earlier had been transferred from the job of MGB director in Krasnoyarsk to Moscow, be appointed minister of state security. At this juncture Ogoltsov begged Comrade Stalin not to do so because, as an honest party member, he knew he was totally unfit for the post. He lacked the necessary experience. Then Stalin suggested that Abakumov be appointed minister. Beria and Molotov remained silent, while Andrei Zhdanov, a Politburo member, enthusiastically supported the move.

Within a week Eitingon and I were summoned to Abakumov. "Almost two years ago," he said, "I made up my mind not to work with you two, but Comrade Stalin said, when I proposed relieving you from your duties, that we should manage to get along with each other. So, we'll work together." At first Eitingon and I were impressed by his honesty and felt relieved. What followed taught us not to feel so comfortable. In a few days we were summoned to the main conference room of the Lubyanka for a meeting of the special commission of the Central Committee of the CPSU chaired by the new party secretary, Aleksei Kuznetsov.

The commission was looking into "criminal mistakes" and deeds of negligence that were committed by the former leadership of the Ministry of State Security. Whenever there was a change of leadership in key power centers such as defense, security, or foreign affairs, the Central Committee appointed a commission to look into the record of the old leadership before passing it on to new officials.

Among claims to be investigated was that Merkulov had stopped criminal proceedings against Trotsky's followers in the 1940s, especially during wartime. Suddenly the old issue of Eitingon's and my suspicious connections with known enemies of the people in the intelligence directorate reemerged. Abakumov directly accused me and Eitingon of "criminal manipulations" — releasing my "mistresses" and friends from jail in 1941 and helping them escape punishment. I was deeply offended that Raisa Sobel, our family friend, was being slandered. I had no mistresses. I became furious and counterattacked, saying, "I will not allow anybody to slander the memory of heroes of the war, men and women who displayed their courage and devotion to the country in the struggle against fascism. In the presence of the representative of the Central Committee, I will prove that the cases against chekists who were released on my initiative after war broke out were fabricated in the criminal tradition of Yezhov."

Kuznetsov, who was chairing the meeting, intervened and said that the matter was closed. He knew me because we had met at the dacha of a mutual friend. The matter was finished, and I left.

As soon as I returned to my office, I summoned Serebryansky, Zubov, Prokupuk, Medvedev, and other officers who had been purged in the thirties and suggested that they immediately retire. They should not draw unnecessary attention to themselves. Zubov and Serebryansky were particularly vulnerable because Abakumov was personally handling their investigations.

In July 1946, for the first time since 1938, I went on an official leave with my wife and children to a Baltic resort in Riga, Mayori. At first we stayed in the military guest house, but then Vilas Lotis, the famous Latvian writer, once people's commissar of security and then prime minister of Latvia, invited us to stay in his residence. When I returned to Moscow I was officially told by Chernov, chief of the Ministry of Security secretariat, that the Fourth Directorate (guerrilla warfare), of which I was chief, was officially dissolved, its functions terminated. Since the directorate no longer existed, I was ordered to submit to the minister suggestions for the use of its personnel. With Molotov heading the Committee of Information and Abakumov the minister of security, I was caught between them.

I was still chief of Department S, in charge of atomic intelligence. From Ogoltsov I learned that Abakumov was annoyed that I still maintained my post on the Special State Committee on Problem Number One and in this capacity had direct access to the Kremlin and to several ministers, but he couldn't relieve me from those duties because the atomic program was not under his jurisdiction.

The new Committee of Information was supposed to amalgamate GRU and MGB intelligence directorates, duplicating the work of Department S, which was in charge of coordinating GRU and MGB agent penetrations and intelligence for nuclear weapons. Where did Department S belong now? How could Department S work for the Committee of Information if it had no roof under which to serve? At the end of 1946 the matter became urgent; I couldn't arrange a meeting with Beria, but finally I got him on the phone. He was then deputy prime minister and a member of the Politburo. I asked Beria in what organizational structure Department S — and, by extension, the Special Second Bureau of the Committee on Problem Number One — should be placed and how its status should be defined. His reply puzzled me.

"You have your own minister for that sort of decision," he said, and hung up. If I still had a minister, he was Abakumov, and I knew that he would not support me.

I immediately suggested that the functions of Department S should be transferred to the Committee of Information. Given the importance of the atomic issue, the director of scientific and technological intelligence should be made personally responsible for it. In this capacity he would have the support of this department for intelligence activities. At my recommendation Lev Vasilevsky was appointed director of science and technology intelligence, but he was kept in this job by Molotov for only six months. As I mentioned earlier, he was purged from the committee and allowed to retire on a pension in 1948 in the wake of the anti-Semitic campaign.

The problem of where I belonged in the intelligence bureaucracy was resolved in September 1946 when the Central Committee decided to appoint me director of Special Bureau Number One for Diversions and Intelligence, under the Ministry of State Security. My mission was to establish an administration that could be quickly reorganized into a major directorate in case of war or if pockets of tension within the Soviet Union erupted in strife. Eitingon was appointed my deputy.

I retained my position as the director of an autonomous unit in the ministry. Abakumov was shrewd enough not to deprive me of the privileges that I had received in the war years. We kept the dacha, and he continued to include me in the list of those who received extra money subsidies from the government and access to special foods. My position changed in one way: I was not regularly invited to attend chief-of-department conferences chaired by the minister, as I had been in the war years.

Thus Abakumov and I kept out of each other's way — until falsifying investigators were on the loose and I received an unexpected phone call from him. "What is this I hear about your sons planning to kill Stalin?" Abakumov demanded.

"What do you mean?" I asked.

"Just what I said," replied Abakumov.

"Do you know how old they are?" I asked.

"What's the difference?"

"Comrade Minister," I replied, "I don't know who told you that, but the truth of the charge is highly unlikely because the younger of my sons is three and the older one is five years old."

Abakumov slammed down the receiver and that was the last I heard from him for almost a year. He never met with me even though I was directly subordinate to him. Questions were decided only by telephone, never in person.

The end of the year 1946 and beginning of 1947 continued the drastic reorganization of the intelligence bureaucracy. Half a year was spent shuffling and dividing agents between the Committee of Information and my bureau. William Fisher, who had worked in the Fourth Directorate under me in the war years, supervising radio communication service, was transferred to the Committee of Information. With the support of Ogoltsov, Abakumov's first deputy, I argued with Molotov's deputy, Fedotov, that my bureau should have its own radio center. The final decision did not make me happy. Both the Committee of Information and the bureau were to jointly use the same radio center. Aleksandr Korotkov, who was appointed chief of the illegals department of the Committee of Information, worked out a plan to use Fisher, who later became famous under the pseudonym Rudolf Abel, as the chief of illegal networks in Western Europe.

The plan came to me for my agreement because it included tasks of penetrating military bases and installations in Bergen, Norway, and in Le Havre and Cherbourg, France. I strongly objected to it because Fisher could have been more valuable working abroad to improve all our illegal radio communications, not risking exposure running agent networks. Illegal radio operators and illegal agents should be husbands and wives or work separately from each other, communicating through a courier, to minimize the risk of getting caught together and compromising the whole network; this key rule was not observed during the war by the Red Orchestra and led to tragic losses. Korotkov was pressing for Fisher to combine the functions of running an agent network and controlling radio operators.

No decision about his trip abroad was made until the end of 1947. I suggested to Fedotov that we send Fisher to both Western Europe and North America to assess what remained of our networks in France, Norway, the United States, and Canada. His mission would be to gain access to military installations, warehouses, and stored supplies of ammunition. We badly needed to know how quickly American reinforcements could appear in Europe in case of a rise in Cold War tension.

Eitingon suggested that Fisher become a naturalized citizen of the United States and set up his own system of radio communications with Moscow. I stressed that he should not trust old sources of information. He should make new confidential contacts and then check people who were used by us in the 1930s and 1940s, but in every case it should be entirely his decision to contact them, meaning they should not be told by us that he would appear in the West.

Major targets for Fisher were on the West Coast of the United States, near the Long Beach military facilities. He was ordered to report the shipment of American military supplies to the Chinese nationalists, at that time still involved in a bitter civil war with the Chinese Communists.

Fisher created a new network that encompassed agent informers in California and MGB illegal officers in Brazil, Mexico, and Argentina posing as immigrants from Czechoslovakia. The informers reported the traffic of military hardware and ammunition from American Pacific ports to the Far East; the team of MGB illegals in Latin America, who regularly came on business pretexts to the United States, were experts in sabotage operations. They had been participants in the guerrilla war against the Germans. They included Vladimir Grinchinko, Mikhail Filonenko, and Trotsky's former secretary Maria de la Sierra, code name

Africa. The MGB officers based in South America, under orders from the Center, could enlist the California informers to implement sabotage operations. Colonel Filonenko and his wife lived in Argentina, Brazil, and Paraguay, posing as Czech business people who had escaped from the Chinese Communists in Shanghai. They established contacts in Chinese communities in California. The Filonenkos could use Chinese in California to put explosives on board American ships carrying military supplies bound for the Far East. To minimize the risk, Filonenko preferred regular visits to being permanently posted in the United States. The order to carry out sabotage against American ships never came.

Another Fisher network used German immigrants on the West Coast. Fisher cleverly enlisted Kurt Wissel, once assistant to Ernest Wollweber, the veteran expert in sabotage operations in prewar Europe. Wissel rose to the sensitive position of senior engineer in an American shipbuilding company, either near Norfolk or Philadelphia, and he had connections in German communities. Through dockers and service personnel looking for additional income, Wissel set up an infrastructure for performing sabotage operations. By 1949 and 1950, he had safe apartments strategically located around port facilities.

At the end of the 1940s there was a temptation to provide Wissel and Filonenko with Soviet-made explosive devices, but I vetoed this proposal because there was no need to expose our people to unjustified danger. When the crisis in the Korean War climaxed in autumn 1950, our experts capable of assembling explosive devices using local materials came from Latin America and stayed in the United States for two months. Their talents were never ordered into use, and they returned safely to Argentina and via Vienna to Moscow.

When Fisher came to Moscow on leave, either Abakumov or Molotov brought up the question of finding Orlov. I vehemently objected, repeating that the Central Committee forbade us to pursue him. Orlov would quickly notice surveillance or any attempts by our agents to approach his relatives. The idea of using Fisher to trace Orlov came from Aleksandr Korotkov, code name Long, who was supposed to act as Orlov's assistant in running the illegal network in France and who knew that in the 1930s there had been an aborted plan to use Fisher as Orlov's radio operator there.

Later Korotkov brought about Fisher's downfall. In 1953 he chose an MGB officer of Finnish descent, Reino Hayhanen, to assist Fisher. Hayhanen was a heavy drinker who broke security regulations and stole

MGB funds. When he was recalled to Moscow, he defected to the United States and betrayed Fisher.[9]

Because we never decided to use our sabotage plans in the United States during the Korean War, Fisher was transferred to the jurisdiction of the illegals department of MGB intelligence, but I continued to have plans for using him. In 1951 or 1952, the new minister of security, Ignatiev, ordered my bureau and the GRU to jointly prepare a plan for subversive operations against American ammunition warehouses and military airfields in case of war or military tension on Soviet borders. We defined one hundred targets for sabotage actions, divided into three categories: military bases deploying the American strategic air force carrying nuclear weapons; military installations containing stocks of munitions and hardware to reinforce the American army in Europe and the Far East; and oil pipelines and fuel supplies for American and NATO

9. Aleksandr Korotkov was an experienced intelligence officer whose father-in-law was a close friend of Orlov, according to P. A. Sudoplatov. "Korotkov was tall, thin, and handsome, with black hair and blue eyes. During two years as an illegal in France he supervised a Turkish assassin in liquidating important Trotskyites and other defectors, including Rudolf Klement and Georgi Agabekov.

"Korotkov returned to Moscow in the uncertain atmosphere of the 1930s purges and attempted to strengthen himself by denouncing the Turk for friendly comments toward the disgraced NKVD leadership. When I read his denunciation letter, I knew Korotkov could not be trusted. Later, when the Jewish purges began, he divorced his Jewish wife, with whom he had two children, to preserve his leading position in the security bureaucracy. He used his position at the end of the 1940s to send the Turk back to Ankara as an illegal rezident to get rid of him, although this man was mortally ill with heart trouble.

"Later, in Korotkov's biographical file, he included that in the course of his career he also participated in dirty work, meaning those two liquidations. In his file he dramatized his biography by stating that the October Revolution brought happiness to the Soviet people but destroyed his family because his father was a high-ranking official of the Novosibirsk Commercial Bank. He had to begin a new life, starting his career as an elevator operator. Then, after marrying well, he studied German, trained in illegal tradecraft, and obtained a post as a junior case officer in the Foreign Intelligence Directorate. In 1940 and 1941 in Germany, Korotkov was deputy rezident and maintained contacts with three principal agents, Corsican, Senior Warrant Officer, and the playwright Adam Kukoff, all leaders of the Red Orchestra network in Germany.

"Korotkov was a witness at Beria's trial, accusing him of suspicious contacts with foreign intelligence. Shortly after that, he received the rank of major general. In the mid-1950s he rose to the position of first deputy director of the KGB intelligence service. He was on good terms with Serov, and frequently played tennis with him. When Shelepin succeeded Serov as KGB director in 1958, he sent Korotkov to East Germany as KGB representative. They told me that he died from a heart attack on the tennis court, playing with Serov in August 1961," Sudoplatov recalled.

(North Atlantic Treaty Organization) forces stationed in Europe, the Middle East, and the Far East near our borders.

By the beginning of the 1950s we had acquired agents with access to military installations in Norway, France, Austria, Germany, the United States, and Canada. The plan was to set up a system of permanent monitoring of any unusual activities around NATO strategic military installations. Fisher, as our chief illegal rezident in the United States, would stop gathering day-to-day political information; he would establish permanent, reliable radio communication with our battle groups. These combat troops on reserve in Latin America were ready to come north through Mexico, disguised as seasonal workers.

Filonenko and Grinchinko expanded their commercial business and offered favorable conditions for employment to seasonal Latin American harvesters. The network of safe apartments and supporting infrastructure was prepared cautiously in the course of two years.

In Europe, Prince Gagarin, our veteran agent who pretended to be an anti-Soviet émigré and who had served in the Vlasov army in World War II, moved from Germany to France. His job was to create an infrastructure for port and airfield sabotage; he was also to organize a combat group that could disrupt the functions of the NATO headquarters command in the suburbs of Paris in case of war or heightened tension. I received a group of experts in oil refining and fuel processing and storage, who analyzed the technical facilities and disposition of major pipelines in Western Europe. We directed our officers and agents to recruit personnel at oil refineries and pipeline installations.

In 1952 I received a briefing that Fisher had become a naturalized citizen of the United States and had settled into a cover life. He claimed to be a man of several professions, an independent artist and painter. He had set up three sites for radio transmissions: between New York and Norfolk, near the Great Lakes, and on the West Coast. That was the last I heard of him before I was arrested and until he was exchanged for Gary Powers, who was serving his term with me in Vladimir jail.[10]

10. Powers and Sudoplatov were in the same cellblock in 1960–1961 but never saw each other. They were escorted separately for exercise. Sudoplatov recalled that his subordinate Lieutenant Colonel Nikolai Zemskov, head of the Special Bureau's American section, came to Vladimir prison several times to interrogate Powers. Sudoplatov recalled, "Zemskov was the son-in-law of my close friend General Drozdov, with whom I worked during World War II, so Zemskov sometimes came to see me to check the validity of information. He asked me to compare data from the end of the 1940s with recently received information about American bases in Norway. There was no reference to the previous intensive work of our agents in Norway at the end of the

In 1952, Minister of State Security Ignatiev, who succeeded Abakumov, and Minister of Defense Marshal Vasilevsky endorsed a plan of action against American and NATO strategic military installations in case of war or aggravation of local conflicts. The plan was signed by me and by the GRU director at that time, General Matvey Zakharov. In the case of a major military alert in Europe, our first move would be to disrupt communications at NATO headquarters, but my plan to place an agent group in Paris unexpectedly met difficulties.

The wartime veteran agent Nikolai Khokhlov, code name Whistler, became unstable and later defected to the West. By profession he was an actor; his fluent German and good appearance had made him a valuable agent for Maklarsky and Ilyin. On the eve of the war, he had reported on the Russian intelligentsia in Moscow. We planned to use him as a courier for an agent network that was to stay in Moscow if the Germans occupied the city, but later he posed as a German officer on leave in Minsk. He made contacts with women servants in the household of Gauleiter Kuba, who was blown up in his bed in Minsk in 1943. Khokhlov and his women friends escaped. I took Khokhlov to Romania, where he stayed for a while to become accustomed to Western life. After returning to Moscow, he was in the MGB reserve for deep agent penetrations, on the secret staff of my bureau, which meant that he received his regular salary as a junior officer while leading the life of a student and an ordinary Soviet citizen. I arranged for him to be accepted at Moscow University without passing exams, and he entered the department of philology. I gave him this special dispensation because his undergraduate studies were interrupted by the outbreak of the war. I could not help him with a bigger apartment, however, when he married and soon had a small son. In 1950, Khokhlov began to travel to the West regularly; I wanted him to familiarize himself with the mode of life in Western Europe. He was supplied with excellent false papers issued in the name of Herr Hofbauer. His case officer was Tamara Ivanova, who was also chief of the section dealing with training of illegals in my bureau. She had successfully worked in Hungary and Austria but was recalled in 1948 because of Stalin's directive at that time to stop recruiting operations and to bring back illegals from Eastern Europe.

Khokhlov as Hofbauer made several trips to Germany, Austria, and

---

1940s in the files of the European department. I was able to refer him to the Special Bureau files, stored separately from the archives of the First Chief Directorate. He left me two kilos of sugar."

Switzerland. Taking advantage of his blond, blue-eyed good looks and his artistic personality, I wanted him to get acquainted with a ballerina of Georgian origin in the Paris Opera. She had been noticed in the company of American military officers and personnel of NATO headquarters. Khokhlov's suave ways could be useful in setting up a group to gather information and, more important for me, to build a reserve infrastructure for combat operations.

He was not informed about these plans and didn't understand what was at stake. To my dismay, he made what he thought was a casual error, but which in my eyes ruined his career as an illegal.

Khokhlov tried to smuggle an accordion purchased in Switzerland into Austria; he was detained by customs, who examined his papers and confiscated his passport for several hours. When he reported the incident in Moscow, it was clear to me that the Hofbauer legend was finished. He had drawn attention to himself in the course of a routine check at the border and now surely was on a list of persons suspected by Western intelligence services. Thus he was naturally unfit for combat operations. He asked me to relieve him from his duties and I did; in his personnel file I stressed my consent for him to leave my bureau.

Unfortunately for him, he was sent to Germany as an interpreter in the local intelligence station, and in 1954, after my arrest, he was assigned to lead a team of assassins to liquidate Georgi S. Okolovich, leader of the Russian nationalist organization that collaborated with the Germans in the war years. Khokhlov was caught and turned by the CIA, who made him famous by using him in an anti-Soviet propaganda campaign. In his publicized story, he portrayed himself as a patriot for the West who made up his mind to surrender to Okolovich and reveal the assassination plan to American authorities. Scandal erupted after his revelations at a press conference in Frankfurt staged by the CIA.

Most striking was his allegation that his wife, Tatiana, urged him not to fulfill the assignment. She was arrested in Moscow and spent a year in jail with her son and then was exiled to Siberia for five years. Khokhlov portrayed her as anti-Soviet, the inspiration for his defection, and as an ardent religious believer, but this was not true. Later Khokhlov claimed that he was poisoned at a cocktail party by the KGB in 1957 and that CIA doctors helped him survive the radioactive thalium used on him.

In May 1992 Khokhlov appeared briefly in Moscow after being amnestied by Yeltsin, but he returned to the United States. Lord Bethel of the European parliament made a request to Yeltsin and with the approval of the procurator's office interviewed me about Khokhlov. His story, with important details omitted, was published in *Novoye Vremya* (*New Times*), a leading Soviet magazine. I was told by one of Khokhlov's last mentors, Colonel Evgeny I. Mirkovsky, who was my former assistant, that Khokhlov did not want to be sent on his last mission. He was sent not to assassinate Okolovich, but to make preparations for the liquidation to be carried out by a team of German agents. Second, Khokhlov objected to a plan of taking his wife and son to Austria, which means that he had no plans to defect. At the press conference, under direction of the CIA, he claimed that he and his wife were dreaming of defection. He created a cause célèbre in the Western press by pleading for Western authorities to intervene and arrange for his wife and son to join him in the West. Mirkovsky assumes that our mistake was to allow him to appear in the West using a passport that was already suspect. We presumed that he was captured and compelled to cooperate, but in this desperate situation he managed to send a postcard to his wife. Although screened by the CIA, it contained a warning signal that he was working under hostile control. His bad luck was that the signal was not understood. Two other agents assigned by us to work with Khokhlov were captured by the Americans because he was forced to reveal them. Our officers controlling Khokhlov evaded the trap set by the Americans in Vienna to capture our station chief, Lieutenant Colonel Saul Okun. Khokhlov was abandoned and forced to play the role that was created for him.

Khokhlov later wrote a book in which he describes ongoing quarrels with the CIA; he portrays himself as a patriotic Russian anti-Communist. He presents himself as an expert in guerrilla operations during the war, but leaves out his unsuccessful intelligence career. His services under special contracts arranged by the CIA to teach antiguerrilla warfare in Taiwan and South Vietnam ended in failure because he had experience only as an illegal agent, recruiter of attractive women, and informer, but not as a man engaged in real combat. He was right in choosing a scientific career, leaving behind his life in intelligence operations. His family suffered from his defection and his depiction of his wife as anti-Communist. She preferred to keep silent and never told her son of his father in the West. Their son became a full professor of biology at Moscow University and traveled to the United States as a scientific expert, but he never met his father until he appeared at his Moscow apartment in May 1992. The family reunion was sad and bitter.

*   *   *

The origins of the Cold War are closely interwoven with Western support for nationalist unrest in the Baltic areas and Western Ukraine. Local MGB organizations and party security organs accomplished most of the antiguerrilla struggle, but Moscow closely monitored these battlegrounds and cooperated by supplying arms and advisers. My long knowledge of the Ukraine brought me into the thick of this battle.

On one occasion, during the summer of 1946, I was summoned to the Central Committee headquarters on Staraya Ploshchad (Old Square), together with Abakumov. There I met Khrushchev, then first secretary of the Ukrainian Communist party, in Kuznetsov's office. Kuznetsov, secretary of the Communist party, was very formal even though he knew me socially. He informed me that the Central Committee had agreed to the suggestion of Comrade Khrushchev to secretly liquidate the leader of the Ukrainian nationalists, A. Shumsky, who was reported by the Ukrainian security service to have established contacts with Ukrainian émigrés. Shumsky was plotting to join the Ukrainian provisional government-in-exile. Besides, he was disrespectful enough to contradict Stalin in conversations with his friends. Shumsky was a well-known nationalist who had been purged during intraparty struggles in the beginning of the thirties. He was denounced in the resolutions of all Ukrainian party congresses. He was sentenced to imprisonment but released because he was partially paralyzed.

Shumsky foolishly had contacted Ukrainian cultural leaders in Kiev and abroad while, still in poor health, he was in internal exile in Saratov. Kuznetsov said that Shumsky overestimated his prestige among Ukrainian émigrés and wrote an arrogant letter to Stalin threatening to commit suicide if he was not allowed to return to the Ukraine. Khrushchev said that according to his information, Shumsky had already bought the railway tickets and was returning to the Ukraine with the purpose of leading an armed nationalist movement or escaping abroad to become the spokesman for traitors against the Soviet Union.

Abakumov then said that since I was an expert in Ukrainian affairs, I should trace Shumsky's connections among the underground and émigrés. He would dispatch a team to Saratov to liquidate him; it was my job to prevent his supporters from knowing that he had been murdered. Grigori M. Maironovsky, head of MGB toxicological research, was called in as a consultant to the hospital in Saratov where Shumsky lay ill and did the job with poison from his laboratory. The execution was made to look like a natural death from heart failure. We were never able to establish any foreign connections for Shumsky.

Our reassurances to Roosevelt before Yalta that Soviet citizens now enjoyed religious freedom did not end our problems with the Ukrainian Catholic church, or Uniates. Our agent in Rome, Joseph Grigulevich, who had acquired Costa Rican citizenship and became ambassador from Costa Rica to both the Vatican and Yugoslavia right after the war, reported that the Vatican would take a strong stand against us because of Moscow's treatment of the Ukrainian Catholic church.

The Uniate church held a unique position; it was subordinated to the Vatican but performed services and rites in the Ukrainian language. The church was headed by Metropolitan Andrew Shepitsky, a Polish count and former high-ranking officer of the Austrian army. He had been appointed head of the Ukrainian Catholic church by the Pope before World War I and had given up his military career. During World War I he collaborated with the Austrian intelligence service. Because his advocacy of Ukrainian catholicism greatly jeopardized Russian interests, he was arrested by the czarist intelligence service and sent into exile. He was released by the provisional government in 1917 and returned to Lvov, where an organization of Ukrainian nationalists had been established under the leadership of Colonel Yevhen Konovalets, my former alleged mentor.

In 1941, when the war broke out and Lvov was seized by the Germans, Shepitsky sent a greeting from the Uniate church to Hitler, proclaiming the liberation of the Ukraine from bolshevism. He went so far as to bless the formation, in November 1943, of the ss Galizien division, a special Ukrainian unit, commanded by German Gestapo officers, which took an oath of loyalty to Hitler. The division was used to punish the population and round up Jews for extermination in the Ukraine, Slovakia, and Yugoslavia. Shepitsky appointed Archbishop Slipi chaplain of this division.

Units of the division were taken prisoner by the British in Italy and Austria, and in May 1947 their leaders were sent to England to sponsor a resistance movement in the Ukraine. The British Secret Intelligence Service used them to accompany parachutists dropped in Western Ukraine in 1951.

In 1944 Shepitsky was old and dying. Concerned with the fate of the Ukrainian Uniate church, he shrewdly dispatched a mission to Moscow, which included his younger brother, Archbishop Slipi, and Archbishop Gabriel Kostelnik. They applied to be received by the patriarch of the Russian Orthodox church, which had never been on good terms with the Catholics. The Presidium of the Supreme Soviet sent them first to the NKVD to clear up the question of collaboration with the Germans. Together with General Stepan Mamulov, the chief of Beria's secretariat, I was ordered to receive this delegation. To their surprise, I addressed them in the Western Ukrainian dialect. I laid out the record of the Uniate church leadership in collaborating with the Germans. At the same time, I was ordered to assure them that, provided they repented and no military crimes had been committed by church officials, they were not liable to prosecution.[11]

Events later developed tragically. After the death of Shepitsky, the metropolitan, in 1945, the conflict among church officials grew bitter. In the Uniate church there had been a strong movement toward unification with the Orthodox church, and the clergymen around Shepitsky who opposed such a union had been seriously compromised by their cooperation with the Germans. Gabriel Kostelnik, motivated by convictions that he had advocated for nearly thirty years, headed the movement for unification. It is frequently said that he was an NKVD agent, but this is groundless. The truth is that his two sons were actively involved in the Bandera guerrilla movement and both died heroically in combat against NKVD troops. Kostelnik assembled a congregation of Uniate clergymen in 1946 who voted for reunification with the Orthodox church; Slipi was arrested and exiled. Reunification was a decisive blow against the Ukrainian guerrilla resistance under Bandera's leadership because the bulk of guerrilla commanders came from the families of Ukrainian clergymen.

In Bandera's last attempt to keep the nationalist movement intact, terror became the common feature of life in Western Ukraine. Local authorities lost control in the countryside. Guerrilla commanders prohibited the conscription of the local population into the Red Army. Bandera's men killed conscripts' entire families and burned their houses to establish guerrilla rule in rural areas. The climax of this campaign came with the assassination of Gabriel Kostelnik on the steps of the

---

11. Sudoplatov's explanations of his activities in Western Ukraine during the late 1940s reflect the Kremlin's belief that the Uniate church was disloyal to the Soviet Union. Stalin considered the Uniate church a seedbed for Ukrainian nationalism and Vatican influence in the Ukraine. The traditional animosity between the Catholic church of Western Ukraine and the Russian Orthodox church reflected the Uniate church's political threat to communism. Their theological differences seemed minor by comparison.

cathedral in Lvov while he was leaving after a religious service. The assassin was blocked by the crowd and shot himself, but he was identified as a member of the terrorist squad personally supervised by Bandera's deputy Roman Shukheyevich, for seven years head of the Ukrainian guerrilla underground. During the war Shukheyevich held the rank of Haupsturmführer in the Gestapo division that liquidated the Polish intelligentsia and the Jewish ghetto in Lvov in July 1941.

Grigulevich's information, received in 1947, that the Vatican was lobbying American and British officials to render assistance to the Ukrainian Catholic church and the guerrilla movement supporting it, was directed not only to Stalin and Molotov but also to Khrushchev in the Ukraine. Khrushchev's response was to ask Stalin to sanction the secret liquidation of the Uniate church leadership in the formerly Hungarian city of Uzhgorod. Khrushchev, together with Savchenko, minister of Ukrainian security, sent an aide-mémoire to Stalin and Abakumov stating that Archbishop Romzha of the Ukrainian Uniate church maintained intensive contacts with guerrilla leaders and secret representatives of the Vatican who sought to obstruct the socialist Ukrainian leadership and to stimulate armed banditry. In conclusion, the memo stated that Romzha and his church had become a stronghold of anti-Soviet activities and presented a serious threat to political stability in the region. Abakumov, who had become minister of state security of the USSR, showed me the memo and warned me not to get involved unless we received a command from Comrade Stalin.

The attack on Romzha was badly handled; Savchenko and his team staged a car accident in which Romzha was only injured and sent to the hospital in Uzhgorod. Khrushchev panicked and appealed to Stalin for help. He claimed that Romzha was about to receive top-level underground couriers from Germany and from the Vatican. My team was dispatched to Uzhgorod to trace these contacts, for I was the one who personally knew all the leadership of Ukrainian nationalists from my days working in Konovalets's headquarters. I spent nearly two weeks in Uzhgorod trying to trace the routes and connections of the couriers who were supposed to appear. Then Abakumov phoned me in Uzhgorod informing me that Maironovsky, head of the toxicological laboratory, together with Savchenko, would arrive by train a week later, with instructions for liquidating Romzha. Stalin agreed with Khrushchev that it was time to clean out the "terrorist nest of the Vatican in Uzhgorod." When Savchenko and Maironovsky arrived, they told me that Comrade Khrushchev had received them in Kiev in his private railroad car at the station, gave precise orders, and wished them every success in the mission. Two days later, in my presence, Savchenko reported to Khrushchev by telephone that everything was in place to carry out the order, and received Khrushchev's blessing. Maironovsky provided an ampule of curare poison to a local MGB agent who worked as a nurse in the hospital, and she delivered the fatal injection.

In Savchenko's presence I telephoned Abakumov to give him the news, and he ordered me to remain and trace Romzha's contacts. We soon learned that the real danger for Khrushchev came from nuns under Romzha's control who had close contact with the wife of Ivan Turinitza, who was both first district party secretary and the head of the municipal administration. Khrushchev knew that Romzha was infiltrating both government and party administrations but didn't know how. Fearing exposure of his ineptitude, Khrushchev initiated Romzha's secret assassination. Savchenko received a promotion, and a year later was transferred to Moscow, where he was appointed deputy chairman of the Committee of Information.

In November 1949 a Ukrainian pamphleteer, Yaroslav Galan, who bitterly attacked the Vatican and Ukrainian Uniate church officials for collaborating with the Germans, was killed with an axe in his apartment in Lvov.

After almost a year of not hearing from Abakumov, I received an unexpected telephone call around 4:00 A.M. "At ten o'clock be ready for an urgent mission at Vnukovo airfield." The airfield is in the vicinity of Moscow.

I arrived at Vnukovo accompanied by Eitingon, who was seeing me off. There I met Abakumov's deputy, Lieutenant General Nikolai Selivanovsky, who made a gesture for me to follow him into the plane. Only when we were approaching Kiev did he announce that we were heading for Lvov. Dense fog prevented our landing there, so we returned to Kiev and took the train to Lvov. Only there, in the train, did Selivanovsky brief me about the terrorist action by Bandera's followers who had liquidated Galan, the pamphleteer. Selivanovsky told me that Comrade Stalin rated the work of the security organs combatting banditry in Western Ukraine as highly unsatisfactory. I was ordered to identify the leadership of Bandera's underground in Lvov and liquidate it. I realized that my fate in the ministry depended on the success of this mission.

In Lvov we went straight to a meeting of the local leadership chaired by Khrushchev, who had arrived from Kiev to personally handle the investigation of Galan's murder. This encounter with Khrushchev turned into a battle of polemics. He was in a bad mood, fearing Stalin's rage for his inability to stamp out the resistance of the armed Ukrainian nationalists. I angered him because I objected to his idea of requiring special internal passports for the inhabitants of Western Ukraine. He also wanted to mobilize young men from Western Ukraine for work in the Donbas coalfields and for vocational training in cities of Eastern Ukraine, far from home. I said that inevitably this discrimination — internal passports — and relocating young men to try to break their ties with their nationalist parents and friends, would only increase resentment. Rather than being drafted, young men would escape to the woods and join the armed resistance. Khrushchev bitterly disagreed with me, suggesting that I should concentrate on beheading the leadership of the armed resistance, not meddling in social policy issues.

My resistance was fruitful; he gave up his idea of introducing special passports for the local population. Conscription plans were mostly abandoned, and amnesty was proclaimed for all those who would give up armed resistance and hand in their arms to militia or security organs. The amnesty was especially effective. In the first week of the new year, 1950, eight thousand armed guerrillas handed in their arms to the local militia. In the great majority of cases they were not prosecuted, and we later established that among the eight thousand guerrillas, five thousand were in the dangerous age group from fifteen to twenty and had run away from home fearing conscription to the coalfields.

We established that the armed resistance was coordinated by Roman Shukheyevich, who had been commander of the ss and Abwehr battalion Nachtangel during the war, and who went underground working for Bandera. He was a bold man, competent in clandestine work, who remained active for seven years after the departure of the Germans. When we looked for him around Lvov, he was receiving medical treatment in the cardiological clinic of an Odessa health resort on the Black Sea. He visited Ukrainian cultural celebrities in Lvov and sent a wreath to the funeral of a well-known person among them. That wreath was an unwise gesture because it was talked about, and our agent, an actress who was a correspondent of *Izvestia*, confirmed his presence in the area. We identified four of his female bodyguards, some of them doubling as his wife.

Armed resistance was popular in the areas around Lvov; I went to a remote village with my assistant Vassili Lebed, the veteran of the Ukrainian nationalist movement who had assisted me in my work against Konovalets in the 1930s. We went to find Lebed's relatives, two nephews who were heading anti-Communist guerrilla detachments. Lebed wanted to convince them to give up the armed struggle. Lebed's own cousin had been shot by a Bandera group for accepting an offer to become the chairman of the local kolkhoz (collective farm), even though they knew that his daughter and two sons were in the anti-Communist underground. The stoicism of the cousin's daughter made a deep impression on me. Although deeply depressed, she accepted the execution of her father as inevitable because he didn't obey the warnings of the resistance.

I stayed in Lvov for half a year. The breakthrough came logically but unexpectedly. Shukheyevich relied too much on his connections from the war years. The family of Gorbavoy, a lawyer and an influential member of the Bandera movement, was interested in reaching a compromise with the Soviet regime. They wanted to dissociate themselves from violence. I found access to Gorbavoy's family and friends, and was able to present my case. I argued that the war should be stopped and we should let people who gave up the armed struggle lead their normal lives. I kept my promise. I personally telephoned Abakumov to free Gorbavoy's niece, who was being held in a prison camp in Russia because she was a relative of a prominent Ukrainian nationalist. She was brought to Lvov two days later by plane and promptly released from custody.

This led Gorbavoy to indicate the areas where Shukheyevich was hiding. We managed to turn to our side Shukheyevich's courier, a soccer player on the local Dynamo team. We didn't prosecute either Gorbavoy or his associate, Academician Kripekevich, whose son was a Bandera activist, on grounds of their repentance.

Shukneyevich made another fatal mistake because his nerves were too strained. When a local militiaman came for a routine check to a house where Shukheyevich was living with one of his bodyguards and her mother, he shot the man and they fled. Our search for him took us to a remote village, where we came across the old woman. Shukheyevich was gone, but this was proof of his recent presence. When she was arrested later, Daria Gusyak, the bodyguard, told us that she had pleaded with Shukheyevich not to shoot her mother when all three fled her house. Her mother had a wooden leg, and he feared she would be a burden to them in the getaway. So they had left her in the village.

Our ambush group remained at Daria's mother's house, and soon I was talking with a young attractive student from the medical institute in Lvov, Daria's niece, who had come to visit her relatives. She gave lectures on the dangers of Ukrainian nationalism as part of her Komsomol duties. During my friendly talk with her, in which I posed as an assistant to the local economic planning administration, I asked her if she had seen Daria recently. She said Daria was staying in the dormitory of her medical institute, occasionally going to the forestry institute to prepare for its entrance exams.

Our surveillance team quickly established Daria's regular routes to a village near Lvov, where she spent hours in the cooperative general store. We assumed Shukheyevich was there. Unfortunately, the young officers shadowing her on March 5, 1950, were not experienced, and they tried to flirt with her. When Lieutenant Revenko extended his hand, saying in Ukrainian that he wanted to make the acquaintance of a charming woman, she sensed the surveillance and shot him on the spot. She was seized, not by my security people but by local people responding to the crime.

My security men took her from her captors within a minute and brought her to the nearest local administrator, the village elder. I was there within half an hour and gave two orders: first, to spread rumors that the woman had shot herself, and the deaths were probably over a love affair; and second, for two men to remain with her while I, with my deputy, General Drozdov, and twenty men ran to the cooperative store to block its escape routes. We surrounded the building, and Drozdov demanded that Shukheyevich lay down his arms, guaranteeing his life on behalf of the Ukrainian socialist government. Automatic fire was the reply. Shukheyevich threw two hand grenades and, accompanied by two women, all armed, attempted to break out. In the combat Shukheyevich and two of our officers were killed.

The organized guerrilla resistance in Western Ukraine collapsed after his death. We soon learned that he had created a dangerous underground network. Six months earlier, in June 1949, Daria, armed with false papers and explosives, had lived for two weeks in the Metropol Hotel in Moscow and patrolled Red Square looking for targets. The archives and records of the Bandera movement were smuggled by the nationalists from Lvov to Leningrad and hidden in the department of archive manuscripts.

The end of the Ukrainian escapade occurred a year later. Ilarion Kamazuk, an MGB operator under my command, and I planted an agent in the surviving Bandera group that made its way from the Ukraine to Czechoslovakia and then to Germany. British intelligence picked them up and carried them to England for training. Our man was introduced to Bandera as an activist close to Shukheyevich. Our agent maintained contact with us while he was in Munich with Bandera, but when they went to England we decided not to risk approaching him. Bandera was concerned with the lack of radio communications with Shukheyevich and was sending his assistant, the chief of Ukrainian guerrilla security service, Eugene Matviyeko, to the Ukraine to restore the movement and to learn the fate of Shukheyevich. Our man's only order while he was in England was to mail a coded postcard to an address in Germany informing us of the Matviyeko group's tentative route back to the Ukraine. He revealed their planned landing near Rovno in Podolia. Special instructions were given to our air defense command not to attack the British plane that was flying from Malta carrying Matviyeko and his team to be parachuted into the Ukraine.[12] We not only wanted to protect our own man, who was with them, we wanted to take them alive.

They were met cordially at a safe apartment by agents working under Raikhman disguised as their local contacts. After enjoying a heavily drugged Ukrainian feast, they peacefully went to sleep and woke up in the internal jail of the Kiev MGB.

In May 1951, now back in Moscow, I was awakened at about three in the morning by a telephone call from Abakumov's secretary and summoned to his office. He and Yevgeni Petrovich Pitovranov, deputy minister of security and chief of counterintelligence, were interrogating Matviyeko. At first I was the interpreter for them, because Matviyeko spoke only in the Western Ukrainian language. That lasted for two hours, and then Abakumov ordered me to work with Matviyeko.

I worked with him for about a month, without using classic interrogation methods. We talked in the office of the director of the internal jail, where Matviyeko watched television. He was surprised when he saw a performance by the Ukrainian opera theater of *Bogdan Chmelnitzky*, about the founder of the Ukrainian national army in the seven-

12. Sudoplatov adds: "About once a month during the late forties and early fifties American and British planes violated our air space; in most cases they were attacked by our fighter planes, and both sides suffered heavy losses in those dogfights. I have no knowledge of any American or British pilots taken prisoner when their planes were shot down over Soviet or neutral territory."

teenth century. The opera was staged in Moscow by Ukrainian artists for a festival called A Decade of Ukrainian Arts. In Poland and in Western Ukraine, Matviyeko had never attended a performance of Ukrainian opera with classic singing in the native language. It was unbelievable for him, and to reassure him that it was not a hoax I took him with an escort to the Ukrainian festival.

After a month of our conversations, he realized that except for the names of some secondary agents, there was nothing we didn't know about Ukrainian emigrant organizations and the Bandera movement. He was taken aback by my recital to him of the biographies of all their leaders, bitter conflicts between them, and details of their lives. I assured him I had no desire to turn him into an agent; for us, I explained, the most important thing was to stop armed confrontation, to stop the carnage inevitable in a guerrilla war. With the sanction of Abakumov, I telephoned Melnikov, first secretary of the Ukrainian Communist party, who succeeded Khrushchev in Kiev, and asked him to receive Matviyeko in Kiev. Melnikov would show him that the Ukraine, and Western Ukraine in particular, were not occupied zones and that citizens were leading a normal life there and didn't want this endless bloodletting.

I didn't meet Matviyeko again; he arrived in Kiev, where he was put under house arrest but was given the chance to move around. The same opportunity to see city life was provided for him in Lvov, where he was housed in an MGB villa. From there he escaped. What an uproar in Kiev and in Moscow! An all-union search was announced. The minister of state security of the Ukraine, future GRU director Petr Ivashutin, immediately ordered the arrest of Matviyeko's handlers. He had casually said goodbye to the soldier on duty at the gate of the villa, who had become accustomed to seeing him come and go accompanied by security officers during the previous ten days, and didn't stop him from going out alone. Three days later Matviyeko turned himself in to the Lvov security agency.

During that time he went into hiding in an apartment of an old acquaintance who had nothing to do with the Bandera movement, claiming that he merely wanted to stay for a week on business from Moscow. He tried Bandera safe apartments and contacts in Lvov that he had not told me about in the course of my interrogations and were not known to the members of his team. To his dismay, this Bandera network was not functioning; two addresses were wrong, and the contacts he thought he had did not exist. They were part of the inflated success of the local movement reported to the exile headquarters in

London and Munich. He was a good enough intelligence operator to perceive that the remaining safe apartments were already under MGB surveillance and were allowed to continue operating as traps for unwary visitors from abroad.

Under these circumstances, he declared his surrender to the local Ukrainian authorities and at a press conference staged by the Ukrainian Communist government denounced the Bandera movement. He used his authority to appeal for national reconciliation. He began a new life as an accountant, married, had three children, and died peacefully in 1974.

Matviyeko's story has new relevance now with the proclamation of Ukrainian independence. In the West it is not realized that after the Bolshevik Revolution, Ukraine received a certain autonomy within the Soviet Union that went further than any sovereignty it had ever enjoyed under Austrian, Polish, or czarist rule. Unlike those in other republics, Ukrainian Communist rulers were always regarded in Moscow as influential junior partners, and cooperation with the enormous republic was considered crucial to the stability of the entire state. That is why the Ukraine retained all the attributes of an independent state: education in the native language, traditional arts and literature, its own Politburo (which was enjoyed by no other republic), its own membership in the United Nations, all of which were unthinkable under other dominations. The Ukraine had never been an independent state, but I still think of myself as a Ukrainian who contributed to the buildup of this partnership within the union. The Ukraine's strength within the union was the prelude to its ability to become an independent state after the collapse of the Soviet Union.

In 1946 the Kurdish leader Mullah Mustafa Barzani and his rebel tribes broke through the Iranian border and entered Azerbaijan. They had been ambushed by the shah's forces and abandoned by British and American supporters. Barzani's task force contained two thousand men with small arms and artillery, accompanied by a thousand family members. The Soviet government first interned them in a camp, where I went to meet Barzani. Abakumov sent me to Baku in 1947 with instructions to offer Barzani political asylum for both troops and families, with temporary settlement in rural Uzbekistan not far from Tashkent. I was presented to Barzani as Matveyev, deputy director of TASS and a spokesman for the Soviet government.

It was the first time I had met a real feudal lord. Barzani gave the impression of being a shrewd politician and military commander. He noted that during the eighty uprisings by the Kurds against Persian, Iraqi, and Turkish rule in the past hundred years, they had applied for help to Russia sixty times and always received some support in arms and ammunition. Therefore, it was natural for them to ask us for assistance in this bitter period when the Kurdish democratic republic was crushed by forces of the shah of Iran, Mohammad Reza Pahlavi.

Barzani's relatives were lured by the shah for negotiations and were hanged by him. Therefore, when the shah invited Barzani, he replied that he would go to Tehran for negotiations only if the shah sent members of his family as hostages to Barzani's headquarters. While preliminary contacts with the shah were under way, Barzani maneuvered the bulk of his forces into the Soviet Union. We were interested in using the Kurds in a campaign to destabilize Western influence in the Middle East. We agreed that Barzani and some of his officers would attend Soviet military academies, and that their settlement in Central Asia would be only a pause in their trek, a time for preparations to liberate Kurdistan in a future armed struggle with the Iraqi and Iranian governments.

Abakumov forbade me to inform the local Communist party boss M. Bagirov about the content of my negotiations with Barzani and especially Stalin's agreement to provide military training. Some of Barzani's men moved from Azerbaijan to Armenia and set up a Kurdish radio broadcasting service.

I returned to Moscow, and Barzani accompanied his disarmed troops and their families to Uzbekistan. Five years later, in March 1952, I was sent to Uzbekistan to meet Barzani near Tashkent, where they had settled. Barzani was displeased with his treatment by local authorities and demanded intervention from the central government in Moscow to resolve his problems. He wanted to preserve autonomous rule over his three thousand tribespeople, who were settled in collective farms around Tashkent. Barzani feared he would lose control.

Our meeting took place at a government dacha. I was accompanied by Major Nikolai Zemskov, my interpreter, who spoke fluent English, as did Barzani. In our second encounter, Barzani described English and American officials who gave bribes to Kurdish nationalists to win their allegiance. He also disclosed his contacts with British intelligence agents who wanted to use his men to influence events in Iraq, Iran, and Turkey.

My plan for the Kurds, endorsed by Minister of State Security Ignatiev, was to train a Kurdish brigade of fifteen hundred men in sabotage techniques so they could overthrow the government of Nuri Said in Baghdad. Such an operation would seriously undermine the prevailing British influence in Iraq. The Kurds also fit into my plans of controlling strategic oil supplies to Europe and the United States from the Middle East. They could slow the flow of oil by destroying pipelines from Iraq and Iran.

Barzani agreed to participate in a political alliance with the Soviet government in return for our full support to an independent Kurdish republic carved from the borderlands of Turkey, Iran, and Iraq. He thought it would be more realistic to set up the Kurdish republic in northern Iraq; the Kurdish regions in Iran and Turkey should be granted autonomy and aligned with the Kurdish republic.

I told Barzani I had no instructions to discuss the details of such an agreement, but we were ready for him to establish a Kurdish government-in-exile. For that purpose my companion Nikolai Manchka, an assistant to Boris Ponomarev, the director of the international department of the Central Committee, offered his assistance in setting up the Democratic Party of Kurdistan in an office of a collective farm ten miles from Tashkent. Manchka explained to Barzani how the municipal clerks of the new Kurdish administration should be subordinated to the central committee of the new party to be chaired by Barzani.

I did not interfere in that conversation, but listened attentively. When the conversation ended two hours later, it was clear to me that the plan was one of the ideological fantasies created in the Central Committee offices on Staraya Ploshchad. Barzani invited me to meet with officers of his staff. We entered a room in which thirty people stood at attention. When we appeared, all of them fell to their knees and crawled toward Barzani, begging his permission to touch and kiss the hem of his gown and his boots. All illusions of democratic Kurdistan evaporated from my mind.

In April 1952, Barzani settled down near Tashkent, surrounded by his family and his countrymen in a large collective farm. When I returned to Moscow with Manchka, it was decided that the Kurds would be given the status of an autonomous area. The Ministry of State Security would provide them military training and help them maintain contacts with their countrymen abroad. Our attempt to infiltrate Barzani's team with our agents and recruit some Kurds was effectively thwarted by Barzani's security service. Zemskov, who had experience dealing with Kurds in Iran, managed to recruit one minor officer while he studied in our military academy, but on his return to Tashkent he disappeared without leaving a trace. We could never contact him or find him. We assumed he was liquidated.

The Kurdish issue involved me for the first time in bureaucratic procedures that required a Politburo decision. Ignatiev ordered me to remain in Manchka's office until the document laying out our proposals on the issue was agreed upon. As a rule, Ignatiev was very polite and attentive, but when I told him I had an urgent meeting with Barzani at his hotel in Moscow, Ignatiev indignantly reproached me for not grasping the political importance of obtaining speedy endorsement from the Central Committee. Ignatiev accompanied Manchka and me to visit Molotov and Vyshinsky to get them to sign the draft. For the first time in all my experience with Molotov and Vyshinsky, both appeared to be old, passive, and exhausted men, but they were persistent in deleting one paragraph of the document. They wanted no reference to the obligations of the Ministry of Foreign Affairs concerning negotiations on the Kurdish issue. They also urged that the matter should be considered at the Politburo as one raised by the Ministry of Security, not as a joint proposal by the Ministry of Foreign Affairs and the Ministry of Security. With these comments in mind, and accompanied by a bodyguard who carried the draft decisions in his briefcase, I suggested to Manchka that we return to my office at Lubyanka to type the final version of the document. Ignatiev agreed.

Then the comedy began. We presented the draft of the decision to Ignatiev and he approved it. What was of more importance to him was the formal letter of transmission of the document, which had to be sent for concurrence to members of the Politburo. Ignatiev three times ordered me and the typist to change the order of the names of the members of the Politburo to whom the document was to be submitted. He asked Manchka whether to circulate the list in alphabetical order or to list members of the external commission of the Politburo first. In this case Comrade Khrushchev should be on the list before Bulganin. Should Comrade Beria be listed before Comrade Malenkov? These and other unheard of nuances astounded me, but Manchka appeared to be an expert in compiling lists and offered his advice to Ignatiev. The typists remained puzzled by the need to redo the documents, which contained no changes except the order of the names of Politburo members.

In the spring of 1953, there was a serious breach of security in my meetings with Barzani. He was undergoing a course of training in a military academy in Moscow at which I was also studying. One day he noticed me there dressed in my lieutenant general's uniform. He winked at me and through a young lieutenant accompanying him as an interpreter said, "I am glad to deal with a representative of the Soviet government who holds high military rank." I wished him every success in passing his exams.

The last time I saw Barzani was on the eve of my arrest. He saw me walking on Gorky Street and was anxious to chat about his problems, but I preferred to avoid him, and before he could reach me I got lost in the crowd.

Barzani was intelligent enough to understand that the future of the Kurds depended on their capacity to manipulate the interests of the superpowers in the Middle East. In retrospect it is clear that the superpowers had no interest in a just solution of the Kurdish problem. The fate of Kurdistan was never regarded in the Kremlin — or in London or Washington — to be a humanitarian issue; access to the oil fields in Kurdistan appeared to be the decisive motive in the cynical policy of both the East and the West. Mikhail Suslov, who succeeded me in working with Barzani, promised all-out support for Kurdish autonomy for overthrowing Nuri Said in Iraq, but in the 1970s we abandoned the Kurds in their struggle. The Americans also promised him support in overthrowing the regime in Baghdad, but withheld it at the critical moment. The Kurds were tragically manipulated.

In the 1950s the purpose of my involvement in Kurdish affairs was to take advantage of the Kurdish movement in the confrontation of the Cold War. For us the setting up of the republic of Kurdistan was an attractive instrument for pursuing our policy in the Middle East. It was a way of undermining British and American interests and positions there. However, the balance of forces was not in our favor.

In the 1960s, when Nuri Said's government was overthrown in a military coup with our support, the Soviet Union acquired allies in the area who were far more important for our geopolitical considerations than the Kurds. The tragedy of Barzani and the Kurdish people is that the interests of the East and the West — and to a certain extent of the Arab States and Iran — are to preserve the Kurds as a deterrent force in the region, a pawn in the interregional struggle among Turkey, Iraq, and Iran. In the 1950s the Kurds were Russia's only allies in the area, but later our strategic alliances with Iraq and Syria became the dominant factor in Middle East politics. A reasonable solution for the Kurds would be international guarantees of limited autonomy. No one in the West or the Arabic states wants the Kurds to control the Mosul oil fields in an independent Kurdish republic.

When I was in jail, I wrote proposals for contacting Barzani when the situation in the Middle East was aggravated in 1963. I was informed that my proposals were accepted, and the Kurds were supplied with ammunition and weapons to defend their areas against punishment expeditions by the Iraqi army. However, our attempts to turn the Kurds into our strategic ally to control who ruled Iraq ended in failure.

RAOUL WALLENBERG, LAB X, AND OTHER SPECIAL TASKS

There are unsolved mysteries involving the Wallenberg family of Sweden. The best known is the case of diplomat Raoul Wallenberg, who was arrested by Soviet military counterintelligence, SMERSH, in 1945 in Budapest and, I believe, executed secretly in Lubyanka jail in 1947. The Wallenberg family had clandestine contacts with representatives of the Soviet government from the beginning of 1944, and while I was not involved with Raoul Wallenberg, I was aware of his family's contribution to our making peace with Finland. The pattern of military counterintelligence reports on Raoul Wallenberg and the family's connection made him a candidate for recruitment. His arrest, interrogation, and death in Lubyanka all fit the pattern of a recruitment effort gone bad. Fear that the attempt to recruit him would be exposed if Wallenberg were released led to his elimination as an unwanted witness.

The Wallenbergs' relationship with the Soviet Union started in 1944, when our rezidentura in Stockholm was instructed to look for influential figures in Sweden who might act as intermediaries between the Soviet and Finnish governments to facilitate the signing of a separate peace treaty between Finland and the Soviet Union. Stalin was concerned that Finland, a German ally since 1941, would sign a peace treaty with the Americans that would not guarantee Soviet interests in the Baltic area; the Americans would not allow us to occupy Finland. In fact, we did not need to occupy Finland; we could keep it neutral through our agents of influence in all of the major Finnish political parties. These agents cooperated with us in return for a guarantee of the preservation of a neutral Finnish role in Europe — a bridge between the Communist and capitalist worlds. This is what came to be known as Finlandization in the 1970s and 1980s.

I remember how in 1938, before the first Soviet-Finnish war, the Winter War, Stalin authorized the transfer of $500,000 to the Finnish Small Farmers party to strengthen a campaign for peaceful settlement with Russia. My good friend Colonel Rybkin, first secretary of the Soviet mission in Finland before the war under the name Yatsev, arranged that transfer. Stalin personally instructed him how to deal with NKVD agents of influence in Finland.

During the war years, Rybkin and his wife were rezidents in Stockholm. Their primary task was to maintain contact with the Red Orchestra network in Germany through Swedish outposts. Rybkin's wife is known in Russia as a writer of children's books, under her maiden name, Zoya Vozkresenskaya. She was known in Stockholm and in Moscow diplomatic circles as Zoya Yatseva. A classic Russian beauty, she spoke German and Finnish fluently.

Rybkin, a tall, well-built man, had a sense of humor and was a good storyteller. He and Zoya were popular on the diplomatic circuit, where one of their missions was to watch for German overtures for a separate peace deal with the United States and Britain without Soviet participation. They were also active in clandestine economic operations. In 1942 Rybkin arranged through an agent, the popular Swedish actor and satirist Karl Earhardt, a deal to supply the Soviet Union with high-tensile steel for the aviation industry. We desperately needed that steel because our metallurgical plants were seized by the Germans in 1941 and our supplies from Siberia were unreliable. The deal was a gross violation of Swedish neutrality, but the Enskilda Bank, controlled by the Wallenberg family, profited handsomely from the exchange of the steel for Russian platinum.[1]

The Wallenberg family was interested in a peaceful Soviet-Finnish settlement because of its capital investments in Finland. Marcus

1. Zoya Vozkresenskaya (Rybkina) memoirs, *Teper Ya Mogu Skazat Pravdu* (*Now I Can Tell the Truth*) (Moscow: Respublica Izdatelzvo, 1993), p. 102, recounts this episode, which is contained in the Wallenberg family file in the KGB archives.

Wallenberg (Raoul's uncle) maintained friendly contacts with Karl Earhardt, and the Center suggested that Earhardt should introduce Zoya to Marcus at a cocktail party.

Zoya charmed Marcus Wallenberg, and they agreed to meet again at a luxurious hotel owned by the Wallenbergs outside Stockholm at Saltsjobaden. Zoya spent a weekend with Marcus Wallenberg planning how to bring together Soviet and Finnish diplomats so that the terms of a separate peace treaty could be discussed. What was important, she said, was that Wallenberg convey to the Finns that the Soviet side would guarantee real neutrality for Finland with a quid pro quo of a limited Soviet military presence in the Finnish Baltic ports in the area of Porkkala.

It took only a week for Marcus Wallenberg to arrange Zoya's first meeting, in February 1944, with the Finnish ambassador to Stockholm, Juho Kusti Paasikivi, who later became president of Finland.[2] Alexandra Kolontai, the Soviet ambassador to Sweden and our first woman diplomat, joined the talks under instructions from Stalin and Molotov. The consultations continued throughout the summer of 1944, and on September 4 a treaty was concluded. TASS reported that the government of Finland had severed its alliance with Hitler and signed an armistice agreement with the Soviet Union.[3]

Thus the detention of Raoul Wallenberg in Budapest in 1945 was not accidental. Stalin and Molotov wanted to blackmail the Wallenberg family; they wanted to use its connections for favorable dealings with the West. In 1945 the Soviet leadership was playing with the "Jewish issue," cynically spreading rumors that an autonomous Jewish republic would be established in the Crimea, not Palestine, in order to mollify our British ally. I received oral instructions from Beria to plant such rumors in the talks I had with American ambassador Averell Harriman when I met with him in 1945 under the cover name Matveyev. My speculations are that Stalin wanted Wallenberg recruited to assist in raising the international capital that Stalin hoped to attract for postwar economic reconstruction, using the bait of a Jewish homeland.

At the time of his arrest by the Red Army in Budapest, Raoul Wallenberg was deeply involved in the evacuation of Jews from Ger-

2. In 1946, succeeding Carl Gustaf Mannerheim.

3. The American government was informed of the secret contacts between the Wallenberg family and Soviet officials in a note to the State Department from the Soviet Embassy in Washington, February 19, 1944. See *Documents of Soviet-American Relations 1941–1945* (Moscow: Politizdat, 1985), vol. 22, pp. 41–42.

many and Hungary to Palestine. We knew he had a heroic image among world Jewish leaders. Wallenberg could not have been detained without direct orders from Moscow. If he was arrested accidentally, as might occur during the fierce fighting in Budapest, local SMERSH authorities were bound to report the incident to Moscow. Now it is known that Nikolai Bulganin, then the deputy commissar of defense, signed the order to detain Wallenberg in Hungary in 1945, and passed it on to Abakumov, head of SMERSH.

After nearly half a century of fruitless investigations by KGB officials and journalists, the file on Wallenberg is now said to have mysteriously vanished. One of my former colleagues, Lieutenant General Aleksandr Belkin, then deputy head of SMERSH, saw the files before they disappeared. He reported that in 1945 all rezidenturas of SMERSH received an *orientirovka* (briefing) identifying Wallenberg as an established asset of German, American, and British intelligence. The instructions were to continuously report Wallenberg's movements to Moscow and to assess and study his contacts with German authorities, both national and local.[4]

I recall that Wallenberg's work in Hungary was given a dubious cast by agent reports from Kutuzov, a Russian émigré in Budapest, a relative of Prince Kutuzov, who had been recruited by us in the 1920s. He worked in the Red Cross mission in Budapest and observed Raoul Wallenberg's movements. Kutuzov reported that Wallenberg was collaborating with German intelligence. In the high-risk business of freeing Jews, it was necessary for Wallenberg to have frequent negotiations with German security officials. Kutuzov's interpretation was that Wallenberg was playing a double game. Thus Wallenberg had left himself open to forced recruitment as our agent: join us or be exposed as a German agent. This was how the plan must have been formulated to recruit Raoul Wallenberg and through him promote the cooperation of his family with Soviet representatives in Scandinavia.

Before he was taken to see the Soviet authorities outside Budapest in January 1945, Wallenberg is reported to have said to a friend, "I'm not sure if I'm going as their guest or their prisoner." Wallenberg was brought to Moscow under guard, but he traveled in a luxury railroad

---

4. Wallenberg was chosen to save Jews in Hungary by the American representative of the War Refugee Board in Stockholm, Iver Iksen, and the chief rabbi of Stockholm, Dr. Marcus Ehrenpreis. He was provided with funds from the American Jewish Joint Distribution Committee to fulfill his task when he arrived in Budapest in July 1944.

car and was treated as a guest.[5] Kutuzov was brought back to Moscow separately. However, he was released and in 1952 allowed to return to the West. He settled in Ireland, where he died in 1967.

Pitovranov, deputy minister of security in those years, told me that Wallenberg's guards provided him with special food from the dining car on the train from Budapest. When he arrived in Moscow, he was kept in the special block of the internal jail reserved for very important persons. He was considered to be a guest, but not allowed on the street to talk to people as he wished.

An effort was made to develop him as an agent, to operate either with his family or with the Swedish government. His interrogators may have bullied him with charges that he was a Gestapo informer or American agent, but that was not the intention from the top. The goal was to recruit him.

It is clear from the archive materials that Wallenberg was held in two jails in Moscow, Lefortovo prison and the internal jail of the Lubyanka. KGB veterans remember that after tough interrogations in Lefortovo, Wallenberg was moved to the second block of the internal jail on Lubyanka Street, where VIPs and foreigners were held who were scheduled for either recruitment or liquidation. Block two of the internal jail gave the appearance of a hotel. The rooms were not cells in the usual sense; they had high ceilings and were equipped with furniture and conveniences. Food was brought there from the NKVD canteen and restaurant, which was far superior to prison fare.[6] During Stalin's reign this was a dangerous place; the office of the Kommandatura of the NKVD, where all death sentences were carried out, was located in the internal jail.

Behind this building, on Varsonofyevsky Lane, and closely linked to the Kommandatura, was the toxicological laboratory. In my time this laboratory was called LAB X in official documents. Its director, Professor Grigori Moiseyevich Maironovsky, was a leading biological scientist who had worked on the impact of lethal gases and the use of poisons in

---

5. Kati Marton, *Wallenberg* (New York: Random House, 1982), p. 158, notes that when Wallenberg arrived in Moscow he was taken to see the newly completed Moscow Metro, the city's prized subway system.

6. Igor Prelin, former deputy director of the KGB press office, who interviewed P. A. Sudoplatov in 1992, described the circumstances and conditions of prisoners held in the Kommandatura section.

combatting malignant tumors. Maironovsky was highly respected in medical circles, but he became a tragic figure.

In 1937 Maironovsky's research group at the Institute of Biochemistry was transferred to the jurisdiction of the NKVD. He became chief of the toxicological research group, subordinated directly to the director of the technical warfare department. They worked for the Kommandatura Service, responsible for guarding NKVD buildings, internal security, and carrying out executions. The research activities of his group had a legal status endorsed by the minister of security, and were governed by him or his first deputy. Yet alongside his research work, Maironovsky carried out death sentences on the direct orders of ministers and commissars of security Beria, Yezhov, and Merkulov. From 1937 until 1947, Maironovsky and his subordinates were used to carry out death sentences and secret liquidations with their poisons. There were special passes into the premises of the laboratory, and even top-level personnel of NKVD had no access or right to enter their building in the Kommandatura compound.

Wallenberg was interrogated by officers of military counterintelligence, primarily Lieutenant Colonel Dmitri Koppelyansky, fluent in German, who was purged from the security service in 1951 because of his Jewish origin. Although Koppelyansky's involvement is stated in the documents, he has denied his role in the case, insisting that he does not remember Wallenberg. However, he is listed in the jail's records as being responsible for interrogating Wallenberg, and he was the officer who called Wallenberg from his cell to his office just one day before his death. Koppelyansky vigorously denies his involvement because he fears to be associated in any way with the Kommandatura and its top-secret cell.

By early July 1947 Wallenberg's case was stalled. Wallenberg had refused to cooperate and he was eliminated, at the same time that the leadership continued to tell the Swedes that they knew nothing of his fate.

Probably, Wallenberg was taken to a supersecret cell known as the *spetsialnie laboratornaya kamera* in the commandant's section of the ministry, a location monitored personally by Maironovsky as chief of the toxicological laboratory.

My best estimate is that Wallenberg was killed by Maironovsky, who was ordered to inject him with poison under the guise of medical treatment. According to witnesses who told me the story, Wallenberg was kept in the second block of the jail, where medical checkups and injections were routine for prisoners. One of the reasons I believe Wallenberg was poisoned is that his body was cremated without an autopsy, under the direct order of Minister of Security Abakumov. An autopsy would have revealed the exact nature of his death. The regulations were that those executed under special government decisions were cremated without autopsy at the Donskoi cemetery crematorium and their ashes buried in a common grave. The authorities have reluctantly admitted that such prominent figures as Yakir, Tukhachevsky, Uborevich, Meyerhold, and others were dispatched in this manner.[7] Since Donskoi crematorium was the only one in Moscow until 1965, it is likely that the ashes of Wallenberg, Yezhov, and Beria are buried in the same common grave.

The record book of all operations undertaken by Maironovsky and his subordinates, which was placed in a sealed envelope marked top secret after the arrest of Beria and sent directly to a special section of the Politburo secretariat, has never been seen again. There is no record of its being removed to another place. There are two witnesses who testified that this top-secret book, in its special envelope, was taken from Lubyanka by Malenkov's chief assistant, Dmitri Sukhanov, who is still alive. I never read the contents, but I saw the envelope, sealed with red wax and marked: "Do Not Open Without the Approval of the Minister." I understood that this record book contained the names of victims, dates of executions, and names of those who carried out the orders to eliminate unwanted persons by poisonous injection. I believe these records still exist.

Some documents have come to light. In June 1993, *Izvestia* published an article by journalist Ella Maxsimova titled, "Wallenberg Is Dead. Unfortunately, There Is Sufficient Proof."[8] In it new details are revealed. She cites documents confirming Wallenberg's stay in Lubyanka and Lefortovo prisons and a memorandum to Molotov discussing the fate of Wallenberg. Molotov, as deputy prime minister and head of the Committee of Information, gave the order for Wallenberg's liquidation. This follows from the letter of Andrei Vyshinsky, who was deputy minister of foreign affairs in this period. What is concealed is that he was also the acting head of the Committee of Information, the coordinating and decision-making body for the intelligence and security agencies.

7. Pyotr Yakir was commander of the Kiev military district before his execution in 1937. I. P. Uborevich was commander of the Byelorussian military district.

8. *Izvestia*, June 3, 1993, p. 5.

This highly significant letter from Vyshinsky to Molotov, dated May 14, 1947, registered number 312-B, signed on May 13, 1947, has been declassified from its top-secret classification. There are no titles on the document, clearly indicating it is an internal memorandum.

To Comrade V. Molotov:

At the end of 1944 the Swedes addressed to the People's Commissariat of Foreign Affairs of the USSR a request to take under its protection the first secretary of the Swedish Mission in Budapest, Raoul Wallenberg. On January 16, (1945) the mission was informed that Wallenberg was found and was taken under protection by Soviet military authorities. On April 24, 1945, the Swedes informed the People's Commissariat of the USSR that among members of their mission who left Budapest, Wallenberg was missing and asked us to locate him. These requests from the Swedish side then were repeated several times both in written form (eight notes) and in oral form (five meetings). On June 15, 1946, the former Swedish Ambassador to the Soviet Union Soderblom was received by Comrade Stalin and asked Comrade Stalin to issue instructions to establish the fate of Raoul Wallenberg.

We several times in oral and written form channeled our requests in 1945 and 1946 to SMERSH and later to the Ministry of State Security for clarification on the fate and whereabouts of Wallenberg. As a result of this, only in February of this year in his talk with Comrade Novikov did Comrade Fedotov[9] inform us that Wallenberg was now at the disposal of the Ministry of State Security and promise to report to you personally on further undertakings of the Ministry of State Security in this case.

As the case of Wallenberg to the present day remains without progress, I request you to direct Comrade Abakumov to submit a summary of the substance of the case and suggestions for liquidation.

The *Izvestia* article raises a question of semantics. The last words of Vyshinsky's letter, *lekvderovat delo,* can mean both "his liquida-

9. K. I. Novikov, of the Ministry of Foreign Affairs, and Peter Fedotov, Molotov's deputy on the Committee of Information and chief of counterintelligence in the MGB.

tion" — that is, Wallenberg's — or "liquidation of this case." The question the article posed is, could Vyshinsky have meant to finish the case that was going nowhere by releasing Wallenberg, or is the use of the word "liquidation" clear enough that he meant physical extinction of the person? Could there have been a tragic misinterpretation of the order?

To me it is clear that this was not a suggestion to close the case, but one to eliminate Wallenberg. The term "liquidation" in such top-secret documents meant physical elimination. Wallenberg had become an unwanted witness, which is clearly implied by Vyshinsky.

The document sent to Stalin and Molotov in 1947 on the fate of Isaac Oggins, an American working for us, contained similar phrasing when Abakumov proposed to eliminate Oggins with no trace of a violent death.

Molotov's comment on the Wallenberg letter is also significant. It is typed in the left-hand corner: "Comrade Abakumov: Report to me. Molotov, May 18, 1947."

This comment was an order to Abakumov to submit a proposal on how Wallenberg was to be liquidated. This was the usual procedure. After the proposal was made and considered, Stalin or Molotov would give oral approval, and Abakumov, the minister, would note in his own handwriting on the proposal "Consent given by Comrade Stalin" — or, in this case, "by Comrade Molotov."

Wallenberg died on July 17, 1947, according to official Soviet documents, but it was not until one month later, on August 18, 1947, that Vyshinsky informed the Swedish ambassador in Moscow that the Soviet government had no information on Wallenberg's fate and that there was no way he could have been detained by Soviet authorities; he had probably perished in Budapest.

Also in June 1993, *Izvestia* for the first time published in full the memorandum from the Soviet government to the Swedish government on the fate of Wallenberg. The draft was compiled by the Ministry of Foreign Affairs and the KGB on January 12, 1957. At that time Dmitri Trofimovich Shepilov was foreign minister and Ivan Aleksandrovich Serov was head of the KGB. The text:

> In accordance with the decision of the Central Committee of the CPSU on May 3, 1956, the Ministry of Foreign Affairs and KGB submit the draft of the answer to the government of Sweden on the question of the Swedish diplomat Wallenberg.

The draft of the decision is attached. For your consideration, (signed) Shepilov and Serov.

Draft aide-mémoire:

In accordance with the request of the government of Sweden, the Soviet government issued instructions to competent Soviet institutions to undertake consideration and verification of materials relating to Raoul Wallenberg received from the Swedish side in the course of Soviet-Swedish negotiations in Moscow in March and April 1956, and in May 1956.

In the process of consideration and verification of these materials the Soviet institutions undertook thorough search of the archives relating to prisoners and in the investigation files, including archives of the Lefortovo and Lubyanka prisons in Moscow and the prison in the city of Vladimir.

However, as a result of these measures no data were found containing information on Wallenberg's stay in the Soviet Union. It was established that no one from the prisons who was questioned knew anything about the person under the name of Wallenberg.

In view of that, competent Soviet authorities undertook a check of all lists of archive documents of auxiliary services in the above-mentioned prisons. [There is a handwritten note that adds several prisons.] As a result of that check, in the archive documents of the medical service of the Lubyanka jail, there was established the handwritten report addressed to the former minister of state security of the USSR Abakumov, which was written by the chief of the medical service of this jail, A. L. Smoltsov, with the following contents:

"I report that prisoner Wallenberg, known to you, unexpectedly died tonight in his cell, presumably from myocardial infarction. In view of your personal instructions on personal supervision of Wallenberg, I request your instructions to whom to entrust the autopsy of the body to determine the cause of death.

signed: Colonel of Medical Service

Smoltsov, July 17, 1947

signed: Chief of Medical Section of the prison"

On this report is a handwritten notation by Smoltsov: "Reported personally to Minister [Abakumov]. The order: cremate the body without an autopsy. July 17, 1947." . . .

The Soviet government sincerely expresses its sorrow on this occurrence and expresses its deep condolences to the government of Sweden and the relatives of Raoul Wallenberg.

Still missing is the mysterious decision of May 3, 1956, on the Wallenberg case by the Central Committee of the CPSU to undertake verification of the case. I believe that at that time they were beginning to destroy documents, because Bulganin and Molotov were still in power and the case directly involved Bulganin, who had his name on the arrest order for Wallenberg.

It was not until February 1957 that the death of Wallenberg in 1947 of a heart attack was officially announced by Deputy Foreign Minister Andrei Gromyko. At that time, Bulganin, who had ordered Wallenberg's arrest in 1945, was the prime minister. Gromyko could not announce the death of Wallenberg without the consent of the Politburo. Thus, there should be a record of the Politburo decision in several files. From my knowledge, File 6 in the KGB archives should contain a secret summary reporting the main facts of Wallenberg's stay in Soviet jails.[10] Khrushchev and his subordinates announced that Raoul Wallenberg was arrested unlawfully by Minister of State Security Abakumov, a criminal, and that he died in detention due to heart failure. Abakumov had been executed for committing this crime, among others, they said. This was a cynical lie, because Abakumov was never accused of detaining Wallenberg. That is clear from Abakumov's indictment, which was recently published in Moscow. Far more interesting is the absence of the report by KGB head Serov to Khrushchev on what really happened to Wallenberg, the secret summary that would have to have been written before Gromyko's statement could be approved by the Politburo.

The last order to investigate the Wallenberg case was given by President Gorbachev to KGB chief Vadim Bakatin in August 1991. The investigation revealed that Wallenberg died in prison and that his file was missing. This investigation was supervised by Professor Vyacheslav Nikonov, the chief of Bakatin's secretariat and grandson of Foreign Minister Molotov. Somewhere in the Ministry of Security there must be a letter from Abakumov to Molotov discussing Wallenberg's detention

10. File 6 in the KGB archives contains orders signed by the commissars and ministers of state security, and their correspondence with the Kremlin leadership.

by the organs of state security. Although the copy of this letter is missing from the KGB archives, it should be recorded with a code number in the book that registers all KGB letters to the government signed by a minister. Therefore, the letter can easily be traced in the Molotov section of the Presidential Archives. The next investigator must look for the letters from Abakumov to Stalin and Molotov that are registered in File 6 of the Central Operation Archives of the KGB. Once the date is established, the search should not prove difficult.

Ivan Serov, chairman of the KGB in 1957, would have written to Khrushchev, requesting permission to destroy Wallenberg's file. The reason for destroying this file is evident: in February 1957 Molotov was still an authoritative and powerful figure in the Soviet establishment, one of the leaders who naturally wanted to destroy evidence of their involvement in scandalous international incidents in the 1930s and 1940s. Serov's letter should be traceable in the Khrushchev section of the Presidential Archives, which I believe were inviolate.

Khrushchev certainly would have done that favor for Molotov; he must have ordered Serov to destroy Wallenberg's file in the KGB archives, but it is likely he kept that letter from Serov to incriminate Molotov later. I remember, after my arrest, how vaguely but persistently my interrogators asked what I knew about Molotov's involvement in secret deals with various prominent Western industrialists and diplomats. At that time I had no idea that these questions were not accidental.[11]

It is possible that a curious researcher will find a second letter from Serov to Khrushchev, in which he must have reported the destruction of KGB files explaining the liquidation of Wallenberg. Even the tightest cover-up cannot anticipate accidents. In April 1992 Wallenberg's diplomatic passport and other personal belongings were accidentally found by a KGB archivist technician who had nothing to do with attempts to reinvestigate the case. They were in an envelope that fell from a huge bundle of unsorted documents in a room that was formerly the main block of the NKVD Lubyanka jail.

The cover-up of Wallenberg's case is similar to efforts to hide the infamous Katyn affair. Aleksandr N. Shelepin, then chairman of the KGB, in

11. When Khrushchev visited Sweden in June 1964, Prime Minister Tage Erlander asked him for specific details about the fate of Wallenberg. Khrushchev blew up and said the Soviet government had given a full reply in 1957. "Do you think we are liars? I will return home immediately," Khrushchev threatened. The Swedish government backed off the search for Wallenberg.

1959 approached Khrushchev for permission to destroy all documentary evidence in the KGB archives that recorded direct instructions to eliminate Polish officer prisoners of war at Katyn Forest, near Smolensk. The revelation of Shelepin's request shows how the records have been pillaged. That such sensitive documents in the KGB archives were destroyed makes me believe that a similar trick was played with the Wallenberg file. However, it would be difficult even for a determined paper shredder to get rid of copies in all the repositories, especially Presidential Archives.

Shelepin's report about the destruction of files of the 21,857 Polish officers executed at Katyn and other prison camps in 1940 was revealed from the top-secret archives only in October 1992, together with Beria's letter to Stalin recommending that Polish officers be executed.[12] Now documents on Katyn have surfaced from the archives, but they are being released selectively.

Parts of the mystery still remain. The release of the documents by President Yeltsin to President Lech Walesa of Poland was incomplete and in the form of photocopies, not original documents. However, the Poles accepted the gesture as a measure of Soviet willingness to recognize Polish sovereignty. The documents released from the KGB archives do not disclose the planning and execution of this criminal operation. Even those active in recruiting Polish officers as agents, such as Vassili Zarubin, had no idea what was in store for the prisoners they did not

12. In a top-secret letter dated March 5, 1940 (see Appendix Five), Beria alleged that the Polish officers in the camps "are attempting to continue their counterrevolutionary activities" and should be tried before special tribunals, which would examine the cases "without summoning those detained and without bringing charges" and "apply to them the supreme penalty: shooting."

In the aftermath of the Molotov-Ribbentrop Pact, while Hitler and Stalin were dividing up spheres of domination in Eastern Poland and the Baltic States, thousands of Polish officers and civilians were interned by the Soviet army. Stalin and his Politburo wanted to decapitate the Polish elite and professional class, and they systematically executed nearly 26,000 prisoners. This was followed by the deportation of 1.2 million Polish civilians to Siberia and Central Asia. The mass graves of Polish officers executed at Katyn in 1940 were discovered in April 1943, and Stalin tried to place the blame for the massacre on the German Army. The Soviet Union denied guilt for Katyn until President Boris Yeltsin released the incriminating documents in October 1992.

On Polish television, October 20, 1992, President Lech Walesa called Yeltsin's action a "test of truth." For a detailed discussion on the issues involved between Yeltsin and Gorbachev and the internal Soviet power struggle, see Louisa Vinton, "The Katyn Documents: Politics and History," *RFE/RL Research Report*, vol. 2, no. 4 (January 22, 1993), pp. 19–31.

take away with them. At the time, I believed the official version, that camps with Polish prisoners fell into the hands of the Germans, who executed them. I was convinced of this by the publication of archive materials that showed some of the victims were shot with German ammunition. Later I thought that probably the officers were buried by the Germans in a common grave with Soviet victims of our prewar purges.

Mikhail Maklarsky, chief of the Byelorussian desk in the guerrilla warfare directorate under my command during the war years, although well known for his talkative character, never revealed to anybody that he was in charge of destroying the registration cards of Polish prisoners of war near Kharkov. Probably he knew about the fate of the Polish officers. I assume Leonid Raikhman knew of their fate, too, because he was in charge of negotiations with Polish authorities when the Polish army was formed in the Soviet Union in the autumn of 1941. In July 1941, a month after the German invasion of the USSR, Stalin amnestied all remaining Polish prisoners of war, who then joined the Polish army under General Anders.

Raikhman, who died in 1991, never revealed to me anything about his involvement with Katyn. I first heard hints that Polish officers were killed by us in 1988, from Major General Vyacheslav Y. Kevorkov, then deputy director of TASS.[13] He said that Valentin Falin, then director of the international department of the CPSU, had come under fire in the 1970s from Yuri Andropov, head of the KGB, because he showed interest in the Katyn affair and suggested the investigation be reopened. I was stunned by Kevorkov's remarks that the highest authority, meaning the Central Committee of the Communist party, was concerned that the truth of Stalin's extermination of the Polish officers might be revealed.[14]

When I was arrested in 1953, I was accused of administering poisons to hundreds of people who had been lured to special safe apartments and

13. Kevorkov is retired from the KGB but still works for TASS in Bonn and Vienna.

14. Among the Katyn documents released to the Polish government on October 14, 1992, were a report to the CPSU Central Committee by Falin dated March 6, 1989, and a joint memorandum by Falin, Foreign Minister Eduard Shevardnadze, and KGB chief Vladimir Kryuchkov dated March 22, 1989. These documents stress the need for resolving the Katyn problem and warn that "the Katyn problem has grown more acute." The March 22 memorandum recommended resolving the problem: "In all likelihood we will not be able to avoid explaining the tragic events of the past to the Polish leadership and Polish society. In this case, time is not our ally. It might be better to explain what really happened and who specifically is responsible for what happened

country houses. These mass murders of persons unwanted by Beria and his accomplices were allegedly concealed and later presented as accidental deaths. Despite these monstrous allegations, no names of my victims were stated in the indictment against me or in the court sentence, contrary to all elementary principles of criminal law. The absence of specific crimes and victims is not accidental, because my carrying out of so-called special tasks, the elimination of double agents and political opponents of Stalin, Molotov, and Khrushchev within the Soviet Union in 1946 and 1947, was done under the direct orders of the government. Beria had nothing to do with these operations. Abakumov, who actually gave the orders on behalf of the government, was not charged with responsibility for these specific cases, in which I indeed carried out the orders. These were extraordinarily important cases, and the facts justifying these executions were well known to the investigating teams and to the government.

In my indictment it is stated that I supervised the work of the top-secret toxicological laboratory, which experimented with poisons on prisoners sentenced to death from 1942 to 1946. I was cleared of that charge because the rules governing the laboratory were found in party and KGB archives; the laboratory was not controlled by me. I could not give orders to its director, Maironovsky, either to use poisons against anyone or to experiment with them.

---

and close the issue there. The costs of this course of action would be lower, in the final analysis, than the damage caused by our own inaction."

It was not until April 1990 that Mikhail Gorbachev acknowledged Soviet guilt, following a script suggested by Falin written at the end of February 1990.

"The following version seems to entail the lowest costs:

"Inform W. Jaruzelski [Poland's president] that, in a thorough review of the relevant archival resources, we did not find direct proof (orders, directives, and so forth) that would allow us to determine the exact date of and the specific culprits in the Katyn tragedy. Meanwhile, . . . indications were found that undermine the credibility of the N. Burdenko Report [the official Soviet version dating from 1944]. On the basis of these indications, the conclusion can be drawn that the death of the Polish officers in the Katyn region was the work of the NKVD and of Beria and Merkulov personally."

The release of the Katyn documents came as the result of fierce political infighting between Yeltsin and Gorbachev. Yeltsin used the release of the documents to make the point that Gorbachev had known of them since 1989 but had remained silent. The Poles chose to ignore the dispute between Gorbachev and Yeltsin. In an interview in October 1992 Walesa said, "What matters to me personally is not the moment Yeltsin chose for the action but the fact that he *did* it, radically changing the entire atmosphere surrounding our relations." Vinton, "The Katyn Documents."

In 1951 Maironovsky was arrested and charged with being part of the Zionist conspiracy to poison top Soviet leaders, including Stalin, in cooperation with Jewish doctors supposedly under the instructions of Abakumov and Eitingon. Mikhail Ryumin, the accuser and notorious anti-Semitic interrogator, extracted fantastic confessions from Maironovsky by beating him almost to death. When Ryumin, a deputy of Ignatiev, was dismissed by Stalin at the end of 1952, the Investigation Department was afraid to formulate the indictment in the way Ryumin had edited it because Maironovsky's testimony was not supported by statements of other prisoners and the arrested doctors.

Maironovsky was widely respected as a scientist, but nobody among the arrested doctors or chekists knew about his secret work. He confessed to experimenting with poisons, under orders, on persons condemned to death by firing squad. Publication of his confession was too risky because he referred to instructions and awards he had received from top members of the Politburo: Beria, Molotov, and Khrushchev, who were still in power. Therefore, his case was sent to a special conference; in absentia he was sentenced in February 1953 to ten years' imprisonment for "unlawfully possessing poisons at home and overstepping his authority under the article of abuse of power." He was not convicted of high treason. In short, he was thrown into jail with a substantial sentence in order to be at hand if needed to testify against victims of further purges.

Maironovsky was sentenced to ten years in prison three weeks before Stalin died. After Stalin's death, when Beria succeeded Ignatiev as security chief, Maironovsky flooded Beria with appeals for his release, mentioning his services in carrying out top-secret orders, including executions. Maironovsky stated that he had personally liquidated a number of the most important enemies of the Communist party and the Soviet government. His case was reopened; Beria wanted to release Maironovsky, but before he could act Beria himself was arrested. The procurator's office promptly used Maironovsky's letters to Beria against him, this time charging him with mass murders, not within the framework of a Zionist conspiracy but within the framework of secret crimes committed by Beria in eliminating his rivals. He was kept in jail until 1961.

I had personal knowledge about four cases, in 1946 and 1947, in which I was ordered to make the executions by Maironovsky look like natural deaths. As I previously related, I was called in to cover up the operation in November 1947 ordered by Khrushchev against Archbishop Romzha of the Uniate church in Western Ukraine. I was also involved, under orders by Khrushchev and Kaganovich, in the operation to eliminate the Ukrainian nationalist A. Shumsky.

A similar action in 1947, this time on direct orders of Bulganin, newly appointed minister of defense, was undertaken by Maironovsky in Ulyanovsk against a Polish engineer of Jewish origin, Samet, who had been interned since 1939. Samet was arranging his defection to Britain while working on secret research on snorkels, which would enable submarine engines to run undetected and allow the vessels to stay submerged for longer periods of time. Eitingon went to Ulyanovsk to plant agents around Samet, and simultaneously Maironovsky silenced him with an injection of poison under the guise of a routine medical checkup. It was necessary to conceal this action, and the local security agency in Ulyanovsk had no experienced personnel for handling the case.

In 1992 General Dmitri Volkogonov presented to the U.S. Congress a list of Americans who perished in the Soviet Union during World War II and the Cold War and expressed Russian president Yeltsin's regrets for their deaths. Volkogonov named Isaac Oggins as a case in point of how the Soviet government feared exposure of its labor camps and penal colonies. Volkogonov said the liquidation of Oggins was ordered because he could have revealed the hardships and suffering of life in Soviet prison camps.

The motive for eliminating Oggins was not so simple. According to news reports, Oggins was erroneously and unlawfully arrested by the NKVD and sentenced to eight years in a concentration camp for anti-Soviet activities. At the same time, it was reported that Oggins had arrived in the Soviet Far East under false Czechoslovakian papers. The reality of his story is this: Oggins was a Communist sympathizer and a member of the American Communist party. He was also a veteran agent of the Comintern and NKVD intelligence in China and the Far East. His wife, Nora, was a member of the NKVD intelligence network in charge of controlling safe apartments in France in the mid-1930s. Oggins was arrested in the Soviet Union in 1938 and began serving his term without attracting attention from the press. In 1939 Nora Oggins returned to the United States. I have every reason to believe that she began to cooperate with the FBI and other government agencies.

After the war, Nora Oggins requested that the American Embassy in Moscow demand Isaac's release, and an American diplomat was given permission to meet with him in Butyrka prison. I knew of Oggins as a minor Comintern-NKVD agent operating in the Far East who came to the Soviet Union in 1938 under false Czech documents, not as an American citizen.

Abakumov suggested Oggins's liquidation because Molotov was concerned about the possibility of his being used as a witness against the American Communist party by the House Un-American Activities Committee. In particular, our intelligence services feared that Nora Oggins's contacts with American officials and her revelations to the FBI would disrupt our agent network in America. Stalin and Molotov made the decision to eliminate Oggins, and in 1947 in the course of a routine medical checkup in prison Maironovsky poisoned him by injection. We were ordered to arrange his funeral in the Jewish cemetery in the city of Penza, two hundred miles from Moscow. Looking back at this episode, I feel sorry for him; but in those Cold War years we did not concern ourselves with what methods were used to eliminate people who knew too much.

Investigations by the procurator's office in 1990 into the use of poisons established that after 1947 these experiments and executions were stopped, and that they resumed without Maironovsky in 1952. I was summoned to the procurator's office together with former KGB general Oleg Kalugin. He was interrogated on the case of Georgi Markov, the Bulgarian dissident poisoned in London in 1978,[15] and I was questioned about Oggins. Kalugin told the procurator that as chief of counterintelligence it was his job to approve measures against agents of Western intelligence services, and he consulted with the Bulgarians on the plan to eliminate Markov. Kalugin revealed that he passed poison from LAB X to the Bulgarian Special Services in Moscow, who administered it to Markov with the tip of an umbrella. The novelty of the method received worldwide media attention. Kalugin was awarded a medal and a Browning automatic pistol from the Bulgarian government for his services.[16]

15. Markov was working for the Bulgarian section of the BBC World Service and was writing articles critical of Bulgarian leader Todor Zhivkov in the Western press. Before he died in October 1978 he told doctors that a stranger had accidentally bumped into him while he was crossing Westminster Bridge in London, poking him with his umbrella. A tiny stab wound and the remains of a highly toxic pellet about the size of a pinhead were found in Markov's right thigh. See Andrew and Gordievsky, *KGB: The Inside Story,* pp. 644–645.

16. On October 30, 1993, Oleg Kalugin arrived in London to participate in a BBC broadcast. He was arrested at Heathrow airport and held for twenty-four hours at the Belgravia police station under investigation by Scotland Yard's antiterrorist unit for

At the procurator's office we both admitted indirectly taking part in those acts, but we both stressed that we took no part in the decisions to liquidate the victims. Kalugin testified that he was a military man fulfilling an order; KGB chief Yuri Andropov regarded Markov as an agent of the British secret service. Under the circumstances of the Cold War, it was logical for Kalugin to obey the order to help the Bulgarians plan the assassination because he was under military discipline. I agreed with his explanation, because I had carried out orders under the same rationale.

Kalugin rightly demanded that strict government control should be imposed on toxicological research work. To my mind, however, this is not only a matter of control; toxicological laboratories are a logical component of technical support services of every security organization. Agents in the years of the Cold War were often equipped with poisons; Aleksandr D. Ogorudnik, a Ministry of Foreign Affairs official who was a CIA agent in Moscow, committed suicide with poison in the course of his arrest in 1977. Before that, he poisoned his woman friend, fearing his own exposure through her. Toxicological service is necessary for security operations. However, the danger is that such a powerful and silent weapon can be manipulated in the interests of authoritarian rule and dictatorship. A secret directive by the government should be circulated to all the staff of toxicological services, strictly defining their functions and forbidding production of disguised poisonous weapons that might be used in an uncontrolled way. Unfortunately, in these delicate security issues, much depends on the honesty and morals of those who give the orders and those who obey them.

Is it justified to administer drugs or nonlethal poisons to a terrorist in order to neutralize him or to safeguard your source of information in a terrorist ring so that you can round up the whole group later? Even a well-planned operation is always subject to fatal error. Strict regulations must rule out individual operational executions by poisoning under any circumstances; legal execution must be reserved for convictions under the criminal code.

Maironovsky, too, was the victim of totalitarian rule. I do not want to whitewash Beria, Stalin, Abakumov, or Ignatiev in these episodes, but it must be noted that the toxicological laboratory preceded them. Investigations in 1968, 1977, and 1990 revealed that this laboratory was

possible involvement in the "poisoned umbrella murder." Kalugin is reported to have denied his involvement, and he was released when the Crown Prosecution Service said it had decided there was not enough evidence to begin proceedings against him.

established not by Beria, but by order of Lenin (it began as a special section — *spetsialne kabinet* — in his secretariat) and was subordinated to the Council of People's Commissars, to the prime minister directly. Probably it was from this laboratory that Lenin asked Stalin to get him poison when he knew he was dying and feared helplessness. In 1937 the laboratory was transferred to the NKVD, and from then on it was subordinated to the people's commissar or minister of state security. The laboratory, from 1960 to 1970, was top-secret Toxicological Laboratory Number 12 in the KGB Research Institute of Higher and Advanced Technologies, according to General Kalugin. Our leaders were always interested in poisons; afterward the doctors who were involved in these experiments were all purged. Professor Nikolai Kazakov, director of the special toxicological laboratory in the 1930s, was purged in Bukharin's trial in 1938, and later Maironovsky met a similar end.

The notoriety of the laboratory continued to fascinate the Soviet leadership. I remember being told in 1988 by KGB major general Vassili Shadrin that Gorbachev became interested in the laboratory after reading former KGB chairman Vladimir Semichastny's stories in *Ogonyok* magazine of hints by Brezhnev that it would be easier to poison Khrushchev than oust him from power. KGB chairman Viktor Chebrikov summoned Semichastny to his office and ordered him to produce a written statement on the experiments with poisons and alleged instructions from Brezhnev in the 1960s, quoting an order from Gorbachev. Semichastny, however, refused to produce any written statement, according to General Shadrin.

The legacy of these tragic events must be taken into account in the making of future policies. History shows that no top-secret decisions, no secret crimes or terrorist plans, can be concealed forever. This is one of the great lessons of the breakdown of the Soviet Union and Communist party rule. Once the dam is broken, the flood of secret information is uncontrollable.

THE JEWS:
CALIFORNIA IN
THE CRIMEA

rom where I sat on the seventh floor of Lubyanka, many sensitive issues crossed my desk demanding action. Perhaps the most politically charged were those dealing with the Jewish question. Not only was my wife Jewish, but many of my most trusted colleagues were of Jewish origin, including my deputy, Leonid Eitingon. He was among the principal figures accused in the 1952–1953 Doctors' Plot and the so-called Zionist conspiracy. Contrary to widespread reports that anti-Semitism was Stalin's main reason for the persecution of Jews, I regard anti-Semitism as Stalin's weapon but not his determining strategy.

In 1944 and the first half of 1945, Stalin's strategic motivation was to use the Jewish issue as a bargaining chip to bring in international Jewish capital to rebuild the war-torn Soviet Union and to influence the postwar realignment of power in the Middle East. Stalin planned to use Jewish aspirations for a homeland to attract Western credits.

Intentions to form a Jewish republic really existed, based on a letter addressed to Stalin from the Jewish Antifascist Committee. The letter, which was to prove a fateful milestone in Jewish life in the Soviet Union, was written by Solomon Mikhoels, a beloved actor of the Yiddish State

Art Theater and a leading member of the committee; Shakhne Epshtein, the executive secretary of the committee; and Itzik Feffer, a popular poet and a member of the committee who accompanied Mikhoels on a speaking tour of the United States from June to December 1943.

This letter, addressed to Stalin and dated February 15, 1944, was later shown to Vyacheslav Molotov by Solomon Lozovsky, deputy foreign minister and supervisor of the Jewish Antifascist Committee. Under Molotov's instructions, he edited the letter, redated it February 21, and readdressed it to Molotov. On February 24 the letter was registered in Molotov's secretariat under the number M-23314 and the same day, with Molotov's notation on it, the letter was redirected to Georgi Malenkov, secretary of the Communist party; Anastas Mikoyan, minister of foreign trade; A. S. Shcherbakov, secretary of the Moscow party committee and chief of the armed forces political directorate; and Aleksei Voznesensky, chairman of GOSPLAN, the State Planning Committee.

Part of the letter, published for the first time in 1993, stated:

> The creation of a Jewish Soviet republic will once and forever, in a Bolshevik manner, within the spirit of Leninist-Stalinist national policy, settle the problem of the state legal position of the Jewish people and further development of their multicentury culture. This is a problem that no one has been capable of settling in the course of many centuries. It can be solved only in our great socialist country.[1]

The letter, whose existence is officially admitted in the journals of the Communist party,[2] is still not declassified and was not shown with the archival material of the Jewish Antifascist Committee that was displayed in Washington, D.C., during President Yeltsin's visit in 1992.

Gregory Kheifetz, our operative who had been successful in atomic espionage, told me that the letter was a proposal with details for a plan to make the Crimean Socialist Republic a homeland for Jewish people from all over the world. This would have required the resettlement of the population still living in the Crimea. In March and April 1944 the Crimean Tatars were forcibly deported from the area; 150,000 people

1. *Literaturnaya Gazeta,* July 7, 1933.
2. *Izvestia CC CPSU,* no. 12, 1989, p. 37.

were moved to Uzbekistan in Central Asja.[3] That the letter and the order to move the Tatars bore virtually the same dates — February 14 and 15, 1944 — was completely coincidental. The order by Stalin to move the Tatars (they were accused of mass collaboration with the Germans) had been signed earlier, but it came to Beria for signature a day before the letter from the Jewish Antifascist Committee was received.

Coordination and execution of Stalin's plans to lure foreign Jewish capital was entrusted to Kheifetz, who orchestrated Mikhoels's trip to America in 1943, while Kheifetz was serving as vice consul in San Francisco. At the time, we were trying desperately to obtain as much aid as possible from America. Before his departure to the United States, Mikhoels was summoned to Beria's office in the Lubyanka and instructed to establish broad contacts in the American Jewish community. Our plan was for him to lay the groundwork for American investment in the metal and coal mining industries in the Soviet Union. It was rumored that Mikhoels might be offered the post of chairman of the Supreme Soviet in the proposed new Jewish republic. Apart from Molotov, Lozovsky, and other high-ranking officials in the Ministry of Foreign Affairs, Mikhoels was the only one aware of Stalin's plans to establish another puppet state in Palestine or the Crimea. Stalin hoped to receive $10 billion in credits for the restoration of the economy after the war.

I did not know the detailed contents of the Jewish Antifascist Committee letter to Stalin. I was informed by Beria that the initiative came from the American side, from American Jewish organizations. I regarded the discussions about an autonomous Jewish republic within the Soviet Union as a probe of Western intentions to give us substantial economic aid after the war. The letter remained in the file for four years, its contents the subject of rumors. Then, in 1948, Malenkov used it as a weapon in Stalin's purge of the Jewish Antifascist Committee and later the old guard in the leadership. Molotov, Mikoyan, Voroshilov, Voznesensky, and finally Beria — because of their Jewish relatives or

---

3. The idea of resettling Soviet Jews in the Crimea first arose in the 1920s. It became a lingering myth, a vast projected scheme that would involve a million acres and 400,000 people. It was to be an answer to the impoverishment of Jews caused by the end of petty trade, and a way of maintaining Jewish national cohesion. Thus even at this early stage it posed the dilemma of whether or not it encouraged nationalism, in conflict with socialist goals. See Nora Levin, *The Jews in the Soviet Union Since 1917* (New York: New York University Press, 1990), vol. 1, pp. 147, 455–456.

their involvement in the discussions of a separate autonomous Jewish republic in the Crimea — were tainted with what had become an outrageous affront to Stalin's control.[4]

In the early 1920s, when the Bolshevik regime was first establishing itself, there was a preponderance of Jewish names in administrative positions at all levels because they had the education to fill these jobs. At this time there were no internal passports in Russia, so people were not officially identified as Jews or other nationalities. In 1922 and 1923 there was a rapid roundup of the leaders of all Jewish and other nationalist underground groups. The Police of Zion organization (Politzi Tzion) was extremely active, for example, and outmaneuvered GPU surveillance teams in Odessa; the Zionists led the secret service officers to a remote cemetery and then turned on them and beat them. Haganah had its origins in Zhitomir in the Ukraine, but the irony is that the Jews who worked in the Ukrainian GPU were put in charge of the operations against the Zionist underground groups. The crackdown included the Jewish Bund, a socialist organization that was a member of the Socialist International. The Jewish Communist party, a splinter group from the Jewish Bund, was also dissolved. This was the Bolshevik policy, to eliminate any political national splinter group in or out of the Communist party. The separatist Ukrainian Communist party was also dissolved. The Communist Party of the Ukraine (Bolsheviks) was the established and approved political party. It was the only party with its own politburo.

The Jewish leadership was either exiled or permitted to emigrate. Before 1928, there was no barrier to emigrating; the procedure for leaving the country was simpler than now. The effect of the loss of these leaders was that Jews no longer had any political organizations and lost their Jewish identity. The Jewish intelligentsia lost its political roots. In 1933 the internal passport system was introduced, and Jews were identified as a national group, even though they had no republic to be their homeland. In every major ministry at this time, Jews held top positions. I scarcely remember the directive of the Central Committee in 1939, after the Great Purge, to look into how many people of any one nation-

4. Molotov and Voroshilov had Jewish wives. Mikoyan and Voznesensky were involved in the discussions of establishing a Jewish homeland in the Crimea. Beria was instrumental in the establishment of the Jewish Antifascist Committee during the war and arranged for Mikhoels's trip to America in 1943.

ality were occupying key positions in sensitive ministries, but it was more potent than I perceived it to be. For the first time, an effective quota system came into being. Fortunately, most of my comrades-in-arms, men and women who became distinguished fighters, agents, and officers during the war, were already in place and were not affected by this directive.

The establishment of the Jewish Autonomous Oblast in Birobidzhan in 1928 was ordered by Stalin only as an effort to strengthen the Far Eastern border region with an outpost, not as a favor to the Jews. The area was constantly penetrated by Chinese and White Russian terrorist groups, and the idea was to shield the territory by establishing a settlement whose inhabitants would be hostile to White Russian émigrés, especially the Cossacks. The status of this region was defined shrewdly as an autonomous district, not an autonomous republic, which meant that no local legislature, high court, or government post of ministerial rank was permitted. It was an autonomous area, but a bare frontier, not a political center.

Before the war, Stalin's government toyed with the idea of using the leaders of the Jewish Socialist Bund, Henryk Ehrlich and Victor Alter, for pursuing Soviet policy goals abroad. General Raikhman, former deputy director of the Second Directorate in charge of counterintelligence, told me in 1970 that these leaders of the bund were arrested in Poland in September and October 1939. When the war with the Germans broke out, they were released in September 1941, summoned to Beria, and offered the opportunity to set up a Jewish anti-Hitler committee. At first it was planned that Ehrlich was to become the head of the committee and Mikhoels was to become his deputy; Alter was to be the executive secretary. This plan was abandoned because these people knew too much about Stalin's intentions to use them for raising money in the West. In December 1941, Alter and Ehrlich were rearrested. No charges were brought against them. Ehrlich wrote to President Kalinin on December 27, 1941, protesting that he was loyal to the Soviet government and eager to cooperate with the NKVD. In his letter he said:

> The main task of the proposed Jewish Anti-Hitler Committee should be intensive propaganda among Jewish communities of the U.S.A. and Britain for rendering the fullest necessary aid to the USSR in its struggle against Hitler's invasion. All of our proposals were fully endorsed by the leadership,

and the NKVD was entrusted to find a suitable place for the committee's headquarters.[5]

Ehrlich never received an answer to his letter. The archives show that in December Beria ordered Ehrlich and Alter placed in solitary confinement and assigned prisoner numbers 41 and 42. It was forbidden to interrogate them or fill in their names on prison registration forms in the Kuibyshev NKVD jail, where they were transferred. General Raikhman later told me that there was a special order to conceal from the personnel of the jail the real names of prisoners 41 and 42. The orders came from Stalin, Molotov, and Beria, but they were strange orders, forbidding the interrogation of the prisoners.

In 1942 American politician Wendell Willkie and William Green, president of the American Federation of Labor, inquired about the fate of Ehrlich and Alter through Soviet ambassador Maksim Litvinov. So did the Polish ambassador to Moscow, Stanislaw Kot. Deputy Foreign Minister Andrei Vyshinsky hinted in his reply to Kot that Ehrlich and Alter were pardoned by mistake; it had been determined that they were secretly conspiring with the Germans. Willkie inquired in late 1942 but received no answer until February 1943. Litvinov was authorized by Molotov to say that on December 23, 1941, Ehrlich and Alter were sentenced to death because in October and November 1941 they "systematically were involved in treasonous activities in their efforts to spread hostile propaganda in the Soviet Union to halt the war and sign a peace treaty with fascist Germany."[6]

This reply was a deliberate lie. By the time it was sent, Ehrlich had committed suicide (May 14, 1942) by hanging himself in his cell. Alter remained in solitary confinement until February 17, 1943, when he was secretly shot on orders from Beria. At the time, I was not aware of their fate. All this happened on the eve of Mikhoels's visit to the United States as head of the Jewish Antifascist Committee.

Only in September 1992 were the true facts of Ehrlich's and Alter's fate revealed from their files in the KGB's weekly newspaper, *Shait y Mech* (*Shield and Sword*). The elimination of Ehrlich and Alter was the first stage in Stalin and Molotov's conspiracy to conceal clandestine informal contacts of the Soviet leadership with influential representatives of the foreign Jewish community. Ehrlich and Alter were removed because Stalin feared their independence and political influence. I believe

5. *Shait y Mech* (*Shield and Sword*), September 3, 1992, p. 13.
6. Ibid.

they were eliminated because their popularity went beyond the boundaries of the Soviet Union. Mikhoels faced the same fate. His successful trip to America immediately made him suspect in Stalin's eyes. He had become a cultural hero for Jews around the world.

The plan to lure American capital was associated with the idea of a Jewish state in the Crimea — what we called California in the Crimea. This idea was widely discussed in American Jewish circles, Kheifetz told me. In particular he mentioned the interest of Eric Johnston, president of the American Chamber of Commerce, who in June 1944 was received by Stalin with Ambassador Averell Harriman to discuss the reconstruction of areas that used to be major Jewish settlements in Byelorussia and resettlement of Jews in the Crimea. Johnston drew a rosy picture for Stalin that long-term American credits would be granted for this purpose to the Soviet Union after the war.

The idea of setting up a Jewish socialist republic in the Crimea was openly discussed in Moscow, not only in the Jewish community but at the administrative level of the government. I remember that in mid-1944 or 1945, at a meeting of the state committee on atomic energy, Borisov, deputy chairman of GOSPLAN, said, "Our resources are too scarce, Comrade Pervukhin. We have just received instruction to look into the financial requirements for creating the infrastructure for a future Jewish republic in the Crimea."

Mikhoels greatly relied on Feffer, a full-time controlled NKVD agent run personally by Commissar of State Security Leonid Raikhman. Occasionally even Beria met with Feffer in a safe apartment to review the Jewish question and encourage the project.

Until June 1945 this plan appeared to be operational and on the way to realization. In preparation for the Yalta Conference, Harriman inquired of me and Novikov, Molotov's aide, how much progress had been made in plans to establish a Jewish republic, in connection with future American credits for this project. I recall seeing reports that Stalin discussed the plan for setting up a Jewish republic in the Crimea and restoring the Gomel area of Byelorussia with American senators who visited the Soviet Union right after the war. He asked them not to confine possible Western credits and technical assistance to these two areas, but to make the aid unrestricted.

Then, in June 1945, after Yalta and after the victory over Hitler, Stalin issued a decree declaring the Crimea to be only an administrative district, not a republic. Before the war the Crimea had been an autonomous republic with strong Tatar representation at government levels. In November 1945, when Harriman tried to reach Stalin through Molotov to discuss economic cooperation, his request for a meeting was rebuffed on Stalin's orders.

Stalin apparently had abandoned the plan for a Jewish republic in the Crimea. "Stalin was of a different opinion on the solution to the problem of the Jewish people. He did not support the idea of a Jewish republic in the Crimea. Without any consequences the [Jewish Antifascist Committee] letter found its place in the archive. It was taken out four years later and was given the matching color of an indictment for dozens of innocent people," writes Arkady Vaksberg in *Literaturnaya Gazeta*,[7] in answer to a reader's inquiry whether the idea of setting up a Jewish republic in the Crimea was Beria's provocation for a campaign against the Jews or whether a letter to Stalin actually existed and was seriously considered.

After the war, Stalin preferred to play another game, which was to penetrate the Zionist movement. Until 1948 Great Britain held a mandate from the League of Nations to administer the territory of Palestine. Stalin and Molotov hoped to assuage the fears of the British that they would be pushed out of Palestine by the founding of a Jewish state there; part of the impetus for a Jewish homeland in the Crimea was to help our British allies. It was held out as a diversion for world Jewish leaders, to confuse the focus on Palestine as a solution to the Jewish problem. When it became clear at the end of 1945 that Stalin was not going to fulfill his earlier hints of a Jewish republic in the Crimea, the British and Americans set up the Anglo-American Committee in Palestine, leaving out the Soviet Union. This was contrary to a previous understanding that there would be joint consultation of the three wartime allies.

Thus in April 1946, Dekanozov, deputy minister of foreign affairs, and Vyshinsky, also a deputy minister, wrote a memorandum to Stalin and Molotov stressing that the Soviet Union had been snubbed. The Palestinian issue would be settled without the Soviet Union. They suggested that the leadership formulate a public policy of looking favorably on a Jewish state in Palestine. Under an alias, with the consent of Molotov, Vyshinsky published an article in the magazine *Novoye Vremya*, affirming the necessity of creating a democratic Jewish state in the territory of the British mandate. Clearly the intention was to

7. July 7, 1993, p. 15.

strengthen the Soviet stand in the Middle East and to undermine British influence among Arab states, who objected to the Jewish state, by showing their inability to stop the Jews.[8]

Concurrent with this political move, I was ordered to send agents to Palestine through Romania in 1946. They were to set up an illegal network that might participate in combat and sabotage operations against the British. I assigned three officers, Josef Garbuz, Aleksandr Semyonov (real name Taubman; he was Grigulevich's assistant in the Lithuanian underground and had helped liquidate Rudolf Klement in Paris in 1938), and Julius Kolesnikov. Garbuz and Kolesnikov had experience in guerrilla warfare in the Ukraine and in Byelorussia, where they had carried out sabotage operations against the Germans.

Semyonov and Kolesnikov settled down in Haifa and built two networks, but they did not participate in any active sabotage operations against the British. Kolesnikov arranged for the shipment of small arms and antitank grenades seized from the Germans in Romania to Palestine. Semyonov attempted to renew contacts with an agent of Serebryansky, who had been planted in the Stern organization, an anti-British terrorist group, in 1937. Garbuz remained in Romania, gathering candidates for settlement in the future Israel.

When the order came to plant agents in Palestine and provide ammunition to the Jewish guerrilla organizations, it became clear to me that while we were ostensibly helping the Jews, the real purpose of our efforts was to set up our own network within the Zionist political and military structure. The Jews were seeking independence and were deeply involved with America. They would not be subject to our influence to the degree that Eastern Europe was, but we felt it important to plant our presence there. Kheifetz told me that as early as 1943 Litvinov, in a message to Molotov from Washington, stressed that Palestine and the creation of a Jewish state would become a major issue in the postwar international order.

It was in the second half of 1946, when Stalin had become disenchanted with Jewish alliances abroad and Jewish demands at home and was feeling isolated by the British-American joint stand in Palestine, that he began to stimulate an anti-Semitic campaign, which culminated in a purge of Jews from the party machinery, diplomatic service, military

8. Anatoli Sudoplatov conversation with a confidential source.

apparatus, and intelligence services. It developed into the infamous Doctors' Plot and Zionist conspiracy charges, in which every Jewish doctor was suspect. The anti-Semitic campaign was a repeat of the purges of the 1930s, another maneuver by Stalin to sweep out all established power centers in the bureaucracy in order to replace them with weaker men and women who would not threaten his supreme hold on the country's leadership.

In October 1946, for the first time, the specter of Jewish bourgeois nationalism as a threat to Communist ideology was raised, in a letter from Viktor Semyonovich Abakumov, newly appointed minister of state security, to Stalin. In the letter he accused leaders of the Jewish Antifascist Committee of engaging in nationalist propaganda, meaning they were putting Jewish concerns above Soviet interests. This was a heavy warning sign. Kheifetz, who had performed so brilliantly in obtaining atomic information for us and establishing high-level contacts in the American Jewish community, was suddenly out of favor. He continued to serve the Jewish Antifascist Committee as its secretary for foreign affairs, but he was forced to sever its contacts with the American Jewish community.

One of the complaints in Abakumov's letter was that the committee intervened on behalf of Jews reclaiming their homes at the end of the war. Thousands of Jews had fled from Kiev, Minsk, Riga, Leningrad, and Moscow during the war to escape annihilation by the Germans. The Nazis had arrived promising to liberate Ukrainians and the Baltic states from "Jewish leadership." This found fertile soil among the nationalists, who seized Jewish property, homes, and apartments. In 1945 the Jews began to return, only to find they had been dispossessed. The government issued instructions regulating the return of the population to their homes.

I remember when Khrushchev, then the secretary of the Ukrainian Communist party, telephoned Usman Usupov, the secretary of the Communist party of Uzbekistan, in 1947, complaining to him that Jews from Uzbekistan "are flying to the Ukraine like crows from Tashkent and Samarkand. I have no space to accommodate them because the city is destroyed. Stop the flow or pogroms will start." I was in Usupov's office at the time, and he told me the story because I had come to him with a request to accommodate three thousand Kurds, headed by Barzani, who had fled to Azerbaijan from Iran. It was dangerous to maintain them in the Caucasus, and we wanted to resettle them in Uzbekistan. To settle the Kurds was easy. Usupov ordered a new Kurdish collective farm to be built, a lot simpler than finding new homes for the displaced Jewish intelligentsia returning to Kiev.

Mikhoels had tried to intervene on behalf of the Jews, acting as the head of the Jewish Antifascist Committee. Abakumov's letter of complaint was meant to show that efforts to protect the rights of Jews to resettle in their former homes were a sign of Jewish bourgeois nationalism; it reflected the annoyance of party officials who were overwhelmed with problems of resettlement. Mikhoels's actions on behalf of displaced Jews not only annoyed Stalin, they made him deeply suspicious of Mikhoels. Imagine, in the Soviet system of discipline, suddenly a man with international reputation and authority begins to act on his own initiative. Mikhoels was doomed.

The situation deteriorated in 1947. I remember the oral instruction from A. Obruchnikov, the deputy minister of state security in charge of personnel, not to enlist Jews as officers in the organs of state security. I could not imagine that this direct anti-Semitic order came from Stalin. I thought it must be Abakumov's initiative. It became clear to me that the grand plan of using our Jewish intellectuals for international cooperation with the world Jewish community had been abandoned. Eitingon, who kept complaining about an anti-Semitic campaign against his relatives in the university and medical services, was convinced that anti-Semitism was an essential element of the government's policy. In hindsight I realize that he understood the situation better than I did.

Beria and Kobulov frequently told me that Stalin enjoyed anti-Muslim and anti-Azerbaijani jokes and anecdotes told to him in the presence of Bagirov, the first secretary of the Azerbaijani Communist party, who was disheartened by Kobulov's imitation of Azerbaijani pronunciation of Russian words. This makes me believe that humor directed at any nationalist group was pleasing to Stalin, and that he was neither anti-Semitic nor anti-Muslim, only opposed to any nationalist enclave of power.

Stalin and his close aides were interested in the Jewish issue mainly to exploit it politically, either for use in a power struggle or for consolidating their power. That's how the flirtation with anti-Semitism started in high party echelons. After Stalin opened an "anticosmopolitan" drive in 1946 and 1947, middle-level personnel and rank-and-file party bureaucracy took anti-Semitism for granted as the official party line. "Rootless cosmopolitans" became synonymous with Jews; it meant that Soviets of Jewish origin shared cultural values with Western Jews and therefore were less than completely loyal to the Soviet Union.

This anticosmopolitan drive coincided with a shift in the power balance around Stalin. Malenkov was demoted and Beria stripped of his position to supervise any activities in the sphere of state security. Rumors began to spread that he and Molotov surrounded themselves with Jews.

Stalin's efforts after the war were focused on extending Soviet hegemony, first over the countries of Eastern Europe bordering the Soviet Union, and then everywhere he was in competition with British interests. He foresaw that the Arab states would turn to the Soviet Union when they were frustrated by British and American support for Israel. The Arabs would appreciate the anti-Zionist trends in Soviet foreign policy. I was told by Vetrov, Molotov's assistant, later ambassador to Denmark, what Stalin said: "Let's agree to the establishment of Israel. This will be a pain in the ass for the Arab states and will make them turn their backs on the British. In the long run it will totally undermine British influence in Egypt, Syria, Turkey, and Iraq."

The Cold War began in earnest in 1946 and 1947, when the illusion of postwar cooperation with the West ended. The wartime policy of treating Britain and America as allies turned into confrontation. The civil war in China was intensifying and tensions were rising in Italy and France because of the political struggle by the Communists to come to power. With the onset of the Cold War, our hopes for obtaining Western Jewish money faded. It became clear to the leadership that it could not rely on the support of the Jewish business community to invest in the reconstruction of the Soviet Union.

The first victim was Mikhoels, who had been at the heart of the discussions to establish a Jewish Crimean republic. Stalin feared that Mikhoels would unleash forces that could not be controlled and would lead to unpredictable political consequences. Stalin feared a truly independent Jewish homeland. Mikhoels had the stature of a leader with world recognition, and Stalin could not risk his developing his own power base.

Mikhoels was murdered in January 1948, under the direct order of Stalin. Probably because Emma was Jewish, the assignment, fortunately, was not given to me. The assassination was carried out by Colonel Lebedev under the operational control of the minister of state security of Byelorussia, Lavrenti Tsanava, and Sergei Ogoltsov, Abakumov's deputy, first deputy minister of state security. Mikhoels was lured to Tsanava's dacha on the outskirts of Minsk, ostensibly to meet leading Byelorussian dramatic artists. There Mikhoels, together with his secretary, V. Golubov, was jabbed with a poisoned needle. Golubov, unknown to Mikhoels, was an MGB informer who had become an unwanted witness because he had brought Mikhoels to the dacha. The two were thrown under the wheels of a truck to make it appear they had been killed on the street in a hit-and-run accident.

When I first heard of Mikhoels's death, I kept my suspicions to myself. I never imagined that Ogoltsov would personally go to Minsk to supervise arrangements for Mikhoels's assassination. I thought that probably Mikhoels was killed by an anti-Semitic gangster who had been told in advance where to find such a notorious defender of the Jewish cause. I could not imagine that such an act, using such poor intelligence tradecraft, could be committed by trained officers. Such a crude execution did not seem to be the work of professionals. (I learned the details only after Stalin's death, when I was appointed by Beria to an MVD commission assigned to investigate the Doctors' Plot and the mysterious death of Mikhoels.)

During most of 1948 I was preoccupied with the Berlin crisis and establishing a Kurdish guerrilla network in Iran, Iraq, and Turkey with the goal of overthrowing the government of Nuri Said and Faisal II in Iraq. This was the period when we were consolidating a Communist takeover in Czechoslovakia, and I flew to Prague with Zubov to meet Beneš, to neutralize his opposition to transferring power to Klement Gottwald.

Emma had become seriously ill in 1947 and retired on a pension from the service. She was wise enough to retire from all operational work in 1940 and was appointed a senior lecturer for training illegals in the NKVD (later MGB) school. Occasionally she was used for contacting important women agents by the leadership of the Second Directorate, but most of the time she tried to avoid attracting attention. It was a happy coincidence that her illness and retirement came at about the time the purge of Jews began in the MVD, MGB, and the Ministry of Foreign Affairs. She retired with the rank of lieutenant colonel in 1949 and was listed in the records under her maiden name, Kaganova.

In 1949 and 1950, when I frequently had to leave Moscow for Prague, Western Ukraine, Azerbaijan, and Uzbekistan, Eitingon, my deputy, took command of Special Bureau Number One for Diversions and Intelligence. He visited Emma and told her that an anti-Semitic campaign was growing in harshness and scope. Eitingon's sister Sonia, a well-known cardiologist and the chief doctor at the polyclinic of the

Stalin Automobile Factory, was fired. Emma's younger sister Elizabeth was denied postgraduate training at a medical institute in Kiev because she was Jewish. I intervened in these cases through a good friend, Andrei Muzichenko, director of the Central Clinical Research Institute of Moscow. In the 1930s he had been an NKVD illegal in France and Austria, but after the purges in 1938 he decided to rely on his diploma as a doctor and left the intelligence business. He offered jobs to Sonia and to Elizabeth, who is still working there.

I was stunned when Gregory Kheifetz was arrested in 1948 or 1949, but neither I nor Eitingon could intervene. We attributed his arrest to Abakumov's anti-Semitic campaign. Almost all the members of the Jewish Antifascist Committee and leading Jewish intellectuals were arrested and tried for the conspiracy to separate the Crimea from the USSR.

An internal power struggle from 1948 to 1952 developed into the public anti-Semitic campaign known as the Doctors' Plot. Although it was known as an anti-Semitic campaign, the Doctors' Plot was not restricted to Jews. Rather it was part of a struggle to settle old scores in the leadership. On one side Stalin, with the help of Malenkov and Khrushchev, was trying to purge his own old guard and Beria. The scapegoats in the alleged Jewish "conspiracy" were to be Molotov, Voroshilov, and Mikoyan, the last of Stalin's Politburo old guard. The truth about the initiation of the Doctors' Plot has never been revealed, even during Gorbachev's glasnost, because it was a vicious power struggle in the Kremlin on the eve of Stalin's death that drew in the entire leadership.

It is generally believed that the Doctors' Plot began with a hysterical letter to Stalin accusing Jewish doctors of plans to murder the leadership by means of maltreatment and poisoning. The notorious letter of Lydia Timashuk, a doctor in the Kremlin Polyclinic, was written and sent to Stalin not in 1952, just prior to the arrest of the doctors, but in August 1948. To her letter, which charged that Academician V. N. Vinogradov was maltreating Zhdanov and others and caused Zhdanov's death, Stalin's reaction had been: *"Chepukha"* — "Absurd." Her letter remained on file for three years without action and was only dug up at the end of 1951 when it became useful as a weapon in the power struggle. All members of the Politburo knew of the letter and had heard Stalin's reaction to it. (Colonel Boris Ludvigov, Beria's chief assistant on matters relating to the Politburo and Council of Ministers, told me this in Vladimir prison.)

I always thought that Abakumov initiated the Doctors' Plot as a continuation of the anticosmopolitan drive. I learned differently in 1990, when the military prosecutor's office consulted me as a witness in the reinvestigation of Abakumov's postwar repressions. Instead of being the promulgator of the Doctors' Plot, he was a target of it. When he was arrested in 1951, he was accused of suppressing evidence of the plot to kill Stalin because he wanted to seize power and become the dictator of the Soviet Union. Abakumov was alleged to rely on Jewish doctors and Jewish sabotage experts in the Ministry of State Security (meaning Eitingon).

For Malenkov and Beria, the goal was to remove Abakumov, and they were prepared to use whatever means were at hand. Malenkov's chief assistant, Dmitri Sukhanov, in spring 1951 received in his office a rank-and-file investigator from the Investigation Department of the Security Ministry, Lieutenant Colonel Mikhail Ryumin, known to be a primitive anti-Semite. This meeting was another fateful turning point for Soviet Jews. Ryumin feared expulsion from the security service because he had received a reprimand for leaving an investigation file on the bus from Lefortovo jail to Lubyanka headquarters. Additionally, he had concealed from the party and from the organs of state security the facts about the kulak (rich land-owning peasants) origin of his father, that his brother and sister had been convicted of thievery, and that his father-in-law had served as an officer in the White Army of Admirial Aleksandr Kolchak.

To his credit, Abakumov knew that the earlier attempts of Ryumin to portray arrested Jewish doctors as terrorists was a prelude to the grand Doctors' Plot, and he curbed Ryumin's efforts for several months in 1950. To save his own career and to serve his anti-Semitic ambitions, Ryumin readily accommodated Sukhanov's demand that he write a letter to Stalin denouncing Abakumov.

Thirty years after these events, my former sister-in-law, Nina Sudoplatova, who worked as a typist-clerk in Malenkov's office — Sukhanov was her immediate boss — told me that Ryumin, a poorly educated man, had to rewrite his letter denouncing Abakumov eleven times. Sukhanov kept him waiting in the reception room for almost ten hours while he conferred with Malenkov on the contents of the letter. Only Sukhanov knows how Ryumin was chosen to denounce Abakumov, and he did not reveal this aspect of the story when he appeared on Russian television in July 1992 to discuss the origin of the Doctors' Plot.

In his denunciation, Ryumin, inspired by Malenkov, stated that

Abakumov instructed the Investigation Department to suppress evidence about a "Zionist conspiracy aimed against leaders of the Soviet government" in the form of terrorist acts.

By that time, a number of well-known Jewish doctors had been arrested for anti-Soviet Zionist propaganda. The most prominent of them, Dr. Yakob G. Etinger, tragically died in jail while being interrogated before Abakumov was arrested in July 1951. Ryumin charged Abakumov with being responsible for Etinger's death by placing him in a cold cell in Lefortovo; he charged Abakumov with attempting to kill the doctor to prevent his revealing other Zionist conspirators. Ryumin took advantage of this and other cases and inflated them into a full-scale Zionist terrorist conspiracy. Out of the files came Timashuk's accusations against Jewish doctors.

Abakumov, more experienced in such intrigues, had been afraid to inflate the Zionist conspiracy case with such gross fabrications. He sensed that Stalin would demand real evidence in such high-risk provocations. Besides, Abakumov knew well that the rule was not to take the initiative in situations created by the top leadership. Jewish doctors treated Stalin and had their own intimate and direct access to Politburo members by virtue of their professional doctor-patient relationships. Thus Abakumov was not enthusiastic about transforming the Jewish Antifascist Committee into a grand conspiracy that would cause tremors at the top and affect key members of the Politburo such as Voroshilov and Molotov, who had Jewish wives, and Kaganovich, who was Jewish. Abakumov's hesitancy contributed to his undoing.

Ryumin was first appointed chief of the MGB Investigation Department and then deputy minister of security; he was given a free hand to manipulate the evidence against Abakumov, and with him out of the way, to unleash the alleged doctors' conspiracy.

The new investigators demanded to know who the members of Abakumov's new government were to be once Stalin was overthrown. Abakumov was also charged with concealing the treacherous crimes of Molotov's wife, Polina Zhemchuzhina. He was accused of covering up her contacts with Israeli politician Golda Meir (then known as Golda Meyerson).

Abakumov vigorously denied any guilt in either suppressing exposure of the doctor's conspiracy or being himself the leader and instigator of the Doctors' Plot through his Jewish subordinates in the Ministry of Security. Abakumov stood firm in his denial despite heavy torture. He became a dying invalid, but still he refused to "confess." The whole case for a Jewish conspiracy in the Ministry of Security then rested on the confessions of Colonel Naum Shvartsman, a former journalist who had never conducted an interrogation but who acted as editor of falsified confessions extracted from prisoners. When Stalin ordered the arrest of the director and three deputy directors of the investigation section, one among them was Colonel Shvartsman, a Jew. He confessed to being Abakumov's deputy in the Jewish terrorist organization that comprised all senior Jewish security officers. Under interrogation Shvartsman confessed that he was instructed by Abakumov to set up a group of Jewish conspirators in the Ministry of State Security to plan terrorist actions against the government.

Shvartsman also "confessed" to having homosexual relations with Abakumov, his son, and the British ambassador. Shvartsman confessed that he had used homosexual contacts with the American double agents Gavrilov and Lavrentiev, who had been planted in the American Embassy compound, to pass orders for terrorist actions to Jewish conspirators.[9]

He knew the machinery of investigation; to escape being beaten he proved he was cooperating by accusing Jewish officials. At the same time he invented unbelievable stories, like being inspired in his terrorist activities by drinking Zionist soup prepared by his Jewish aunt, or sleeping with his stepdaughter, or having homosexual relations with his son. He wanted to be sent for psychiatric examination, and that was recommended by deputy military prosecutor Colonel Uspensky. However, when his testimony accusing thirty Jewish top officials of terrorism was reported to Stalin, Stalin told Ignatiev and Ryumin, "You are both fools. That scoundrel is playing for time. No need for any expert opinion. Arrest the whole group immediately." (Ludvigov told me this in jail.)

Stalin ordered the arrest of all Jewish colonels and generals in the Ministry of Security. A total of some fifty senior officers and generals were arrested, including Eitingon, Raikhman, and deputy minister of security Lieutenant General Belkin. Retired colonel Maklarsky, who had become a successful scriptwriter of popular espionage films, was also arrested because Shvartsman fingered him. Colonel Andrei Sverdlov, son of the first Soviet president, was arrested, along with two deputy ministers of state security suspected of Jewish connections, Lieutenant General Selivanovsky and Lieutenant General Pitovranov.

9. Shvartsman confirmed this in 1953, when the cases of the doctors and Jewish security officers were reopened. Kiril Stolyarov, *Golgotha* (Moscow: Krasnoye Proletari Izdatelzvo, 1991), pp. 14–15.

They were arrested together with their direct Russian subordinates. New blood was hired in the Investigation Department; totally incompetent people from the Central Committee, like Konyakhin and Nikolai Mesetsov (who later, under Brezhnev, became head of the state radio and television service and ambassador to Australia), became investigators. They beat prisoners almost to death. Ryumin arrested all Jewish doctors who were accused of working on orders from Abakumov. I was astonished by the charges of the Doctors' Plot because Professor Aleksandr Feldman, one of the accused terrorists, was our trusted family doctor, to whom I always sent flowers on state holidays.

Eitingon's sister Sonia was supposed to be the courier between the academicians and her brother, planner of the assassinations. Abakumov was supposed to have named the insurgency cabinet. The new trio of Ryumin, Mesetsov, and Konyakhin placed Abakumov in a special refrigerated cell in Lefortovo. All prisoners except Eitingon, Raikhman, Abakumov, and Yakob Matusov, an MGB section chief, confessed.

At first I was not aware of the scope of the MGB purge because arrests were never announced, and it took several weeks to grasp the full extent of the scourge. I sensed something was seriously wrong when I tried to contact Colonel Shubnikov, chief of the American section in the Counterintelligence Directorate, and found he was unavailable, despite my need for information from him about an agent he was running.[10] Only he had the information, and I could not trace him. Although I was chief of the Bureau for Diversions and Intelligence and a lieutenant general, no one could or would explain to me the whereabouts of Shubnikov. Indignantly, I telephoned Pitovranov, chief of counterintelligence, only to find that he, too, had disappeared and was unreachable. At that point it became clear to me that we had begun to repeat the pattern of the prewar mass purges. Both men had been taken to Lefortovo prison.

In 1951, when Abakumov was arrested, I remember receiving a telephone call from Ryumin, who had just been appointed chief of the MGB Investigation Department. He said that he had "serious incriminating materials against Eitingon and his sister Sonia." Eitingon was in Lithuania on a mission for three months, so I asked for the file on the case to be brought to my office. Within an hour Ryumin appeared with a thin file. There were no depositions against Eitingon, but there was a sum-

10. The Secret Political Department, which Shubnikov also headed, was included in the Counterintelligence Directorate.

mary of agent reports alleging that Sonia Eitingon refused to provide medical aid and consultations to Russians, and treated only Jews. I told Ryumin this was not convincing to me and I still regarded Eitingon as a reliable senior operations officer. Ryumin retorted, "The Central Committee found this evidence quite convincing." He snatched the file and left in a huff.

The situation in the Ministry of State Security was confused and uncertain. Abakumov, the minister, was under arrest and being held in Matrosskaya Tishina prison while the procurator's interrogation built the case against him. No successor as minister of state security had been appointed. When I called First Deputy Minister Ogoltsov and asked him to discuss the case of Eitingon's sister, he replied: "This is a political matter to be discussed in the Central Committee." He told me he would refuse to sign any document or give any discretionary orders before the new minister was appointed.

I had no alternative but to telephone Semyon Ignatiev, then a secretary of the Central Committee with responsibility for the MGB and MVD. He was a member of the Central Committee commission established by Stalin to reorganize the ministry after Abakumov's arrest. I had appeared before the commission, and I must admit that I criticized the mistakes of the leadership of the ministry in conducting intelligence and counterintelligence operations abroad, in Western Ukraine and in Central Asia. At that time Ignatiev said that he was always available for contact on pressing issues. When I telephoned him, he appeared eager to receive me at the Central Committee headquarters on Staraya Ploshchad.

I told him that I was concerned with the attempt to slander Eitingon and his sister and ascribe to them nationalist sympathies. Ignatiev summoned Ryumin with the file. In my presence Ryumin incoherently quoted two depositions against Eitingon and Sonia, charging them with "hostility to the Soviet government." The agent summary against Sonia was never mentioned.

"As Communists we must evaluate people by what they do, not by the rumors that are spread about them," I said. "Here is what Eitingon did as the organizer of the assassination of Trotsky in Mexico and as the organizer of an effective intelligence network abroad, and his role in acquiring atomic intelligence."

Ryumin remained silent, and Ignatiev stopped me and said, "Let's leave Eitingon and his family in peace." After the meeting with Ignatiev, I felt reassured that Eitingon and his sister would be all right.

304304

304 304

304 304

About one month later Ignatiev was appointed minister of state security, and on his direct order in October 1951 Eitingon was arrested at Moscow's Vnukovo airport when he returned from Lithuania. He had just succeeded in rounding up the leadership of the anti-Soviet underground there. His stepdaughter Zoya Zarubina phoned me at home to tell me that Eitingon had been detained in her presence when she went to meet him at the airport. I did not know how to respond this time. Emma suggested I remain silent. In my office the next morning, I asked Zoya to prepare her letter of resignation from the service. That Eitingon was her stepfather was not mentioned on her registration card. I immediately telephoned the rector of the Institute of Foreign Languages, Varvara Pivovarova, whose sister had worked under me as a translator in the MGB atomic intelligence bureau, to take on Zoya as an instructor on his staff. The important thing was to sever her contacts with the security system before anyone became aware of her relationship to Eitingon. Most people naturally knew her as the daughter of retired general Vassili Zarubin, who was divorced in 1925 from Zoya's mother before she married Eitingon.

In a few days I had the opportunity to meet Ignatiev at a staff meeting. He privately reproached me. "You were mistaken about Eitingon. What do you think of him now?" he asked me.

I still remember my prompt reply. "My assessment of people and their deeds is always in agreement with the party line," I said. The party would eventually vindicate me.

Here I must speak of my illusions. I always regarded the Doctors' Plot and the Zionist conspiracy as pure fabrications by scoundrels like Ryumin who were reporting to incompetent people like Ignatiev. Each time I met Ignatiev he appeared to be totally out of his depth in handling whatever was reported to him. His judgment was appalling. For him an agent report was a revelation, and he could be influenced by what he read without bothering to have it cross-checked for accuracy. He could be convinced of anything.

Ignatiev was absolutely unfit for the job. One morning, in the midst of an operational conference with more than ten people present in his office, he became hysterically annoyed by a telephone call from the commandant of the MGB, General Blokhin. I remember that he shouted into the phone: "You should act in accordance with the law. Don't bother me." Then he hung up and told us, "I can't stand these regular telephone calls from Blokhin demanding I sign the orders for carrying out death sentences in accordance with internal MGB regulations. Why should I get involved in that? Why should I sign these orders? He should act in accordance with the law." Nobody answered. We sat in embarrassed silence.

Ignatiev could be easily manipulated to fabricate cases against innocent people. Only later did I realize he was fulfilling orders that came from the top — from Stalin, Molotov, Malenkov, and others.

When TASS announced that well-known doctors and academicians were accused of a Zionist conspiracy to kill Stalin and the Politburo by injurious medical treatment, I believed it was a provocation, a continuation of the anti-Semitic campaign which had begun earlier, combined with the criminal incompetence of Minister of State Security Ignatiev. I looked into the files accusing Eitingon of training the doctors to perform terrorist acts against Stalin and the government. For that purpose, the indictment charged, Eitingon kept in his office samples of mines and explosives disguised as electrical appliances. These were the usual equipment for his special field of expertise.

Moscow was flooded with rumors about attempts of Jewish doctors and pharmacists to poison ordinary citizens, and about coming pogroms. I was worried when our two children, then about nine and twelve, came home from school with these rumors. Emma and I were in a difficult position; it was dangerous to instruct children of high-ranking security officials to contradict brazen anti-Semitic remarks, because they would draw attention to themselves by inspiring debates. They would definitely be noticed by the local party administration, which monitored every sphere of public life. Add to this that they were going to school with Malenkov's and Kaganovich's sons, which meant that the school was under constant surveillance. Even as children they could not make political statements saying that Stalin and Lenin were always against anti-Semitism; this would be misinterpreted and would become twisted.

Emma and I told them to say that in conditions that demand absolute vigilance, it was bad to spread rumors because they inspire "provocations." We all had to stick to the version of events printed in *Pravda*, the party newspaper, where there were no hints of pogroms or eradication of the Jewish nation. Wrath over treacherous, monstrous crimes of individual terrorists was understandable, we told the children, but spreading rumors meant playing with fire, and playing into the hands of enemies of our country. I wondered how this would sound at Pioneer meetings at school. Then the director of the school telephoned Emma and thanked her for the children's proper upbringing. He was in a difficult position because there were many Jewish children and teachers in his school, known for teaching subjects in English. He told Emma that the children's statement at the Pioneer meeting, that spreading rumors was a provocation, brought cheers and helped to calm the heated situation.

Later, in Vladimir jail, when I shared a cell with Colonel Ludvigov, he revealed to me things I could hardly believe. He told me that Stalin had written on the minutes of one doctor's interrogation: "Put them in handcuffs and beat them until they confess."

In the final period of the Zionist conspiracy in 1952, it ballooned out of its organizers' control. Ryumin and Ignatiev joined the minister of state security of Georgia, Nikolai M. Rukhadze, to accuse Beria of concealing his Jewish origin and fabricating a conspiracy against Stalin in Georgia. Beria was next on the list for elimination by Stalin. The Crimean conspiracy case, which had dragged on since 1948, was resolved in August 1952, with the execution of all arrested members of the Jewish Antifascist Committee and former deputy foreign minister Lozovsky. Kheifetz was kept alive to testify against Beria and Molotov when they would be accused of initiating the Crimean proposal and stimulating informal contacts with American Jewish communities.

My knowledge comes from the files on Abakumov's case that I read forty years later in the military prosecutor's office, forty volumes thick. I always believed that Ryumin was investigating the doctors' case to the day of Stalin's death, but Stalin was shrewd enough to realize that the plot portrayed by Ryumin was too primitive to be believed. He could not supply the details to make credible the story he was creating out of whole cloth. Ryumin was fired from his job by Stalin himself on November 12, 1952, for "being incapable of adequately fulfilling his duties." He was reappointed to the post he held before joining the security service, a rank-and-file accountant in the State Control Commission. He had earlier been a junior accountant in the Archangelsk cooperative union. At the peak of the anti-Semitic campaign, not Ryumin but Mesetsov, Konyakhin, and Ignatiev were in charge of the criminal interrogation and beating of the doctors. They were never prosecuted or charged with any crimes when the whole fabrication was exposed; they were promoted by Khrushchev and Malenkov to responsible Central Committee posts as a reward for faithfully following orders.

At the end of February 1953, on the eve of Stalin's death, I noticed a growing uncertainty in the behavior of Ignatiev, and my intuition told me that the whole anti-Semitic drive was about to end. The time was coming for the investigators to become unwanted witnesses and be purged. After Stalin's death, Beria accused Ignatiev of deceiving the party and fired him.

One important element not revealed is that among those investigated in the MGB for allegedly taking part in the Jewish conspiracy was Maironovsky, head of the MGB toxicological laboratory. In 1951 he was arrested and named a principal figure in the Doctors' Plot because he knew all the accused academicians and worked closely with them. He was a notable personality in Moscow medical circles.

According to Ryumin, Maironovsky was acting under the direction of Eitingon in an effort to kill the leadership. Ryumin did not realize that he was treading on dangerous ground, since Maironovsky's work was top secret and carried out on Stalin's orders. Maironovsky confessed to everything he was asked, including that he was Emma's nephew, but then Ignatiev sensed that Ryumin had gone too far. Ignatiev decided that Maironovsky should be kept out of the main case against the doctors. On February 14, 1953, he was convicted by a special conference of the MGB and sentenced to ten years in prison for criminal possession of poisons.

Stalin's death brought the end of the Doctors' Plot, but anti-Semitism remained a potent force. Beria initiated the exposure of the fabrications that had gripped the country in a paranoic spasm of fear, and began to rehabilitate the arrested doctors, but truth did not bring him friends at the top. In May 1953, two months after Stalin's death, Zoya Zarubina, who had become a dean of the Moscow Institute of Foreign Languages and a party secretary, heard at a confidential party meeting that Beria was concealing his Jewish origins. He was arrested two months later.

The Doctors' Plot greatly damaged the general image of the medical profession in Russian society and created distrust toward doctors. After the exposure of the falsity of the plot, rival groups in the medical community found themselves in a difficult position. My friend Professor Andrei Muzichenko, director of the Moscow Central Clinical Research Institute, told me that the government stood in the middle of any conflict in the medical community because it was the only source of financial support in the whole system of medical care. The message to all bureaucrats was to avoid any professional controversy, because one could not predict where the chips would fall; they could be picked up by the leadership and used politically in an unpredictable fashion that could bring Lubyanka into action. This created a dampening effect on creative controversy. It postponed government decisions on priority of resources for health care. The fear still persists that clashes of opinion on medical and other professional issues will cause Lubyanka people to investigate and report to the government their assessments of the arguments and the availability of incriminating materials against principal rival groups. No one knows how any argument will come out and what factors will decide it.

It is rumored now that a plan existed for deportation of Jews from Moscow on the eve of Stalin's death. I never heard of it; if such a plan existed it could be easily traced in the archives of state security and of the Moscow party committee, because it would have required large-scale preparations. Deportation operations are very difficult to carry out, especially if they are not concealed beforehand. There would have been some sort of top-secret directive, endorsed by the government at least one month before the start of such an operation. Therefore, I believe that it was only a rumor, probably based on comments by Stalin or Malenkov assessing the outrage of public opinion against Jews associated with the Doctors' Plot. When righteous remarks are made at a high level suggesting that "Soviet workers and peasants are justified in demanding deportation of Jewish criminals," a vicious tradition develops.

Even with this anti-Semitic atmosphere, started by Stalin and continued by Khrushchev, there remained the "selective" approach in which a closed group of Jewish intellectuals and highly qualified professionals were allowed to make their careers in the Soviet establishment; but the Zionist plot and the fall of Beria put an end to the employment of Jews in influential posts of the intelligence service or in the Central Committee. As far as I knew, the Committee for State Security (KGB) in the 1960s and 1970s employed only two Jewish rank-and-file case operators, for use against Zionist organizations. The presence of large numbers of Jews in the intelligence services, which had been the case from the Revolution to 1948, came to an end.

From the point of view of Soviet thought, the idea of establishing a Jewish republic with foreign support sounds ridiculous. It would constitute a basic interference in party and state affairs. Such a move would be regarded in Soviet terms as suspicious business because of the foreign involvement it would bring about in our closed society. In fact, that's what happened. For me at the time, sounding out Harriman on the idea of a Jewish republic was part of my instructions from Beria to ascertain America's intentions and the seriousness of its commitment to the idea. I knew that probes of this nature often led nowhere but were standard intelligence operational procedure. I could not imagine at the time that to be associated with such discussions would turn into a kiss of death.

The tragedy was that in a closed society like the Soviet Union, the establishment of the state of Israel in 1948 made the Jews appear to be the only significant national group with a foreign-based homeland. This automatically placed the whole national group under suspicion of potential divided loyalties, especially after Israel defeated the Arabs in the 1948 war of independence. The pride that followed the Jewish military victory revitalized the cultural consciousness of Soviet Jews, which had been destroyed in the twenties. The Jews and the Germans, since they had foreign-based homelands, were not allowed to form their own constituent republics in the Soviet Union with their own legislatures. Discrimination against all ethnic groups was harsher if they had potential support from overseas. Greeks, for example, were deported from the Caucasus to Uzbekistan.

What had begun as another purge of the bureacracy and a sweeping away of failed policies had gotten out of hand. Stalin's use of anti-Semitism, antinationalism, and anti–bourgeois cosmopolitanism for his usual political juggling had turned into license for leaders who harbored old hatreds against Jews. For Stalin anti-Semitism was a tool, an opportunistic weapon; but in the hands of his subordinates it became a revival of an age-old tradition, pure hatred of Jews. Unfortunately, it was a legacy that remained and flourished after his death. The acceptance within the leadership of anti-Semitic policies finally stripped the government of an entire population of public servants who had supported the Revolution and worked for the establishment of Soviet power. When the country came upon hard times and disintegrated, the flower of this educated leadership and their children had emigrated to Israel and the West.

FINAL YEARS UNDER STALIN, 1946–1953

he appointment of Abakumov as minister of state security by Stalin in 1946 initiated shifts in the power balance among Stalin's subordinates. At the time, Stalin's real purpose was carefully masked and we thought the new appointments to the Kremlin leadership — Andrei Zhdanov brought to Moscow from Leningrad, Aleksei A. Kuznetsov placed on the Central Committee, and M. I. Rodionov named as prime minister of the Russian Federation — were personnel shifts of a routine nature. This was not the case. Stalin was once again putting new people into power in order to maintain his own supremacy by setting up rival groups. Zhdanov became second to Stalin in making party and government decisions.

Two episodes shed new light on the power struggle. One was a case of corruption in the aviation industry; the second, which emerged from the first, was the demotion of Marshal Zhukov and other World War II heroes. It began with a case against Marshal of Aviation A. A. Novikov and People's Commissar of the Aviation Industry A. I. Shakhurin for covering up aircraft defects that caused flight accidents.

As chief of military counterintelligence in 1945, Abakumov first reported letters and complaints from test pilots disclosing shoddy production standards. When he was appointed minister of state security, he opened the official case against the manufacturers of defective aircraft and the military officials who concealed these faults. The issue was very sensitive because of American air superiority right after the war. Stalin was outraged when his son Vassili, an air force officer, and Abakumov reported that senior industry officials were deliberately concealing defects in equipment in order to win promotions for fulfilling production quotas. Malenkov, in his position on the Politburo, was responsible for the aviation industry, and had received a gold medal, Hero of Socialist Labor, for his outstanding work in wartime production.

The investigation revealed a deliberate attempt to conceal the number of fatal air crashes. Accidents were ascribed to pilot error rather than equipment failure. Before the war, severe punishment was the precedent for airplane failure. When Valery Chkalov, the pilot who flew nonstop to America over the North Pole, was killed in a plane crash in 1938, the plane designer, Nikolai Polykarpov, and the officer in charge of Chkalov's security were arrested. Polykarpov was kept at his job under house arrest, but the security officer was shot for failing to find the defects in the plane's construction, which led to the death of a national hero.

According to Abakumov, who recounted the conversation at a conference of senior Ministry of Security officials in July 1946, Stalin told him: "The guilt [of Novikov and Shakhurin] is established. What measure of punishment do you suggest?"

Abakumov replied without hesitation: "They should be shot."

"It is very easy to shoot people; it is more difficult to make them work. We should make them work," said Stalin, unexpectedly. They were sentenced to ten years in prison, where Stalin extracted confessions from them.

Stalin had ulterior motives for keeping them alive. From the confessions of Novikov and Shakhurin emerged a case against Marshal Zhukov and Malenkov.

Just before Stalin relinquished his self-appointed wartime position as minister of defense in 1946, he used these confessions to fire Marshal Zhukov as his deputy minister and commander of the Soviet ground forces. Order number 009 on June 9, 1946, signed by Stalin, documented charges against Zhukov for "lack of modesty," "overweening personal ambition," and "ascribing to himself the sole role in the implementation of all major wartime military operations including those in which he played no role at all." Zhukov was demoted to commander of the Odessa military district. The order also stated that "Marshal

Zhukov, feeling embittered, decided to group around himself failed, discontented commanders who had been relieved from their posts, thus putting himself into opposition to the government and to the High Command."[1]

This charge was based on the testimony of Marshal Novikov, who under interrogation denounced Zhukov. In his letter to Stalin he portrayed Zhukov's ambitions and reported that he had "anti-Stalinist conversations with him." Marshal Novikov also claimed that Zhukov "helped me to conceal my origins in the family of a czarist policeman."[2]

The disgrace and demotion of Zhukov by Stalin had far-reaching consequences. It was the opening of a campaign to demote the heroes of the Great Patriotic War and rid himself of potential rivals. Soon Admiral N. G. Kuznetsov, commander of the navy, was demoted, and in the resulting reshuffle Nikolai Bulganin emerged as the new defense minister. Bulganin was incapable of handling the massive problems of demobilizing and restructuring our armed forces. I met him casually in the Kremlin several times when I attended the conferences of the chiefs of intelligence services. His incompetence was striking. Bulganin was confused about such elementary concepts as the rapid deployment of forces, state of alert, and strategic military installations. He did not understand that sabotage against logistical storage facilities was far preferable to direct strikes at airfields. Bulganin argued with me and General Matvey Zakharov that instead of blowing up American fuel storage areas at Innsbruck in Austria, it would be more impressive to blow up American aircraft on airfields in Germany and France. He said this would destroy American morale and the Americans would be afraid to use their bases in Europe.

Bulganin was notorious for avoiding decisions. Letters requesting urgent action remained unsigned for months. The entire secretariat of the Council of Ministers was furious with his style of work, especially when Stalin left him in command while he vacationed in the Caucasus. Beria personally appealed to Stalin to release urgent strategic raw materials for the atomic project that were being held up in Bulganin's secretariat. In response, Stalin entrusted his deputy prime ministers with the right of signing urgent enactments, thus bypassing Bulganin. At the same time, Stalin ordered his deputies to provide Bulganin with support, assis-

1. *Sovershenoye Sekretno* (*Top Secret*) (Moscow), no. 2, 1993, p. 11.
2. Ibid.

tance, and constructive help. It was all a smokescreen for keeping power in his own hands, yielding a little authority here and there among weak men.

Bulganin's appearance was deceiving. Unlike Khrushchev or Beria, Bulganin was always smartly dressed and looked like an old nobleman, with well-groomed gray hair and a goatee. Later I learned he was a heavy drinker and an admirer of ballerinas and singers from the Bolshoi Theater. He was a man without any political principles, only the obedient servant of any leader. His aristocratic bearing was used by Stalin, who made him first deputy to the Council of Ministers, and then by Khrushchev, who appointed him to succeed Malenkov as prime minister. Then, in 1957, when Bulganin sided with Malenkov, Molotov, Kaganovich, and Voroshilov in their attempts to oust Khrushchev, Nikita Sergeyevich strongly denounced him at the party meeting: "He was Stalin's *stukach* [stool pigeon]. For this Stalin made him marshal of the Soviet Union," Khrushchev said. "Naturally, after unmasking his antiparty and treacherous behavior, we stripped him of this rank and demoted him to colonel general." (My former deputy, Colonel Lev Studnikov, who was present at the meeting, told me this.)

In March 1958 Bulganin was appointed director of the Central Bank, then three months later exiled to the economic administration in Stavropol, where an unknown Mikhail Gorbachev was beginning his career. Bulganin eventually retired on a pension, and I met him in downtown Moscow in the early 1970s, standing on line to buy a watermelon.

When Stalin made Bulganin minister of defense he achieved his goal of making himself the arbiter between real commanders of the armed forces — such as Vasilevsky, Zhukov, Shtemenko, Konev, Rokossovsky, and Bagramyan — and Bulganin, for whom they had no respect. Bulganin would never take responsibility for any serious decision even within his competence, yet the others could not bypass him. Thus neither side, the real leaders or the figurehead, could act independently. This stimulated rivalry among the military, for whom there was no longer a clear-cut hierarchy.

Abakumov arrested the generals of Zhukov's staff in Germany on charges that at first seemed nonpolitical: embezzlement of funds and illegally confiscating furniture, paintings, and jewelry from Germany and Austria. Recently published archives show that confessions were extracted from them that Zhukov had made anti-Stalinist statements. In 1944, during the war, Stalin had ordered Bogdan Kobulov, Beria's deputy, to install listening devices in Zhukov's Moscow apartment. The technical surveillance of Zhukov's and Admiral Kuznetsov's apartments[3] never yielded the hoped-for statements against Stalin. However, a group of prominent marshals and generals were thrown into prison and some of them shot because of their casual criticism of Stalin recorded by listening devices in their apartments or from confessions under duress.

Zhukov and Kuznetsov maintained their dignity, admitting their mistakes openly; Zhukov repented that he had awarded an Order of the Red Star to the famous singer Ruslanova. Although in wartime he had the right to do so, in peacetime only the Supreme Soviet could award such a medal.

Two generals, Grigori Kulik and Nikolai Rebalchenko, were shot in 1950. The others served prison terms and were released after Stalin's death. Novikov and Admiral Kuznetsov were reinstated in 1952, and after Stalin's death all charges against them were dropped. Zhukov continued to be commander of the military districts in Odessa and Siberia, and in 1952 Stalin made him a candidate member of the Central Committee. Only after Stalin's death was he summoned back to Moscow and appointed first deputy minister of defense.

Zhukov, understandably, was ill disposed to all security operations and the entire staff of the Ministry of Security. For him it made no difference who was in charge of his surveillance, Beria, Abakumov, or Kobulov; they were all voyeurs into his private life. The bugging of Zhukov's apartment ceased in 1953 after Stalin's death, but was resumed by Khrushchev in 1957 and continued by Brezhnev until Zhukov's death in 1974. Even in retirement Zhukov remained, in the mind of Khrushchev and Brezhnev, a potential threat, the military hero who might lead a coup against them, or be the choice of the military to replace them.[4]

Viktor Semyonovich Abakumov, born in 1908, was the minister of state security from 1946 to 1951. He was tall, with a full head of dark hair and a sensuous face. Although he had no education, he rose to the top through shrewdness and ruthlessness. His chekist career specialized in

---

3. The recently published file on Marshal Zhukov is named Gordetz — Arrogant Man — in KGB archives.

4. Transcripts of tapes of Zhukov's conversations appear in *Voyenniye Arkhivi Rossii* (*Military Archives of Russia*) (Moscow), no. 1, 1993, p. 231.

technical support for operations, not running agents; he arranged safe apartments, cars, schedules. Later, in the purges of the thirties, he became an interrogator and made his name under Kobulov, Beria's deputy. Just before the war, Abakumov was promoted to the rank of deputy commissar of internal affairs in charge of investigations. When Mikheyev, the director of SMERSH, killed himself after both his legs were blown off by German bombs in Kiev, Abakumov, then only thirty-four years old, was chosen by Stalin to replace him. In this capacity Abakumov was responsible for ensuring the political reliability of troops and combatting German espionage in the armed forces, and he gained competency in security issues. He could not be compared to Beria in professional ability, but his native intelligence set him apart from ordinary party apparatchiks.

In December 1945 Beria was relieved from his post as commissar of internal affairs, which he had held since 1938. He ceased to be supervisor of security and intelligence operations both at home and abroad, except where they touched on his job as manager of the Special State Committee on Problem Number One.

When Abakumov was appointed minister of state security in 1946, replacing Merkulov, he was not close to Beria. On the contrary, Stalin instructed Abakumov to compile incriminating materials against all power centers, including Beria. After Abakumov proved that Malenkov had full knowledge of defects in aviation production that had been concealed from the government, Malenkov received a party reprimand, demotion, and temporary exile to Kazakhstan in 1947. He was purged from the Central Committee secretariat and his duties were taken over by Aleksei Kuznetsov, Zhdanov's protégé. Abakumov and Kuznetsov soon became friends.

Stalin, however, allowed Malenkov to return to Moscow after two months and appointed him deputy prime minister. Beria in this period strongly supported Malenkov and let it be known that they often lunched together. Abakumov was reporting to Stalin Malenkov's and Beria's sympathy for the discharged heads of aviation production and navy officers. Abakumov got access to militia reports on the abuses of Beria's bodyguards, who picked up young women and teenagers on the street and brought them to Beria, which provoked outrage from husbands and parents.

Stalin's lineup emerged as follows: Beria and Malenkov together were on good terms with Pervukhin and M. Z. Saburov, top economic managers, who formed one competing group. They promoted their own people to influential positions in the government. A second group, later identified as the Leningrad faction, included Voznesensky, first deputy of Stalin and head of GOSPLAN; Zhdanov, second secretary of the party and head of ideology; Kuznetsov, secretary of the Central Committee, in charge of personnel; Rodionov, prime minister of the Russian Federation; and Aleksei Kosygin, deputy prime minister in charge of light industry and finance. The second group nominated their people to be secretaries of district party organizations. Kuznetsov promoted M. Popov, a former aviation plant director, to be Moscow district party secretary in 1946, and Popov became a Politburo member. Zhdanov encouraged him to control government ministers by having them elected to the Moscow party committee. Zhdanov and Kuznetsov's idea was to ensure double control over these men through Popov and through the Central Committee (similar to Yeltsin's maneuvers when he became secretary of the Moscow party committee in 1985). These actions, in which city and national government came under control of the same politicians, upset the Politburo's balance of power.

In this way government ministers, equivalent to cabinet members, could be manipulated without interference from Beria, Pervukhin, and their faction. When Zhdanov died in 1948, Popov demanded that the ministers, as party members, be subordinated to him, as head of the Moscow party committee. Malenkov interpreted Popov's request as a conspiracy, the setting up of an independent power center in the Moscow party organization. His report to Stalin was seconded by the ministers, who complained that Popov was interfering in their day-to-day affairs of state. Khrushchev, who was viceroy in the Ukraine but attended weekly Politburo meetings in Moscow, was sympathetic to Beria and Malenkov's faction. Like Malenkov, Khrushchev had been demoted at the urging of Zhdanov. In 1946, after a bad harvest, Khrushchev was dropped from first secretary of the Ukrainian Communist party to prime minister of the Ukraine. There was such bad blood between the factions that Stalin took the precaution of placing innocuous and unaligned men like Bulganin in his office when he took a vacation.

Stalin relished this factional fight; he knew it would leave his power uncontested. Stalin also correctly sensed that the power struggle between factions of his old guard brought about an opportunity to get rid of them. He could substitute a young generation of local party officials who had no national experience.

With these warring factions safely under Stalin's domination, he and Zhdanov initiated the anticosmopolitan campaign to wipe out Western ideological influence in the intelligentsia. Another of Stalin's purposes was to consolidate his newly acquired power in Eastern Europe and make his hold there equal to the repressive control he enjoyed internally.

Concurrently, Israel's victory in its war of independence greatly strengthened awareness among Soviet Jews of their cultural identity. Israel presented a new magnet for emigration. The anticosmopolitan campaign quickly turned anti-Semitic. Now the banner was against "rootless cosmopolitans," meaning Jews who had Western ties or ideas and might not hold the Soviet Union first in their hearts.

Finally, this campaign provided Stalin with an excuse to be rid of the leaders of the Jewish Antifascist Committee. They were pressing for the fulfillment of promises made during the war, promises that they had conveyed to Jewish leaders abroad. Their connections to influential people in the West were sufficient reason to make them targets for Stalin.

A year after Churchill's speech at Fulton, Missouri, in 1946, declaring confrontation and ideological war with communism, Stalin decided to tighten further ideological control of the party and the society, stamping out any sympathy, envy, or support for the West. The Cold War was on, and the immediate effect was a chill in all aspects of Soviet intellectual life. This set off a series of so-called scientific discussions in biology, philosophy, economic theory, literary criticism, and linguistics. Both Kremlin factions took advantage of the campaign for their own interests, trying to point out the ideological divergences of their rivals. This was not simply taking sides with Jews (cosmopolitans) against loyal Soviets; rather, the issue was a fundamental reshuffle of scientific and artistic personnel in the interests of the division of power at the top.

The case of biology is notorious. In the 1930s a smoldering argument in the field of genetic science broke out of the academy and into politics. On one side were world-known biologists pressuring the government to finance further research in plant and human genetics. Opposing them were the group led by Trofim Lysenko, who speculated on Marxist ideology, boldly asserting that plants, animals, and humans could be changed by factors in their material environment. He gave incredible examples to prove the impact of the external environment on the human race, claiming that Tatars had slanted eyes in response to their evolution under desert conditions facing centuries of sandstorms. He presented a vision to the government of the perfection of food supply through the services of Communist science. By altering conditions of agriculture, he would bring about a new era of abundance. He claimed that the mainstream biologists were the prisoners of bourgeois capitalist mentality and their work in genetic science should be terminated. He fought openly against the genetic scientists as obstacles to progress. Lysenko claimed that he was applying Marxist ideology when he initiated a purge against these scientists. Molotov, who was then prime minister, supported Lysenko.

A decade later, his promises had failed to materialize. A new debate opened with articles in scientific journals criticizing Lysenko and his followers. Prominent scientists wrote letters to the Central Committee revealing the serious consequences of Lysenko's mistakes. Molotov was no longer in charge of science.

Zhdanov arranged to have his son Yuri, who for a time was married to Stalin's daughter, Svetlana, become chief of the department of science in the CPSU Central Committee, and together they supported Lysenko's critics. Zhdanov was acting on Abakumov's information, signed by General Raikhman, saying that "trusted agent sources in the scientific biological community report that Academician Lysenko is trying to deceive the government, by reporting his alleged achievements in agro-biology, which are untrue." Letters from respected scientists established that Lysenko's dominance in agro-biological science since the 1930s, and his strong opposition to any research in genetics, was detrimental to scientific progress.

Ludvigov told me how Zhdanov manipulated the situation to enhance his own power. Zhdanov was no supporter of academic freedom; he was not concerned with the intellectual issues, but rather with exerting his power. His moves against Lysenko were useful in pursuing his own interests, to place his people in control of science and technology.

When Zhdanov died in 1948, his son was demoted in rank but stayed in the Central Committee, and the official line in science policy became once again sympathetic to Lysenko and his drive against genetic science. Unfortunately, published archival materials on the fate of genetics in the 1940s don't mention that sudden changes in official attitude toward supporters of genetic science coincided with and were caused by cardinal changes in the party leadership supervising scientific developments.

At the end of the 1940s, I became close friends with Anna

Tsukanova, deputy director of the personnel department of the Central Committee, in effect Malenkov's deputy. Raisa Sobel, a close friend of Emma's, who worked in the intelligence directorate prior to 1938, was also a friend of Anna Tsukanova.

I knew that Emma and Raisa had a friend named Anna, but I did not meet her until the three women invited me for lunch one day at the Ararat restaurant in downtown Moscow near Lubyanka. The custom for every high-placed government official was to have under the glass top of his desk a list of telephone numbers of high-ranking officials in the Central Committee, Council of Ministers, and most important ministries. Thus their full names were familiar to me. When I arrived at lunch with the three women and learned Anna's full name, I realized that she was Malenkov's deputy. I immediately took to her plump good looks and her long dark braid tied in a bun, the image of a Russian provincial beauty. It was the beginning of our long friendship. Anna and I talked to each other as true colleagues who understood each other's terms of reference; we both had access to secret material, so we felt free to discuss our work. Together we were an island of trust in a sea of suspicion. We are still friends more than forty years later.

Through Anna, I learned the real mechanism of power plays in the Soviet system. Anna frequently said that the policy of Comrade Stalin and his follower Comrade Malenkov was to ensure permanent rotation of high-ranking party and security officials throughout the country, not allowing them to stay in office for more than three years. She also was the first to reveal to me that the participation in ideological campaigns by party and government officials was the criterion for appointments. This was the way in which party cadres were tested.

I was shocked to learn from Anna that the Central Committee did not always prosecute corruption reported by the Party Control Commission and security organs. Stalin and Malenkov preferred to reproach an errant high-ranking official rather than prosecute him, but if the man landed in the wrong power group, then the incriminating evidence was used to demote or purge him. Another major reason for prosecution was failure to meet production or harvest quotas.

Anna revealed to me that the leadership was aware of the heavy toll of every ideological drive, but the ends, Malenkov said, justified these "permitted costs." This criminal justification for the adverse costs of the purge campaigns and ideological drives was the fatal mistake of the rulers. The purge of rival leadership, of Jewish doctors and scientists, of agronomists and biologists who opposed first Lysenko and later Khrushchev in his Virgin Lands campaigns,[5] of dissenters in the cultural sphere, robbed the country of vital talent. In the long run, these negative costs undermined the system.

Anna did not realize how much she revealed to me concerning the true state of power relationships when she said that the Central Committee was aware of "negative elements" — meaning fabricated accusations — in the anticosmopolitan campaign. She was sure that in time these mistakes would be corrected.

It was from her that I learned of Stalin's initiative to clean out the Georgian party organization. She said that everybody in the Central Committee was afraid to suggest personnel changes in the Georgian party because the subject was so close to Comrade Stalin's roots that they might overstep what was acceptable to him. She and I believed that Stalin was responding to corruption in Georgia. How naive we were. We now know from archive documents that the so-called Mingrelian Affair marked the last upheaval and criminal purge of Stalin's rule.

In the final period of his rule, the small circle of leadership included Malenkov, Bulganin, Khrushchev, and Beria, with Stalin busy stimulating rivalry among them. In 1951 Beria fell out of favor. Stalin ordered listening devices installed in Beria's mother's residence, correctly sensing that Beria would not allow himself or his wife any anti-Stalinist comments, but his mother, Martha, living in Georgia, might have Mingrelian nationalist connections. This Mingrelian tribe from which Beria came was historically on bad terms with the Gurieli, the Georgian minority that Stalin trusted most. The Mingrelian Affair was, in fact, based on fabricated accusations of a conspiracy to secede from the Soviet Union. Stalin's underlying motive was simply to get rid of Beria. Stalin cruelly chose Beria to purge his most trusted associates. To keep up the ruse that Beria himself was still trusted, Stalin gave Beria the rare honor of addressing party and state activists on the occasion of the thirty-fourth anniversary of the October Revolution, on November 6, 1951.

5. The Virgin Lands campaign in 1954 was a massive effort to open vast tracts of steppe lands for grain production, mainly in Kazakhstan, where 90 million acres — more than the whole cultivated area of England, France, and Spain — were initially plowed by half a million "volunteers" organized into huge state farms. After initial but costly success, the experiment had to be curtailed because of soil erosion that rapidly turned the land into a dust bowl.

In 1947, four years before the Georgian purge began, Stalin had appointed General Rukhadze minister of state security of Georgia. In the war years he had been chief of SMERSH in the Caucasus. His anti-Beria inclinations were known. On Stalin's personal instructions, Rukhadze, assisted by the infamous Ryumin, collected incriminating evidence against Beria and the circle around him. At first it only amounted to routine monitoring of Beria's relatives in Georgia. Beria did not hide from Stalin or Molotov that his wife's uncle, N. Djordania, was the minister of foreign affairs in the exiled Georgian Menshevik government in Paris; nor that her nephew had collaborated with the Germans when he was a prisoner of war and served us as a double agent.

At the end of the 1930s and again after the war, Soviet intelligence penetrated Georgian émigré groups in France. The most successful NKVD officer in this effort was Vardo Maximalishvili, Beria's secretary, who before her mission to Paris had been trained by Emma.

At this time it was rumored in the closed circles of the government that Beria's son Sergei would soon marry Svetlana Alliluyeva, Stalin's daughter, after she divorced Zhdanov's son. According to Beria's secretary Ludvigov, who told me the story in Vladimir jail, Nina, Beria's wife, and Beria himself strongly opposed the marriage. Beria had no illusions; he knew that the marriage would be used against him by his rivals in the Politburo. He shrewdly observed Stalin's failing strength. If Beria were attached to Stalin by family ties, he would lose out when Stalin eventually died.

This created a personal conflict between Stalin and Beria, and explains why in 1951 Stalin instructed General Rukhadze to proceed with the investigations of corruption among Georgian officials of Mingrelian origin. In Georgia, Mingrelians supplied the majority of bureaucratic personnel in the security service and procurator's office. They were also powerful in the party machinery.

Stalin ordered Rukhadze to find proof and extract confessions showing connections between Mingrelians in Georgia, Turkey, and Paris. All he had to say was, "These Mingrelians, they are totally unreliable. I don't want to be surrounded by people with dubious connections abroad." That was enough for Rukhadze to know that he must fabricate a conspiracy.

It all began during Stalin's vacation in Abkhazia, in northwest Georgia, in 1951. He received Rukhadze at his dacha and suggested intensification of the anticorruption drive against Mingrelians who tried to suppress evidence against their kinsmen. "And while you are at it, you should think about sabotage operations in Turkey and Paris," Stalin said. Rukhadze reminded Stalin that the Georgian security organs had no experience in foreign operations and would need assistance from the Center. Stalin promised his personal help.

Soon after this encounter, Rukhadze attended a dinner party at which, after heavy drinking, he boasted that he had links with Stalin, who had given him instructions for sabotage operations in Turkey and France. Also present at the dinner was the Georgian minister of the interior, Bzyava, a Mingrelian himself, who the next day wrote a letter to Minister of Security Ignatiev in Moscow denouncing Rukhadze's behavior at the dinner. Ignatiev reported the letter to Stalin, who had him show the letter to Rukhadze and destroy it in his presence. Ignatiev warned Rukhadze that even though he still was in favor with Stalin, he should curb his excessive behavior. Bzyava, nonetheless, was soon arrested.

Rukhadze's next move was to arrest the former minister of security of Georgia, A. N. Rapava, Procurator General V. I. Shonia, and Academician P. A. Sharia, a member of the credential board of the USSR parliament, the Chamber of Nationalities, and formerly a deputy director of foreign intelligence in the NKVD. All were accused of contact with émigré organizations through NKVD agent Gigelia, who had returned from Paris with a French wife in 1947 after ten years abroad. Gigelia and his wife were arrested on Stalin's orders and tortured in an attempt to make him confess his part in the plot, despite her immunity to arrest as a French citizen.

Thus began the purge of the Georgian leadership, men close to Beria. Beria's agent Vardo and her husband were arrested in Moscow. The anticorruption drive in Georgia was now transformed into accusations of a Mingrelian plot to secede from the Soviet Union, first to become an autonomous region, then to ally itself with Turkey. Stalin had gone to these extreme measures first because of his personal grudge against Beria, and second to deprive Beria of his power base in the Georgian government and party.

Stalin began this drive in 1951, soon after a notable increase in Beria's popularity due to his success in managing the atomic project and setting off the second test blast. Stalin knew that the second blast was Beria's pride because it did not copy the American 1945 design but was a Soviet creation. Rather than promote his protégé for his success, Stalin now wanted a man more under his thumb to run the program.

Cynically, Stalin appointed Beria to chair the party commission that would look into the Mingrelian divergence. Stalin sent Beria to Tbilisi to crack down on Mingrelian nationalism and fire his closest associate, Party Secretary Kandida Charkviani, who was replaced by Beria's archenemy, A. I. Mgeladze, Stalin's appointee. Beria also closed down the Mingrelian newspaper.

At the very moment that Beria was being feted in Moscow, and was invited to address the all-government and party meeting for celebration of the anniversary of the October Revolution, a team of interrogators were dispatched to extract confessions from arrested Mingrelians that would implicate Beria and his wife, Nina. The Mingrelians never broke. They spent a year and a half in jail, subjected to sleep deprivation and other tortures, and were released by Beria only after Stalin's death. Eight months before Stalin died, he had Rukhadze arrested because he had failed to extract any confessions. Officially, he was charged with deceiving the party. He had boasted once too often about his closeness to Stalin and their telephone conversations and personal correspondence in the Georgian language.

Now, forty years later, Kiril Stolyarov, a writer digging in the procurator's archives, briefed me on the Mingrelian Affair. He has cleared up the episode that confronted me in Georgia in 1951 or 1952 when I was ordered by Ignatiev to visit Tbilisi. I was to assess the potential of the local Georgian intelligence service and assist in their preparations to kidnap the leaders of the Georgian Menshevik exile community in Paris, relatives of Beria's wife, Nina Gegichkori. I was told that the initiative in the operation came from Tbilisi, from General Rukhadze, and was endorsed personally by Stalin. Rukhadze insisted that Georgian agents undertake this operation. With that in mind, he arrived in Moscow, was received by Ignatiev, and then flew back to Tbilisi, inviting me to join him on the plane. I preferred the train and I followed him. My instructions were to report personally to Ignatiev.

What I found in Tbilisi depressed me. The only capable agent with good connections in France, Gigelia, was in prison, charged with being a Mingrelian nationalist. Rukhadze's agents were not reliable; they even refused to talk with me in the Russian language. Rukhadze's deputy, who planned the mission to Paris, had never been abroad. He actually believed that bringing a basket filled with Georgian wine and shashlik and serving it to a party of Georgians at the most fashionable restaurant in Paris would automatically win the good graces of Georgian émigrés for the newcomers from Tbilisi. They also proposed sending a cultural delegation to Paris, but it was clear that this grandiose plan only concealed Rukhadze's desire to take his wife to Paris, representing the Tbilisi Conservatory. She was a modest woman and a good singer. The plan was absurd.

The team from Moscow who were interrogating Mingrelians joyfully told Rukhadze that they were close to establishing the connection between Beria's family and imprisoned secessionists. Then I noticed that under a glass plate covering Rukhadze's desk was a portrait of the young Beria, one among the enemies on his most-wanted list. Rukhadze was an ally of Abakumov, who as early as 1946 started his campaign to compromise first Beria's former subordinates in the security service and then Beria himself.

The amateurish adventurism of Rukhadze frightened me and I hurried back to Moscow to report to Ignatiev. He and his first deputy, Ogoltsov, listened attentively but pointed out that the matter had to be considered by the highest authority because Rukhadze maintained a personal correspondence with Stalin in the Georgian language. Stalin, however, understood that Rukhadze and Ryumin were dangerous: the questions they posed to Abakumov and Mingrelian associates of Beria, instead of probing simply for confessions of treason, displayed unusual interest in high party and government intrigues. Abakumov complained in his letter to Beria and Malenkov on October 11, 1952, that Ryumin asked questions on internal Politburo relations derived from top-secret memoranda sent to Stalin.

Clearly, the purge and prosecution of Abakumov and the Mingrelians had gone too far. It was decided to sacrifice Ryumin and Rukhadze. Rukhadze was soon imprisoned in Lefortovo jail; Ryumin was relieved from his duties in November 1952 and arrested after Stalin's death. He would have fallen even if Stalin had lived.

After Stalin died, Beria kept Rukhadze in prison but released his victims. Rukhadze and Ryumin, both in custody, bombarded Beria with pleas for their release, addressing him as "Great Man." Three months later, when Beria was arrested by Khrushchev and Malenkov, these pleas implicated them in Beria's alleged conspiracy. Thus Rukhadze went on trial in Tbilisi in 1955, together with his earlier victims, who were now rearrested for their connections to Beria. The Mingrelians Rapava, Shonia, and Sharia got it in the neck twice, first from Stalin and again from Khrushchev. The leadership in Tbilisi and in Moscow both wanted to be rid of them.

Subjective motives and ambitions in the late 1940s and early 1950s played a far more significant role in political events than it seemed at the time. We who watched and suffered the results later came to the conclusion that the party leadership — Stalin and those who succeeded him — used such banners as anticorruption, de-Stalinization, perestroika, and antialcoholism to purge their opponents and rivals. They aimed to consolidate absolute power or to replace their staffs with new figures. They relied on incriminating information from the Party Control Commission and the security service. The standard rule was to collect dirt against everyone and then manipulate this evidence. I was both the instrument and the victim of this system.

Abakumov had reported personally to Stalin, and the information he provided served Stalin by compromising all top officials. After the death of Zhdanov the equilibrium of power-sharing that had given stability to the previous period ended. Stalin hadn't allowed Zhdanov to get rid of Malenkov totally when he was compromised in the aviation scandal; instead he simply demoted him, leaving him still an influential member of the Politburo. Stalin made Malenkov responsible for correcting past mistakes in the aviation industry, knowing that Malenkov would do his utmost, fearing further exposures. Thus he remained in place, a counterbalance to Zhdanov, whose followers would soon pay the price.

From Anna Tsukanova I learned the most striking facts about the Leningrad Case, in which all the followers of Zhdanov, all competitors of Malenkov and Beria, were convicted and shot. In 1949 we did not know the monstrous charges against them. At that time, Anna told me only that Kuznetsov and Voznesensky were removed from their posts because they were involved in fraud connected with party elections at the Leningrad city conference. Kuznetsov's friendship with Abakumov did not save him; Stalin tested Abakumov's loyalty by forcing him to purge his friend.

We must recall what is often overlooked, the mentality of idealistic Communists in the late forties and early fifties. The worst crime that Anna and I could conceive of for a high-ranking party or government official was high treason, but no less was that of falsifying secret party ballots. Party business was sacred, especially internal party elections by secret ballot, which were rightly regarded as the most effective instrument of intraparty democracy. It was the only lever the rank and file had for controlling our leaders. Therefore, when Anna told me that the

Leningrad party leadership had falsified party elections at the district conference, these men were finished in our eyes.

The actual details of the Leningrad Case were kept secret from mid-level party activists; even Anna did not know the extent of the accusations. Now we know that the accusations included attempts to split the Communist party by establishing a rival power center in Leningrad to counter the Russian federative government and the all-union Council of Ministers. Those arrested were also charged with stealing individual property left in besieged Leningrad during the war. One of the accused, Ya. F. Kapustin, was charged with espionage, but that could not be substantiated.

These accusations were fabricated, motivated by the ongoing power struggle among Stalin's aides. Malenkov, Beria, and Khrushchev had an obvious motive — enhancing their own power — in doing away with the Leningrad group. They feared that the young Leningrad team would succeed Stalin after his death. We now know that there were indeed falsifications in counting the secret ballots in 1948 in Leningrad, but in no way were the accused men guilty. The entire Politburo, including Stalin, Malenkov, Khrushchev, and Beria, unanimously passed a resolution ordering Abakumov to arrest and prosecute the Leningrad group, but contrary to Khrushchev's memoirs and the textbooks of party history, Abakumov did not initiate this case. True, his subordinates fabricated it under his instructions, but Abakumov acted on official party directives.

At first all those arrested were accused of minor crimes; Voznesensky, for instance, with the loss of documents in his secretariat and with nepotism because he allowed his younger brother and sister to be appointed to various posts in Leningrad. Indirectly, Mikoyan was seriously implicated, because one of his sons was married to Kuznetsov's daughter.

The Leningrad Case remained secret until Stalin's death, and even I, although director of an autonomous department in the security service, had no idea of the fate of those who perished in obscurity.

The head of the Leningrad security service, General Kubatkin, was purged and shot in a separate trial. Now the documents of the Leningrad affair are partly published. Blood is on the hands of all Politburo members of that period, because they endorsed the death sentence for the defendants three weeks before the proceedings in the Leningrad court began.

                    *   *   *

The Leningrad Case coincided with a sharp demotion of Molotov, who although he retained his position as a Politburo member, was relieved in March 1949 from his post as foreign minister and replaced by Vyshinsky. Molotov was seriously damaged by the arrest of his wife, Polina Zhemchuzhina, a Jew, who was charged first with abuses of power in the cosmetics and textile trust that she directed, and then with loss of secret documents (which may, in fact, have been stolen at Stalin's direction). Under the orders of Stalin and his interrogators, to compromise her in the eyes of her husband and the Politburo, two officials in her ministry were compelled to confess that they were having sexual relations with her. She first spent a year in jail, then was placed under house arrest in Alma-Ata, Kazakhstan, where she was kept under close surveillance because she had met Golda Meir before the October Revolution or in the years of the Civil War.

Stalin wanted her confessions to compromise Molotov. Her arrest was kept secret, and I learned about it just before Stalin's death when Pavel Fitin, then the minister of security of Kazakhstan, complained to me how hard it was to be personally responsible for surveillance of Zhemchuzhina. Top-level officers of the ministry were inquiring about her, wanting to know about her Zionist connections and revelations she made while in exile in Kazakhstan. Fitin was summoned by Sergei Goglidze, first deputy minister of security, and understood from his questions and the order to transfer her to Lubyanka that the purpose was to implicate Molotov in Zionist connections. Fitin was upset that the alarming changes in the leadership could affect all those who had worked with Molotov.

We didn't know at that time, October 1952, that Stalin was openly attacking Molotov and Mikoyan at Central Committee plenary sessions. At those meetings Stalin denounced Molotov and Mikoyan as conspirators. He accused Molotov of giving in to blackmail and pressure from imperialist circles, implying that Zhemchuzhina, although he did not mention her name, was close to the Zionist conspiracy.

Right after the plenary session, Molotov was compelled to return to Stalin's secretariat the original documents of the Molotov-Ribbentrop Pact, which included the secret protocols. Since that day until they were published in 1992, they were kept in the secret archives of the Politburo. I do not rule out that Stalin's idea was to implicate Molotov with charges of pro-German sympathies or capitulating to Hitler during their secret negotiations.

*   *   *

In September 1950 Viktor Drozdov, the Ukrainian deputy minister of security, was transferred to Moscow. We had known each other almost thirty years. Emma and his wife were friends, and when I was in Lvov tracking the Ukrainian nationalist Shukheyevich, I lived in Drozdov's villa not far from the city. In Moscow, he was put in charge of Special Bureau Number Two, which was set up to undertake secret surveillance and kidnapping operations against Stalin's enemies — both real and, as I now see, imagined.

Originally, Abakumov and Ogoltsov planned to put my Bureau for Diversions and Intelligence in charge of these operations internally and abroad, with Drozdov as my deputy, since Eitingon was out of favor. This did not suit Abakumov, and he arranged the division of labor so that Drozdov was in charge of internal operations. He had no connections in Moscow and was trusted to execute these most delicate special tasks. Drozdov's first assignment was to monitor the security of our listening program to ensure the devices had not been detected. Drozdov revealed to me that in 1942 Stalin ordered Kobulov, Beria's deputy, to install listening devices in the apartments of Marshals Voroshilov, Budyonny, and Zhukov. Later, in 1950, Molotov and Mikoyan were added to the list. There were also grand plans to ensure secret bugging of all telephone conversations in Central Committee headquarters. This was accomplished only in Brezhnev's time, when the technology became available.

Drozdov was lucky not to be involved in any kidnapping operations on Stalin's behalf, but twice his men were borrowed by the Counterintelligence Directorate to accost and assault foreign diplomats and Russian writers meeting with them on the street. The first thing Beria did when he took over the security service after Stalin's death was to fire Drozdov because he knew too much about internal intrigues and because he was on bad terms with Kobulov. Drozdov's firing at age fifty was a blessing in disguise; otherwise he would have gone down with Beria and joined him in another world.

Next came the arrest of Abakumov himself. In his last year as minister of security, especially in the last nine months, he was totally isolated from Stalin. The Kremlin diary of Stalin's visitors shows that Abakumov was not granted an audience with Stalin after November 1950; on July 12, 1951, he was arrested. For Stalin, Abakumov knew too much. For me, his fall was a thunderbolt.

In May or June 1951, when for the last time I spent some hours in Abakumov's office, he looked very sure of himself. He showed no indecisiveness in running the daily affairs of the ministry. Only later did I learn from my cellmate Mamulov that in the last months of 1950 Abakumov tried to establish closer relations with Mamulov, who was known to have direct access to Beria. Mamulov told me that Abakumov asked him to arrange an audience with Beria, claiming that he was always loyal and never took part in intrigues against Beria. This request by Abakumov was fruitless.

Abakumov was accused of delaying investigations of important crimes and suppressing evidence about the double role of agents Gavrilov and Lavrentiev, homosexuals planted in the American Embassy compound. Ryumin claimed that Abakumov did not report that the pair were suspected of working for the CIA station in Moscow.

Certainly, Abakumov had a number of fabrications and false forced confessions on his conscience, but it is also true that first the procurator's office and then Ryumin were accusing him of crimes he never committed. He was never a politician and could never have conspired to seize power; he was devoted to Stalin and believed in him.

At first I didn't realize the consequences of Abakumov's fall; Abakumov and I had often disagreed and it seemed to me that the party leadership wanted to correct serious mistakes. The Politburo commission comprising Beria, Malenkov, Ignatiev, and Matvey Shkiratov (chief of the Party Control Commission) initially seemed interested in auditing the efficiency of counterintelligence and intelligence operations. Soon it became clear that Abakumov's dismissal and arrest marked the beginning of a new purge. As a result of his arrest, Malenkov strengthened his position, because Stalin promoted his onetime secretary and later chief of personnel of the Central Committee, Semyon Denisovich Ignatiev, to the post of minister of state security. With the removal of both Abakumov and the Leningrad faction, Malenkov and Ignatiev, in alliance with Khrushchev, emerged as a new power center in the leadership.

After a conference with Ignatiev and his deputies, I returned to my office in a gloomy mood. They had a different purpose than I did for our active operations — liquidations. For me, they had to be logical actions taken to prevent serious damage to our agent networks or to our interests. They, on the other hand, were planning to assassinate old people, leaders of émigré groups in Germany and Paris. They would use agents code-named Cabbage and Cabbage Core, who were assigned to watch retired general Kapustiansky, a Ukrainian nationalist who had been promoted to his rank by the czar. He was in his seventies, no longer active, but Ignatiev's group was eager to report his liquidation to impress the government. I strongly opposed this plan and convinced Ignatiev to cancel it, arguing that the old man's death would deprive us of control over his mail, our most important source of regular information on the émigrés.

I recall that Ignatiev signed a directive to our overseas rezidenturas ordering them to intensify agent penetration into Menshevik organizations, branding them one of our main adversaries. This was in 1952, thirty-five years after the Revolution. I protested vigorously that our rezidentura in Vienna was busy penetrating American military installations in Europe and had no time or personnel to track down Mensheviks. Ignatiev, despite support for his directive by his two aides, said, "The directive is good, but you are telling the truth. Let's withdraw it."

Emma and I were disturbed by the random arrests. The growing tension was evident in both the anti-Semitic drive and in power intrigues in the ministry. Emma correctly sensed that although she was a retired officer and attracted no interest of interrogators, those who were arrested — Raikhman, Eitingon, Matusov, Sverdlov — were questioned about her. When Anna came to visit us, it was the first time in my life that I began to discuss with Emma prospects and possibilities of finding a new job. Being a senior officer in a service run by an incompetent minister, whose aides included adventurers and careerists like Ryumin, would inevitably snare you in a net of trouble. I had just received the diploma of the military academy, for which I had worked evenings for five years, and this certificate of higher education gave me hope of finding a new job in the military or party machinery. Anna agreed to help me.

In 1952 Stalin did not take his usual vacation in the Caucasus. One morning I received an unexpected phone call from Malenkov announcing that the Central Committee had entrusted me with a very important mission and Comrade Ignatiev would brief me in detail. Ignatiev soon summoned me to his office in Lubyanka where, strangely, he was alone. After greeting me in a very solemn manner, Ignatiev said, "The highest authority is very much concerned with the prospects of the formation of an anti-Bolshevik bloc of nations whose chairman will be Kerensky. This initiative of the American reactionaries should be decisively severed and the leadership of the anti-Bolshevik bloc should be decapitated before its activities can develop."

I was ordered to promptly prepare an operational plan for action in Paris or in London. Within a week, however, I told Ignatiev that an immediate operation was too risky, because the man in Paris I had in mind for the action, Nikolai Khokhlov, was under suspicion. His papers had been examined by the Austrian police at his last border crossing, and he was now on the watch list. We could not even use him for another less prominent operation, helping the Georgian Security Ministry foil the Mingrelian secession conspiracy by kidnapping Beria's wife's relatives in Paris.

Our illegal task force in Paris was headed by Prince Gagarin, whose main responsibility was to find the vulnerable approaches to NATO headquarters in Fontainebleau and be ready to blow up its communications facilities and military alert system in case of extreme confrontation or war. The presence of this task force was reported to Stalin and Malenkov on several occasions. I asked Ignatiev if we should reorient this group to liquidate Kerensky when he attended the founding meeting of the proposed Anti-Bolshevik Bloc of Nations.

Ignatiev, never a risk taker, said the matter would have to be decided by the highest authority. A day or two later, I received a TASS report stating that the formation of an anti-Bolshevik bloc had been thwarted by the Ukrainian nationalists and Croatian émigrés, who refused to have a Russian, Kerensky, as the head of their organization.

The next morning, without comment, I sent the TASS report to Ignatiev so he would understand that Kerensky was no longer a threatening rival to the Soviet Union. He responded by calling a conference in his office attended by the Security Ministry leadership. Ignatiev reproached the intelligence directorate for recommending initiatives without taking into consideration the internal rivalries within the anti-Communist groups.

Ignatiev said that Comrade Malenkov was particularly concerned that we not divert our efforts from combatting the main adversary, the United States. This remark was the watershed: concern with émigré organizations was put where it belonged, in the past. We had new, much more powerful enemies.

After this meeting Ignatiev suggested we prepare proposals for the reorganization of foreign intelligence work in the Ministry of Security.

Stalin personally took charge of the reorganization. Under his initiative and leadership, the Politburo, on December 19, 1952, transformed the First Directorate (foreign intelligence) of the Ministry of Security into the First Chief Directorate and recommended that the chief of intelligence should hold the rank of deputy minister. It was a momentous change; it meant that foreign intelligence operations would have an expanded budget, increased manpower, and heightened prestige.

I was not invited to the Kremlin for the discussion presided over by Stalin, but Malenkov came to the ministry at the end of 1952 and formally announced the decision, which he described as a plan for creating "a grand intelligence network abroad." Malenkov quoted Stalin: "The work against our main adversary is impossible without adhering to the principle of a grand intelligence network. It is not necessary to set up our intelligence strongholds in the United States, but we should act decisively against the Americans, first of all in Europe and in the Middle East. We should use new opportunities opened up by the intensification of Chinese emigration to the United States. The vulnerability of America is the multinational structure of its population. We must look for options in exploiting minorities. No foreign-born American, while serving as our agent, should be asked to work against his own country of origin. You should make maximum use of immigrants from Germany, Italy, and France in the United States by convincing them that by helping us they are working for the countries of their birth."

As 1953 began, I was deeply worried about the reshuffle in the structure of the ministry initiated by Stalin. I knew I was on the list of 213 persons, including top-level officials, whose names were connected with the Jewish Antifascist Committee and the Doctors' Plot. Anna told me that Colonel Vladimir Sokolev, a deputy director of the Investigation Department of the ministry, went through transcripts of interrogations and wrote summaries of why people were named either by the interrogator or the prisoner. Based on the incriminating charges, Malenkov was replacing the top positions in the government and party machinery, demoting people or sending them out of Moscow. The object was to install new men who were unaware of the mechanisms of power and who would follow harsh instructions without hesitation.

This administrative purge soon became bloody. Lieutenant General Vlasik, chief of the Kremlin guards and Stalin's security, was sent to Siberia as the head of a camp and then secretly arrested there. Vlasik was charged with suppressing the famous letter from Timashuk that set the Doctors' Plot in motion, suspicious ties with agents of foreign intelligence, and a secret conspiracy with Abakumov.

Vlasik was mercilessly beaten and tortured. His desperate appeals to Stalin protesting his innocence went unanswered. Vlasik was forced to confess his negligence of duty, that he allowed dubious people to attend official ceremonies in the Kremlin, Red Square, and the Bolshoi Theater which were attended by Stalin and members of the Politburo, putting them at risk. Vlasik remained in prison until 1955, when he was sentenced for the embezzlement of funds for the Yalta and Potsdam conferences and then granted amnesty. Despite support from Marshal Zhukov, his appeals for rehabilitation were denied.

The dismissal of Vlasik did not mean that Beria managed to change Stalin's personal bodyguards. In 1952, after the arrest of Vlasik, Ignatiev was appointed chief of the Kremlin guards department in addition to his post as minister of security.

All rumors that Stalin was assassinated by Beria men in his bodyguard are unfounded.[6] It was impossible for anyone in Stalin's internal circle to move against him. He was a sick old man with accelerating paranoia, but until his last day he was in strong control. When he twice openly announced his desire to retire, first after the big victory celebration in the Kremlin in 1945, and again at the plenary session of the Central Committee in October 1952, he was only manufacturing a ruse to reshuffle his aides.

As part of the process of redirecting the focus of our intelligence activities, Malenkov told me to think about how to utilize the recall of our adviser to China, Kovalov, who had reported to the Central Committee the Chinese leadership's attempts to recruit agents from among Soviet specialists working there. Comrade Stalin, said Malenkov, decided to send a copy of this report directly to Mao Tse-tung, announcing that we had recalled our adviser because we had full trust in the Chinese leadership. At the same time, Kovalov was appointed to a responsible job in the Council of Ministers. Malenkov ordered me to consult with him on setting up an illegal network in the Far East to gather information on China. Malenkov emphasized that the network should be independent

6. Ronald Hingley, *The Russian Secret Police* (New York: Simon and Schuster, 1970), p. 313, states that the death of Major General Pyotr Kosynkin, deputy chief of the Kremlin bodyguard, in January, signaled a power struggle between the old and new generations in Stalin's Kremlin surroundings.

of old sources that might be known to the Chinese from the Comintern years.

On February 20, 1953, in this atmosphere of intensified activity, I was summoned to Ignatiev's office, where Goglidze, his first deputy, and Konyakhin, deputy chief of the Investigation Department, were waiting. Ignatiev said we were going to the Kremlin. It was late in the evening; Ignatiev, Goglidze, and Konyakhin entered Stalin's study, and I was left alone in the reception room for about an hour. Then Goglidze and Konyakhin left and I was asked to enter. While waiting, I thought over this Chinese business, for which I was not prepared. The order had come only two or three days earlier, and I had no experience in the Far East. It occurred to me to suggest the use of Eitingon, who had worked in China in the 1920s and had smuggled out of China a group of our advisers who had been arrested. The advisers, including Mikhail M. Borodin (the father of Red China),[7] had all been charged as enemies of the Chinese people. For safely getting them out, Eitingon was awarded the Order of the Red Banner in 1926 or 1927. Now he was in jail.

I entered Stalin's study feeling agitated until I looked at him. I was startled to see a tired old man. Stalin had changed greatly. His hair was thinner, and although he had always spoken calmly and slowly, now he talked with difficulty and his pauses between sentences were longer. His appearance confirmed rumors that he had suffered two strokes, one after the Yalta Conference and the other after his seventieth birthday, in 1950.

Stalin began by discussing the reorganization of foreign intelligence. Ignatiev asked my view on whether there was a need to preserve two independent foreign intelligence directorates in the Ministry of Security. My Bureau for Diversions and Intelligence would either remain independent or be folded into the First Chief Directorate. I explained that for diversion operations against strategic NATO and American bases surrounding our frontier, we must constantly coordinate our efforts and maintain a state of readiness. No matter what the form of organizational control, it would be necessary to establish priorities.

Rapid deployment forces for special tasks such as sabotage require

7. Mikhail Markovich Borodin (1884–1952) emigrated to America and belonged to the American Socialist party before returning to Russia in 1917. From 1918 he worked as an agent of the Communist International. He was invited to China by Sun Yat-sen in 1923 and served as a senior adviser to the Kuomintang until 1927. Borodin was arrested in 1949 during the anti-Semitic purge and died in 1952 in prison while under interrogation.

support and communications units. I stressed that the success of our sabotage operations against the Germans had depended heavily on the quality of our agent network preestablished in the vicinity of the bases to be attacked. I said, "In accordance with the Central Committee directive passed by Abakumov in 1948, we were ready to blow up the American fuel depot in Innsbruck, Austria. We dispatched not only a task force equipped with special explosives, but our agent there had direct access to the facilities. Therefore, we were perplexed with Abakumov's abrupt order to cancel the operation, which could have seriously hampered the American airlift to Berlin."

Stalin did not comment. There was an awkward pause for several minutes. Then Stalin said, "The bureau for diversion work abroad should be retained as an autonomous unit, subordinated directly to the minister. It will be a necessary instrument for causing serious damage and losses to the enemy if war breaks out. Comrade Sudoplatov should also be made a deputy chief of the intelligence directorate so as to be aware of capabilities and developments in intelligence operations, to utilize them for the purpose of sabotage."

Stalin asked me if I had met Nikolai Mironov, General Aleksei A. Yepishev's deputy in the personnel department of the ministry, suggesting that he should be promoted to head the First Chief Directorate. I replied that I had met Mironov only once, when under the minister's orders I had briefed him about the general duties of the Bureau for Diversions and Intelligence.

There was another awkward pause. Stalin handed me a handwritten document and asked for my comments. It outlined a plan to assassinate Marshal Tito. I had never seen it before, but I thought the handwriting might be that of Pitovranov, deputy minister of state security.

I had heard that Pitovranov was married to Malenkov's niece. He was tall and handsome with the look of a distinguished academician. In 1939, after graduating from the Institute of Communications, where he was the secretary of the party committee, Pitovranov was promoted to the security service and during the war became chief of the important NKVD office in Gorky district. Pitovranov was a capable bureaucrat; he never bothered himself with minor details at the lower level. For a short time he had been imprisoned by Ryumin. Although he was a hunting companion of Eitingon's, Pitovranov arranged for Eitingon's arrest in October 1951 at Vnukovo airport. Only two days later, Pitovranov was himself arrested, as an accomplice of Abakumov, and placed in a cell opposite Eitingon. I heard later that Pitovranov appealed to Stalin from his cell, saying he had been detained in a treacherous attempt by Ryumin to wreck our operations against prominent émigrés in the West and Marshal Tito in Yugoslavia. He was released and returned to his office after a month's medical leave in Archangelskoye Military Sanatorium for the high command.

The suggestions in this document for ways to liquidate Tito were childish and naive, I told Stalin, and reflected dangerous incompetence in planning and execution of an assassination or a combat operation. The letter to Stalin stated:

> The Ministry of State Security asks permission to prepare and organize a terrorist act against Tito with the use of illegal agent Max — Comrade Joseph Romvaldovich Grigulevich — citizen of the USSR, member of the CPSU from 1950 (summary is attached). Max, using a Costa Rican passport, is our agent in Italy, where he has managed to gain the confidence of and become a member of the diplomatic corps of South American countries. He befriended Costa Rican officials and businessmen visiting Italy. Using these connections Max, in accordance with our instructions, managed to be appointed to the post of ambassador extraordinary and plenipotentiary of Costa Rica in Italy and simultaneously in Yugoslavia. While fulfilling his diplomatic duties in the second half of the year 1952, he twice visited Yugoslavia, where he was well received. He had access to the social group close to Tito's staff and was given the promise of a personal audience with Tito. The post held by Max at the present time makes it possible to use his capabilities for undertaking active operations against Tito. In the beginning of February this year, Max was recalled by us to Vienna, where we arranged a meeting with him under conditions of clandestine cover. In the course of discussing Max's capabilities, we posed the question: In what way could he be most useful, taking into account his position? Max suggested an effective undertaking against Tito. We discussed with him how he imagines this could be accomplished. As a result, the following possible options emerged for carrying out a terrorist act against Tito:
>
> 1. To order Max to attain a personal audience with Tito, in the course of which he would spray a dose of bacteria of

lung plague that would guarantee the death of Tito and all those present. The spray should be administered from a noiseless mechanism which would be camouflaged as part of Max's clothing. Max himself would not be aware of the substance of the preparation; to save Max's life, he would be inoculated in advance with an antiplague vaccine.

2. During Tito's expected trip to London, Max would be sent there with the task of using his official position and good personal relations with the Yugoslav ambassador to Great Britain, Welebit, to be invited to the reception hosted by Welebit at the Yugoslav Embassy there. The terrorist act would be committed by a noiseless shot from a weapon camouflaged as personal belongings. Simultaneously he would spray tear gas to cause panic among those present and create an atmosphere favorable for Max to escape unseen.

3. Take advantage of an official reception in Belgrade at which members of the diplomatic corps are invited. The terrorist act would be carried out as in the second option and entrusted personally to Max as a diplomat accredited to the Yugoslavian government.

4. To entrust Max to prepare the conditions for handling through one of the Costa Rican representatives a gift of jewelry to Tito in a box which when opened would activate a mechanism that instantly released a lethal poison gas.

It was suggested to Max to once again consider the situation and submit the proposals for most effectively carrying out the mission against Tito. The methods of communication with him are agreed upon. It is also agreed that he will be given further instructions later. We consider it expedient to use Max's capabilities to carry out a terrorist act against Tito. Max, by his personal qualities and experience in intelligence work, is fit for the accomplishment of such a mission. Your approval is requested.[8]

Stalin had written no notes on the document. The letter was not signed, but it seems to me that it was written by Pitovranov, because he supported this plan when we discussed it two or three days later in the ministry. In Stalin's office, looking into his eyes, I said Max was unfit for

8. Quoted by Dmitri Volkogonov in *Izvestia* on June 11, 1993.

that kind of mission, because he had never taken part in any combat operation. He was used in the operation against Trotsky in Mexico, as well as against a police informer in Lithuania, but only to prepare access, not to take part in the actual assault. I said that it didn't follow from the document that the approach to Tito was guaranteed because, whatever we thought of him, we must regard him as a serious adversary who was engaged in combat operations in the war years and definitely would not panic.

I referred to our agent Val, who was a major general — Momo Jurovich — in Tito's bodyguard. His reports suggested that Tito was always on the alert because of the internal situation in Yugoslavia. Unfortunately Val, due to internal intrigues not unlike our own, had fallen out of Tito's favor and was now imprisoned.

I suggested it would be wiser to take advantage of the discord in Tito's entourage. I tried to think of a way to bring Eitingon in to take charge of the field operation, because he was admired by Grigulevich and had worked with him abroad for two years. I noticed that Ignatiev was unhappy with my remarks, but I suddenly felt confident, because my mentioning a highly placed source in Tito's security machinery impressed Stalin.

However, Stalin cut me off and, addressing Ignatiev and me, said that the matter should be rethought, taking into account internal conflicts in the Yugoslav leadership. Then he turned to me and said that although the mission was important for consolidating our position in Eastern Europe, and for the future of the Balkans, I should take enough time to avoid the kind of minor mistakes that were made in Mexico. This would be the first target who was not an émigré or an agent of dubious loyalty, but a head of state. All my hopes of raising the issue of Eitingon's involvement evaporated.

The next day in the ministry, I was given the case file (liternoye delo) named Carrion Crow, which contained dirt against Tito and his connections, going back to his Comintern days in Moscow. There were weekly reports from our rezidentura in Belgrade. The files contained idiotic instructions, signed by Molotov, to look for Tito's connections with profascist groups and Croatian nationalists. In the files I found no serious access to Tito's inner circle that could bring our agents within striking distance.

When I was summoned to Ignatiev's office the next day, four of Khrushchev's men — Deputy Ministers Serov, Savchenko, Vassili Ryasnoi, and Yepishev — plus Pitovranov were there, and I immediately felt uncomfortable, because I had previously discussed such delicate matters only with Beria, Stalin, and my immediate superior. I was the only professional intelligence officer among those present. How could I tell them that their plan was childish? I couldn't believe it when Yepishev lectured for fifteen minutes about the political importance of the mission. Then Pitovranov intervened, supported by Savchenko, saying that Grigulevich was totally fit for the job and pointing to his agent file, which contained a letter Grigulevich had been forced to write to his wife, explaining the ideological motivations for his sacrifice.

I realized my reservations and warnings would have no effect, so I said that as a party member I felt it was my duty to tell them and Comrade Stalin that in peacetime combat operations we could not send an agent to his certain death. The operational plan had to include the possibility of escape. I could not agree to a plan in which the agent, who had no combat experience, would be given the order to kill a heavily guarded target and in which there would be no chance to study the surrounding situation. It was bad tradecraft. Ignatiev closed the meeting by summing up the arguments and saying that we must all think, think, and think again on how to fulfill the party's orders.

This turned out to be my final operational meeting with Ignatiev and Yepishev. Within ten days, Ignatiev put all senior officers and all combat units on the alert, and confidentially informed heads of departments of Stalin's illness. Two days later, Stalin died and the plan was dropped.

Meanwhile, my efforts to find a new position outside the Security Ministry seemed to be bearing fruit. With Anna's help, I forwarded to the Central Committee information received from our rezidentura in Vienna about American and British plans to kidnap the secretary of the Austrian Communist party, Fuerenburger. I was summoned to Central Committee headquarters to discuss this information. A few days after I talked about this matter with Suslov, in the first days of March 1953, Anna told me in confidence that I was being considered for the vacancy of deputy chief of the newly formed International Commission of the Central Committee. I would be in charge of illegal connections with foreign Communist parties. Emma and I were delighted with this prospect, which could put an end to my service in the security machinery just when tough new times were approaching.

But the speedy turn of events drastically changed my fate. On

March 5 Stalin died, and the same day, late in the evening, Beria was appointed minister of the enlarged Ministry of Internal Affairs (MVD), which now comprised both the militia and the security apparatus (MGB). I attended Stalin's funeral and saw the incompetence with which Serov, Goglidze, and Ryasnoi controlled the traffic and the crowds. Before I could reach the House of Columns to stand in the delegation of my ministry, a cordon of trucks blocked the way, so that we had to crawl across the seats of the trucks' cabs. The arrangements for every delegation attending the funeral was equally mismanaged. These were stupid, minor inconveniences, but tragically, hundreds of mourners were killed in the crush of unregulated crowds.

The chaotic crush of mourners nearly mowed down my children. They were normally picked up by car from school in Sokolniki, then the outskirts of Moscow, and driven to our apartment downtown, a distance of ten miles. Occasionally, I accompanied them to school, using the metro from Kirov station, ten minutes' walk from our house. When in the ministry we received the disturbing news of the number of people killed in the disorderly marches of mourners at Trubnaya Square not far from our house, and also that all traffic was blocked, I realized the children would try to return from school on their own.

I feared my enthusiastic Pioneers would be tempted at Kirov station to join the mourning columns passing the station on their way to the House of Columns, where Stalin lay in state. I called Emma and learned that the driver had already left for the school. I quickly left the ministry, took the metro, and intercepted my children and two schoolmates on the staircase of the Sokolniki subway station. I led them home, then called the officer on duty at my secretariat to accompany two other ten-year-old boys from my apartment to their own, which was situated in the vortex of the swirling crowds near the House of Columns. For three years I had been the chairman of the parents' committee at school, and thus I knew the telephone numbers of all students' families; I called to assure the parents that their children were safe.

At the time of his death and funeral, my grief for Stalin was sincere; to my mind, his atrocities were merely mistakes committed with the participation of his incompetent ministers.

The day after Stalin's funeral, I realized that a new epoch had begun. Beria's secretary telephoned me at 6:00 P.M. announcing that the new Hozyain had left the office, leaving no instructions to await his return. From this moment on, I could leave work every night at six, a sharp change from years of working until two or three in the morning, when Stalin and the Ministry of Security finally called it a day.

A sweeping reorganization of the ministry began; Beria's first deputy, Kruglov, who had worked with him in the Central Committee in the 1930s and had been minister of the interior for the past seven years, became Beria's first deputy in the enlarged MVD. Goglidze, who had been involved unwillingly in the Mingrelian Affair, was demoted to head military counterintelligence. Kobulov, Beria's protégé, who had been demoted by Abakumov to an obscure post in the administration of foreign property, returned to Lubyanka to become Beria's deputy. Serov, a Khrushchev man, retained his position as first deputy minister to Beria. Ryasnoi and Savchenko, who, like Serov, had worked with Khrushchev in the Ukraine, were assigned to lead the First Chief Directorate. Fedotov, always neutral and disciplined, who briefly followed Fitin at the Foreign Intelligence Directorate and then worked in the Committee of Information, was reinstated to his wartime status, chief of counterintelligence. Beria appointed Lieutenant General Nikolai Sazikin, once my deputy in Department S and an assistant in Beria's secretariat for the past seven years, as chief of the Secret Political Directorate.[9] Gorlinsky was assigned to head the economic and industrial counterintelligence service. Pitovranov, protégé of Malenkov, released by Stalin from prison in December 1952, became a deputy to Fedotov, a comedown from his former status as a deputy minister under Abakumov.

Parallel with these speedy appointments by Beria was the denunciation of the accusers of the Zionist conspirators. Eitingon, Raikhman, Selivanovsky, Belkin, Shubnikov, and other high-ranking officers arrested on charges of concealing or abetting the Zionist conspiracy were released at the end of March 1953. The archives disclose that Zhemchuzhina's case was closed by Beria himself on March 23, but she was actually released the day after Stalin's funeral, on the occasion of Molotov's birthday, the ninth of March. Beria instructed Meshik, who had worked in the administration of the atomic project and was now inspector general of the enlarged ministry, to look into the cases of Eitingon and Raikhman, and hasten the necessary formalities for their release.

Eitingon's release proved to be especially difficult. He told me that

9. This became the ideological witch-hunt service of the ministry and its successor, the KGB.

the main method of torture used on him was sleep deprivation, but his bleeding ulcer saved him. Ryumin wanted to keep him alive and present him as a terrorist villain, so he patiently waited while Eitingon recuperated on his cot in his cell. Eitingon was the only prisoner under Ryumin's interrogation who refused to sign even one protocol of interrogation, so Meshik spent ten days reconstructing the case without confessions to work from. Only because the two men had worked together in the war years was Meshik able to get Eitingon to sign the necessary papers for his release. While waiting for the paperwork, he and other generals awaiting formal release were allowed to sleep, read, and order good meals from the MVD canteen.

Eitingon later told me how he expected nothing good when he was summoned into the interrogation room after Stalin's death, of which he knew nothing. To his surprise, he found there not Goglidze, Konyakhin, or Mesetsov, his interrogators, but Kobulov, whom he knew had been fired from the security service six years earlier. He immediately sensed that big changes had occurred. He accepted Kobulov's explanations because Kobulov had only one question to ask, whether or not Leonid was willing to continue his service after release. He wasn't up to par, he said, but was willing to keep working. Then Kobulov told Eitingon that Stalin had died and Kobulov was speaking on behalf of Beria, recently appointed head of the enlarged Ministry of the Interior, and he, Kobulov, was his deputy in charge of investigation and counterintelligence. Kobulov promised that although the formalities would take several days, Eitingon could rest comfortably while he waited to be released. Eitingon suggested that during his comfortable internment he no longer be isolated from the other members of his "terrorist team" and they be allowed to join him.

Or, Eitingon added, he should be placed away from the interrogation block so he would not have to hear the screams of the prisoners subjected by Ryumin to "active methods of investigation." Kobulov announced that Ryumin was himself under investigation for the atrocities he committed. The first order of Beria as minister was to banish all beatings and tortures of prisoners held either in Lubyanka or Lefortovo.

Then Kobulov pressed a button and the guard entered the interrogation room to escort Eitingon back to his cell. Showing off for Kobulov, the guard ordered Eitingon to place his hands behind him, standard treatment of prisoners. Kobulov immediately intervened, cursing the guard and ordering him to treat Eitingon as a major general of the security service, with necessary respect, not in custody but under house arrest. This finally convinced Eitingon that he was not being subjected to Kobulov's talent as a subtle manipulator.

Beria ordered me and other top-ranking generals to check the falsified evidence of the Zionist conspiracy. What startled me most was that Zhemchuzhina, Molotov's wife, had maintained clandestine contacts through Mikhoels and Jewish activists with her brother in the United States. A letter to her brother dated October 5, 1946, before she was arrested, was purely Communist in outlook but otherwise nonpolitical. As an intelligence officer, I immediately understood that this letter was sanctioned by the top leadership with the purpose of establishing an informal confidential channel for future use. I couldn't imagine that Zhemchuzhina would write such a letter without permission. In her testimony she had denied that she had attended a synagogue service in Moscow in March 1945 devoted to Jews who had died in the war. Four independent witnesses placed her there. The diplomatic corps was also represented. Surely Molotov encouraged her to go because it was useful to have American observers see his wife there after the Yalta Conference, but as she was his wife, his instruction was oral, without record. Later, she did not want to implicate him so she denied the episode, but it was used against her and against him in the anti-Semitic campaign and in ousting him from power.

My contacts with Harriman on plans for a Jewish republic in the Crimea flashed through my mind; from the testimonies of Zhemchuzhina I realized that similar probes had been carried out simultaneously by her, by Mikhoels, and by an American journalist, Goldberg, a man close to the World Jewish Congress, who was editor of a New York daily newspaper.[10] All of these were discussing the possibility of setting up "California in the Crimea." These revelations convinced me that my approach to Harriman was only one in a series of probes discussing how

10. Ben Zion Goldberg, of the New York Yiddish daily *Der Tog*, had visited the Soviet Union to report on the condition of Jews since the establishment of the Jewish autonomous region in Birobidzhan in 1928. He served as president of the American Committee of Jewish Writers, Artists, and Scientists, which hosted Mikhoels and Feffer's visit to the United States in 1943. He revisited the Soviet Union in 1946 and reported favorably on the work of the Jewish Antifascist Committee. See Levin, *The Jews in the Soviet Union Since 1917*, vol. 1, pp. 457–458.

to use the Jewish question in the broader context of Soviet-American relations.[11]

When I discussed with Beria what role Zhemchuzhina might play in resuming informal contacts with the international Jewish community, he told me the question of Zhemchuzhina's role in probes on Jewish issues was closed once and forever.

Instead, he pointed to Ivan Maisky, who he said was a far more important figure. Academician Maisky, former ambassador to London and deputy minister of foreign affairs, then in his seventies, had a distinguished career. He had been a Menshevik leader who opposed Lenin, but later made a remarkable career in the Soviet diplomatic service. He was also accused in the Zionist conspiracy. Absurd charges against him were fabricated, saying that Jewish organizations abroad were seeking to have him nominated minister of foreign affairs of the new government after Abakumov seized power.

Beria said Maisky was the ideal man to present to the West our new foreign policy. He could handle high-level informal contacts to promote our striking turnaround in policy after Stalin's death. Beria said, "As you knew Maisky in the war years, before Yalta, and your wife became friendly with his wife, you should be prepared to work as a team in the future." Beria ordered me to seek Maisky's help in intelligence probes with Western politicians.

Fedotov, who was looking into Maisky's case, advised me not to meet with him. "Pavel Anatolievich, from my very first encounter with him, when I formally announced to him 'You are in the office of counterintelligence chief General Fedotov, who is ordered to reconsider absurd charges brought against you and the circumstances of your unlawful arrest,' he started to confess to me that he was first a Japanese spy, then a British spy, and then an American spy." Maisky tried to convince Fedotov of his guilt, to avoid torture, deprivation of sleep, and being put into a punishment cell. He refused to believe that Stalin was dead and buried in the Lenin Mausoleum; he said this was a provocation to compromise him. Fedotov suggested that we postpone any discussion of substantive intelligence and diplomatic issues with him for two or three weeks. Fedotov, under Beria's orders, transferred him to the rest-reception room behind his office, where Maisky could see his wife and

11. The interrogation of Zhemchuzhina on January 26, 1949, is reproduced in Ekaterina Vassileva, *Kremlovskie Zhony* (*Kremlin Wives*) (Moscow: Terra, 1992), p. 341.

where a documentary film on Stalin's funeral was shown to him. Since he was deeply implicated by the testimony of executed members of the Jewish Antifascist Committee, he was kept under house arrest while those cases were reconsidered.

The three-week delay proved to be near fatal, because the case was not closed, as it was for others, in May 1953. When Beria was arrested, Maisky, to whom Malenkov and Molotov were ill disposed, was living comfortably in Lubyanka with his wife in the room behind Fedotov's office. Maisky was then accused of plotting with Beria to become his minister of foreign affairs and was thrown back in jail, where he had a nervous breakdown.

Later, Emma met his wife in the reception room of Butyrka prison, where Maisky and I were both being held. Madame Maisky said she was leading a fantastic life, because although all Maisky's money and government bonds were confiscated, her own bonds for the last five years remained intact and one of them had won the government lottery, yielding her 100,000 rubles (when one ruble equaled four U.S. dollars). She became a rich woman. When she met Emma at the jail, where she brought a food parcel for her husband, the same way Emma did for me, she could not at first remember where she had seen Emma before. "Was it in Paris, in London, or a reception in the Kremlin?" she asked. Emma smiled and reminded her it had been at the dacha of Yemolyan Yaroslavsky, which was near our dacha, and at Yaroslavsky's apartment downtown.

After four years in jail, Maisky was finally put on trial for being an accomplice to Beria's attempts to seize power. Maisky denied the charges, and the military court, at which Viktor Zorin served as his defense attorney, could not establish his guilt. Anatoli Gorsky (rezident in London when Maisky was ambassador) was called to testify to the treacherous relations between Maisky and Beria, but he changed his earlier testimony and did not support the charge. The guilt was reduced to abuse of power as an ambassador, because he had sent reports from London not only to the Ministry of Foreign Affairs but to Beria as well; the standard rule had now become an offense. He was also charged with being criminally fond of the Western style of life and agitating for Western manners in the staff of the Soviet compound in London, and in Moscow. Maisky was sentenced to ten years in prison, four and a half of which were already served; he was soon amnestied because Molotov and Malenkov were ousted from their influential positions in 1955, although they remained in the Politburo until 1957.

Maisky resumed the life of an academician, a senior research fellow in the Institute of History. He published his memoirs, never mentioning his misadventures and unhappy encounter with intelligence operations. He received full rehabilitation only in the early 1970s, not long before his death.

The Maisky case is but one of many. In 1993, after a thorough study of the documents, Russia's chief archivist, Rudolf Pikoya, wrote:

> Russian historians do not know postwar history. We lived in the epoch but had no idea of what was really going on. Even specialists in this period did not know much. Histories of the fifties and sixties and real life existed in parallel lines, without intersecting. Let's look at the well-known repressions of 1952 and 1953 called the Doctors' Plot. In reality, such a case simply did not exist. The case was really against Abakumov. This was just an ordinary vicious power struggle in which simple people were unhappily involved.

> Or take another example, the well-known villain Lavrenti Beria. It was absolutely clear that he was made a bloody symbol of arbitrariness. Let us remember what post Beria held in the second half of the 1940s, deputy prime minister of the USSR, neither minister of security nor minister of internal affairs. Only now is it definitely established that the Ministry of Security was compiling compromising evidence against Beria. In the beginning of the 1950s, listening devices were installed even in his mother's apartment. Stalin personally organized the Mingrelian Affair, which could be used to bring Beria down.

> I do not deny Beria's villainous qualities, but it was he who unleashed massive rehabilitation for Stalin's victims. As soon as Beria was arrested, the well-known architect of spring, Nikita Sergeyevich Khrushchev, reinstated Semyon Denisovich Ignatiev, the man who was the real fabricator of the Doctors' Plot, as a member of the Central Committee of the Communist party. Khrushchev reinstated him at the plenary session saying that "expulsion of Ignatiev from the Central Committee was done under a denunciation known to be slanderous." What sort of known slanderous denunciation? Did Khrushchev mean the decision of the Presidium of the Central Committee, where it was stated that Ignatiev and the Ministry of Security falsified

the Doctors' Plot? Thus reinstatement of Ignatiev meant rejection of rehabilitation for victims of unlawful repression.

In the documents, Khrushchev emerges not as a figure of light, but as the organizer of murders of Ukrainian nationalists in the forties. In this he closely collaborated with Minister of Security Abakumov. In 1944 the younger brother of Kobulov, who was close to Beria and who was the NKVD officer in charge of the Ukraine, wrote a letter where he stressed that Khrushchev encouraged massive repressions in the Ukraine and never lifted a finger to save anybody. Khrushchev was an experienced tactician who seized power behind Malenkov's back and then excluded him.

Khrushchev's speech at the Twentieth Party Congress, in 1956, in which he revealed a long list of Stalin's crimes in a secret session of the Communist party leadership, was part of the power struggle. Khrushchev managed to create a different understanding and interpretation of the principle of collective leadership, which was supported by Malenkov. In party terminology, collective leadership was when the chairman of the Council of Ministers presided over meetings of the Presidium of the Central Committee. Khrushchev was the main figure as secretary of the Central Committee. But behind this dispute, the main issue was: which is more important — the party or the state? Khrushchev completed the transformation of our society into the party state, completing the trend started under Lenin and retained by Stalin. In the years of Khrushchev's rule, the party machinery led the country, annihilating the Ministry of Security and Marshal Zhukov and subordinating to its rule the Council of Ministers, the government. The party machinery ran the state and continued to do so until August 1991.[12]

The case of Jewish plotters in the security service was finally closed sometime in the middle of May 1953, when Andrei Sverdlov and Yakob Matusov were released. Maklarsky and Kheifetz, however, remained in custody in the prison hospital, virtually under house arrest. Because of their poor state of health, it was impossible to finish the bureaucratic

12. *Nezavisima Gazeta (Independent Newspaper)*, March 31, 1993, p. 5.

procedures necessary for their formal release. Sverdlov had been accused with Maironovsky and Matusov of, under the leadership of Eitingon, concealing poisons to be used against the leadership of the country. Now Sverdlov was appointed by Beria to be chief of the section in charge of investigation and checking of anonymous letters. His colleague Matusov, whose diary provides the most interesting chronology of the purges from 1930 to 1950 in the Secret Political Department, was released in 1953 but not reinstated in the security machinery. He died in 1970. Emma used Matusov's unpublished diary, supplied by his wife, to document her appeals on my behalf.

In 1963 Matusov and Sverdlov were summoned by the deputy chairman of the Party Control Commission, Zinovy Timofeyevich Serdiuk, a Khrushchev protégé, who demanded that Sverdlov stop writing letters to the Central Committee on behalf of Matusov, because the party now would prosecute both of them for spreading rumors and above all for their unlawful punishment of the famous writer Aleksandr Solzhenitsyn.

Sverdlov and Matusov vigorously protested that they had not falsified this case. Solzhenitsyn's letter criticizing the Soviet system and Stalin personally for lack of military talent was intercepted during the war by military censorship, which initiated the case against him. In the conditions of war, all statements and criticism of military command were regarded to be at least suspicious. Serdiuk cut them short and said that from the evidence the Party Control Commission had, Solzhenitsyn had always been a staunch Leninist. Serdiuk showed them the letter written by Solzhenitsyn to Khrushchev on February 24, 1956, asking for his rehabilitation, after having served a term of eight years in prison camp, from 1945 to 1953. Solzhenitsyn was rehabilitated in 1957, but Serdiuk demanded from Sverdlov and Matusov written explanations of the facts in Solzhenitsyn's appeal to Khrushchev. Solzhenitsyn's letter had stated:

> . . . I was from my childhood years brought up in the spirit of Leninism, . . . I without any hesitation supported and shared the policy of our party and the Soviet state. My harsh statements in these letters against the personality cult that dominated at that time, against the unlimited flattery of one man to the detriment of the creative spirit of Marxism-Leninism, were regarded as a crime. The personality cult is now decisively condemned. I really was concerned with the state of our economic

and historical sciences, and linguistics. That was the backbone of my letters, but now from the rostrum of the Twentieth Party Congress, Comrades Khrushchev, Mikoyan, and other members of the Central Committee admitted exactly the unsatisfactory state of these sciences. There were no other objective data for my conviction. I ask, fully rehabilitate me and return my combat awards.[13]

Sverdlov received a party reprimand but continued his work as senior research fellow in the Institute of Marxism-Leninism, where he was transferred after being expelled from the security service following Beria's arrest. Matusov's expulsion from the party was confirmed forever. It was officially announced that this decision would never be reconsidered, but he was left in peace and allowed to pursue his literary career. He died peacefully at the end of the 1960s. He was a remarkable man who often gave Emma legal advice while I was in jail.

Abakumov was not released. Beria and Malenkov had grudges against him. He was accused of falsifying the case against Zhemchuzhina. At that moment, I didn't care about Abakumov, I had my own grudges against him, but I learned from Raikhman that Abakumov denied the charges implicating him in the Zionist conspiracy despite torture by Ryumin. Raikhman told me that he behaved as a man with a strong will. In 1990 I was called as a witness when his case was reopened by the military procurator's office; I changed my opinion of him, because whatever atrocities he committed, he paid the price for them in jail. He was subjected to unbelievable suffering and managed not to yield to his torturers. He struggled for life and defended the scientific Jewish community, which was implicated in the fabricated Zionist plot. His firmness and courage made it possible in March and April 1953 to release in a speedy manner all the doctors detained in the so-called plot.

It was clear that the case against the doctors had no validity. The procurators needed Abakumov's, Raikhman's, or Eitingon's confession, not one of which they got.

However, Beria and Malenkov had decided to do away with Abakumov. At a conference of senior officials in Beria's office, Beria officially announced that although the accusations against Abakumov in the Zionist conspiracy were dropped, he was under investigation for embez-

13. Solzhenitsyn's letter appeared in Yakob Matusov's unpublished diary and in Solzhenitsyn's rehabilitation file, which was examined by Kiril Stolyarov in the Office of the Military Prosecutor, file 4N-083/49.

zlement of government funds, abuse of power in decorating his apartment, and more serious, for falsifying the case against the former leaders of the Aviation Ministry and air force and against Polina Zhemchuzhina.

Solomon Braverman, deputy chief of Abakumov's secretariat, who was arrested at the same time as Abakumov, provided false testimony against his former boss under torture. In jail he was ready to slander everyone he knew.

Happily, neither Eitingon nor I was on Beria's list of Abakumov's accomplices, because we were only indirectly involved in four cases — Samet, Shumsky, Oggins, and Romzha.

As soon as Eitingon was released, on March 23, 1953, he was hospitalized for his ulcer and general exhaustion. He pleaded with me to arrange the immediate release of his sister Sonia, who had been arrested together with him in 1951, and was sentenced by the Moscow District Court in closed session to ten years' imprisonment for mistreatment of patients and being a Zionist plotter.

Sonia had at first been sentenced to eight years, but the Jewish procurator, Daron, who supervised the investigations in the Ministry of Security, fearing accusations of sympathy to other Jews, insisted on a longer term. I took advantage of my next audience with Beria to present a letter on her behalf from Eitingon. Luckily for Sonia, Beria's first deputy, Sergei Kruglov, was present in Beria's office. When I tried to explain her case, Beria interrupted me, handed the letter without putting his initials on it to Kruglov, and said, "Arrange her release immediately."

I followed Kruglov to his office, where he dictated a short letter to the Supreme Court: "Undertaken by the Ministry of Internal Affairs, verification of the accusations against Sonia Isakovna Eitingon revealed that the case was fabricated and proofs of her guilt falsified. The ministry finds it expedient to ask the Supreme Court to annul the sentence and close the case against her on the grounds of corpus delicti. (Signed) S. Kruglov, First Deputy Minister of Internal Affairs."

I monitored the transfer of the letter to the Supreme Court and tried to speed up the formalities for her release. Although the decision of the Supreme Court was signed within three weeks, it took another week to transfer it to the administration of the camp where she was held. I personally telephoned the director of the camp, urging her prompt release, but he reported that she was in hospital undergoing an appendectomy. Using my position, I gave the order to take her out of prison and put her in a hospital for free citizens as soon as the operation was over.

It was her luck that Kruglov, not Beria, signed the letter for her release. Within weeks Beria was arrested, and his mark on the letter would have kept her in jail for at least another two years, when the other prisoners held on charges of the Zionist conspiracy and agitation were released. Sonia's case was one of the first in the wave of rehabilitation that Beria initiated after Stalin's death.

We now know that even this wave, which seemed to us like a benign correction of past mistakes, was motivated by a reshuffle of the leadership balance of power, in Beria's favor.

A new charter for the Communist party had been endorsed by the Nineteenth Party Congress in 1952, before Stalin died. Under this charter there was only one leading organ, the Presidium of the Central Committee, now greatly enlarged. The Politburo, which had contained only eleven members, was abolished. The new Presidium contained twenty-five people, including the old guard of Molotov, Kaganovich, and Voroshilov, and relatively young figures like Brezhnev, Nikolai Chesnokov, and Suslov.

However, real power was concentrated in the Bureau of the Presidium, unknown to the public, which was elected by the last plenary session presided over by Stalin in October 1952. It consisted of Stalin, Malenkov, Beria, Khrushchev, Bulganin, Saburov, Pervukhin, and Ignatiev. It didn't contain Voroshilov, Kaganovich, Molotov, and Mikoyan, influential figures of the old guard, who by this time had been stripped of real power. The new bureau was dominated by Stalin and the young generation.

In a plenary session of the Central Committee on April 2, 1953, barely a month after Stalin's death, Beria exposed Stalin's and Ignatiev's abuses in fabricating the Doctors' Plot, carefully deleting all reference to Abakumov's involvement. Ignatiev had been Beria's principal enemy in the Mingrelian case, and now Beria, with the support of Khrushchev, ousted him. This was the first, unprecedented attack on Stalin, three years before Khrushchev's world-shaking report to the Twentieth Party Congress. Beria's motives were not only to restore justice but to get rid of Ignatiev, who right after Stalin's death was elected secretary of the Central Committee to supervise organs of state security. This move by Beria coincided with Khrushchev's interests to lessen the influence of Malenkov, because Ignatiev had always sided with Malenkov and worked under him in the Central Committee. The removal of Ignatiev is overlooked by our historians, but this was the decisive initial shift in the balance of power in the Politburo that greatly strengthened Khrushchev's position in the Central Committee, leaving him the only man with Presidium rank and rank of secretary of the Communist party.

During the last year of Stalin's rule, Khrushchev had used his alliance with Malenkov to consolidate his standing in the party. He had secured the rare privilege of addressing the Nineteenth Party Congress. Having vanquished his faction's rivals in a series of purges, he set out to place his men in strategic government and party positions. It is seldom noted that Khrushchev managed in the final year of Stalin's rule to install four trusted allies in the top-level hierarchy of the Ministry of State Security — Deputy Ministers Serov, Savchenko, Ryasnoi, and Yepishev. The first three had worked with him as chiefs of the security service in the Ukraine. The fourth served under him as secretary of the district party committee in Odessa and Kharkov, in charge of personnel.

Right after the April 1953 plenary session, Malenkov was relieved of his post in the party secretariat. Thus his position in the leadership now depended entirely on his alliance with Beria. He didn't understand that; he overestimated his authority, still living with the illusions that he was second to Stalin in the party and that all the men around him, including the Presidium, were interested in being on good terms with him. Compared with the Stalinist years, the behavior of the members of the Presidium became independent, each wanting to play his own role. Thus the scene was set for Khrushchev's ascent to replace Stalin in the paramount power seat.

T W E L V E

THE FALL
OF BERIA AND
MY ARREST

Within twenty-four hours of Stalin's death, the Ministry of State Security and the Ministry of Internal Affairs were combined under Beria's sole command. On March 10, 1953, Beria set up four groups in the enlarged Ministry of Internal Affairs (MVD) to review the falsified cases of the Doctors' Plot, the Jewish Antifascist Committee, the Mingrelian Affair, and the cases against security officers arrested on Stalin's orders.

The press statement issued by the MVD concerning the release of imprisoned doctors was worded differently from the decision of the Central Committee. Beria's statement used harsher language condemning the arrest of the doctors. However, proposals to rehabilitate the executed members of the Jewish Antifascist Committee were turned down by Khrushchev until 1955, and rumors spread by the Central Committee secretariat about Beria's Jewish connections continued until then. In the beginning of April 1953, Khrushchev issued a directive to the party organization not to

353

comment on the MVD's press release and not to discuss anti-Semitism at party meetings.[1]

On April 2, 1953, Beria sent a circular to the Council of Ministers stating that Mikhoels was slandered and was criminally killed on the orders of Abakumov by a team headed by Ogoltsov, Tsanava, Lebedev, and five junior operators. He demanded that the edict issued by the Presidium of the Supreme Soviet to decorate these people with the Order of the Red Banner and the Red Star be canceled, and that Ogoltsov and Tsanava as executors of the action be arrested and charged with murder. However, Tsanava was not arrested until six months later, and then not for his part in killing Mikhoels but as a member of the Beria gang. The awards were taken away from Ogoltsov and his team, but they were not charged with any criminal action, and he was expelled from the party in 1954. No one was ever prosecuted for the murder of Mikhoels. Their only punishment was that they had to return their medals.

In April 1953 I noticed certain changes in Beria's behavior. He openly criticized his colleagues in the Presidium while making telephone calls to Malenkov, Bulganin, and Khrushchev in my presence and that of other senior officers. He addressed them with the familiar *ti*, not the formal *vyui*. In the presence of the chief of the Ideological Department and the chief of counterintelligence, he recalled how he had saved the writer Ilya Ehrenburg from Stalin's wrath. Beria said he received the order from Stalin to arrest Ehrenburg as soon as he arrived from France in 1939. When Beria returned from the Kremlin to his office, he received a cable from the NKVD station in Paris, signed by the station chief Lev Vasilevsky, praising the political contributions of Ehrenburg. Instead of obeying Stalin's order, Beria in his next audience with Stalin showed him

---

1. This was revealed at the Conference on Jews and Jewish Life in Russia and the Soviet Union, held in Moscow April 26–28, 1993, and attended by Anatoli Sudoplatov.

Vladimir Naumov, an aide to Aleksandr N. Yakovlev (Gorbachev's senior political adviser), reported that on April 13, 1953, Khrushchev, Suslov, P. N. Pospelov, and Nikolai Shatalin sent a memorandum of the CPSU secretariat to the members of the Presidium, summarizing the letters received by *Pravda* commenting on rehabilitation of doctors accused in the Doctors' Plot. Ten percent of those who wrote wanted their letter of denunciation of the doctors returned. Fifteen percent expressed surprise and a lack of understanding of what was going on. Fifteen percent raised the question of an anti-Semitic trend in state policy, which was incompatible with true socialism. Thirty-five percent expressed their disagreement with the defense of Jews and departure from the line of Comrade Stalin against the doctors.

Vasilevsky's cable. Stalin muttered: "If you like this Jew so much, go on working with him."

One day I went to Beria's office and heard Beria arguing on the phone with Khrushchev. "Look, you asked me to find a way to liquidate Bandera [the Ukrainian nationalist leader], and at the same time your petty crooks in Kiev and Lvov are preventing real work against real opponents." Beria's harshness with his top colleagues puzzled me, because previously he had not allowed himself such liberties in confrontations when in the presence of subordinates.

In May 1953 Grigulevich was recalled to Moscow for two reasons: to check whether or not he had been exposed by Aleksandr Orlov's revelations in a series of *Life* magazine articles published in April, and, if he was still secure, to use him in an intelligence probe of the Vatican, planned by Beria, to move toward the unification of Germany and normalization of relations with Yugoslavia. Grigulevich was to test the waters and report the Yugoslav leadership's attitude toward the Soviet Union.

My position in the spring of 1953 was unclear. Bogdan Kobulov, Beria's deputy, suggested to him that I be made chief inspector of the ministry. This would have made me the supervisor of instructions to all the territorial security offices in the Soviet Union. I did not like this idea, because it would have made me responsible for the performance of district officials and involved me in personality conflicts and rivalries. Kruglov, first deputy to Beria, suggested instead that Eitingon and I, while retaining our posts in the Bureau of Diversions and Intelligence, should be assigned as deputies to the newly created Ideological Department. Our assignment would be to crush the nationalist underground in the Soviet Union, especially in the Baltic republics.

I agreed to this proposal, but I never started the new job. Within a week, Beria suggested I succeed Fedotov as chief of counterintelligence. However, the next day, when Fedotov and I came to Beria's office, Kobulov was present and he unexpectedly suggested my appointment as minister of security in the Ukraine or, to arrange a better life for me, as chief representative of the MVD in Berlin. Knowing Kobulov as a master of intrigue, I said I could not agree for personal reasons. I pleaded Emma's state of health and her need for medical attention in Moscow. I suggested that Kobulov's younger brother, Amayak, then chief of the department of prisoners of war, be sent to Germany instead of me.

I think Kobulov wanted me out of the ministry and out of intelligence because I knew too much about his and Beria's operations against Georgian émigrés in Paris. I was also aware of their family connections, that the nephew of Beria's wife, a certain Shavdia, had been taken prisoner by the Germans and acted as our double agent, cooperating with the Gestapo in Paris. In 1945 he returned to Moscow and then to Tbilisi. In 1951, Stalin ordered his arrest as a Mingrelian nationalist and Nazi collaborator. He was sentenced to twenty-five years at hard labor, and although Beria did not release him from jail when he took over the security service, his relationship to a convicted Georgian criminal remained a potentially harmful blot on Beria's family history.

Beria agreed with my refusal to leave Moscow. Within a week, I was appointed chief of the newly created Ninth Department of the MVD, reporting directly to the minister. The Ninth Department — or Bureau for Special Tasks, as it was more commonly known — had its own special-purpose brigade, responsible for sabotage operations abroad. While no one described it as such, the new job was in line with Stalin's earlier recommendation that I become a deputy director of the First Chief Directorate, to be better able to mobilize resources in an emergency situation.

We began a reassessment of our foreign and domestic priorities after Stalin's death. Beria made only two attempts to change our domestic situation. I was involved in preparing two memoranda giving details of the mistakes by local party and security organizations in executing national policies in the Ukraine and in Lithuania. Beria stressed the necessity of moving local people into leading positions, and appointing Russian nationals to deputy positions. The memoranda revealed unjustified deportations and repressions against ethnic groups who were not involved in any anti-Soviet activities. Beria suggested that the republics establish their own systems of medals and awards to build local pride. He stressed the need to encourage the spread of native cultural traditions and languages. In particular, he was concerned with developing a new generation of intelligentsia that would be sympathetic to socialist ideas.

This led to some awkward moments. The newly appointed minister of the interior of Lithuania, in all innocence, forwarded to Beria a memorandum in Lithuanian, creating an uproar in the secretariat since nobody could read it. Besides, when the minister came to Moscow to see Beria, he was unable to report the details of a very delicate radio deception game with British intelligence because he had lost his briefcase in the MVD guest house on Kolpachney Lane where he was staying. Later it was rumored that he had lost it on purpose. As a former party official and city manager, he did not want to work in the security system, and, indeed, he was given another job, in the economics administration of the Lithuanian government.

Unfortunately, Beria's memorandum on mistakes made in the Ukraine coincided with conflicts between the newly appointed minister of the interior, Pavel Meshik, and local party and MVD officials. Meshik was intent on ousting Khrushchev's protégé Timofei Strokach, who had been fired from the security service in 1941 for failing to save the NKVD file in Kiev when the Germans surrounded the city. In addition, Meshik quarreled with the local party bosses Z. T. Serdiuk and Pyotr Shelest. Serdiuk had tried to take over the house used for the MVD children's kindergarten, to make it into his own home. Serdiuk ordered his personal bodyguard into the kindergarten, but Meshik intervened, placing his own armed men in the disputed building. Shelest, as secretary of the Kiev party district, had commandeered a fire brigade boat to go hunting and never returned it.

Although everyone else spoke in Russian, Meshik addressed a plenary session of the Ukrainian Central Committee arrogantly and in Ukrainian, suggesting to the shocked Russians, including the first secretary, Melnikov, that they should all learn Ukrainian. He was enthusiastically supported by the Ukrainian writer Aleksandr Korneichuk, who also spoke in Ukrainian and who praised Beria for his support.

Meshik proudly told me of these escapades in pursuing an ethnically correct national policy. I told him he was a fool. I introduced Meshik to Andrei Muzichenko, once our agent in Paris, who had experience in dealing with Ukrainian nationalists. We decided to send him to Kiev as Meshik's deputy. He could distinguish real terrorists from nationalist storytellers, and would help avoid unnecessary clashes. Muzichenko had to delay his trip to Kiev because, at Khrushchev's request, Beria ordered that Bandera's sisters, in exile in Siberia, be brought to Moscow and put under house arrest in a safe apartment. Muzichenko was to try to persuade them to transmit a message to Bandera in Germany that might get him to meet our agent.

Muzichenko was still in Moscow when Beria and Meshik were arrested. Not yet confirmed in his new post as the Ukraine's deputy minister of the interior, he was saved from being arrested with them. He simply stopped coming to work and resumed his job as director of the Moscow Clinical Research Institute. He was interrogated twice by the procurator's office about Beria's and Meshik's alleged plans to revive bourgeois nationalism in the Ukraine, but he was experienced enough

to reply that he had only just been offered the job and had not begun work.

Beria's initiatives and release of imprisoned doctors unfortunately coincided with an ill-planned amnesty for ordinary criminals. More than one
million prisoners — thieves, crooks, and hooligans who were sentenced
to less than five years — were released simultaneously from jails and
labor camps. This flooded our cities with riffraff, for which the police
were totally unprepared. An uproar spread through the country, and
there were clashes in the streets. Within a few days, Beria put all his
deputies and directors of key departments of the Ministry of Internal
Affairs on alert, making each responsible for public order in a district.
Beria used MVD troops for patrolling Moscow and for a mass search of
attics and underground hideaways. Disorder was promptly crushed, and
all recently amnestied criminals were exiled from Moscow. No doubt
the amnesty and the disruptions weakened his standing in public
opinion.

Abakumov remained in jail, despite the release of senior operational
officers arrested for conspiring with him. Chiefs of his secretariat and
principal interrogators in the Investigation Department were not freed.

Beria put an end to the Mingrelian investigation started two years
earlier by Stalin. He released secretaries of the Georgian party committee
M. I. Baramia and Sharia and former minister of security Rapava, who
had not yielded under severe torture and who refused to make false
confessions. However, the chief instigator of the affair, Rukhadze, who
under Stalin's orders fabricated the case, and who installed listening
devices in Beria's mother's houses in Abkhazia and Tbilisi, was kept
in jail.

Khrushchev helped Beria end the Mingrelian case. Beria personally
went to Tbilisi after the Presidium revoked the charge of nationalism
against the Georgian party organization. The man who intrigued against
Beria, Mgeladze, was relieved of his post as first secretary of the Georgian party. With Khrushchev's blessing, Beria made the former chief of
his secretariat in Moscow, Stepan Mamulov, chief of the Georgian party
personnel department, then in the midst of an intraparty purge. Later,
Mamulov told me that it was not Beria but Khrushchev who instructed
him to carry out the bloodless purge. The irony was that he was to get
rid of those who had deceived Stalin by writing slanderous letters to
Moscow about Beria's and Malenkov's association with Georgian

Mensheviks and nationalists. Actually it was Stalin who ordered these letters written in the Georgian language, to incriminate Beria. We learned later that the cabal of Stalin, Rukhadze, and Mgeladze had discussed what the content of the letters should be.[2]

Beria's Mingrelian origins in Georgia were troublesome throughout his career and finally proved fatal. His cordial relations with Malenkov abruptly ended in May 1953 because of a personal strain that developed inadvertently between them. A Georgian playwright, Gregori Mdivani, who knew Beria, came to his office and handed Ludvigov, chief of Beria's secretariat, a memorandum claiming that Malenkov, the new prime minister, had plagiarized his report to the Nineteenth Party Congress. Malenkov had supposedly used material from a speech by a czarist minister stating that governments are in need of literary masterpieces, more Gogols and Shchedrins, to raise the spiritual atmosphere of the society.[3] The charge of plagiarism in party documents was a serious matter, especially during the power struggle after Stalin's death. Beria indignantly ordered Ludvigov to ignore the memorandum and to end his associations with "Georgian scoundrels," but the memo found its way from Beria's secretariat to Malenkov's office, and the damage was done.

These intrigues occurred just when Beria launched another initiative, this time involving my office. He called a meeting of heads of intelligence services, GRU and MVD, bitterly attacking Ryasnoi, head of the First Chief Directorate, who had been promoted by Khrushchev. Beria accused Ryasnoi of primitive and ineffective methods. Stalin's instructions to annihilate minor figures in émigré circles were of no practical use for a great power, he said.

2. Mgeladze rose to become first secretary of the Abkhazia party organization. He was the man who served Stalin on vacation in Abkhazia, just as Gorbachev later came to prominence when he served Brezhnev, Suslov, and Andropov on their vacations in the Caucasus.

3. Nikolai Vasilyevich Gogol (1809–1852), Ukrainian by origin, is regarded as the father of the Realist school in Russian literature. He is best known for *Dead Souls,* a novel portraying the foibles of the serf-owning gentry who suffer with what he called "the laughter through tears invisible to the world." N. Shchedrin (1826–1889) was the pen name of Mikhail Yevgrafovich Saltykov, a satirical writer who was exiled for calling attention to the contradictions of social and economic inequality in Russian life. Allowed to return to St. Petersburg in 1855, he continued to write satires of the gentry and rising bourgeoisie. His novel *The Golovlyov Family* is considered a masterpiece.

Beria stressed that our priority was to set up a strong base for intelligence operations. In Germany we should use the remnants of our old networks, such as the surviving network of the Red Orchestra in Hamburg; the illegals should be strengthened in countries bordering the United States. Beria also referred to the necessity to instruct the Ministry of Foreign Affairs, the Ministry of Foreign Trade, TASS, and all other institutions to provide support for intelligence activities. He emphasized the need for two parallel intelligence services, one in the Ministry of Internal Affairs and the other in the Ministry of Defense: one for the regular gathering of information and one for special operations in case of danger to the state. His arguments were a repetition of Stalin's instructions; the only new element was that assassination orders were canceled.

Beria ordered me to report to him within a week — together with GRU head General Zakharov; the chief of naval intelligence operations, Vorontsov; and Marshal Golovanov, chief of the long-range bombing task force — on recommended measures to neutralize American strategic air superiority and nuclear bomber bases. He wanted a plan to incapacitate the American military supply line to Europe, including ports and air bases.

The following week, when we assembled in his spacious office in the Kremlin, Admiral N. G. Kuznetsov, chief of the navy, was present. He thanked Beria for rehabilitating the good name of his assistant, Vice Admiral Goncharov, who had died in 1948 under interrogation, accused of sharing anti-Stalinist views with Kuznetsov. All Kuznetsov's senior aides had been arrested in 1948, and Kuznetsov himself demoted to rear admiral and reassigned to the Pacific fleet, based in Vladivostok. However, three years later, Kuznetsov wrote Stalin a long letter proposing a strategic overhaul of the Soviet navy, including a program of research for the construction of nuclear submarines and aircraft carriers. Kuznetsov's plan called for a drastic change in the balance of surface ships and submarines. Stalin endorsed Kuznetsov's ideas and reinstated him as commander in chief of the navy, even though his former deputies remained in prison. I had always held Kuznetsov in high regard because I knew him during the war, when he was a dynamic and outstanding leader, respected in the security service. Thus, Kuznetsov set the tone for the meeting.

I was ready with a plan for illegal networks to regularly monitor approximately 150 main Western strategic installations in Europe and the United States. Admiral Kuznetsov brought a different perspective to the meeting. He said emergency operations should be classified according to the features of modern warfare; he said modern military conflicts tended to be short-lived and decisively resolved. He brought into the discussion the concept of preemptive strikes, a new feature of modern warfare. Based on my draft, he asked the question, Where would our priorities lie, given our limited resources — in a preemptive strike, wiping out three or four carriers anchored in Atlantic ports or the Mediterranean; or in blowing up naval bases, preventing the flow of troops? With his naval perspective, he argued that in the long term, depriving the Americans and British of their superiority in aircraft carriers would change the balance of naval power in our favor, making our submarines more effective everywhere. General Zakharov, who later became chief of the general staff, remarked that the issue of preemptive strikes against strategic installations of the enemy was a novel approach in the art of warfare, and he suggested pursuing this issue seriously.

Marshal Golovanov, chief of the strategic air force, intervened, saying he saw no answers to these questions of priorities in the intelligence plans. In a state of war, due to limited resources, it would be realistic to assume our retaliatory ability would be limited to no more than one or two strikes against any of the enemy's strategic installations.

I followed Zakharov, citing examples of World War II and our limited experience in the Korean War, in which our illegal rezidenturas were equipped only to monitor and supply information. Their combat experience was confined to kidnapping and assaults on individuals who possessed vital information or were targeted enemies. The new demands of nuclear warfare required a total revision of our concept of guerrilla warfare. I told the meeting that there was a need not only for individually trained agents, but also for mobile strike forces, attached to every major illegal rezidentura, capable of attacking nuclear weapons storage depots or bases where aircraft with nuclear weapons were stationed. We all remembered that it had worked well against the Germans in 1941 and 1942; however, we had been successful only because the Germans were operating on hostile territory and we had strong agent networks. I pointed out that our analysis of World War II and the Korean War showed that attacks against supply lines, especially when communications were extended, might be strategically more important than direct hits on military targets. Although the latter are impressive in causing immediate panic, the long-range impact of disrupting supply lines is stronger. Direct military targets are heavily guarded and in a rapid assault it is possible to destroy only two or three installations.

My idea to substitute guerrilla operations for our limited air and naval strike force capacity was attractive to the military leadership. There was no disagreement in the room.

Therefore, I summed up, the Bureau for Special Tasks (Ninth Department) should contain specific units and sections to deal with the qualitatively different tasks of sabotage, guerrilla warfare, and agent intelligence tradecraft. The preparation of sabotage operations required an enlarged agenda on a scale we had never faced before. Special Tasks should be ready to act on direct instructions of the government and maintain close relations with the general staff. It should have at its disposal special-purpose troops and fully equipped naval and air force units. In short, I said, what was needed was a far-reaching decision by the government. Being a realist, I demanded first of all that an independent radio communications center be attached to my department. I was currently sharing communications with the First Chief Directorate.

Beria listened carefully and then said he was glad that I had followed his recommendation and concluded my postwar training in the military academy. Everybody laughed. But Beria had not yet visualized how this new reorganized and enhanced service would be coordinated. Should it be a combined task force of all the armed services? If so, it might repeat the bad experience of the Committee of Information, an amalgamation of the MGB and GRU under Molotov at the end of the 1940s. Molotov initiated operations in response to foreign policy demands and ignored the needs of independent military intelligence. The committee created bureaucratic obstacles.

General Zakharov then suggested that special service operations should be set up in all the armed forces and in the Ministry of Internal Affairs, but priority agent activities should be assigned to my department. At the same time, there should be a permanent working group of deputy directors of the GRU, MVD, and naval and air force intelligence to coordinate strategic priorities in carrying out sabotage operations.

Beria agreed, and closed the meeting by suggesting that within a month the specific structure of the new coordinating group should be reported to him. In the meantime, he would strengthen my bureau with resources and personnel, especially with experts in communications, weapons technology, oil refining, and transportation.

The next day Beria summoned me and Kruglov, his first deputy, and ordered Kruglov to provide me additional personnel and equipment. We decided to assemble one battalion of troops from the MVD and our frontier troops to become a special-purpose force specializing in intelligence gathering and sabotage. This would be similar to the brigade I had commanded during the war years, which had been disbanded by Abakumov in 1946. Beria and Kruglov approved my request to recall to active duty our experts in intelligence and guerrilla operations, including atomic espionage. Vasilevsky, Zarubin and his wife, Serebryansky, Afanasiev, Sam Semyonov, and Taubman, all of whom had been purged from the service and forced to retire, returned to Lubyanka as high-ranking members of the enlarged Ninth Department of the MVD.

I consulted Marshal Golovanov on testing our ability to strike at NATO bases in Western Europe; the idea was to send a probe mission of bombers capable of attacking strategic installations, to see if they were detected by enemy radar. We had already secured, from a Dutch air force officer stationed at NATO headquarters, a "friend or foe" radar detection device used to differentiate approaching planes. We decided to test whether or not we could foil the Western device by attaching our sample to a bomber. The reconnaissance bomber took off from Murmansk at the end of May 1953 and made a circular tour along the northern end of Norway and Great Britain, approaching NATO strategic military and port installations within striking distance. The plane returned undetected.

The idea for the probe came from my office, in coordination with the Strategic Air Force. Our liaison man with the general staff was Colonel Zimin; he reported the success to me and I forwarded it to Beria. I received word that Generals Shtemenko and Zakharov on the general staff were impressed.

Also in May 1953, Beria ordered the first test of the Soviet hydrogen bomb. He used his authority as first deputy prime minister to begin preparations for the test, without asking for approval from the Presidium or from Prime Minister Malenkov.

Beria's initiatives concerning Germany and Yugoslavia reflected the confusion in the collective leadership under Malenkov. The idea of German unification did not originate with Beria; in 1951 Stalin himself strongly supported this necessary eventuality, but with due consideration given the Soviet Union's interests. (The issue was discussed right up to the building of the Berlin Wall in 1961.) A questionnaire approved by Ignatiev before Stalin's death was sent to all intelligence stations abroad, asking for views on the matter. Prior to the May Day celebrations in 1953, Beria ordered me to prepare top-secret intelligence probes to test the feasibility of unifying Germany. He told me that the Kremlin believed that the best way to strengthen our world position would be to create a neutral, unified Germany run by a coalition government. Germany would be the balancing factor between American and Soviet interests in Western Europe. This would mean concessions from us, but the issue could be resolved by compensating the Soviet Union, actually blackmail money for demoting the Ulbricht government from its central role to a peripheral one. East Germany, the German Democratic Republic, would become an autonomous province in the new unified Germany.

Beria's plan was to use the German contacts of Olga Chekhova, Prince Janusz Radziwill, and Joseph Grigulevich to spread rumors that the Soviet Union was ready to make a deal on German unification. Then we would monitor the reactions in the Vatican, in American German policy circles, and from influential people around West Germany's chancellor, Konrad Adenauer. By putting out these feelers, Beria hoped to begin negotiations with the Western powers.

By that time, Zoya Rybkina was working for me as chief of the German intelligence section, and she was to go to Berlin and Vienna to set up probes that we hoped would be followed by talks. Beria warned me that this project was top secret and Molotov's office and the Ministry of Foreign Affairs were to act only at the second stage, after talks had begun. Beria had to resort to the intelligence services because there were no diplomatic lines of communication with West Germany.

Events in Germany soon got out of Soviet control, in part because of Beria's initiative. (Most of this information concerning the events and debates over German policy that took place among both Soviet and GDR leadership groups during May–June 1953 I learned from Zoya Rybkina.) In May we summoned to Moscow General Wollweber, minister of security of the GDR, who reported a serious split in the East German leadership, as a result of Walter Ulbricht's statement that the ultimate goal of East Germany was to build a state run by a proletarian dictatorship. Ulbricht's indiscreet remarks provoked heated discussions about German democratic traditions, and greatly annoyed Moscow. Our political counselor to Ulbricht, former ambassador to China Pavel Yudin, was reprimanded. Molotov suggested that the Presidium of the Central Committee adopt a resolution announcing that the proclaimed goal of *accelerated* construction of socialism in Germany was erroneous. But Beria — pushing for a unified, neutral Germany — said we didn't need a permanently unstable socialist Germany whose survival relied on the support of the Soviet Union.

Molotov strongly disagreed, and soon a commission of Beria, Malenkov, and Molotov was set up to work out the future Soviet policy for East Germany. The commission was to define the terms of settlement for unification, with the aim of extending reparation payments from Germany for ten years. The money would be invested in badly needed modernization and extension of our highway and railway systems, which would allow us to move troops back and forth freely. Beria was obsessed with the idea of getting about $10 billion, the same amount that had been expected from the international Jewish community, to rebuild the Soviet Union. The plan was to strengthen our position in both the German Democratic Republic and Poland, where economic chaos was causing thousands of refugees to flee to West Germany. Without unification, we would have to supply them with cheap raw materials and food in the coming ten years, before collectivized agriculture and industrialization would bear fruit.

On June 5, 1953, Vladimir Semyonov, the newly appointed Soviet High Commissioner, arrived in Germany and announced our decision to slow socialist construction and seek unification. Semyonov later told Zoya Rybkina that the German leaders begged for two weeks' time to elaborate their own political line based on Moscow's decision. Semyonov said he told them that in two weeks their state could be reduced to an autonomous region in a reunified Germany. From June 5 onward, the German government was paralyzed; rumors were afloat that Ulbricht was doomed.

In Moscow, General Wollweber and Colonel Ivan Fadeykin, our deputy rezident in Berlin, described to me the growing unrest in Germany, resulting from economic hardship and paralysis in the government bureaucracy. Ulbricht, together with other GDR leaders, was called to Moscow in early June, and we informed them of our new policy, approved by the Presidium on June 12. "Measures to Create a Healthy Political Situation in the GDR" contained Molotov's statement that at present, accelerating the implementation of socialism in Germany was not advantageous. Other provisions of this document ordering Ulbricht to change his policies were close to Beria's views. (Although there are references to this document in official publications, no one can now find the document itself.)

While I did not attend the meeting with the East German delegation — at which Beria, Malenkov, Khrushchev, Molotov, Semyonov, and General Grechko (commander of Soviet troops in Germany) were present — I later learned that Ulbricht strongly disagreed. Therefore, Beria, Malenkov, and Khrushchev decided to remove him.

The outburst of strikes and riots that occurred on June 17 may have resulted from the rebel leaders thinking that the government could not respond. Another theory is that Ulbricht provoked the uprising by refusing to meet the demand for increased pay for the striking workers. I believe both factors were involved. There was an illusion that Ulbricht's government was not supported by the Russians, who it was believed would not move against the strikers. When the revolt took place, Beria ordered Grechko and Semyonov to crush it with Red Army troops. The result was tragic, with thousands of deaths, but Beria didn't abandon his idea of unification. With a show of force, he hoped our chances for compromise with the Western powers would be strengthened. The West would lose its illusions that Soviet rule could be driven out by popular uprising.

Zoya Rybkina was dispatched to Berlin with instructions to meet Olga Chekhova to start the intelligence probe on prospects of unification. She and I had no idea that two days later Beria would be ousted. She went on with her mission and met Chekhova on June 26, the day Beria was arrested. The next day, she reported to me by secure telephone that the contact was resumed; without giving her any explanation, I ordered her prompt return to Moscow by military plane.

This was easier said than done, because General Grechko was instructed by Moscow to arrest all recently arrived top officials of the Soviet security service. Amayak Kobulov, just appointed MVD representative in Germany, and Sergei Goglidze, who had recently been appointed chief of counterintelligence by Beria and had come to Berlin to help crush the revolt, were arrested and returned to Moscow under armed guard. All means of travel were put under military control of Grechko. Zoya thus had to ask Grechko, who never took women seriously, for transportation back to Moscow. She declined to tell him her top-secret mission, referring only to my instructions to return immediately; Grechko had no idea who I was or who this security service female colonel could be, so he sent her back under guard. The same guards, GRU officers, escorted her to my office. She was lucky, because the GRU officers knew her from her frequent visits to Germany and advised Grechko not to arrest her. They knew that for the past five years she had been head of the German desk at the Committee of Information and then at the intelligence directorate. She was also lucky that the mission was an oral assignment, without written orders. Beria's probe for the unification of Germany was aborted before it began. On June 29 the Presidium canceled its new East German policy.

A similar story occurred with Yugoslavia. Beria convinced Malenkov of the necessity of reconciliation with Tito. The scheme for assassinating him was abandoned; instead, Beria proposed that Colonel Sergei Fedoseyev, his representative, should approach the Yugoslav leadership with plans for restoring cooperation between our two countries. Fedoseyev was chosen for the mission because he was young and energetic, an experienced security officer just promoted to become a deputy chief of the MVD intelligence directorate. I knew him in the war years, when he headed counterintelligence in the Moscow district NKVD administration and provided valuable assistance for radio games. From 1947 he worked in the Committee of Information, and because he didn't travel to the West he was not a known figure. Beria appointed him rezident to Belgrade, and Malenkov endorsed this plan, which was officially documented.

Unaware of his mission, I was busy with a parallel probe directed at reconciliation with Tito. Grigulevich, instead of being ordered to assassinate Tito, was now summoned to Vienna and then Moscow to discuss with Beria the options for improving our relations with Yugoslavia. This was another stillborn probe because of Beria's arrest. Grigulevich was now tagged a security risk because he could be identified abroad since publication of Orlov's articles in *Life* magazine. Grigulevich never returned to his home in Italy, and the Costa Rican government, for whom he served as ambassador to the Vatican and Yugoslavia, lost all trace of him. He reemerged in Moscow in the 1960s, as a leading Latin American scholar. Fedoseyev never got to Belgrade either, because he had not yet left when Beria was detained.

Beria also had plans to reshuffle the Hungarian leadership. He put forward Imre Nagy as a candidate for prime minister. Since the 1930s Nagy had been a full-time NKVD agent, code-named Volodya, whose services were considered highly valuable. Beria's idea was to have Nagy, his own man, in a key position in the Hungarian leadership. Nagy would be amenable to instructions from Moscow.

On June 5, Emma and I sent our children to Kiev on vacation with our relatives, and we moved to the dacha. Meshik, minister of the interior of the Ukraine, provided a place in the government rest house for the children and my niece, who was helping take care of them. I had no reason to be on the alert. The number of street crimes resulting from the amnesty was decreasing and I found nothing abnormal in the ministry or my office. I had nothing special to report to Beria or his first deputy, Kruglov, and nobody bothered me with new assignments.

I was not aware of the growing tension in the leadership. But when I advised Beria that Zoya Rybkina had departed for Germany on her probe mission and told him of my long-term plans to renew our wartime contacts in Germany, using part of the Red Orchestra in Hamburg and our connections with IEG and Thyssen leaders in German industrial circles, I noticed that he was distracted.

On June 26, on my way home from work to the dacha, I found the highway blocked by tanks, but I thought the column was simply a routine military movement badly coordinated with traffic police. The next day, when I appeared in my office, it was clear something drastic had happened. The portrait of Beria that normally hung in my reception room on the seventh floor had been removed. The officer on duty reported that it had been taken by a man from the Kommandatura. He made no comments and asked no questions. The ministry was calm. Contrary to widespread rumors, there were no orders shifting MVD troops to Moscow. Within an hour, Kruglov summoned me to the conference room, where all the heads of directorates and departments and all the deputy ministers, except Bogdan Kobulov, were assembled. Kruglov and Serov were at the head of the table. Kruglov told us that Beria, due to provocative, antigovernment actions undertaken in recent days, was arrested and detained under orders of the government. Kruglov said he had been appointed minister of internal affairs, and he instructed us to remain calm and carry out his orders. We were told to report personally to him all examples of Beria's provocative moves. Serov interrupted to announce that he remained in the post of first deputy minister. He announced the detention of Kobulov, his brother Amayak, and Sergei Goglidze for criminal association with Beria. Also detained, Serov said, were Pavel Meshik, minister of the interior of Ukraine; Rafael Sarkisov, chief of Beria's bodyguards; and Ludvigov, chief of Beria's secretariat. We were stunned. Kruglov closed the meeting quickly, saying he would report to Comrade Malenkov that the Internal Affairs Ministry and its troops were firm in their loyalty to the government and the party.

I hurried to my office and summoned Leonid Eitingon. We both realized that a purge would follow. However, we were naive enough to believe that Kruglov, in making up the list for arrests, would take into consideration the service's professional requirements. While we were not close to Beria, not considered part of his inner circle, two months earlier Beria had invited Eitingon and me to work under him. Eitingon was more of a realist than I. He correctly sensed that the Jewish team recently reinstated in the ministry would be the first to go.

I telephoned the party secretary of the Ninth Department and summoned him to my office. I informed him of Kruglov's announcement that Beria was now an enemy of the people. He stared at me in disbelief. I urged him to be vigilant but calm and to warn the party members against spreading rumors. Kruglov had demanded that the arrest of Beria and his accomplices be kept secret until a formal public announcement was made.

The list of those detained puzzled me, because it included not only influential figures, but also minor ones like Sarkisov, who had headed Beria's bodyguards but whom Beria had fired three weeks before. Moreover, when Sarkisov had then been made deputy director of the bureau that handled internal surveillance, kidnapping, and other special tasks, the head of this department, Colonel Prudnikov, refused to accept him. Kobulov, Beria's deputy, told Prudnikov, a veteran of guerrilla warfare and a Hero of the Soviet Union, "First, who are you to dispute the minister's orders? Second, don't worry. Sarkisov will soon be out of Moscow. He is not a threat to your career." Clearly, Sarkisov was out of favor and certainly not Beria's accomplice. This indicated that the decision to arrest Beria was made earlier, when Sarkisov was still close to him, or by people who were not aware that Sarkisov had been discharged.

Beria's arrest, ordered by Malenkov, resulted from a power struggle at the top of the government. Still, I could not imagine that Beria had challenged Malenkov, with whom he seemed on excellent terms. As soon as Beria was detained by the military on June 26, 1953, all the members of his secretariat who knew about the memo accusing Malenkov of plagiarism in his report to the Nineteenth Party Congress were promptly arrested and imprisoned. Only after Khrushchev's ouster, eleven years later, were they amnestied.

The next thing I did was to report to Kruglov's secretariat that I was going to visit my sick mother, who had been seriously ill for two weeks. I telephoned Emma at the dacha and invited her to lunch downtown after my visit to the hospital. Emma was more worried than I; she was sure that the arrest list yet to come would include me. As the director of a sensitive department, well known to Malenkov, Molotov, and Khrushchev, I could not escape their attention. All we could do was lie low, take no initiatives, and bring our children back from Kiev. Emma telephoned my brother, director of a food-processing plant in Kiev, and instructed him to send the children back to Moscow immediately, using his own connections, strictly forbidding him to take favors from Ukrainian security headquarters. She referred obliquely to "the man with whom you had lunch," meaning Pavel Meshik, whose arrest was not yet announced. At the hospital, fortunately, I ran into Ivan Agayants, chief of a regional department, who was not aware of what was happening. Meeting him there confirmed that I truly had left the office to visit my sick mother.

That evening Emma and I visited my eldest sister, informing her confidentially of the turn of events and the threat of our arrest. We used their telephone to contact Kiev again, and my elder brother, Grigori, confirmed that he was sending the children and my niece home to Moscow by train the next day. As a plant director, he was able to book the tickets and make the arrangements on his own. We agreed that my eldest sister, Nadezhda, would meet the children at the station and bring them to her apartment in case Emma and I were detained. I was sure Emma would be arrested with me or shortly thereafter.

That same day, I learned that Bogdan Kobulov was arrested when he was summoned to Central Committee headquarters on Old Square to discuss personnel appointments. Meshik was detained in Kiev when he visited the Central Committee headquarters. Amayak Kobulov and Goglidze were arrested in Germany by General Grechko and returned to Moscow under guard.

The next important information I received — two days later — was from my younger brother, Konstantin, a minor official in Moscow's counterintelligence office. His wife, Nina, was a typist in Malenkov's secretariat and worked in the Kremlin. Konstantin revealed that Beria had been arrested by Zhukov and several generals at a meeting of the Presidium of the Central Committee and was detained by the Ministry of Defense, not the MVD. Konstantin said that everyone in the Kremlin was nervous that day because Nina's immediate boss, Sukhanov, chief of Malenkov's secretariat, had ordered the staff to stay out of the corridors for three hours, during the crucial Presidium meeting. From Konstantin I learned that a dozen armed generals — which was unprecedented — appeared in the Kremlin, summoned by the Presidium. At the orders of Serov and Kruglov, first deputies of Beria, they substituted the generals for the usual guards. Among them was young Brezhnev, then chief of political administration of the navy. Konstantin, quoting Nina, also told me that in addition to the arrests announced, two others were detained, the chief of the Bodyguard Department, Major General Sergei F. Kuzmichev, and chief of the Special Records Department, Major General Arkady Gertzovsky. I strongly urged Konstantin not to tell anyone that he had such a highly placed source of information in Malenkov's office. The best thing was to pretend he knew nothing.

Konstantin's information deeply impressed and concerned me; the Kremlin power struggle had acquired dangerous proportions. Even under Stalin, it was strictly forbidden to enter the Kremlin armed; the only armed personnel were the guards. What a precedent for Minister of Defense Bulganin to bring his team of armed generals and officers, with weapons hidden from the guards. What if there had been an accident with all these guns? The consequences could have been tragic and unpredictable. Fortunately, Beria's arrest and detention appears to be the only example in Soviet history when a group of officers with hidden weapons entered the Kremlin and risked confrontation with the guards. The explosive potential of this episode was that the officers with hidden weapons did not know the purpose of their assignment. They had been ordered to the Kremlin with their personal arms by the minister of defense, without explanation. I learned later that Marshal Zhukov only learned about the plan to arrest Beria a few hours before the event.

Ludvigov was taken into custody at a soccer match by two high-ranking MVD officers who were waiting for him at the exit of Dynamo Stadium. They formally announced he was under arrest and took him to Butyrka prison. Later, in jail, he told me that initially he believed Beria had ordered his arrest, and he was surprised when his interrogators told him the next day that he was charged in Beria's conspiracy against the Soviet government. He believed this charge was a provocation to trap him into confessions that Beria would use to get rid of him. He thought at first that because he was married to Mikoyan's niece and Beria knew Mikoyan intimately enough to argue with him at times, Beria wanted to compromise him. Soon enough the procurator's office convinced him that the charges against him and Beria could result in a firing squad.

Sarkisov was arrested while on leave and was also convinced that it was on Beria's orders.

❊   ❊   ❊

It was clear that Khrushchev was the string puller in this coup. Beria was arrested not by Serov or Kruglov, deputy chiefs of the security forces, but by the military, who reported directly to Bulganin. Bulganin was known to be Khrushchev's man ever since they worked closely together in the 1930s as party secretaries and leaders of the Moscow municipal administration. The fact that Beria was held by military authorities, somewhere in their headquarters, made it clear that Khrushchev controlled his case.

Later I learned that the military, under Bulganin's orders, took the unprecedented step of not allowing Kruglov, the newly appointed chief of security forces, to interrogate Beria. Malenkov, formally still prime minister and head of the government, had ordered Beria's arrest, but in reality he had no control of the case. Thus, Malenkov, because he had been close to Beria in the previous ten years, was also doomed.

Khrushchev's account in his memoirs of the reasons for Beria's arrest are unconvincing.[4] It is now established that Beria never plotted to seize power and overthrow the collective government. He had no power base within the bureaucracy to entertain such an idea. His initiatives showed that he wanted a determining voice in both internal and foreign policy. Beria was exploiting his long personal ties with Malenkov, putting him in awkward isolation from the other members of the Presidium of the Central Committee. Beria's position depended entirely on Malenkov's strength and support. Beria annoyed Malenkov by purging Ignatiev in alliance with Khrushchev; Ignatiev was Malenkov's man, and supervised the party security machinery. Malenkov overestimated his own popularity; he didn't perceive that Beria's support was crucial to his own position because Beria, Pervukhin, Saburov, and Malenkov represented the relatively younger generation in the ruling Presidium. The old group — Molotov, Voroshilov, Mikoyan, Kaganovich — deprived of real power under Stalin, was hostile to this young generation that came to power after the purges of the thirties. The two generations had an uneasy equilibrium; the public prestige of the older leaders was higher than that of Malenkov, Khrushchev, and Beria, who in the eyes of the public had been servants of Stalin's power and instruments of his repressions rather than beloved heroes.

Khrushchev was effectively maneuvering between the two groups; he supported Beria to weaken Malenkov when Ignatiev was compromised in the Doctors' Plot. He supported Beria again to oust Malenkov

4. See *Khrushchev Remembers* (1970), pp. 321–341.

from his powerful job as secretary of the Central Committee of the Communist party. To me it is now clear that Khrushchev took advantage of the dissatisfaction with Beria's new activism to initiate his destruction. In 1952 the post of general secretary of the party was abolished, leaving Khrushchev first among equals; to become the supreme leader he had to get rid of Malenkov as head of the government. The best way was to remove Malenkov's real power base, his alliance with Beria and control over the security machinery. This would promote Khrushchev's own men to positions of control in the security service.

The archives demonstrate that Khrushchev seized the initiative from the beginning. Under his direction the Presidium fired the procurator general, Safonov, and recalled Khrushchev's protégé Roman Rudenko from the Ukraine, to appoint him procurator general of the Soviet Union, formally entrusting him on June 29 with the investigation of Beria's case. To appreciate the dynamics of the case against Beria, it is important to understand that his investigators were mainly the same men who had supervised the proceedings against the alleged Zionist conspirators. I never believed that Beria plotted to seize power, a belief that has now been confirmed by Kiril Stolyarov, a scholar who saw Beria's file. In Beria's indictment no orders, specific dates, or instructions are mentioned. There are not even indications of where the "plotters" met, or what their plan was; on the contrary, the file reveals that he was busy with affairs with women. Stolyarov asked me: How could a man intent on seizing power spend all his free time with his mistress on the day he was supposed to have carried out his coup? There is no record of who his coplotters were or what forces he planned to use in the takeover.

The accusations are supported only by Beria's "treacherous initiatives" in national policy, moves toward reconciliation with Yugoslavia and betraying the cause of socialism in Germany. Stolyarov told me that the plot theory included Beria's desire to contact the British intelligence service; the procurator drew this conclusion because Beria ordered the end of the investigation against Ivan Maisky, ambassador to Great Britain, who was accused of spying for the British. In the indictment, Maisky was supposed to have been in line to assume the post of foreign minister in Beria's government. Another Beria initiative, the order to prepare for a hydrogen bomb test, was not rescinded; preparations continued through June, during his arrest, and the test took place in August.

One of the principal accusations against Beria was that he was the agent of the Azeri (Azerbaijani) nationalist intelligence service in 1919, during the Civil War. As the agent of these anti-Bolsheviks he allegedly established clandestine contacts with British intelligence in Baku and was sent by them as an undercover agent to penetrate the Bolsheviks. The indictment stated that Beria eliminated all witnesses to his treacherous behavior in the Civil War in the Caucasus and slandered the memory of the revered Bolshevik Sergo Ordzhonikidze, a Georgian hero and close friend of Lenin and Stalin. Later, in the fifties and up to the August 1991 coup attempt, all leaders from Khrushchev to Gorbachev claimed that Ordzhonikidze was a victim of Stalin and Beria because he strongly opposed the purges of the 1930s. However, undisclosed documents in the archives tell a different story. According to a chief of Beria's secretariat, Mamulov, Ordzhonikidze personally prepared a summary in his own handwriting and sent it to the Party Control Commission, confirming that Beria was sent by the Communist party to work among Azeri nationalists in an attempt to penetrate their intelligence service. His work was of particular value for the Bolshevik underground network in Baku in 1918–1920. This document is in the Beria file of the Presidential Archives. Also in this file are documents that illustrate Ordzhonikidze's personal conflicts with Stalin; he intervened on behalf of individual victims, but there is no evidence that he opposed the purges in principle.

In January 1991 the minutes of the plenary session of the Central Committee on the Beria case were unexpectedly published in *Izvestia CC CPSU*, the news bulletin of the committee. The speeches of Molotov, Malenkov, Khrushchev, Mikoyan, and others reveal that the charges against Beria were based solely on intrigues in the leadership. The charges arose from rumors that the members of the Presidium themselves had spread. The minutes contain no hard evidence, just imprecise remarks such as, "I thought," or "I didn't trust him from the very beginning."

Following the arrest of Beria, in late June or early July, Malenkov appointed Nikolai Shatalin, secretary of the CPSU Central Committee, to act as first deputy of the minister of internal affairs, in charge of security. I quickly reported to him the scope of my work against American strategic installations and asked for instructions, hoping to show that I was involved in serious and professional operations, not power intrigues. I asked him to sanction further probes into the state of NATO readiness, but he replied, "I'm not here to decide anything. I will sign no documents or resolutions." He returned my written summary without comments.

When Beria's arrest was made public and it was formally announced that the Central Committee had expelled him from the party as an enemy of the people, a party meeting of the MVD leadership was called. Malenkov and Shatalin presented explanations for Beria's arrest that sounded amateurish and childish to every security professional assembled in the hall. The audience listened in silence to the revelations of Shatalin that, in order to deceive Beria, the Presidium of the Central Committee knowingly endorsed false decisions and orders. This was unprecedented in the country and the party. No leader had ever admitted that he was involved in or would condone such a practice. Everyone believed that under no circumstances would the leadership pass a false directive to deceive party activists, however good the cause. I was naive enough to suppose that under Stalin it had been different; we thought that level of official cynicism was impossible. Shatalin continued, saying that the Central Committee leadership and Comrade Malenkov, together with true war heroes — referring to Marshal Zhukov and Generals A. Batitsky and Kirill Moskalenko, who had helped carry out the arrest — had performed a heroic duty. "It was not so easy to plan and carry out the arrest of such a villain." Eitingon, Raikhman, and I were sitting near one another and simultaneously exchanged knowing glances. We understood that there was no Beria conspiracy; the reality was an anti-Beria plot in the leadership.

Following Shatalin's remarks, Pitovranov, deputy chief of counterintelligence, and General A. Obruchnikov, deputy minister in charge of personnel, denounced Raikhman, Eitingon, and me as untrustworthy. These two men were not our enemies; they were simply doing what they were told. Pitovranov attacked me for being surrounded by odious characters such as Eitingon, and suspicious figures like Serebryansky and Vasilevsky, who had previously been arrested or purged from intelligence work. My attempts to respond to these accusations were blocked by Serov, Kruglov's deputy, who was in charge of the meeting.

Only in 1991 did I learn that Pitovranov simply repeated word for word what Kruglov had said at the plenary session in the Kremlin. Unlike Serov, Kruglov was not a key player in the plot against Beria; he was so frightened for himself that he lost half his body weight during these extraordinary days. I was deeply upset by the meeting, but still hoped life in the ministry would soon return to normal.

Shatalin reported the political shortsightedness and total incompetence of a section chief in counterintelligence, Colonel Potapov, who, while meeting his informers on the eve of Beria's arrest, praised the political genius and shrewdness of Beria. Shatalin quoted a letter from an informer in the Institute of Foreign Languages, Oleg Troyanovsky.[5] Potapov turned pale when Malenkov asked, "Is this man here?" Potapov stood up but was utterly unable to comment. Serov intervened and said that irresponsible men who made such antiparty statements could not be allowed to attend confidential party meetings, and Potapov was escorted out of the hall. Fortunately, he was too minor in rank to be prosecuted and was dismissed with a party reprimand.

After the meeting I went to work every day but did nothing sub-stantial. According to my diary notes, this meeting occurred on July 15, and on August 5 I was summoned to Kruglov's office and ordered to bring the agent file of Ivan Stamenov, the Bulgarian ambassador to Moscow whom I had run as an agent during the war years. With no explanation he ordered me to accompany him, bringing this file, to Instantsiya (the highest authority, the code word for the Kremlin). Dressed in our military uniforms, we drove in through the Spassky gate and turned right to the familiar building of the Council of Ministers. I found myself in the same corridor where, in February 1953, I had last seen Stalin. This time I was received in a unique manner. Kruglov and I immediately realized that something unusual and unprecedented was about to take place. The chief of Malenkov's secretariat, instead of invit-ing the minister and his subordinate into the room, as was the practice with Stalin, ordered Kruglov to remain in the reception area while I was told to enter Stalin's former office alone, carrying the Stamenov file.

Khrushchev, Molotov, Malenkov, Bulganin, and Voroshilov were seated around a table. Although Malenkov, as prime minister, was con-sidered to be the head of the leadership, it was Khrushchev who greeted me and offered me a seat. The rule was to call everybody comrade and then use their name, but Khrushchev said, "Good day, Comrade General. You look like the model of a freshly minted general. Take a seat.

"Comrade Sudoplatov," he continued in the formal manner of a party official, "you know that we arrested Beria for treacherous activi-ties. You worked with him for many years. Now Beria writes to us say-ing he wants to talk with us. But we don't want to talk to him. We have

5. Later Khrushchev's personal interpreter, ambassador to Japan, and ambassador to the United Nations, Troyanovsky denounced his case officer Potapov to Malenkov for praising Beria, and demanded a full investigation into the atrocities of provocateurs like Potapov in the security service.

summoned you to clarify some of his conspiratorial actions. We expect you to be candid in your answers."

There was a pause, and I replied, "It is my party duty to present the true facts to the party leadership." I explained that I was really shocked by the unmasking of Beria as an enemy of the people and said, "I was shortsighted to learn about his conspiracy against the government only from the official announcement." Then Malenkov spoke up, demanding that I explain my involvement in secret attempts of Beria to establish contact with Hitler right after the outbreak of the war, so as to start peace negotiations on the basis of territorial concessions.

I answered that Stamenov was our veteran agent, and when the war broke out Beria summoned me on July 25 to meet with Stamenov. I was to use him to spread disinformation among the diplomatic corps in Moscow that a peace settlement, based on territorial concessions, was possible with the Germans. I pointed out that Beria had planned to meet Stamenov but Molotov forbade him to do so. Stamenov was to convey these rumors on his own initiative, from "a highly placed source," to impress the Bulgarian czar. No written order was placed in his file. I had arranged, with Molotov's permission, to get Stamenov's wife a job in the Institute of Biochemistry of the Academy of Sciences. The rumor had gone nowhere; our interception service, which had access to all Stamenov's ciphers and diplomatic mail, detected no messages to Sofia reporting these rumors. The disinformation operation was dropped.

Malenkov interrupted me and suggested that I write an explanatory note immediately. With that, I was ordered to leave the room and to prepare a written statement in the reception office. Meanwhile, Kruglov was called in, and when Malenkov's secretary reported that I had finished my written explanation, I was invited into the room once again.

Beria's statement covering this episode says: "I received from Stalin an order to create through Stamenov conditions that could allow the Soviet government to maneuver and win time for collecting forces." Beria continued, "The aim of this operation was to plant disinformation in the hope of impeding the German offensive and further movement of the German fascist troops."[6]

Khrushchev read aloud my explanation, written on one page. Molotov remained silent and Khrushchev again took the initiative, asking me to tell them the substance of my work under Abakumov and Beria

6. P. A. Sudoplatov learned from Stolyarov that Beria's statement is included in his case file, The Criminal Case Against Beria, vol. 6, pp. 230, 231.

in the postwar years. Here I think I made a fatal mistake. After outlining planned operations against NATO military bases, I was asked by Khrushchev to report on secret liquidations. I started with the assassinations of Konovalets and Trotsky, then special operations in Minsk and Berlin during the war years. I listed four postwar cases — Oggins, Samet, Romzha, and Shumsky — and in each instance mentioned who had initiated these actions. I said that all these actions were taken with the approval and knowledge not only of Stalin but also Molotov, Khrushchev, and Bulganin. Khrushchev corrected me, addressing the Presidium, saying that in most of the cases the initiative came from Stalin and our foreign comrades. An awkward pause lasted a minute. Then I was unexpectedly relieved when Bulganin supported these operations as being against what he called sworn enemies of socialism. Khrushchev finished the interview, addressing me. "The party has no grudges against you. We trust you. You are to continue your work. You will shortly be asked to prepare a plan for liquidating the Bandera leadership of the Ukrainian fascist movement in Western Europe, which is arrogantly insulting the leadership of the Soviet Union."

With this, Khrushchev indicated he was finished with me, and Kruglov nodded to me to leave and wait for him in the reception room. I waited uneasily for almost an hour and a half. I didn't believe a word of Khrushchev's assurances. Malenkov's hostile manner and Molotov's silence were ominous. The Stamenov agent file (code name Chesary — Caesar — because Stamenov had been recruited in Rome in 1934, when he was a third secretary of the Bulgarian Embassy) was not returned to me, but remained with the Presidium of the Central Committee. I had watched Molotov and Bulganin thumb through the file carefully while I was talking.

I was deeply worried. A very real possibility existed that Kruglov would emerge from the meeting with an order to arrest me. Finally Kruglov came out and signaled me to follow him. In the car, he told me to submit immediately a handwritten report of all liquidations known to me, at home and abroad, that were ordered by, carried out, or canceled by Beria, Abakumov, and Ignatiev.

When I arrived in my office, I considered his instructions and, after preparing a handwritten list of all known special tasks, showed the paper to the secretary of the party for the Ninth Department, Colonel Lev Studnikov. In my report I emphasized that I was listing only those cases personally known to me and with which in some way I had been involved. I asked Studnikov to take it to Kruglov's secretariat. I wanted to be sure there would be a witness to the document, because by that time a rumor was spreading in the ministry that my department was responsible for secret, mass killings at the instigation of Beria.

After Kruglov's secretary confirmed that my sealed report had been delivered by Studnikov, I left for my dacha to consult with Emma. Although we tried to remain optimistic, Emma was correct in assuming that at the worst I was now being considered an accomplice of Beria's by the new leadership.

In two or three days, I learned from Konstantin, my younger brother, that my name had begun to appear in the minutes of interrogations of Beria, Kobulov, and Maironovsky. On the Kremlovka — the direct phone line from the Kremlin — I received a call from Rudenko, the procurator general, requesting me to appear in his office "to clarify some essential facts known to you." Before going to the ornate procurator's office at 15 Pushkin Street, I told myself that I would not commit suicide and would fight to the end. I was in no way a conspirator with Beria or even part of his personal entourage.

When I arrived at Rudenko's office I met army general Ivan Maslennikov, a Hero of the Soviet Union, who was just leaving. We nodded to each other, and I could see that he was grim. As first deputy minister of the interior, he had commanded the ministry's troops, and during the war he had won his gold Hero of the Soviet Union medal as a commander at the front. I always regarded him highly: the first order he signed after the war was to provide free admission to military schools for the children of chekists who had perished during the war.

Present in Rudenko's office was Colonel of Justice Tsarigradsky, who did not utter a word but diligently transcribed Rudenko's questions and my answers. Rudenko told me he had been instructed by the Central Committee to formalize my explanations and to include them in the Beria case. In particular he was concerned that all references I had made to Stalin and Molotov in my account of the Stamenov episode be omitted. Instead, he suggested, there should only be references to Beria giving instructions and orders, with Beria referring to orders received from the highest authority. I did not protest, because for anyone aware of the party rules, this was standard procedure. In my memos to the minister I would never write that I was proposing some action on the instructions of Comrade Khrushchev or Malenkov. The rule was to state that the highest authority (Instantsiya on Russian documents) believed it expedient to undertake this or that measure.

From the very beginning, I did not like the way Rudenko asked questions, such as, "When did you receive the criminal order from Beria to initiate a probe of a secret peace with Hitler?" I protested, noting that such terms as "criminal orders" had not been used by Comrades Malenkov and Khrushchev when they questioned me and listened to my explanations. I only learned about the criminal acts of Beria from the official announcement. I was an operational officer who could not imagine that the man appointed by the government to run the security service was an unmasked criminal.

As a result, Rudenko was not pleased with the minutes of our meeting. Although he remained polite, he reproached me for being too formal and bureaucratic in exposing an archenemy of the party and the government. I walked back to the Lubyanka in a black mood, reconstructing the meeting and imagining what it foreshadowed. Nothing good, I thought. I was absolutely right. As soon as I returned to my desk, I was faced with ominous developments.

Aleksandr Panyushkin, an overconfident but passive bureaucrat who had not acquired any competence in intelligence operations despite his experience in the field as both ambassador and rezident in China and then in Washington in the early 1950s, was appointed head of the First Chief Directorate.

I was in the first deputy minister's office when Ivan Serov told me of the appointment. Serov said that the Ninth Department would no longer be independent, but would be part of the First Chief Directorate under Panyushkin. This clearly contradicted Khrushchev's assurances that I would continue to work as before. Panyushkin and Serov tried to extract from me as much as they could about the operational plans of the department. Although they confirmed I was still a deputy chief of the directorate, they surprisingly suggested that I might want to go on leave — to take a rest in a ministry sanatorium. I agreed, but said that since the school year was about to begin, I would go after putting my children in school. I left.

As I thought over their offer to go on leave, it occured to me that they might prefer to arrest me quietly outside the Lubyanka. When I reached my office on the seventh floor, I was shocked to learn that Maslennikov had shot and killed himself in his study only an hour earlier. I learned later that Maslennikov had been interrogated about Beria's alleged plan to have him move the MVD troops under his command into Moscow to arrest government leaders. No such plan existed, and Maslennikov decided to take his own life rather than face torture or imprisonment. It was his way of maintaining his honor.

By that time Eitingon, Elizabeth and Vassili Zarubin, Serebryansky, Afanasiev, Vasilevsky, and Sam Semyonov had all been relieved of their posts and suspended without pay. Eitingon and Serebryansky were later arrested. The others were forced to retire on pension, still in their forties and early fifties. Semyonov, a hero of atomic espionage, was expelled without a pension. Zoya Rybkina was purged six months after my arrest. She became a case officer running agents in the Siberian Gulag, by which she earned her pension as a police officer. She retired in 1955, not from the intelligence service but from the police. At our last meeting, Serov had not raised the issue of these people, and I preferred not to mention them.

The situation was grave. Emma made sure I had no access to arms at home; she would not allow me to end my life to avoid arrest and save the family from deportation to Siberia. Meanwhile, at our flat we met Raikhman, who had been fired by Serov a week after formal charges against Beria were announced. Raikhman said his wife, the ballerina Lepishinskaya, who had contacts with people around Khrushchev, reassured him that the purge would be limited to those arrested with Beria and would not embroil midlevel bureaucrats. He was sure that he and Eitingon would only be forced to retire. We both chose to believe this might be so, because we had not been close to Beria, and the men who had been, Kruglov and Serov, were still in a strong position.

Raikhman's forecast proved to be incorrect.

A few days later, on August 21, I remember it was a Friday, my intuition told me something was really wrong. I received a telephone call from the secretary on duty in the minister's secretariat, asking me if I was planning to call Eitingon to my office to clarify some minor issue. It startled me that a junior officer, a lieutenant colonel, would inquire about a matter so far from his competence. Eitingon phoned me, saying that he was invited to the ministry personnel department, but his ulcer was bothering him so he was staying home sick. I told him I had no idea why they were asking him to come in, but within an hour, while I was listening to routine reports from Studnikov, Major Pavel Buychkov, my secretary, appeared and informed me that three men with a top-secret directive from the minister were demanding to see me. I ordered Studnikov to leave, and Buychkov brought the visitors in.

I recognized Colonel Mikhail Gordeyev, deputy chief of the department for carrying out arrests and detentions in major cases. He had arrested Voznesensky, a member of the Politburo; Aleksei Kuznetsov, secretary of the Central Committee; Shakhurin, minister of the aviation industry; and others. I simply asked if they had all the formalities signed for my detention. Gordeyev confirmed this, saying that they were fulfilling Kruglov's order and that the arrest warrant was signed by Serov. I suggested we leave through the back door rather than through the reception room, so as not to agitate my staff.[7] They agreed, despite the fact that this was a gross violation of the law. I was supposed to sign the protocol for the search of my office and be present while it was conducted. I became agitated and now cannot remember anything that happened on the way to the jail cell in the basement of Lubyanka. Without formalities, I filled out a registration card and was locked into a cell as prisoner number 8.

It all happened before lunch, and soon they brought soup, but I couldn't swallow it. I had a terrible headache and found my regular pills in my jacket pocket. They hadn't even searched me beyond looking for an obvious weapon. I forced myself to use the soup to swallow the headache pills, and began to collect my thoughts. The door opened and two guards hurriedly escorted me to the administration block, where I was searched, and everything was removed from my possession, including necktie, pills, and notebooks. The guard took off my Swiss chronometer wristwatch, bought fifteen years earlier in Belgium, and then put it in the handkerchief pocket of my jacket. He escorted me to a prison van, and at the last moment snatched the watch from my pocket. This petty theft ended what was left of my chekist idealism. How such an act could occur in the security service occupied my thoughts, even though I was coming to understand that I was about to be eliminated. Then I decided to see if I could take advantage of the loss of my watch.

I was taken to Butyrka jail, where the formalities of a search were repeated, and found myself in an ordinary solitary confinement cell. It was no different from the Finnish jail where I had spent a few months in my youth. My first interrogation came the same night. I was confronted by Rudenko and Colonel of Justice Tsarigradsky, who was again taking notes. There was no need for introductions. Rudenko bluntly announced that I was arrested as an active participant in Beria's conspiracy to seize power. I was one of the most trusted persons who

7. P. A. Sudoplatov adds that John Barron, in *KGB: The Secret Work of Soviet Secret Agents* (New York: Bantam Books, 1974), p. 419, "incorrectly asserts that I was handed a letter and as I reached to receive it 'two officers grabbed his arms and wrenched them behind his back, then dragged him away to Vladimir prison.'"

worked for him. He charged I was an accomplice of Beria in secret deals with foreign powers against the Soviet government. I was also charged with being the organizer of terrorist activities planned by Beria against the government and persons hostile to him.

To the interrogators' dismay, I replied by strongly protesting the outrageous practices in the jail under their supervision. I stressed that I had received no list of belongings taken from me; I had not signed such a list. Contrary to the law, I was not present at the search of my office, and such blatant violations of the law had logically ended with the theft of my watch.

There was a pause. They stared at me in disbelief. Rudenko said he would order his subordinates to explain what had happened. While he was still befuddled, I pressed further, categorically protesting being interrogated at night, contrary to the rules. Here he cut me short, saying, "There is no need to bother with the rules while interrogating archcriminals who kill innocent Soviet people, plan to overthrow the government, who themselves observed no formalities in NKVD practice. Beria, you, and your group will be treated in the same manner."

Forty years later, Colonel General Dmitri Volkogonov, adviser on archives to President Yeltsin, showed my son Anatoli the minutes of this first interrogation, which Rudenko hurriedly sent to Malenkov early in the morning on August 22, 1953.[8] There was no reference to my protests, but the document did reflect that I had admitted no charges; it also reported my statement that I had learned about Beria's treacherous activities only from the official announcement, and that I had not heard of any plot in the Ministry of Internal Affairs.

To Rudenko's credit, he sent the minutes to Malenkov without comments. There were no falsifications nor any fabricated confession. The time had not yet come for that. However, the next morning, the duty officer came to my cell with a list of my belongings and asked me to sign it. I noticed that my Swiss chronometer was on the list, and the officer told me that it had been found. After lunch I was summoned again for interrogation. It was the same team of Rudenko and Tsarigradsky. At first, Rudenko politely asked about my personal biography. I emphasized that I had no connection with Beria prior to his appointment to the NKVD central office in 1938.

Then Rudenko sprang his proposal that I testify to the treacherous activities of Beria. These included alleged plans for a secret deal with

8. P. A. Sudoplatov identifies this document as interrogation number 207/August 22, verified as authentic by Major of Justice Yuryeva.

Hitler through Stamenov, a scheme to use the "English spy Maisky" to establish clandestine relations with Winston Churchill, and secretly planning to poison the Soviet leadership. "To expose these schemes," Rudenko concluded, "is your party duty."

"I was not aware of such monstrous crimes," I replied. I told Rudenko that I had explained to Comrade Khrushchev and the Presidium that my contacts with Stamenov never included discussions of a secret deal with Hitler. The last time I spoke to Maisky was in 1946, and I had had no contacts with him when he was under detention. The memorandum analyzing his contacts by our British section was a routine procedure in intelligence work, channeled to me and other bureau directors.

As for my involvement in terrorist plans, the possibility of such an accusation had never crossed my mind. On the contrary, at the risk of my life throughout thirty years of my career, I had protected the Soviet people and government from sworn enemies of the Soviet regime.

Rudenko cut me short, accusing me of not fulfilling Malenkov's and Stalin's order to do away with such anti-Soviet figures as Kerensky. He said Beria, as an additional part of his treachery, canceled the government's order to kidnap his relatives in Paris and bring them to Moscow, because he naturally feared that his pro-Western sympathies would be exposed. "Have no illusions that some positive work that you and Eitingon did abroad many years ago will save you," Rudenko warned me. "The party and the government have entrusted me to offer you the opportunity to cooperate in unmasking Beria's crimes. I am authorized to tell you that the extent of your cooperation will be taken into account in deciding your fate. Currently you are prisoner number eight in the group of fifty of Beria's conspirators who have been detained. If you do not cooperate, we will crush you and your family."

Over the preceding fifteen years of purges and show trials, I had heard a lot about the technique Rudenko was using. Vannikov, Beria's deputy on the atomic project, had told of a similar method of interrogation used against him when he was arrested in 1941 under Stalin's orders and mistakenly charged with sabotage. Vannikov was tortured until, under the pretext of cooperating with the party, he confessed that he had been involved in sabotage. From the files of the executed and imprisoned intelligence officers that I had reviewed in 1941, I knew that although their fate was sealed, the only way to maintain one's innocence for history was to deny involvement in dubious activities. Yet, to save myself and my family, I could not allow myself to make any skeptical comments on whether or not Beria's conspiracy really existed. There-fore, I said I was ready to cooperate about any facts that were known to me, but I had no knowledge either of a plot or other concrete exam-ples of Beria's criminal orders. The order to abandon the plans to kidnap leading Georgian emigrants in Paris had not come from Beria, but as a directive of the government. This order had been repeated in the pres-ence of Kruglov, who was a member of the Central Committee, and the matter had not been raised either at a meeting of the Presidium or with Kruglov, one month after Beria's arrest.

That was my final meeting with Rudenko. The next day I was left alone. Shortly thereafter, interrogations continued, but now only with Tsarigradsky, who formally charged me with conspiring with Stamenov to make a secret peace with Hitler, with organizing the Administration for Special Tasks for secret assassinations ordered by Beria of people hostile to him and of leaders of the government. He also charged me with conspiring to commit these murders with special poisons that could not be detected. He said I had used Maironovsky (falsely alleged to be my relative, and who had been arrested earlier) to kill dozens of people hostile to Beria in safe apartments.

I was also accused of participation in Beria's plot to seize power and of such minor offenses as withholding information from the government about his plans to defect from the Soviet Union in 1947 and 1948. As for Beria's plans to escape to the West in a bomber from Murmansk if his conspiracy failed, I pointed out that the air force was not under my control and I could in no way be instrumental in such a plan. This was an obvious distortion of our successful probe of NATO air defenses in a flight that originated in Murmansk. When I met Colonel Zimin, our general staff liaison, almost forty years later in the KGB hospital, he was in his eighties and he revealed the flight almost ended his career. The procurator's office interpreted this flight, which Beria approved as first deputy prime minister but did not report to Prime Minister Malenkov, as Beria's plan to use the Murmansk air base for an escape to the West if his attempt to overthrow the government failed.

Shtemenko, as the initiator of these "treacherous plans," was forced to retire from the army, a colonel general still in his forties. He was spared by Khrushchev and Malenkov because they did not want high-ranking army officers put on trial in connection with the Beria case. He was called back almost fifteen years later by Brezhnev to prepare plans for the military invasion of Czechoslovakia, which he did superbly and won his fourth star. Zimin was questioned but left alone.

I was also charged with impeding the plan to liquidate Tito in "a cowardly and treacherous manner." My protests and demands to counter the charges were ignored.

Tsarigradsky began to manipulate my biography, using as incriminating evidence the cases of Shpigelglas, Maly, and other officers who had been purged as enemies of the people. He tried to portray me as their accomplice and said that Beria, knowing the incriminating evidence, had preferred not to unmask me but instead to recruit me in his organization, thus deceiving the government and the party when I received high awards for my work. Beria, he said, concealed from the Central Committee and the government that as early as 1938 to 1941 there was incriminating evidence against me in the Investigation Department of the NKVD.

I was also accused of secretly mining government dachas and out-of-town residences on the instructions of Beria during the war years and preserving these mines as the means of eliminating government and party leaders. My deputy during the war years, Colonel Mikhail F. Orlov, who was the chief of staff of the Administration for Special Tasks and later commanded the Special-Purpose Brigade, was summoned to the MVD. When I was arrested Orlov had been fired, but he was now recalled to assist an MVD team and officials from the procurator's office to check the government residences near the Minsk highway and find the land mines allegedly placed there on Beria's orders to blow up the leadership. Although the search continued for a year and a half, nothing was ever found.

In reality, I had supervised the planting of land mines on and near highways to block the German tank advance in October 1941, during the battle for Moscow. But after the German advance stalled, the mines were removed under strict control and in accordance with a detailed plan. Apparently, Khrushchev and Malenkov believed the story that was invented by the procurator's office or generated through false, forced confessions. The search teams also looked for treasures that Beria had allegedly hidden in caches near his dacha or in an MVD safe house outside Moscow, but nothing was found.

I was not beaten, but after an interrogation that lasted two or three hours, I was given supper and then escorted once again to the interrogation room, where teams of younger officers kept me awake until 5:00 A.M. repeating standard questions: "Do you confess? . . . Do you admit your involvement in Beria's treacherous crimes?" The teams changed frequently, and I was forced to stay awake and respond to their accusations. The junior officers did not appear to be instructed to pursue any details of the case but were simply depriving me of sleep.

After about a month and a half of this treatment, it was apparent to me that my confession was not that important to Tsarigradsky. However, I was aware that some of the prisoners, such as Bogdan Kobulov, were playing for time. Tsarigradsky confronted me with excerpts from Kobulov's interrogation which made it clear that while avoiding talking about serious matters, such as espionage and deals with foreign agents, he was throwing them scraps. Kobulov said that my staff was full of suspicious people from whom "you could expect any criminal act." Kobulov, an experienced interrogator, was trying to create the impression that he was cooperating and might be of use in the future. As for me, this option was unacceptable. I realized that I would be at the top of the list of those to be eliminated, since the accusations against me rested on facts that the leadership chose to interpret not for what they were, but as evidence of a conspiracy.

Throughout the interrogation period, I was alone in my cell. No witnesses or alleged accomplices confronted me, but I sensed that I was being kept not far from other key figures in the case. For example, Merkulov's gait was familiar to me and I recognized it when he was escorted to interrogation. I knew that Merkulov had been close to Beria in the Caucasus and later in Moscow, but had not worked with him for eight years, since he was dismissed as security minister. This led me to believe that Rudenko was instructed to eliminate people who had been involved with Beria in the past, even if they no longer were. I also knew that Merkulov had suffered a heart attack shortly after Stalin's death and was seriously ill. It would have been impossible for him to play any role in a conspiracy had Beria been planning one.

At that point I decided to follow Sergei Shpigelglas's instructions for illegals who are caught red-handed with no way to deny their guilt: gradually stop talking, gradually stop eating. Do not announce a hunger strike; just place the remains of your meals in the waste bucket. In two or three weeks, you will find yourself in a state of total prostration, at which point you should refuse to accept any food. It will be two or three weeks before a doctor examines you, diagnoses exhaustion, and orders you hospitalized and placed on intravenous feeding.

I knew that Shpigelglas was broken in Lefortovo prison. He had been subjected to intravenous feeding for two months. For me, Kamo

Petrosyan was the example. He was the head of an underground battle group that, under Lenin's orders, robbed a bank in Tbilisi in 1907 and brought the money to Europe. There Petrosyan was captured by the German police when his men tried to change 250,000 rubles (about $250,000 then) into German, Swiss, and French currency. The czarist government demanded his extradition, but Petrosyan resisted passively by creating the impression that he had fallen into a stupor. A panel of the best German psychiatrists could not agree on a diagnosis, but pointed to his definite physical and mental deterioration. That saved Petrosyan. After four years in a German mental hospital, he was extradited to Russia "to continue medical treatment" in a Russian prison hospital, from which he managed to escape. He went to work for Beria in the Caucasus after the Revolution broke out, and was killed in a car accident in 1925 in Tbilisi.

The crucial moment, Petrosyan had told young chekists, was enduring the terrible pain of a spinal tap used to break your stupor and bring you back to your normal senses. If you passed this test, any panel of psychiatrists would certify that you were totally unfit for interrogation or any type of court hearing. By late autumn, I was gradually losing my strength. Tsarigradsky tried to trick me, saying that not everything was lost in my case; my past accomplishments would be taken into account by the authorities. But I did not reply to a single question he asked me. I remained passive and uninterested. My genuine despair was so terrible that at one point I threw a full metal soup plate at my jailer. Soon a doctor appeared, but as I did not answer any of his questions, she suggested that I be transferred to the hospital block for examination.

I was carried on a stretcher to the hospital block and left in the corridor outside the doctors' office. Suddenly a group of three or four inmates working as orderlies appeared and began shouting threats — "Let's do away with this police dog" — and began to beat me. I was too weak to respond, and lay limp trying to limit the damage of their blows. The attack lasted for several minutes, and I had the feeling I was being observed by doctors in the adjacent room. Soon the jailers returned and drove off my tormentors, who, it seemed clear, had been instructed not to hit me in the head.

I was placed in the hospital and fed intravenously. I do not remember much of what happened because I was in a semiconscious state. I do recall the dreaded spinal tap was given to me within a few days. I managed to bear the pain and not cry out. Now, from notes that Emma kept, it is clear that I remained in Butyrka prison hospital mental ward being fed intravenously and by forced feeding for more than a year. I managed to survive because of Emma's clandestine support, which I recognized within two or three months. Every week food packages arrived, and the medical orderlies opened the packages in my presence in an effort to interest me in the fresh fruit, smoked salmon, caviar, tomatoes, cucumbers, and roast chicken. I sensed that the food was not a prison provocation. It was not similar to the way VIP prisoners were offered food to encourage them to talk. From the way the chopped fish was prepared, I guessed that only Emma's mother could have done it. I was filled with joy to think that the family was all right. Tsarigradsky had told me that my family had given me up as an enemy of the people. The real breakthrough occurred several months later.

A nurse in Butyrka unexpectedly said, "Pavel Anatolievich, I see you do not eat tomatoes." Looking into my eyes, she said, "The tomato juice I will make for you will strengthen you, and people say it is absolutely necessary for your survival." This established, although never spoken in words, informal and friendly relations between us. Whenever she was on duty, this nurse would sit near me and open a book to read. Held to the back cover of the book she was reading one day was a newspaper announcement of Abakumov's execution. This indicated to me that Beria and all the ranking officials arrested with him had been executed. I noticed among the names of those executed the names of minor clerks, far junior in rank to me. It indicated that no mercy awaited me. The game continued.

I opposed the forced feeding, occasionally by the friendly nurse, but more often by others. In this struggle I frequently fainted, but through this nurse I learned what was happening outside. She read her book, and on the back cover again placed newspaper clippings with important information about the fate of the so-called Beria Gang. I understood that the first chapter in the Beria case was finished.

I was lucky not to have been arrested in the first wave with Beria. The wives of that group, which included Beria, Goglidze, Kobulov, Meshik, and others, were interned and exiled. Soon after my arrest, my neighbor Vera Spector, the wife of Mark Spector, with whom Emma worked in Odessa in the 1920s, signaled Emma to meet her at the rear stairway of the house. She told Emma: "Mark sends greetings and asked me to tell you that the government has abolished the law allowing the Ministry of Internal Affairs or any other institution to administratively exile members of families of enemies of the people without a court decision. Stand firm and refuse to move out of Moscow unless they produce a court order."

Although Emma was harassed and ordered to confine the family to one room in our five-room apartment, she refused, saying she would only obey a court order. Emma had her own income, her pension, which was 2,500 rubles a month, a significant amount at that time. She appeared every week in the Butyrka reception room, and I knew of her presence through the transfer of food and minor sums of money to my account. Crucially important was her meeting with Mark Spector, a retired security service colonel, who was very shrewd. He had been the chief of naval counterintelligence during the war and for a year had been the head of Merkulov's secretariat. He had suffered a heart attack and retired in 1946 and now worked as deputy chairman of the board of Moscow lawyers.

He did not talk with Emma in our apartment house but at the Ministry of Security polyclinic, so that it appeared their meetings were by chance. He had always been sympathetic to me and understood the absurdity of the charges against me. When he heard rumors that I was in a desperate condition and dying, he worked out a scheme for Emma's indirect contact with me. He arranged for Emma to meet at the polyclinic with Grigori Volkonsky, with whom Emma and I had once worked in Kharkov.

Volkonsky was now deputy chief of the main prison administration, which included the Butyrka jail. When he learned of my near critical condition, Volkonsky suggested that Emma appear on a prearranged date in his reception room at Butyrka with the cover story that she did not believe her husband was alive and wanted to know why the administration of the jail demanded, against prison rules, luxury foods for him. She was bringing everything but wine and brandy at the request of the doctor.

Volkonsky stressed that she should come at a specified time so he could then summon a recently appointed medical nurse to his office. She was a young, sentimental woman in her twenties who had just started work; she was idealistic and susceptible to recruitment and development. "It's your job to work with and develop her," Volkonsky told Emma.

The young nurse, Maria Yakovlevna Kuzina, was not a member of the security staff, although it was her duty to report all abnormal contacts with prisoners. Emma was to tell the young nurse the story of a slandered Bolshevik war hero and seek her sympathy. Volkonsky would give Emma only three or four minutes to explain the case in his presence before he cut her short.

Within a month, the plan worked. Volkonsky summoned Maria Yakovlevna to his office, asking her, in the presence of the wife of the prisoner, to report his condition. Then Emma made her appeal for fair medical treatment for me, a man who had risked his life in the underground fighting the Nazis. She pleaded with both Volkonsky and the nurse to save my life for a fair trial. This interview was surely being taped and made part of my file, but it would not attract the attention of the procurator.

After Volkonsky confirmed that Maria had been deeply moved by my plight, Emma then found the telephone number of this young woman and made contact with her. That was how Emma established clandestine and friendly relations with Maria Kuzina, the kind nurse who force-fed me and brought me news. Emma supplemented her income. They remained close for nearly fifteen years. Maria and I never spoke, but she would grasp my hand gently after placing a clipping on the back cover of her book.

This routine continued for six months, and then unexpectedly I was placed on a stretcher and taken by a special medical van with guards to the railway station. It was winter 1955. A year and a half had passed since my arrest. I was escorted by Maria and two armed guards dressed in civilian clothes into a sleeping compartment on the train. I had no idea where we were going. It was night, but I saw a name plate on the railroad car: Moscow-Leningrad. A normal sleeping compartment for four people was booked for us. The guards locked me in with Maria and left us after the train started to move, saying they would be back in thirty minutes. I lay on the lower bunk and Maria handed me an article from *Pravda* on the finale of Beria and Abakumov's conspiracy. In the latest fabrication, Abakumov was branded an accomplice of Beria's. Even more important, the article contained the news that Malenkov had been relieved as prime minister and replaced by Bulganin. Khrushchev, the first secretary of the party, had announced this major reshuffle.

This news did a little to raise my spirits. Now that Khrushchev had ousted Malenkov, the vague hope arose that I might somehow exploit that situation to my own advantage. I was sure that the compartment was bugged and therefore did not comment on the article or speak to Maria, who again pressed my hand compassionately. Soon the guards returned in high spirits and, exhausted from the strain and uncertainty of being moved, I fell asleep.

We were met by a medical ambulance at the Leningrad station and I was taken to the infamous Kresti prison, which in czarist times was for preliminary detention and investigation. The old wing of the prison had been turned into a mental hospital. The formalities were strict. Maria disappeared, and I was examined by the chief psychiatrist, Lieutenant Colonel of Medicine Petrov, who later supervised the "medical treatment" of the human rights dissident Vladimir Bukovsky. Even in my time, the prison was filled not only with common thieves but with political prisoners, some of whom were in detention for more than fifteen years.

Petrov seemed satisfied with the examination and placed me in a ward with General Sumbatov, the chief of the supply administration of the security service, and Sarkisov, the former chief of Beria's bodyguards. I sensed that the ward was bugged. These two men appeared to be mentally ill. Sarkisov, a former textile factory engineer in Tbilisi, kept complaining that the false charges of treason against him prevented implementation of a speeded-up five-year-plan for the textile industry with a new machine he had invented. He asked the doctors to help him expose Procurator Rudenko, who was sabotaging his efforts to increase textile production and become a hero of socialist labor.

Sumbatov sat on his bed crying and babbling that Beria's treasures were buried at the Council of Ministers dacha in Zhukovka, outside Moscow, and had not been smuggled abroad. Soon his screams increased. At first I thought this was his reaction to injections, but when he died, after being taken from our ward, we learned he had suffered unbearable pain from cancer.

The stay in Leningrad nearly crippled me. I underwent a second spinal tap, not administered as brutally as in Butyrka, but it seriously damaged my spinal column, crushing one disc. I lost consciousness and only intravenous feeding brought me back. Emma appeared in Leningrad a week after my arrival there; that saved me, because she was able to enlist the help of a strong network of friends, former security people. Most helpful was Emma's uncle, Isaac Krimker, a charming personality who moved from one profession to another and performed brilliantly in whatever he did. This resourceful relative arranged regular delivery of food parcels specially prepared for a liquid diet, and put Emma in contact with a nurse who had access to my ward. The nurse knew that there were listening devices within reach of any conversation and that it was dangerous to bring me information. Emma and Krimker devised a coded letter addressed to the nurse's relative, which she allowed me to read and which contained all the news of the outside world.

Thus Emma let me know that "the old man," meaning Stalin, was exposed at the gathering of "the collective farm," meaning the Twentieth Party Congress. I learned from her that "the accounting officers," meaning those purged together with me, were in bad health; that conditions on "the farm were the same," but she had enough money and contacts to carry on. I was confused by her message that "no one can predict when Lev Semyonovich will recover from TB." That turned out to be the name of a real man; it was a precaution in case the letter was seized, to give news about a real person that could be verified. I thought that Lev Semyonovich was a code name for me, that the authorities regarded me as genuinely ill and I should stay there and play for time.

Repeated injections left me in an unstable state of misery. The separation from Emma lasted until the end of 1957, when she was allowed to visit me in response to appeals from her to the procurator and the director of the jail. In December 1957 we had seven meetings, with my interrogator Tsarigradsky and two doctors present. I didn't utter a word, but at the second meeting I couldn't control my tears. Emma kept talking, telling me that the family was well, that Raikhman was amnestied, that Eitingon got a twelve-year sentence, that no one believed my guilt, that she was still surrounded by old friends, that I should begin to eat. I didn't answer her. Their purpose in allowing the meetings was to bring me out of my stupor.

A month later I resumed eating solid food; my front teeth were broken from forced feeding, but I began to recover, and to answer simple questions. The conditions of my stay promptly improved; I received a soldier's meals instead of prison fare. In addition, I had food parcels from Emma. Gradually I recovered, and in April 1958, Lieutenant Colonel Petrov announced that I was fit for further interrogation. I was transferred by prison van to the railway station and in an ordinary criminal holding car sent to Moscow and to the familiar block at Butyrka.

I immediately sensed that the political situation had changed drastically. Within days I received visits from three warders and the administrator of the prison wing, all former soldiers of the Special-Purpose Brigade during the war years, who came to greet and encourage me. They openly cursed Khrushchev for eliminating the special pay usually given for military rank in the Ministry of Internal Affairs, which put them in a second-grade position compared with the army and frontier troops.[9] They were also indignant that Khrushchev delayed for twenty years repayment of government bonds that all officers were required to buy with a ten percent to twenty percent portion of their salaries. I was not sure how to respond, but I thanked them for their moral support and for the privilege of shaving myself, the first time in five years.

9. The three components of salaries for military and police personnel were administrative duty, military rank, and years of service. Khrushchev eliminated payments for military rank for personnel in the Ministry of Internal Affairs, including prison guards and militia. Brezhnev restored these payments in 1968, but only at 75 percent of other armed services.

THE TRIAL

oon I was summoned for interrogation. This time I
learned that Tsarigradsky was not handling my case.
He had been replaced by Rudenko's special assistant,
Preobrazhensky, who worked together with Senior
Investigator Andreev. Preobrazhensky, in his fifties,
had a crippled leg, and it affected his personality, making him dour and withdrawn. His bitterness was in
contrast to the attitude of Andreev, about forty, who
was always well dressed and often joked cynically
about the accusations against me. Preobrazhensky
had prepared false transcripts of my interrogations. I
refused to sign them and crossed out the lies he had
created to incriminate me. Then he tried to blackmail me, saying he
would add a new accusation: simulating madness. Calmly, I said: "I
have no objections, but you will have to annul the two findings of the
medical commission, which both conclude that I was comatose and was
totally unfit for interrogation." I pointed out that Tsarigradsky and
Rudenko, by depriving me of sleep for more than three months, and
placing me in a windowless cell, had caused this condition.

Andreev was different. He transcribed the interrogation sessions
without altering my answers. I sensed that he had become sympathetic
toward me when he realized that I had nothing to do with Mikhoels's

murder in 1948 or experiments in the toxicological laboratory on people
condemned to death. The substance of my case was clear, Andreev said,
but a prison term was inevitable considering the leadership's attitude
toward people who had worked with Beria. He predicted a sentence of
fifteen years.

Preobrazhensky pressed me, but I refused to budge, and soon he
announced, "Your case is finished." For the first and only time, I was
given the four volumes of my case to examine. The indictment was written on two thin pages. I noted that Andreev had kept his promise to
drop, because of lack of evidence, the charges that I had conspired with
Beria to seize power. Also absent were earlier accusations of mishandling
the assassination operation against Marshal Tito and withholding information on Tito's conspiracy against the Soviet Union in 1946. Beria's
fantastic escape plans to the West from a special air force base in
Murmansk with the help of General Shtemenko were no longer part of
the case against me. Maironovsky was no longer incorrectly mentioned
as my relative. Nevertheless, the indictment presented me as a villain
who conspired with enemies of the people against the party and the
government from 1938 onward. To support this case, they added the
charges made against the officers whom I had urged be freed from prison
at the beginning of the war — Shpigelglas, Serebryansky, and others —
although, except for Serebryansky, all of these men had since been rehabilitated. Legally these accusations were invalid, but that did not seem
to matter.

Three charges remained from the original indictment:

One. Secretly conspiring with Beria to make a separate peace with
Hitler in 1941 and to overthrow the Soviet government.

Two. As Beria's man, responsible for the Administration for Special
Tasks, I had carried out secret assassinations of people hostile to Beria
by administering poisons and then covered up the deaths by making
them appear to be accidental.

Three. From 1942 to 1946, I supervised the work of the toxicological laboratory that tested poisons on people condemned to death.

There were no references to specific cases or examples. The accusations were confirmed only by the materials in the case file and by the
fact that Eitingon, my deputy, had already been convicted of high treason in 1957. Eitingon had been released in March 1953, after Stalin's
death, but was rearrested in August of the same year, soon after Beria's
downfall. He was serving twelve years in prison. The indictment con-

cluded that I should be tried by the Military Collegium of the Supreme Court in a closed hearing. There was no need for a procurator or a defense lawyer.

I recalled that Emma had told me in Leningrad that the holding of secret trials, introduced after Kirov's murder, was now prohibited by law. Raikhman was amnestied because he had managed to avoid a secret trial. I was in a difficult position. How could I tell Preobrazhensky that I knew of changes in the law when I was supposed to have been comatose in Leningrad?

I asked Preobrazhensky to justify the closed court procedure; the indictment should say that I was about to be subjected to a closed secret trial in violation of the law. He said there was no need for such details in the indictment; he formally turned down my appeal for a defense lawyer. I requested a copy of existing regulations for trials, but this, too, was rejected in writing by Preobrazhensky. Andreev was more sympathetic. He told me it would be naive to expect a lawyer to defend me, since my fate and the method of dealing with me had already been decided.

I then appealed to the deputy director of the jail, my former subordinate during the war years. A guard came to my cell to tell me that my request for court regulations was rejected but the deputy director would hear my complaints on the conditions of my imprisonment. When I was brought to the deputy director's office, which I assumed was bugged, there was no sign of recognition between us. He told me that my request was turned down, but pointed to the regulations for conditions of imprisonment on his table and suggested that I examine them before writing a formal appeal. I sensed something unusual in his gesture. The volume of standard rules for prisoners had attached to it a summary of the rights of prisoners. This contained what I needed: that the Presidium of the Supreme Soviet of the USSR, in its April 30, 1956, decree, had abolished closed trials without defense lawyers in cases of high treason.

My formal appeal for a lawyer had been deliberately ignored, most likely on orders from the highest authority, Khrushchev, who by that time was head of the party and the government. I decided to wait and plead for a defense lawyer at the court itself.

The investigation concluded with an awkward meeting. Preobrazhensky suddenly demanded that I write a special summary of the way Molotov was involved in the Stamenov probe. This puzzled me, and I wondered if Molotov was out of favor. I knew nothing of the "antiparty group" purged in 1957, which included Molotov, Malenkov, and Kaganovich. My summary clearly impressed Preobrazhensky, especially the information that Molotov had arranged a position in the Institute of Biochemistry of the Academy of Sciences for Stamenov's wife. I also recalled that Molotov had been consulted about the gifts Stamenov gave to the Bulgarian czarist family. This deposition strengthened my hope that despite a secret hearing I would be kept alive as a witness against Molotov.

I sent thirty-three appeals, bombarding Khrushchev, Rudenko, the chairman of the Supreme Soviet, Serov — now chairman of the KGB[1] — and others with requests for a lawyer and protesting gross falsifications in the charges against me. I did not receive a single answer.

Normally when a high-level investigation was completed, the case was forwarded to the Supreme Court. Within a week, or a month at the most, I should have received notice of when my case was to be tried. Three months went by with no word. Only in the beginning of September 1958 was I officially informed that my case would be considered by the Military Collegium on September 12 in closed session without procurator or defense lawyer. I was transferred to the internal jail at Lubyanka and then to Lefortovo prison. Years later I learned that General Borisoglevsky, chairman of the Military Collegium, sent my case back to the procurator's office three times recommending additional investigation. Three times it was returned to him refusing his request.

It seems to me now that, although my fate was sealed, nobody wanted to ignore the formalities in the self-righteous period after Stalin's death and Khrushchev's revelations of his crimes at the Twentieth Party Congress. Later I learned that my appeals to Serov and Khrushchev, in which I referred to our meetings in the Kremlin and operational cooperation during and after the war, inspired prompt action. A senior case officer from my former department, Colonel Pavel Aleksakhin, was sent to the procurator's office to remove all records from my file involving Khrushchev in our secret tasks against Ukrainian nationalists. Colonel Aleksakhin was an experienced intelligence officer who, when shown the indictment against me, openly told the military procurator that the charges were fabricated. Junior officers agreed with him and complained that the orders to press the case came from the top.

1. The KGB, Committee for State Security, was established in 1954, downgrading the security apparatus from an independent ministry to a state committee formally attached to the Council of Ministers, in an attempt to keep it under political control.

Aleksakhin took three sealed envelopes of unexamined operational materials from my safe. The procurator's office assured Aleksakhin that there were no references to Khrushchev in the four volumes of my criminal case. Aleksakhin gave the envelopes to Serov and never saw them again. I cannot remember everything that was in my safe, but I know for certain that there were records of the official requests for the elimination of Oggins, Shumsky, Romzha, and Samet, made by the highest authority, which was then Stalin, Molotov, Malenkov, Khrushchev, and Bulganin.

Later, when Aleksakhin joined two other intelligence officers in appealing my case, he referred to this episode. In 1988, when he wrote his final appeal on behalf of my rehabilitation, Aleksakhin was told to remain silent and not further compromise the party by digging up such unpleasant matters.

For the trial I was taken in a prison van to the headquarters of the Supreme Court, on Vorovsky Street. I was not handcuffed, and the KGB guards who escorted me were ordered to wait in the reception room of the deputy chairman of the Military Collegium, outside the courtroom, contrary to normal procedure. I was dressed in civilian clothes. I entered not a courtroom but a well-appointed office with only five people present. The desk of the chief was in a corner, and a conference table was used for the hearing. At the head of the table was Major General Kostromin, who introduced himself as deputy chairman of the Military Collegium. Two other judges were Colonel of Justice Romanov and Vice Admiral Simonov. Two secretaries were present, one of them Major Afanaysev, who later was one of the secretaries at the Oleg Penkovsky treason trial.

It was a long table. I was seated at one end and the three judges at the other end. Kostromin formally began the procedure by announcing the names of the judges, and asked if I had any objections to the composition of the court. I said I had none, but I protested the closed session and the gross violation of my basic constitutional right to legal counsel. Due to the serious illness I had suffered, I could not defend myself properly. Kostromin was stunned when I said that the law forbade closed sessions and made a defense attorney mandatory in cases where the death penalty was possible under the criminal code. The judges looked at him with concern, especially the admiral. Kostromin indignantly announced that the session would adjourn to consider my appeal but I had no right to question the legality of the court. He asked the secretary to accompany me to the reception room.

The recess lasted about an hour, during which I unexpectedly got to see the witnesses against me. The first one to appear in the reception room was Academician G. Muromtsev, who had been chief of the military bacteriological laboratory in the NKVD and Ministry of Security until 1950. I scarcely knew him and had never worked with him except to send him intelligence materials received from the West about developments in bacteriological warfare. Another witness was Maironovsky, who was escorted to the reception room by guards, looking pale and haunted. Dressed in shabby clothes, he looked like he had just been brought from jail. Clearly, the poison laboratory would be a major part of the case against me.

Maironovsky began to weep the instant he saw me. He didn't expect me to be sitting in an armchair in a good suit with a necktie. The secretary ordered the guard to remove him to the corridor, and ran to report to Kostromin. The secretary quickly returned and escorted me back to the judges, who were waiting to resume the trial. Kostromin, in full uniform, said that my claim of illegality about the procedure was rejected by the chairman of the Supreme Court of the USSR by special enactment just received by government telephone call. If I chose not to respond to the charges, he would continue the trial without me. He said the Supreme Court, as the highest authority in the USSR, had the right to establish procedures of hearings in cases of top importance to the state. He asked if I pleaded guilty, and I categorically denied all of the criminal charges. Then he announced that two witnesses who were to testify against me as Beria's accomplice, both of them former security officials, could not appear in court due to bad health. Two others, Academician Muromtsev and the convicted Maironovsky, were in the adjacent room ready to testify.

Kostromin stated that the court was not convinced by Beria's assertion at his preliminary investigation that I was not his man and was only fulfilling orders passed to me by him on behalf of the government. On the contrary, Beria's statements, he said, were intended to conceal high treason. The court would not consider my arguments in this regard. The Stamenov episode was mentioned only in a general way; Kostromin stressed that high treason was clear, but new facts, showing that Beria had discussed contacting Stamenov with other members of the leadership, would be considered in the form of an aide-mémoire to the court. I protested the definition of this authorized intelligence probe as high treason, and denied that we had made attempts to establish clandestine contacts in secret from the government, since Molotov not only knew of the contacts, but had sanctioned them; but this was ignored. Moreover, I told the court that Comrade Khrushchev himself, on the fifth of August, 1953, five years earlier, had told me that he found no evidence of misdeeds or guilt on my part in this episode.

The chairman turned pale and forbade me to mention Khrushchev. The secretaries immediately stopped transcribing the proceedings. I also turned pale, became agitated, and was unable to control myself. I told the judges they were trying a man who had been sentenced to death by fascists and the pro-German Ukrainian nationalist organization, who had risked his life for the government. "You are putting me on trial in the manner of your predecessors, who sentenced heroes of Soviet intelligence to the firing squad on slanderous charges." I referred to Artuzov, Shpigelglas, Maly, Serebryansky, and other lost friends. Kostromin was taken aback and Vice Admiral Simonov blanched.

After a short pause, Kostromin remarked, "No one has prejudged you to a death sentence here. We want to establish the truth." Muromtsev was then called as a witness and listened as his five-year-old testimony was read to the court. Then, to the dissatisfaction and surprise of the judges, he stated that he could not confirm his previous testimony. He didn't remember any episode of my involvement in the work of the secret bacteriological research laboratory that he headed. Next Maironovsky was called in. He testified that he had consulted me on four cases. With the permission of the chairman, I asked him whether he was subordinated to me, whether the four cases were experiments or combat operations, and from whom he had received the instructions for these specific actions. To my surprise, the admiral intervened, supporting me. What had been a well-planned scenario erupted in disorder. Maironovsky, answering that he had never worked for me, began to weep. Through his tears he said that these were indeed top-secret combat operations, not experiments, and he named Khrushchev and Molotov as the source of his instructions. He first told of meeting Molotov in the Committee of Information headquarters, and then, to the wrath of the chairman, mentioned meeting Khrushchev in the railroad carriage on his way to Uzhgorod. The chairman of the court cut him short, saying that the evidence from him was clear. He pressed a button to call the guards, who appeared and rushed Maironovsky out. I didn't see him again for three years, when we met in the courtyard of Vladimir prison.

The judges were taken aback. They now had evidence that these

"terrorist acts" were combat operations, carried out against sworn enemies and opponents of the regime under direct orders of the government,
and not under my initiative. I also pointed out that I was not the
commanding officer in any of these operations, because in each case
designated representatives of the government — First Deputy Minister
Ogoltsov and Minister of Security of the Ukraine Savchenko — were
present and the local security organs were subordinated to them. I asked
to have them called as witnesses and demanded to be told why these
men had not been indicted for commanding these operations. Once
again, the judges were uneasy. I knew that in the minutes of the investigation against me, facts about victims of the Cold War, the period from
1946 to 1953, were sketchy. The theme of the charges, repeated over
and over, was that Maironovsky, with my assistance, killed people hostile to Beria. The judges were clearly not prepared for the real facts: these
murders were sanctioned by leaders higher than Beria.

Kostromin quickly recovered and summed up the hearing. He said
that they were not indicting me for these four episodes but were inclined
to believe that I was in charge of other secret operations against Beria's
enemies. He said rumors of atrocities committed at my dacha were serious. I asked for one single fact showing that I had committed any terrorist act against the government or Beria's enemies. Kostromin sternly
answered that Beria's case was closed and it had been established that
he had committed such acts, and because I worked for him I was also
guilty. However, the court did not at this moment have the pertinent
evidence before it. With that he closed the case and gave me a chance to
make a final statement. I was brief, and pleaded innocence. I warned the
court that punishing me furthered the interests of Ukrainian fascists,
imperialist intelligence services, and Trotskyites abroad. I demanded the
right, under the law, to read the minutes of the hearing and add my own
notes and sign them, but this was denied.

Kostromin announced a recess before sentencing. I was ushered out
to the reception room, where I was offered tea and sandwiches. The
admiral came out to speak to me, and shook my hand, soothing me with
assurances that everything would be all right. He said I had behaved like
a man. I was led back into Kostromin's office. The judges rose and
Kostromin read the handwritten sentence, which was a direct repetition
of the indictment from the procurator's office, with one addition: "The
Court does not find it necessary to apply the highest measure of punishment, the death sentence." The sentence was fifteen years in jail; the

sentence was final, without the right to appeal. It was now autumn of 1958, so I had already served five years since my arrest in 1953.

All strength left me. I had expected the outcome but was still shocked. I nearly fainted, and sat down. Before long I was back in the internal jail of Lubyanka. A terrible headache overtook me, and the guard gave me medication. I was still feeling miserable when I was brought to Serov's office on the third floor, formerly Beria's domain. He looked at me sternly and offered a seat. "Listen carefully," Serov said. "You will have plenty of time to think over your position. You will be sent to Vladimir prison. If you recollect any dubious acts and directives of Molotov and Malenkov in intelligence operations, let me know, but don't mention Nikita Sergeyevich. If you remember what I tell you, you will be kept alive and eventually amnestied." In spite of my terrible headache, I nodded in agreement. I never saw him again.

I was transferred to Lefortovo prison and two days later met with Emma and my younger brother, Konstantin. I wept on their shoulders and they comforted me. We concealed our joy that I would be transferred to Vladimir prison, in the city where Emma's younger sister Cecilia lived, married to Aleksandr Komelkov, senior official of the Ministry of Interior's administration of the district. He was deputy director of traffic police. Cecilia and Aleksandr lived in the same apartment block with all the chief wardens of Vladimir prison and were on friendly terms with them. Soon my younger son, Anatoli, would come to spend his summer vacations in Vladimir with Aleksandr's family and become close to Yuri, a boy his age, son of the prison commandant, Colonel Mikhail Kozik. Olga, the daughter of Kozik's deputy, played with them.

Emma was lucky not to have been arrested while I was under preliminary investigation, as had the wives of other officials in the Beria case. She wisely severed all relations with security acquaintances and friends. Our friends outside the security world supported us, particularly Mariana Yaroslavskaya. Her father, Yemolyan, had been secretary of the Central Committee from the 1920s through the 1940s. He was informally the ideological watchdog of the party. Through her, Emma made a new group of friends who were painters, sculptors, and scientists. Anna Tsukanova, transferred by Khrushchev after the fall of Malenkov to the post of deputy minister of culture, kept up her usual support and assistance. Anna advised Emma to keep out of the case. Therefore, Emma's appeals for just consideration of her husband's case to Khrushchev and Malenkov always began with a disclaimer, saying she was unaware of the charges. She made copies of my letters to her from abroad, in which I had written her that despite the risks I was facing I was ready to sacrifice my life for the cause of the government and the Communist party. She sent the letters to Khrushchev and Malenkov to prove that they were persecuting a sincere Bolshevik, wholly devoted to the same ideals as they were. She collected from thirteen of my co-workers, including Heroes of the Soviet Union, sworn statements certified by district party committees that I was a devoted Communist. She forwarded these statements to the procurator's office of the Military Collegium of the Supreme Court, requesting that the signers be called as witnesses. When I learned about her activities, I understood the hesitancy of the judges and the fact that my sympathetic interrogator, Andreev, contrary to the rules, had evaded signing the indictment.

Two scandals in the handling of the Beria case slowed the search for incriminating evidence against members of the detainees' families. Beria's daughter-in-law was the granddaughter of the writer Maksim Gorky, an icon of the USSR, and although she divorced Beria's son when he was arrested with his mother and exiled to Siberia, the connection was an embarrassment to the state. Second, the upper levels of government were shaken by revelations that Dmitri Sukhanov, chief of Malenkov's secretariat of the Presidium of the Central Committee, who cooperated in the actual arrest of Beria, had stolen eight gold watches, a gold badge, and bonds and cash amounting to more than 100,000 rubles from Beria's safe, including his prize for successfully running the Soviet nuclear program.

In the years preceding my trial, the governing classes in Moscow buzzed with rumors about the theft and trail of evidence leading to the thieves. At the time of Beria's arrest, and the detention of his staff, his and their safes, as a matter of course, were emptied by the authorities. By law, there should have been a careful accounting of the contents. Instead, Military Procurator Uspensky and Sukhanov, assisted by Aleksandr M. Puzanov (an official of the Central Committee and future ambassador to Bulgaria), kept no list of the confiscated wealth of these men.

One of the arrested men's wives, first imprisoned, then released but purged from her job and only means of livelihood, had a list of the numbers of the bonds belonging to her husband. These were the bonds that every high-ranking officer was required to purchase monthly; every calendar quarter a lottery was conducted, awarding a large sum of money to the winning bondholder. Sukhanov included in the indictment against this woman's husband instructions for confiscation of his money, but because he was not actually a security officer, nor convicted of high treason but of failing to report Beria's alleged criminal intentions, the court threw out the confiscation instruction. The woman then pressed the court for the return of her family money, which she needed to support her children while her husband was in jail. At first her appeals fell on deaf ears, then Khrushchev ordered Serov to trace her bonds. A woman appeared at a bank with one of the missing bonds, to claim the lottery money that had been announced for that bond number. It turned out that she was a typist for Sukhanov.

She was detained, and Sukhanov had to admit the theft from Beria and his subordinates, for which he was sentenced to ten years in prison. This scandal, although not publicly announced, was talked about and undermined the prestige of Beria's case handlers. Interest in the Beria case and even in his infamy began to dissipate.

This affected Emma's status in Moscow in a positive way. In danger of losing her own colonel's pension, she learned to sew. She soon became a popular seamstress for cultural figures, her new friends, and made good money at it. When Khrushchev cut military pensions, she could still support our two children and her mother. The MVD wanted to take away our downtown apartment, but couldn't lawfully deprive a war veteran, Emma herself, of her home. Anna Tsukanova, now deputy minister of culture, supported Emma in her fight with the supply department of the MVD, claiming that I was not legally convicted of any crime, was undergoing medical treatment in hospital, and therefore could not be deprived of my apartment. Their next step was to raise the rent, but Emma was in the lucky position to be able to pay it without arguing.

In 1956 and 1957 she learned that the purge of security officers that had swept away Beria and me was over. Witnesses who knew too much had been shot, including the false accusers. Raikhman, because of the intervention of his wife, the ballerina, was only charged with abuse of power, and promptly amnestied. Maisky also was released from jail. Emma learned that Khrushchev had ordered about one hundred retired generals and colonels who had served in the security service purged from the party and stripped of military rank. They had either been involved in purges of the 1930s or knew too much about party intrigues. The big change now was that although they lost their pensions and party membership, they were not imprisoned or shot. Among those purged in this manner were two heroes of atomic espionage, Major General Ovakimian, who in 1942 and 1943 was coordinator for NKVD atomic intelligence operations in the United States, and my deputy Lev Vasilevsky, accused only of being too close to Beria.

The change in mood in Moscow was evidenced by Vasilevsky's success in reestablishing himself in the party, using his past connections with Bruno Pontecorvo, by then an academician in Moscow, to appeal to Khrushchev. He became, together with Anatoli Gorsky, former rezident in London and Washington, a translator of adventure stories from English and French that flooded the Russian children's book market. Other security officers, with the support of Viktor Ilyin, the former purged NKVD ideological commissar, who after rehabilitation in 1954 became secretary of the Moscow Union of Writers, began new careers as writers and journalists. Rehabilitation meant the dropping of all charges and the right to reinstatement to one's former position. Practically this was impossible, but it did allow people to start their lives again and receive a higher pension.

My term in Vladimir prison fortunately coincided with a liberalization of prison policy by Khrushchev. I was permitted four parcels of food supplies a month. Although at first I often felt dizzy and lost consciousness because of terrible headaches, I soon began to regain my strength. I was kept in solitary confinement, but I was not totally isolated and had access to newspapers and radio broadcasts and the jail library.

Vladimir prison was remarkable by all standards. It was regarded as the stronghold where important prisoners were kept in the vicinity of Moscow, having been built by Czar Nicholas at the beginning of the century. Under Soviet rule it played the same role. Because it was only 150 miles from Moscow, prisoners held there were brought to Moscow for additional interrogation. The irony was that I was held in the second block of the prison, which I had twice visited to call on captured German generals serving their terms there. At that time I was shown the famous cell that was kept vacant in honor of one of the founders of the Red Army, Mikhail V. Frunze, who served his term there for guerrilla warfare against the czar.

The prison consisted of three blocks, accommodating a total of about three hundred inmates. After 1950 it was expanded and its three blocks were rebuilt to handle eight hundred prisoners. The normal regimen was strict. We were awakened at 6:00 A.M. and had meals in our cells. Poor food was handed to us through a slot in the heavy metal cell door. Hunger was a constant companion, evident in the dullness of the prisoners' eyes. At first, after breakfast my bed was placed upright and locked to the wall so that there was no place to lie down. I could only sit on a chair fixed to the cement cell floor. We were permitted to walk for thirty to forty-five minutes each day in the "box," a high walled room of about twenty square meters, open to the sky, with a guard present. Only one hour was allowed for rest after lunch, when the bed was unlocked by the guard. There was no toilet in the cell, only a bucket, and prisoners had to ask the guard to escort them to the toilet. (I have heard that now toilet facilities have been installed in the cells.) The lights remained on all night, although we were permitted to go to sleep at 10:00 P.M.

After several days, I noticed a sympathetic attitude toward me by the prison administration. They took me out of solitary and put me in the prison hospital, which allowed me one glass of milk a day and, even more important, the right to stay in bed and rest all day. I soon found out that among my fellow prisoners were former officials well known to me. They included Wilhelm Munters, the former Latvian minister of foreign affairs; during the takeover of Latvia in 1940, I had brought him out to teach at Voronezh University. Another was V. V. Shulgin, the target of NKVD intelligence abroad for twenty years, the former deputy chairman of the Duma under the czar; when the Red Army liberated Belgrade in 1945, he had been captured and returned to the Soviet Union to stand trial for anti-Soviet activities during and after the Civil War. A certain Vasiliev, actually Stalin's son Vassili, was kept three or four cells from me and continued to create trouble even while in prison. When his wife, the daughter of Marshal Timoshenko, came to visit him he attacked her with his fists and demanded that she apply to Khrushchev and Voroshilov to release him. Maironovsky was also with us, sentenced to ten years. He had been in Vladimir since 1953 and was a shell of his former self.

To save himself Maironovsky, broken by jail beatings and hoping for release, had testified against Beria, Merkulov, and Abakumov, providing the evidence for their indictment for secret murders but without specific names of victims. Beria, Merkulov, and Abakumov had been shot while Maironovsky continued to serve his term, occasionally appearing as a witness for the procurator's office.

In my trial he admitted that he never fulfilled orders from me for experiments with poisons or for executions, and that he was not my subordinate. For this I am thankful to him, as well as for his risky work in the war years, when he changed ampules with poisons in the shirt collars of German terrorists who were drugged to sleep by him, so that they could not commit suicide while under arrest. These were parachutists who came to what they believed were safe apartments, and disarming them was a dangerous job even though they were drugged.

Sometimes Maironovsky and I met in Vladimir prison, and I advised him that he should appeal for support to scientists in the medical community, whom he knew and who had high respect for him. When Maironovsky was released in December 1961, he was supported for rehabilitation by Academician Nikolai Blokhin, president of the Academy of Medical Sciences. Two days after he appeared in Khrushchev's reception office in Central Committee headquarters and left his appeal to him, mentioning the episode of their encounter aboard Khrushchev's train in Kiev in late 1947, he was detained by the KGB. Maironovsky was promptly decertified as a professor of medicine, deprived of his scientific degree, and forced to live in exile in Michachkala, a small seaport on the Caspian Sea. There he worked as the head of a chemical laboratory. Unfortunately for him, he had become an unwanted witness for Khrushchev. Maironovsky was naive to appeal to Khrushchev for help by recalling their meeting before Archbishop Romzha's liquidation in Uzhgorod. Maironovsky should have realized that Khrushchev, now in power, wanted to erase the record of such earlier activities.

Occasionally Maironovsky visited Academician Blokhin in Moscow, hoping to restore his career, but on the eve of a meeting they had planned to discuss results of his experiments with malignant tumors, Maironovsky died mysteriously. The diagnosis for the cause of his death was ironically the same as for Wallenberg and Oggins, cardiac insufficiency.

There was in Vladimir prison a small, exclusive club of former NKVD leadership, led by Leonid Eitingon, who had arrived in March 1957 with half his twelve-year sentence served. Others included Stepan Mamulov, former chief of Beria's secretariat and deputy minister of internal affairs, in charge of gold mining. Although he was an Armenian, Mamulov had been the secretary responsible for personnel of the Communist party of Georgia. Academician Pyotr Sharia, who was also a Communist party secretary in Georgia, had once served as deputy chief of the intelligence directorate. After being released from jail on charges of being a Mingrelian nationalist he was, due to his bad luck, appointed as Beria's chief on foreign policy issues with the military rank of major general. He got caught in the net with Beria. Colonel Boris Ludvigov, chief of Beria's secretariat in the Ministry of Internal Affairs, was arrested because he knew too much about his boss and his sexual behavior. Ludvigov was married to Mikoyan's niece, which helped him get out of jail ten days after Khrushchev was ousted, in 1964. He was amnestied by a special decree, signed by Mikoyan, who three months earlier had been appointed chairman of the Supreme Soviet. Mikoyan also amnestied his distant relative Sarkisov, chief of Beria's bodyguards and the man responsible for procuring women for Beria.

Other members of the prison community were two women, Daria Gusyak and Maria Dydik, the illegal couriers of the Bandera underground whom I helped capture in the shootout with their leader, Shukheyevich. With us was also a close friend of the poet Vladimir Mayakovsky, Vladimir Brik (nephew of publisher Osip Brik), caught by the KGB in an attempt to flee to the United States. Maksim Steinberg, our NKVD illegal rezident in Switzerland in the thirties who refused to return during the purges, had come back to Moscow with his wife, Elsa, after Stalin's death, lured by a false amnesty. He had been sentenced to fifteen years, she to ten, for high treason.

Emma brought the children to visit three months after my arrival in Vladimir, wisely deciding not to let them see me while I was in poor condition. My hands trembled and my emotions went out of control when she arrived. Colonel Kozik, director of the jail, authorized two extra meetings with Emma, in addition to the regular monthly meeting. Just before Kozik retired in 1959, he arranged for me to meet in his office with my brother-in-law, Aleksandr, who briefed me on the current conditions of the Ministry of Internal Affairs and KGB. Knowing who was in power, and who was out, what were the instructions and priorities of the new KGB chairman, Aleksandr Shelepin, gave me hope that I might contribute advice based on my expertise. From that could come amnesty and rehabilitation, perhaps a fate similar to that of the generals and officers released by Stalin and Beria in 1939 and 1941.

Despite my desire to be left alone, solitary confinement ended after a year, and I shared a cell first with Brik, then with Steinberg, and later with the governor of Smolensk under the Germans, V. Minshagin. Our relations were polite but distant. Although they were interesting people, their previous roles in and knowledge of the Soviet state were minor and I stayed aloof from them.

After half a year in Vladimir, I began bombarding the Supreme Court and the procurator's office with appeals to reconsider my case. From Emma I learned that she had appealed twice to Khrushchev and the Supreme Court to allow a lawyer to participate in the court hearings, but her request was denied. She brought me copies of her appeals, and I sent a protest saying that by law the sentence was invalid because I had been denied defense assistance, and that although promised, I had not been shown the minutes of the hearing. That meant I was being held in jail illegally.

I received one answer, signed by Lev N. Smirnov, deputy chairman of the Supreme Court, saying there were no reasons to reconsider the case. There were no answers to my next forty appeals. My cellmates, especially Eitingon, laughed at my judicial maneuvers. "Laws and power struggles are incompatible," Eitingon said. The breakthrough came in 1960, when I was summoned to the prison director's office. Eitingon was just leaving as I entered. Instead of the director, I found a tall, handsome, fashionably dressed man in his fifties who introduced himself as investigator in charge of special tasks of the Party Control Committee.[2] His name was Herman Klimov, and on the desk were the volumes of my case and my personal KGB dossier. He said that the Central Committee had ordered him to examine the case because it contained no information about Molotov's involvement in Beria's secret intelligence operations abroad; and, more important to him, no names of Beria's kidnapping and assassination victims inside the country.

He produced a summary, from the Party Control Committee to the Central Committee, of secret murders and kidnappings ordered by Beria with the approval of Stalin. It was signed by Rudenko's deputy, D. Salin. The summary stated that the procurator's office had established that Beria ordered the secret killing of a former Soviet ambassador to China, B. Luganets, together with his wife, and of Madame K. Simonich-Kulik, wife of Marshal of Artillery Kulik, who had been shot on Stalin's orders in 1950. The procurator's office had learned of these acts while prosecuting Beria and the men who had carried out the kidnappings and killings.

---

2. The Party Control Committee (KPK) was the special investigatory administration of the CPSU, directly responsible to the first secretary. In the Stalin years it was called the Party Control Commission.

The summary also said the procurator's office had reliable information that other secret murders were committed on Beria's orders at home and abroad, but found it impossible to establish the names of the victims because Eitingon and I had concealed all traces of these operations. For several years, Eitingon's and my poor physical state had impeded the investigation. Klimov demanded, on behalf of the party, complete exposure of the operations in which I had participated. He was bothered by the discrepancy between oral charges that I had helped murder Mikhoels, and the procurator's unwillingness to put them in writing. Klimov was surprised to learn from me that I had nothing to do with Mikhoels's murder. He wanted to clarify these murky events before the next party congress, to be held in 1961.

We talked for more than two hours, going through my entire file and dossier, page by page. I did not deny my involvement in special tasks, but pointed out that the procurator had been hesitant to report my case clearly because the operations described were still regarded as top secret, and in each case they implicated leaders now in power. The authority of the Communist party leadership was at stake if my operations, conducted with their approval years earlier, were not justified. Klimov was persistent in verifying details and was visibly impressed when I informed him that there existed in the Ministry of Security a system of accountability for every operation involving my staff with Maironovsky's laboratory.

Klimov then acknowledged that I could not have given orders to Maironovsky or received poisons from him. The charter of the laboratory, endorsed by three NKVD/MGB chiefs, Beria, Abakumov, and Ignatiev, prevented this. He said with considerable emotion that this document automatically proved my case. If the charter had been attached to my file, the charges against me and Eitingon could not have been sustained, but the document was stored in the Central Committee and KGB archives, where it remains to this day.

I explained to him that all four cases known to me — Oggins, Romzha, Shumsky, and Samet — were not only sanctioned by the Central Committee, but were reported back to them after completion. The reports, compiled by Sergei Ogoltsov, were kept in a special file, sealed in a large envelope. After each operation the seal was removed, a new handwritten page added, and the envelope resealed. On this envelope was a stamp, "Not to be opened without sanction of the Minister, (signed) Ogoltsov." Klimov listened carefully and took notes while we had tea and sandwiches during the meeting.

Klimov stayed several days. He had a typewriter sent to my cell, and I wrote out answers to all his questions. They covered the history of intelligence operations; details of instructions from Beria, Abakumov, Ignatiev, Kruglov, Malenkov, and Molotov; and my successes in guerrilla warfare against the Germans and atomic espionage. Finally, at Klimov's suggestion, I typed another appeal for rehabilitation and release. Following his recommendation, I did not mention Khrushchev, but stipulated that all my orders came from the Central Committee. Klimov assured me of my inevitable release and reinstatement in the party. He made similar promises to Eitingon.

I learned later that the interest in my case was twofold. One aspect was the desire to peer into Stalin's crimes and secrets. Second, the release of Ramon Mercader from prison in Mexico and his return to Moscow sparked initiatives by Dolores Ibarruri and leaders of the French and Austrian Communist parties to get Eitingon and me out of prison. Interest in Beria and his crimes was fading.

Klimov's visit to Vladimir greatly improved Emma's situation in Moscow. The newly appointed chief of the KGB, Aleksandr Shelepin, sent to the Party Control Committee a positive summary of Eitingon's and my careers which concluded that the Committee for State Security (KGB) "has no incriminating evidence at its disposal against Sudoplatov and Eitingon implicating them in crimes committed by the Beria group." Such an endorsement sent a signal to experienced bureaucrats that a move was under way to rehabilitate us. In 1960 the Party Control Committee officially opened Eitingon's and my files.

This coincided with a KGB search in the United States for a Jewish family that had emigrated from Poland in 1939 via Russia to the United States. This was the family that Emma had helped flee from Western Ukraine after they were evacuated from Warsaw in 1939. A relative of theirs came to Moscow as a tourist in 1960 and inquired at *Izvestia*, trying to locate Emma, who had told the family she worked there. When the KGB heard about this, it contacted Emma with the idea of recruiting the relative for use in America. There was no longer a threat to Emma's remaining in our apartment. Emma was asked to report to Lubyanka several times to discuss preparing the apartment as a safe house for meeting the visiting relative. Nothing came of the attempt to develop the relative, but Emma began to use the apartment as a safe house.

The Ideological Department became interested in using Emma again to attract young intellectuals. Her former NKVD intelligence tradecraft students and Lieutenant Colonel Dmitri Ryabov involved her in disciplining the poet Yevgeny Yevtushenko. Rather than reprimand and punish Yevtushenko for drunken adventures or recruit him as a full-time informer, Emma suggested, they should use the same methods as were employed in the 1930s with creative artists.[3] Friendly confidential relations should be established, and Emma recommended he be sent to the World Youth Festival in Finland as a Soviet delegate. Yevtushenko's behavior improved, and he became a supporter of the new Communist ideas promoted by Khrushchev in the name of Lenin. The popular poet began reporting to Colonel Ryabov the ideological deviations of writers who were critical of his work.

Emma also arranged to help a friend's son, Boris Zhutovsky, a talented graphic artist, who had become an outspoken critic of Khrushchev's cultural policies. Emma set up a meeting at the apartment with Ryabov, to whom Zhutovsky explained that his remarks had been misunderstood. He wrote a report on the internal conflicts in the Painters Union, claiming he was always supportive of Communist policies. His report reached the Ideological Department of the Central Committee, which saw to it that he continued to receive proper guidance from young Lubyanka officers.

The flirtation between Emma and the KGB soon came to an end. Procurator Rudenko torpedoed the move to rehabilitate me. The building that contained our fine flat was taken over from the KGB by the Ministry of Foreign Affairs and became the residence of the Polish Trade Mission. Emma and the children, with Anna's support, received a pleasant but smaller apartment, far from downtown Moscow. It was not too far for Mercader and Caridad to come and visit. It was around this time that the children finished high school, and thanks to Zoya Zarubina, now dean of the Institute of Foreign Languages, and Varvara Pivovarova, rector of the institute, they began to study there.

That year, 1961, marked for the children the end of all illusions that the authorities would eventually admit a mistake had been made in my case.

3. They included Count Aleksei Tolstoy, a well-known writer and figure in Russian cultural life, who became a pillar of Stalin's cult of personality; Mikhail Golodny, a talented young poet, who was the first to implicate Zinoviev and Trotsky in verse for inspiring Kirov's assassin; Iona Prut, a popular Moscow playwright, later arrested as a Zionist conspirator and released only after Stalin's death.

After Klimov received Emma at Central Committee headquarters and told her that both Eitingon and I were innocent victims in the Beria case, and that he was urging reconsideration to the highest authorities, she understood that my fate was now in Khrushchev's hands, that my case was not stalled in the bureaucracy but rather a decision had been made at the top to keep me in prison.

Klimov was indirect in his language, but stressed the need for Emma to keep up the appeals campaign. He told her, "It is essential for you and anyone else making these appeals to refer to the materials available in the Party Control Committee and KGB files." He added, "You should demand parallel analyses of the material kept in both the main criminal case file and the supervisory file (*nabludatelnoye delo*), because all your appeals, positive testimony, and documents contradicting the indictment are kept there."

He said, "For example, the indictment states that Sudoplatov, prior to the war, set up the Administration for Special Tasks to fulfill Beria's special orders. Parallel to that he headed the Directorate for Guerrilla Warfare from 1942 to 1946, the Fourth Directorate. But in the supervisory file are extracts from the documents establishing the Administration for Special Tasks, which show that it was one and the same as the guerrilla warfare unit." This clearly contradicted the indictment.

At our next meeting Emma described her interview with Klimov. By that time Eitingon had become my cellmate, and we spent long hours discussing how to expedite our appeals. Emma, the realist, encouraged me to prepare for a new career as a translator. She brought me and Eitingon stacks of German, French, Polish, and Ukrainian books, both novels and history, that kept us busy. The prison director had orders to keep me and all other high-ranking security officers isolated from other prisoners, and thus we were exempted from manual labor, which would have meant contact with other prisoners. We knew that Gary Powers and Greville Wynne[4] were in an adjacent cellblock, but we never saw them.

In 1961 prison conditions began to deteriorate; the allowed number of five-kilogram food parcels was reduced from four to one a month, and then to one in six months. The stringency resulted from new prison

4. Greville Wynne was a British businessman who served MI-6 as a liaison and courier for Colonel Oleg Penkovsky, the GRU officer who spied for the West from 1960 to 1962. Wynne and Penkovsky were arrested in September 1962. Penkovsky was executed and Wynne sentenced to ten years in prison. Wynne was exchanged for convicted Soviet spy Gordon Lonsdale, aka Konon Molody, on April 22, 1964.

rules promulgated by Khrushchev to fight the growing crime rate that resulted from his liberalization and worsening economic conditions. In September 1961, during the Twenty-second Party Congress (which exposed additional details of Stalin's crimes), ten food rioters from the small city of Murom were secretly tried and shot in Vladimir prison. Visits by relatives were reduced from one a month to one in six months, but I received censored mail from Emma every day. The prison administration changed from friends to strangers. In 1962 I suffered a mild heart attack when, during a period of prison repairs, five former NKVD generals were required to occupy one cell.

Quarrels and disputes were restricted to chess games, but I never took part. Sometimes tempers flared, as when Ludvigov remarked that he had never imagined Beria to be such a villain. Eitingon retorted, "Let's not be childish. We know who named their children Lavrenti in his honor." The others smiled sheepishly. Usually Eitingon and I simply listened to their revelations of the inner workings of the Politburo under Stalin, Beria, Malenkov, and Khrushchev. Tactfully, we did not remind them that under pressure they had admitted their guilt in "not exposing Beria, the enemy of the people."

Eitingon and I, in an effort to attract attention to our appeal, devised and wrote, for Khrushchev's consideration, operational proposals to establish a Soviet counterforce to President Kennedy's newly created Green Berets. Our letter was favorably endorsed by Shelepin, then secretary of the CPSU Central Committee in charge of security and intelligence operations. The letter landed on the desk of General Ivan Fadeykin, my successor as chief of the Ninth Department (for special operations abroad) in the First Chief Directorate of KGB. He dispatched an officer, Major Vasiliev, to contact us for organizational details and to reward us with two kilograms of sugar. Thus our initiative brought into being KGB Spetsnaz, the special training center for guerrilla operations in the First Chief Directorate, later known as Alpha Group, which stormed the Amin Palace in Kabul in 1979, setting off the Afghan war.

Inspired by our success and the moral support of the KGB, we sent further proposals to Khrushchev, suggesting that contacts be resumed with the Kurdish leader Barzani, to be a counterforce to the irascible Iraqi dictator, General Abdul Karim Kassem. We received a visit from Colonel Shevchenko, chief of the Vladimir district KGB office, who informed us that the leadership was utilizing our suggestions. This time we were rewarded with the right to receive food parcels once every three months instead of every six.

More important, Shevchenko authorized our first meeting with a defense lawyer, Evgeni Zorin, a close friend of Emma's who had served with her in the Odessa GPU in the 1920s. He was the first outsider to lay eyes on Eitingon's and my sentences by the Military Collegium, which had never been publicly announced. In his opinion, my case was hopeless unless the highest authority reversed it. For Eitingon he saw some possibility to amend the sentence because he had been in jail for eighteen months under Stalin. Raikhman's sentence had been reduced because the eighteen months were counted. Zorin believed a legal mistake had been made in not crediting Eitingon with this time served, and he appealed directly to the Military Collegium. He hoped that since Kostromin, chairman of the court at the time of the trial, had died, no one would be embarrassed by admitting the minor legal error. Zorin's appeal was turned down, but Zoya Zarubina successfully intervened. The niece of the chairman of the Military Collegium was struggling unsuccessfully to enter the Institute of Foreign Languages; Zoya reversed her failure, and in return the student's well-placed uncle reconsidered Eitingon's appeal.

In December 1963 the Military Collegium announced that Eitingon's term in jail would include the eighteen months served prior to Beria's arrest, shortening his stay. Just before that, Eitingon nearly died of an intestinal tumor. Zoya, using her leverage with students whose parents were high-ranking officials, gained access to the jail for a top-ranking surgeon, a colleague of Eitingon's sister Sonia. He operated on Eitingon and saved his life.

Before the operation, Eitingon appealed to Khrushchev with a farewell letter to the party. He asked Khrushchev how he could allow the imprisonment of loyal party members whose innocence had been established by the Party Control Committee, and who had carried out an important mission for the Communist cause in Mexico. Ramon Mercader, Trotsky's assassin, had recently returned and received a gold medal, Hero of the Soviet Union, for this operation. (Thirty years later, General Volkogonov was stunned when he came across Eitingon's letter while perusing the archives.)

I met with Colonel Vassili Ivashensko, the deputy director of the KGB Investigation Department, who came to the prison to interview us concerning the amnesty of a fellow prisoner, a talented mathematician, R. Pimenov. Ivashenko, whom I knew previously, told us that although there was no chance for our cases to be reconsidered by the present leadership, we definitely would be released when our terms ended. Stalin's practice of keeping important witnesses in jail forever or doing away with them appeared to have ended.

The first test would be the release of Academician Sharia, scheduled for June 26, 1963. He had been arrested on the same day as Beria in 1953. We arranged that Sharia, if released, on his way home to Tbilisi would contact Eitingon's family or mine to tell them, "I am going to lead a new life."

We waited impatiently for the signal. We still doubted, despite assurances, that Sharia would be permitted to return home. In two weeks, confirmation came from Emma that Professor Pyotr Sharia had paid her a short visit. She remembered an imposing, self-assured philosophy lecturer at the NKVD school, but now she met a small, subdued old man. Sharia remained mentally vigorous and became a professor of philosophy in the Georgian Academy of Sciences, where he worked until his death in 1983.

In 1964 Leonid Eitingon was released. He rejoined his second wife, Olga Naumova, and began to work as a senior editor in the Foreign Languages Publishing House. Ludvigov was released after Khrushchev's ouster and began working as the assistant to the chief inspector of the Central Statistical Office. Emma had the illusion that I, too, could be amnestied, but her appeal was rejected.

Mamulov and I became cellmates. We had lived in the same apartment house before our arrests and our children played together, so there was much to discuss. Meanwhile, Eitingon was again becoming an unwanted witness, now for Brezhnev, who did not want to be bothered with old unfinished and embarrassing business. The authorities were outraged when, during the celebrations of the twentieth anniversary of the victory over Hitler, Brezhnev received a petition from twenty-four NKVD/KGB veterans, including Rudolf Abel (the name William Fisher had used since 1957) and five Heroes of the Soviet Union, asking the leadership to reconsider Eitingon's and my cases. Two Central Committee officials received the delegation who signed the petition. The new men around Brezhnev relied on Procurator General Rudenko's summary of my case, which said that I, as director of the Administration for Special Tasks, set up by Beria and consisting of his most trusted aides, had committed terrorist acts against his enemies. All of the petitioners protested, saying that they, too, were members of the Administration for Special Tasks, and in no way were they people trusted by Beria. They demanded

that specific crimes and terrorist acts be named to substantiate my indictment and sentence. This encounter ended inconclusively, but three
months later, on the eve of the Twenty-third Party Congress, the same
petitioners, joined by former Comintern activists and foreign Communists who were part of World War II guerrilla detachments, presented a
new petition. This time they charged Rudenko with fabricating the case
against me and Eitingon.

The pressure for reconsideration of my case was building. The former minister of defense of Bulgaria, who had served under Eitingon in
China in the 1920s, approached Suslov on our behalf, but Suslov was
furious. "The cases have been decided once and forever by the Central
Committee. This is entirely our internal affair," said Suslov, the Politburo member responsible for foreign policy and some aspects of security
and intelligence. Middle-level personnel in the Central Committee prepared an amnesty for me because I had become an invalid after two
strokes, and blind in my left eye, but it was turned down on December
19, 1966, by Nikolai Podgorny, chairman of the Presidium of the
Supreme Soviet.

A petition for clemency was submitted to the Presidium by the KGB,
but it was turned down. The official decree of rejection referred to a
petition signed by Emma, which shook Emma's fragile serenity. She was
hospitalized with heart trouble and nervous exhaustion. My younger
son, Anatoli, a postgraduate student in economics at Moscow State University, appeared at the Central Committee and the Supreme Soviet with
his party membership card to plead my case. At first, minor officials
refused to take him seriously, but he showed them the official enactment
of the Presidium of the Supreme Soviet, signed by the chief of Podgorny's
secretariat, and demanded to be received by a senior official.

Anatoli was firm but reasonable. He referred to the Party Control
Committee file on the case and the authority of the chief of the secretariat of the Committee, Herman Klimov, who had told him of my innocence and said it was all right to refer to him. The Central Committee
officials passed him on to the Presidium of the Supreme Soviet, where
he was received by Mikhail Sklarov, chief of the reception office of the
Presidium. Anatoli explained my case to Sklarov, a calm, gray-haired
official with long years of experience in the party. Anatoli was twenty-
three years old and had just received his party card after serving as a
Komsomol leader. "As a party member I ask you for a clear and sincere
answer. How could the highest authority ignore proofs of the innocence
of a man who devoted his whole life to the party and the state? How

could the Presidium ignore the appeal of Heroes of the Soviet Union on my father's behalf?" implored Anatoli. Most embarrassing to Sklarov was Anatoli's question asking why the Supreme Soviet rejection referred to an appeal from my mother, which was not submitted, instead of identifying it correctly as an appeal from the KGB.

Sklarov studied Anatoli carefully and told him: "I know your father to be an honest man — I worked with him in the Kharkov Komsomol — but the decision of his case is final. No one will review it again. You know too much about sensitive issues that you should have nothing to do with. I assure you that no one will interfere with your academic career if you behave in a reasonable manner. Your father will be released when his term ends in a year and a half. Think of how to support your family. I wish you success in that endeavor."

Anatoli stifled the urge to vomit and breathed deeply. He realized that difficult times faced him; he would have to conceal his family's feelings about the criminal hypocrisy of the leadership. Emma, when she recovered, was deeply concerned that Anatoli's appeal might cause real trouble, so she trained him in counterintelligence tradecraft. He learned to detect surveillance and telephone bugs, to avoid being developed into an informer, and how to identify informers around him. His short course included detecting the key questions used in standard intelligence analysis. This proved useful in avoiding dangerous political discussions and remaining clear of circles critical of the government. Anatoli was warned never to meet foreigners alone, but only in an official capacity and only when accompanied by a witness.

On August 21, 1968, the day after the invasion of Czechoslovakia, I was released. I was driven to Moscow by my brother-in-law. I received back my watch, still working, and 80,000 rubles' worth of government bonds, which I had purchased from my monthly pay over the years. It took until 1975 to receive the money, which by then, due to the currency reform, was worth 8,000 rubles.

Our apartment was full of relatives waiting to greet me when we returned from Vladimir. Being at home seemed like a dream. Freedom was joyful, but I had trouble sleeping because I was used to having the lights on all night. When I walked, I kept my hands behind my back, as I had been required to do in the prison yard. Crossing the street seemed an unsurmountable task; the distance appeared so huge after fifteen years in a small cell.

Soon old friends such as Zoya Rybkina, Raisa Sobel, and Eitingon came to visit. Even people with whom I was not on close terms — Ilyin, Vasilevsky, Semyon Semyonov, and Fitin — came to pay their respects. They brought me proposals for starting a literary career as a translator from German, Polish, and Ukrainian into Russian. I signed two contracts with the Children's Publishing House to translate novels from German and Ukrainian. Ilyin, now secretary of the Moscow Union of Writers, and Raisa Sobel arranged for me to be admitted to the trade union of literary translators. After publishing three books, I received the right to a literary pension, 130 rubles a month, the highest civilian pension, but less than the 200 rubles a month Emma received as a retired security service lieutenant colonel.

After a month of freedom, I suffered a heart attack, but I recovered after two months in the hospital. Emma opposed making any appeals for my rehabilitation. She argued that I should not attract attention to myself. She feared that the strain of discussions with procurators and party officials would bring on a fatal heart attack. When Emma was out shopping, I typed appeals to Yuri Andropov, then head of the KGB, and the Party Control Committee. The KGB telephoned and said in a friendly manner that it would assist me by providing documents, but my case was not its to resolve. The KGB did guarantee my residence in Moscow despite my being a released dangerous criminal. Otherwise my status automatically placed me under police supervision with no right to permanent residence in Moscow. I surprised the local police officer who checked on me when I produced a new internal passport provided by the KGB, stamped by the chief of the militia directorate of the USSR Ministry of the Interior. After that I was left alone.

I kept busy with literary work and led a normal life in the 1970s. The honorariums from translations and my royalties as a coauthor (under the pen name Anatoli Andreev) with Raisa Sobel supplemented our pensions and allowed us to live comfortably. In all, I translated and wrote fourteen books. Among them were four volumes of reminiscences of guerrillas who fought under my command during the war. I occasionally met with former chekists at Lev Heselberg's photo studio on Kuznetsky Bridge Street, under the shadow of the main Lubyanka headquarters. The studio was well known for Lev's excellent portrait work. He was also a good host in a back room where Eitingon, Raikhman, Fitin, Abel, Molody, and other former illegals gathered for drinks and sandwiches. Emma strongly disapproved of my occasional visits there.

Abel, who had supported me, complained that he was being used as a museum exhibit and deprived of real work. The same was true of Konon Molody, aka Gordon Lonsdale, whom I had never met before. Eitingon and Raikhman looked at me with disapproval when I did not drink with them. I slipped away when they began cursing the government and KGB leadership. These were different times from Stalin's, but it was hard for me to believe that KGB colonels still in service could drop in for a drink and openly berate the Brezhnev leadership, KGB rules, and injustices with impunity.

Abel told me the story of his arrest when he attempted to recover $30,000 hidden in a Brooklyn, New York, safe apartment, for which he would have to account to the Center. We both agreed that it had been stupid of him to return for the money; it cost a great deal more in lawyers' fees when he was arrested by the FBI. But he had feared that if the money were left behind he would be suspected of stealing it.

Lonsdale, code-named Ben, was equally indignant that he had been ordered to study at the Institute of Oriental Languages in London, which was staffed by intelligence officers from the United States, Great Britain, and Israel. He was convinced that the original suspicions of MI-5, British counterintelligence, were confirmed by his attendance at this institute, where so many students were intelligence officers. He said it was also unwise for the Center to have put him in touch with a British agent who worked in Eastern bloc countries under diplomatic cover. It was a violation of tradecraft for an illegal rezident to directly contact an agent who worked in an Eastern bloc country under official cover; such an agent was automatically on his own country's list for constant checks. At any rate, our meetings and these complaints ended in 1980, when Heselberg's studio was demolished and a new KGB building replaced it.

My literary work mattered more and more to me. It was a path to reestablishing myself in society. My novel on Kossior,[5] *Horizons*, written together with Raisa Sobel and edited by Emma, received official endorsement in a *Pravda* review. The book was reprinted several times and brought us considerable income. More important were my publications about the war. I received reviews under my pen name in *Pravda* and other official newspapers, one of which, ironically, emphasized that "the

5. S. V. Kossior, a member of Stalin's Politburo, was first secretary of the Ukrainian Communist party until his recall and arrest in 1938. Khrushchev replaced him in the Ukraine.

Administration for Special Tasks of NKVD played a historic role in the organization of guerrilla activities in the war." In 1976, after these reviews, I renewed my appeals for rehabilitation. I argued that the Central Committee and *Pravda* had acknowledged that the Administration for Special Tasks and its officers were heroes, while my criminal file charged that Special Tasks was Beria's terrorist organization.

Companions like Heselberg and Fitin were dying off; witnesses who could prove our innocence were disappearing. In 1976 Eitingon and I enlisted Mercader and Dolores Ibarruri to once again raise my case before Andropov and the Party Control Committee, likening the injustice done to us to immorality in the party. Andropov and Arvid Pelshe, who now headed the Party Control Committee, compiled a summary of the cases in 1977, which stated that there was a lack of proof that we were involved in Beria's crimes. By that time Serebryansky had been rehabilitated, fifteen years after he had died in prison under interrogation; his case was easier because it did not have to come to court. It merely needed an enactment by the military procurator. Our cases had to come before the Politburo, in the form of Pelshe's summaries, which were signed by Klimov; before Baturin, deputy senior investigator of the military procurator's office; and before Volkov, director of the KGB Investigation Department. However, Suslov, the party ideologue, stated that there was no need to reopen settled issues. Our cases had been decided long ago.

As a consolation, on Pelshe's direct orders, Eitingon and I received the right to be treated in the Kremlin polyclinic. When Pelshe met with the two of us in the presence of his first deputy, Ivan S. Gustov, in August 1977, he said he was greeting heroic intelligence officers, but for the time being our cases could not be decided. We would have to wait for another party congress for reconsideration of our cases.

In 1978 Ramon Mercader died in Cuba, where he was working as a counselor in the Ministry of Internal Affairs at the invitation of Fidel Castro. His body was secretly shipped to Moscow. I was in a health sanatorium with Emma, and Eitingon could not reach me. The KGB, in a cowardly manner, tried to bury him secretly without informing Eitingon, but Mercader's widow, Raquelia, staged a row and telephoned Leonid, who attended the funeral without me.

Eitingon became fatally ill from his ulcer and died in the Kremlin clinic right after the next party congress, in 1981, to which we had also appealed but received no reply. Throughout the eighties, especially on the eve of Brezhnev's death in 1982, I kept bombarding the Central Committee with appeals. The last witnesses still alive joined in my efforts in 1984, 1985, and 1988, appealing first to Konstantin Chernenko, who did not live long after taking office,[6] then to Gorbachev and Aleksandr Yakovlev, referring to the conclusions of my innocence established by the Andropov-Pelshe commission. These appeals were edited by Mikhail Sklarov, still chief of the reception office for the Presidium of the Supreme Soviet, who as an experienced bureaucrat knew how to arrange the files for ready endorsement by Gorbachev. General secretaries came and went but Sklarov was still on the job.

Klimov told me that the matter was ready for settlement in 1984, but then Chernenko died and there was no answer from Gorbachev or Mikhail Solomentsov, chairman of the Party Control Committee, who then became chairman of the Special Commission for Rehabilitation of Victims of Political Repression.[7] My daughter-in-law's father, a deputy minister of the coal mining industry, was on friendly terms with Solomentsov, and urged him to seek a favorable decision by the Party Control Committee. Solomentsov reported the case to Gorbachev, who refused reconsideration of any petitions during that period. Iogon Steiner, deputy secretary general of the Austrian Communist party, a former illegal of the Administration for Special Tasks, demanded in 1988 that his and other prominent Communists' names should be cleared of slanderous accusations against them in Sudoplatov's file. He was listened to politely, but no action was taken. I was summoned to the procurator's office in 1988, where I was told that my case would not be reconsidered. I was handed an official reply signed by Procurator General Aleksandr Rekunkov, addressed to me and to the Central Com-

6. Konstantin Chernenko succeeded Yuri Andropov as general secretary of the Communist party in early 1984 and after his death in March 1985 was in turn succeeded by Mikhail Gorbachev.

7. This commission was established by Mikhail Gorbachev in October 1987 and headed by Solomentsov. In 1988 he was replaced by Yakovlev, Gorbachev's senior adviser. The commission was a Politburo decision-making administration with the right to endorse recommendations of the KGB, the procurator's office, and the Supreme Court to drop criminal charges against victims of repression. All major cases were first examined by the commission, and after its endorsement the Supreme Court formally annulled its previous verdicts. The commission was eliminated by Gorbachev in 1990. Under President Yeltsin the Commission on the History of Political Repression, chaired by Yakovlev, has only a consultative and research status.

mittee. The reply contained a serious error: it stated that I was convicted as the accomplice of both Beria and Abakumov, even though there had never been any mention of Abakumov in my indictment.

In 1986 Emma was eighty-one years old and her health had begun to deteriorate. At first she seemed merely to be weaker than her usual sturdy and realistic self, but we soon learned that she had Parkinson's disease. As a veteran she was entitled to preferential treatment in the KGB hospital. Two former co-workers in the KGB helped me get permission to move into the hospital room with Emma. For the final two months, I stayed with her and watched her life end slowly. She died in September 1988, and her ashes are interred in the wall in the Donskoi Monastery cemetery near to those of Grigulevich, Eitingon, and Abel. Raisa Sobel died a month before Emma. Zoya Rybkina lived another three years.

The three survivors of our great but tragic intelligence adventures are Zoya Zarubina, Anna Tsukanova, and I. Zoya and I, as veteran intelligence officers, attended the Victory Day celebrations on May 9, 1993, with our children and grandchildren. Anna and I are getting old, and it is harder to get together, so we talk on the telephone. Zoya is still active, lecturing as far away as Australia.

After Emma's death my health grew worse, and my son Anatoli appealed to Vladimir Kryuchkov, first deputy KGB chairman under Chebrikov, to hospitalize me, which he granted. Later I was treated for another two months in the Central Committee sanatorium.

The ruling administration in the mideighties was ambiguous about my case. On the one hand, believing the case against me to have been fabricated, they invited me to lecture to young officers on the history of illegal operations. They paid well for these lectures at KGB headquarters and for my notes. I participated in a KGB conference to study the history of intelligence operations in Germany, held at Yasenevo, the intelligence headquarters in the outskirts of Moscow. In 1986, on the eve of Gorbachev's meeting with President Reagan in Reykjavik, I wrote a memo for the KGB leadership recounting our experience at Yalta. On the other hand, I was still not rehabilitated.

Glasnost was then everywhere, and my son pressed my case by hiring a lawyer, which shocked the Party Control Committee and the procurator's office. The lawyer compiled a letter accusing the procurator's office of deception, referring to the Abakumov mistake. The lawyer's request for the case records was turned down. The following year, the country fell into crisis.

For Valentin Falin, then secretary of the CPSU Central Committee in charge of foreign policy issues, I wrote a memorandum on the history of German-Soviet relations before the war. I wrote another on the government's handling of nationality policy, including Jewish issues. He thanked me for the material but gave no tangible support for my rehabilitation.

Gorbachev was interested in how the orders were prepared and transmitted for liquidations and assassinations. I received a visit from Major General Shadrin, KGB official in charge of special missions, but I turned down his request to write a description of how we handled such tasks. I explained that full reports were in the archives of the Central Committee. I told him that I personally prepared two handwritten reports on the operations in Mexico and Rotterdam, for which I was responsible. Other reports were handwritten by the senior officers directly in charge of the operations — such as Ogoltsov, Savchenko, Tsanava, and Abakumov — for Molotov and Vyshinsky when they headed the Committee of Information. It was news to him that the GRU also liquidated its double agents and defectors, and that Major General Markelov was in charge during the postwar years. I said they should consult him on those matters. I assume he informed Falin of our meeting.

At the peak of perestroika in 1990, I learned from a high-ranking KGB source that Mikhail Sergeyevich Gorbachev was displeased with the way democratization had gotten out of control. In autumn 1990 the KGB and armed forces were directed to prepare a plan for martial law. The order coincided with a doubling of salaries for all military personnel.

I received strong moral support from KGB major generals Vyacheslav Kevorkov and Nikolai Gubernatorov, who took advantage of the appointment of former ideological watchdog General Ivan Abramov as deputy procurator general of the USSR to examine my file in his office. They reported that the four volumes contained at best rumors, no concrete evidence against me. More important, in the party archives they found a draft of a Politburo decision "To agree with the proposal of the Party Control Committee, KGB, on rehabilitating Sudoplatov and Eitingon, following from the newly established circumstances and no proof of their involvement in crimes of the Beria group, taking into account their contribution in the victory over fascism in the war, and solution of the atomic problem."

This emboldened me, and my son decided to take advantage of the fact that Ramon Mercader had been buried as a Hero of the Soviet Union, while I remained a criminal. My rehabilitation was supported not only by the KGB but by high-ranking figures in the Central Committee. With glasnost I had a new, potent weapon, the press. I wrote a letter to KGB chief Kryuchkov and one to the commission investigating political repressions, stating that I would reveal to the press that current investigations were concealing the truth of the real mechanism of these purges. I asked Kryuchkov to channel to the procurator's office copies of the documents of my real work. That would expose the fraud against me.

The KGB responded promptly. I was informed by the deputy director of the KGB personnel department that all the documents I enumerated in my letter were certified by the KGB and had been sent to the procurator's office with their recommendation to analyze them and treat them as new evidence in my case. I was invited to the military procurator's office, where I was told that my case was reopened. They were also reviewing the case of Abakumov and his group. The reinvestigation took a year. I got the impression that it was done under secret instruction from Gorbachev.

Strange things began to happen. Beria's file was removed from the procurator's office and placed in Gorbachev's secretariat. Then Beria's file vanished. Soon after, I was bitterly attacked in *Moskovskiye Novosti* (*Moscow News*)[8] with quotations from Beria's indictment, alleging that I organized secret murders by poisoning people lured to KGB safe apartments in Moscow, Ulyanovsk, Saratov, and the Carpathian Ukraine. I was being attacked as Beria's accomplice, with no mention of my real career in the intelligence service. The editorial board then asked readers to supply any information they had about these episodes or other facts connected with Sudoplatov, because there was a dearth of specific names and cases in Beria's file. Who was killed, at home and abroad? There was no reaction from the public. In his editorial notes to the article, Yegor Yakovlev, then the editor of *Moskovskiye Novosti*, concluded that a law was needed to regulate special operations and the use of poison laboratories, by both the CIA and KGB.

8. June 17–24, 1990, pp. 8–9.

His editorial remarks were a follow-up to former KGB general Oleg Kalugin's revelations that such a laboratory still existed in the KGB and that the CIA tested drugs on its own people. This time the public was shocked. Yakovlev reported that all attempts by the press to find out the identity and career of Sudoplatov ended in failure. I was portrayed as an unknown murderer. The October 1990 *Moskovskiye Novosti* article said that Maironovsky was a victim of Stalinist repression. Maironovsky, the article said, had a reputation as a scientist in Moscow and probably slandered himself under interrogation. The article also contained severe criticism of the way the Beria case was handled, "in the Stalinist manner," without concrete accusations, which still left doubts about the validity of accusations against me and Eitingon.

I sensed that my rehabilitation case would drag on because no one in power was willing to reveal in print the truths that would compromise Khrushchev's liberalization, now being portrayed as the model for their own reforms. Decisions of the earlier leadership to eliminate political opponents like Trotsky and Shumsky, the Ukrainian nationalist, had not been brought up again for discussion in the press, nor had they been repudiated by Gorbachev and Aleksandr Yakovlev. They could not permit themselves to expose Khrushchev, either as an accomplice to Stalin or as organizer of his own secret political murders. The heroic memory of the Twentieth Party Congress, in which Khrushchev exposed Stalin's crimes, would have been stained. The delegates at the congress and the members of the Central Committee knew about his and their participation in Stalin's crimes. Thus, if my case were brought into the daylight, the entire party leadership under Khrushchev would be exposed as having used Beria and the men who worked under him as scapegoats for themselves. Gorbachev's leadership would then be held responsible for concealing the guilt of the mentors who had brought them to power.

Ironically, at the time of the appeals for my rehabilitation, Gorbachev received a strange missive. Three generals who participated in Beria's arrest wrote a petition to Gorbachev on April 3, 1985, demanding medals as Heroes of the Soviet Union, which they had been promised for the clandestine and risky operation. On April 19, 1985, the secretary of the Central Committee forwarded this letter to Gorbachev. Thus, while Solomentsov, chairman of the Party Control Committee, was making the case for my rehabilitation, the generals were requesting their awards. Gorbachev turned down both applications. The generals were reminded that on January 28, 1954, they had received the Order of the

Red Banner for their work. In 1985 the Central Committee said it "does not find it expedient to return to this matter."[9]

Beria and his enemies in the leadership had identical morals. I agree with the writer Kiril Stolyarov, who said that the only difference between Beria and his rivals was the amount of blood they spilled. However, we must give them all their due. Despite their crimes, Beria, Stalin, Molotov, and Pervukhin succeeded in transforming the Soviet Union from a backward agrarian hinterland into a superpower armed with sophisticated nuclear weapons. While committing equally monstrous crimes against their opponents and innocent bystanders, Khrushchev, Bulganin, and Malenkov contributed much less to the transformation of the USSR. Unlike Stalin, they greatly weakened the state through their own power struggles. Gorbachev and his aides, governed no less by personal ambition, caused the crumbling of the state. Gorbachev and Yakovlev behaved like traditional party bosses, exploiting the name of democracy to strengthen their own power base. They were naive as statesmen and under the illusion that they were capable of outmaneuvering their rivals and preserving their power. They accomplished nothing in domestic policy or in foreign affairs. In 1989 Gorbachev moved Erich Honecker out of power in East Germany, hoping to strengthen socialism, but it backfired. He and Shevardnadze were incapable of negotiating economic concessions from the West in return for the withdrawal of the Soviet Union from Eastern Europe.

During this period Colonel General Dmitri Volkogonov, who was writing biographies of Stalin and Trotsky, called me.[10] In June 1989 Volkogonov managed to reach me in Peredelkino at the dacha of Zoya Rybkina, where I was staying. I had been warned to be cautious in my revelations to Volkogonov, but I decided to meet him because he had

9. From the Archives of the Central Committee, Document 1502, Top Secret File. In *Rodina*, July 4, 1992, pp. 62–63. (*Rodina* magazine publishes materials and documents from party archives.) Archive documents reveal that Beria's case was so sensitive, so extraordinary, that his sentence was carried out not by a rank-and-file executioner, but by a three-star general of the Red Army, A. Batitsky. This was intended, says P. A. Sudoplatov, to prevent any revelation of the deliberations and decision making by Khrushchev and his leadership in eliminating Beria.

10. Volkogonov was deputy chief of the Main Political Administration of the Soviet army, in charge of psychological warfare against the American armed forces in the 1970s and 1980s. He became director of the Institute of Military History of the Ministry of Defense in 1986.

access to the archives and could present the story of past atrocities and triumphs in a clear, unfiltered light. Cautiously, and with natural mistakes because of his official position and subordination to military authority, he opened a new chapter in Russian historical studies.

Volkogonov promised to support my rehabilitation in exchange for my cooperation. When we met on November 4, 1989, I suggested that Volkogonov correct his account of the Stamenov episode, which had just appeared in *Oktyabr,* a literary journal. He claimed in the article that Stalin had personally met Stamenov, which I knew was untrue. I myself had handled the probe to plant disinformation among Nazi diplomats, feeling out the Germans' desire for a peace settlement in 1941. When Volkogonov's book appeared, the episode was not corrected. He sticks to the version that Stalin and Molotov planned a separate Brest-Litovsk type peace treaty with Hitler, using as his source references to discussions in the Politburo.[11]

The Politburo might have discussed this intelligence operation. As I have already explained, my orders were to plant disinformation about a possible peace with Hitler, using Stamenov as the source for the rumor. Beria and Molotov assumed that Stamenov would actively use this false information to enhance his image with the czar of Bulgaria. However, he chose not to report it to Sofia. I had not ordered him to do so; had I insisted, he could not have refused, because he was a controlled NKVD agent. But my instructions were to suggest the rumor, not order him to transmit it.

I led Volkogonov straight to the Trotsky file in the KGB and Central Committee archives, a feat he could not have accomplished alone. Even if you are a top government official with the right to look at top-secret files, the whereabouts of any single piece of paper requires searching through a jungle. He could not know, for example, that Trotsky's own archives, stolen from Paris in 1937, were not where they should have been, but were actively used by the International Department of the Central Committee of the CPSU.

Since the August 1991 attempted coup, there has been an undisciplined rush to lay hands on secret Communist party archives with the intent to use and sell them for films, research projects, and popular books. Although Volkogonov acknowledged my help in the introduction of his book on Trotsky, it appeared without his showing me the manuscript. That is perhaps why, for the first time, my code name and identity

11. Volkogonov, *Stalin: Triumph and Tragedy,* pp. 412–413.

in the operation against Konovalets were revealed.[12] The result, in 1992, was an indictment against me by the Ukrainian procurator's office. The Ukrainian indictment was dropped by the military procurator's office in June 1993 because it was established that Konovalets's terrorist organization had formally declared a state of war against the Soviet Union, which lasted from 1919 to 1991.

In printing my name publicly in his book on Trotsky and telling of my real role in World War II guerrilla operations and atomic espionage, Volkogonov's history, though faulty, at least restored my identity. For many years my name had been a blank space in Soviet history, missing from all the accounts of heroic deeds my colleagues accomplished in the war against Hitler, under my leadership. It was Volkogonov who planted with my son the idea of telling the story of my life, which gives me the chance to set the record straight.

In 1991 the military procurator's office came to the conclusion that Abakumov's case was fabricated and that although he was guilty of unlawful repressions he was not guilty of high treason or crimes against the party. They recommended that the indictment against him should be amended to change the basis on which he was prosecuted. Abuse of power and falsification of criminal evidence were his actual crimes and according to law warranted the same punishment. The implication of the procurator's recommendation was that those above him were equally guilty of these abuses.

The procurator took a new approach to Eitingon's and my cases. The record showed that we did not initiate liquidations or assassinations, nor did we fabricate false evidence against any victims. Thus, we had acted according to military discipline, taking our orders from legal directives of the government. The formal charges against us, abetting Beria in treason and planning terrorist acts against the government and Beria's personal enemies, were repudiated by the documents. Chief Military Procurator General Pavel Boriskin formally closed our cases and stated that if, before his retirement, he had not rehabilitated us, then the archives would show that he was another guilty participant in covering up the truth about the Kremlin power struggles in the 1950s. Four months after the August 1991 attempted coup, within days after the dissolution of the Soviet Union in December, and two days before his

12. Volkogonov, *Trotsky* (Moscow: Novosti, 1992), vol. 2, pp. 303–305.

retirement, Boriskin made his peace with history. He endorsed the decision to rehabilitate Eitingon and me. He also dismissed the murder charge against Kalugin for Markov's liquidation in London, since Kalugin was fulfilling his military duty.

My rehabilitation was no longer a political matter, but only a minor event in the history of the disintegration of the Soviet Union. The military procurator's office was no longer obliged to consult the highest authorities of the Communist party on how to handle my case. A new generation that had been raised to power by the old generation, but not implicated in the atrocities of Stalin's and Khrushchev's authoritarian rule, was now the leadership. The icon of Khrushchev, useful in the new reform religion of glasnost and perestroika, lost its glow. In the tense atmosphere of the former Soviet Union, brought about by the lack of a new political tradition and culture to replace the old, and by a gridlock in the economy, hatred toward me persists only among those who would prefer that all witnesses to the old order disappear. Then there would be no one who could correct the record or tell where the truth is hidden in the archives.

The Soviet Union — to which I devoted every fiber of my being and for which I was willing to die; for which I averted my eyes from every brutality, finding justification in its transformation from a backward nation into a superpower; for which I spent long months on duty away from Emma and the children; whose mistakes cost me fifteen years of my life as a husband and father — was unwilling to admit its failure and take me back as a citizen. Only when there was no more Soviet Union, no more proud empire, was I reinstated and my name returned to its rightful place.

Despite my rehabilitation, my medals have not been returned to me; let no one forget that I, too, have been a victim of political repression.

STALIN'S VISITORS, JUNE 21 AND JUNE 22, 1941

ENTRIES FROM
KREMLIN LOGBOOK
(EXCERPT)

This excerpt from *Izvestia CC CPSU* (*News of the Central Committee, Communist Party of the Soviet Union*), no. 6, 1990, confirms Sudoplatov's contention that Stalin, contrary to Khrushchev's claims in his memoirs, was not immobilized by panic after the German invasion of the Soviet Union on June 22, 1941, but rather received a steady stream of visitors at his Kremlin study. (The translation omits the T., which stands for Tovarich — Comrade — before each name.)

The Logbook Entries of the People Received by J. V. Stalin * *
June 21–28, 1941

The logbooks of J. V. Stalin's visitors from 1927 to 1953 are kept in the CC [Central Committee] CPSU archives [in Moscow]. Below are some entries made by the receptionists on duty during eight days — from the evening of June 21 to June 28, 1941 (the next entry is dated July 1, 1941). These records give the visitors' names and the duration of their stay in Stalin's study in the Kremlin. Among the visitors are members of the Politburo of the Central Committee of the Communist Party of the Soviet Union, CC CPSU, other important Communist party and government members, and top military commanders. . . .

21 June 1941

1. Molotov   18.27–23.00
2. Voroshilov   19.05–23.00
3. Beria   19.05–23.00***
4. Voznesensky   19.05–20.15
5. Malenkov   19.05–22.20
6. Kuznetsov**** 19.05–20.15
7. Timoshenko   19.05–20.15
8. Safonov   19.05–20.15
9. Timoshenko   20.50–22.20
10. Zhukov   20.50–22.20
11. Budyonny   20.50–22.00
12. Mekhlis   21.55–22.20
13. Beria   22.40–23.00***
The last ones left 23.00

22 June 1941

1. Molotov	Enter	5.45
	Exit	12.05
2. Beria	Enter	5.45
	Exit	9.20
3. Timoshenko	Enter	5.45
	Exit	8.30
4. Mekhlis	Enter	5.45
	Exit	8.30
5. Zhukov	Enter	5.45
	Exit	8.30
6. Malenkov	Enter	7.30
	Exit	9.20
7. Mikoyan	Enter	7.55
	Exit	9.30
8. Kaganovich	Enter	8.00
	Exit	9.35
9. Voroshilov	Enter	8.00
	Exit	10.15
10. Vishnevsky	Enter	7.30
	Exit	10.40
11. Kuznetsov	Enter	8.15
	Exit	8.30
12. Dimitrov	Enter	8.40
	Exit	10.40
13. Manuilsky	Enter	8.40
	Exit	10.40
14. Kuznetsov	Enter	9.40
	Exit	10.20
15. Mikoyan	Enter	9.50
	Exit	10.30
16. Molotov	Enter	12.25
	Exit	16.45
17. Voroshilov	Enter	[11].40
	Exit	12.05
18. Beria	Enter	11.30
	Exit	12.00
19. Malenkov	Enter	11.30
	Exit	12.00

. . . .

**The logbook does not have a name. The title has been provided by the editors.
***As it is in the document. Ed.
****Clearly the People's Commissar of the Navy of the USSR, N. G. Kuznetsov. Ed.

Из тетради записи лиц, принятых И. В. Сталиным **
21—28 июня 1941 г.

В архиве ЦК КПСС хранятся тетради записи лиц, принятых И. В. Сталиным с 1927 по 1953 г. Ниже приводятся записи, сделанные дежурными в приемной в течение 8 дней — с вечера 21 по 28 июня 1941 г. (следующая запись датирована 1 июля 1941 г.). В них зафиксированы фамилии посетителей и время их пребывания в сталинском кабинете в Кремле. Среди посетителей члены Политбюро ЦК ВКП(б), партийные и государственные деятели, высшие военачальники.

Эти записи упомянуты в статье Л. М. Спирина «Сталин и война» (Вопросы истории КПСС, 1990, № 5, с. 101—102). Однако при цитировании автор допустил неточность, указав, что 22 июня к И. В. Сталину прибыли Г. Димитров и С. А. Лозовский. В записи посетителей указано, что вместе с Г. Димитровым на приеме был Д. З. Мануильский.

21-го июня 1941 г.

1. т. Молотов	18.27—23.00	
2. т. Ворошилов	19.05—23.00	
3. т. Берия	19.05—23.00 ***	
4. т. Вознесенский	19.05—20.15	
5. т. Маленков	19.05—22.20	
6. т. Кузнецов ****	19.05—20.15	
7. т. Тимошенко	19.05—20.15	
8. т. Сафонов	19.05—20.15	
9. т. Тимошенко	20.50—22.20	
10. т. Жуков	20.50—22.20	
11. т. Буденный	20.50—22.00	
12. т. Мехлис	21.55—22.20	
13. т. Берия	22.40—23.00 ***	
Последние вышли	23.00	

22 июня 1941 г.

1. т. Молотов	вход в 5.45 м.	выход 12.05 м.
2. т. Берия	вход 5.45 м.	выход 9.20 м.
3. т. Тимошенко	вход в 5.45 м.	выход 8.30 м.
4. т. Мехлис	вход в 5.45 м.	выход 8.30 м.
5. т. Жуков	вход в 5.45 м.	выход 8.30 м.
6. т. Маленков	вход 7.30 м.	выход 9.20 м.
7. т. Микоян	вход в 7.55 м.	выход 9.30 м.
8. т. Каганович Л. М.	в 8.00 м.	выход 9.35 м.
9. т. Ворошилов	вход 8.00 м.	выход 10.15 м.
10. т. Вышинский	вход 7.30 м.	выход 10.40 м.
11. т. Кузнецов	вход в 8.15 м.	выход 8.30 м.
12. т. Димитров	вход 8.40 м.	выход 10.40 м.
13. т. Мануильский	в 8.40 м.	выход 10.40 м.
14. т. Кузнецов	вход 9.40 м.	выход 10.20 м.
15. т. Микоян	вход 9.50 м.	выход 10.30 м.
16. т. Молотов	вход в 12.25 м.	выход 16.45 м.
17. т. Ворошилов	вход в [11].40 м.	выход 12.05 м.
18. т. Берия	вход 11.30 м.	выход 12.00 м.
19. т. Маленков	вход 11.30 м.	выход 12.00 м.

___

* Далее текст обрывается. По смыслу: «связи не имеем». Ред.
** Тетрадь не имеет названия. Заголовок дан редакторами. Ред.
*** Так в документе. Ред.
**** Видимо, нарком ВМФ СССР Н. Г. Кузнецов. Ред.

Entries from Kremlin Logbook, June 21 and June 22, 1941. Pages from an article in Izvestia CC CPSU, *no. 6, 1990.*

Страница из тетради записи лиц, принятых И. В. Сталиным 22 и 23 июня 1941 г.

ATOMIC ESPIONAGE DOCUMENTS, 1941–1946

FROM THE ARCHIVES OF THE FOREIGN INTELLIGENCE SERVICE OF RUSSIA (EXCERPTS)

The following documents, from the archives of the Foreign Intelligence Service of Russia, appeared in *Voprossi Istorii Estestvoznania i Tekhniki* (*Questions of History of Natural Science and Technology*) (Russian Academy of Science, Moscow), no. 3, 1992, pages 107–134. They were published and distributed to libraries throughout Russia and then withdrawn from circulation because of the secrecy of the technical data they contain on building an atomic bomb. The pages translated and reproduced here were obtained from a public library where the magazine was briefly in circulation. They reveal the extent of Soviet espionage and the direct questions that Soviet scientists were able to ask and have answered by Soviet intelligence officers in England, the United States, and Canada.

Material deemed too technical or of limited interest has been omitted from the translations, and Documents 12 and 13 have been omitted in their entirety on the recommendation of a senior American scientist because of their detailed and still-classified nature. Material interpolated in the documents by the Russian editors of *Voprossi Istorii* is enclosed in angle brackets ⟨ ⟩ and omissions made by them are indicated by ⟨. . .⟩. Our interpolations in the translated excerpts are enclosed in square brackets [ ], and omissions are indicated by [. . .].

The translation conforms to the Russian original in placing commentary on and reference notes to the individual documents following

Document 14. The commentary is frequently useful in putting the documents in context; these notes begin on page 463. Dates in the documents have been rendered in normal American style (e.g., 16.IX.41 is translated as September 16, 1941).

A representative sampling of the pages that appeared in *Voprossi Istorii* are reproduced here. A complete copy of the documents as published in *Voprossi Istorii* has been turned over to the library of the Hoover Institution, Stanford University, Palo Alto, California, so that qualified experts can consult them in full in the original.

Materials from the Archives of the Foreign Intelligence Service of Russia

Document No. 1

TOP SECRET

Report

on No. 6881/1065 of September 25, 1941, from London

VADIM[1] has relayed a report from Leaf[2] about a meeting of the Uranium Committee[3] of September 16, 1941. The meeting was chaired by Boss.*

The meeting was advised of the following.

The uranium bomb may conceivably be developed in the course of two years, particularly if the Imperial Chemical Industries[4] company is obliged to manufacture it under a crash program.

A representative of the Woolwich arsenal, FERGUSSON, declared that the fuse for the bomb can be designed within several months. There is no need or possibility to obtain the minimal velocity of the relative movement of the mass of explosive at 6 thousand feet per second. The explosion will be produced prematurely. But even in that case the force of the explosion will be infinitely greater than that of conventional explosives. [. . .]

Three months ago the Metropolitan Vickers company was issued an order for designing a 20-stage apparatus, but the permission for that was granted only recently. The execution of this order is set as a top priority.

The Imperial Chemical Industries company holds a contract for the production of uranium hexafluoride, but it has not yet been started. Fairly recently a patent was issued in the United States for a simpler production process employing uranium nitrate.

At the meeting it was also reported that data about the best type of diffusion membranes can be obtained in the USA.[5]

The Chiefs of Staffs Committee at their meeting on September 20, 1941, made a decision to immediately launch construction in Britain of a plant to manufacture uranium bombs.

Vadim requests an appraisal of Leaf's materials on uranium.

Correct: (signature) Potapov

*Henkey (handwritten). [Probably Sir Maurice Hankey, secretary of the Committee for Imperial Defense.]

Document No. 2

TOP SECRET

Report

on No. 7073, 7081/1096 of October 3, 1941, from London

VADIM informs about a report, received from Leaf, which was submitted to the War Cabinet on September 24, 1941, on projects of the Uranium Committee.

The report touches on the following issues:

The calculation of the critical mass depends on determining the fission cross section of the uranium 235 nucleus. It is assumed that the amount of the critical mass lies between 10 and 43 kilograms. This amount was determined on the basis of general information about the properties of U-235 and the impact of high-velocity neutrons on atoms of other elements.[6]

The production of uranium hexafluoride has been developed by Imperial Chemical Industries, which has already obtained 3 kilograms of the substance. The production of F-235* is effected by way of diffusion of uranium hexafluoride in a gaseous state through a number of membranes which are grids of the finest wire.

The designing of the separation plant poses significant problems. [. . .]

It is assumed that the entire separation factory will require 19,000** 10-stage units, due to which the territory of the plant should be upwards of 20 acres.

The overall amount of uranium hexafluoride should be not more than 0.5 tons per day. Therefore, the chemical division of the plant is to occupy only a small part of it.

It is reported that, besides the tremendous destructive effect of the uranium bomb, the air at the site of the explosion will be saturated with radioactive particles, capable of destroying everything living that may fall under the impact of these particles.

Correct: (signature) Potapov

*Clearly, U-235.
**Obviously a typing error — not 19,000 but 1,900.

Document No. 3

KZ-4   TOP SECRET
USSR   Copy No. 1
PEOPLE'S COMMISSARIAT
FOR INTERNAL AFFAIRS
"   " MARCH 1942
MOSCOW

The State Committee for Defense of the Union SSR
To Comrade STALIN

In a number of capitalist countries, in connection with work under way on the fission of the atom nucleus with a view to obtaining a new source of energy, research has been launched into the utilization of the nuclear energy of uranium for military purposes.

In 1939 extensive research work was started in France, Britain, the United States, and Germany to devise a method of the utilization of uranium for creating new explosives. The work is being conducted in the conditions of a high degree of secrecy.

From top-secret materials, enclosed, obtained by the NKVD through intelligence gathering and characterizing the activities of the Uranium Committee on the issue of the nuclear energy of uranium, it is evident that:

a) The British War Cabinet, taking stock of the possibility of Germany successfully tackling this task, has been paying a great deal of attention to the problem of utilizing nuclear energy for military purposes.

b) The War Cabinet's Uranium Committee, headed by the well-known British physicist J. P. THOMSON, coordinates the work of prominent British researchers, engaged in utilizing the nuclear energy of uranium, both with regard to theoretical and experimental, and to purely applied development, i.e., the production of uranium bombs of high destructive power.

c) The research is based on the utilization of one of the isotopes of uranium, U-235, with its capacity for effective fission. Used for that is uranium ore, whose most significant resources are found in Canada, the Belgian Congo, the Sudetes [Czechoslovakia], and Portugal.

d) The French scientists HALBAN and KOWARSKI, who emigrated to Britain, have devised a method of separating the uranium 235 isotope through the use of uranium oxide, treated with heavy water.

The British scientists Professor PEIERLS and Dr. of Physics BEIS[?], have developed a way of separating the reactive isotope U-235 with the help of a diffusion apparatus, designed by Dr. SIMON, which was recommended for practical utilization in obtaining uranium that is used for manufacturing the uranium bomb.

e) Alongside a number of British research institutions, taking a direct part in mastering the industrial method of separating U-235 are the Woolwich arsenal, as well as the Metro-Vickers Co. and the Imperial Chemical Industries concern. The concern provides the following estimate of the progress achieved in the method of obtaining U-235 and of manufacturing uranium bombs:

"Research into the utilization of nuclear energy for uranium bombs has reached a stage when the work should be lent a large scale. The problem can be resolved and the necessary production plant can be built."

f) The Uranium Committee is pressing for cooperation with relevant research institutions and organizations in the United States (the Du Pont company), confining itself to theoretical problems alone.

The applied aspect of the development project is based on the following principal provisions, corroborated by theoretical calculations and experimental results, namely:

Prof. R. PEIERLS of Birmingham University has theoretically established the critical mass of U-235 to be 10 kilograms. A smaller than critical quantity of the substance is stable and completely safe, while in a mass of U-235 in excess of 10 kilograms there emerges a progressive fission reaction, producing an explosion of colossal power.

In designing the bomb, its core should consist of two halves, whose sum total should exceed the critical mass. For obtaining the maximum force of the explosion of the two halves of U-235, according to Prof. FERGUSSON of the Research Department of the Woolwich arsenal, the velocity of the movement of the masses should lie within 6,000 feet per second. In the event the velocity is decreased, the chain reaction of the fission of uranium nuclei and the power of the explosion lose in intensity, but still exceed the force of conventional explosives manifold.

Prof. TAYLOR has calculated that the destructive power of 10 kilograms of U-235 should be equal to 1,600 tons of TNT.

The whole complexity of the production of uranium bombs lies in separating the active part of uranium, U-235, from other isotopes, manufacturing a shell of the bomb that would preclude disintegration, and in securing the necessary velocity of the movement of the masses.

According to Imperial Chemical Industries (ICI), the separation of U-235 isotopes will require 1,900 of the devices designed by Dr. SIMON, worth 3,300,000 pounds sterling, while the cost of the entire production facility will run into 4.5–5 million pounds.

In the event of the production of 36 bombs a year by one such plant, the cost of one bomb will amount to 236,000 pounds sterling, as compared to the cost of 1,500 tons of TNT at 326,000 pounds sterling.

A study of materials devoted to the development of the uranium problem for military application in Britain leads to the following conclusions:

1. The Supreme Military Command of Britain considers fundamentally resolved the question of the practical utilization of the nuclear energy of uranium (U-235) for military purposes.

2. The Uranium Committee of the British War Cabinet has devised the preliminary theoretical basis for designing and building a plant for the production of uranium bombs.

3. The biggest scientific and research organizations and major companies in

Britain have joined their efforts and potentials and geared them to the development of the uranium 235 problem, which is subject to a regime of special secrecy.

4. The British War Cabinet is deliberating the question of a decision of principle on launching the production of uranium bombs.

Proceeding from the importance and urgency of the practical utilization of the nuclear energy of uranium 235 for the Soviet Union's military purposes, it would be expedient to:

1. Examine the question of setting up a Scientific Consultative body of experts, affiliated with the State Defense Committee of the USSR, for the coordination, study, and direction of the efforts of all scientists and research organizations of the USSR, engaged in the problem of the nuclear energy of uranium.

2. Confidentially advise prominent specialists of NKVD materials on uranium with a view to evaluating and utilizing them.

Note:

Dealing with atomic nuclear fission in the USSR have been Academician KAPITSA at the USSR Academy of Sciences, Academician SKOBELTSIN [formerly] at the Leningrad Physics Institute, and Prof. SLUTSKY at the Kharkov Physical Technical Institute.

PEOPLE'S COMMISSAR OF INTERNAL AFFAIRS OF THE UNION SSR (L. BERIA)

Document No. 4

USSR **DEPUTY CHAIRMAN** **OF THE COUNCIL OF PEOPLE'S** **COMMISSARS** **M. G. PERVUKHIN** **MOSCOW — KREMLIN**	<u>**TOP SECRET No. P-37ss**</u> " " April 1943

To Deputy People's Commissar of the USSR NKVD Comrade V. N. Merkulov

Enclosed please find a report by Prof. I. V. Kurchatov about materials on the uranium problem.

Requesting your orders on additional clarification of questions raised in the report.

Upon utilization the material is to be returned to me.

(signature) Pervukhin
April 8

[*Document continues on page 446.*]

Original pages from the Russian article translated in Appendix Two. These pages include the letter from Beria to Stalin advising him of the progress being made on an atomic bomb.

ние 20-ступенчатого аппарата, но разрешение на это было дано только недавно. Намечается обеспечение выполнения этого заказа в порядке 1-й очереди.

Фирма «Империал Кемикал Индастриес» имеет договор на получение гексафторурана, но так давно в США был выдан патент на более простой процесс производства с использованием нитрата урана.

На совещании было сообщено, что о лучшем типе диффузионных мембран можно получить в США.

Комитетом Начальников Штабов на своем совещании, состоявшемся 20.IX.41 г., было вынесено решение о немедленном начале строительства в Англии завода изготовления урановых бомб.

Вадим просит оценку материалов «Листа» по урану.

           Верно: (подпись) Потапов

*Хенки (вписано от руки)

СОВ. СЕКРЕТНО

Документ № 2

СПРАВКА
на № 7073, 7081/1096 от 3.X.41 г. из Лондона

ВАДИМ сообщает о полученном от «Листа» переданном Военному Кабинету 24.IX.41 г. докладе о работах Уранового Комитета.

В докладе освещаются следующие вопросы.

Определение критической массы урана зависит от определения поперечного сечения ядра урана-235 (fission cross section). Предполагается, что величина критической массы находится в пределах от 10 до 43 кг. Эта величина определялась на основании общих сведений по свойствам U-235 и действии быстрых нейтронов на атомы других элементов.

Получение гексафторурана (гексафлюороурана) разработано фирмой «Империал Кемикал Индастриес», которая уже получила 3 кг этого вещества. Получение F-235* осуществляется диффузией гексафторурана в парообразном состоянии через ряд мембран, представляющих собой сетку из тончайшей проволоки.

Проектирование сепарационного завода представляет большие трудности, т. к.:

1) Гексафторуран разрушает смазочные вещества. Поэтому, возможно, потребуется разработка специальной конструкции вещества. Но даже в этом случае потребуется установка газовых затворов.

2) Гексафторуран подвергается разложению в присутствии водяных паров. В присутствии даже незначительного количества влаги гексафторуран действует разрушающе на аппаратуру.

3) Процесс происходит при вакууме 0,4 мм, в связи с чем потребуется наличие возможно меньшего количества соединений в аппаратуре.

4) Конструкция и установка мембран должны быть таковы, чтобы обеспечить полное отсутствие вибрации мембран.

5) Возможность утечки и загрязнения сальников.

Предполагается, что для всего сепарационного завода в целом потребуется 19.000** 10-ступенчатых агрегатов, в связи с чем территория завода должна быть более 20 акров.

Общее количество гексафторурана будет не более 0,5 тонны в день, следовательно, химическая часть завода будет занимать только небольшую его часть.

Сообщается, что завод будет насыщен радиоактивными частицами, умерщвляющими все живое, что попадет под действие этих частей.

           Верно: (подпись) Потапов

*очевидно, U-235.
**очевидно, опечатка — не 19.000, а 1.900.

СОВ. СЕКРЕТНО
Экз. № 1

Документ № 3

К3-4
СССР
НАРОДНЫЙ КОМИССАРИАТ
ВНУТРЕННИХ ДЕЛ
"__" марта 1942 г.
г. Москва

ГОСУДАРСТВЕННЫЙ КОМИТЕТ ОБОРОНЫ СОЮЗА ССР
товарищу СТАЛИНУ

В ряде капиталистических стран в связи с проводимыми работами по расщеплению атомного ядра с целью получения нового источника энергии было начато изучение вопроса использования атомной энергии урана для военных целей.

В 1939 году во Франции, Англии, США и Германии развернулась интенсивная научно-исследовательская работа по разработке метода применения урана для новых взрывчатых веществ. Эти работы ведутся в условиях большой секретности.

Из прилагаемых совершенно секретных материалов, полученных НКВД СССР в Англии агентурным путем, характеризующих деятельность Уранового Комитета по вопросу атомной энергии урана, видно, что:

а) Английский Военный Кабинет, учитывая возможность успешного разрешения этой задачи Германией, уделяет большое внимание проблеме использования атомной энергии урана для военных целей.

б) Урановый Комитет Военного кабинета, возглавляемый известным английским физиком Г. П. ТОМСОНОМ, координирует работу видных английских ученых, занимающихся вопросом использования атомной энергии урана, как в отношении теоретической, эксперментальной разработки, так и чисто прикладной, т. е. изготовления урановых бомб, обладающих свойством большой разрушительной силой.

в) Эти исследования основаны на использовании одного из изотопов урана, U-235, обладающего свойством эффективного расщепления. Для этого используется урановая руда, наиболее значительные запасы которой имеются в Канаде, в Бельгийском Конго, в Судетах и в Португалии.

г) Английские ученые ХАЛЬБАН и КОВАРСКИЙ, эмигрировавшие в Англию, разработали метод выделения изотопа урана-235 путем применения окиси урана, обрабатываемого тяжелой водой.

д) Английский ученый, профессор ПЕЙЕРЛС и доктор физических наук БАЙС, разработали способ выделения реактивного изотопа U-235 при помощи диффузирующего аппарата, сконструированного д-ром СИМОН, которая и рекомендовал для практического использования в деле получения урана, идущего для изготовления урановой бомбы.

д) В освоении производственного метода выделения U-235, помимо ряда научно-исследовательских учреждений Англии, непосредственное участие принимают Вульвичский арсенал, а также фирмы «Метро—Виккерс», химический концерн «Империал Кемикал Индастриес». Этот концерн дает следующую оценку состояния разработки метода получения U-235 и производства урановых бомб.

«Научно-исследовательские работы по использованию атомной энергии для урановых бомб достигли стадии, когда необходимо начать работы в широком масштабе. Эта проблема может быть разрешена и необходимый завод может быть построен.

е) Урановый Комитет добивается кооперирования с соответствующими научно-исследовательскими организациями и фирмами США (фирма Люлюн), ограничиваясь лишь теоретическими вопросами.

Прикладная сторона разработки основывается на следующих главных положениях, подтвержденных теоретическими расчетами и экспериментальными работами, а именно:

Профессор Бирмингамского Университета Р. ПЕЙЕРЛС определил теоретическим путем, что вес 10 кг U-235 является критической величиной. Количество этого вещества меньше критического, устойчиво и совершенно безопасно, в то время как в массе U-235, большей 10 кг, возникает прогрессирующая реакция расщепления, вызывающая колоссальной силы взрыв.

При проектировании бомб активная часть должна состоять из двух равных половин, в своей сумме превышающих максимальную критическую величину. Для производства максимальной силы взрыва этих частей U-235, по данным профессора ФЕРГЮССОНА из Научно-исследова-

сов. секретно 6
Экз. № 1

СССР
НАРОДНЫЙ КОМИССАРИАТ
ВНУТРЕННИХ ДЕЛ
____ марта ____ 194_ г.
№ _____
г. Москва

ГОСУДАРСТВЕННЫЙ КОМИТЕТ ОБОРОНЫ
СОЮЗА С.С.Р.

товарищу СТАЛИНУ

В ряде капиталистических стран в связи с проводимыми работами по расщеплению атомного ядра, с целью получения нового источника энергии, было начато изучение вопроса использования атомной энергии урана для военных целей.

В 1939 году во Франции, Англии, США и Германии развернулись интенсивные научно-исследовательские работы по разработке метода применения урана для новых взрывчатых веществ. Эти работы ведутся в условиях большой секретности.

Из прилагаемых совершенно секретных материалов, полученных НКВД СССР в Англии агентурным путем, характеризующих деятельность Уранового Комитета по вопросу атомной энергии урана видно, что:

а) Английский Военный Кабинет, учитывая возможность успешного разрешения этой задачи Германией, уделяет большое внимание проблеме использования атомной энергии урана для военных целей.

б) Урановый Комитет Военного кабинета, возглавляемый известным английским физиком Г.П. ТОМСОНОМ,

тельского отдела Вульвичского арсенала, скорость перемещения масс должна лежать в пределах 6.000 футов/секунду. При уменьшении этой скорости происходит затухание цепной реакции расщепления атомов урана и сила взрыва значительно уменьшается, но все же во много раз превышает силу взрыва обычного ВВ.

Профессор ТЕЙЛОР пояснил, что разрушительное действие 10 кг U-235 будет соответствовать 1.600 тонн TNT.

Вся сложность производства урановых бомб заключается в трудности отделения активной части урана — U-235 от других изотопов, предохраняющих [...] распадение, и получения необходимой U-235 [...]

По данным концерна «Империал Кемикал Индастриз» (ICI), для отделения изотопа U-235 потребуется 1.900 аппаратов системы д-ра СИМОНА стоимостью в 3.300.000 фунтов стерлингов, а стоимость всего предприятия выразится суммой в 4,5—5 миллионов фунтов стерлингов. При производстве таким заводом 36 бомб в год стоимость одной бомбы будет равна 236.000 фунтов стерлингов по сравнению со стоимостью 1.500 тонн TNT в 326.000 фунтов стерлингов.

Изучение материалов по разработке проблемы урана для военных целей в Англии приводят к следующим выводам:

1. Верховное Военное командование Англии считает принципиально решенным вопрос практического использования атомной энергии урана (U-235) для военных целей.

2. Урановый Комитет Английского Военного Кабинета разработал предварительную теоретическую часть для проектирования и постройки завода по изготовлению урановых бомб.

3. Усилия и возможности наиболее крупных научно-исследовательских организаций и крупных фирм Англии объединены и направлены на разработку проблемы урана-235, которая особо засекречена.

4. Английский Военный Кабинет занимается вопросом принципиального решения об организации производства урановых бомб.

Исходя из важности и актуальности проблемы практического применения атомной энергии урана-235 для военных целей Советского Союза было бы целесообразно:

1. Проработать вопрос о создании Научно-Совещательного органа при Государственном Комитете Обороны СССР из авторитетных лиц для координирования, изучения и направления работ всех ученых, научно-исследовательских организаций СССР, занимающихся вопросом атомной энергии урана.

2. Обеспечить секретное ознакомление с материалами НКВД СССР по урану видных специалистов с целью дачи оценки и соответствующего использования.

Примечание:

Вопросами расщепления атомного ядра в СССР занимались академик КАПИЦА — в Академии наук СССР, академик СКОБЕЛЬЦИН — Ленинградский физико-технический институт и профессор СЛУЦКИЙ — Харьковский физико-технический институт.

НАРОДНЫЙ КОМИССАР ВНУТРЕННИХ ДЕЛ СОЮЗА С.С.Р. (Л. БЕРИЯ)

Документ № 4

С.С.С.Р.
ЗАМЕСТИТЕЛЬ ПРЕДСЕДАТЕЛЯ
СОВЕТА НАРОДНЫХ
КОМИССАРОВ
М. Г. ПЕРВУХИН
МОСКВА—КРЕМЛЬ

СОВ. СЕКРЕТНО № П-37сс
« » апреля 1943 г.

Заместителю Народного Комиссара НКВД СССР товарищу Меркулову В. Н.

При сем направляю записку профессора Курчатова И. В. о материалах по проблеме урана.

Прошу дать указание о дополнительном выяснении поставленных в записке вопросов.

По использовании материал прошу вернуть мне.

(подпись) Первухин
8/IV

СОВЕРШ. СЕКРЕТНО

Заместителю Председателя Совета Народных Комиссаров Союза ССР
т. Первухину М. Г.

Произведенное мной рассмотрение материала показало, что получение его имеет громадное, неоценимое значение для нашего Государства и науки.

С одной стороны, материал показал серьезность и напряженность научно-исследовательской работы в Англии по проблеме урана, с другой — дал возможность получить весьма важные ориентиры для нашего научного исследования, миновать многие весьма трудоемкие фазы разработки проблемы и узнать о новых научных и технических путях ее разрешения.

В дальнейшем приводятся соображения по отдельным разделам материала.

These pages show letters from Kurchatov evaluating American work on uranium for the atomic bomb and listing American laboratories and scientists to be targeted for further intelligence acquisitions.

3. Изучение свойств элемента ЕкаОсм[4], [6]

В заключение необходимо отметить, что вся совокупность сведений материала указывает на техническую возможность решения всей проблемы урана в значительно более короткий срок, чем это думают наши ученые, не знакомые с ходом работ по этой проблеме за границей.

Естественно возникает вопрос о том, отражают ли полученные материалы действительный ход научно-исследовательской работы в Англии, и не являются ли задачей которого явилась бы дезориентация нашей науки. Этот вопрос для нас имеет особенно большое значение потому, что по многим важным разделам работы (из-за отсутствия технической базы) мы не в состоянии произвести проверку данных, изложенных в материале.

На основании внимательного ознакомления с материалом у меня осталось впечатление, что он отражает истинное положение вещей.

Некоторые выводы, даже те из них весьма важные разделы работы, мне кажутся сомнительными, некоторые из них мало обоснованными, но ответственными за это являются английские ученые, а не доброкачественность информации.

Это письмо будет передано Вам Вашим Помощником т. А. И. Васиным, у которого находятся подлежащие уничтожению черновые записи к письму.

Содержание письма никому, кроме него, не может быть пока известно.

г.Москва   Зав.лабор.
7.03.43   Профессор Курчатов

Документ № 5

СОВЕРШЕННО СЕКРЕТНО

Заместителю Председателя Совета Народных Комиссаров Союза ССР
т.Первухину М. Г.

В материалах, рассмотрением которых занимался в последнее время, содержатся отрывочные замечания о возможности использовать в «урановом котле» не только уран-235, но и уран-238. Кроме того, указано, что, может быть, продукты сгорания ядерного топлива в «урановом котле» могут быть использованы вместо урана-235 в качестве материала для бомбы.

Имея в виду эти замечания, я внимательно рассмотрел последние из опубликованных американцами в «Physical Review» работ по трансурановым элементам (эка-рений-239 и эка-осмий-239)[1] и смог установить новое направление в решении всей проблемы урана — Перспективы этого направления необычайно увлекательны.

§ 1

«Урановый котел» и роль трансурановых элементов

«Урановый котел» представляет собой систему из обычного урана, смешанного с каким-либо веществом, замедляющим нейтроны (простой водой, тяжелой водой или графитом). Вопрос о том, можно ли создать на этой основе (т. е. без выделения изотопов урана) «урановый котел», сейчас еще остается открытым.

Кажется почти несомненным, что, применяя простую воду в качестве замедлителя, не удастся решить задачу, но есть указания, что использование тяжелой воды приведет к положительному результату.

Предположим, что «урановый котел» создан.

Всегда допускалось, что в «урановом котле» полезным окажется лишь легкий изотоп

урана — уран-235, входящий в количестве $\frac{1}{140}$ в обычный уран. Остальной же уран — уран-238, — входящий в количестве $\frac{139}{140}$, будет бесполезным, так как попадание в него замедленного нейтрона не дает большого выделения энергии и испускания вторичных нейтронов.

Таким образом, считалось, что в «урановом котле» удастся использовать лишь $\frac{1}{140}$ часть всего заложенного в него урана.

Это заключение, однако, может оказаться совершенно неверным, если детальней проследить за теми изменениями, которые в «урановом котле» будут происходить с ураном-238.

Хотя попадание замедленного нейтрона в уран-238 и не дает большого выделения энергии и испускания вторичных нейтронов, атомное ядро урана-238 в результате попадания в него нейтрона испытывает некоторые изменения и превращается в уран-239. Этот элемент неустойчив и через 20 минут (в среднем) сам собой превращается в 93-й элемент (не существующий на Земле) — элемент, которому присвоено название эка-рений. Оказывается, что, хотя эка-рений несколько и более устойчив, чем уран-239, но также имеет малую длительность существования (в среднем около двух дней) и сам собой превращается в 94-й элемент — элемент, которому присвоено название эка-осмий.

Дальнейшие превращения эка-осмия пока не установлены, так как он в течение довольно длительного промежутка времени будет сохраняться и накапливаться в «урановом котле».

По всем существующим сейчас теоретическим представлениям попадание нейтрона в ядро эка-осмия должно сопровождаться большим выделением энергии и испусканием вторичных нейтронов, так что в этом отношении он должен быть эквивалентен урану-235. Таким образом, в «урановом котле», где «деление энергии идет сначала только за счет урана-235, будет способный к ядерному горению.

В свете этих предположений уран-238 не будет бесполезным, а, в конечном счете, будет сожжен в «котле», правда, не прямым путем, а через ряд превращений, ведущих к эка-осмию-239.

§ 2

Трансураны и урановая бомба[2]

Если в действительности эка-осмий обладает такими же свойствами, как и уран-235, его можно будет выделить из «уранового котла» и употребить в качестве материала для «эка-осмиевой» бомбы. Бомба будет сделана, следовательно, из «высшего» материала, исчезнувшего на нашей планете.

Как видно при таком решении всей проблемы отпадает необходимость разделения изотопов урана, которая используется как топливо и как взрывчатое вещество.

Заключение

Разобранные необычайные возможности, конечно, во многом еще не обоснованы. Их реализация мыслима лишь в том случае, если эка-осмий-239 действительно аналогичен урану-235 и если, кроме того, так или иначе может быть пущен в ход «урановый котел». Кроме того, развитая схема нуждается в проведении количественного учета всех деталей процесса. Эта последняя работа в ближайшее время будет мной поручена проф. Я. Б. Зельдовичу.

До сих пор в нашей стране работы по эка-рению-239 и эка-осмию-239 не проводились. Все, что известно в этом направлении, было выполнено проф. Мак-Милланом, располагавшим наиболее мощным циклотроном в мире в лаборатории проф. Лауренса (Калифорния, Беркли).

Последняя работа Мак-Миллана была напечатана в номере «Physical Review» от 15 июня 1940 г. Из данных этой статьи видно, что Мак-Миллан получил уже довольно большие количества эка-осмия-239 и в состоянии изучить его свойства.

Более поздних публикаций нет.

Мы в Союзе не сможем полностью изучить свойства этого элемента ранее середины 1944 года после восстановления и пуска наших циклотронов. (Вопрос о возможности проведения некоторых предварительных исследований еще в 1943 году будет обсужден мной с акад. Хлопиным и т. Флеровским.) Таким образом, является весьма важным узнать объем и содержание сведений в Америке о 93-м (эка-рении) и 94-м (эка-осмии) элементах.

Можно с несомненностью утверждать, что соответствующий материал имеется у проф. Мак-Миллана и, вероятно, в ряде других лабораторий, располагающих работающими циклотронными установками.

В связи с этим обращаюсь к Вам с просьбой дать указания Разведывательным Органам выяснить, что сделано в рассматриваемом направлении в Америке. Возможными точками работы могут явиться следующие:

1. Radiation Laboratory, Department of Physics, University of California, Berkely, California (здесь работает проф. Мак-Миллан).
2. Sloane Physic Laboratory, Yale University, New Haven, Connecticut.
3. University of Michigan, Ann Arbor, Michigan.
4. Pupin Physics Laboratory, Columbia University, New York, New York (здесь работает знаменитый итальянец Ферми, всегда интересовавшийся 93-м 94-м элементами.
5. University of Rochester, Rochester, New York.
6. Palmer Physical Laboratory, Princeton, New Jersey.
7. Bartol Research Foundation, the Franklin Institute Swarthmore, Pennsylvania.

Подлежат выяснению следующие вопросы:

а) происходит ли деление (fission) атомного ядра 94-го элемента (эка-осмия-239) под действием быстрых или медленных нейтронов;
б) если происходит, то каково сечение деления (отдельно для быстрых и медленных нейтронов);
в) происходит ли спонтанное (самопроизвольное) деление атомных ядер 94-го элемента (эка-осмия-239) и каков период полураспада по отношению к этому процессу;
г) какие превращения испытывает во времени 94-й элемент (эка-осмий-239).

Помимо этого, важно было бы знать, каково содержание проводившихся сейчас с циклотронными установками работ.

О написании Вам этого письма не говори никому. Соображения, изложенные в § 1, § 2, § 3 известны проф. Кикоину и проф. Алиханову.

проф. Курчатов
22.03.43 г.

Экземпляр единственный

Документ № 6

СОВ. СЕКРЕТНО

Заместителю Председателя Совета Народных Комиссаров Союза ССР
т. М. Г. Первухину

Мною рассмотрен прилагаемый к сему перечень американских работ по проблеме урана. Направляю Вам результаты этого рассмотрения и прошу Вас дать указания ознакомить с этими результатами т. Кафтанова С. В. и т. Овакимяна Г. Д.

Сведения, которые было бы желательно получить из-за границы, подчеркнуты синим карандашом.

проф. Курчатов

Экз. единств.
Москва 3.07.43

В рассмотренном перечне американских работ содержится 286 названий: 39 из них (57, 95, 125, 143, 256, 257, 258, 281, 286, 287, 288, 289, 290, 291, 292, 293, 296, 297, 317, 318, 328, 330, 367, 385, 170, 254, 259, 72, 73, 74, 75, 79, 81, 82, 83, 86, 87, 100 и 102) являются отчетами, содержание которых неизвестно; содержание 10 работ (38, 112, 118, 148, 301, 309, 315, 331, 380, 252) остается для меня мало ясным. Анализ остальных 237 работ дается ниже.
<...>

29 работ по уран-графитовому котлу

(11, 12, 21, 55, 134, 142, 232, 277, 284, 294, 305, 308, 310, 316, 342, 344, 347, 350, 351, 353, 354, 356, 357, 362, 384, 387, 390, 394, 338).

Основные результаты американских работ по уран-графитовому котлу нам известны по материалам, полученным из Америки.

Эти материалы, однако, дают лишь краткое изложение общих результатов исследования и не содержат тех важных технических подробностей, потребовавших для уточнения кропотливой работы большого количества разнообразных специалистов — физиков, химиков и инженеров:

— Fermi, Well, Anderson, Szillard, Huiban, Wigner, Wheeler, Davis, Burton, Christy, Weinberg, Howe, Yeveteil, Spedding, Newson, Sullivan, Volgi [крд] Young, Williamson, Snell, Brolley, Nedrel, Wilkins, Creatz, Summons, Gladrow, Teller.

Необходимо отметить, что в Америке по этому разделу обсуждаются детали таких вопросов (температура стенок, охлаждающих трубок, диффузия продуктов деления в уране при температуре 600—1000° и т. д.), которые характерны для технического проекта, а не отвлеченной физической схемы.

Это лишний раз убеждает в серьезности попыток американских ученых осуществить в ближайшее время подобного уран-графитовый котел.

Естественно, что получение подобного технического материала по этой системе из Америки является крайне необходимым.

14 работ по 93-му и 94-му элементам

(22, 33, 45, 68, 135, 136, 146, 151, 152, 278, 296, 306, 386, 392).

В полученных из Америки данных содержатся довольно подробные сведения о физических свойствах 93-го и 94-го элементов: указаны характер распада, энергии вылетающих частиц, период полураспада, сечение деления медленными нейтронами и ряд других данных.

Из отдаления видно, однако, что некоторые результаты работ по изучению этих элементов в полученных до сих пор материалах. Особенно интересна в этом смысле работа Сиборга и Сегре <...> посвященная изучению деления 94-го элемента нейтронами.

По своим характеристикам по отношению к действию нейтронов этот элемент подобен урану-235, для которого деление под действием быстрых нейтронов пока еще не изучено. Данные Сиборга для эка-осмия-94-239 представляют, таким образом, интерес и для проблемы осуществления бомбы из урана-235.

Получение сведений о результатах этой работы Сиборга и Сегре представляется поэтому для нас особенно важным.

Интересны попытки американских физиков обнаружить 94-й элемент в природе в урановых рудах. По всей вероятности, эти работы (146, Search for elements 94 and 93 in nature, Presence of 94-239 in Pitchblende, Seaborg Pearlman 13.4.42, 228 Search for elements 94 and 93 in nature, Presence of 94-239 in [крд] Bonner, Seaborg,) привели к отрицательным результатам, но убедиться в этом было бы необходимо. В том случае, если бы на самом деле на земле сохранился 94-й элемент, можно было бы рассчитывать выделить его из руд и осуществить «эка-осмиевую» бомбу, не осуществляя ядерного котла.

Проведение работ по определению эка-осмия в рудах у нас в СССР пока невозможно, так как работ по химии 93-го и 94-го элементов у нас до сих пор не производилось. Лаборатория № 2 наметила начать работы по химии 93-го и 94-го элементов в июле 1943 года, поручив их Б. В. Курчатову.
<...>

To Deputy Chairman of the Council of People's Commissars of the Union SSR
Com. M. G. Pervukhin

The examination of the materials I have done shows that <u>obtaining them has immense, indeed invaluable importance for our State and science.</u>

On the one hand, the materials furnished evidence of the importance and intensity of the research work in Britain on the uranium problem; on the other, they provided a chance to obtain most important guidelines for our own research, enabling us to bypass many very labor-consuming stages of the problem's development and to learn about new scientific and technological ways of tackling it.

Below please find deliberations on individual parts of the materials.

I. Separation of Isotopes

The most valuable part of the materials relates to the task of isotope separation.

1. Adopted as the only rational way of resolving it is the separation of isotopes with the help of diffusion through a fine-holed membrane. The preference of the diffusion method to the centrifuge method has come as a surprise to our physicists and chemists. Common here was the view whereby the potential of the centrifuge method is by far superior to that of the diffusion method, which was considered practically inapplicable for the separation of heavy metals isotopes. In conformity with that point of view, only research with the use of the centrifuge (Lange method)[1] was envisaged at the initial stage of the effort regarding the uranium problem.

The materials have prompted us, alongside the centrifuge method, to also include the diffusion separation method in our research schedule.

The theoretical provisions outlined in the materials on separation through diffusion are a manifestation of profound research work, including a detailed examination of all the units of the machine proposed by Simon.[2] The materials contain calculations of:

a) the number of stages of the machine; b) the size of the working surfaces of the grids through which diffusion takes place; c) velocities and dimensions of the rotor of the centrifugal gas blower; d) the time frame for the establishment of the necessary equilibrium in the machine; e) the ratio of the circulating gas stream to the outgoing stream, and a number of other parameters. All of this major work is yet to be corroborated by our theoretical scientists, but, so far as I can judge, it must have been carried out by a group of prominent scientists who based their profound and formidable calculations on explicit physical premises. These calculations and other data contained in the materials hold out the promise of completely re-creating the layout of the machine and the plant (it will be submitted to you at a later date). Upon verification (and the reconstruction of part of the theoretical calculations in the materials) by Soviet theoretical scientists, it is conceivable that we, too, will develop a model of an installation for the separation of isotopes by way of diffusion. <u>In this way, the data contained in the materials provide for bypassing an initial stage in launching here in the Soviet Union a new and vastly important direction of work on the problem of isotope separation.</u>

Besides calculations on isotope separation by diffusion methods, the materials contain some experimental data and information about a work plan on manufacturing the machines and designing the plant. In that regard the information is less systematic, and it would be desirable to obtain additional data.

It would be very important to learn:

1) What clearances are allowed between the moving and nonmoving parts of the machine in the following units:

a) between the rotor impeller and the partition, dividing individual stages of the machine (a1 on drawing 1);

b) between the shaft of the rotor and the edge of the partition (a2 on drawing 2);

c) between the wall of the rotor and the edge of the baffle plate (a3 on drawing 2).

2) What material is used for the grids on the model.

3) What is the thickness of these grids, the size of the holes, and the ratio of the area of the holes to that of the entire grid.

4) Have lubricants been found resistant to UF6 and what are they?

5) Has any better solution been found to the problem of lubrication than the bringing of the shaft out through the labyrinth gland to a bearing which is in an atmosphere free of UF6 with the blowing of inert gas through the gland to the machine. If there is no such solution, it would be important to obtain more detailed information on the design of the labyrinth gland.

2. The materials contain a brief analysis of the applicability of the thermodiffusion method, the centrifuge method, the mass spectrography method, and the evaporation method for uranium isotope separation:

a) the thermodiffusion method is considered to be of little effect because of major power intensity. This conclusion is corroborated by calculations of Prof. Ya. B. Zeldovich,[3] executed on our instructions in March 1943;

b) the centrifuge method is considered hardly suitable for the separation of major quantities of uranium 235 due to the need for building plants of high circumferential velocities of rotation. This assumption may be contested; a final conclusion can be drawn after studying the equipment being currently developed by researchers at Prof. Lange's laboratory;

c) the mass spectrography method and the method of isotope separation through evaporation are likewise considered inapplicable to uranium. The correctness of this view is being ascertained by laboratory researchers Prof. Artsimovich and Prof. Kornfeld.[3]

II. The Problem of Nuclear Explosion and Combustion
Data relating to this part of the materials are also of substantial interest.

This relates primarily to the claim, contained in the materials, about the feasibility of effecting nuclear combustion in a mixture of ordinary uranium oxide (or metallic uranium) and heavy water. That, too, is unexpected for Soviet physicists and runs counter to the accepted point of view.

We have considered it proven that without isotope separation it is impossible to achieve nuclear combustion in a mixture with heavy water. That conclusion was based on calculations of Prof. Yu. B. Khariton[3] and Prof. Ya. B. Zeldovich, who in their theory showed that the development of a chain reaction in the mixture of uranium and heavy water requires that the cross section of the capture of thermal neutrons by nuclei of heavy hydrogen is not in excess of 3×10^{-27} cm^2.

Not a single physicist in the Soviet Union (due to the absence of relevant technological facilities — powerful cyclotrons and major quantities of heavy water) has determined the above-mentioned cross section, and, in the course of reviewing and analyzing this entire problem, we applied the magnitudes of cross sections as determined by the American researchers Alvarez, Burst, and Harkins in their research into the radioactive disintegration of the hydrogen isotope with the mass of 3. According to data by Alvarez, Burst, and Harkins, the value of appr. 10^{-26} cm^2 was envisaged for the cross section of the absorption of low-velocity neutrons by heavy hydrogen, i.e., greater than the limit which, according to calculations by Prof. Yu. B. Khariton and Prof. Ya. B. Zeldovich, could still provide for the development of a chain reaction. In this way we came to the conclusion that a reaction was impossible to achieve in a mixture of uranium and heavy water.

As is evident from the materials, on the basis of direct experiments with major quantities (180 kg) of heavy water, including the entire world reserves (for 1939) of this substance, Halban and Kowarski[2] came to an opposite conclusion, which of course has tremendous fundamental importance. Halban and Kowarski have, according to the materials, achieved the formation of 1.05–1.06 secondary neutrons per a single primary neutron, i.e., have materialized the conditions of a progressive chain process.

We see that the conclusions drawn by Soviet physicists about the properties of the uranium–heavy water system are in glaring contradiction to the conclusions of Halban and Kowarski, and it should be said that Halban and Kowarski have all the advantages of a direct experiment as compared to calculations, which also contained a number of intermediary links.

For technical reasons we are unable to re-create the experiment of Halban and Kowarski, since the Soviet Union possesses a mere 2–3 kg of heavy water, and alternative ways are therefore necessary to corroborate the absolute credibility of the conclusions drawn abroad.

The materials point out that Halban and Kowarski intended to continue their experiments with still greater amounts of heavy water in America, where allegedly the production of this substance has in recent years been streamlined in major quantities and on a very large scale.

The re-creation of experiments with still greater quantities of heavy water is of course essential, since the formation in the system of 1.05–1.06 neutrons per one primary neutron is very close to the threshold value (1), at which a chain reaction is altogether impossible. During a transfer to major quantities of heavy water the diffusion of neutrons from the system is going to be hampered, the ratio of the number of secondary neutrons to the number of primary neutrons should increase, and the results of the experiment should be more convincing.

It would therefore be highly important to find out whether Halban and/or Kowarski traveled from Britain to America (in 1941–1942) and whether they conducted experiments with uranium in a laboratory with major reserves of heavy water. It would be very important to learn, if experiments of this kind have indeed been conducted in America, what quantities of uranium and heavy water were used in them and what was the ratio of the number of secondary neutrons to the number of primary ones.

All the studies conducted and publicized so far of uranium-moderating substance systems have been carried out with homogeneous mixtures of these components (most often with water solutions of uranium salts or with suspensions in water of minute particles of its oxide). It is conceivable that lower requirements to the cross section of the thermal neutrons capture by heavy hydrogen and oxygen will occur in the event the system is not homogeneous and the uranium will be concentrated inside a mass of heavy water in blocs of acceptable size, positioned at some optimal distance from each other.

It would therefore be important to learn: 1) what form of a uranium–heavy water system — homogeneous (with dispersed distribution of uranium) or nonhomogeneous (with blocs-concentrated distribution of uranium) — has been found more rational; and 2) what form of system — homogeneous or nonhomogeneous — were experiments in America conducted with.

The materials say that Halban and Kowarski have taken 7 patents related to the uranium–heavy water system, and it is conceivable that some of them deal with issues of the distribution of uranium. That is why it would be important to find out the contents of Halban's and Kowarski's above-mentioned patents.

Besides, I believe it necessary to carry out with the help of our Soviet scientists a theoretical analysis of comparative properties of homogeneous and nonhomogeneous mixtures of uranium and heavy water and am planning to entrust the execution of this analysis to Prof. Yu. B. Khariton and Prof. Ya. B. Zeldovich.

As mentioned above, on the basis of works published by the American physicists Alvarez, Burst, and Harkins, the cross section of the absorption of low-velocity thermal neutrons by nuclei of the heavy isotope of hydrogen turns out to be equal to appr. 10^{-26} cm^2. The experiments were conducted by Alvarez, Burst, and Harkins in 1940–1941, published in the form of Letters to the Editor in the "Physical Review" magazine, and contain a number of assumptions whose legitimacy could be made clear only by reviewing all the details of the work. Most probably the American physicists have in recent years been continuing their work on the absorption of low-velocity neutrons by heavy hydrogen and oxygen, and it would therefore be important to find out the value, accepted in America currently, of the cross section of the absorption of low-velocity thermal neutrons by heavy hydrogen and oxygen[4] and to have even the minimum of information about how the latest, most accurate specifications of these values were reached.

With regard to materials devoted to the problem of the nuclear explosion and combustion, besides examining data on the uranium–heavy water system, they also contain important remarks on the use as material for a bomb of an element with the mass number 239, which should be formed in the "uranium pile" as a result of the absorption of neutrons by uranium 238. I have previously scrutinized the issue and described the analysis in a special letter in your name.[5]

A great deal of attention is paid in the materials to the physical processes that are to take place in the uranium bomb. The conclusions contained in the materials are generally in accord with the calculations that were carried out on the matter by our scientists.

III. Physics of the Fission Process

In this regard there is hardly any fundamentally new information for Soviet physicists, but some of the data cited deserve a closer look.

1. It was very important for us to learn that Frisch confirmed the phenomenon, discovered by the Soviet physicists G. N. Flyorov and K. A. Petrac, of spontaneous fission of uranium, a phenomenon which can in the mass of uranium create initial neutrons leading to the emergence of an avalanche process. Due to this phenomenon it is impossible, until the very moment of explosion, to keep the entire bomb charge of uranium in one place. Uranium should be divided into two parts which at the moment of explosion should be brought together at a high relative velocity. This way of activating the uranium bomb is reviewed in the materials and is likewise not new to Soviet physicists. A similar method was proposed by our physicist G. N. Flyorov; he calculated the necessary approach velocity of the two halves of the bomb, and the results obtained are in perfect agreement with those cited in the materials.

2. The materials contain data on the number of secondary neutrons (2–3) per fission and, in addition, attached to one of the reports is a curve, belonging to Chadwick, for the distribution of secondary neutrons by energy values. The materials, however, contain no indication of which isotope of uranium (uranium 235 or uranium 238) these data and the Chadwick curve bear on. Nor is it clear whether these experiments were conducted with high- or low-velocity neutrons. In the event the data relate to the fission of atomic nuclei of uranium 235 with low-velocity thermal neutrons, they alter nothing in the much-publicized picture of the release of secondary neutrons.

Published in 1939 and 1940, works by Joliot, Halban, and Kowarski in France; Anderson, Fermi, Zinn, and Szilard in America; as well as some research conducted in my laboratory, yield the same values of the number of secondary neutrons per fission and approximately the same general picture of their distribution by energy values. If, however, the data of the materials on the release of secondary neutrons relate to uranium nuclei fission by high-velocity neutrons, they have a vast significance, since I know of no indisputable serious work on the matter. It is therefore important to ascertain whether the data, contained in the materials on the number and energy distribution of secondary neutrons, relate to low- or high-velocity neutrons, and to obtain at least brief data on the execution of the experiments. Besides, it would be of substance to receive fresh data on the matter, which is of cardinal importance to the entire problem.

3. The determination of the minimal size of the bomb of uranium 235 requires, besides data on the number and energy of secondary neutrons, information on the cross section of the fission of uranium 235 ⟨. . .⟩ nuclei by neutrons in the interval of 0.1–10 million electronvolts.

On the experimental side, the question of cross sections of the fission has been studied only for a fairly small region of the energy of neutrons while, according to theory, the possible dependance of ⟨. . .⟩ on the energy of neutrons in the entire region of energy is represented by the curves a and b on drawing 3. The curves in drawing 3 are plotted in logarithmic coordinates.

The materials contain indications that measurements of ⟨. . .⟩ were made in the interval of energy from 200 to 800 kev. At that values were obtained $(2–3.10^{-24}$ $cm^2)$, lying on the red path on drawing 3 (circles on this drawing).

As is evident from the drawing, one of the two theoretical options can in this way be singularly determined, which is of vast importance for estimating the size of the bomb. It would be extremely important to obtain more detailed information on staging experiments toward the determination of ⟨. . .⟩ for uranium 235.

As the materials state, research in the course of which the above-mentioned results were obtained, was conducted with ordinary uranium, but the materials also reported about an intention to repeat it on a compound of separated uranium 235 which was to be prepared by Prof. Neer in America. There is every reason to believe that experiments on a compound of pure uranium 235 have by now been carried out and it is critical to be advised of the obtained values of the fission cross section of ⟨. . .⟩ for the entire energy interval.

Considering the fact that in this refined research mistakes are often committed in calculating the final results from the data of measurements, it would be very desirable to obtain, besides the final results, also at least the most cursory information on staging the experiment which, in particular, would report on which nuclear reactions were employed in these experiments for neutron generation.

Conclusion
The materials, as shown above, compel us to review our notions with regard to many aspects of the problem and set forth three directions of work which are new for Soviet physics.

1. Separation of the uranium 235 isotope through diffusion.
2. Execution of nuclear combustion in the uranium–heavy water mixture.
3. Study of the properties of EkaOs238/94.[6]

It should be pointed out in conclusion that the overall mass of data contained in the materials points to the technical feasibility of the entire uranium problem being resolved much sooner than our scientists believe, who are not familiar with the progress of work on the problem carried out abroad.

Naturally, the question arises whether the materials obtained reflect the real progress of research in Britain, and are not a contrivance designed to mislead our research. This question has particular significance for us because with regard to many important spheres of work (due to the absence of the technological base) we are so far unable to verify data contained in the materials.

A close scrutiny of the materials suggests that it does reflect the real state of affairs.

Some of the conclusions, even on very important aspects of the work, seem dubious to me, others poorly substantiated, but responsible for that are British researchers, but not reliability of the information.

This letter will be handed over to you by your aide A. I. Vasin, who also holds draft notes for it which are to be destroyed.

The contents of the letter cannot so far be known to anybody but him.

Moscow   Head of laboratory
March 7, 1943   Professor Kurchatov

Document No. 5

To Deputy Chairman of the Council of People's Commissars of the Union SSR
Com. M. G. Pervukhin

The materials which I have had an opportunity to examine lately contain fragmented remarks on the possibility of using not only uranium 235 but also uranium 238 in the "uranium pile." In addition, it is claimed that products of combustion of the nuclear fuel in the "uranium pile" may perhaps be used instead of uranium 235 as material for the bomb.

With those remarks in mind, I have closely studied the latest of the works, published by Americans in the "Physical Review," on transuranium elements (eka-rhenium 239 and eka-osmium 239)[1] and have been able to establish a new direction in tackling the entire uranium problem — a direction conditioned by the peculiarities of transuranium elements.

The prospects of this direction are unusually captivating.

§1
The "Uranium Pile" and the Role of Transuranium Elements

[. . . .]

§2
Transuraniums and the Uranium Bomb[2]

[. . . .]

Conclusion

The unusual possibilities reviewed above are of course in many ways unsubstantiated. Their realization is only feasible in the event eka-osmium 239 is indeed analogous to uranium 235 and, in addition, in the event the "uranium pile" can in this or that way be rendered operational.

Besides, a ramified scheme is in need of a quantitative accounting of all the details of the process. I intend to charge Prof. Ya. B. Zeldovich with this latter job in the near future.

No research into eka-rhenium 239 or eka-osmium 239 has been carried out in our country so far. Everything that is known in this regard has been accomplished by Prof. McMillan, who was in command of the world's largest cyclotron, at Prof. Lawrence's laboratory (Berkeley, California).[3]

McMillan's latest work was published in the "Physical Review" of June 15, 1940. It is evident from the data contained in the article that McMillan has obtained fairly large quantities of eka-osmium 239 and is in a position to study its properties.

There are no more recent publications on this score.

We in the Soviet Union will not be able to study the properties of this element in earnest before the middle of 1944, after our cyclotrons are rebuilt and put into operation. (I intend to discuss the possibility of carrying out some preliminary research as soon as 1943 with Acad. Khlopin and Com. Flyorov.)[4] The main point is the need to learn about the quantity and contents of data in America about the 93rd (eka-rhenium) and 94th (eka-osmium) elements.

It can be contended without a shade of doubt that relevant materials are available to Prof. McMillan and are probably possessed by a number of other laboratories that have operating cyclotron units.

In this connection I am asking you to instruct Intelligence Bodies to find out about what has been done in America in regard to the direction in question. Possible locations of the work may include the following:[5]

1. Radiation Laboratory, Department of Physics, University of California, Berkeley, California (Prof. McMillan works here).

2. Sloane Physics Laboratory, Yale University, New Haven, Connecticut.

3. University of Michigan, Ann Arbor, Michigan.

4. Pupin Physics Laboratory, Columbia University, New York, New York (the famous Italian Fermi works here, who has always been interested in elements 93 and 94).

5. University of Rochester, Rochester, New York.

6. Palmer Physical Laboratory, Princeton, New Jersey.

7. Bartol Research Foundation, the Franklin Institute, Swarthmore, Pennsylvania.

The following questions need to be cleared:

a) does fission of the atomic nucleus of the element 94 (eka-osmium 239) take place under the impact of high- or low-velocity neutrons;

b) if so, what is the cross section of the fission (separately for high-velocity and low-velocity neutrons);

c) does spontaneous fission of atomic nuclei of element 94 (eka-osmium 239) take place and what is its half-life in relation to this process;

d) what transformations in time does element 94 (eka-osmium 239) undergo.

Besides this, it would be important to know about the contents of work being carried out currently with cyclotron plants.

I have informed no one about writing this letter to you. Ideas put forth in §1, §2 and §3 [sic] are familiar to Prof. Kikoin and Prof. Alikhanov.[6]

Prof. Kurchatov
March 22, 1943

Only copy

Document No. 6

To Deputy Chairman of the Council of People's Commissars of the Union SSR
Com. M. G. Pervukhin

I have reviewed the list, enclosed, of American works on the uranium problem.

I am forwarding the results of this scrutiny to you and asking for your instructions that S. V. Kaftanov and G. B. Ovakimian be advised of these results.

Underlined in blue pencil are data that it would be desirable to obtain from abroad.

Prof. Kurchatov

Only copy
Moscow, July 3, 1943

The list of American works examined by me includes 286 titles: 39 of them (57, 95, 125, 143, 256, 257, 258, 281, 286, 287, 288, 289, 290, 291, 292, 293, 296, 297, 317, 318, 328, 330, 367, 385, 170, 254, 259, 72, 73, 74, 75, 79, 81, 82, 83, 86, 87, 100 and 102) are reports whose contents are unknown; the contents of 10 works (38, 112, 118, 148, 301, 309, 315, 331, 380, 252) remain not very clear to me. An analysis of the remaining 237 works is offered below. ⟨. . .⟩

29 works on the uranium-graphite pile

(11, 12, 21, [. . .] 390, 394, 338.)

The principal results of American works on the uranium-graphite pile are familiar to us from materials received from America.

These materials, however, provide only a brief outline of the overall results of the research and do not contain very important technical details; more precise definition requires painstaking work of a great number of various specialists — physicists, chemists and engineers:

Fermi, Weil, Szilard, Halban, Wigner, Wheeler, Davis, Burton, Christy, Weinberg, Howe, Everett, Spedding, Newton, Sullivan, Voigt, [unclear], Young, Williamson, Snell, Brolley, Nedrel, Wilkins, Creatz, Gladrow, Teller.[1]

It must be noted that with regard to this sphere of the work in America, details of such questions are being discussed (temperature of the walls of cooling tubes, the diffusion of uranium fission products at temperatures of 600–1000 degrees) as are characteristic of a technological project, rather than an abstract physical notion.

That goes to prove once again that attempts by American researchers are very serious to execute a uranium-graphite pile in the near future.

Naturally, the acquisition of detailed technical information from America with regard to this system is necessary in the extreme.

14 works on elements 93 and 94

(22, 33, 45, [. . .] 306, 386, 392.)

The data received from America contain fairly detailed information on the physical properties of elements 93 and 94; described are the character of the disintegration, the energy of outgoing particles, the half-value period, the cross section of fission with low-velocity neutrons, and a number of other data.

The list of contents shows, however, that some of the results of research into these elements are not covered in the materials obtained thus far. Of particular interest in this regard is the work by Seaborg and Segre[2] ⟨. . .⟩ devoted to the fission of element 94 eka-osmium with high-velocity neutrons. [. . .]

Information on the results of this work by Seaborg and Segre is therefore of particular importance to us.

Also of interest are attempts by American physicists to discover the element 94 in nature in uranium ores. Most probably these efforts [. . .] have yielded negative results, but it should be necessary to get confirmation of that. In the event element 94 was indeed preserved on Earth, we could count on separating it from ores and build the "eka-osmium" bomb without having to execute the nuclear pile.

Similar efforts to spot eka-osmium in ores here in the USSR are impossible for the time being, since no research into the chemistry of elements 93 or 94 has been conducted here so far. Laboratory No. 2 has set itself the task of launching research into the chemistry of elements 93 and 94 in July 1943, and charged B. V. Kurchatov with carrying it out.[3] ⟨. . .⟩

The contents show that research into the uranium problem has received a powerful impetus in America.

Americans have lately been very reluctant about reporting their data to Britain, their volume of work being incomparably greater than in Britain. That is why the exchange of information yields little to America in technical terms, but leads to the divulgence of secrets.

Since quite a few foreigners are working in Britain on the uranium problem, and since the Americans fear that after the war the results of the work will be reported by those foreign scientists to their Governments, the Americans see a loss rather than any gain from their participation.

It is evident from the information above that here in the Soviet Union research into the uranium problem (of course, on a scale that is far from sufficient) has been conducted in most of the directions along which it has been developing in America, too.

But with regard to two directions
1) uranium–heavy water pile[4]
2) separation of uranium isotopes through electrolysis
work in the Soviet Union has not been started.

I believe it would be expedient to launch work in both these directions and, in my view, the first of them requires serious attention.

The execution of the uranium–heavy water pile is somewhat more complicated than the execution of a pile of a mixture of uranium with carbon, since that requires mastering the production, which is new to us, of heavy water in very big quantities (several tons). Besides, the uranium–heavy water pile does not permit a very great increase in temperature, and its work will be further complicated by the disintegration of water under the impact of radiation.

However, this system at the same time possesses one very important advantage over the uranium-graphite pile. It requires for its execution not 50, but 1–2 tons of uranium, an amount we will have already in 1943, while the time it will take for our country to accumulate 50 tons of uranium seems absolutely unclear at this stage.

The latter of the above-mentioned directions probably does not offer extensive prospects, but, in my view, research into the separation of uranium isotopes through electrolysis should still be launched here with the help of researchers whose efforts cannot be utilized in other directions of work on the uranium problem.

July 4, 1943
Moscow

Document No. 7

NK-4	**TOP SECRET**
USSR	<u>Copy No. 1</u>
PEOPLE'S COMMISSARIAT	
FOR STATE SECURITY	
February 28, 1945	
No. 1103/M	

To The People's Commissar of the Interior of the Union SSR
Comrade L. P. Beria

NKGB USSR presents intelligence information herein on the progress of work toward the creation of an atomic bomb of great destructive power:

Research carried out by leading scientists of Britain and the USA on the utilization of inner atomic energy for the creation of an atomic bomb has shown that this type of weapon should be considered practicable, and that the problem of building the bomb is at the present time confined to two main tasks:

1. The production of the necessary amount of fissionable elements, uranium 235 and plutonium.

2. The development of a system of activating the bomb.

In accordance with these tasks the following centers have been set up in the USA:

1. a) Camp 1, also known as Camp X, in Oak Ridge, 35 km from Knoxville, Tennessee. The construction of a plant is under way there for the production of uranium 235. Two billion dollars has been allocated on the construction of the plant, and about 130,000 people are employed. The overall supervision of the construction of the plant has been delegated to Kellex company, a specially set up subsidiary of

the well-known New York–based design company M. V. Kellog. The contract for the construction has been granted to the Jones Construction company; besides, other prominent companies have been involved: Du Pont, Carbide and Carbon Chemical Co. All the work on the construction of the plant has been given the code name of Clinton Engineering Works.

Under the plan the first phase of construction is to be completed in 1945. Overall, the construction will take about 3 years.

b) Camp W, near Hanford, Washington, on the Columbia River. An installation belonging to the Du Pont company there produces element 94, or plutonium.

2. Camp 2, or Camp Y, is situated in the township of Los Alamos, 70 km northeast of the small city of Santa Fe, New Mexico. The camp is managed directly by the War Ministry. Research and experimental work is conducted here on the development of the bomb itself. Camp 2 is isolated from the outside world. It is situated in a deserted locality, on top of a mountain plateau. Close to 2,000 people live in the camp, surrounded by a wire fence and having a special security system. The people have good living conditions: comfortable apartments, sporting grounds, a swimming pool, a community club, etc. Mail communication with the outside world is under control. Employees are allowed to leave the camp only on special permission of the military authorities. There are several proving ranges around the camp, the closest of them being Anchor Ranch, 5 miles from Los Alamos.

The latest research data on the effectiveness of the atomic bomb contribute to a new notion of the scale of destruction. According to calculations, the energy of an atomic bomb weighing close to 3 tons is to be equivalent to the energy of 2,000–10,000 tons of conventional explosives. It is believed that the explosion of an atomic bomb will be accompanied by not only the formation of an air shock, but also by high temperatures and a powerful radioactive effect, and that, as a result, everything living within the radius of 1 km will be destroyed.

Two ways of activating the atomic bomb are being developed:

1. The ballistic method and
2. The implosion method.

No time frame of any certainty is available for the production of the first bomb, since research or design work has not yet been completed. It is suggested that the production of such a bomb will require one year at least and 5 years at the most.

As for bombs of a somewhat smaller capacity, it is reported that within a mere few weeks one can expect the production of one or two bombs, for which Americans already have the necessary amount of the active substance. This bomb will not be so effective, but it will still have practical significance as a new type of arms, by far superior to existing ones in its effectiveness. The first experimental "combat" explosion is expected in 2 or 3 months.

In connection with the overall problem of the utilization of intranuclear energy of uranium, the question of the availability and scale of uranium ore deposits in each of the countries acquires a particularly important role.

We are in possession of the following data on the issue:

The principal deposits of uranium ore are situated in the Belgian Congo, Canada, Czechoslovakia, Australia, and Madagascar.

Canadian ore is being mined by the Canadian Radio and Uranium Corp. in Port Hope, Ontario, and has been used by both the British and the Americans. There was an intention on the part of the Canadian government to nationalize uranium mines. But Americans blocked the move by having taken over Canadian mines, even though they are largely depleted by now.

Americans have in addition secured unlimited control over the mining of uranium ores in the Belgian Congo. The position of the British in the Belgian Congo is much weaker, since the industrial elite of that colony are leaning toward the Americans and are disposed in a separatist way, stating their case in favor of secession as an independent state.

Deposits of uranium ore in Czechoslovakia are situated in the Sudeten region, in the vicinity of Joachimstahl on the southern slopes of Erzgebirge, 20 km north of Carlsbad.

According to our intelligence data, the British allegedly intended to conclude an agreement with the Czechoslovak government in London on developing these deposits.

PEOPLE'S COMMISSAR OF STATE
SECURITY OF THE UNION SSR
(V. MERKULOV)

Document No. 8

TOP SECRET

Report on Materials Accompanying Document No. 1/3/3920

of March 5, 1945, from the "Atomic Bomb" Section of the Report.

The materials pose a great deal of interest: alongside methods and schemes developed by us it also points to potentialities that have not been reviewed here so far. These include: 1) the utilization of uranium-hydride 235 instead of metallic uranium 235 as the explosive in the atomic bomb; 2) the use of implosion for activating the bomb.

I

The utilization of uranium-hydride 235 instead of uranium 235, as the materials suggest, is based on a great degree of probability of the absorption of low-velocity neutrons by uranium, which provides for diminishing the critical mass. The introduction of hydrogen, however, retards the entire process and may drag it out to impermissibly long periods of time. Besides, because of the low density of the substance, the critical mass needs to be increased. Therefore, it is far from obvious that the use of uranium-hydride instead of uranium will yield that significant (almost 20-fold) gain with regard to the mass, which the materials suggest.

The proposal in question can only be gauged after a stringent theoretical scrutiny of the matter.[. . .]

It seems exceptionally important to establish whether the system described was studied through calculation or by way of an experiment. If the latter, that would mean that the atomic bomb has already been executed and that uranium 235 has been separated in major quantities. The materials contain a remark that seems to suggest that. In describing the implosion method it is pointed out that no experiments have yet been carried out with active material, but they are to be staged within months.

In light of the above, the top-priority task of exceptional importance is to obtain several tens of grams of uranium, strongly enriched with uranium 235 from laboratories, whose materials are being studied here.

II

The implosion method makes use of the phenomenal phenomena [probably "pressures" — tr.] and velocities that emerge during an explosion. The materials indicate that this method provides for increasing the relative velocity of particles to 10,000 meters per second if pressure symmetry is ensured and that, consequently, this method should be preferred to the "discharge" method. It is difficult to give such a conclusion a final assessment, but the implosion method is undoubtedly of immense interest, is fundamentally correct, and should be subjected to close scrutiny both theoretically and experimentally.

The materials contain stimulating remarks with regard to the insulation substance for the atomic bomb. They are in conformity with the views that have also been widespread here in recent time. Our designs also suggest the use of beryllium for insulation, though in its metal form, and not an oxide, which is what the materials propose.

(signature) KURCHATOV
March 16, 1945

Document No. 9

TOP SECRET

Report on Materials to Letter No. 1/3/2382 of February 7, 1945

⟨. . .⟩

The materials contain general ideas with regard to the uranium-graphite pile, which view uranium hexafluoride as the cooling medium. (Materials received earlier contained some data on this system.)

The uranium-graphite pile, incorporating a mass of graphite and tubes of uranium, through which liquid uranium hexafluoride flows, as the materials quite correctly suggest, possesses a number of advantages over other designs of uranium-graphite piles.

In particular, the task of separating plutonium is rendered much easier in this system, and requirements to the cooling system are greatly simplified. Satisfactory cooling can be achieved at velocities of the flow of liquid uranium hexafluoride through the pipes at a mere 1.5 meters per second. The basic drawback of the new system is the great amount of uranium required, 250 tons, compared to 50 tons required by other systems using these piles.

(signature) KURCHATOV
March 16, 1945

Document No. 10

TOP SECRET

Preliminary Report on Materials Accompanying Document No. 1/3/6134
of April 6, 1945

The materials are of great value. They contain data: 1) on atomic characteristics of the nuclear explosive; 2) on details of the implosion method of activating the atomic bomb; 3) on the electromagnetic method of uranium isotope separation.

I. Atomic Characteristics of the Nuclear Explosive
Of exceptional importance in this section are data on the spontaneous fission of heavy nuclei, containing a confirmation of a report received earlier on a lesser probability of the spontaneous fission of uranium 235 in comparison with uranium 238. The probability of this process in the case of plutonium 240 is strikingly high.

The table, giving the values of the number of fission neutrons per fission, does not specify whether $v = 2.47$ for uranium 235 was obtained for fission with high- or low-velocity neutrons. Nor is there the v value for uranium 238 fission with high-velocity neutrons.

It would be important to obtain additional data on these issues.

§6 of this section provides a table of vast importance, giving the magnitudes of the cross section of the fission of uranium 235 and plutonium 239 with high-velocity neutrons of various energies. This table of precise values of the cross section provides for dependably defining the critical dimensions of the atomic bomb. It is only thanks to this that it is possible to recognize that the formula for the critical radius (p. 4) can indeed be correct with the accuracy of up to 2 percent as the text suggests. [. . .]

II. Details of the Implosion Method of Activating the Bomb
The biggest in volume, this section of the materials describes the implosion method of activating the bomb, which we found out about only recently and are just starting to work on.

However, we have already realized all of its advantages in comparison to the collision discharge.

The materials received provide: 1) a diagram whereby the propagation of the detonation wave in the explosive and the deformation of the insulation material can be viewed; 2) a description of the compression of the body by the implosion and of the implosion itself.

All these are very valuable data, but of particular substance are indications with regard to conditions conducive to achieving symmetry of the implosion effect, which is crucial to the very essence of the method.

Described are interesting phenomena of the irregular impact of the air shock. Very valuable are indications that these irregularities of impact can be done away with by proper positioning of the detonators and the use of interlayers of explosives of various effects.

The same section of the materials explores important issues of experimental technology involving explosives and the optics of implosion [explosion? — tr.] phenomena.

Considering the fact that research into this method has not made any progress here, it is now impossible to formulate pertinent questions that would require additional information. That could be done later after a serious analysis of the materials in question.

I would consider it necessary to show the relevant text (from p. 6 to the end with the exception of p. 22) to Prof. Yu. B. Khariton. ⟨. . .⟩

April 7, 1945   (signature) KURCHATOV
Only copy

Document No. 11

TOP SECRET

Report on Materials Accompanying Document No. 1/3/22500
of December 25, 1944

⟨. . .⟩

II. Uranium-Graphite Pile

Reviewed are water-cooled and helium-cooled systems.

Water-Cooled System
The uranium-graphite water-cooled pile is the simplest technological form of executing the pile. We have not been developing this system so far, since we are not sure that, due to absorption in water, the multiplication factor in the system will

amount to more than one. The same uncertainty is also voiced in the materials which, moreover, point to two other technological problems related to the use of water cooling: the chemical impact of water on uranium and the dangerous mechanical tensions in uranium emerging due to big temperature gradients.

Despite all that, as the materials suggest, a blueprint of such a pile has still been developed. Under the design the pile consists of a large graphite bloc, going through which are tubes of uranium with the internal diameter of 10 mm and walls 7.5 mm thick. The water coolant circulates in the tubes.

It is evident from the materials that a decision was taken to abandon the design and the entire project of a uranium-graphite water-cooled pile. The decision was taken in August 1942 and the point of view with regard to this system could have changed in the meantime. It would be important to find out how things are today, whether work on a high-yield uranium-graphite water-cooled pile unit has been renewed and what the results of this work are.

Helium-Cooled System
There are no fundamentally new indications with regard to this system, since we have previously received more recent reports of the same laboratories, but some individual efforts are still extremely interesting. [. . .]

Certain technological details of manufacturing graphite forms for casting uranium grids for the pile and the techniques of plating uranium with a protective layer of metal should be of use to us.

Judging by the time frame, mentioned in the materials, of the deliveries of graphite and metallic uranium, it was back in late 1942 that major work was carried out on the construction of a 100,000 kilowatt helium-cooled reactor. At that, it was envisaged that the reactor could be commissioned in 1943, even though there were doubts voiced about the feasibility of the schedule. One and a half years have gone by since the time limit envisaged, and the reactor should by now be operational. It is vitally important to obtain data on the progress of work with this system.

III. Uranium–Heavy Water Pile
Calculation data are provided on the uranium–heavy water reactor. It is noted that the minimal quantity of heavy water for the pile is equal to 3–4 tons. If ordinary water is used for cooling, the necessary quantity of water should be increased and will amount to 6–8 tons with 5 percent of ordinary water in the cooling system. ⟨. . .⟩

April 11, 1945   (signature) KURCHATOV
Only copy

[Documents 12 and 13 are omitted in their entirety.]

Document No. 14

TOP SECRET
PERSONAL

To Comrade V. S. Abakumov

Materials, with which Com. Vasilevsky acquainted me today, on questions of:

a) American work on the superbomb;
b) some specific features in the work of atomic piles in Hanford seem plausible to me and present a great deal of interest for our domestic effort.

(signature) KURCHATOV

December 31, 1946
Only copy

Reference Notes

To Documents No. 1–2

Each of the two documents contains a typewritten page. Both documents are the earliest evidence of Soviet intelligence being aware of the start of extensive work abroad toward the development of the atomic bomb.

Document No. 2 has a handwritten note in the lower right-hand corner: "Reference: a copy of the extract from the translation of this report into Russian and Academician Kurchatov's comments on its value are in the 2nd volume of the intelligence file 'Enormous,' pp. 20–38." "Enormous" is the name for the file on the Soviet atomic project. Kurchatov was probably acquainted with it in early 1943 (re Document No. 4 and notes to it).

1. Vadim — alias of the head of Soviet intelligence ring in London, A. V. Gorsky.
2. Leaf — alias of Donald Maclean, a high-placed official of the British Foreign Office, who cooperated with Soviet intelligence.
3. The Uranium Committee of the British War Cabinet was, judging by Document No. 3, headed by the prominent British physicist J. P. Thomson, and coordinated work on the atomic project, code-named Tube Alloys.[. . .]
4. Imperial Chemical Industries (ICI) — Britain's biggest corporation, which was the principal industrial contractor on the British atomic project, whose directorate was headed by its representatives W. Eckers and M. Perrin.
5. Document No. 1 provides evidence of British scientists possessing a clear-cut plan toward the construction of the uranium 235 atomic bomb, which they had planned to achieve with the help of the diffusion method of separating uranium isotopes.
6. The initial estimate of the critical mass was exaggerated 2- to 8-fold.

To Document No. 3

The document consists of five typewritten pages. Page 1 carries three hand-written notes:

a) "Copy destroyed. Apr 5. Signature" (probably of deputy head of department for scientific and technical intelligence L. R. Kvasnikov, who from 1943 to 1945 was in charge of the Soviet intelligence network in New York).

b) "An accompanying document in a different version has been handed to Com. Beria for directing materials to Com. Stalin." A. A. Yatskov notes that "no copy of the 'different version' has been found in the file; it must have remained in Beria's archive."

c) "Leaf (Maclean), received in late 1941." Probably refers to the principal source, on whose information the document was compiled. The information was probably not exhausted by Documents No. 1 and No. 2.

J. P. Thomson, R. Peierls, H. Halban, L. Kowarski, F. Simon, and others mentioned in the document are prominent British physicists, some of them emigrants from France and Germany, who took an active part in the British atomic project.[. . .]

This document is one of the first instances of the official reaction of the Soviet leadership at government level to intelligence information about work on the development of the atomic bomb in the West. The choice of specialists on issues of "atomic nuclear fission," recommended in the note for consultations and for an appraisal of relevant intelligence materials, turned out to be unsuccessful[. . . .]

To Document No. 4

The document consists of 14 standard typewritten pages, authored by I. V. Kurchatov. Attached to it is a typewritten accompanying note by Deputy Chairman of the Council of People's Commissars M. G. Pervukhin [. . .] to Deputy People's Commissar of the Interior V. N. Merkulov. [. . .] The horizontal underlines, preserved in the publication, were drawn by Kurchatov.

1. [. . .] There are disparities in the initials of Lange, a researcher at the Kharkov UFTI (Ukrainian Institute of Physical and Technical Studies), who emigrated from Germany. In [some] recollections [. . .] he is referred to as K.A. [. . .] while other data have his initials as F.F. [. . .]

2. F. Simon, L. Alvarez, W. Harkins, H. Halban, L. Kowarski, O. Frisch, J. Chadwick, G. Anderson, E. Fermi, V. Zinn, L. Szilard, F. Joliot[-Curie], A. Neer — outstanding specialists in nuclear physics. [. . .]

3. Of Soviet scientists most often mentioned in the document are researchers of the Kurchatov Laboratory No. 2, Ya. B. Zeldovich, Yu. B. Khariton, and G. N. Flyorov, as well as L. A. Artsimovich, M. I. Kornfeld, and F. F. Lange. [. . .]

4. The cross section of absorption, disintegration, dispersal, etc., [. . .] is the basic magnitude for carrying out calculations of nuclear interaction and is determined by way of experiment. That is why the most oft repeated question in this and subsequent notes by Kurchatov is that of the magnitude of cross sections of the various nuclear processes.

5. A very important point, related to the idea of the utilization of element 239 (eka-osmium), which can be obtained in a uranium pile from uranium 238, for the

atomic bomb. [. . .] The materials mentioned by Kurchatov and devoted specifically to this problem are not yet known to us.

6. [. . .] These novel approaches dramatically altered the course of the Soviet program. [. . .]

To Document No. 5

The document is a note of eight handwritten pages from Kurchatov to Pervukhin. The note is written in Kurchatov's hand and contains his detailed "appraisal" of Soviet intelligence information on the British and U.S. uranium projects. . . . The fundamental significance of the document [is that] it makes clear that in resolving the problem Kurchatov was inclined to place the principal stake on the plutonium bomb and, consequently, on the uranium pile working on natural uranium.

1. Eka-rhenium 239 and eka-osmium 239 are isotopes of neptunium and plutonium, respectively. [. . .]

2. For the first time here the "course was taken" toward the "eka-osmium" (i.e., plutonium) bomb, and it was stressed that its development rendered unnecessary the entire program related to uranium isotope separation.

3. E. M. McMillan, an American physicist who in 1940 together with F. Abelson synthesized the first transuranium element neptunium 239 (eka-rhenium) and that same year together with G. Seaborg and others obtained plutonium 239 (eka-osmium).

E. Lawrence, an American physicist, winner of the Nobel Prize (for designing and improving the cyclotron).[. . .]

The fusion of these transuranium elements was achieved with the help of the then biggest cyclotron, built at Lawrence's laboratory in Berkeley.

4. V. G. Khlopin, an outstanding Soviet radiochemist, member of the Academy, since 1939 the director of the Radium Institute. Obviously, Kurchatov was referring to the institute's cyclotron, which was planned to be used for the fusion of transuraniums. Khlopin made a significant contribution to the solution of the uranium problem in the USSR, in particular, by developing the technology for the separation of plutonium from the uranium mass. [. . .]

5. Information about the laboratories, listed here, can also be gleaned from a number of books on the American atomic project (see [. . .] R. Rhodes, *The Making of the Atomic Bomb,* [New York,] 1986).

6. The list of questions, related wholly to plutonium, once again points to the planned reorientation of the entire Soviet program to the development of the "pile" and the plutonium bomb as top-priority tasks.

Alongside the already mentioned Zeldovich, Flyorov, Khariton, and others, I. K. Kikoin and A. I. Alikhanov formed the nucleus of the newly set up Laboratory No. 2. [. . .]

To Document No. 6

The document presents a fairly detailed analysis (24 pp.) of a "list of American works on the uranium problem," done by I. V. Kurchatov. As the "notes" of March 7 and 22, this document is written in his hand. Published in part.

1. Most of those on the list are prominent American specialists in nuclear physics, radiochemistry and related branches.[. . .]

2. G. Seaborg, a prominent American specialist on transuranium elements, won the 1951 Nobel Prize for chemistry for the discovery of plutonium 239.

E. Segre, a prominent Italian specialist in nuclear physics and chemistry, made a contribution to the discovery and study of plutonium 239. Won the Nobel Prize for the discovery of the antiproton (1959). [. . .]

3. Boris Vasiliyevich Kurchatov, physicist and radiochemist, author of a number of works on the physics of dielectrics, ferroelectrics, and semiconductors, and on nuclear physics and chemistry, brother of I. V. Kurchatov. Employed by Laboratory No. 2 since 1943. It was indeed under B. V. Kurchatov's management that the first laboratory (1944) and reactor (1947) quantities of plutonium were obtained and its chemical properties studied.

4. It follows from this remark that 1943, even probably its first half, saw the choice with regard to the "Uranium pile" made in favor of the uranium-graphite version. True, the choice was not yet final. Though possessing many advantages, that version required much greater quantities of uranium than the "heavy water" pile. Both these versions were reviewed by Kurchatov. [. . .]

To Document No. 7

The document makes the first mention of the implosion method[. . .]. The margins of the document carry notes, possibly made by Beria.

To Documents No. 8–11

Document No. 8 is a handwritten note by Kurchatov.

It contains two parts. The first discusses the possibility of replacing metallic uranium with uranium-hydride [. . .]. That part is also of interest because in it for the first time Kurchatov draws the conclusion (with a high degree of probability) that Americans already possess significant amounts of uranium 235 and, consequently, the atomic bomb.

The second part for the first time in Kurchatov's notes reviews the implosion method.

It also speaks of the coincidence of the American and Soviet choices with regard to the "insulation substance for the atomic bomb," namely, beryllium (or its oxide).

Document No. 9 contains an analogous conclusion, also dated March 16, 1945. Published here is only that section relating to the uranium-graphite pile. [. . .] Kurchatov notes [. . .] that this method requires 5 times more uranium than other systems of the uranium-graphite pile. [. . .]

Document No. 10 presents yet another of Kurchatov's reports. Published is the greater part of the document (everything except the concluding section, devoted to the electromagnetic method of isotope separation). Particularly worthwhile in the first section of the document ("Atomic Characteristics of the Nuclear Explosive") is the high appraisal by Kurchatov of the accurate data on cross sections of the fission of uranium 235 and plutonium 239, which provided for dependable calculation of the critical dimensions of the uranium and plutonium bombs. The second section, devoted to the implosion method, stresses the need for involving Yu. B. Khariton in the effort.

Document No. 11, which is Kurchatov's handwritten report on intelligence materials of December 1944, analyzes various materials, including works on the uranium-graphite and uranium–heavy water reactors. It is that part of the document that we are publishing. It is worth mentioning that in his reports Kurchatov tried to underscore achievements by Soviet nuclear physicists, too. In this document, discussing the calculations of the progress of reaction in the pile with the use of regulatory rods of cadmium or boron, he noted that the Americans had in these calculations been taking stock of delayed neutrons, "whose substantive regulating role was first pointed out by Prof. Khariton and Prof. Zeldovich in 1940."

To Documents No. 12–14

[Documents 12 and 13 are omitted in their entirety.]

Document No. 14 is a small handwritten note by Kurchatov. It is worth noting that [Colonel Lev] Vasilevsky is mentioned in it [. . . .]

Comments prepared by V. P. Vizgin

TECHNICAL ASPECTS OF THE AMERICAN ATOMIC BOMB PROJECT

NOTES FROM KURCHATOV'S PRIVATE ARCHIVE

These handwritten notes, the first three by Soviet physicist Igor Kurchatov and the last by Academician I. K. Kikoin, are representative documents from Kurchatov's archive in the Ministry of Atomic Energy in Moscow. They reveal the close cooperation of Kurchatov, representing the Soviet scientific establishment, with Soviet intelligence. These notes, which have been declassified and made available for a biography of Kurchatov by journalist Igor Morozov, complement the materials in Appendix Two and are published here for the first time. They indicate the high degree of scientific detail obtained by Soviet intelligence officers and their ability to provide answers needed by Kurchatov and his team to proceed with a Soviet atomic bomb.

Document 1

TOP SECRET
1944

Conclusion on "Overview of the Uranium Issue," ref. letter No. 1/3/16015 dated 16.09.44 [September 16, 1944]

The "Overview of the Uranium Issue" is an <u>excellent summary</u> of the latest data on the main theoretical and salient aspects of the issue.

Most of the data were known to us from the more detailed articles and reports received in the summer of 1944. It is necessary to point to the coincidence between the data of those reports and the overview in question. However, this overview contains two new and extremely important essential indications:

1) of the feasibility of a reactor from a mixture of regular water and metallic uranium, and

2) of the existence of radiational capture of neutrons by uranium 235 and plutonium 239, and a deviation from the i/v law in the capture of slow neutrons.

The feasibility of a reactor from a mixture of regular water and metallic uranium was ruled out earlier, because according to measurements by the British that we knew from materials we received earlier, that system's reproduction factor was equal to 0.95. Adoption of a heterogeneous system with a special setup described in the review (cores having 2.8 cm in diameter, the distance between core centers being 3.5 cm) could increase the factor to a greater-than-one value, but this can only be found out with a large quantity of metallic uranium.

So far we cannot make that experiment. Since the feasibility of a system including regular water and metallic uranium facilitates extremely the task of creating a reactor and obtaining plutonium in that way, it would be of exceptional importance to have more detailed information about the system.

Some experiments conducted at Laboratory No. 2 of the USSR Academy of Sciences might suggest that capture of neutrons by uranium 235 does not conform with the i/v law. The overview in question contains definite indications of those deviations and of the radiational capture of neutrons by uranium 235 and plutonium 239. It appears to be surprising that the radiational capture cross section of plutonium 239 reaches approximately the same values as the same isotope's fission cross section. This is in most dramatic contradiction to Bohr's theory of the fission phenomenon.

It would be important therefore to receive more detailed data on the issues, and to find out about experiments finding 3 neutrons per each fission of a plutonium atom by a thermal neutron.

There is an extremely interesting remark on page 9 of the "Overview" about studies conducted at Laboratory V to determine the various physical properties of uranium 235 and plutonium (fission, elastic and inelastic scattering) in the context of manufacturing the bomb.

It would be very useful to have information about the conduct of those studies at Laboratory V and the results obtained.

The paper in question makes no mention of the magnetic method of isolating uranium 235, while it would be extremely desirable to have detailed information about that method.

I. Kurchatov

24.XII.44 [December 24, 1944]
City of Moscow
Only copy

Document 2

In the following letter from Kurchatov's personal archive, the scientist writes about the same espionage report to which he refers in Document 11 in Appendix Two. His comments are dated April 11, 1945.

DATA FOR 1944–45   **TOP SECRET**

Conclusion on Materials with Accompanying Document No. 1/3/22500 dated 25 December 1944

A very rich and in many respects instructive material. It contains theoretically important directions, descriptions of technological processes and analysis methods, and gives an idea of the rates of work at individual laboratories and possible dates when atomic installations may be put into operation.

On the basis of tentative examination, the following is a brief account of the material and an analysis of its contents:

1. technological and chemical issues;
2. the "uranium-graphite reactor";
3. the "uranium–heavy water reactor";
4. The works of one of the laboratories in the period from March 1943 to June 1944;
5. miscellaneous works.

It will now be possible to better evaluate the method's merits and drawbacks.

On the basis of theoretical data, there are no grounds to believe that in this respect there will be any difficulties in implementing the bomb, because according to the general concept the value of D_0 should be expected to be 10^{-13} sec.

An attempt is being made to determine D_0 experimentally; however, it would be interesting to know the latest results of the work with the electron multiplier.

Note should be taken of the second study to which serious attention is given in the reports: a study of the processes caused by fast neutrons in the metallic uranium mass. We learned for the first time that they use the same methods abroad as those I used as early as in 1940, and that there are reasons to expect the development of a chain in the spherical mass of the metal with a radius of 60–70 cm. We came to the same conclusion last year judging by calculations based on my suggestion. It was very interesting for us to learn that the chain process in the mass of metallic uranium is examined by foreign laboratories too. For comparison, it would be important to obtain the papers (referred to in the reports) by Szilard and Feld, who made estimates of neutron multiplication in a mass of pure metallic uranium.

The reports contain some data relating to cross sections of neutron interaction with uranium, lead, oxygen, light and heavy hydrogen, the behavior of uranium hexafluoride in a gas discharge, the viscosity of various mixtures made up of uranium hexafluoride and other gases, the thermal properties of uranium hexafluoride and its chemical effect on various materials. All these data will be useful to us in our current work.

Pages from the personal archive of Igor Kurchatov. The two pages above are in Kurchatov's hand; the page at right is by I. K. Kikoin.

V. Miscellaneous Papers

a) Two types of reactors are examined theoretically, consisting of regular water and uranium cores enriched with uranium 235. (I will give a separate conclusion on those systems later.)

b) Descriptions are given of experiments to determine the content of uranium 235 in enriched uranium using the fragments method also developed by us for that purpose.

c) Descriptions are given of experiments to isolate uranium 234 through uranium X from a mixture of regular uranium isotopes. The role of uranium 234 in the overall spontaneous fission effect is shown to be insignificant. That is very interesting and agrees with the data on spontaneous fission for other uranium isotopes.

d) Descriptions are given of experiments to determine the cross section of plutonium fission by slow neutrons. Earlier we knew only the results of those experiments, while here they are described in detail. It is very valuable because it permits judgment about the validity of the results.

e) Descriptions are given of experiments to determine the presence of plutonium and neptunium in uranium ores. The plutonium and neptunium content is shown not to exceed 10^{-6}–10^{-7} share of percent.

f) Descriptions are given of experiments with neutrons emerging as a result of spontaneous fission. The number of neutrons is shown to be 2.6 ± 0.5 per fission. The work has been performed well, and its results agree with the data recently obtained by us using other methods.

I. Kurchatov

11.04.45 [April 11, 1945]
Only copy

Document 3

Gaik Ovakimian was the director of the American department of NKGB in 1945, after his being expelled from New York.

Only copy

To Comrade G. B. Ovakimian

The accompanying note dated April 6, 1945, came with exceptionally important material on the implosion method.

Considering that it is a special material, I ask for your permission to admit Prof. Yu. B. Khariton into the work on its translation (from the 2nd half of page 2 to the end, with the exception of page 22).

Prof. Yu. B. Khariton is engaged with the design of a uranium bomb at the laboratory and is one of our country's biggest researchers of explosive phenomena.

Until now he has not been familiarized with the materials even in Russian, and only I have orally informed him of the probability of spontaneous uranium 235 and uranium 238 fission and about the general principles of the implosion method.

I. Kurchatov

30 April 1945

Document 4

I. K. Kikoin was a physicist on Kurchatov's inner research team. This undated note gives another example of the kinds of intelligence materials provided to Soviet scientists for analysis and the inferences they were able to draw from them.

The materials dated 30.VII are <u>very interesting and important</u> because they indicated that at least part of the plant is already functioning and operating.

The text of those materials (3 pages) gives a description of a small chart showing the locations of plant buildings. The chart is pasted on a larger drawing also representing the locations of plant buildings. The description says that the small chart is a plan of the buildings not shown on the larger drawing. It says that these buildings are completely fenced off; an external description is given of what can be seen from outside. That brief description is suggestive of what it could all be about. The textual and graphic materials (especially the latter one) are <u>extremely important</u> as they give some idea of the scale of the structures. <u>Any amplification of that material would be of extreme importance and of great help.</u>

Kikoin

Only copy

FIRST AMERICAN ATOMIC BOMB TEST

LETTER TO BERIA,
JULY 10, 1945
(EXCERPT)

This letter, based on cables dated June 13 and July 4, gives details of how the bomb was built for the first American atomic test. It demonstrates how close Soviet intelligence officers in the United States were to the Manhattan Project. Its most detailed technical secrets were transmitted to Moscow before the first American atomic test explosion, which took place at Alamogordo on July 16, 1945.

Reproduced here with translation is part of the first page of the letter as it was published in *Kurier Sovietski Razvedke* (*Courier of Soviet Intelligence*), Moscow, 1991. The notation as to sources in the upper left refers to Bruno Pontecorvo (Mlad, or Youngster) and Klaus Fuchs (Charles). In the upper right, the number 361 has been crossed out and replaced by 114, an example of how documents can be reshuffled over time.

Partial first page of letter to Beria, July 10, 1945, giving details on the first American atomic bomb, soon to be tested in New Mexico. Reproduced from Kurier Sovietski Razvedke.

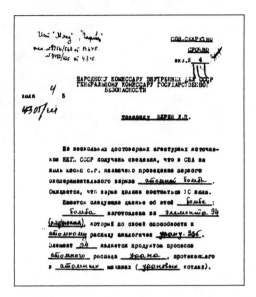

Sources: "Mlad," "Charles"

Cables numbered 18956/568 June 13, 1945
9482/625 July 4, 1945

TOP SECRET
URGENT
Copy 4
No. 114

July 10, 1945
No. 4305

People's Commissar of Internal Affairs of the USSR

Commissar General of State Security

Comrade Beria, L. P.

From several reliable agent sources NKGB USSR received data that in the USA in July this year the first experimental explosion of the atomic bomb is scheduled. It is expected that the explosion will take place on the tenth of July.

The following data is available about this bomb:

The bomb is produced from the element 94 (plutonium), which according to its susceptibility to atomic decay is similar to Uranium 235. Element 94 is the product of the process of atomic decay of Uranium which takes place in atomic reactors (uranium reactors). . . .

BASIS FOR THE KATYN FOREST MASSACRE
LETTER FROM BERIA TO STALIN, MARCH 5, 1940

This letter to Stalin reveals that Beria recommended the execution of Polish officers and other prisoners on the grounds that they were "hardened and uncompromising enemies of Soviet authority." The letter was endorsed for action with the signatures of Stalin, Kliment Voroshilov, Vyacheslav Molotov, and Anastas Mikoyan. In the margin was written "Kalinin, in favor," and "Kaganovich, in favor." The letter clears up the fifty-year-old mystery of who gave the order to massacre 25,700 Polish prisoners taken in the aftermath of the Molotov-Ribbentrop Pact.

The translation below appeared in *RFE/RL Research Report*, vol. 2, no. 4 (January 22, 1993), p. 22, and is used by permission.

TOP SECRET
5 March 1940

USSR People's Commissariat for Internal Affairs
March 1940
Moscow

To Comrade Stalin:

A large number of former officers of the Polish Army, former employees of the Polish police and intelligence agencies, members of Polish nationalist, counterrevolutionary parties, members of exposed counterrevolutionary resistance organizations, escapees, and others, all of them sworn enemies of Soviet authority [and] full of hatred for the Soviet system, are currently being held in prisoner-of-war camps of the USSR NKVD and in prisons in the western oblasts of Ukraine and Belarus [Byelorussia].

The military and police officers in the camps are attempting to continue their counterrevolutionary activities and are carrying out anti-Soviet agitation. Each of them is waiting only for his release in order to enter actively into the struggle against Soviet authority.

The organs of the NKVD in the western oblasts of Ukraine and Belarus have uncovered a number of counterrevolutionary rebel organizations. Former officers of the Polish Army and police as well as gendarmes have played an active, leading role in all of these organizations.

Among the detained escapees and violators of the state border a considerable number of people have been identified as belonging to counterrevolutionary espionage and resistance organizations.

14,736 former officers, government officials, landowners, policemen, gendarmes, prison guards, settlers in the border region [*osadniki*], and intelligence officers (more than 97% of them are Poles) are being kept in prisoner-of-war camps. This number excludes soldiers and junior officers.

They include:

Generals, colonels and lieutenant colonels—	295
Majors and captains—	2,080
Lieutenants, second lieutenants, and ensigns—	6,049
Officers and junior officers of the police, border troops, and gendarmerie—	1,030
Rank-and-file police officers, gendarmes, prison guards, and intelligence officers—	5,138
Government officials, landowners, priests, and settlers in border regions—	144

18,632 detained people are being kept in prisons in western regions of Ukraine and Belarus (10,685 of them are Poles).

They include:

Former officers—	1,207
Former intelligence officers of the police and gendarmerie—	5,141
Spies and saboteurs—	347
Former landowners, factory owners, and government officials—	465
Members of various counterrevolutionary and resistance organizations and various counterrevolutionary elements—	5,345
Escapees—	6,127

In view of the fact that all are hardened and uncompromising enemies of Soviet authority, the USSR NKVD considers it necessary:

1. To instruct the USSR NKVD that it should try before special tribunals
   1) the cases of the 14,700 former Polish officers, government officials, landowners, police officers, intelligence officers, gendarmes, settlers in border regions, and prison guards being kept in prisoner-of-war camps.
   2) and also the cases of 11,000 members of various counterrevolutionary

*First page of Beria's
March 5, 1940, letter
to Stalin proposing the
execution of Polish
prisoners. The large
underlined signature is
Stalin's. Reproduced by
permission from* RFE/
RL Research Report,
*vol. 2, no. 4 (January
22, 1993), p. 23.*

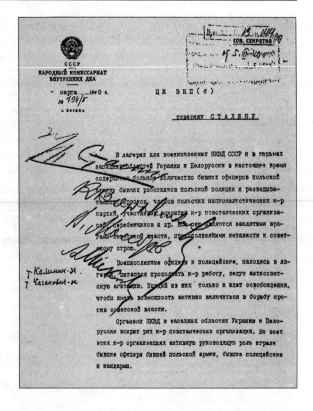

organizations of spies and saboteurs, former landowners, factory own-
ers, former Polish officers, government officials, and escapees who
have been arrested and are being held in prisons in the western oblasts
of Ukraine and Belarus and apply to them the supreme penalty:
shooting.

2. Examination of the cases is to be carried out without summoning those
detained and without bringing charges; the statements concerning the conclusion of the investigation and the final verdict [should be issued] as
follows:

    a) for persons being held in prisoner-of-war camps, in the form of certif-
icates issued by the Administration for the Affairs of Prisoners of War
of the USSR NKVD;

    b) for arrested persons, in the form of certificates issued by the NKVD of
the Ukrainian SSR and the NKVD of the Belarusian SSR.

3. The cases should be examined and the verdicts pronounced by a three-per-
son tribunal consisting of Comrades Merkulov, Kobulov, and Bashtakov.

People's Commissar for Internal Affairs of the USSR

L. Beria

REHABILITATION DOCUMENTS OF PAVEL SUDOPLATOV

APPEAL TO THE CENTRAL COMMITTEE, 1982 (EXCERPT), AND CERTIFICATE OF REHABILITATION

In 1982 Pavel Sudoplatov submitted to the Central Committee a seven-page letter outlining his career and contributions to the Soviet Union, appealing for restoration of his and Leonid Eitingon's rank, decorations, and rights. Sudoplatov was granted his document of rehabilitation, but not until the collapse of the Communist party, when verification of his account was no longer subject to political distortion. Rehabilitation documents were prized by ex-prisoners of jails and the Gulag because they restored civil rights and pensions to them and their families. It was important to rehabilitate the dead as well, because these certificates restored both reputations and family benefits. They are symbolic of the still-incomplete attempt of Russia to come to terms with the repression and crimes of Communist rule.

To: Com. Yu. V. ANDROPOV, CC CPSU POLITBURO MEMBER, CC CPSU SECRETARY; Com. K. I. CHERNENKO, CC CPSU POLITBURO MEMBER, CC CPSU SECRETARY; Com. A. Ya. PELSHE, CC CPSU POLITBURO MEMBER, CHAIRMAN, CC CPSU PCC; Com. V. V. FEDORCHUK, CHAIRMAN, USSR KGB

A Civil War participant and a CHEKA veteran appeals to you with this request for help and rehabilitation since the CC CPSU Party Control Commission has conducted its investigation and established my noncomplicity in the crimes committed by former leaders of the NKVD-MVD and the MGB of the USSR.

In 1934, after ten years of operative work, I became an undercover intelligence officer of the OGPU and, under orders from the CC CPSU, carried out abroad secret assignments of the combat nature. In 1935, I succeeded in infiltrating the leadership of the fascist Ukrainian Nationalist Organization (OUN) and had meetings with its leaders in Berlin, Vienna, Paris, Belgium, Holland, Finland, and Estonia. The party and the government appreciated my work by giving me my first Order of the Red Banner. In the same year, 1937, I received a new assignment of the Party Central Committee which involved the founder and the leader of the OUN, E. Konovalets. I arranged a secret, eye-to-eye meeting with Konovalets in a foreign country and destroyed him in May 1938; I returned home safely in July that year.

In 1939, under party orders, Eitingon and I organized a combat operation in Mexico, and carried it out successfully. While giving awards for this mission to me, Eitingon, and the Spanish woman Caridad Mercador, Com. M. I. Kalinin repeated the promise Eitingon and I had heard already at the CC CPSU headquarters: "The Party will never forget what you have done, and will help and support not only you but your families as well." . . .

At the beginning of the Great Patriotic War, following the instructions of the CC CPSU, the NKVD formed the Special Group placed under my command. The group's task was to develop a partisan (guerrilla) movement, to create a special intelligence network, to carry out acts of sabotage, and to eliminate the traitors who had deserted to the enemy. Sometimes the military command used Special Group troops in combat operations. . . . But our major objective was fighting in the enemy rear, for which we were praised by the party and the government and also by such military commanders as Comrades Rokossovsky (see his cable to the NKGB), Zhukov, and others.

Due to the expansion of the Special Group operations, it was transformed into the Fourth Directorate with special army units attached to it. . . .

While the war was still on, in addition to my work at the Fourth Directorate, I was appointed chief of a bureau at the Special Committee of the USSR Council of People's Commissars involved in atom bomb research. My duties included gathering intelligence data (on atomic secrets) and practical application at home of the information thus obtained. A separate department "S" of the USSR NKGB, which was under my command, served as the bureau's working instrument. In this capacity, I took part in the sessions of the Special Committee and in those of the Council for Science and Technology. . . .

I shall omit the details of my work in this area. It is described by Doctor of Technical Sciences, Professor N. S. Sazykin in his letter to the president of the Soviet Academy of Sciences Com. Aleksandrov and to the USSR KGB. I shall only say that Department S rendered considerable help to our scientists by giving them the latest materials on atom bomb research, obtained from such sources as the famous nuclear physicists R. Oppenheimer, E. Fermi, K. Fuchs, and others. When an accident happened at one of the Soviet nuclear projects, into which hundreds of millions of rubles had been invested, and our scientists found it difficult to repair the situation, Department S assigned one of its staff, a young physicist, to go to Denmark and meet with the world-known physicist Niels Bohr; the information he brought back enabled us to eliminate the damage, bring the facility back to normal, and thus speed up the building of the nuclear bomb. . . .

I appeal to you with the request to rehabilitate myself and Eitingon, to restore

Не буду останавливаться на подробностях этой моей работы. Они изложены доктором технических наук, профессором Сазыкиным Н.С. в письме, направленном президенту Академии Наук тов.Александрову и в КГБ СССР. Скажу лишь, что отдел "С" оказал существенную помощь нашим ученым, ознакомив их с новейшими материалами по атомной бомбе, источники – известные физики-атомщики Р.Опенгеймер, Э.Ферми, К.Фукс и др. Когда у нас, в СССР, произошла авария на одном из атомных проектов, в который вложены были уже сотни миллионов рублей и наши ученые оказались в затруднении как выправить положение, Отдел "С" послал в Данию, на встречу с всемирноизвестным физиком Нильс Бором, молодого физика, сотрудника нашего отдела и тот привез информацию, позволившую ликвидировать аварию, восстановить нужное производство и тем самым ускорить создание атомной бомбы.

В период "холодной войны", в 1946 году, когда вокруг нас стали создаваться военные базы, противники и западные державы активно поддерживали воинствующих националистов и их банды на Украине,Белоруссии и Прибалтике, по указанию ЦК КПСС, в МГБ СССР была создана СПЕЦСЛУЖБА во главе со мной. Перед нами была поставлена задача: выполнять специальные задания партии и правительства, создавать на военных базах врага агентурно-диверсионный аппарат. Во вне, Спец.служба готовила операцию против Саида Нури, одного из инициаторов Багдадского пакта, бывшего иракского премьера, проводившего реакционную проанглийскую политику. Действовать против него мы решили из Турции, для чего создали под соответствующим прикрытием наш опорный пункт во главе с полковником Волковым Н.В опытным закордонным разведчиком, успешно действовавшим в тылах фашистских войск во время войны. В тогдашней, не нейтральной Австрии тов. Е.И.Мирковский – герой Советского Союза подготовился к проведению диверсионной операции на американской военной базе. Все было готово, однако по указанию обе инстанции операции были отложены.

Оуновские бандиты, при поддержке США и Англии, погубили на Украине тысячи и тысячи советских людей, партийных, советских работников. Среди них: генерал армии тов.Ватутин, польский революционер и генерал т.Сверчевский, писатель т.Галан, священик Костельник Гавриил,сыгравший серьезную роль в воссоединении униатов с православием. ОУН готовила, но не успела осуществить тер.акты в Москве, для чего приезжала в столицу и жила в "Метрополе" оуновка Дарья Гусяк. ОУН предполагала взорвать памятник Ленину в Киеве и произвести взрывы в Полтаве на местах Полтавской битвы. ЦК КПСС потребовал применения решительных мер для пресечения деятельности украинских националистов. Мне было поручено выехать во Львов и "сосредоточиться" на розыске и уничтожении Шухевича Романа – главаря банд и националистического подполья. Шухевич настолько уверовал в свою неуловимость, что дважды, под чужой фамилией, под охраной своих голо-

A page from Sudoplatov's 1982 appeal to the Central Committee. The first paragraph outlines the atomic espionage activities of Department S.

our party membership and to return to us our military ranks and decorations, as well as to give Eitingon's widow, Yevgenia Orefjevna Puzirova, born in 1906, . . . her pension as the wife of a major general.

(signed) Pavel Anatolievich Sudoplatov

Delivered to the reception of CC CPSU, July 20, 1982

ПРОКУРАТУРА
Союза Советских
Социалистических республик

ГЛАВНАЯ
ВОЕННАЯ ПРОКУРАТУРА

· 12 , февраля 199 2 г.

№ 3-40039-55   СПРАВКА О РЕАБИЛИТАЦИИ

103160, Москва. К-160

Выдана бывшему генерал-лейтенанту НКВД-МВД СССР Судоплатову
Павлу Анатольевичу, 1907 года рождения, осужденному 12 сентября
1958г. Военной коллегией Верховного Суда СССР по обвинению в
совершении преступления, предусмотренного ст.ст.17-58-I"б" УК
РСФСР к 15 годам лишения свободы (арестован 21 августа 1953г.)
в том, что он в соответствии с п."а" ст.3 Закона Российской
Федерации "О реабилитации жертв политических репрессий" от 18
октября 1991г. реабилитирован.

ПОМОЩНИК ГЛАВНОГО ВОЕННОГО ПРОКУРОРА
полковник юстиции

Н.Л.Анисимов

Procurator
Union of Soviet Socialist Republics
Chief Military Prosecutor
12 February 1992
No. 3-40039-55
103160 Moscow. K-160

CERTIFICATE OF REHABILITATION

Issued to the former Lieutenant General of NKVD Pavel Anatolievich Sudoplatov, born in 1907, convicted on 12 September 1958 by the Military Collegium of
the Supreme Court for committing the crime in accordance with article 17-58-1 of
the Criminal Code of the Russian Federation to fifteen years of imprisonment
(arrested 21 August 1953). He is rehabilitated in accordance with paragraph A,
article 3 of the law of the Russian Federation on the rehabilitation of political repressions of 18 October 1991.

Assistant to the Chief Military Prosecutor
Colonel of Justice
N. L. Anisimov

I N D E X

Rosenbergs' role in, 177, 191, 213, 214, 215–17
Soviet codebooks and, 218–19
Soviet scientists and, 183–84, 446–56
structure of intelligence bureaucracy and, 184–85, 240
Sudoplatov's assessment of, 211
transfer of contacts in, 186–88
uncovering and arrest of sources in, 207–8, 208n-9n, 212, 213–20
on U.S. capability to fight nuclear war, 209, 210
Attlee, Clement, 210
Austria, 225, 245
Austrian Communist party, 339
aviation industry, corruption in, 310–11, 315, 325
Azerbaijan, 259, 260, 294, 295
Azeri (Azerbaijani) nationalists, 373–74

Bagirov, M., 260, 295
Bagramyan, I. Kh., 313
Baibakov, Nikolai, 205
Bakatin, Vadim, 275
Balitsky, V. A., 12, 61
Balodis, Janis, 100
Baltic states, 98–102, 117–18, 236, 249, 266, 294, 355
Molotov-Ribbentrop secret protocols and, 97n, 98, 99
Soviet strategic interests in, 98
see also specific states
Bandera, Stepan, 15–16, 105, 132, 251–52, 355, 357
liquidation of followers of, 253–59, 378, 409
Bandrovska, Wanda, 109
Baramia, M. I., 358
Baranovsky, Jaroslav, 24, 28–29
Barcza, Margarete, 144
Bardaiev, N., 144
Barkovsky, Vladimir Borisovich, 173n, 207
Barth, Albert, 139, 140, 142
Barthou, Louis, 15
Barzani, Mustafa, 259–64, 294, 415
Sudoplatov's meeting with, 260–61
Batitsky, A., 375, 428n
Baturin (investigator), 422
Beck, Ludwig, 225
Bednyy, Demyan, 52
Belgium, 119
agent networks in, 138, 139
Belkin, Aleksandr, 137, 139, 268, 301, 302, 341
Beneš, Edvard, 62–63, 120, 223

power transferred to Gottwald by, 233–35, 297
Tukhachevsky purge and, 90–93
Ukrainian nationalists and, 104, 106
Bentley, Elizabeth, 217–18, 228n
Berenzon, Abram, 43
Berezantsov, Professor, 156–57, 158
Berezhkov, Valentin, 145, 146
Beria, Lavrenti Pavlovich, xxii, 25, 36, 126, 129, 134–35, 221, 238, 240, 262, 267, 271, 295, 315–16, 348, 352, 353–87, 417, 424, 426, 428, 434
Abakumov and, 162, 163, 329, 349–50
Adamovich's disappearance and, 107–9
appearance and demeanor of, 39, 40
appointed Yezhov's deputy, 40, 41
arrested by military, 370–71, 372, 375, 427–28
assessments of, 5, 428
atomic projects and, 175, 178, 179, 181, 182, 183, 185–86, 188, 199–209, 211, 312, 322, 439–41, 456–58, 464, 466, 474–75
Baltic states and, 99–100, 101
case against, 373–74
Caucasus campaign and, 148, 149, 150, 151
in Civil War, 373–74
Doctors' Plot and, 297, 298, 299, 307, 341, 342, 343, 350, 351, 353, 358
as economic administrator, 204–5
in events leading to German invasion, 118, 122–24, 125
executions by poison and, 279, 280, 284, 385, 396, 400, 402, 407, 411
first hydrogen bomb test and, 363, 373
German unification and, 363–66, 368, 373
governing of republics and, 356–58
Hungarian leadership and, 367
Ilyin affair and, 162, 163, 164
intelligence services overhauled by, 359–63
Jewish issues and, 287–88, 289, 290, 291, 292, 296, 306, 307, 309, 344–45, 353, 354
Kapler beating and, 152
Katyn Forest massacre and, 277, 279n, 476–78
Leningrad Case and, 325, 326
Malenkov's relationship with, 352, 359, 372